Encyclopedia of Junk Food and Fast Food

Advisory Board

ENCYCLOPEDIA OF JUNK FOOD AND FAST FOOD

Andrew F. Smith

GREENWOOD PRESS
Westport, Connecticut • London

Library of Congress Cataloging-in-Publication Data

Smith, Andrew F., 1946–
Encyclopedia of junk food and fast food / Andrew F. Smith.
p. cm.
Includes bibliographical references and index.
ISBN 0-313-33527-3 (alk. paper)
1. Junk food—Encyclopedias. 2. Convenience foods—Encyclopedias. I. Title.
TX370.S63 2006
641.5—dc22 2006012113

British Library Cataloguing in Publication Data is available.

Library of Congress Catalog Card Number: 2006012113
ISBN: 0-313-33527-3

First published in 2006

Greenwood Press, 88 Post Road West, Westport, CT 06881
An imprint of Greenwood Publishing Group, Inc.
www.greenwood.com

Printed in the United States of America

The paper used in this book complies with the Permanent Paper Standard issued by the National Information Standards Organization (Z39.48–1984).

10 9 8 7 6 5 4 3 2 1

This encyclopedia is dedicated to America's youth— particularly Amanda, Connor, Ethan, Julia, Luke, Meghanne, Owen, Peter Max, Reilly, and Stephanie, who have assisted in completing this work. May you make wise decisions as you balance your food and beverage choices throughout your lives.

Contents

Preface ix

Acknowledgments xiii

List of Entries xv

List of Entries by Topic xix

Introduction xxv

Chronology xxxi

The Encyclopedia 1

Glossary 293

Selected Bibliography 297

Resource Guide 303

Index 307

Preface

My first trip to McDonald's was in 1955, when I was nine years old. I can still remember the visit, for there was nothing else like McDonald's at the time: it was fast, convenient, and inexpensive. It was spotlessly clean, the equipment was shiny, the outside and inside were brightly lit, workers scurried about in military-like precision, and very unusual arches stuck out of the building. At that time, McDonald's only served hamburgers, cheeseburgers, French fries, and beverages. The outlets had no indoor tables, so customers ate in their cars. Because we ate most meals at home, eating in the car was an unusual experience. Like many baby-boom Americans, I've had a love affair with fast food ever since.

Full disclosure also forces me to also admit that I also loved junk food—Cracker Jack, Fritos, various fruit pies, and Hostess Sno Balls frequently appeared in my lunch box. I've always loved ice cream and soft drinks. I must admit that one of the joys of going to the movies in my youth was the ability to buy a snack—usually hot buttered popcorn and a soda. Despite these comments, I hasten to add that my consumption of fast food, junk food, and soft drinks was not a daily occurrence in my youth.

These memories were surely the beginning of my lifelong fascination with junk food, fast food, and soft drinks. This fascination continued long after my consumption of these products declined. While my interest in them initially sprang from childhood memories, today, as a food historian, I am concerned with what roles these foods play in larger social, historical, cultural, and culinary contexts and what this tells us about what it means to be an American.

Fast food and junk food did not just suddenly appear and immediately dominate American culinary world. I have tried to place these phenomena into a broader historical setting, for the directions these industries have taken clearly reflect wider trends. For instance, fast food did not just materialize in the twentieth century. For hundreds of years, Europeans have commented upon the speed with which Americans eat. Speed of eating is part of a much broader societal change in America—the commodification of time. Benjamin Franklin coined the phrase "Time is money," and this has applied to many different aspects of our lives. Eating quickly meant that the diner had more important things to do—why waste time preparing food and cleaning up afterwards? Eating at fast food outlets and other restaurants is simply a manifestation of the commodification of time coupled with the relatively low value many Americans have placed on the food they eat.

Likewise, Western civilization has had a love affair with sugar and chocolate for almost 500 years. For most of this time, these products were considered luxuries and few could easily afford to buy them or buy products made from them. Due to improvements in technology and agriculture, the price of sugar and chocolate declined greatly during the nineteenth century, such that most Americans could easily afford to buy sweets and chocolates.

Generic American soft drinks, such as root beer, originated in the late eighteenth century and rapidly expanded during the second half of the nineteenth century. At first, soft drinks were considered medicinal; many of America's most famous sodas, including Hires Root Beer, Moxie, Coca-Cola, Pepsi-Cola, and Dr Pepper, were invented by medical professionals in drugstores. Soft drinks were products of the medical profession but they became popular largely due to the temperance movement that touted alternatives to alcoholic beverages.

While this encyclopedia focuses upon junk food and fast food, it is clear that these phenomena are part of the much broader economic, social, and cultural milieu. The rise in consumption of these foods is directly correlated with the increase in Americans' disposable income and the rise of the two-income family after World War II. As disposable income increases, so does the consumption of junk food and fast food. Likewise, the growth of multinational food companies, the rapid expansion of franchises and chains, and the concentration of agriculture and food production are systemic, not just phenomena of the fast food and junk food industries.

This encyclopedia is intended to be the primary balanced source for information about fast food and junk food. It focuses specifically on national fast food franchises and commercial junk food targeted at youth. Junk food is defined as those commercial products, including candy, bakery goods, ice cream, salty snacks, and soft drinks, which have little or no nutritional value but do have plenty of calories, salt, and fats. While not all fast foods are junk foods, most are. Fast foods are ready-to-eat foods served promptly after ordering. Some fast foods are high in calories and low in nutritional value, while other fast foods, such as salads, may be low in calories and high in nutritional value.

My motivation in producing this encyclopedia is not just an indulgence in good old memories of junk foods eaten, or an academic interest in what these foods can tell us. My motivation is also based on a deep concern with the effects fast food and junk food have upon the United States and the world. Fifty years ago, on my first visit to McDonald's, the sign out front proudly announced "Over 1 million hamburgers sold." As of January, 2006, the sign said "Over 99 billion hamburgers sold." Many other statistics demonstrate the vast increase in the consumption of other fast food, sodas, and junk food. As industries, they are extremely important in America. Most fast food and junk food tastes good, which is why people buy them. They are also inexpensive and conveniently available in grocery stores, kiosks, vending machines, and fast food outlets. Hundreds of millions of people buy junk food, soft drinks, and fast food every day.

Cumulatively, these simple transactions have resulted in numerous problems in America and the world, including destruction of the environment, proliferation of trash and waste, the concentration of industry, and the growth of factory farms, to name a few. Simultaneous with the growth of fast food and junk food has been a tremendous increase in obesity. Today, an estimated 61 percent of Americans are deemed overweight. As a result, the Centers for Disease Control (CDC) has estimated that 248,000 Americans die prematurely due to obesity; other medical professionals believe that this figure is low and believe that many more people die prematurely due to illnesses related to obesity.

An even more ominous statistic indicating that this may get worse is that the percentage of children and adolescents who are obese has doubled in the last 20 years. Today, 25 percent of American children are now classified as overweight, according to the CDC. This should come as no surprise, for junk food and fast food are heavily marketed to America's youth, who consume vast quantities of both.

This encyclopedia is aimed at the general reader and students who are interested in junk food and fast food. The entries in it are listed in alphabetical order. Overview entries, such as those on Fast Food, Chains, and Soda/Soft Drink explain the term, give an overview, and describe its significance. Specific entries, such as those on Snickers, Hires Root Beer, and Coca-Cola, give brief histories of these products and note their significance. Each entry contains cross-references in **bold** type to other entries in the encyclopedia and a list of suggested readings at the end. Following the introduction, there is a chronology of key junk food and fast food events and people. At the back of the encyclopedia are a glossary and a resource guide of books, films, and Web sites. This encyclopedia is fully indexed.

Acknowledgments

I would like to thank the dozens of people who have helped with this encyclopedia, including the Advisory Board consisting of Ken Albala, Gary Allen, Joseph Carlin, Barbara Haber, Cathy K. Kaufman, and Bruce Kraig. All have kindly reviewed parts of the manuscript and I have greatly appreciated all their comments. I would also like to thank Barry Popick, whose research has been used liberally throughout this work. I would also like to acknowledge Greenwood Press, especially my editor, Wendi Schnaufer, who has responded to my many questions and has offered excellent comments regarding the text and organization of the encyclopedia. I also want to thank Kelly Fitzsimmons for her excellent photography.

List of Entries

A&W Root Beer
Advertising
AFC Enterprises
American Junk Food and Fast Food in Other Countries
Animal Rights Movement
Anti-unionization
Arby's
Architecture and Design
Arthur Treacher's
Automats, Cafeterias, Diners, and Lunchrooms
Automobiles
Baby Ruth
Bakery Snacks
Barq's Root Beer
Baskin-Robbins
Battle of the Burgers
Beef Jerky
Ben & Jerry's
Beverages
Big Boy
Bit-O-Honey
Blimpie International, Inc.
Blue Bell
Boston Market
Bovine Growth Hormone (BGH)
Boycotts
Breakfast Fast Foods
Breyers
Bugles
Burger King
Butterfinger
Cadbury
Cadbury Schweppes
Caffeine
California Pizza Kitchen
Canada Dry Ginger Ale
Candy
Caramels
Carbohydrates
Carhops
Carl's Jr.
Carvel Corporation
Center for Science in the Public Interest (CSPI)
Cereals (Breakfast)
Chains
Chanukah Candy
Charities
Cheese-based Snacks
Cheetos
Chewy Candy
Chicken
Chicken Delight
Chicken McNuggets
Chips Ahoy!
Chocolate
Chocolate Chip Cookies
Chocolate Confections
Cholesterol
Christmas
Chuck E. Cheese Pizza
Church's Chicken

Cinnabon
Clark Bar
Coca-Cola Company
Cola
Cola Wars
Collectibles and Americana
Condiments
Conformity
Consumerism
Controversies
Convenience Foods/Drinks
Cookies and Crackers
Corn Chips
Corporate Concentration
Corporate Sponsorships and Programs in Schools
Cracker Jack
Crime
Dairy Queen
Deep-fried Mars Bars and Twinkies
Del Taco
Diabetes
Diet Soda
Dieting
Dips
Disclosure
Discrimination
Domino's Pizza
Doritos
Doughnuts
Dove Bar
Dr Pepper
Dreyer's/Edy's Ice Cream
Drive-ins
Drive-thrus
Drumsticks
Dunkin' Donuts
Easter Candy
Efficiency
Egg Fast Food
Elderly
Employment
Entrepreneurs
Environment
Escherichia coli
Eskimo Pie
Exploitation
Exposés
Extruded Snacks
Factory Farming
Fair Food
Famous Amos
Fast Food
Fast Food and Snack Food Associations
Fast Food Nation
Fats
Film
Fish and Chips
Fish as Fast Food
Food Pyramid
Foodborne Illnesses
Fortune Cookies
Fosters Freeze
Franchising
French Fries
Fried Chicken
Frito Bandito
Frito-Lay
Frito-Lay Corn Chips
Frozen Pizza
General Foods Corp.
General Mills, Inc.
Genetically Modified Organisms (GMOs)
Ginger Ale
Girl Scout Cookies
Globalization
Goldfish
Good & Plenty
Good Humor
Graham Crackers
Gross-out Candy
Gum
Gummi/Gummy Candy
Häagen-Dazs
Halloween
Hamburgers
Happy Meal
Hard Candy
Hardee's
Health Concerns
Hershey, Milton S.
Hershey Company
Hershey's Chocolate Bar
Hires Root Beer
Hollywood, Movie Tie-ins, and Celebrity Endorsements

Hostess
Hot Dog
Hyperactivity
Ice Cream
Iconography
Ilitch, Mike
Injury
In-N-Out Burger
Jack in the Box
Jell-O
Jelly Beans
Junior Mints
Junk Foods
Just Born
Karcher, Carl N.
Keebler
Kellogg Company
Kentucky Fried Chicken (KFC)
Ketchup
Klondike Bar
Kool-Aid
Kraft Foods
Krispy Kreme
Kroc, Ray
Lawsuits
Licorice
LifeSavers
Little Caesar's Pizza
Little Debbie
Lobbying
Locations
Lollipops and Suckers
Long John Silver's
M&M's
Mad Cow Disease
Marriott Corp.
Mars, Forrest
Mars, Frank
Mars, Inc.
Mary Jane Candies
Mascots, Logos, and Icons
McDonaldization
McDonald's
McLibel
Meatpacking Industry
Memoirs
Menus
Mexican Food
Mike and Ike
Milk Duds
Milk Shakes, Malts, and Ice Cream Sodas
Milky Way
Minimum Wage
Monaghan, Tom
Moon Pie
Mounds Bar
Mountain Dew
Moxie
Mr. Peanut
Mrs. Fields Cookies
Music
Nabisco
Nachos
Nathan's Famous
National Confectioners Association
Neighborhoods
Nestlé SA
New England Confectionery Company
Newspapers
Nutrition
Nutritional Guidelines
Nuts
Obesity
Occupational Safety and Health Administration (OSHA)
Oh Henry!
Onion Rings
Orange Crush
Oreos
Packaging
Panda Express
Patriotism
PayDay
Penny Candy
Pepperidge Farm
PepsiCo
Peter Paul Candy Company
PEZ
Physicians Committee for Responsible Medicine
Pizza
Pizza Hut
Politics of Junk Food
El Pollo Loco
Popcorn
Popeyes

Popsicle
Pop-Tarts
Potato Chips
Powdered Mixes
Power and Energy Bars
Pretzels
Pricing
Pringles
Protests
Push-ups
Quiznos Sub
Radio
Redenbacher, Orville
Reese's Peanut Butter Cups
Regional Fast Foods
Ritz Crackers
Ronald McDonald
Root Beer
Rowntree's of York
Roy Rogers
Royal Crown Cola
Rules
Salmonella
Salt
Sanders, Harland
Sandwiches
Sbarro
Schools
Schweppes
Seasonal Candy
Secret Formulas
7-Eleven
7-Up
Shakey's Pizza
Signage
Slogans and Jingles
Slow Food
Slurpee
Snack Foods
Snickers
Soda/Soft Drink
Soda Fountains
Sonic
Sports Drinks
Sports Sponsorships
Street Vendors
Subs/Grinders
Subway
Suckers
Sugars
Supermarkets
Supersizing
Suppliers
Sweet Popcorn
Taco Bell
Tang
Tastee-Freez
Tater Tots
Taxing Snack Food
Teen Hangouts
Television
Theaters
Thomas, Dave
3 Musketeers
Tie-ins
Toblerone
Tombstone Pizza
Tootsie Roll
Toys
Training
Tricon Global Restaurants
Twinkies
Uniforms
Unilever
Urban Blight
U.S. Department of Agriculture (USDA)
Valentine's Day Candies
Vegetarianism/Veganism
Vending Machines
Vernor's Ginger Ale
Violence
Waste
Wendy's International
White Castle
White Tower
Wienerschnitzel
Wimpy
Winchell's Donut House
Wrigley Co.
York Peppermint Patties
Yum! Brands, Inc.

List of Entries by Topic

Bakery Goods

Bakery Snacks
Chips Ahoy!
Chocolate Chip Cookies
Cinnabon
Cookies and Crackers
Doughnuts
Dunkin' Donuts
Famous Amos
Fortune Cookies
Girl Scout Cookies
Hostess
Keebler
Krispy Kreme
Little Debbie
Moon Pie
Mrs. Fields Cookies
Oreos
Pepperidge Farm
Pop-Tarts
Snack Foods
Twinkies
Winchell's Donut House

Beverages

A&W Root Beer
Barq's Root Beer
Beverages
Cadbury Schweppes
Canada Dry Ginger Ale
Coca-Cola Company
Cola
Cola Wars
Convenience Foods/Drinks
Diet Soda
Dr Pepper
Ginger Ale
Hires Root Beer
Kool-Aid
Mountain Dew
Moxie
Orange Crush
PepsiCo
Powdered Mixes
Power and Energy Bars
Root Beer
Royal Crown Cola
Schweppes
7-Up
Slurpee
Soda/Soft Drink
Soda Fountains
Sports Drinks
Sugars
Tang
Vernor's Ginger Ale

Candy

Baby Ruth
Bit-O-Honey
Butterfinger
Cadbury
Cadbury Schweppes
Candy

Caramels
Chanukah Candy
Chewy Candy
Chocolate
Chocolate Confections
Christmas
Clark Bar
Deep-fried Mars Bars and Twinkies
Easter Candy
Good & Plenty
Gross-out Candy
Gum
Gummi/Gummy Candy
Halloween
Hard Candy
Hershey's Chocolate Bar
Jelly Beans
Junior Mints
Junk Foods
Just Born
Licorice
LifeSavers
Lollipops and Suckers
M&M's
Mars, Inc.
Mary Jane Candies
Mike and Ike
Milk Duds
Milky Way
Mounds Bar
Nestlé
New England Confectionery Company
Oh Henry!
PayDay
Penny Candy
PEZ
Reese's Peanut Butter Cups
Ritz Crackers
Rowntree's of York
Seasonal Candy
Snack Foods
Snickers
Sugars
3 Musketeers
Toblerone
Tootsie Roll
Valentine's Day Candies
Wrigley Co.
York Peppermint Patties

Companies and Corporations

Advertising
American Junk Food /Fast Food in Other Countries
Cadbury
Cadbury Schweppes
Charities
Coca-Cola Company
Corporate Concentration
Corporate Sponsorships and Programs in Schools
Frito Bandito
Frito-Lay
General Foods Corp.
General Mills, Inc.
Hershey Company
Just Born
Keebler
Kellogg Company
Kraft Foods
Marriott Corp.
Mars, Inc.
McDonald's
McLibel
Nabisco
Nestlé SA
New England Confectionery Company
PepsiCo
Peter Paul Candy Company
Ronald McDonald
Rowntree's of York
7-Eleven
Unilever

Fast Food

A&W Root Beer
AFC Enterprises
Arby's
Arthur Treacher's
Blimpie International, Inc.
Boston Market
Breakfast Fast Foods
Burger King
California Pizza Kitchen

Carl's Jr.
Chicken
Chicken Delight
Chicken McNuggets
Chuck E. Cheese Pizza
Church's Chicken
Cinnabon
Condiments
Convenience Foods/Drinks
Del Taco
Domino's Pizza
Drive-thrus
Egg Fast Food
Fast Food Nation
Fast Food
Fish and Chips
Fish as Fast Food
French Fries
Fried Chicken
Frozen Pizza
Hamburgers
Happy Meal
Hardee's
Hot Dog
In-N-Out Burger
Jack in the Box
Junk Foods
Kentucky Fried Chicken (KFC)
Ketchup
Little Caesar's Pizza
Long John Silver's
McDonald's
Menus
Mexican Food
Milkshakes, Malts, and Ice Cream Sodas
Nathan's Famous
Onion Rings
Panda Express
Pizza
Pizza Hut
El Pollo Loco
Popeyes
Quiznos Sub
Regional Fast Foods
Ronald McDonald
Roy Rogers
Sbarro
Shakey's Pizza
Sonic
Subs/Grinders
Subway
Taco Bell
Tombstone Pizza
Wendy's International
Wimpy
White Castle
White Tower
Wienerschnitzel

Health and Nutrition

Bovine Growth Hormone (BGH)
Caffeine
Carbohydrates
Cholesterol
Diabetes
Dieting
Escherichia coli
Fats
Food Pyramid
Foodborne Illnesses
Health Concerns
Hyperactivity
Injury
Mad Cow Disease
Nutrition
Nutritional Guidelines
Obesity
Salmonella

Ice Cream

Baskin-Robbins
Ben & Jerry's
Blue Bell
Breyers
Carvel Corp.
Dairy Queen
Dove Bar
Dreyer's/Edy's Ice Cream
Drumsticks
Eskimo Pie
Fosters Freeze
Good Humor
Häagen-Dazs
Ice Cream

Klondike Bar
Popsicle
Push-ups
Tastee-Freeze

Issues and Special Topics

Animal Rights Movement
Anti-unionization
Architecture and Design
Automobiles
Battle of the Burgers
Boycotts
Cereals (Breakfast)
Collectibles and Americana
Conformity
Consumerism
Controversies
Convenience Foods/Drinks
Corporate Sponsorships and Programs in Schools
Crime
Disclosure
Discrimination
Efficiency
Elderly
Employment
Entrepreneurs
Environment
Exploitation
Exposés
Factory Farming
Fair Food
Fast Food Nation
Film
Food Pyramid
Genetically Modified Organisms (GMOs)
Globalization
Hollywood, Movie Tie-ins, Celebrity Endorsements
Iconography
Lawsuits
Lobbying
Mascots, Logos, and Icons
McDonaldization
McLibel
Meatpacking Industry
Memoirs
Minimum Wage
Music
Neighborhoods
Newspapers
Occupational Safety and Health Administration (OSHA)
Packaging
Patriotism
Politics of Junk Food
Pricing
Protests
Radio
Rules
Sandwiches
Schools
Secret Formulas
Signage
Slogans and Jingles
Sports Sponsorships
Street Vendors
Supermarkets
Supersizing
Suppliers
Tater Tots
Taxing Snack Food
Teen Hangouts
Television
Theaters
Tie-ins
Toys
Training
Uniforms
Urban Blight
U.S. Department of Agriculture (USDA)
Vegetarianism/Veganism
Vending Machines
Violence
Waste

Organizations

Center for Science in the Public Interest (CSPI)
Fast Food and Snack Food Associations
National Confectioners Association
Physicians Committee for Responsible Medicine
Slow Food

People

Hershey, Milton S.
Ilitch, Mike
Karcher, Carl N.
Kroc, Ray
Mars, Forrest
Mars, Frank
Monaghan, Tom
Redenbacher, Orville
Sanders, Harland
Thomas, Dave

Restaurants and Drive-ins

Automats, Cafeterias, Diners, and Lunchrooms
Big Boy
Carhops
Chains
Drive-ins
Franchising
Locations
Tricon Global Restaurants
Yum! Brands, Inc.

Salty and Other Noncandy Snacks

Beef Jerky
Bugles
Cheese-based Snacks
Cheetos
Corn Chips
Cracker jack
Dips
Doritos
Extruded Snacks
Frito-Lay Corn Chips
Goldfish
Graham Crackers
Jell-O
Mr. Peanut
Nachos
Nuts
Popcorn
Potato Chips
Pretzels
Pringles
Salt
Snack Foods
Sweet Popcorn

Introduction

For the first 200 years of European settlement, most Americans lived on farms and were culinarily self-sufficient. They grew, raised, or produced almost everything they ate. Those who were well-off acquired a few luxuries, such as coffee, tea, sugar, and spices. Until the second half of the nineteenth century, most food was sold as commodities—there were few brand-named products and most of those were too expensive for most Americans. Likewise, few Americans ate outside the home. No fast food chains existed, and neither did hamburgers, hot dogs, pizza, Hershey bars, Snickers, French fries, potato chips, Oreos, or Nachos; none of these foods became important until almost the mid-twentieth century. While fast food and junk food—foods with high calories and little nutritional value—were mainly twentieth-century inventions, a number of important shifts were underway in America in the nineteenth century that created the preconditions necessary for the subsequent rise of junk food and fast food.

Technology, Transportation, and Protest

It is easy to see where America's junk food culinary revolution began: It started with the improvement of technology related to milling flour. Until the early nineteenth century, farmers grew, harvested, and stored wheat at their farms. When they wanted flour, they took their grain to small local mills where the grain was milled into flour. This was usually not bolted (sifted), so the bran remained in the flour. This pattern began to change in 1785 when Oliver Evans built a new type of mill near Wilmington, Delaware. He had studied existing mills and concluded that he could design a mill such that wheat could be taken directly from a wagon or boat, cleaned, ground, dried, cooled, sifted, and packed without the intervention of a human operator. His revolutionary design was improved over the next few decades. By the 1820s, mills using these new methods could process grain cheaply and, just as important, the flour that came out was sifted and was therefore much whiter than previously. However, there was a catch: The new mills required expensive new equipment and therefore the up-front costs for constructing these mills were much higher. But the advantages were that the new mills could process more grain in less time and with less labor.

Two important principles emerged from this type of milling that continued to affect all subsequent food production, eventually including those related to junk food and fast food. First, technology decreases labor costs, and second, improved technology can speed up the processing of products. The result was that mills produced lower-priced goods for consumers but made more profits for the owners through increased volume.

Mills built on these principles were themselves revolutionary, but these technological changes were amplified by improvements in transportation. Until the early nineteenth century, most Americans lived along the Eastern seaboard. This began to change with the construction of the Erie Canal, which connected the Hudson River with the Great Lakes, thus opening up central New York state and the Midwest to additional commerce. This meant that low-cost wheat could be grown, harvested, and milled in central New York and easily shipped through the canal, down the Hudson, and then to other parts of the United States. Because the mills constructed in central New York used the new technology, the cost of that state's flour was much lower. Cheap flour from central New York flooded markets throughout the United States.

Cheap flour affected all parts of the United States, but it particularly affected New England, where growing wheat had always been difficult. When New England wheat growers were undersold by wheat imported through the Erie Canal, Sylvester Graham, a minister, began advocating the consumption of locally produced wheat, regardless of its higher price. Graham wanted to save the family farms in New England and he was suspicious of the origins of food coming from hundreds of miles away. He also believed that white flour coming from the new mills was unhealthy. Graham failed in his efforts to preserve New England's family farms, and many New England farmers emigrated West settling in central New York and the Midwest. Graham had launched America's first food protest movement and the issues he raised, such as the healthfulness of food and the loss of family farms, have been controversial ever since. In many ways, today's concerns with fast food and junk food can be traced to Sylvester Graham's first food protest movement.

Through canals and railroads Americans moved westward, particularly after 1869 when the transcontinental railroad was completed. A national railroad network made it possible to grow or process foods in California and ship them thousands of miles to East Coast markets. Railroads also made it possible for food processors to centralize their operations in particular locations (such as meatpacking in Chicago or making ketchup in Pittsburgh) and ship their products throughout the nation. Other twentieth-century transportation innovations, such as the Panama Canal, contributed to shifting food production and processing from local activities to global businesses.

Civil War and Industrialization

Even more culinary changes resulted from the Civil War (1861–1865). During the war, Union forces were spread over thousands of miles. This created a logistical nightmare for those trying to supply these forces with fresh, wholesome food. One solution was to manufacture canned goods and ship them by railroad to the armies in the field. The costs of canning and bottling declined during the war as manufacturers gained experience with mass-production techniques and soldiers became familiar with canned and bottled products. When they returned to civilian life after the war, they wanted these commercial products. The industrialization of American food had begun, and one eventual result was the manufacture of low-cost food decades before junk foods were invented.

Railroad construction and the Civil War also contributed to general industrialization and urbanization. Americans moved from farms into cities. As cities grew larger and as factories were often built a great distance from where workers lived, feeding workers became a problem. Most workers just brought food with them and ate it in the factory. As disposable income increased and time to prepare food decreased, workers opted to eat food prepared by others. Vendors pushed lunch carts to factory gates and sold foods that could easily be carried away and eaten. As their businesses grew, vendors increased the size of their carts so that customers could stand inside, which was particularly important during inclement weather; this was the beginning of the diner. Vendors acquired property around the gates of factories or near subway or trolley stops and traded up to stationary buildings with inside seating, where possible.

Workers had minimal time to eat and factory owners concluded that it would be better for their operations if workers did not leave the premises to eat. Many factories therefore built cafeterias which permitted workers to eat quickly and return to work. Whether one ate out of a lunch box or from a lunch cart or in a cafeteria, the amount of time spent eating significantly decreased.

Before the Industrial Revolution most women stayed at home, and preparing meals was one of their responsibilities. When America began to industrialize, however, women began to join the work force. At first, these were mainly single women who left their jobs when they married. During the twentieth century, however, the number of married women who worked began to increase. As disposable income increased, it became more common for families to purchase foods prepared and served by other people. By the early twentieth century, America was ripe for the junk food and fast food revolutions.

Invention of Junk Food

Junk foods, such as peanuts, popcorn, and Cracker Jack, have been sold at fairs and by pushcart operators throughout the nineteenth century. It was a minor part of the food that Americans consumed. Medical authorities resolutely condemned it and many were opposed to snacking between meals, claiming that it ruined one's appetite. The first commercially successful junk food was Cracker Jack, created by Frederick and Louis Rueckheim in 1896. The major reason for its success was advertising. Within a decade of its national launch, Cracker Jack quickly became the most popular confection in America, and by 1916 it was the best-selling confection in the world. Other confections followed Cracker Jack's lead, and Americans began to buy branded confections.

The Federal Role in Agriculture and Pure Food

The U.S. Bureau of Agriculture was established in 1862; it was upgraded to the U.S. Department of Agriculture (USDA) in 1889. The Department established experimental research programs to assist farmers in improving their crops. Because the USDA was mainly interested in increasing the yield of crops, it encouraged the growth of large farms that produced great quantities of food more efficiently. As a result, the number of small family farms decreased as they were outstripped in terms of production by large farms. The USDA and the large farms focused on crops and varieties that could be produced efficiently and transported hundreds of miles to market, such as lettuce that stayed crisp and peaches that would not bruise. Lower prices for agricultural products encouraged the growth of food processors and manufacturers.

In the late nineteenth century, many processed and manufactured foods contained so-called adulterants, such as cyanide, bleach, borax, and sawdust, some of them dangerous. Although Sylvester Graham and Dr. John Harvey Kellogg were concerned about these problems, they failed in their efforts to make the food supply safer. By 1900, impure processed foods injured thousands of Americans annually. England, Canada, and other countries had passed pure food laws during the nineteenth century. Other countries refused to import certain American foods they considered unsafe. Dr. Harvey Wiley, a medical doctor and former chief chemist for the USDA, worked for almost 30 years to make food safer. Though his efforts, legislation to create the Pure Food and Drug Act became law in 1906, though it was bitterly opposed by many commercial food processors.

The effects of the federal activities in agriculture and food safety were significant. As Americans became confident that processed foods were safe, sales of such foods soared and these products (and the techniques used to make them) spread to other countries. One result of the work of the USDA was a dwindling of the great diversity of foods grown on family farms. Another effect was the decline in the price Americans paid for their food—a trend that continues today. According to the U.S. Department of Agriculture, Americans spend about nine percent of their disposable income on food, which is less than any other people around the world. As food prices dropped, producers needed new ways to reach wider markets, and one solution was advertising.

Advertising and Marketing

Commercial foods were usually little-known outside their place of origin. To increase sales, manufacturers needed to advertise. The first food company to package and advertise its product nationally was the American Cereal Company, and the product was Quaker Oats. Although the manufacturer had no connection to the Quakers, it trademarked the name and created the icon of the Quaker man. The company ran special trains around the United States with signs promoting Quaker Oats; men dressed as Quakers gave away free samples. The company also invented the notion of premiums, which were placed in the cereal boxes. Similar tactics would be employed by other food manufacturers. America's first junk food producer, the Cracker Jack Company, launched advertising campaigns that used toys to target children, claimed that Cracker Jack had healthful contents, and promulgated grand slogans. These campaigns were so successful that they were emulated by other fast food and junk food manufacturers.

The Automobile and the Invention of Fast Food

The automobile appeared in America in the 1890s, but it was mainly a luxury toy for the rich until Henry Ford mass-produced his first Model Ts in 1908. Inexpensive cars were suddenly available and, although World War I slowed their construction, after the war automobile sales skyrocketed. By 1920 there were 9.2 million cars, trucks, and buses in the United States. Cars freed commuters from the hassles of public transportation and made it easier for many Americans to drive when they traveled.

Automobiles encouraged the development of a new type of restaurant with simple menus and faster, more convenient service. As automobile ownership became available to the lower middle class, the market for fast food developed. To attract drivers, restaurants needed to be highly visible, which meant creating distinctive architecture that could easily been seen as different from its surroundings. It also meant large advertising expenditures, and that restaurants needed places for cars to park. To attract attention of passing motorists, drive-ins created a new type of architecture to really stand out. During the second half of the twentieth century, the fast food industry expanded alongside the interstate highway system, with outlets clustering around off-ramps.

Stiff competition also encouraged the lowering of prices to attract customers. Lower prices dictated the types of food that could be served. Whereas extensive menus required extensive raw materials and storage space, limited menus kept inventory ordering to a minimum. Various foods were served but the heart of the limited menu was food that could be prepared easily, quickly, and cheaply. Chicken and hamburgers, for example, required little space for preparation, and specialization kept required equipment to a minimum. A simple menu of easily prepared food meant that less employee training was required for preparing the food and the food could be served relatively quickly. Fast service meant that volumes could increase and prices could be lowered, while profits could be maintained. Customers would not have to wait long, the turnover would be rapid, and eating area space could be limited.

The 1950s

With the end of World War II, servicemen returned and began to seek job opportunities, marry, and start families. A number of those servicemen launched doughnut shops, ice cream parlors, and fast food establishments. Low-interest, federally guaranteed home loans helped millions of veterans acquire new homes. America's fertility rate had been declining prior to the baby boom after World War II. During the 1950s, many veterans and their families moved into suburbs. As suburbs began to grow, supermarkets, convenience stores, and fast food chains moved into the suburbs to service baby boomers' families. Wages increased by 30 percent during this decade and disposable income increased. With additional income, families could more easily eat outside the home.

Fast Food

Fast food, an invention of the early twentieth century, was partly a response to the rise of the automobile. Although fast food had been around for decades, the McDonald brothers carried the concept to its ultimate implementation. Their efficient operation permitted them to speed up service and lower prices. The surprise effect was how quickly fast food would become a large proportion of the American diet. McDonald's and other fast food chains successfully targeted the suburbs for their operations. It was not until the 1950s that the hamburger and French fries became the iconic American meal.

Beginning in the 1960s, American fast food began to spread around the world, challenging local and national cuisines in foreign lands. Fast food entrenched the idea of eating outside the home, which contributed to the explosion of restaurants in subsequent years; it taught Americans to enjoy eating out, and it usually catered to different ethnic and class groups, thus sustaining a widely fragmented and heterogeneous society. Elitists have always looked down on fast food, criticizing how it tastes and regarding it as another tacky manifestation of American popular culture. Consumers enjoy the low cost, convenience, and taste of fast food.

Fast Food and Junk Food Today

Sales of junk food and fast food have dramatically increased over the past 50 years. Today, they are multibillion-dollar businesses, which directly and indirectly employ hundreds of thousands of workers. These industries exert major influences upon the lives of every American. The purpose of this encyclopedia is to explore the history and social influence of fast food, soft drinks, and junk food.

Chronology

1783 Jean Jacob Schweppes improved a process for manufacturing carbonated water and formed the Schweppes Company in Geneva, Switzerland. In 1792 Schweppes moved the company to England. Soda at that time was considered a medicinal beverage. During the nineteenth century, the Schweppes Company began manufacturing Schweppes Tonic Water.

1825 The Erie Canal was completed, linking the Midwest to the East Coast. This enabled the transportation of wheat and flour from western New York state and later the Midwest. The flood of white flour into New England created America's first culinary protest movement, led by Sylvester Graham, who believed that low-cost white flour was destroying New England life. His solution was to use only locally grown, unbolted wheat. He created what would be later called Graham flour.

1847 Joseph S. Fry & Sons of Bristol, England combined cocoa powder with sugar and added cocoa butter to produce a thin paste that could be shaped in a mold and be consumed as a solid. This discovery launched a revolution that converted chocolate from being used mainly for hot beverages and for baking to being a component of chocolate candy.

1862 In the United States, the Bureau of Agriculture was established in 1862; in 1889, the Bureau became the Department of Agriculture (USDA) with cabinet rank. The USDA administers thousands of programs related to food and agriculture, including programs on food safety and nutrition.

1866 James Vernor, a Detroit pharmacist, introduced Ginger Ale, which is considered America's first commercial carbonated soft drink.

1867 Charles Feltman, a pushcart vendor on Coney Island, New York, began selling sausages on white rolls. These are considered the first hot dogs.

1869 The transcontinental railroad was completed, connecting California with the East Coast. This and other railroads permitted foods to be shipped throughout the United States. After the invention of the refrigerated railroad car, seafood was easily transported to inland cities hundreds of miles from the ocean, and beef was easily brought from the Midwestern stockyards to cities all over America.

1871 Thomas Adams of New York invented America's first chewing gum, which he began to manufacture. Others followed in his footsteps.

1876 At the Centennial Exposition held in Philadelphia, James W. Tufts and Charles Lippincott constructed a building with a 30-foot soda fountain and dozens of soda dispensers ready to refresh thirsty fairgoers. After the Exposition closed, Tufts and Lippincott made a fortune selling soda fountains to drugstores around the nation. By 1908 there were an estimated 75,000 soda fountains in the United States.

Hires Root Beer was the first soft drink to be mass-produced for public sale in Philadelphia.

In Switzerland, Henri Nestlé, a milk expert, went into business to produce milk chocolate. In 1879, the Nestlé Company produced its first chocolate bar.

Augustin Thompson, an itinerant pharmacist in Lowell, Massachusetts, concocted Moxie Nerve Food, which was later converted into Moxie, a soft drink.

1877 The American Cereal Company, headed by Henry D. Seymour and William Heston, developed and trademarked a new product they called Quaker Oats. They packed their product in cardboard boxes bearing the reassuring image of an elderly Quaker and promoted it via an advertising campaign in 1882, making it the first processed food to be advertised nationally.

1885 Charles Alderton, employed at Morrison's Old Corner Drug Store in Waco, Texas, invented a beverage called Dr Pepper.

1886 Dr. John S. Pemberton invented Coca-Cola in Atlanta, Georgia. Pemberton considered it a cure for headaches and addiction to morphine, he sold it as a medicine in drugstores. The business was sold to Asa Chandler, who began selling the syrup to other druggists and soda fountain operators who, in turn, mixed it with soda. Today, Coca-Cola is sold in more than 200 countries and territories.

1890 Chemist Wilbur O. Atwater analyzed the nutritional components of food (protein, fat, and carbohydrates) and measured the caloric value of each.

1892 William Painter's invention of the crown bottle cap made it possible to seal bottles easily and cheaply. The bottling of soft drinks was greatly enhanced by improved glass bottles that could keep the carbon dioxide in and would not shatter during the manufacturing process.

1893 At the Columbian Exposition in Chicago, Milton S. Hershey, a caramel maker in Lancaster, Pennsylvania, bought chocolate-making machinery from a German exhibitor; when he returned home, he launched the Hershey Chocolate Company. In 1898 he sold his caramel company and concentrated on chocolate manufacturing. After years of experiments, in about 1900 he finally produced what he called a Chocolate Bar. The Hershey Company quickly became America's largest chocolate manufacturer, a title it still holds more than 100 years later.

The Quaker City Confectionery Company of Philadelphia first produced Good & Plenty candy.

William Wrigley, Jr. began manufacturing Juicy Fruit and Wrigley's Spearmint gums in Chicago. Today, the company is the world's largest maker of chewing and bubble gum.

1895 Charles W. Post, a patient at the Battle Creek Sanitarium in Battle Creek, Michigan, offered to go into business with Dr. John Harvey Kellogg (who ran the sanitarium) to market the sanitarium's products, but Kellogg declined. Post later established the Postum Cereal Company (later renamed General Foods Corporation) and began producing Grape Nuts, the first commercial cold cereal. His success encouraged dozens of other companies to begin manufacturing cereal in Battle Creek.

1896 Frederick and Louis Rueckheim of Chicago launched Cracker Jack, America's first junk food. By 1916 it was the best-selling confection in the world.

William A. Breyer, who had sold ice cream on a retail basis since 1866, began wholesaling it in Philadelphia. Breyers Ice Cream Company became one of America's largest manufacturers of ice cream.

1897 Cadbury Brothers began manufacturing milk chocolate. In 1919, Cadbury merged with Joseph S. Fry & Sons, another major English chocolate maker. The company continued to grow globally throughout the twentieth century. In 1969 Cadbury and Schweppes merged to form Cadbury Schweppes.

1898 The National Biscuit Company (NBC), the forerunner of Nabisco, was created and the company launched a new product called Uneeda Biscuits. Uneeda Biscuits was the first cracker advertised nationally in America. In the same year, NBC began manufacturing Graham Crackers, although the crackers contain ingredients (such as sugar and preservatives) that Sylvester Graham would have strongly opposed.

William Entenmann opened his first bakery in Brooklyn, New York. His business flourished and, in the 1950s, the company began to expand throughout the East Coast, selling its goods through grocery stores as well as through its bakeries. Today, Entenmann's is one of America's largest pastry makers and is the nation's second-largest doughnut maker.

Pepsi-Cola was invented by Caleb Bradham, a pharmacist in New Bern, North Carolina, although the formula would be revised over the years.

1900 Frank Woodward, owner of the Genesee Pure Food Company in LeRoy, New York, bought the formula for flavored gelatin. He marketed it under the name Jell-O.

1904 Canadian John J. McLaughlin perfected a recipe for Pale Dry Ginger Ale. The label for the bottle included a map of Canada with a beaver, which is the national symbol of Canada.

1905 Tootsie Rolls were manufactured in New York City by Leo Hershfield, who brought his recipe from Austria. Named after his daughter, Tootsie, it was the first penny candy to be individually wrapped.

Chero-Cola, later reformulated and released as Royal Crown Cola, was created in Columbus, Georgia.

1906 Congress passed the Pure Food and Drug Act.

Dr. John Harvey Kellogg established the Battle Creek Toasted Corn Flakes Company, later renamed Kellogg's. He named his younger brother, Will K. Kellogg, president of the new company.

1908 Milton S. Hershey introduced almonds into the Hershey Company's chocolate bar; the bar had been introduced in 1900 but he continued to revise the formula until 1905.

1912 Nabisco introduced Oreo Biscuits to compete with the Hydrox Biscuit Bonbons rolled out in 1908 by the Loose-Wiles Biscuit Company of Kansas City, Missouri. Oreos became America's best-selling cookie.

1912 The Stephen F. Whitman Company, founded in Philadelphia in 1842, created the Whitman Sampler which consisted of chocolate-coated candies, complete with an identifying chart inside the lid.

1916 Nathan Handwerker, a Polish shoemaker, opened a hot dog stand on Coney Island, New York. His business thrived and later became Nathan's Famous, Inc.

1919 Taggart Bakery introduced chocolate cupcakes, minus the vanilla filling and the icing fillip. The company was renamed Hostess Cup Cakes in 1925. These were the first national pastry.

Roy Allen launched a root beer stand in June of 1919, in Lodi, California; three years later Allen took on a partner, Frank Wright. They combined their initials and formally named the beverage A&W Root Beer.

Peter Paul Halajian and associates founded the Peter Paul Candy Manufacturing Company in New Haven, Connecticut. They later created two famous chocolate bars, Mounds in 1920 and Almond Joy in 1946.

1921 A White Castle hamburger stand opened in Wichita, Kansas. It was the beginning of America's first fast food chain.

The Eskimo Pie, first named I-Scream, was invented by Christian Kent Nelson, of Onawa, Iowa.

1922 Mars, Inc., formed. It released the Milky Way chocolate bar (1923), followed by Snickers (1930) and 3 Musketeers (1932).

1923 Frank Epperson invented Epsicles—ice pops on wooden sticks. He later changed the product name to Popsicle.

1924 A&W Root Beer in Sacramento, California, and the Pig Stand in Dallas, Texas, became the first-known food franchises.

The Washburn Crosby Company (a forerunner of General Mills, Inc.) acquired the Wheaties cereal brand and began advertising it as The Breakfast of Champions.

1927 PEZ was introduced in Austria as a peppermint breath mint for smokers; in 1948 its unique plastic dispensers were introduced into the United States.

Kool-Aid was introduced in a powdered form in Hastings, Nebraska. Chemist Edwin Perkins was inspired by Jell-O to make a concentrate product, which could be easily manufactured, distributed, and converted into a beverage.

Southland Ice Company opened a convenience store in Dallas, Texas, which was later called 7-Eleven. Today, 7-Eleven is the world's largest convenience store chain, with more than 29,000 stores worldwide (11,000 of which are in Japan).

1928 Reese's Peanut Butter Cups were invented by Harry Burnett Reese, a former employee of the Hershey Chocolate Company, who founded the H. B. Reese Candy Company. They were sold in five-pound boxes for use in candy assortments. Ten years later, Reese marketed these cups separately for a penny apiece. They remain one of America's most popular candy bars.

Bubble gum was invented by Walter E. Diemer, who experimented with different ways of making chewing gum until he found one that stretched more easily and was less sticky.

1929 7-Up was invented by Charles Leiper Grigg of St. Louis, Missouri. Within 10 years, 7-Up was the third-best-selling soft drink in the world.

The General Foods Corporation was created when the Postum Company, the maker of Post cereals, went on a buying spree, acquiring such brands as Baker's chocolate, Maxwell House coffee, and Jell-O. It later acquired Kool-Aid and introduced Tang, an orange-flavored beverage powder.

1930 Jimmy Dewar, manager of a Continental Baking Company bakery in Chicago, invented a banana creme-filled cake that could be sold year-round at the price of two for a nickel. He named it Twinkies. During World War II the banana filling was replaced with a vanilla creme filling.

Mars, Inc., released the Snickers chocolate bar. It quickly became America's most-consumed candy bar, a position it has held ever since.

1932 Elmer Doolin, an unemployed salesman, began manufacturing Fritos (corn chips) in his kitchen. He was successful in selling them and he quickly opened a factory in San Antonio, Texas, to increase production. Fritos were the first commercially produced corn chips.

1934 The National Biscuit Company (later renamed Nabisco) test-marketed Ritz Crackers. They were so successful that the company released them nationally the following year.

Thomas Carvel, a salesman who sold ice cream at fairs and beach resorts, opened a retail ice cream shop in Hartsdale, New York. Carvel

Corporation franchised its operation after World War II and became a major East Coast ice cream chain.

1937 Vernon Rudolph launched Krispy Kreme doughnuts in Winston-Salem, North Carolina.

Margaret Rudkin of Fairfield, Connecticut began a small business baking preservative-free, whole-wheat bread. She named her business Pepperidge Farm.

1938 Herman W. Lay introduced Lay's potato chips; they became the best-selling potato chip in America.

1940 Sherb Noble, an ice cream store owner, acquired a Dairy Queen franchise and opened his first outlet in Joliet, Illinois. The soft-serve ice cream had been perfected by Alex McCullough and F. J. McCullough, owners of the Homemade Ice Cream Company in Green River, Illinois.

M&M's candy was introduced by Forrest Mars, the son of the founder of Mars, Inc., who had established a chocolate manufacturing company with Bruce Murrie, the son of the president of the Hershey Company. Because both of their last names started with M, they called their new company M&M. They named their first product after their company, which later merged with Mars, Inc.

1941–1945 During World War II, confectioners lobbied for candy to be declared "good for the troops," and M&M's became part of military rations, as were Tootsie Rolls, Wrigley's chewing gum, and Hershey bars.

1946 Irvine Robbins and his brother-in-law, Burt Baskin, formed a partnership to create Baskin-Robbins, which sold premium ice cream. As of 2005, there were about 2,500 Baskin-Robbins stores in the United States and a similar number in 50 other countries.

1948 Richard and Maurice McDonald created a radical new fast food operation in San Bernardino, California. The brothers created an efficient assembly line to make hamburgers and French fries, and it provided customers with fast, reliable, and inexpensive food. The brothers began franchising their operation in 1953. The following year, the McDonalds signed an agreement with Ray Kroc to franchise their operation nationally.

Harry and Esther Snyder launched their first In-N-Out Burger operation in Baldwin Park, California.

Verne H. Winchell founded Winchell's Donut House in Temple City, a suburb of Los Angeles, California. As of 2005, Winchell's Donut House had about 200 stores, mainly in Western states.

1950 Bill Rosenberg of Quincy, Massachusetts, changed the name of his doughnut shop to Dunkin' Donuts. He began franchising his operation in 1955.

Sugar Pops were introduced by the Kellogg Company (cereal makers had determined that children preferred sweet cereals). Other sugared cereals were soon released, including several by the Kellogg Company, and General Mills introduced Trix in 1954.

Jack in the Box was started by Robert O. Peterson in San Diego. As of 2005, Jack in the Box was the fifth-largest hamburger chain in America and had 1,670 outlets nationwide.

Leo Maranz went into partnership with Harry Axene in Chicago to create Tastee-Freez.

1952 Harlan Sanders, a restaurant owner in Corbin, Kentucky, sold his first Kentucky Fried Chicken franchise.

Hyman Kirsch introduced the first diet soft drinks, No-Cal ginger ale and root beer. Kirsch's success was followed by many other diet sodas, including Royal Crown Company's Diet Rite Cola; the Coca-Cola Company's Tab, and Diet Coke, Cadbury Schweppes's Diet 7-Up, and PepsiCo's Diet Pepsi.

Al Tunick founded Chicken Delight in Illinois. He decided to market his cooking method through small take-out stands and was the first fast food chain to offer home delivery. He began franchising his operation, and it grew quickly.

In 1952 George W. Church, Sr., a retired incubator salesman, conceived and launched Church's Fried Chicken to Go in downtown San Antonio, Texas. As of 2005, Church's had 1,334 outlets—100 in Mexico and the rest in the United States, where it is the third-largest chicken franchise chain.

1954 James McLamore and David R. Edgerton Jr., launched their first Insta-Burger-King outlet in Miami, Florida. They later acquired the company and change its name to Burger King. It became the second-largest hamburger fast food chain in the world.

M&M, Inc. introduced Peanut M&M's, which become the most popular confection in America.

1956 Carl's Jr. was launched by fast food pioneer Karl Karcher of Anaheim, California. In 2004, CKE Restaurants had more than 3,400 outlets.

Leo Stefanos, a candy store owner, invented the Dove Ice Cream Bar—ice cream dipped in rich chocolate. In 1985, Mars, Inc., acquired the Dove Bar brand and the following year began to market it nationally.

The first Sonic drive-in opened in Shawnee, Oklahoma. Today, there are almost 3,000 Sonic drive-ins across the United States; it is the only national fast food chain to retain carhops as an integral part of its operations.

1958 Frank Carney and his brother Dan opened a pizza parlor in Wichita, Kansas. Six months after the Carneys opened their first restaurant, they opened a second. Within a year there were six Pizza Hut outlets. The brothers began franchising Pizza Hut in 1959. Pizza Hut popularized pizza as a fast food in America.

Tang Breakfast Beverage Crystals was introduced nationally by General Foods Corporation, but did not become popular until the National Aeronautic and Space Administration (NASA) popularized it on their Gemini flights in 1965.

1959 The Frito Corn Chip company merged with Lay's, creating Frito-Lay, Inc., with headquarters in Dallas, Texas. The merged company continued to grow; six years later Frito-Lay merged with the Pepsi Cola Company, creating PepsiCo.

Mike and Marian Ilitch opened a small pizzeria, named Little Caesar's Pizza Treat, in Garden City, Michigan. The company is now the world's largest carry-out pizza chain. Little Caesar's ranks eleventh among restaurant chains in America.

Gennaro and Carmela Sbarro opened an Italian grocery store in Brooklyn, New York, that launched the Sbarro chain of Italian restaurants. As of 2005, Sbarro operated 960 restaurants in the United States and 26 other countries.

1960 Reuben Mattus formed a company to sell a premium ice cream, Häagen-Dazs. The brand was a success, and others imitated Mattus. By 2005, Häagen-Dazs was sold in 54 countries.

McKee Foods launched the Little Debbie pastry line, which started with an Oatmeal Creme Pie. As of 2005, Little Debbie cakes manufactured by McKee Foods were the best-selling cakes in America.

1961 Brothers Tom and James Monaghan purchased a Dominick's pizza store in Ypsilanti, Michigan. In 1965 Tom renamed the business Domino's Pizza. By 2006, the company expanded even more and currently has more than 8,000 outlets—5,000 in the United States and 3,000 in 50 other countries.

Ray Kroc bought out the McDonald brothers' hamburger franchise company and began a massive expansion of McDonald's operations. By 2006, there were more than 30,000 McDonald's outlets throughout the world.

John Galardi opened the first Wienerschnitzel hot dog stand in Newport Beach, California. Today it is the largest hot dog chain, with more than 360 outlets in the United States.

1962 Joseph, Ronald, Frances, and Joan Simek, owners of the Tombstone Bar in Medford, Wisconsin, began making small frozen pizzas (Tombstone Pizzas) in a small factory next to their tavern for distribution to local bars and taverns. Rose Totino of Totino's Italian Kitchen in Minneapolis claims to have also done this in the same year (Totino's Pizzas).

1963 Jean Nidetch and Albert and Felice Lippert formed Weight Watchers. Other weight-loss programs, such as the Weight Losers Institute, NutriSystem, and Jenny Craig, followed Weight Watcher's example.

Nabisco released Chips Ahoy!, currently America's best-selling chocolate chip cookie.

1964 Harland Sanders sold his Kentucky Fried Chicken franchise business to John Y. Brown and Jack Massey for $2 million. There were more than 600 franchises at that time. He became a spokesman and goodwill ambassador for Kentucky Fried Chicken, and the Col. Sanders image became synonymous with the company.

Pop-Tarts were introduced by the Kellogg Company. Pop-Tarts have a sugary filling sealed inside two layers of a pastry crust, which are thin enough to fit into toasters. Country Squares, a competitive product introduced by Post Cereals, failed to take off but Pop-Tarts sales were extremely successful. As of 2005, there were 32 flavors of Pop-Tarts.

The brothers Forrest and Leroy Raffel launched the first Arby's in Boardman, Ohio. It specialized in roast beef. Today, there are more than 3,400 Arby's restaurants worldwide.

Blimpie (subs and salads) was launched by Tony Conza, Peter DeCarlo, and Angelo Baldassare in Hoboken, New Jersey. As of 2004, there were almost 1,600 Blimpie locations across the United States and in more than 10 other countries.

1965 Frederick DeLuca of Bridgeport, Connecticut opened a sandwich shop in Milford, Connecticut. It would become Subway, which today has become the second-largest fast food franchise in the world with more than 24,000 locations in the United States and 82 other countries.

1966 Doritos, invented by Arch West, were launched by Frito-Lay, Inc. They were America's first commercial tortilla chip.

1969 Procter & Gamble introduced Pringles Potato Chips made from dehydrated and reconstituted potatoes. Pringles are cut into a uniform size and shape, allowing them to be packaged in a long tube.

Cadbury and Schweppes merged to form Cadbury Schweppes. As of 2005, Cadbury Schweppes was a leading global confectionery company, the world's second-largest manufacturer of chewing gum, and the world's third-largest soft drink company.

Dave Thomas opened the first Wendy's (hamburgers and chicken) outlet in Columbus, Ohio. In 1970, Thomas began expanding his operation in other cities in Ohio. In 1972, the first out-of-state Wendy's was opened in Indianapolis, Indiana. Wendy's went from nine outlets in 1972 to 1,818 six years later.

Long John Silver's Fish 'n' Chips was launched by Jerrico, Inc. of Lexington, Kentucky. In 2005, it was the largest fast food fish chain in America.

1971 The Center for Science in the Public Interest (CSPI) was formed in Washington, D.C. It is one of America's most influential consumer advocate organizations.

1972 Al Copeland opened a fast food (chicken and biscuits) restaurant called Popeyes in New Orleans, Louisiana. Popeyes has more than 1,800 restaurants in the United States and 27 international markets.

1975 Wally Amos opened the Amos Chocolate Cookie Company on Hollywood's Sunset Boulevard, Los Angeles, California. Today, sales of Famous Amos cookies are reported at about $100 million per year.

El Pollo Loco began as a roadside chicken stand in Guasave on Mexico's Pacific Coast. In 1980, it opened first outlet in the United States in Los Angeles, California. As of 2005, the company had 330 outlets in Arizona, California, Illinois, Nevada, and Texas.

1977 Plastic soda bottles made with polyethylene terephthalate (PET) were invented by Nathan Wyeth, who worked for DuPont Corp. Previously, soda beverages stored in plastic exploded. Wyeth developed a stronger system of molding plastic, enabling DuPont to produce a light, clear, and resilient bottle.

Nolan Bushnell created Chuck E. Cheese's Pizza Time Theatre, the first of which opened in San Jose, California. As of 2005, there were 498 Chuck E. Cheese outlets, which operate in 48 states and 4 countries.

Debbi Fields opened a cookie store in Palo Alto, California. Mrs. Fields Cookies began franchising in 1990; as of 2005, the company has more than 700 locations in 11 countries.

1978 Ben Cohen and Jerry Greenfield opened Ben & Jerry's Homemade Ice Cream and Crêpes in South Burlington, Vermont. In August 2000, Ben & Jerry's was purchased by the Unilever conglomerate.

1980 7-Eleven, the world's largest convenience store operation, began selling 32-ounce Big Gulp beverages; at that time it was the biggest beverage cup on the market. In 1988, 7-Eleven introduced the giant 64-ounce Double Gulp. It was the first retailer to introduce self-serve fountain drinks and today it sells almost 33 million gallons of fountain drinks annually worldwide.

People for the Ethical Treatment of Animals (PETA) was founded and today has a membership of 850,000. PETA members regularly campaign for animal rights and attack fast food chains for their treatment of animals before and during slaughter.

1981 The first Quiznos Sub restaurant was opened in Denver, Colorado. By 2004 the chain had more than 3,000 outlets in the United States and 15 other nations.

1985 Rick Rosenfield and Larry Flax opened the first California Pizza Kitchen (CPK) in Beverly Hills, California. CPK created unusual-flavored pizzas, such as its BBQ Chicken, that differed greatly from traditional American pizza.

1992 The U.S. Department of Agriculture released a Food Guide Pyramid which recommended a hierarchal—and therefore controversial—dietary pattern based on breads, cereals, rice, pasta, fruits and vegetables, and dairy products. It also recommended that consumption of high-fat processed meats be limited and that only two to three servings of meat, poultry, fish, beans, eggs, and nuts be consumed daily.

1993 Max Shondor, a Florida-based natural food restaurateur, introduced soy-based Boca Burgers; he subsequently expanded his line to include other flavors as well as meatless breakfast patties and nuggets. Similar products are now sold in some fast food chains.

1997 Tricon Global Restaurants, Inc., a PepsiCo spin-off, was created to manage fast food chains, including Kentucky Fried Chicken, Pizza Hut, and Taco Bell. In 2002, Tricon announced the acquisition of Long John Silver's and A&W All-American Food. Tricon changed its name to Yum! Brands, Inc. in 2003.

2005 The U.S. Department of Agriculture released MyPyramid, based on its revised Dietary Guidelines for Americans. MyPyramid recommends twelve different food pyramids based upon age, sex, and physical activity.

2006 After extensive pressure from consumer groups, the three major soft drink companies, Coca-Cola, PepsiCo, and Cadbury Schweppes agreed to ban sweet sodas from sale in schools.

A

A&W Root Beer Roy Allen, who refurbished old hotels, met a pharmacist who had perfected a recipe for making **root beer**. Allen bought the recipe and on June 20, 1919, opened a root beer stand in Lodi, California, offering frosty mugs of root beer for a nickel. Shortly thereafter, he opened more stands in Stockton and Sacramento, one of which may have been a **drive-in**. In 1920, Frank Wright, an employee at the Stockton stand, became Allen's partner; they combined their initials and called the company A&W Root Beer. Additional A&W stands were opened throughout California, Utah, and Texas. Allen eventually bought out Wright, trademarked the A&W Root Beer logo (a bull's eye and arrow), and began to **franchise** the **chain**; thus, A&W became one of the first **fast food** franchise chains in the country. Franchisees paid a small licensing fee, displayed the A&W logo, and bought root beer syrup from Allen. Other than these connections, little commonality existed among franchisees—no common **architecture**, no common **menu**, and no common procedures or national **advertising**.

Some A&W Root Beer franchises began selling food, including **hamburgers** and **hot dogs**, along with root beer. Some early A&W Root Beer stands were drive-ins, featuring tray-boys and tray-girls, later renamed **carhops**, who brought orders to customers in their cars outside.

The Depression affected franchises differently. Some went out of business, but others opened more new stands. In 1933, A&W had 170 outlets; by 1941, it had 260 stands nationwide. The war years between 1941 and 1945, on the other hand, were a very difficult time for A&W. There were labor shortages and **sugar** shortages, and by the time the war ended many franchises had closed. After the war, however, A&W rapidly expanded. During the 1950s, Roy Allen sold the business to a Nebraskan, Gene Hurtz, who formed the A&W Root Beer Company. Within ten years, the number of A&W outlets had increased to more than 2,000. In 1956, an A&W Root Beer outlet opened in Canada, followed by Guam and the Philippines.

A&W went through many ownership changes beginning in 1960, when the chain was sold to the J. Hungerford Smith Company, which had manufactured the concentrate for the soda almost since the beginning. Three years later, both companies were sold to the United Fruit Company (later renamed United Brands Company). Within United Brands, the company changed its name to A&W International. In 1971, United Brands formed A&W Beverages, Inc., and test-marketed A&W Root Beer in bottles and cans in California and

A&W Root Beer. © Kelly Fitzsimmons

Arizona. The product was well-received and was subsequently distributed nationally, along with sugar-free, low-sodium, and caffeine-free versions. In 1974 the company introduced its **mascot**, The Great Root Bear.

In 1975, franchisees formed the National Advisory Council of the National A&W Franchisees Association (NAWFA), which was the first time that franchisees had a voice in the formation of their contract. A standard menu for each restaurant was created in 1978. The new A&W Great Food Restaurants included salad bars and **ice cream** bars, among many other innovations. At the same time, A&W Restaurants, Inc., a wholly owned restaurant franchise subsidiary, was formed.

A. Alfred Taubman, the shopping mall and real estate tycoon, purchased A&W Restaurants, Inc. in 1982, and he opened new franchises in malls and shopping centers. The company also began expanding its operation to include A&W Hot Dogs and More restaurants. By the mid-1980s, the company had expanded its operations into several Southeast Asian countries, with an office in Malaysia serving as the headquarters of A&W's international operations. In October, 1993, A&W Beverages, Inc. became part of Cadbury Beverages, Inc. Today, the A&W Beverages continues under the ownership of Plano, Texas-based Dr Pepper/Seven Up, Inc., the largest non-cola soft drink enterprise in North America and the largest subsidiary of London-based **Cadbury Schweppes**.

In 1994, A&W Restaurants, Inc. was purchased by Sagittarius Acquisitions, Inc., which in 1999 merged with **Long John Silver's** to form the Yorkshire Global Restaurants based in Lexington, Kentucky. By 2001, A&W had 970 restaurants (780 in the United States and 190 in other countries), and 121 joint establishments with Long John Silver's. Tricon Global Restaurants (later renamed **Yum! Brands, Inc.**) acquired A&W Restaurants in 2002.

SUGGESTED READING: A&W Root Beer Web site: www.awrootbeer.com/hist_hist.htm; Anne Cooper Funderburg, *Sundae Best: A History of Soda Fountains* (Bowling Green, OH: Bowling Green State University Popular Press, 2002); John A. Jakle and Keith A. Sculle, *Fast Food: Roadside Restaurants in the Automobile Age* (Baltimore: Johns Hopkins University Press, 1999); Philip Langdon, *Orange Roofs, Golden Arches: The Architecture of American Chain Restaurants* (New York: Knopf, 1986).

Advertising In the early days of commercial food production, virtually all such foods were little-known outside their place of origin. To increase sales, manufacturers needed to advertise. Before companies could advertise their products, they needed an attractive name and visually appealing **packaging** with trademarks, icons, and colorful designs.

The first food company to package and nationally advertise its product was the American Cereal Company, which made Quaker Oats. Although the company was unrelated to the Quaker religion, it trademarked the name and created the icon of a male Quaker, which was placed on boxes of the **cereal**. The company ran special trains with advertising signs on the sides of the train cars and with men dressed as Quakers giving away free samples. The company invented the notion of premiums, which were placed in the box. The National Biscuit Company, the forerunner of Nabisco, used similar tactics with its national promotion of Uneeda Biscuits in 1898.

Similar promotions would be employed by subsequent **junk food** manufacturers, such as the Cracker Jack Company. The company applied for a trademark on the name **Cracker Jack** on February 17, 1896. Thirty-six days later the trademark was issued. Shortly thereafter, manufacturer launched promotional and marketing campaigns in Chicago, soon followed by New York and Philadelphia. In each of these cities, the manufacturer placed advertisements in newspapers, announcing that Cracker Jack was a new confection, not yet six months old, that "made the most instantaneous success of anything ever introduced." It was called the "1896 sensation," along with its **slogan** "The More You Eat the More You Want." From Chicago, where the Cracker Jack was produced, the company shipped tons of the confection by train to each city. More advertisements reported that Cracker Jack was "the greatest seller of its kind." The company continued to advertise, claiming that their product was "a healthful, nourishing food-confection" and that it was the "standard **popcorn** confection" by which all others were judged. It began placing toys in every box and it became, as its 1913 advertisement proclaimed, "the world's most famous confection." By 1937 the Cracker Jack Company declared itself the producer of "America's oldest, best known and most popular confection."

Advertising campaigns to sell Cracker Jack were so successful that they encouraged others to invent new confections, and they engaged in advertising campaigns similar to those developed by Cracker Jack—using toys to target children, claiming healthful contents of the junk food, and creating grand slogans; these all became common in the advertising of fast food and junk food manufacturers.

Other manufacturers went in for dramatic stunts. For instance, Otto Y. Schnering of Chicago, inventor of the **Baby Ruth** candy bar in 1920, was extremely successful because of his unusual promotions. He chartered an airplane and dropped the candy bars by parachute over the city of Pittsburgh. He later expanded his drops to cities in more than 40 states. At the same time, the company launched a promotional campaign that placed four-color advertisements in national magazines. These proclaimed that Baby Ruth was the "sweetest story ever told" and that it was "the world's most popular candy." Promotional stunts became less effective when **radio** became popular in the late 1920s.

Most junk food companies advertised extensively to promote their products. An exception was America's largest **chocolate** company, the **Hershey Company**, which stopped advertising during the 1930s to save money during the Depression. During World War II, chocolate was rationed and was mainly sent to American armed forces. However, Hershey's competition advertised extensively after the war. For instance, **Mars, Inc.**, the maker of **M&M's**, started with radio spots, billboards, and standard promotional print ads in national newspapers and magazines; sales increased to $3 million by 1949. In 1950 the company hired Ted Bates & Co., an advertising firm in Chicago, to help figure out how to market its products, while the Hershey Company saw no need for marketing at all. The M&M's slogan "Melts in your mouth, not in your hands" was an instant success, and the cartoon characters Mr. Plain and **Mr. Peanut** were added in 1954. When Mars's advertising began to cut into Hershey's profits in the 1970s, Hershey's finally decided to begin advertising again. One of Hershey's greatest advertising successes came in 1981, when Universal Studios approached Mars, Inc., to use M&M's in its movie, *ET, The Extra-Terrestrial.* Mars turned Universal Studios down, and Universal approached Hershey's, which produced Reese's Pieces. Universal and Hershey's came to an agreement in which Reese's Pieces were used in the movie and Hershey agreed to promote *ET* with $1 million worth of promotions. When the movie was released, sales of Reese's Pieces skyrocketed. Today, junk food manufacturers spend billions of dollars on advertising, much of it targeted at children.

Fast Food

During the 1920s, **White Castle**, the first **fast food chain**, advertised in newspapers. It was slow to value radio advertising but did have promotions on radio during the 1930s. Most of its advertising was targeted at working class. This changed during the 1950s, when White Castle sponsored a children's television show, *The Cactus and Randy Show.*

McDonald's did little national advertising in the 1950s. In 1959, a Minneapolis McDonald's operator, Jim Zein, began running radio advertisements and his sales skyrocketed. Based on this success, **Ray Kroc** encouraged other franchisees and managers to launch their own campaigns. Following this directive, two Washington, D.C., franchisees, John Gibson and Oscar Goldstein, began sponsoring a children's **television** show, called *Bozo's Circus*. This resulted in the creation of **Ronald McDonald**, the McDonald's corporate clown icon who appeared on local Washington, D.C. television commercials beginning in 1963. During the following year, he appeared on national television on Thanksgiving. The company has regularly used Ronald McDonald its advertising campaigns and, like the Quaker Oats man, people dressed as Ronald McDonald make personal appearances throughout the nation. According to *Advertising Age*, Ronald McDonald is the second-best American advertising icon of the twentieth century. Through extensive advertising, McDonald's became the nation's largest fast food chain during the 1970s.

Led by McDonald's, all national fast food chains have engaged in extensive television advertising campaigns. McDonald's campaign slogan "You Deserve a Break Today" was selected as the best advertising campaign of the twentieth century by *Advertising Age*. Other significant advertising campaigns have included **Burger King**'s "Burger King, Home of the Whopper" and "Have It Your Way," and **Wendy's** "Where's the Beef?"

Soft Drinks

Soft drink companies, such as the **Coca-Cola Company**, **PepsiCo**, and **Dr Pepper/** Seven Up, Inc., engaged in massive advertising through billboards and print sources, such as newspapers and magazines, during the early twentieth century. Today, soft drink manufacturers spend billions of dollars annually on advertising. In the United States alone, these marketing efforts generated more than $57 billion in sales in 2004. Coca-Cola paid the Boys & Girls Clubs of America $60 million in 1998 to market its brand exclusively in over 2,000 facilities, and ads selling soft drinks now run on Channel One, the commercial television network with programming shown in classrooms almost every day to eight million middle, junior, and high **school** students. These companies place advertisements in prominent locations in schools—on school buses, on posters in hallways, and on calendars, book covers, and even mouse pads. Teenagers drink twice as much carbonated **soda** as milk; as a result only 19 percent of girls get the recommended amount of calcium. PepsiCo's campaign "Pepsi-Cola Hits the Spot" was rated by *Advertising Age* as the second-most successful advertising campaign of the twentieth century.

Marketing to Children

Children have been targeted by junk food and soda manufacturers since the early twentieth century. The Cracker Jack Company, for instance, inserted toys in their product boxes, and gum manufacturers placed baseball and other sports cards in their packages.

Television greatly expanded the ability of advertisers to reach children. Children are more vulnerable to commercials, which they view less critically than adults. Children's programs, especially on Saturday mornings, meant that advertisers could market directly to the age group of their choice. By the 1960s, advertisers had identified children as a separate market, and fast food chains joined junk food and soda companies in targeting children. Today, the average American child sees more than 10,000 food advertisements (most related to junk food, fast food, and soda) each year on television. In a 1996 study, Sue Dibbs counted more than 200 junk food advertisements in just one Saturday morning's set of cartoon shows.

In addition to television advertising, fast food chains also created child-oriented characters, such as Ronald McDonald, and began offering meals made especially for children, such as **Happy Meals** with toys and the creation of playgrounds for children. Chains then acquired endorsements from prominent sports, movie, and television figures. Finally, the companies developed movie **tie-ins** and made special arrangements with theme parks such as Disneyland, which has had a long history of selling fast food and junk food. **Frito-Lay** sponsors park attractions, such as the steel roller coaster ride California Screamin at Disneyland and Cracker Jack Stadium at Disney's Wide World of Sports complex in Orlando, Florida.

Fast food, junk food, and soft drink companies advertise their products in a variety of other ways, as well. The Munchkin Bottling Company has soft drink logos placed on baby bottles. There are spin-off products such as lunch boxes and clothing, and many companies sponsor kids' clubs.

Children themselves have little buying power but they do have pester power. Busy parents simply take the easy way out and give in to children's constant pestering. In addition, advertisers believe that childhood experiences will be remembered throughout a lifetime. Brand loyalty begins early in life.

Due to the effectiveness of advertising targeted at children, several countries, including Sweden, have banned advertisements on television and radio programs targeted at children under the age of 12. Belgium has prohibited commercials during children's programs and Australia has banned advertisements during television programming targeted at preschoolers. Calls for similar bans in the United States have regularly been put forth.

SUGGESTED READING: Amanda Barnett-Rhodes, "Sugar Coated Ads and High Calorie Dreams: The Impact of Junk Food Ads on Brand Recognition of Preschool Children," Master's thesis, University of Vermont, 2002; Sue Dibb, *A Spoonful of Sugar. Television Foos Advertising Aimed at Children: an International Comparative Study* (London, UK, Consumers International 1996); Thomas Hine, *The Total Package: The Evolution and Secret Meanings of Boxes, Bottles, Cans, and Tubes* (New York: Little, Brown and Company, 1995); Steve Roden and Dan Goodsell, *Krazy Kid's Food! Vintage Food Graphics* (Köln, Germany: Taschen, 2002); Jackson Lears, *Fables of Abundance: A Cultural History of Advertising in America* (New York: Basic Books, HarperCollins, 1994).

AFC Enterprises In 1989, **Popeyes** acquired **Church's Chicken**. Four years later, America's Favorite Chicken Company, was created as the parent company for both restaurant **chains**. Its name was subsequently changed to AFC Enterprises, Inc. In 2004, AFC operated 3,896 restaurants, bakeries, and cafés in the United States, Puerto Rico, and 30 other countries using the brand names Church's Chicken, **Cinnabon**, Chicken & Biscuits, Popeyes, Seattle's Best Coffee, and Torrefazione Italia Coffee. In 2004, the Atlanta-based Arcapita Inc., bought Church's Chicken from AFC Enterprises, Inc., which also sold Cinnabon and Seattle's Best Coffee to Focus Brands, Inc.

SUGGESTED READING: AFC Enterprises Web site: www.afce.com

American Junk Food and Fast Food in Other Countries **Junk food** and soft drink manufacturers moved into other countries as quickly as possible. America's first commercial junk food, **Cracker Jack**, for instance, was introduced into the United Kingdom in 1897 and into Canada in 1901. Planters Peanuts opened its first international facility in Canada and the United Kingdom during the Depression. In 1932, **Forrest Mars**, the son of the founder of **Mars, Inc.**, opened a factory in Slough, England, and rapidly expanded into Europe. After World War II the company expanded throughout the world.

Soda manufactures followed a similar pattern. **Coca-Cola** was exported to the United Kingdom in 1909, and the company began bottling operations in other countries. After the fall of the Berlin Wall in 1989, the Coca-Cola Company began to invest heavily in Eastern Europe. Coca-Cola was a relatively neutral import to China and today it is the favorite drink of Chinese children. As the twentieth century closed, Coca-Cola had begun to construct many new bottling facilities in Africa. PepsiCo was much slower to internationalize. PepsiCo opened operations in Japan and Eastern Europe in 1966 and in the Soviet Union in 1974, thanks to Vice President Richard Nixon, who visited Moscow in 1959 and introduced the Soviet leader to Pepsi-Cola. Today, Coca-Cola and PepsiCo, the two largest soft drink companies in the world, manufacture hundreds of different soft drink brands, which are sold in every country in the world with the exception of North Korea.

Fast Food

American **fast food chains** typically first opened their first non-U.S. operations in Canada and then launched outlets in other countries. **Dairy Queen** opened its first Canadian outlet in 1953. It was followed by many others, such as **A&W Root Beer** (1956), **Chicken Delight** (1958), **McDonald's** (1967), and **Shakey's** (1968).

After World War II, Germany was occupied by American military forces. It was one of the first European nations to become a target for American fast food chains. A&W Root Beer opened an outlet in Germany in 1962, followed by McDonald's (1971) When the Berlin Wall fell in 1989, McDonald's rushed into the former East Germany. Today, Ronald McDonald is commonly known throughout Germany. Only German potatoes and beef are used in their outlets. McDonald's has co-branded with Wal-Mart Stores, Inc. and now has outlets in the Wal-Mart stores. Germany became one of the McDonald's most successful operations.

Since Japan was also occupied by American armed forces it was relatively easy for American fast food operations to open outlets in Japan. **Kentucky Fried Chicken** and **Dunkin' Donuts** opened their first Japanese **franchises** in 1970, followed by Dairy Queen (1971), McDonald's (1971), **Church's Chicken** (1979) and **Arby's** (1981). The convenience store chain **7-Eleven** opened its first store in Japan in 1974. Today, there are more than

11,000 7-Eleven stores in Japan—6,000 more than there are in the United States. When China opened up to fast food operations, Kentucky Fried Chicken was the first American fast food chain to open outlets there, and today it is the most-recognized foreign brand in China, more so than Coca-Cola, **Nestlé SA**, and McDonald's. When the McDonald's restaurant opened in Beijing, thousands of people waited in line for hours to eat there. American fast food operations have also expanded throughout Latin America. In Brazil, McDonald's is the nation's largest employer.

The Middle East and Africa have also seen the growth of fast food chains. McDonald's, for instance, had only 11 outlets in these regions in 1991; by 2001, there were 546 outlets. Much of the growth in the Middle East occurred shortly after the end of the Gulf War in 1991. For instance, when McDonald's opened an outlet in Kuwait, the line of cars waiting to drive through was seven miles long. When a Kentucky Fried Chicken outlet opened in the city of Mecca, it grossed $200,000 during a single week. Despite these frequently repeated statistics, fast food represents a very different lifestyle than many Muslims in the Middle East want, as Benjamin R. Barber pointed out in his thoughtful *Jihad vs. McWorld* (1996).

Localization

To attract people in other countries to their establishments, McDonald's and other fast food operations have offered variations on the American **menu**. Espresso and cold pasta are offered in Italy. McHuevos (poached eggs in buns) are sold in Uruguay. Frankfurters (large sausages) are offered at McDonald's in Germany. **Vegetarian** burgers are offered in the Netherlands and India, and McLaks (salmon **sandwiches**) are offered in Norway. This process of localization has been very successful. Today, there are more than 1,000 McDonald's restaurants in Germany and Japan, and the number of restaurants in China and other Asian countries is rapidly expanding. By 1994, McDonald's generated more revenue from non-U.S. sales than from American outlets. Today, there are 30,000 McDonald's outlets worldwide. More than half—17,000—are outside the United States.

It is not just the menus that have been localized, but also procedures. McDonald's outlets in other countries do not necessarily follow American fast food patterns. In Rio de Janeiro, for example, waiters serve food with champagne in candle-lit restaurants; in Caracas, Venezuela, hostesses seat customers, take orders, and deliver meals; and in South Korea McDonald's employees seat customers at tables occupied by others during crowded times.

Attraction to American Fast Food

There are a number of reasons why American fast food operations have been so successful in other countries. In other countries, fast food outlets appeal particularly to the busy, upwardly mobile middle classes. Customers are attracted to their **efficiency**, reliability, predictability, cleanliness, and public toilets. Then again, American-style fast food outlets are less expensive than other food establishments in many countries. Finally, customers flock to American fast food operations because of their association with the United States. Fast food is considered an exotic American import in many countries, at least during its first few years of being offered. Fast food outlets also symbolize safety, convenience, fun, familiarity, sanctuary, modernity, culinary tourism, and connectedness to the world.

To many people throughout the world, American fast food represents affluence and innovation, and reflects what is considered the good life of the United States. To critics, these same chains represent the bloated lifestyle in the United States and American domination of the world.

SUGGESTED READING: Benjamin R. Barber, *Jihad vs. McWorld* (New York: Ballantine Books, 1996); George Cohon, *To Russia with Fries* (Toronto: McFarlane, 1997); Bert Fragner, "The Meyhane or McDonald's? Changes in Eating Habits and the Evolution of Fast Food in Istanbul," in Sami Zubaida and Richard Tapper, *Culinary Cultures of the Middle East* (New York: I. B. Tauris, 1994); Sidney Mintz, "Fast Food Nation: What the All-American Meal Is Doing to the World," *Times Literary Supplement* (September 14, 2001: 7–9); Tony Royle, *Working for McDonald's in Europe: The Unequal Struggle?* (New York: Routledge, 2001); Tony Royle and Brian Towers, *Labour Relations in the Global Fast Food Industry* (New York: Routledge, 2002); James L. Watson, ed. *Golden Arches East: McDonald's in East Asia* (Stanford, CA: Stanford University Press, 1997); Er Yu, "Foreign Fast Foods Gobble up Chinese-Style Fast Foods," *Chinese Sociology & Anthropology* 31 (Summer 1999): 80–87.

Animal Rights Movement Concern for the humane treatment of animals was heightened in 1824 when the first organization dedicated to the prevention of cruelty to animals was founded in London. It later became the Royal Society for the Prevention of Cruelty to Animals. It encouraged the enforcement of existing laws and **lobbied** for the passage of new laws for the humane treatment of animals. In the United States, The American Society for the Prevention of Cruelty to Animals was launched in 1866; local humane societies care for abandoned and stray animals. Throughout the twentieth century, local humane societies have encouraged the proper care of animals, opposed cruelty to animals, and provided shelters for stray or unwanted animals.

Animal rights came to the cultural forefront in the United States in the 1970s, when many new organizations focusing on specific aspects of animal welfare and animal rights emerged. These diverse groups campaign against the production and use of animals for fur, trapping, hunting, whaling, the killing of dolphins in the fishing industry, and the display of animals in zoos and aquariums. The largest animal rights organization is the People for the Ethical Treatment of Animals (PETA), founded in 1980, which has membership of 850,000.

In 2004, PETA released a video taken at Pilgrim's Pride, a **Kentucky Fried Chicken** supplier in West Virginia. The video depicted animal cruelty. Pilgrim's Pride fired several employees and began a workforce **training** program to prevent animal cruelty in the future. Another victory for animal rights groups was when **McDonald's**, in 2000, made a policy decision to purchase its eggs only from poultry producers who adopt more humane production practices.

Many animal rights organizations are opposed to the **fast food** industry and the meatpacking industry that supports it. Some animal rights advocates are also **vegetarians** who oppose the consumption of all meat, poultry, fish, and seafood, which are the mainstays of the fast food industry.

SUGGESTED READING: Harold D. Guither, *Animal Rights: History and Scope of a Radical Social Movement* (Carbondale, IL: Southern Illinois University Press, 1998); Tina Volpe, *The Fast Food Craze: Wreaking Havoc on Our Bodies and Our Animals* (Kagel Canyon, CA: Canyon Publishing 2005); People for the Ethical Treatment of Animals Web site: www.peta.org

Anti-unionization An important reason for the financial success of **fast food** operations has been the fact that their labor costs are low. Most workers are part-time employees who are paid hourly wages without medical or other benefits. At most **chains**, employee wages are set by local managers according to local laws and conditions. Managers are encouraged to keep labor costs down and some companies have rewarded managers with a bonus when they have reduced employee wages. This sometimes has led to abuse. Some managers, for instance, have required employees to work "off the clock" if they wished to retain their jobs. In this way, outlets do not have to pay overtime wages. This practice is, of course, against the law, but many employees (who are often teenagers, recent immigrants, or others in desperate need of a job) are too timid to challenge such illegal practices.

Despite these conditions, labor unions have yet to succeed in organizing workers in the fast food industry. A major reason for this failure has been the anti-union activities of fast food executives.

As Eric Schlosser notes in his book ***Fast Food Nation*** (2001), it has been almost impossible for unions to gain a foothold in the fast food industry. The high turnover rates of employees at fast food chains, the part-time nature of the work, the low economic status of fast food workers, and the decentralized way that fast food chains have established wages have made it difficult to organize workers. Schlosser also reports that chains have gone to extraordinary lengths to keep labor unions from organizing workers at their outlets. During the 1970s, **McDonald's**, for instance, sent a so-called flying squad of experienced managers and corporate executive to outlets where union activity was suspected. To prevent unionization, employees may be forced to take lie detector tests administered by the company; if workers refuse, they can be fired. Other outlets have been closed down rather than permit union participation to be ratified. In Germany, McDonald's has fired employees who sympathize with unions. Other chains have followed similar tactics, and labor unions have yet to make a breakthrough in a major fast food chain.

SUGGESTED READING: Tony Royle and Brian Towers, *Labour Relations in the Global Fast Food Industry* (New York: Routledge, 2002); Eric Schlosser, *Fast Food Nation: The Dark Side of the All-American Meal* (New York: Houghton Mifflin, 2001); Stuart Tannock, *Youth at Work: The Unionized Fast-food and Grocery Workplace* (Philadelphia: Temple University Press, 2001).

Arby's In 1949, Forrest Raffel and his younger brother Leroy of Youngstown, Ohio, bought their uncle's restaurant equipment business, which they renamed Raffel Brothers, Inc. While engaged in designing and building foodservice facilities, the Raffels analyzed **fast food** establishments and concluded that there was a niche in the market for an upscale, nonhamburger fast food **chain**. They decided that roast beef **sandwiches** would be an ideal centerpiece for a new fast food chain. Their first choice for a name for their new restaurant was Big Tex, but that name was already taken. Instead, they spelled out the initials of Raffel Brothers (RB) to produce Arby's.

In 1964, the Raffels launched the first Arby's in Boardman, Ohio. Their chuckwagon-style buildings, their giant 10-gallon hat sign, and their natural wood and stone décor evoked the Old West. The original **menu** offered 69-cent roast beef sandwiches, **potato chips**, and iced tea. Their menu was later expanded to include other food items and **beverages**. In 1991, for instance, the chain introduced a light (diet) menu, including seven meals under 300 calories. The brothers **franchised** their first operation within a year of opening their initial establishment.

Arby's charged more for their food items than did their fast food **hamburger** competitors, and they also created a more luxurious interior. The company hoped to attract more affluent customers. Their success encouraged other fast food chains to begin to target upscale customers. **Burger King** and **McDonald's**, for example, expanded their menus (introducing more costly items) and began to create more pleasant eating environments.

In 1976 the **Royal Crown Cola** Company of Atlanta, Georgia, purchased the Arby's business. The first overseas Arby's opened in Tokyo in 1981 and by 1988 there were more than 2,000 Arby's outlets worldwide. Today, there are more than 3,400 Arby's restaurants worldwide. In 1996, the company purchased TJ Cinnamons Classic Bakery, which specialized in **breakfast** foods, snacks, and desserts. The first dual-branded Arby's/TJ Cinnamons restaurant opened in 1997.

SUGGESTED READING: John A. Jakle and Keith A. Sculle, *Fast Food: Roadside Restaurants in the Automobile Age* (Baltimore: Johns Hopkins University Press, 1999); Philip Langdon, *Orange Roofs, Golden Arches: The Architecture of American Chain Restaurants* (New York: Knopf, 1986); Arby's Web site: www.arbys.com

Architecture and Design Prior to the early twentieth century, restaurants were embedded within larger structures, such as hotels, or they were freestanding buildings that were similar in appearance to surrounding structures. In small towns, everyone knew where the restaurants were. In larger towns and cities, they were easy to spot when people walked or rode horses down streets.

The arrival of the **automobile** altered the structure of certain restaurants. With automobiles, Americans were able to travel more easily to other communities, and they did so at a much faster speed. To attract drivers, **chain** restaurants needed to be highly visible; their architecture was used to **advertise** the chain. This meant creating distinctive architecture that could easily been seen as being different from surrounding buildings. This required large signs and places for cars to park.

To attract attention of passing motorists, **drive-ins** needed a new type of architecture to stand out. Unusual designs, such as those appearing to be windmills, teapots, barrels, castles, oranges, derbies, milk cans, cartons, and **ice cream** cones, predominated. Some were A-frame construction; some had zigzag roofs; and still others had golden arches and large doughnuts. Many were topped with towers and flashing signs. In addition, many structures sported bright neon lights so they would be easily visible at night, and bright colors so they would be easily seen during the day.

At first, these new, outlandish structures provided entertainment for those viewing them. Yet it soon became apparent that most were of flimsy construction to keep costs down, many had dirt driveways and unpaved parking areas, and all lacked landscaping. Many placed large signs on top of or in front of their establishments. By the 1920s, tens of thousands of such stands crowded cities and highways, particularly at crossroads. With stiff competition, chain restaurants needed even more outlandish designs, signs, and gimmicks.

Stiff competition also encouraged the lowering of prices to attract customers. Lower prices dictated the types of food that could be served. Whereas extensive **menus** required large quantities of raw materials and storage space, limited menus kept ordering to a minimum. Various foods were served but the heart of the menu was food that could be prepared easily, quickly, and cheaply. **Chicken** and **hamburgers**, for example, required little space for preparation, and specialization kept required equipment to a minimum. Less equipment and limited menus had another advantage: employees needed a minimum of **training**. Faster service also meant that more customers could be served, prices could be lowered, and profits could be increased. Customers would not have to wait long, the turnover would be rapid, and the eating areas could be smaller.

The predecessors of **fast food** chains—diners, cafeterias, automats, and other restaurants—could be located in almost any type of building and their architectures were diverse. **White Castle** made a major break with this diverse architectural tradition by requiring that all their outlets be constructed exactly the same way. The first White Castle outlets had seats for only three customers and the buildings themselves were only 10-foot by 15-foot rectangles. Their unusual castle-like structures were easily spotted by passersby. The inside and outside of the outlets were predominately white in color; this was intended to reassure customers than the food served at White Castles was safe. To reinforce this message, employees were instructed to regularly clean the inside to ensure a spotless environment. In addition, the outlets were configured in such a way that customers could watch their food being prepared. The reasons for these innovations had much to do the deep concern many Americans had about the safety of hamburger and the quality of food served outside the home. The 1906 publication of Upton Sinclair's *The Jungle*, which describes in nauseating details the conditions in the meatpacking plants—including dead rates being ground into sausage—outraged the public and made them fearful about what ground meat contained. By the end of the 1920s, other fast food chains made similar efforts to appear sanitary and convince customers that their food was safe to eat. Chain restaurants also began to follow the principle of chain-wide architectural uniformity.

This model was improved upon by Maurice and Richard McDonald, who created another architectural model after World War II. By the late 1940s, the limitations of drive-in restaurants had become apparent. Teenagers lingered at drive-ins and scared away older customers. **Carhops** were often more interested in socializing than in selling food. In addition, the brothers were interested in reducing employees to a minimum to reduce expenses and increase profits. They designed a new type of drive-in where customers ordered and picked up food at a window and ate the food in their car or took it off the premises. They constructed a few picnic tables and uncomfortable chairs for the walk-up trade or for those who did not want to eat in their cars, but their goal was to discouraging loitering. The McDonald brothers did not want customers to stay long; hence, newspaper boxes, candy machines, telephones, pinball machines, cigarette machines, jukeboxes, and other similar entertainments were prohibited. In addition, **McDonald's** outlets were designed with a considerable amount of glass on the front, giving customers the ability to watch the preparation of the food.

The McDonald brothers carefully designed the inside of the building so that their limited menu—hamburgers, **French fries**, **sodas**, and **milk shakes**—could be efficiently made and distributed to customers. The outside of the building was also revolutionary. It included a slanted roof with two golden arches protruding through the roof. Parking lots were constructed so that customers could eat their orders on the premises but would not be served by carhops. During the 1950s and early 1960s, this design typified all of their outlets. McDonald's began to reconsider its "one size fits all" design in 1964 when its first outlet in downtown Washington, D.C., opened. Inner-city fast food outlets needed tables and chairs for customers, and there was little room for parking lots. McDonald's began a period of experimentation in its architectural design.

Other fast food chains developed their own designs. **Arby's** used natural woods and stone walls with an Old West décor. At first, **Kentucky Fried Chicken** (KFC) used existing buildings, merely adding KFC signs and the likeness of the honorary colonel. In 1953, a new, uniform structure was adopted, although this did not become standardized in the chain until 1966. **Wienerschnitzel** used A-frames with a hole in the center to permit drive-thru windows. In addition, fast food chains developed mascots that were usually constructed outside. Bob's **Big Boy**, for instance, placed an 8-foot statue of the "big boy" outside of its restaurants, dressed in red-and-white checked overalls and carrying aloft a triple-decker burger. McDonald's put Speedee on its single-arched sign and later created **Ronald McDonald**. **Burger King** created a little king and **Pizza Hut** promoted an Italian chef tossing dough in the air.

By the mid-1960s, the novelty of eating in the car had worn off. Burger King was the chain that challenged the traditional McDonald's architectural design. To combat insect problems, Burger King placed screens on its covered patios; these screens were then replaced with walls of glass, making it possible for that area to be heated and air-conditioned for the comfort of customers in cold winters or in the heat of summers. It was a simple step to enclose these patios so that customers could eat inside year-round. By 1967, the company needed a new design that incorporated these changes, and removed its "handlebars" that had mimicked McDonald's golden arches. In addition, the new design included an internal dining area where customers could eat.

Following Burger King's success, McDonald's developed a new design of its own in 1968. The new design included indoor dining areas intended to encourage families with children to come in and discouraged teenagers from congregating outside. As the new designs proved successful, older designs were phased out.

There were other reasons for the changes in fast food architecture. At first, garish designs were novelties that attracted attention, but after a while reactions set in against novelty. Flamboyant designs were unwelcome in many communities. Several local building commissions, for example, forced McDonald's to change its building design. Some municipalities objected to McDonald's design because the arches still burst through its roof; others considered their slanted roof an eyesore. Building commissions often refused permission to build restaurants near **schools**, churches, and hospitals. As a result, McDonald's removed the golden arches that had been promoted by the McDonald brothers, and shifted to the "M" as the company's symbol. The company redesigned its outlets to include brick walls and mansard roofs, and changed its red-and-white exteriors to dull-brown brick and plate-glass facades. In the 1970s, McDonald's installed larger and softer seats and enlarged their tables to make their restaurants more family-friendly. Other chains also subdued their architecture, decreased the size and garishness of their signage, and eliminated exotic color schemes.

SUGGESTED READING: Paul Hirshorn and Steven Izenour, *White Towers* (Cambridge, MA: MIT Press, 1979); John A. Jakle and Keith A. Sculle, *Fast Food: Roadside Restaurants in the Automobile Age* (Baltimore: Johns Hopkins University Press, 1999); Philip Langdon, *Orange Roofs, Golden Arches: The Architecture of American Chain Restaurants* (New York: Knopf, 1986).

Arthur Treacher's **Fish and chips**—battered and fried fish with **French fries**—has been a popular meal in England since the mid-nineteenth century. It is a surprise that fish and chips took so long to become a popular fast food in America. The first fish and chip **chain** was Arthur Treacher's Fish & Chips, which was launched in March, 1969. Arthur Treacher was a British actor who came to the United States in 1928. During the 1960s, he frequently appeared on Merv Griffin's **television** show. Treacher licensed his name and image to the National Fast Food Corporation, which was renamed OrangeCo in 1971, when the company acquired citrus groves in Florida and began producing orange concentrate. The company incorporated the **fast food** chain and also purchased the recipe for fish and chips from Malin's of Bow, a restaurant in London, which purportedly invented (in the 1860s) the combination of deep-fried whitefish and fried potatoes seasoned with a sprinkling of malt vinegar.

The first Arthur Treacher's Fish & Chip's restaurant opened in Columbus, Ohio, in 1969. It featured Atlantic cod; other items, such as fried shrimp, clams, and **chicken**, as well as hush puppies and cole slaw, were later added to the **menu**. Arthur Treacher served as a spokesperson for the company in its early years. In the 1980s, the price of Atlantic cod skyrocketed and the company suffered. More interested in making orange concentrate, OrangeCo sold Arthur Treacher's in 1978 and the troubled company changed hands repeatedly. In 1998, a partnership was formed with Pudgie's Famous Chicken, Miami Subs, and **Nathan's Famous**; in selected locations, the Arthur Treacher's menu is served at these **franchises**.

SUGGESTED READING: John A. Jakle and Keith A. Sculle, *Fast Food: Roadside Restaurants in the Automobile Age* (Baltimore: Johns Hopkins University Press, 1999); Arthur Treacher's Web site: www.arthurtreachers.com/about-at.htm

Automats, Cafeterias, Diners, and Lunchrooms In the nineteenth century, few restaurants served food that workingmen could afford. As America industrialized, food delivery systems were invented to meet this new demand, including lunch wagons and diners. The first lunch wagon was launched by Walter Scott of Providence, Rhode Island, in 1872. He parked his wagon at a downtown intersection and sold sandwiches to night workers through a service window. Lunch wagons improved over the years. Some wagons created a place for customers to stand inside at a counter, which was particularly helpful in inclement weather. Next came stools so customers could sit and eat their food. In 1897, Thomas Buckley began mass-producing lunch wagons.

A diner in Pennsylvania. © Kelly Fitzsimmons

The diner evolved from the lunch wagon. Patrick Tierney of New Rochelle, New York, upgraded the wagon into something resembling a railroad dining car. Customers at first sat on stools located along a counter; later versions offered booths for customers and waitresses to service tables. The diner was basically a small restaurant, not much different from a main street or highway café. Its advantage was its modular construction. It was relatively inexpensive to build, buy, and maintain. If a particular site proved unsuccessful, the diner could easily be disassembled and moved to another location. Various restaurants, such as **White Castle** and **White Tower**, employed diner concepts. For instance, **fast food** restaurant chains are based on modular construction of their outlets.

Another way of serving food efficiently was the self-service cafeteria, where the customers emulated an assembly line. They picked up trays, utensils, and napkins, proceeded down a long counter containing foods in trays heated by hot water. Customers picked the foods that they wanted and placed them on their trays, while employees punched the customer's tickets, noting which foods the customers took. Customers then sat at a table and ate the food. When finished, customers presented the punched ticket at the door, paid the bill, and departed. Cafeterias appeared almost simultaneously in the Midwest and the West and East coasts during the late nineteenth century. California became known as the "cafeteria belt," although it was in the South that the cafeteria became a culinary institution.

Early cafeterias were often operated by the Young Women's Christian Association (YWCA) and other nonprofit groups for the poor and workingmen. By 1906, however, they were being run as profit-making enterprises. The key to a cafeteria's success was the scale of its operation. It required a bigger investment and a greater volume of customers than did other restaurants. It also required more space for a larger kitchen to prepare the food and an increased seating capacity. Cafeterias were widely adopted in factories as a means of quickly serving food to workers; cafeterias were also commonly operated in other institutional settings, such as schools, hospitals, and military installations.

Another attempt to industrialize the food system was the automat, which dispensed food through banks of windows. The idea had been perfected in Europe and was in use in the United States by the late nineteenth century. The most famous **chain** of automats was started in 1902 by Philadelphians Joseph Horn and Frank Hardart, who ordered the mechanisms from a German firm that installed food **vending machines** in European train stations. In automats, food was prepared in advance and placed in glass compartments so that customers could see what they were getting. To remove the food, customers were required to place coins in slots and turn a knob, which opened the glass doors. The food could be sandwiches, salads, or desserts. Heated or refrigerated compartments provided hot and cold food. Empty compartments could then be filled by workers who prepared food behind the row of machines.

By 1912, Horn and Hardart had four establishments in Philadelphia and began opening automats in New York City. By 1950, the company operated 50 automats. Within 30 years, all except two would be closed, the firm having converted most of its operations to **Burger King** outlets.

Yet another means of feeding working class peoples emerged—the lunchroom. Most lunchrooms were mom-and-pop establishments that sold candy, baked goods, and other products. By the 1920s, lunchroom chains began to develop in large cities. Most chains had only two or three establishments. These shared a name and were advertised as a system. Large chains might also have had central food distribution and preparation. One such chain was W. F. Schrafft's, launched by Frank Shattuck in 1898 as a **candy** store in Boston. By 1915, Schrafft's had extended its operation to New York City and Syracuse. By 1922, the chain had 22 stores.

Fast food chains, which emerged during the 1920s, incorporated aspects of automats, cafeterias, and lunchrooms. Some emulations failed, such as White Tower's experiment with its Tower-O-Matic restaurants, which tried to imitate Horn and Hardart's automats by serving hamburgers and other fast foods in machines. However, similar to cafeterias but unlike full-service restaurants, fast food operations were self-service. Unlike lunch wagons but similar to cafeterias, fast food outlets were permanent structures. Similar to lunch wagons but not to cafeterias and restaurants, fast food chain customers stood in line to order food, employees packed the order, and gave customers the food. Similar to lunch wagons and food stands but unlike diners and cafeterias, early fast food chain menus were limited and customers did not eat the food inside the outlet.

SUGGESTED READING: John Baeder, *Diners* (New York: Abrams, 1995 [revised and updated]); Lorraine B. Diehl and Marrianne Hardart, *Automat: The History, Recipes, and Allure of Horn & Hardart's Masterpiece* (New York: Clarkson Potter, 2002); Richard J. Gutman, *American Diner, Then and Now* (New York: HarperPerennial, 1993); John A. Jakle and Keith A. Sculle, *Fast Food: Roadside Restaurants in the Automobile Age* (Baltimore: Johns Hopkins University Press, 1999); Philip Langdon, *Orange Roofs, Golden Arches: The Architecture of American Chain Restaurants* (New York: Knopf, 1986).

Automobiles During the twentieth century, profound social and cultural changes affected the way Americans lived, and the automobile was a primary catalyst in these changes. Automobiles appeared in America in the 1890s but they were mainly luxury toys for the rich. When Henry Ford mass-produced his first Model Ts in 1908, inexpensive cars were suddenly available. World War I slowed their manufacture, but after the war automobile sales skyrocketed. By 1920 there were 9.2 million cars, trucks, and buses in the United States. Cars freed commuters from the hassles of public transportation. This tidal wave slowed during the Depression and World War II, but it was off again in the 1950s. One of the many results of America's infatuation with the automobile was the construction of new kinds of restaurants that were more accommodating to motorists. This meant that new restaurant sites had to be developed, new building designs and new types of signs created, and new **menus** developed.

Specifically, automobiles encouraged the development of a new type of restaurant with simple menus and faster, more convenient service. As automobile ownership became more available to the lower middle class, the market for **fast food** developed. The first fast food outlets were initially built at mass transportation hubs—trolley and bus stops and subway exits—and near large factories. These early outlets had little or no parking space for customers. But subsequent fast food **chains** evolved around the automobile: **Drive-in** restaurants, for example, were constructed to attract motorists. At drive-ins, customers ate in their cars, frequently served by **carhops**. As the owner of one of the earliest drive-ins, the Pig Stand in Dallas, Texas, stated that people were just too lazy to get out of their cars. Cars also offered more privacy and were more relaxing for families with small children.

In addition to changing the place where customers ate their food, the automobile had many other influences on fast food. Owners of drive-ins believed it was necessary to construct memorable (frequently gaudy) **architecture**, and a profusion of large, flashing signs emerged that could attract passing motorists. Automobiles also encouraged standardization of design so that a passing motorist could easily spot a particular fast food establishment. Fast food outlets quickly discovered that good locations for their establishments were on busy highways, particularly at important crossroads.

Thousands of drive-ins were constructed along the nation's highways, but travelers were often leery of eating at them. Unless customers had previously eaten at a particular drive-in, it was difficult to determine whether the food was good or safe to eat. Fast food chains gave travelers confidence that the quality of food offered in one city would be the same in another location. Automobile travel favored large restaurant chains.

After World War II, automobiles became affordable for even the American working class. There were 15 million cars in 1945 in America; there were 40 million by 1950; and 55 million by 1957. With the baby boom in full swing after the war, new families began moving to less-expensive, newly constructed houses in suburbs around cities. Expressways or freeways were constructed, connecting urban centers to the suburbs. The interstate highway system was created by the Federal Aid Highway Act, which passed in 1956. This new highway grid encouraged so-called white flight from inner urban areas. As the suburbs grew, fast food establishments began constructing outlets intended to attract new families living in there. The growth of chains, such as **McDonald's**, **Burger King**, and **Kentucky Fried Chicken**, can be directly traced to the growth of suburbs.

The construction of interstate highways made long-distance travel affordable for families. Fast food outlets were intentionally constructed at off-ramps, making it relatively easy for drivers to eat and resume travel. Highways had indirect effects on fast food, as well, such as causing dislocations. For example, a major highway was constructed in the 1950s that circumvented Corbin, Kentucky, where **Harland Sanders**'s restaurant was located. This meant that most automobile traffic now bypassed his restaurant; it failed and he sold his assets at auction. At 65 years of age, Sanders hit the road, selling **franchises** for his Kentucky Fried Chicken recipe.

Although most fast food establishments now have indoor dining, many Americans continue to eat in their cars. The popularization of the **drive-thru** window made it easier for drivers to order and then eat in their cars, usually while driving. Eating in cars was such a common activity that during the 1990s car manufacturers began to install cup-holders in dashboards so that drivers could more easily rest their drinks and avoid spilling them. As fast food beverages became larger, so did the cup-holders. In 1990, an estimated 57 percent of all sales in fast food restaurants are purchased through drive-thru windows, according to John A. Jakle and Keith A. Schulle. This has increased subsequently as many drivers eat their food in their cars.

SUGGESTED READING: John A. Jakle and Keith A. Sculle, *Fast Food: Roadside Restaurants in the Automobile Age* (Baltimore: Johns Hopkins University Press, 1999); Philip Langdon, *Orange Roofs, Golden Arches: The Architecture of American Chain Restaurants* (New York: Knopf, 1986); Eric Schlosser, *Fast Food Nation: The Dark Side of the All-American Meal* (New York: Houghton Mifflin Company, 2001).

B

Baby Ruth In 1916, Otto Y. Schnering founded a bakery in Chicago. Along with the bakery, he launched a small **candy** department, which was so successful that the bakery was soon discontinued. Schnering changed the name of the company to reflect his new emphasis, using his mother's maiden name to create the Curtiss Candy Company. One successful product was the Kandy Kate, a bar that had a pastry center topped with nuts and coated with **chocolate**. In 1920, Curtiss changed the formula of the candy bar to peanuts covered with nougat and chocolate, and changed the name of the confection to Baby Ruth. Within two years of its creation, the Baby Ruth was sold nationwide.

Its popularity convinced Babe Ruth, the baseball player, to form his own company, called the George H. Ruth Candy Co. When the Curtiss Candy Company heard that he planned to launch the Babe Ruth Home Run Bar, it sued Babe Ruth for breach of copyright. In the legal proceedings, lawyers for Curtiss maintained that their Baby Ruth candy bar was named after President Grover Cleveland's daughter, Ruth. Many observers then and now consider this oft-repeated story a myth, and with good reason. Ruth Cleveland was born on October 3, 1891 and died of diphtheria 13 years later. Cleveland himself died in 1908. When the Baby Ruth bar was introduced, 16 years after Ruth Cleveland's death, few youthful candy buyers would have remembered her but virtually everyone would have known Babe Ruth, who was then the nation's most popular baseball player. Nevertheless, the Curtiss Candy Company won the suit. When Babe Ruth was informed, he reportedly retorted, "Well, I ain't eatin' your damned candy bar anymore."

Whatever the reasons for the name, Baby Ruth was extremely successful, mainly due to Schnering's promotional ability. He chartered an airplane and dropped the bars by parachutes over the city of Pittsburgh. He later expanded his drops to cities in more than 40 states. At the same time, the company began a promotional campaign that placed four-color **advertisements** in national magazines. These proclaimed that Baby Ruth was the "sweetest story ever told" and that it was "the world's most popular candy."

These promotional efforts proved successful and Schnering had to build another factory, then another, to keep up with demand for Baby Ruths. These plants consumed five or six train carloads (about 150,000 pounds) of peanuts every day. By 1927, the Curtiss candy-making facilities were the largest of their kind in the world. The plants operated 24 hours a day, and Curtiss operated a fleet of 54 five-ton trucks, which brought in raw materials and distributed finished candy bars. By the late 1920s, Baby Ruth had

Baby Ruth candy bar. © Kelly Fitzsimmons

become the best-selling five-cent confection in America. This position was solidified in 1929, when Curtiss began sponsoring the CBS **radio** program *The Baby Ruth Hour*.

The Curtiss Candy Company was sold to Standard Brands in 1930, which promptly decreased advertising for Baby Ruth candy bars. Mars, Inc., began manufacturing **Snickers** in 1930, and sales of Baby Ruths were eclipsed by this new confection. The Baby Ruth brand was acquired by Nabisco in 1981 and by the **Nestlé SA** Food Corporation in 1990. The Baby Ruth candy bar remains among America's most-consumed confections.

SUGGESTED READING: Ray Broekel, *The Chocolate Chronicles* (Lombard, IL: Wallace-Homestead Book Company, 1985); Andrew F. Smith, *Peanuts: The Illustrious History of the Goober Pea* (Urbana, IL: University of Illinois Press, 2002); Tim Richardson, *Sweets: A History of Candy* (New York: Bloomsbury, 2002).

Bakery Snacks Many pastries were made commercially and sold on the local level, such as **Moon Pies** which were invented in 1917 in Chattanooga, Tennessee, and TastyKakes, invented about 1914 in Philadelphia.

The first national commercial pastry was Chocolate Cup Cakes (1919), which was reportedly invented by the Indianapolis-based Taggart Bakery, which also made Wonder Bread. The Continental Baking Company purchased Taggart in 1925 and looked for a brand name for its cake products. It settled on the name **Hostess**. The Hostess Chocolate Cupcakes did not acquire their characteristic white creme filling until after World War II. In 1930, the Continental Baking Company produced **Twinkies**, and subsequently launched coconut-covered Sno Balls in 1947. It also produced Ding Dongs, a flat **chocolate** cake first marketed in 1967, which was similar to Ring Dings, produced by Drake's Cakes.

Newman E. Drake baked pound cakes in Brooklyn, New York, in 1888. He expanded his operations to reach outstate New York, New England, and Florida. Drake's Cakes produced Yodels, a chocolate-frosted, creme-filled Swiss roll, and Ring Dings, a chocolate covered, creme-filled chocolate cake. When Hostess released its Ding Dongs, Drake's sued for copyright infringement and Hostess was required to change the name to Big Wheels in areas where Drake's cakes were sold.

The Interstate Brands Corporation (IBC) released its Dolly Madison line of commercial pastries in 1937. The Dolly Madison brand also includes Zingers (creme-filled cakes), Gems (miniature doughnuts), Angel Food and Pound Cakes, and a variety of breakfast items, such as Sweet Rolls, Dunkin Stix, and Pecan Rollers. In 1995, IBC acquired the Continental Baking Company and changed its name to Interstate Bakeries Corporation, but kept its initials. IBC acquired Drake's in 1998. The low-**carbohydrate** diet craze of the early twenty-first century, coupled with a major business slowdown, caused IBC to declare bankruptcy in 2004.

The McKee Bakery Company (later renamed McKee Foods) of Chattanooga, Tennessee, launched the **Little Debbie** brand in 1960. The best-selling Little Debbie products include Swiss Cake Rolls, Nutty Bars Wafer Bars, Oatmeal Creme Pies, and Fudge Brownies. As of 2005, Little Debbie cakes manufactured by McKee Foods are the best-selling cakes in America, followed by Hostess.

William Entenmann opened his first bakery in Brooklyn, New York, in 1898. He made small cakes, breads, and rolls. His business flourished, and in the 1950s the company began to expand throughout the East coast, selling its goods through grocery stores as well as through its bakeries. In 1961, the company moved to Bay Shore, Long Island. It discontinued making bread and concentrated on pastries. Today, Entenmann's is one of America's largest pastry makers and is the nation's second-largest **doughnut** maker. The Entenmann's brand is now owned by George Weston Bakeries, a subsidiary of a Canadian firm, which also owns Thomas's English Muffins.

Many companies made fruit pies (actually, turnovers) and doughnuts, which are sold in grocery stores. **Krispy Kreme** doughnuts are the best-selling doughnuts in grocery stores, followed by those manufactured by Entenmann's and Dolly Madison.

SUGGESTED READING: Dolly Madison Web site: www.dollymadison.com; Hostess Web site: www.twinkies.com; McKee Foods Web site: www.mckeefoods.com

Barq's Root Beer Edward Charles Edmond Barq, proprietor of Biloxi Artesian Bottling Works in Biloxi, Mississippi, began manufacturing root beer about 1898. By 1902, the name of the company had been changed to Barq's Bottling Works. By 1937, the company had 62 bottling plants in 22 states, mainly in the South. In 1976, John Koerner and John Oudt bought the company from the Barq family and moved its headquarters to New Orleans. In 1995, Barq's was purchased by the **Coca-Cola Company**, which expanded the line to include diet root beer, French Vanilla Créme and Red Créme Soda, and Barq's Root Beer Floatz. Today, Barq's is one of the best-selling root beers in America.

SUGGESTED READING: Barq's Web site: www.barqs.com

Baskin-Robbins In 1945, Irvine Robbins opened the Snowbird Ice Cream Store in Glendale, California. Robbins advertised that it served 21 flavors of **ice cream**. His brother-in-law, Burt Baskin, opened an ice cream parlor called Burton's in the Los Angeles area. The two formed a partnership in 1946 to create Baskin-Robbins, which sold premium ice cream. They began to **franchise** their operation, and within three years the **chain** had grown to eight stores. In 1953, the company **advertised** that its stores served 31 flavors of ice cream. The idea of a number was borrowed from Howard Johnson's motel and restaurant chain's 28 flavors of ice cream. But the Baskin-Robbins number was higher so customers could consume a different flavor every day of a month. The company also regularly created new treats that celebrated holidays or special events, such as the moon landing in 1969, when the company released a Lunar Cheesecake. One franchise even tried **ketchup** ice cream, but it was not a great success, even for ketchup aficionados.

Unlike **soda fountains**, Baskin and Robbins intentionally created a place in which customers would not hang out. Most customers ate their ice cream outside of the store; for those who wanted to eat inside, each outlet had a few uncomfortable chairs so that customers would not stay long.

The chain continued to expand, and the first non-California franchise was launched in Phoenix, Arizona, in 1959. Burt Baskin died in 1967 and the company was sold to the United Fruit Company, which continued running it until 1973, when it was sold to the London-based J. Lyons & Co., Ltd. In 1979, Baskin-Robbins was purchased by Allied Breweries. In 1990 Baskin-Robbins was bought by Allied Lyon, which sold it to Pernod Ricard. Pernod Ricard then sold the chain to a private equity group. As of 2005, there were about 2,500 Baskin-Robbins stores in the United States and a similar number in 50 other countries.

SUGGESTED READING: Anne Cooper Funderburg, *Chocolate, Strawberry, and Vanilla: A History of American Ice Cream* (Bowling Green, OH: Bowling Green State University Popular Press, 1995); Baskin-Robbins Web site: www.baskinrobbins.com

Battle of the Burgers In the 1980s, **Burger King**, the second-largest **hamburger chain** in the world, began a massive **advertising** campaign in hopes of catching up with **McDonald's**. Burger King commercials included **slogans** such as "Battle of the Burgers" and "Aren't You Hungry for a Burger King Now?" in 1982. This was followed with commercials focusing on "broiling versus frying" in 1983 and "The Big Switch" in 1985. Other burger chains responded with advertisements of their own. In some commercials, Burger King claimed that its hamburgers were more popular than either McDonald's or **Wendy's**. Both companies sued Burger King for false advertising and Burger King settled out of court. The Battle of the Burgers, as this was called, resulted in Burger King increasing its market share at the expense of McDonald's and Wendy's.

SUGGESTED READING: John A. Jakle and Keith A. Sculle, *Fast Food: Roadside Restaurants in the Automobile Age* (Baltimore: Johns Hopkins University Press, 1999).

Beef Jerky In prehistoric times, Native Americans dried thin strips of buffalo and other meats, and early European settlers adopted these practices, but beef jerky (from the Spanish *charque*) came in its familiar form to the United States from Mexico, where many of the traditions of the Old West originated. Beef jerky was made commercially in the United States beginning in the early twentieth century but did not become an important commercial product until the late twentieth century. An early jerky maker was the Oberto Sausage Company, launched in Seattle in 1918. It has expanded the beef jerky product line to include jerky crisps and **pizza** sticks. Its Oh Boy! snacks are today distributed by **PepsiCo**'s **Frito-Lay** division. Another commercial jerky manufacturer, Fernando's Foods Corporation, was acquired by ConAgra in 1998. Beef Jerky is a ready-to-eat, low-fat, low-calorie **snack food**, which is one of the reasons for its commercial success.

SUGGESTED READING: Mary T. Bell, *Just Jerky: the Complete Guide to Making It* (Madison, WI: Dry Store Publishing, 1996); A.D. Livingston, *Jerky: Make Your Own Delicious Jerky and Jerky Dishes Using Beef, Venison, Fish, or Fowl* (Guilford, CT: Lyons Press, 2001).

Ben & Jerry's Ben & Jerry's premium **ice cream** was a dream come true for Ben Cohen and Jerry Greenfield, who took a correspondence course in ice cream making from Penn State University. They invested $12,000 to turn a former gas station into an ice cream plant, and in 1978 opened Ben & Jerry's Homemade Ice Cream and Crêpes in South Burlington, Vermont. Supermarket sales soared, but then they ran into a problem. Distributors started to refuse to accept Ben & Jerry's ice cream because the makers of **Häagen-Dazs**, a subsidiary of the Pillsbury Company, required that distributors choose only one brand to sell. Ben & Jerry's filed a **lawsuit** against Pillsbury, running an advertising campaign asking, "What is the Doughboy afraid of?" and encouraging a **boycott** of all Pillsbury subsidiaries, including **Burger King**. Pillsbury settled out of court; it agreed to stop intimidating grocery stores and Ben & Jerry's agreed to end its anti-Pillsbury promotion campaign. Partly because of the publicity surrounding the court case, Ben & Jerry's drew national attention.

Ben & Jerry's ice cream. © Kelly Fitzsimmons

Ben & Jerry's became known for its innovative flavors and strange names, such as Cherry Garcia (named after rock star Jerry Garcia). At a time when mix-ins were innovative in ice cream making, Ben & Jerry's mixed chunks of nuts and fruit into their ice cream. The company was also popular for its use of natural ingredients and its eco-friendliness. Its ice cream cartons were made from recycled paper, and farmers who supplied dairy products to the company pledged that the latter were free of **bovine growth hormone** (BGH).

Their success encouraged Cohen and Greenfield to take the company public to raise more capital for additional growth. This raised funds for expansion but also made it possible for investors to take control of the company, which is what happened. Cohen and Greenfield attempted to regain control of the company that they founded, but their attempt failed. In August, 2000, Ben & Jerry's was purchased by the **Unilever** conglomerate. Other Unilever ice cream brands include **Dove** and **Breyers**. In 2002, the **Center for Science in the Public Interest** accused the company of using artificial flavors, hydrogenated oils, and other factory-made substances that were not natural. Ben & Jerry's removed the All Natural tagline from their promotional materials.

SUGGESTED READING: Ben & Jerry's Web site: www.benjerry.com; Anne Cooper Funderburg, *Chocolate, Strawberry, and Vanilla: A History of American Ice Cream* (Bowling Green, OH: Bowling Green State University Popular Press, 1995); Fred Lager, *Ben & Jerry's, the Inside Scoop: How Two Real Guys Built a Business with Social Conscience and a Sense of Humor* (New York: Crown Publishers, 1994).

Beverages The consumption of water is essential for human life. Throughout history, in rural areas water was easily accessible through rivers, wells and springs. In cities, water was usually provided by public pumps placed at intervals along the streets. Until the mid-nineteenth century, the relationship between sanitation and drinking water was not understood and, hence, consuming water (particularly in cities) often caused illness.

One early solution was to combine water with alcohol. Although it was not understood until almost the twentieth century, alcohol killed many of the germs present in the water. In American colonial times, the most important American beverages were beer and hard cider made from apples. Where apples could not be grown, perry made from pears was a common alcoholic beverage. The consumption of alcohol increased in the late eighteenth and nineteenth centuries as the price of rum declined. Wine did not become an important beverage in America until the late twentieth century.

There were many other beverages in America besides alcoholic ones. Tea was America's most important hot beverage, but this slowly changed during the early nineteenth century as the price of coffee declined. Hot and cold **chocolate** were minor beverages until massive commercial advertising promoted them during the 1930s.

Cows were imported into the New World shortly after European colonization began, and milk was also consumed, particularly by children. During the nineteenth century, milk was a proven disease-carrier and mothers were urged to boil it before giving it to their children. Milk did not become a safe beverage until the late nineteenth century. Beginning in the early twentieth century, milk producers launched major promotional campaigns touting the healthful qualities of milk. As a result, milk is now an important beverage for children and adults in America.

From the 1820s onward, groups advocating temperance began to fight against the consumption of alcoholic beverages. Alternatives to alcoholic beverages began to appear in the mid-nineteenth century. These included fruit juices, such as **root beer** and Welch's Grape Juice, which was invented for temperance ministers who chose not to use wine in their religious services. When soft drinks appeared in the late nineteenth century, they were adopted by the temperance movement, as were **soda fountains**, which were intended as replacements for bars and taverns. Early soft drinks were produced by druggists and were considered medicinal. Hence, **Coca-Cola** and Pepsi-Cola were created by medical professionals who operated drug stores.

In 1927, Edwin Perkins, head of the Perkins Products Company of Hastings, Nebraska, invented **Kool-Aid**, a powdered fruit-flavored beverage that was sold in paper packets, thus reducing expenses. Customers were only required to combine the powder with water and sugar.

During the early twentieth century, thousands of citrus orchards were planted in California and Florida and, when the medical establishment discovered the importance of vitamin C that was contained in citrus fruits, the consumption of orange juice dramatically increased. Frozen orange juice became popular during the 1940s and powdered orange drinks, such as **Tang**, were popular in the 1950s.

Coffee was the most common beverage consumed in the United States until the 1960s, when soft drinks became America's beverages of choice.

SUGGESTED READING: John Hull Brown, *Early American Beverages* (Rutland, VT: Charles E. Tuttle Company, 1966); Edward Emerson, *Beverages, Past and Present: An Historical Sketch of their Production, Together with a Study of the Customs Connected with Their Use.* Two vols. (New York: G. P. Putnam's Sons, 1908); A. W. Noling, comp., *Beverage Literature: A Bibliography* (Metuchen, NJ: The Scarecrow Press, 1971); John J. Riley, *A History of the American Soft Drink Industry. Bottled Carbonated Beverages 1807–1957* (Washington, D.C.: American Bottlers of Carbonated Beverages, 1958).

Big Boy In 1936, Robert Wian opened a 10-stool diner called Bob's Pantry in Glendale, California. It was successful and Wian enlarged his establishment to become a combination coffee shop and **drive-in**. At the time, **White Castle**'s **hamburgers** were small, single-patty **sandwiches**. Wian bid for attention by splitting a sesame-seed bun lengthwise into three parts and placing two pieces of meat between the slices. It was originally called the Fat Boy, but the name was changed promptly to Big Boy. In 1937 Wian changed the name of his restaurant to Bob's Big Boy. Its icon was a plump boy with red-and-white-checkered overalls with the words "Big Boy" spread across his chest. In his hand he carries a large, triple-decker hamburger. The company constructed 12-foot statue of the Big Boy that stood in front of each restaurant in the chain. The flagship meal at Bob's was the Combo, consisting of a Big Boy hamburger, fries, and a small salad.

Wian expanded his operation and new units generally included coffee shops with interior seating as well as drive-in service. He also **franchised** his restaurant. The cost to set up a full-service Big Boy restaurant was $250,000, a very costly sum in the 1940s and 1950s. One unusual arrangement was that franchisees were free to substitute their own name for "Bob's." Hence, the Frisch Company opened Frisch's Big Boy restaurants throughout the Midwest, and Azar's Big Boy restaurants could be found in Colorado. These were not integrated operations but their contractual relationships funneled Wian royalties (2 percent of gross sales) in exchange for the use of the Big Boy logo and the triple-decker sandwich. The company also prepared and distributed to franchisees comic books, coloring books, and games to entertain children at its restaurants.

By the 1960s, Big Boy found it hard to compete with the large, lower-priced fast food operations such as **McDonald's**, **Burger King**, and **Wendy's**. In 1984, the company attempted to revitalize by doing away with the Big Boy statues and logo. Customers complained and the company invited customers to vote on whether to retain the Big Boy; they overwhelmingly voted to retain it.

The **Marriott Corporation** bought the Big Boy chain in 1967. A franchise operator, Elias Brothers, had purchased it in 1987 and moved the company headquarters to Livonia, Michigan. It declared bankruptcy in 2000, and Robert Liggett acquired it and renamed it Big Boy Restaurants International. He also moved the headquarters to Warren, Michigan. Today, the company has about 500 Big Boy restaurants in the United States and Japan.

SUGGESTED READING: Big Boy Web site: www.bigboy.com/history1.asp; Philip Langdon, *Orange Roofs, Golden Arches: The Architecture of American Chain Restaurants* (New York: Knopf, 1986).

Bit-O-Honey Produced by the Schutter-Johnson Company of Chicago in 1924, this confection consisted of six small, individually-wrapped blocks of taffy, each containing an almond; the bite-size portions were enclosed in a wrapper to resemble a candy bar. In the 1950s and 1960s, the product's advertising featured a jingle that went "Bit-O-Honey goes a long, long way—if you have one head, it'll last all day." Today, Bit-O-Honey is manufactured by the **Nestlé SA** Food Corporation.

SUGGESTED READING: Ray Broekel, *The Great America Candy Bar Book* (Boston: Houghton Mifflin Company, 1982); Tim Richardson, *Sweets: A History of Candy* (New York: Bloomsbury, 2002).

Blimpie International, Inc. In 1964, Blimpie was launched by Tony Conza, Peter DeCarlo, and Angelo Baldassare in Hoboken, New Jersey. The name *blimpie* was a derivative of the blimp, which was long and tubular. The **sandwich** was akin to the submarine or hoagie. Sandwich prices ranged from 35 to 95 cents, considerably more than fast food hamburgers at the time. Blimpie sandwiches can include meats, cheese, and a variety of vegetables. As the meat is not fried, they are considered healthier than **hamburgers**.

As of 2004, there were almost 1,600 Blimpie locations across the United States and in more than 10 other countries. Headquartered in Atlanta, Georgia, Blimpie International is owned by an investment group, the Kahala Group, which owns nine other restaurant **chains** including Ranch One. The Kahala Group franchises smaller chains, such as Pasta Central, Maui Tacos, and Smoothie Island. Blimpie has co-branded with other companies, most notably Texaco gas stations. Blimpie International has also developed dual branding partnerships with **Dunkin' Donuts** and **Baskin-Robbins**, in which Blimpie submarine sandwich units will be added to some locations. Blimpie's is the third-largest submarine sandwich chain after **Subway** and **Quiznos**.

SUGGESTED READING: Tony Conza, *Success: It's a Beautiful Thing: Lessons on Life and Business from the Founder of Blimpie International* (New York: Wiley, 2000); Blimpie Web site: www.blimpie.com

Blue Bell Creameries The Brenham Creamery Company was launched in Brenham, Texas in 1907 and began producing **ice cream** four years later. The acquisition of trucks in the 1920s made it possible for the company to expand to other southwestern states, including Oklahoma, Louisiana, Mississippi, Arkansas, Kansas, Missouri, and New Mexico. In 1930 the company changed its name to Blue Bell Creameries, Inc. By 1936 Blue Bell was equipped with refrigerated trucks and freezers, which made it possible to sell ice cream to retail outlets. Blue Bell Creameries has become known for its innovative flavors and products. It was the first company to combine cookie dough with ice cream; its Cookies 'n' Cream was introduced in 1979. In 1995, it introduced bite-size frozen snacks, from frozen ices to **chocolate**-dipped cones. The company continued to expand its operations and in the 1990s it became the nation's third-largest ice cream manufacturer, behind **Breyers** and **Dreyer's/Edy's**. Blue Bell now manufactures other frozen snacks, such as **Snickers** and Nestle's Crunch ice cream bars, as well as **Eskimo Pies**.

SUGGESTED READING: Paul Dickson, *The Great American Ice Cream Book* (New York: Atheneum, 1973); Gail Gibbons, *Ice Cream: The Full Scoop* (New York: Holiday House, 2006).

Boston Market In 1985, Arthur Cores and Steven Kolow launched Boston Chicken in Newton, Massachusetts, specializing in rotisserie **chicken** and side dishes in a cafeteria setting. The company was sold to George Nadaff in 1989, and during the next four years 35 new locations were opened in the Northeast. In 1995, Boston Chicken's menu expanded to include turkey, ham, and meatloaf, and the name was changed to Boston Market. The **chain** grew rapidly during mid-1990s. In 1999, H. J. Heinz began producing Boston Market Home Style Meals, frozen dinners with side dishes. In 200l, **McDonald's** Corporation purchased the chain, which consisted of 751 restaurants. Outlets were upgraded and a new format, the Rotisserie Grill restaurant, was launched in 2003. Boston Market is part of the McDonald's subsidiary Golden Restaurant Operations, which also includes Donato's Pizza and Chipotle Mexican Grill.

SUGGESTED READING: Boston Market Web site: www.bostonmarket.com

Bovine Growth Hormone (BGH) Bovine growth hormone is a naturally occurring hormone in cattle which regulates growth and milk production. A genetically engineered form, recombinant bovine growth hormone (rBGH), is administered to cows in the

United States to accelerate maturation and increase milk production by 5 to 15 percent. Cows treated with rBGH secrete other substances in their milk, one of which is a known carcinogen. Residue of rBGH has also been found in meat products, such as the **hamburger** in **fast food chains**, which is made from cows no longer producing enough milk, and some evidence has shown that rBGH has detrimental effects on the human body. Based on this evidence, 25 European nations have banned rBGH, as have Canada, Australia, New Zealand, and Japan.

SUGGESTED READING: Physicians for Social Responsibility, Oregon Chapter, Web site: www.oregonpsr.org/csf/rbgh_fact_sheet.doc

Boycotts Boycotts of **junk food** and **fast foods** have been called for and conducted for a variety of reasons. One of the longest-running boycotts is of **Nestlé** products. During the 1970s, consumer groups working in developing countries became concerned about the lack of breast-feeding and the increase in infant mortality. They concluded that the cause of 1.5 million infant deaths annually was unsafe (unsanitary) bottle feeding. These groups targeted Nestlé, the largest seller of infant formula in the developing world. In 1988, groups such as the International Baby Food Action Network called for a boycott of all Nestlé products, which has continued to this day. Those engaged in this long-running boycott believe that their actions have drawn attention to infant mortality in the developing world and that, in response. Nestlé has changed some of its infant formula business practices.

Other boycotts have been organized by one business against other business. **Ben & Jerry's ice cream**, for instance, found that potential distributors refused to accept their products because the makers of **Häagen-Dazs**, a subsidiary of the Pillsbury Company, required that distributors choose only one brand to sell. Ben & Jerry's sued Pillsbury and launched an **advertising** campaign against Pillsbury asking, "What is the Doughboy afraid of?" and encouraged a boycott of all Pillsbury subsidiaries, including **Burger King**. (The legal case was settled out of court and Ben & Jerry's ended their boycott). In this case, publicity surrounding the court case and the boycott gained Ben & Jerry's national visibility.

Other boycotts have been based on religious motivation. Boycotts of American fast food **chains** in Arab countries have been launched by those who want to protest American support of Israel. Due to these calls for boycotts, Burger King was forced to withdraw its Whoppers from a food court in an Israeli settlement in the West Bank. Burger King was then denounced by pro-Israel groups in the United States. As a direct result of these calls for boycotts, the **McDonald's** franchise in Saudi Arabia announced that a donation of 26 cents from each burger sold would be given to Palestinian children's hospitals.

Still other boycotts have been organized by those concerned with worker rights. For example, in 2001 the Coalition of Immokalee Workers (CIM) launched a national boycott of **Taco Bell**, one of the largest buyers of Florida tomatoes, demanding that the company address problems of the workers in the Florida tomato fields. This groups organized the Taco Bell Truth Tour, which drove across the country to the Taco Bell headquarters in Southern California. About 75 workers went on a hunger strike. The company settled with the farm workers in May 2005. In another example, some universities in the United Kingdom, the United States, and Ireland have boycotted **Coca-Cola** products for concerns over human rights violations at its plants in Colombia.

Specific boycotts have been urged due to particular practices of fast food and junk food businesses. **Kentucky Fried Chicken** has been boycotted by People for the Ethical Treatment of Animals (PETA) for its cruelty in processing and slaughtering chickens. The boycott gained visibility when actress Pamela Anderson joined PETA's boycott. In 2004, PETA released a video of cruelty to chickens at Pilgrim's Pride, one of Kentucky Fried Chicken's suppliers in West Virginia. As a result of the video, several employees were fired and Pilgrim's Pride launched a training program for its employees on how to treat animals.

Many other boycotts have been recommended. Eric Schlosser, author of ***Fast Food Nation*** (2001), urged a boycott of all fast food, soda, and junk food operations in **schools**, no matter how much corporate money is offered to schools to sell or advertise their products at the schools and at school functions.

Finally, boycotts have been called for due to international politics. In 2003, when American-led coalition forces attacked Iraq, opposition members in the Indian Parliament demanded a countrywide boycott of American businesses, such as Coca-Cola, **PepsiCo**, and McDonald's.

SUGGESTED READING: Eric Schlosser, *Fast Food Nation: The Dark Side of the All-American Meal* (New York: Houghton Mifflin Company, 2001); Baby Milk Action Web site: www.babymilkaction.org; The International Baby Food Action Network Web site: www.ibfan.org; People for the Ethical Treatment of Animals Web site: www.peta.org

Breakfast Fast Foods During the 1920s, **White Castle chains** were open 24 hours a day but they had no special breakfast offerings—just their normal menu of **hamburgers** and **beverages**. During World War II, meat was rationed and **fast food** chains experimented with different types of food. Bruce LaPlante, a White Castle manager in the St. Louis, Missouri, area, invented a fried egg **sandwich**, but it was not adopted systemwide and it was discontinued after the war.

This changed with the arrival of **doughnut** shops, such as **Winchell's Donut House** (1948) in Los Angeles and **Dunkin' Donuts** (1950) in Quincy, Massachusetts. These establishments sold mainly coffee and doughnuts before noon. Over the years, they have increased their breakfast offerings by including buns, biscuits, croissants, bagels, and egg dishes.

Most hamburger, **chicken**, and **hot dog** fast food chains did not serve breakfast until the 1970s. **Jack in the Box** began serving breakfast in 1971 with the introduction of its Breakfast Jack, and its breakfast menu was expanded to include omelets and an Eggs Benedict sandwich. **McDonald's** developed a version of Jack in the Box's Egg Benedict and created the Egg McMuffin in 1973. At the time, English muffins were not big sellers nationally. The Egg McMuffin popularized and created a major new market for muffins. The Egg McMuffin was followed by a complete breakfast line at McDonald's in 1976, that eventually included the Breakfast Burrito and the Big Breakfast. This created a second wave of fast food breakfast foods as many other chains began offering different breakfast foods. **Burger King** championed the Croissant Breakfast Sandwiches, French Toast Sticks, and Cini-Minis; **Carl's Jr.** created the Breakfast Burger; and Jack in the Box now sells breakfast combos and they rolled out its Meaty Breakfast Burrito in 2005.

In addition to the breakfast foods served at fast food chains, a whole series of fast breakfast foods have been commercially produced for serving at home. **Tang**, for example, was a fast food substitute for fresh-squeezed orange juice. Fast breakfast foods, such as Kellogg's Eggo Frozen Waffles (launched in 1954) and **Pop-Tarts** (1964), have been important breakfast foods since the 1970s. Ready-to-eat breakfast and **cereal** bars, such as Kellogg's Special K Breakfast Bars and Nutri-Grain Bars, and General Mills's Milk 'n Cereal Bars, became an important fast foods in the early twenty-first century.

SUGGESTED READING: David Gerard Hogan, *Selling 'em by the Sack: White Castle and the Creation of American Food* (New York: New York University Press, 1997).

Breyers In 1866, William A. Breyer began selling **ice cream** in Philadelphia. He opened a retail ice cream store in 1882 and began wholesaling it in 1896. Breyer's sons incorporated and expanded the business. The company's logo is a sweetbriar leaf. Breyers Ice Cream Company became a division of the National Dairy Products Corporation in 1926. The company was acquired by Kraft Foods, Inc., and then in 1996 by **Unilever**, which combined it with the Gold Bond-**Good Humor** Ice Cream Company. In 1993, the company was renamed Good Humor-Breyers Ice Cream Company.

SUGGESTED READING: Anne Cooper Funderburg, *Chocolate, Strawberry, and Vanilla: A History of American Ice Cream* (Bowling Green, OH: Bowling Green State University Popular Press, 1995).

Bugles In 1965, **General Mills** test-marketed a new product called Bugles. It was an extruded, corn-based snack shaped like a cone. The test was successful and in the following year General Mills began distributing and promoting Bugles nationally along with two other snacks, Daisy*s and Whistles, both of which were subsequently discontinued. In 2004, General Mills launched a new product line based on Bugles, which includes the flavors of Chile Cheese, Nacho Cheese, Original, Salsa, Smokin' BBQ, and Southwest Ranch.

SUGGESTED READING: General Mills Web site: www.generalmills.com

Burger King In 1952, Matthew Burns of Long Beach, California, invited his stepson, Keith G. Cramer, who owned a **carhop** restaurant in Daytona Beach, Florida, to fly out to California and visit **McDonald's**, the new **fast food** operation in San Bernardino, California. Burns and Cramer acquired the rights to George Read's Miracle Insta-Machines, one of which made multiple **milk shakes**; the other was the Insta-Broiler, which cooked twelve burgers simultaneously in wire baskets so that the patties could be cooked on both sides simultaneously. Four hundred burgers could be turned out in an hour with one machine. The cooked patties slid into a container filled with sauce, and then they were ready to be placed on toasted buns. In 1953, Cramer opened the Insta-Burger King in Jacksonville, Florida. His burgers sold for 18 cents apiece and they were a great success.

Two franchisers, James McLamore and David R. Edgerton, Jr., launched several Insta-Burger-King outlets in Miami beginning in 1954. Unlike most of the other fast-food **entrepreneurs** who had limited education, Edgerton and McLamore both held degrees from Cornell University's School of Hotel Administration. Nevertheless, they were unable to make a profit, so they began to experiment. They disposed of the Insta-Broiler and created a flame broiler, for which **Burger King** became famous. They also introduced the Whopper hamburger, which they sold for 37 cents—a risky venture because McDonald's hamburgers sold for 15 cents at the time. The Whopper was an instant success and it became the company's signature product. The tag line "Burger King, Home of the Whopper" appeared in many of the company's **advertisements**. When the Jacksonville Insta-Burger-King **chain** had financial troubles, Edgerton and McLamore acquired the national rights to the system and they launched Burger King of Miami. They began a massive **franchising** effort in 1961.

McLamore and Edgerton franchised Burger King throughout Florida and eventually throughout the nation. To improve managers' skills, they opened Whopper College in 1963, two years after McDonald's had started Hamburger University. They created a Burger King character, attired in royal robe with a crown. It was intended to assure children that Burger King was a fun place to eat, and paper crowns have been used as promotional devices ever since. To combat insect problems, Burger King began installing screens on its ordering areas and patios. These were later replaced with glass, with air-conditioning added later. Indoor eating areas became integral to Burger King outlets by 1967, a year before McDonald's created indoor dining. In some outlets, Burger King experimented with **drive-thrus**, along with separate staffs to run them. This proved too costly and was discontinued, only to be later reinstalled.

Burger King failed to adequately regulate its franchises, and significant inconsistencies developed among them. In 1964, the company created a consistent image for all Burger King outlets. It began to enforce speed, cleanliness, and quality standards, which were controlled by frequent, unscheduled visits by the parent company inspectors. Sales rebounded to such an extent that in 1967 the company was acquired by the Pillsbury Company. Pillsbury ended the use of the little king logo, but it was later revived. Pillsbury also began a massive promotional campaign, with **slogans and jingles** such as "Have it Your Way" and "America Loves Burgers and We're America's Burger King." In the 1980s, Burger King launched an advertising campaign called the "**Battle of the Burgers**," which improved its market share vis-à-vis McDonald's.

As the company began to open franchises in other countries, it changed its name to Burger King International. Pillsbury was itself acquired in 1987. Eventually, Burger King was sold to an equity sponsor group composed of the Texas Pacific Group, Bain Capital, and Goldman Sachs Capital Partners.

As of 2004, Burger King operated more than 11,000 outlets—7,000 in the United States and 4,000 in 61 other countries and territories worldwide. Approximately 90 percent of its restaurants are owned by independent franchisees.

SUGGESTED READING: John A. Jakle and Keith A. Sculle, *Fast Food: Roadside Restaurants in the Automobile Age* (Baltimore: Johns Hopkins University Press, 1999); Burger King Web site: www.bk.com; Anne Cooper Funderburg, *Sundae Best: A History of Soda Fountains* (Bowling Green, OH: Bowling Green State University Popular Press, 2002); Harvey Levenstein, *Paradox of Plenty: A Social History of Eating in Modern America* (New York: Oxford University Press, 1993); Philip Langdon, *Orange Roofs, Golden Arches: The Architecture of American Chain Restaurants* (New York: Knopf, 1986); James W. McLamore, *The Burger King: Jim McLamore and the Building of an Empire* (New York: McGraw-Hill, 1998).

Butterfinger In 1926, Otto Schnering, owner of the Curtiss Candy Company of Chicago, invented the Butterfinger **candy** bar, consisting of an orange-colored, peanut-butter-flavored filling covered with **chocolate**. According to the brand's Web site, the name Butterfinger was selected through a public contest, which is a bit strange because at the time (as now) *butterfinger* was used by sports fans to describe an athlete who lets a ball slip through his fingers. The Curtiss Candy Company was sold to Standard Brands in 1930, then was sold to Nabisco in 1981. In 1990, the brand was acquired by the **Nestlé** Food Corporation.

SUGGESTED READING: Ray Broekel, *The Chocolate Chronicles* (Lombard, IL: Wallace-Homestead Book Company, 1985); Andrew F. Smith, *Peanuts: The Illustrious History of the Goober Pea* (Urbana, IL: University of Illinois Press, 2002); Tim Richardson, *Sweets: A History of Candy* (New York: Bloomsbury, 2002); Nestlé Web site: www.nestle.com

C

Cadbury In 1824 John Cadbury opened a store in Birmingham, England, which sold coffee and tea. Cadbury, a Quaker, was a strong supporter of temperance and believed that manufacturing alternatives to alcohol **beverages** was important. In 1831, Cadbury began manufacturing cocoa for drinking **chocolate**. By 1866, Cadbury Brothers was producing eating chocolate. In 1879 Cadbury launched a new community called Bournville which produced handmade bonbons, chocolate-covered nougat, and other chocolate candies. Cadbury also constructed houses for workers in Bournville and implemented novel labor practices, such as paid holidays and vacations, insurance programs, and night schools for its employees. Cadbury began producing milk chocolate in 1897. In 1919, Cadbury acquired Joseph S. Fry & Sons, another major English chocolate maker. The company continued to grow globally throughout the twentieth century. In 1969 Cadbury and **Schweppes** merged to form **Cadbury Schweppes**.

SUGGESTED READING: Iolo Aneurin Williams, *The Firm of Cadbury, 1831–1931* (London: Constable and Co., 1931); Cadbury Schweppes Web site: www.cadburyschweppes.com

Cadbury Schweppes In 1969, **Cadbury** and **Schweppes** merged to form Cadbury Schweppes. Since then, Cadbury Schweppes has acquired many other companies, including Mott's (1982), Canada Dry (1986), **Hires Root Beer** (1989), **A&W Beverages** (1993), **Dr Pepper** and **7-Up** (1995), Hawaiian Punch (1999), Orangina (2002), and the Snapple Beverage Group (2003). It also acquired Adams Confectionery, which included brands such as Halls, Trident, Dentyne, and Bubbas Bubblegum. As of 2005, Cadbury Schweppes was a leading global confectionery company, the world's second-largest manufacturer of **gum**, and the world's third-largest manufacturer of soft drinks.

SUGGESTED READING: Iolo Aneurin Williams, *The Firm of Cadbury, 1831–1931* (London: Constable and Co. Ltd., 1931); Cadbury Schweppes Web site: www.cadburyschweppes.com

Caffeine Caffeine is a bitter alkaloid common in tea, coffee, **cola**-based soft drinks, and in cacao from which **chocolate** is made. It is the most commonly used drug in the world. Low doses of caffeine act as a mild stimulant to the nervous system. High doses of caffeine affect the brain and skeletal muscle and alleviate fatigue. Many people consume products that contain caffeine in order to stay alert. The effects of caffeine vary, but in general it increases the heart rate and blood pressure; excessive intake can result in restlessness, insomnia, and heart irregularities. Caffeine consumption has also been associated with hypoglycemia, osteoporosis, kidney stones, female infertility, gastritis, Crohn's disease, and attention deficit disorder with hyperactivity (ADHD). Heavy caffeine use can also lead to dependence, which can result in insomnia, headaches, and fatigue upon withdrawal. Caffeine is not recommended for children under 12. Over the past 25 years, however, children and teenagers have greatly increased their caffeine intake, generally through the consumption of soft drinks such as **Coca-Cola** and Pepsi-Cola. Estimates suggest that children and teenagers, on average, consume more than 64 gallons of soft drinks per year. The caffeine content of 12 ounces of cola-based soft drinks varies from 80 milligrams (Jolt) to 45.6 milligrams (Diet Coke) to 41 milligrams (**Dr Pepper**) to 37.5 milligrams (Pepsi-Cola).

SUGGESTED READING: B. S. Gupta and Uma Gupta, eds., *Caffeine and Behavior: Current Views and Research Trends* (Boca Raton, FL: CRC Press, 1999); Bennett Alan Weinberg and Bonnie K. Bealer, *The World of Caffeine: the Science and Culture of the World's Most Popular Drug* (New York: Routledge, 2001); "Children Increasingly Consuming Caffeine," *Caffeine* (May–June 1998) at: www.ndsn.org/mayjun98/caffeine.html

California Pizza Kitchen In 1985, Rick Rosenfield and Larry Flax opened the first California Pizza Kitchen (CPK) in Beverly Hills, California. Rosenfield and Flax created unusual-flavored **pizza**, such as BBQ **chicken**, that differed greatly from traditional American pizza. The CPK also serves pasta, salads, **sandwiches**, soups, and desserts. Its "lite" toppings are attractive to health-conscious consumers. It was acquired by **PepsiCo** but was subsequently spun off. As of 2004, there were 156 CPK full-service restaurants in the United States. In addition, the company created smaller ASAP outlets, which offer fast service with a pared-down menu. CPK pizzas are also available in the frozen food sections of many supermarkets. The company **franchises** internationally but not in the United States. The founders have released two cookbooks; the profits generated are given to **charities**.

SUGGESTED READING: Larry Flax and Rick Rosenfield, *The California Pizza Kitchen Cookbook* (New York: Macmillan USA, 1996); Larry Flax and Rick Rosenfield, *California Pizza Kitchen Pasta, Salads, Soups, and Sides* (New York: Morrow, 1999); John A. Jakle and Keith A. Sculle, *Fast Food: Roadside Restaurants in the Automobile Age* (Baltimore: Johns Hopkins University Press, 1999).

Canada Dry Ginger Ale In 1890, Canadian John J. McLaughlin opened a factory in Toronto for manufacturing carbonated water. He sold carbonated water to drugstore owners, who mixed it with fruit juices and flavoring to sell at their **soda fountains**. McLaughlin, a pharmacist, also developed recipes for **soda** drinks and in 1890 he created McLaughlin Belfast Style Ginger Ale, which was a dark, sweet beverage. He bottled this product and sold it at fairs and at beaches. The label included a map of Canada with a beaver, which is the national symbol of Canada. By 1904, McLaughlin had perfected a recipe for Pale Dry Ginger Ale. In 1922, he trademarked the name Canada Dry. The following year, P. D. Saylor and Associates purchased the company and formed Canada Dry Ginger Ale, Inc.

Sales of Canada Dry Ginger Ale increased in the United States, especially during Prohibition. The company also expanded to other countries. By 1918, the company had bottling plants in 14 other nations. The company expanded its product line during the 1950s, selling various other soft drinks, and it was one of the first soda companies to produce a sugar-free soda.

The company changed hands several times, but was acquired by **Cadbury Schweppes** of London in 1986. Cadbury Schweppes Americas Beverages (CSAB) is a subsidiary division of Cadbury Schweppes headquartered in Plano, Texas. It includes the following brands: **7-Up**, **Dr Pepper**, **RC Cola**, **A&W Root Beer**, and Diet Rite soft drinks, as well as Snapple, Mott's Apple Juice, Sunkist Soda, Hawaiian Punch, and Slush Puppie frozen drinks. Cadbury Schweppes is one of the largest soft drink manufacturers in North America.

SUGGESTED READING: Cadbury Schweppes Web site: www.dpsu.com/canada_dry.html

Candy Candy is a generic term for sugar-based confections. European candy makers immigrated to America in colonial times and brought their candy-making trade with them. Early American candies included comfits, which were sugar-coated **nuts** and glazed fruits. **Sugar** candies were expensive in colonial times and only became widely accessible during the nineteenth century when sugar prices sharply declined. These were hard candies, such as barley candy, jawbreakers, **lollipops**, and lemon drops, that were sold generically by grocers as penny candy. As the century progressed, additional candies became common, such as **licorice**, taffy, and **caramels**.

Candy Companies

During the nineteenth century, there were more than 300 candy manufacturers in America. Many more companies were launched during the twentieth century. In Chicago, for instance, Emil J. Brach opened a candy store in 1904. Brach began manufacturing inexpensive caramels and later expanded to include peanut and hard candies By the 1930s, Brach's was one of America's leading bulk candy manufacturers. In the same city, the Ferrara Pan Candy Company started in 1908. In Chattanooga, Tennessee, the Trigg Candy Company was launched by William E. Brock in 1906. It produced bulk **penny candies** as well as peanut brittle and fudge. It later expanded its line to include marshmallow and jelly candies. It changed its name to the Brock Candy Company. It claims to have been the first American manufacturer of **gummi candies**. In Tacoma, Washington, Harry L. Brown, owner of a small candy store, went into business with J. C. Haley in 1912 to manufacture candy. Their signature product, Almond Roca, was invented in 1923. Today, Brown & Haley is one of America's largest wholesaler of boxed **chocolates**.

Chocolate Companies

Several chocolate makers began operations in America in the eighteenth century, including one begun by James Baker, which initially produced chocolate for drinking. During the nineteenth century, European confectioners determined how to convert chocolate, previously served mainly as a **beverage**, into a confection. Companies that specialized in making chocolate were launched, such as **Cadbury** and **Rowntree**'s **of York** in England, **Nestlé**, and Tobler in Switzerland. American chocolate makers learned from Europeans how to make milk chocolate and convert it into candy.

Stephen F. Whitman Company, founded in Philadelphia in 1842, created America's first packaged confection, Choice Mixed Sugar Plums. The company produced its Whitman Sampler, consisting of chocolate-coated candies, in about 1912. The box's inside lid included a chart for identifying each chocolate. Many chocolate companies were launched during the nineteenth and early twentieth centuries. Ghirardelli's, founded in 1852 in San Francisco, began producing handmade chocolates. In 1921, Charles See opened up a candy shop in Los Angeles. See used the image of his wife, Mary See, to serve as his store's icon. See's Candies expanded throughout California. Candy salesman Russell C. Stover went into business with Christian Nelson to **franchise** the making of **Eskimo Pies** in 1921. The **ice cream** bar was a tremendous success but the franchise business was not, and Stover left the partnership and moved to Denver where he opened a candy store. Stover began manufacturing candy and slowly expanded his operation. In 1931 the headquarters was moved to Kansas City, Missouri. Today, Russell Stover candies are sold through 40,000 retail stores throughout all 50 states, Canada, Puerto Rico, Mexico, Australia, and the United Kingdom.

All chocolates were made by hand until **Milton S. Hershey**, a caramel maker in Lancaster, Pennsylvania, began producing chocolate candies in 1894. During the next six years, he experimented with making milk chocolate, which he used to produce the Hershey Chocolate Bar in about 1900. The **Hershey Company** dominated chocolate candy production in the United States for the next 50 years, and it remains the largest American chocolate producer today.

Despite the low cost of Hershey's chocolate bar (5 cents), it was not immediately consumed by many Americans. Chocolate makers learned from Hershey and began producing chocolate bars. The Standard Candy Company of Nashville, Tennessee, produced the first combination candy, called the Goo Goo Cluster (1912), which contains caramel, marshmallow, roasted peanuts, and milk chocolate. The **Clark Bar**, composed of ground roasted peanuts covered with milk chocolate, was the first nationally marketed combination candy bar and its success induced numerous others to produce comparable products. The **Butterfinger** candy bar was released in 1926. **Mars, Inc.** released many candies, including the **Milky Way** bar followed by **Snickers**, **3 Musketeers**, and **M&M's**. Thousands of candy bars have been manufactured since then.

Concentration in the Candy Industry

In 1945, an estimated 6,000 companies manufactured candy in the United States. Today, this number is greatly reduced. Many companies could not compete with the large conglomerates; other companies were acquired. For example, the Hershey Company acquired the H. B. Reese Candy Company, maker of **Reese's Peanut Butter Cups**, in 1963. In 1977 Hershey acquired Y & S Candies, makers of Twizzlers. In 1988 Hershey purchased **Peter Paul** brands and in 1996 Hershey bought Leaf North America, maker of **Good & Plenty**, Jolly Rancher, Whoppers, Milk Duds, and PayDay. In 2000, the company acquired the Bubble Yum brand.

In 1972, See's Candies was sold to Warren E. Buffett's investment group, Berkshire Hathaway Inc., which also owns International **Dairy Queen** and many other companies. In 1993, Russell Stover Candies, Inc. bought out Whitman Chocolates. In 1972, the Brock Candy Company purchased Schuler Chocolates of Winona, Minnesota, and in 1990 it acquired Shelly Brothers of Souderton, Pennsylvania. In 1993, Brock Candy Company was acquired by E. J. Brach Corp, its biggest competitor. Today, Brach's is owned by Barry Callebaut, a Swiss company, which is one of the world's leading makers of chocolate. In 1990, The **New England Confectionery Company** (NECCO) purchased the Stark Candy Company, which made **Mary Jane Candies**. NECCO acquired the Clark Bar in 1999. The Nestlé Food Corporation acquired Butterfinger and **Baby Ruth** in 1990 and today owns many other candy brands worldwide.

Today, the United States has a $23 billion candy market and candy sales have continued to increase despite concern with **junk food** and **obesity** in America.

SUGGESTED READING: Joël Glenn Brenner, *The Emperors of Chocolate: Inside the Secret World of Hershey and Mars* (New York: Broadway Books, 2000); Tim Richardson, *Sweets: A History of Candy* (New York: Bloomsbury, 2002); candy industry Web site: www.candyindustry.com

Caramels Caramels are a chewy, sweet confection, often square in shape, traditionally composed of **sugar**, cream, butter, and flavorings. Historically, the Arabs may have invented the process of making caramels, but caramels were widely consumed throughout the world. Caramels were expensive until the late nineteenth century, when the cost of sugar declined. Caramels, a softer version of toffee, became popular in the United States during the mid-nineteenth century. Caramel was consumed as a **candy** and was used to coat other confections such as candy apples on a stick, which were sold at fairs, circuses, and sporting events.

Many companies began manufacturing caramels in the United States during the nineteenth century. As a promotional tool, caramel candy manufacturers began giving away baseball cards in 1888, a practice that continued through the 1930s. In the late nineteenth century, there were three major caramel manufacturers in the United States. All three were located in Pennsylvania: Breisch-Hine Company of Philadelphia, the P. C. Wiest Company of York, and Lancaster Caramel Company owned by **Milton S. Hershey**, who had learned how to make caramels while apprenticed to a caramel maker in Denver. Hershey had established his caramel company in 1886 and it became one of the most important caramel manufacturers in America. In 1898 Hershey's two major competitors, Breisch-Hine and P. C. Wiest, merged to form the American Caramel Company. They wanted to form a caramel monopoly and asked Hershey to join them. When he refused to do so, they offered to purchase his caramel manufacturing company for $1 million. Hershey accepted their offer and refocused his energy on manufacturing **chocolate**.

Caramel was easy to make and many others jumped in to making it: the American Caramel Company eventually floundered. Other caramel manufacturers emerged, such as the United States Caramel Company, but most failed. One exception was the York Caramel Company, founded in 1914; it has thrived ever since. In 1975 the company was sold to the Howard B. Stark Company, which renamed it York Candy Kitchens. The company was sold again in 1982 to Robert Lukas, who changed the company's name to Classic Caramel Company. It remains one of the largest caramel manufacturers in America. Other large manufacturers include **Kraft Foods** and Brach's Confections. In addition, caramel is used as an ingredient in many other candies, including Almond Kisses, Cow Tales, Goo Goo Clusters, **Milk Duds**, Slo Pokes, Sugar Daddies, Sugar Babies, TWIX Caramel Cookie Bars, and **Snickers**, the most popular candy bar in the United States.

SUGGESTED READING: Ray Broekel, *The Great America Candy Bar Book* (Boston: Houghton Mifflin Company, 1982); Tim Richardson, *Sweets: A History of Candy* (New York: Bloomsbury, 2002).

Carbohydrates Dietary carbohydrates are a large group of chemical compounds that include simple **sugars**, such as fructose and glucose, starches, glycogens, fibers, cellulose, and dextrin. Carbohydrates are one of the major dietary components. They supply energy to the body and, if present in excess, they are stored as **fat**. Complex carbohydrates are ultimately broken down into glucose, which is an essential nutriment for the brain as well as for blood cells and tissue. Glucose enters the cells according to need. The agent that controls this is the hormone insulin. **Diabetes** occurs when the regulatory mechanism fails. Low-carbohydrate diets, such as the Atkins and South Beach diets, are based on the reduction in the consumption of carbohydrates.

SUGGESTED READING: Ann-Charlotte Eliasson, ed., *Carbohydrates in Food,* 2nd ed. (Boca Raton, FL: CRC Press, 2006); Walter Gratzer, *Terrors of the Table: The Curious History of Nutrition* (New York: Oxford University Press, 2005).

Carhops As more **automobiles** appeared on America's streets during the early twentieth century, the restaurant business began to change to meet new needs. **Soda fountain** operators, for instance, began offering curb service for customers by 1910. Motorists stopped in front of their stores, honked their horns, and soda fountain employees called curbies rushed out to take orders and deliver them. When **drive-ins** developed in the 1920s, orders were taken and food was subsequently delivered on trays, and customers ate in their cars. In small drive-ins, the cook might also perform these functions. As drive-ins became more popular, boys and girls were hired to act as servers. They were variously called tray boys, tray girls, or tray trotters because they carried trays to the cars. At first, the tray was simply handed in through the car window, to be placed on the customer's lap. Sometimes people drove off with the trays, and a lap tray was hardly convenient for the driver, so new trays were developed that fastened to the outside of the car.

By the 1930s, the name changed to carhops, which purportedly referred to their practice of hopping up on cars' running boards. Carhops usually had their own entrance to the kitchen so they would not walk through restaurant seating areas. Other restaurants had their own kitchens and different **menus** for carhops. By the 1930s, young women (usually pretty) were selected to be carhops, and they were required to wear outlandish costumes, such as those that made them look like cheerleaders or majorettes—complete with boots, short skirts, and unusual hats. Others dressed in costumes that were themed to the drive-in, such as cowgirls or kilted Scottish lasses. Carhops occasionally navigated around drive-ins on roller skates. Because they earned their money from tips and small commissions on each item they sold, carhops were especially solicitous of their customers. In February, 1940, the cover of *Life* magazine featured Jeanette Hall, a shapely teenager who was a carhop at Prince's restaurant in Texas. She had been selected Carhop of the Year. Dressed as a majorette with epaulets, a plumed hat, and cowboy boots, she glamorized the carhop's job. After World War II, an enterprising Milwaukee drive-in operator gave carhops walkie-talkies, which increased the number of orders carhops could handle and decreased the number of carhops needed.

The heyday of the carhop lasted from the 1930s to the mid-1950s. Carhops were featured in the 1973 film *American Graffiti.* Filmmaker George Lucas heard that the original Mel's Drive-in in San Francisco was to be demolished, so he leased the site for filming. In the film, carhops skated around the parking lot, picking up orders and flirting. By the time movie premiered, Mel's Drive-in had been demolished.

The carhop era began to fade in 1948, when Maurice and Richard McDonald designed a **fast food** restaurant that did not need carhops. The McDonald brothers figured that carhops were more interested in flirting than in selling food, and that teenage boys, who were attracted to the carhops, kept away more desirable customers—suburban families. The **McDonald's** self-service model required that patrons leave their cars, pick up their own orders, carry them back to their cars, and dispose of their own garbage. This reduced expenses, speeded up service, and attracted suburban families.

As the McDonald's self-service model became almost universal in the fast food industry, carhops quickly disappeared.

Today, carhops are featured at **Sonic** restaurants, and some older **chains** such as Bob's **Big Boy** restaurant in Burbank, California, feature carhops on occasion.

SUGGESTED READING: Jim Heimann, *Car Hops and Curb Service: A History of American Drive-In Restaurants, 1920–1960* (San Francisco: Chronicle Books, 1996); Philip Langdon, *Orange Roofs, Golden Arches: The Architecture of American Chain Restaurants* (New York: Knopf, 1986); *Life Magazine,* February 26, 1940.

Carl's Jr. In 1956, Carl's Jr. was launched by the restaurateur **Carl Karcher** of Anaheim, California. After a visit to the **McDonald's** operation in San Bernardino, California, Karcher decided to develop a **fast food chain** of his own. They were mini-versions of the restaurant that he owned, and hence he called them Carl's Jr. Initially, two outlets were opened in Anaheim and nearby La Brea. Within 10 years, the company had 24 outlets in southern California. To supply its franchisees, Carl's Jr. began purchasing foodstuffs, processing them, and delivering them to outlets.

The company incorporated as Carl Karcher Enterprises, Inc. (CKE) in 1966. Two years later, the company began an expansion plan that created an enlarged version of Carl's Jr. restaurants, complete with larger dining rooms, attractive **architecture**, and music. The main menu items were **hamburgers**, **hot dogs**, **French fries**, and malts. By 1975, the company had about 100 outlets in California. In 1981, the company went public. CKE sold Carl's Jr. **franchises** nationwide. The company began to diversify its menu to include **breakfast** items and a **chicken sandwich**. During the 1990s, Carl's Jr. joined with Green Burrito, which CKE eventually acquired. It also acquired **Hardee's**, La Salsa Fresh Mexican Grill, and Taco Bueno. The corporation has also co-branded with Texaco, and many Carl's Jr. outlets are now inside Texaco gas stations. In 2004, CKE Restaurants had more than 3,400 outlets.

SUGGESTED READING: Carl Karcher and B. Carolyn Knight, *Never Stop Dreaming: The Story of Carl Karcher Enterprises* (San Marcos, CA: Robert Erdmann Publishing, 1991); B. Carolyn Knight, *Making it Happen: The Story of Carl Karcher Enterprises* (Anaheim, CA: C. Karcher Enterprises, 1981); Eric Schlosser, *Fast Food Nation: The Dark Side of the All-American Meal* (New York: Houghton Mifflin Company, 2001).

Carvel Corporation In 1934 Thomas Carvel, a salesman who sold **ice cream** at fairs and beach resorts, opened a retail ice cream shop in Hartsdale, New York. The following year, he perfected an electric freezer and later a formula for making soft ice cream. He was operating three stores when World War II started. After the war, he formed two companies—the parent company, Carvel Corporation, and the Carvel Dari-Freeze Stores, which he began to **franchise**. Within five years, he had generated 125 franchise stores from Maine to Florida. As part of the franchise package, he included plans for a Carvel structure with a glass front which leaned forward under a roof that pitched upwards toward the street. To help franchisees get off the ground, he established the Carvel College of Ice Cream Knowledge, which was referred to as Sundae School.

One of the most important reasons for the success of Carvel franchises was their **locations**. Carvel believed that the best place was on a secondary highway where traffic moves along at a slow speed; there also had to be a large enough population in the local area so that the store could generate repeat customers. To help make site decisions, so-called location engineers were called in. They used counters to determine the number of cars and people who passed by a given location.

Carvel stores sold hundreds of products, from dime ice cream cones to expensive ice cream cakes for weddings. The company continued to diversify its **menu**. As a novelty, Carvel introduced an ice cream sandwich which had ice cream between two **chocolate chip cookies**. This was a success and Carvel continued to combine ice cream with bakery goods, including ice cream cakes such as the Cookie Puss.

In 1992, Carvel began distributing its ice cream to supermarkets. In 2001, the company was sold to Roark Capital Group, a private equity firm, and three years later it was acquired by FOCUS Brands.

SUGGESTED READING: Carvel's Web site: www.carvel.com; Anne Cooper Funderburg, *Chocolate, Strawberry, and Vanilla: A History of American Ice Cream* (Bowling Green, OH: Bowling Green State University Popular Press, 1995); John A. Jakle and Keith A. Sculle, *Fast Food: Roadside Restaurants in the Automobile Age* (Baltimore: Johns Hopkins University Press, 1999); Philip Langdon, *Orange Roofs, Golden Arches: The Architecture of American Chain Restaurants* (New York: Knopf, 1986).

Center for Science in the Public Interest (CSPI) Formed in Washington, D.C. in 1971, the Center for Science in the Public Interest is one of America's most influential consumer advocate organizations. One of its founders, Michael Jacobson, concentrated on food additives and **nutrition**. Jacobson popularized the term **junk food** in 1972, to describe the empty calories present in many **snack** and **fast foods**. By 1977, CSPI focused almost exclusively on food issues, publishing nutritional analyses and critiques. Its *Nutrition Action Healthletter* is the largest-circulation health newsletter in North America.

CSPI has published numerous reports on fast food (*Fast-Food Guide*), junk foods (*What Are We Feeding Our Kids?*), **soda** (*Liquid Candy*), and **salt** (*Salt Assault: Brand-Name Comparisons of Processed Foods* and *Salt: The Forgotten Killer*). CSPI has been particularly concerned with corporate **advertising** targeted at children. CSPI's work has led to several Congressional hearings. As a result, major fast food **chains** have made changes to their operations and many have introduced more healthful foods. CSPI has about 900,000 members.

SUGGESTED READING: Michael F. Jacobson and Sarah Fritschner, *Fast-Food Guide,* 2nd ed. (New York: Workman Publishing, 1991); Michael F. Jacobson and Bruce Maxwell, *What Are We Feeding Our Kids?* (New York: Workman Publishing, 1994); Michael F Jacobson, *Liquid Candy: How Soft Drinks are Harming Americans' Health,* 2nd ed. (Washington, D.C.: Center for Science in the Public Interest, 2005); Michael F. Jacobson with Jessica Emami and Stephanie Grasmick, *Salt Assault: Brand-Name Comparisons of Processed Foods* (Washington, D.C.: Center for Science in the Public Interest, 2005); Michael F. Jacobson *Salt: The Forgotten Killer* (Washington, D.C.: Center for Science in the Public Interest, 2005); Center for Science in the Public Interest Web site: www.cspinet.org

Cereals (Breakfast) In 1877, Henry D. Seymour and William Heston developed and trademarked a new product, rolled oats. All consumers had to do was add hot water to the rolled oats in order to eat them. Because most Americans did not eat oats at that time, the company decided to launch a major **advertising** campaign. To promote sales, the company packed its rolled oats in cardboard boxes bearing the reassuring image of an elderly Quaker and promoted their new product via a national advertising campaign in 1882, making it the first cereal to be advertised nationally. The campaign was so successful that the company changed its name to the Quaker Oats Company in 1901.

In 1863, Dr. James C. Jackson, a vegetarian who operated the Dansville Sanitarium in Dansville, New York, advocated eating healthy food. He took graham flour, baked it, and broke it up into small pieces. This was the first breakfast cereal, and he called it granula. One of the patrons of Jackson's spa was Ellen White, who later formed the Seventh-Day Adventist church. The Seventh-Day Adventists launched a health asylum of their own in Battle Creek, Michigan. In 1876, John Harvey Kellogg became its director. Kellogg visited Jackson's spa and liked granula. Upon his return, Kellogg duplicated Jackson's formula and began selling it. Evidently Jackson threatened to sue him, so Kellogg changed the formula and called his new product granola.

Some of the cereal choices at the American supermarket. © Kelly Fitzsimmons

Kellogg tried to develop more grain-based **vegetarian** options for the guests of his spa. Countless variations of granola were created. He added water to ground corn, which he then rolled into small flakes on trays, which were then cooked. He called the resulting thin, wheat-flaked cereal granose. He similarly rolled and cooked cornmeal and ended up with corn flakes. Both of these cereals were served to patients at the sanitarium.

Charles W. Post, a patient at Kellogg's sanitarium, proclaimed that Kellogg's nine-month health regimen had changed his life. In 1895 Post offered to go into business with Kellogg to market the sanitarium's products, but Kellogg declined. Post then established the Postum Cereal Company (later renamed **General Foods Corporation**) and began producing Grape Nuts, which was a slight variation on Jackson's granula and Kellogg's granola. Post's success convinced Kellogg to commercialize his own products.

In 1906, John Harvey Kellogg established the Toasted Corn Flakes Company (later renamed the **Kellogg Company**) and selected his younger brother, Will K. Kellogg, president of the new company. Will took over the company and launched a major promotional campaign and developed many new cereals. Others followed Post's and Kellogg's examples and more than 40 new cereal companies were established during the early years of the twentieth century in Battle Creek, Michigan.

In 1921, Wheaties was accidentally discovered by a Minneapolis health clinician. The cereal was pitched to the Washburn Crosby Company (later renamed **General Mills**), which acquired the cereal and began advertising it as The Breakfast of Champions. This became one of the first food companies to advertise on **radio**. In the 1930s, the company introduced "Jack Armstrong, the all-American boy" to radio listeners, played by Jim Ameche.

The Postum Cereal Company responded in 1934 when they licensed the rights from Walt Disney to a popular new movie character, Mighty Mouse, who was prominently displayed on Post Toasties boxes and on Post advertisements. Mighty Mouse also appeared on many other products marketed to children

Beginning in the 1920s, cereals, which originated in the health food movement, began to evolve. The new addition was **sugar**. Kellogg's introduced Rice Krispies in 1928.

They consisted mainly of sugar and rice. The elves—Snap, Crackle, and Pop—were derived from a radio advertisement. They were among the first **mascots** developed for advertising cereals. After World War II, cereal makers determined that children preferred sweet cereals and began to add sugar to their products. Kellogg's introduced Sugar Pops in 1950 and Frosted Flakes in 1952. The original Frosted Flakes mascot was a kangaroo but this was later changed to Tony the Tiger. Kellogg's bought the licensing rights for the Superman comic book character, who appeared on Frosted Flakes boxes during the 1950s. Frosted Flakes is the second-largest selling cereal in America today.

General Mills introduced Trix, which contains 46 percent sugar, in 1954. Its advertising slogan, "Trix are for Kids," was introduced in 1960s. John Holahan, vice president of General Mills, invented Lucky Charms in 1963. It has regularly changed over the years, adding new shapes and flavors. Its mascot is the leprechaun, who first appeared in advertisements in 1964. In 1979, General Mills also offered a sugar-coated version of its Cheerios—Honey Nut Cheerios—which is among the top-selling cereals today.

Cereal manufacturers have extended their cereal lines to include confections. Commercial Rice Krispies Treats were first marketed in 1995. Made by Kellogg's, they are packaged in individual servings and are intended as a dessert for lunch boxes. Recently, Snapple and Fruit Loops have co-branded to produce Snapple Candy and Snapplets hard candies. Kellogg co-branded with Brach's Confections to produce Fruit Loops snacks.

Today, ready-to-eat breakfast cereals are served in 9 out of 10 American households. Cereals, which started as a health food, are a major contributor to sugar in the American diet, especially to the diets of children.

SUGGESTED READING: Scott Bruce and Bill Crawford, *Cerealizing America: The Unsweetened Story of American Breakfast Cereal* (Boston: Faber and Faber, 1995); Gerald Carson, *Cornflake Crusade* (New York: Rinehart & Company, Inc., 1957); Ronald D. Michman and Edward M. Mazze, *The Food Industry Wars: Marketing Triumphs and Blunders* (Westport, CT: Quorum, 1998); Horace B. Powell, *The Original Has This Signature—W. K. Kellogg* (Englewood Cliffs, NJ: Prentice-Hall, Inc., 1956).

Chains Chains are multiple restaurants owned by one company, or **franchises** that are licensed by the same parent company. The first restaurant chain in the United States is credited to English immigrant Frederick Henry Harvey, creator of Harvey Houses. He briefly owned a restaurant in St. Louis, Missouri, which failed during the Civil War. At the time, railroads were rapidly expanding westward. Prior to the invention of the Pullman dining car, railroads had limited food options. Working in cooperation with railroad companies, Harvey opened restaurants along the train routes. It was the first large chain of eating houses that could assure customers of quality and service at each outlet.

Small restaurant chains operated in cities. Cafeterias, for instance, often had more than one outlet in a particular city. The initial advantage of a chain was that ingredients and equipment could be acquired in bulk and some foods could be prepared en mass, thus reducing the costs. The first large, urban restaurant chain was developed by John R. Thompson, whose cafeterias in Chicago featured white tile for purity, bright electric lights, and gleaming dining rooms.

Fast food operations adopted techniques from existing restaurant chains. **White Castle** was the first fast food chain; it borrowed Thompson's cafeterias' white tiles and lights, but not the dining rooms. Initially, all of its outlets were owned by the company. **White Tower**, a White Castle clone, operated by franchising. Franchises could expand quickly, but the company-controlled outlets had more consistency. Most subsequent fast food chains were based on franchising.

Beginning in the 1950s, franchising drove the fast food chains to the forefront of the restaurant industry. Today, chains dominate America's eating-out patterns and chain-affiliated outlets outnumber independent restaurants. Larger-scale operations meant cost savings in the procurement, preparation, and distribution of food. Expanding chains generated more profit than stagnant chains, and unsuccessful chains, such as Burger Chef, were often cannibalized by other chains. Among the larger fast food chains are **McDonald's**, **Kentucky Fried Chicken**, and **Burger King**.

SUGGESTED READING: Charles Bernstein and Ron Paul, *Winning the Chain Restaurant Game: Eight Key Strategies* (New York: John Wiley & Sons, 1994); John A. Jakle and Keith A. Sculle, *Fast Food: Roadside Restaurants in the Automobile Age* (Baltimore: Johns Hopkins University Press, 1999); Philip Langdon, *Orange Roofs, Golden Arches: The Architecture of American Chain Restaurants* (New York: Knopf, 1986); H. G. Parsa and Francis A. Kwansa, eds., *Quick Service Restaurants, Franchising, and Multi-unit Chain Management* (New York: Haworth Hospitality Press, 2002).

Chanukah Candy Chanukah, the Festival of Lights, celebrates a Jewish victory in 164 B.C.E. Traditionally, Chanukah is celebrated with the giving of gifts, particularly money or gelt. Jewish colonists and immigrants brought this celebration to America in colonial times. In the 1920s, merchandisers promoted their wares as ideal Chanukah gifts. The Loft Candy Company, for instance, sold **chocolates** wrapped in gold foil to simulate Chanukah gelt. Barton's, which was founded in 1938 by Steven Klein in Manhattan, also made kosher chocolates for Chanukah and other Jewish holidays. The Loft Candy Company acquired Pepsi-Cola in 1931, and it was later merged into **PepsiCo**. Barton's was purchased by Cherrydale Farms in 2001.

Charities Among the earliest contributors to charity was **Milton S. Hershey**. Because he and his wife did not have children, they decided to establish an industrial **school** for orphans and poor boys. Now called the Milton Hershey School, it began on small scale in 1909; after his wife's death, Hershey gave his entire fortune (estimated at $60 million) to a trust for the school. Unlike subsequent contributors to charity, Hershey did not **advertise** his largess; it was only revealed five years after he made the contribution. Today, the 10,000-acre school serves 1,050 boys and girls of diverse backgrounds. Many of its graduates have gone on to Ivy League universities. Thanks to Hershey's gift, the school is one of the most well-endowed in the nation. The school today owns 31.4 percent of **Hershey Company** common stock.

On the **fast food** side, all major fast food **chains** have established charitable foundations. One of the most visible charitable programs is the **Ronald McDonald** House for parents of children in hospitals. The **PepsiCo** Foundation focuses on health and wellness, youth development, and higher education. The **Arby's** Foundation, established in 1986, has focused on Big Brothers Big Sisters of America, which has helped children from primarily single-parent homes by matching them with adult volunteers. In 2001, **Domino's Pizza** focused on the Make-A-Wish Foundation, which grants the wishes of children with life-threatening medical conditions. The Ingram-**White Castle** Foundation gives scholarships to college students.

In the soft drink world, Claud A. Hatcher, founder of **Royal Crown Cola**, established the Pichett-Hatcher Education Fund in 1933. By 1968, this fund had assets of almost $5 million and was one of the largest student loan funds of its kind in America. Other soft drink companies have established company foundations. The **Coca-Cola** Foundation, for instance, also stresses education. Its programs include a scholars program that gives two-year college scholarships to high school seniors and provides extensive funding for many other causes.

Most large fast food chains, **junk food** manufacturers, and **soda** makers give to charity. Like most large business, they believe that it is their civic duty to support charities. This demonstrates that these corporations are good neighbors, and many corporations receive positive visibility due to their contributions. Most of these types of foundations have focused on children or youth.

SUGGESTED READING: Tim Richardson, *Sweets: A History of Candy* (New York: Bloomsbury, 2002); John F. Halbleib, *Milton S. Hershey* ([Hershey, Pa.?]: J. F. Halbleib, [2004]); Hershey's Web site: www.hersheys.com; McDonald's Web site: www.mcdonalds.com/corporate; Coca-Cola Foundation Web site:www.coca-colascholars.org; PepsiCo Foundation Web site: www.pepsico.scholarshipamerica.org; Burger King/McLamore Foundation Web site: www.burgerking.ca/en/1124/1140.php

Cheese-based Snacks The first commercial cheese-based snack were Cheez-It crackers, which were introduced in 1921 by the Sunshine Biscuit Company. They have been a very successful brand ever since, so much so that many other companies have tried to make similar crackers. Today, Cheez-It crackers are a brand of the **Kellogg Company**, which has extended the brand to include many different flavors.

During the 1930s, **extruded snacks** were invented by an animal feed technician, Edward Wilson. His commercial product, Korn Kurls, became popular after World War II. During the 1940s, the Frito Company began experimenting with extruded snacks and in 1948 they released **Cheetos**, which were cheese-flavored. Other companies began manufacturing cheese puffs, which was a generic name for extruded snacks with a cheese covering. Yet another cheese-based snack, **Goldfish**, a small orange-colored, cheese-flavored cracker shaped like a fish, was released by **Pepperidge Farm**, a subsidiary of the Campbell Soup Company.

In the 1980s, **Frito-Lay** introduced other cheese-flavored products, such as Puffed Balls. Many other companies have manufactured products with cheese flavors.

SUGGESTED READING: Cheese-It Web site: www.kelloggs.com/cheez_it/

Cheetos. © Kelly Fitzsimmons

Cheetos During the late 1940s, the Frito Company invented Cheetos, which were marketed by H. W. Lay & Company in 1948. This extruded corn snack is covered with an artificially colored powdered cheddar cheese. The two companies merged in 1961, forming **Frito-Lay,** Inc. The merged company greatly increased its promotion for Cheetos, which acquired a **mascot** named Chester Cheetah. Today, the Cheetos product line has been extended to include many other snacks, including Crunchy Cheetos, Cheetos Puffs, Cheetos

Twists, Cheetos Paws, Cheetos Whirls, Flamin' Hot Cheetos, and Flamin' Hot Cheetos con Limon.

Although similar products are manufactured by other companies, Frito-Lay's Cheetos dominate the puffed snack market with sales twice as high as all the other top 15 products combined. Cheetos are sold in Belgium, Brazil, China, Greece, Hungary, Indonesia, Mexico, Poland, Spain, Turkey, United Kingdom, and many other countries. The Cheetos mascot, Chester Cheetah, has taken on a life of its own, as it now stars in video games, such as *Chester Cheetah: Wild Wild Quest.*

SUGGESTED READING: PepsiCo Web site: www.pepsico.com

Chewy Candy Chewy candies have been common in the United States since the early twentieth century. Henry Heide, a German immigrant who arrived in New York in 1866, founded the Henry Heide Candy Company in 1869. The company made almond paste for bakeries, but during the early twentieth century it began to make chewy, gum arabic-based candies. Its products included Jujubes, named for the juju **gum** that was the main ingredient, which were produced before 1920, and Jujyfruits, which were first made in 1920 (each box contains an assortment of fruit-shaped candies). Both products became famous, particularly when they were sold in movie **theaters**. The Henry Heide Candy Company was acquired by the **Hershey Company** in 1995. Farley's & Sathers Candy Co., Inc. acquired the Heide brand products from Hershey in 2002.

Gummi bears. © Kelly Fitzsimmons

Another type of chewy candy, Gummi Bears, was developed in Germany during the 1920s. In 1982, the German candy company Haribo first marketed **gummi candy** in the United States. Trolli, another German gummi candy manufacturer, introduced gummi worms into the United States during the 1980s and they have remained popular ever since. Edible gelatin is the basic ingredient in gummi candy. Gummi candies are softer and easier to chew than Jujyfruits or Jujubes. In 2000, the convenience store chain **7-Eleven** introduced gummi candies in a plastic cup, called the Candy Gulp. It was intended to fit into the cup-holders in cars, making it possible to drive and eat gummi candy at the same time. It became 7-Eleven's best-selling confection.

SUGGESTED READING: Joël Glenn Brenner, *The Emperors of Chocolate: Inside the Secret World of Hershey and Mars* (New York: Broadway Books, 2000).

Chicken Chickens likely originated in Southeast Asia but they were disseminated widely in prehistoric times. Chickens, along with dogs and pigs, eventually appeared in Europe, Africa, Asia, and the Pacific islands, including Easter Island, but do not appear to have reached the New World until the arrival of the Europeans 500 years ago.

Since the chicken's introduction to the English colonies in North America in the seventeenth century, it has been America's most important fowl. Its mild, neutral flavor can be combined with any number of seasonings and ingredients. Inexpensive and plentiful, chicken lends itself to a variety of cooking methods and recipes. For example, chicken can be roasted or baked, fricasséed, deviled, fried, hashed, or sautéed, made into soups, broths, gumbos, and gravies, and incorporated into pies, puddings, and croquettes. Cold chicken can be served in salads and **sandwiches**. Poultry can be stuffed with bread, grains, forcemeat, or vegetables, or served with special gravies and sauces, such as oyster and curry sauces. Virtually all parts of the chicken, including necks, gizzards, feet, hearts, and livers, are consumed in various ways.

Recipes for preparing chicken for the table abound in cookbooks from the early nineteenth century to today. These include barbecued chicken, chicken pot pie, chicken and dumplings, Chicken Maryland, Brunswick stew, jambalaya, gumbo, and chicken á la king. Chicken was particularly important in the American South. Prior to the Civil War, many slaves were permitted to keep chickens and they elevated the technique of frying chicken to an art form. After the Civil War, migrations of African-Americans out of the South contributed to making Southern Fried Chicken a national dish during the twentieth century.

Poultry was used as a cheap food for servants and slaves, but domesticated and wild birds also appeared on the tables in America's most elegant restaurants. Nineteenth-century cookbooks provide an abundance of recipes for barnyard fowl and wild ducks and geese, as well as blackbirds, larks, quail, grouse, guinea fowl, peafowl, pigeons, plover, widgeons, and other game birds. They contain instructions for buying poultry and for preparing home-grown or purchased birds for the oven or pot. Roasting was a basic method of preparation, but there are also recipes for fricassées, stews, ragouts, pot pies, and hashes. There are directions for making chicken broth or stock as well as heartier soups, and plenty of sauces and stuffings or dressings for specific birds.

Today, chicken remains the dominant poultry in America and the world. In addition to the traditional ways of preparing chicken in the home, **fast food** establishments have commercialized specific chicken dishes, such as the fried chicken served at **Kentucky Fried Chicken**, and **Chicken McNuggets** served at **McDonald's**. Likewise, **Burger King** and **Wendy's** have introduced chicken items on their **menus**. In addition, chicken burgers are served at many **hamburger** establishments, "chicken dogs" are sold in supermarkets throughout America, and many manufacturers have included chicken in their frozen dinners. Other purveyors of fast food chicken include **Church's Chicken, Chicken Delight**, and **Popeyes**.

Chicken is generally eaten by practitioners of most religions. The problems that have emerged with chicken include ***salmonella*** bacteria, the intensive rearing practices, and the lack of flavor. Today, chicken is the most-consumed meat in the United States. Americans eat an average of 67 pounds of chicken per year.

SUGGESTED READING: Page Smith and Charles Daniel, *The Chicken Book* (San Francisco: North Point Press, 1982); USDA Web site: www.ers.usda.gov/Publications/ldp/Oct05/ldpm13502/; Steve Striffler, *Chicken: the Dangerous Transformation of America's Favorite Food* (New Haven: Yale University Press, 2005).

Chicken Delight A. L. "Al" Tunick, a scrap iron dealer, acquired some deep-fryers from a restaurant that was going out of business. In the early 1950s, the restaurant had used the fryers mainly to make **French fries**. At that time, chicken was not considered **fast food**; it was usually pan-fried, steamed, or oven-roasted, and all of these methods took too long for fast food. Deep-fryers cooked the chicken faster, but the device Tunick had run into was even faster. It deep-fried chicken under pressure, thus greatly reducing the time spent in cooking. To exploit this, Tunick founded Chicken Delight in 1952 in Illinois. He decided to market his method through small take-out outlets and his was the first fast food **chain** to offer home delivery. He began **franchising** his operation, and it grew quickly. This growth was abetted by its **advertising**: its **slogan** "Don't Cook Tonight, Call Chicken Delight" became a household phrase and the company became one of the biggest fast food operations in the United States. Tunick expanded into Canada in 1958 and by the mid-1960s Chicken Delight of Canada, Ltd. had more than 50 outlets. When Tunick sold the company to Consolidated Foods in 1964, his chain had hundreds of outlets.

But all was not well with the chain. Tunick had required that franchisees purchase all their equipment and packaging from him. Franchisees took the company to court, challenging this practice. The case was won by the franchisees and the franchiser's main source of revenue declined, as did the entire chain.

Otto Koch purchased his first Chicken Delight franchise in 1969. Koch acquired additional franchise locations and in 1976 bought Chicken Delight of Canada, Ltd. He began to rebuild the franchise system. He updated stores, advertised extensively, and shored up the Chicken Delight brand image. He also diversified the menu by including ribs and **pizza**. Koch acquired the Chicken Delight operations in the United States and Chicken Delight International, Inc. in 1979.

SUGGESTED READING: Chicken Delight Web site: www.chickendelight.com

Chicken McNuggets During the 1970s, **chicken** consumption had greatly increased in the United States, largely due to **fast food chains** such as **Kentucky Fried Chicken**, **Chicken Delight**, and **Church's Chicken**. At the same time, the medical profession praised the healthful benefits of chicken as opposed to **hamburgers**. This caused a stir in the hamburger fast food industry. In 1979 Fred Turner, **McDonald's** chairman, wanted to sell a chicken product that could easily be eaten while a customer was behind the steering wheel of a car, so he requested that a chicken processor create a finger-food without bones. It took six months to develop McNuggets, small pieces of reconstituted chicken held together by stabilizers that were breaded, fried, frozen, and shipped to the outlet, where they were reheated.

Chicken McNuggets. © Kelly Fitzsimmons

The original McNuggets contained ground chicken skin in addition to chicken meat and were fried in oil. When the McNuggets were tested by McDonald's technicians, six of the McNuggets had twice as much as fat as a Big Mac. The skins were eliminated and the improved McNuggets weighed in at 16.3 grams fat compared to 32.4 grams for the Big Mac. McDonald's contracted with Tyson Foods to maintain an adequate supply of chicken. When Chicken McNuggets debuted in 1983, they were an immediate success. Other fast food chains came up with their own McNuggets-type clones, such as **Burger King**'s Chicken Tenders.

There were good reasons for the success of McNuggets. They tasted good and were easy to chew. Many customers thought they were a healthy alternative to hamburgers, but this was not true. McNuggets were cooked in beef tallow and contained a large amount of fatty acids. When this information became public, McDonald's switched to vegetable oil and added beef extract to McNuggets during manufacturing to retain their familiar taste. McNuggets were particularly popular among young people.

McNugget's helped change not only the American diet but also the system of raising and processing poultry. In 1980, most chickens were sold whole; today about 90 percent of chickens sold in United States have been cut into pieces to produce cutlets or nuggets. In 1992, the American consumption of chicken for the first time surpassed that of beef. Due to the McNuggets, McDonald's is the nation's second-largest chicken seller, after Kentucky Fried Chicken.

SUGGESTED READING: David Gerard Hogan, *Selling 'em by the Sack: White Castle and the Creation of American Food* (New York: New York University Press, 1997); Eric Schlosser, *Fast Food Nation: The Dark Side of the All-American Meal* (New York: Houghton Mifflin Company, 2001); Gerry Schremp, *Kitchen Culture: Fifty Years of Food Fads, from Spam to Spa Cuisine* (New York: Pharos Books, 1991).

Chips Ahoy! In 1963, **Nabisco** released Chips Ahoy!, a small, hard **chocolate chip cookie**. Nabisco needed to promote this product and came up with a great idea. Nabisco had repeatedly claimed that every 18-ounce bag of Chips Ahoy! has at least 1,000 chocolate chips. As a promotional activity, Nabisco created the Chips Ahoy! 1,000 Chips Challenge, which asked the public to figure out the most creative way to confirm there are a least 1,000 chocolate chips in every bag. This led to numerous studies to count the actual number of chips in each bag. Nabisco has regularly expanded the Chips Ahoy! product line to include Peanut Butter Chips Ahoy!, Chips Ahoy! Cremewiches, and Chips Ahoy! Ice Cream. In 1994, Nabisco introduced a lower-**fat** version. Nabisco has also released Chips Ahoy! Cookie Barz, which are bar-shaped cookies topped with a layer of **chocolate** creme, covered in fudge, and sprinkled with chocolate chips. Chips Ahoy! are America's favorite chocolate chip cookie. In 2002, the **7-Eleven** chain of convenience stores collaborated with Nabisco to create plastic cups filled with Chips Ahoy! These cups fit into car cup-holders so the product can be consumed by drivers and passengers while the car is underway.

SUGGESTED READING: Chips Ahoy! Web site: www.nabiscoworld.com/cookieguys

Chocolate Chocolate is made by a process of fermenting, roasting, and grinding seeds of the cacao tree (*Theobroma cacao*). Chocolate is a complex combination of about 1,200 chemicals, none of which is dominant. Theobromine, a bitter, colorless alkaloid found in chocolate, is a mild stimulant that acts primarily on the muscles. Cacao also contains small quantities of **caffeine**.

Cacao is a New World plant. In pre-Columbian times, the indigenous peoples of Central America figured out how to bring out the rich flavor of cacao beans through a complicated process that involved fermenting and roasting the seeds. The Spanish conquistador Hernán Cortéz found the Aztec aristocracy consuming vast quantities of cacao combined with cornmeal, chilies, and spices to produce a frothy, bitter **beverage**. Cacao was introduced into Spain, where the ground beans were converted into a hot beverage by adding **sugar**, hot water, and spices. From Spain, this beverage was disseminated throughout Europe. European colonists brought cocoa into North America in the seventeenth century. In colonial times, cocoa beans were imported from the Caribbean and were used only for making hot cocoa. It was not until the nineteenth century that Europeans figured out how to make eating chocolate. Chocolate candies were made by hand and only the well-to-do were able to acquire them. **Milton S. Hershey** began to mass-produce chocolates in the twentieth century, and shortly thereafter **chocolate confections** became affordable by virtually every American. In 1912, Goo Goo Clusters, manufactured by the Standard Candy Company of Nashville, Tennessee, created the first chocolate combination **candy**. It was followed by the **Clark Bar**, composed of ground roasted peanuts covered with milk chocolate. This was the first combination candy bar and its success induced numerous others to produce combination bars. An estimated 100,000 different chocolate candies have subsequently been produced.

White chocolate is made from cocoa butter, milk solids, sugar, and (usually) vanilla. Because it contains no cocoa solids, it is not a true chocolate.

Today, cocoa can only be grown in a limited number of tropical nations; the biggest producers are the Ivory Coast, Brazil, Ghana, and Indonesia. For the past century, reports have persisted that child labor has been used on cocoa farms, particularly in West Africa. It has been estimated that cocoa plantations in Ivory Coast have as many as 15,000 child slaves, according to Tim Richardson, author of *Sweets: A History of Candy*.

Another problem related to cocoa production has been concern for the destruction of the rainforests. Environmental groups have accused cocoa producers of destroying millions of acres of rainforests, particularly in the Ivory Coast, Indonesia, and Brazil.

Because chocolate is extremely important economically, large commercial companies have established research facilities to improve cocoa production. **Mars, Inc.,** for example, has developed a research facility in Brazil, called M&M/Mars Almirante Center for Cocoa Studies. Although the United States leads the world in chocolate production, the Swiss consume more chocolate on a per-capita basis.

SUGGESTED READING: Carole Bloom, *All About Chocolate: The Ultimate Resource to the World's Favorite Food* (New York: Macmillan, 1998); Joël Glenn Brenner, *The Emperors of Chocolate: Inside the Secret World of Hershey and Mars* (New York: Broadway Books, 2000); Ray Broekel, *The Great America Candy Bar Book* (Boston: Houghton Mifflin Company, 1982); Sophie D. Coe and Michael D. Coe, *The True History of Chocolate* (New York: Thames and Hudson, Inc., 1996); Marcia Morton and Frederic Morton, *Chocolate: An Illustrated History* (New York: Crown Publishers, 1986); Tim Richardson, *Sweets: A History of Candy* (New York: Bloomsbury, 2002); Mort Rosenblum, *Chocolate; A Bittersweet Saga of Dark and Light* (New York: North Point Press, 2005); Alex Szogyi, ed., *Chocolate: Food of the Gods* (Westport, CT: Greenwood Press, 1997); Michael Turback, *Hot Chocolate* (Berkeley, CA: Ten Speed Press, 2005).

Chocolate Chip Cookies The invention of the chocolate chip cookie has been attributed to Ruth Wakefield, who bought a tourist lodge named the Toll House Inn in Whitman, Massachusetts in the early 1930s. Wakefield, a nutritionist by training, gained local fame for her desserts that were served at the Toll House. According to tradition, she invented the chocolate chip cookie by accident. While preparing Butter Drop Do cookies, she found herself without baker's chocolate, a required ingredient. She substituted a **Nestlé** semisweet chocolate bar cut up into bits. Baker's chocolate would have completely melted, but the small pieces of semisweet chocolate only softened.

Capitalizing upon the success of homemade chocolate chip cookies, in 1939 Nestlé began manufacturing Tollhouse Morsels packaged with Ruth Wakefield's cookie recipe printed on the back. **Nabisco** introduced **Chips Ahoy!** in 1964. It is the best-selling chocolate chip cookie in America. Fresh-baked chocolate chip cookies have been commercialized by **Mrs. Fields** and **Famous Amos**, and both companies now have a line of cookies that are sold in grocery stores.

Chocolate chip cookies made it into the presidential race in 1992. Hillary Clinton, the wife of the Democratic candidate for president, Bill Clinton, made a notorious remark that she was not going to stay home and bake chocolate chip cookies. This wound up with Hillary Clinton and Barbara Bush, the wife of the incumbent president George Bush, submitting their recipes for chocolate chip cookies to *Family Circle* magazine, which sponsored a bake-off using the recipes.

SUGGESTED READING: Wally Amos with Leroy Robinson, *The Famous Amos Story: The Face That Launched a Thousand Chips* (Garden City, NY: Doubleday, 1983); Karen Lehrman, "Beware the Cookie Monster," *New York Times,* July 18, 1992, Section 1: 23.

Chocolate Confections Cacao, a product of the New World, was imported into Europe in the sixteenth century and became popular during the following century as a **beverage**. European chefs tried to make solid **chocolate** in the late eighteenth century. Although the bars were hard, dry, and too crumbly to be eaten as a solid, they were perfect to dissolve in hot water for a hot beverage. In 1815, a Dutchman named Coenraad Van Houten developed a hand-operated machine that pressed out much of the **fat** content from cacao. He then dried it, ground it into powder, and then treated the powder with alkaline salts (potassium or sodium carbonates) to make the resulting product soluble in water. This process produced Dutch chocolate, which was dark in color and mild in flavor. Van Houten patented the process in 1828. Continued experimentation with Van Houten's process created powdered cocoa, which led to the large-scale manufacture of chocolate powder. In 1847, Joseph S. Fry & Sons in Bristol, England, which had been making drinking chocolate since 1728, combined cocoa powder with **sugar** and added cocoa butter to produce a thin paste which could be shaped in a mold and be consumed as a solid.

Fry's confection was grainy, but others raced to improve the new confection. **Cadbury** brought out its own version a few years later, and the other European firms did likewise. Daniel Peter of Vevey, Switzerland, experimented for eight years before finally perfecting his method. In 1876, he created an alliance with Henri Nestlé, a milk expert, to produce milk chocolate. In 1879, they produced **Nestlé** chocolate. Simultaneously, Jean Tobler launched a company that later marketed the **Toblerone** chocolate bar. Rodolphe Lindt of Berne, Switzerland, invented conching, a process that refined chocolate. More cocoa butter was added and the result was used as fillings for chocolate candies such as bonbons.

Other companies tried to duplicate these confections, and each kept secret the way that it made its chocolate. Different methods produced unique flavors. For instance, Swiss chocolate has been characterized by an aromatic flavor with a smooth texture. Swiss and Germans preferred milk chocolate, such as produced by Toblerone, Lindt, and Milka. The Italians tended to prefer dark chocolate, such as made by Baci.

Chocolate making progressed slowly in North America. Cocoa was imported by the mid-seventeenth century but it remained a luxury item for almost two centuries. Although it hardly compared with the sales of less-expensive tea and coffee, hot chocolate became a relatively common American beverage by the early nineteenth century. Hotels and restaurants offered hot chocolate for breakfast and supper. Many wealthy women adopted the French custom of breakfasting upon rolls and hot chocolate. In the American Southwest, chocolate was popular among Mexican-Americans who imported it from Mexico.

After the Civil War, Americans began using chocolate in a variety of ways in chocolate cakes, blancmanges, creams, cream pies, custards, éclairs, jumbles, macaroons, puddings, soufflés, syrups, and tarts. By the 1880s, chocolate was also used to make frappés, **ice cream**, and syrups for **soda fountains**. Confectioners used it in making chocolate drops, bonbons, and chocolate-coated nuts. Fudge (a combination of sugar, butter, and milk) appeared in women's colleges in the late nineteenth century. Fudge making became a widespread fad at the turn of the twentieth century and was sold by many confectioners.

When the price of sugar and cocoa dropped during the nineteenth century, chocolate confections became popular. With the help of immigrants who brought candy-making skills from Europe, a fledgling chocolate industry began to emerge in the late nineteenth century. By the 1870s, chocolate-covered candy and chocolate **caramels** were popular in America. Chocolate manufacturers included Walter Baker in New England, Domingo Ghirardelli in California, and Walter M. Lowney in Boston. They produced handmade chocolate confections and none produced chocolate on a large enough scale to make it affordable to most Americans.

In 1893, **Milton S. Hershey**, a caramel maker from Lancaster, Pennsylvania, created the **Hershey Chocolate Company**. In 1900, he devoted his attention solely to chocolate manufacturing. With mass-production, the price of chocolate candies decreased, and by the early twentieth century chocolates were affordable to most Americans. Hershey's success encouraged others to begin manufacturing chocolate confections.

World War I impacted the production of chocolate bars, when the U.S. Quartermaster Corps sent them to American soldiers, many of whom ate their first chocolate bars in this milieu. Chocolate candies soon dominated candy production in the United States. Otto Schnering of Chicago created the **Baby Ruth** candy bar in 1916; by 1925 it was the most popular candy bar in America. A decade later he invented the **Butterfinger**. In 1920 George Williamson, also of Chicago, invented the **Oh Henry!** candy bar. Ernest Wilson of San Francisco manufactured Wilsonettes—chocolate-covered peanuts. In 1923, he packaged 150 of them in a box and charged a nickel for it. Similarly, in 1925 the Blumenthal Chocolate Company of Philadelphia began manufacturing Goobers, another chocolate-covered peanut candy that is still sold in movie theaters. **Frank Mars** in Minneapolis began manufacturing candy bars in 1925. Since then, more than 40,000 different brands of chocolate candies and bars have been manufactured in the United States.

SUGGESTED READING: Carole Bloom, *All About Chocolate: The Ultimate Resource to the World's Favorite Food* (New York: Macmillan, 1998); Joël Glenn Brenner, *The Emperors of Chocolate: Inside the Secret World of Hershey and Mars* (New York: Broadway Books, 2000); Ray Broekel, *The Great America Candy Bar Book* (Boston: Houghton Mifflin Company, 1982); Marcia Morton and Frederic Morton, *Chocolate: An Illustrated History* (New York: Crown Publishers, 1986); Mort Rosenblum, *Chocolate: A Bittersweet Saga of Dark and Light* (New

York: North Point Press, 2005); Tim Richardson, *Sweets: A History of Candy* (New York: Bloomsbury, 2002); Alex Szogyi, ed., *Chocolate: Food of the Gods* (Westport, CT: Greenwood Press, 1997).

Cholesterol Cholesterol, a crystalline substance found in animal tissue, is manufactured in the human liver and is a significant constituent of body cells and metabolic processes, such as synthesizing vitamin D, repairing cells, and the production of hormones. Cholesterol is transported through the bloodstream by lipoproteins, which are coagulated proteins with **fat**. There are three types of cholesterol: high-density lipoproteins (HDL), low-density lipoproteins (LDL), and very-low-density lipoproteins (VLDL), which are an intermediate stage in the development of LDL. LDL, commonly known as the bad cholesterol, contributes to arterial plaque. People with high serum cholesterol, such as contained in LDL, are more likely to suffer from a variety of coronary heart diseases. Heredity plays an important part in cholesterol levels, as does the consumption of certain foods. Dietary cholesterol is abundant in meat and dairy products; it is also present in high concentrations in many processed and deep-fried foods, such as **French fries** and **fried chicken**. Considerable medical evidence suggests that a significant reduction in consumption of such foods results in a modest increase in life expectancy.

SUGGESTED READING: Walter Gratzer, *Terrors of the Table: The Curious History of Nutrition* (New York: Oxford University Press, 2005); Jean P. Kovala, ed., *Cholesterol in Atherosclerosis and Coronary Heart Disease* (New York: Nova Science Publishers, 2005).

Christmas Today, Christmas is one of the most important sacred days in the Christian calendar. By Christian tradition, St. Nicholas was known for his good works related to children. His feast day, December 6, has been celebrated throughout Europe for centuries. In Holland, Dutch children put their shoes by the fireplace for St. Nicholas, who rides his horse on rooftops and drops candy down the chimneys into the children's shoes. When the Dutch settled in New Amsterdam (now New York), they brought these traditions with them. It was not until the early nineteenth century that Christmas began to be observed throughout the United States. Some of the traditions surrounding Santa Claus can be attributed to Clement Clarke Moore's poem, "The Night Before Christmas," which mentions stockings being filled by Santa Claus.

Several different types of Christmas candies were made in the nineteenth century. These included butterscotch, **chocolate**, lemon and cream **caramels**, creme **sugar** birds and animals, cream pears, cream mice, cream babies, **jelly beans**, and many other varieties. It was not until 1847 that candy canes became part of American Christmas celebrations. This type of candy is attributed to August Imgard of Wooster, Ohio, who reportedly decorated Christmas trees with paper ornaments and **candy** canes. It was not an immediate commercial success, although candy makers handmade candy canes on a small scale. They were difficult to make and transport. This changed in the 1950s, when candy cane machines automated production and packaging innovations made it possible to make a commercial success of their production. Bob's Candies, Inc. of Albany, Georgia, quickly became the largest producer of candy canes. In 2005, Bobs' Candies was acquired by Farley's & Sathers Candy Company, Inc. of Round Lake, Minnesota. In addition, large candy manufacturers including **Mars**, **Hershey**, and **Nestlé** make their own brands in special colors and packages. According to the **National Confectioners Association**, which has strongly supported the tradition of giving candy at holidays, Americans spend approximately $1.4 billion on candy at Christmas

In addition to candy sales, fast food and soda companies have used Christmas themes to promote their products. The **Coca-Cola Company**, for instance, has produced Christmas/holiday labels for its bottles. Its commercials featuring Santa Claus been credited with inventing the modern image of Santa Claus as a jolly old man with a white beard dressed in red-and-white garments.

SUGGESTED READING: Stephen Nissenbaum, *The Battle for Christmas: A Social and Cultural History of Christmas That Shows How It Was Transformed from an Unruly Carnival Season into the Quintessential American Family Holiday* (New York: Alfred A. Knopf, 1996); Cathy Kaufman, "The Ideal Christmas Dinner," *Gastronomica* 2004;4:17; Jack Santino, *New Old-Fashioned Ways: Holidays and Popular Culture* (Knoxville, TN: The University of Tennessee Press, 1996).

Chuck E. Cheese Pizza Nolan Bushnell, who had worked as a games division manager of an amusement park, developed the video game called *Pong* in 1971. The following year, Bushnell and Ted Dabney founded Atari, which was sold to Warner Communications in 1976. While working for Warner Communications, Bushnell created Chuck E. Cheese's Pizza Time Theatre, the first of which opened in 1977 in San Jose, California. It featured **pizza**, 100 video games, and animated entertainment with life-sized robots, such as Chuck E. Cheese with his trademark cigar.

Bushnell eventually left Atari and bought Pizza Time Theatre from Warner Communications. He began marketing the Pizza Time Theatre concept and by 1983 there were more than 200 outlets in the United States. Robert L. Brock, president of Topeka Inn Management, signed a co-development agreement with Bushnell that gave Brock exclusive franchising rights for Pizza Time Theatres in several states. Topeka Inn Management created a subsidiary called Pizza Show Biz to help launch the new **franchises**.

Brock declared the co-development agreement void and in 1980 opened the ShowBiz Pizza Place in Kansas City, Missouri. It was similar to Pizza Time Theatre. Bushnell sued Brock for breach of contract. The lawsuit was settled out of court, with ShowBiz paying Pizza Time Theatre a portion of its profits for 14 years.

During the late 1970s, both Pizza Time and ShowBiz enjoyed success and both restaurants rapidly expanded their operations. However, in the 1980s Pizza Time's profits plunged and in 1984 the company filed for bankruptcy; ShowBiz Pizza Place bought it out. During 1986 profits began to increase and ShowBiz outlets were remodeled to resemble Chuck E. Cheese characters. The company changed its name to CEC Entertainment. Inc. and it is now headquartered in Irving, Texas. As of 2005, there were 498 Chuck E. Cheese outlets, which operate in 48 states and four countries.

Chuck E. Cheese mascot. © Kelly Fitzsimmons

SUGGESTED READING: Philip Langdon, *Orange Roofs, Golden Arches: The Architecture of American Chain Restaurants* (New York: Knopf, 1986); Chuck E. Cheese Web site: www.chuckecheese.com

Church's Chicken In 1952, George W. Church, Sr., a retired incubator salesman, launched Church's Fried Chicken To Go in downtown San Antonio, Texas. It was a low-overhead operation that sold only take-out, but what was distinctive about Church's was that it served larger **chickens** than did its competitors.

At first, Church only sold **fried chicken**; **French fries** and jalapeños were added in 1955. Church launched new outlets, but when he died in 1956 only four outlets were open. Family members took over the operation and by 1962 the **chain** had grown to eight locations in San Antonio. The company began an expansion beyond San Antonio. The Church family sold the company in 1968 and in the following year Church's Fried Chicken, Inc. became a publicly held company. At the end of 1969, more than 100 Church's restaurants were in operation in seven states. Between 1969 and 1974, Church's grew by an additional 387 restaurants.

International expansion began in 1979 with the establishment of the first Church's in Japan. The company subsequently established locations in Puerto Rico, Canada, Malaysia, Mexico, and Taiwan, under the brand name Texas Chicken. In addition to its chicken, Church's also served fried okra, cole slaw, mashed potatoes, corn on the cob, and honey butter biscuits. In 1981, Church's merged with **Popeyes**. In 1992, America's Favorite Chicken Company, since renamed **AFC Enterprises Inc.**, became the parent company of Church's Chicken. In 2004, the Atlanta-based Arcapita Inc. bought Church's Chicken from AFC Enterprises, Inc. As of 2005, Church's had 1,334 outlets—100 in Mexico and the rest in the United States, where it is the third-largest chicken **franchise** chain.

SUGGESTED READING: John A. Jakle and Keith A. Sculle, *Fast Food: Roadside Restaurants in the Automobile Age* (Baltimore: Johns Hopkins University Press, 1999).

Cinnabon In 1985, Cinnabon opened its first outlet in the SeaTac Mall in Seattle. It only served Cinnabon rolls and a few **beverages**. It expanded its operation into other high-traffic venues, such as shopping malls, airports, train stations, and travel plazas. Cinnabon had systemwide sales of approximately $205.5 million in 2001. As of 2002, the company operated and franchised 603 bakeries in 43 states, Puerto Rico, and 26 countries. Since 2005, Cinnabon's parent company has been FOCUS Brands, Inc.

SUGGESTED READING: Cinnabon Web site: www.cinnabon.com

Clark Bar In 1886, David Clark launched the D. L. Clark Company in Pittsburgh. In 1917 he produced a 5-cent bar composed of ground roasted peanuts covered with milk **chocolate**. It was the first so-called combination bar consisting of chocolate and other confections. It was at first simply called Clark but was later renamed the Clark Bar. The Clark family continued to manage the D. L. Clark Company, makers of the Clark Bar, until 1955, when it was sold to the Beatrice Foods Company, which operated the company. Leaf, Inc. acquired the confectionery division of Beatrice foods in 1983. When Leaf, Inc. announced plans to move the **candy** operations from Pittsburgh, the city protested. The candy plant and rights to the Clark Bar were sold to Michael Carlow, and D. L. Clark became part of the Pittsburgh Food and Beverage Company. The company slowly declined in sales and market position and, in February, 1995, Pittsburgh Food and Beverage filed for bankruptcy. In June, 1995, Jim Clister purchased the D. L. Clark Company, renaming it Clark Bar America. This also went bankrupt and was acquired by the **New England Confectionery Company** in 1999.

SUGGESTED READING: Ray Broekel, *The Chocolate Chronicles* (Lombard, IL: Wallace-Homestead Book Company, 1985); Tim Richardson, *Sweets: A History of Candy* (New York: Bloomsbury, 2002); Andrew F. Smith, *Peanuts: The Illustrious History of the Goober Pea* (Urbana, IL: University of Illinois Press, 2002).

Coca-Cola Company During the early 1880s, Atlanta druggist John Stith Pemberton experimented with various **beverages** to be used for medicinal purposes. Vin Mariani, a coca wine developed in Europe, had been introduced into the United States; by the 1880s, it was one of the most popular patent medicines in Europe and the United States. Pemberton tried to clone it. In 1884 he released Pemberton's French Wine Coca but he discontinued making it the following year, when Atlanta passed temperance legislation preventing the manufacturing or sale of alcohol in the city. Pemberton went back to the drawing board and in 1886 he came up with a new medicine consisting of coca leaves and kola nut extract, sugar, and other ingredients. The result was a syrup that he called Coca-Cola. The original formula did include coca derivatives such as cocaine, which at the time were neither illegal nor unusual for patent medicines. Pemberton considered it a cure for headaches and for morphine addiction, and he sold it as a medicine in drugstores. Pemberton's health failed in 1887 and he sold his business to Willis Venable, who mixed the Coca-Cola syrup with **soda** water and served it as a "brain tonic and intellectual soda fountain beverage." Soda water gave Coca-Cola a sparkling, bubbling effervescence. Shortly after making this change, Venable sold the business to Asa Chandler, who began selling the syrup to other druggists and **soda fountain** operators, who mixed it with soda and sold it as a soft drink for 5 cents.

In 1890, Chandler sold a total of 9,000 gallons of Coca-Cola syrup. He plowed most of his profits back into his business and his efforts paid off. As sales began to increase, he trademarked the name Coca-Cola in 1893. Bottling of the beverage began in 1894, but it was not until 1899 that the company licensed a bottling company in Chattanooga as its exclusive bottler. Sales reach 281,000 gallons of syrup annually. By 1900, Coca-Cola's revenues topped $400,000 per year.

There were several reasons for this early success. One was Chandler's decision to **franchise** the bottling operation and his decision massively advertise his product. This made it possible for the Coca-Cola Company to concentrate on making the syrup and not have to engage making or distributing bottled beverages. Syrup was easily transported and the company could maintain its secret formula. Local druggists or bottlers then combined the syrup with soda. Chandler quickly developed a national distribution system. Chandler's **advertising** associated what he called his "soft" drink with the temperance movement that opposed the production and sale of liquor. During this time Chandler spent more than 25 percent of Coca-Cola's annual budget on advertising. By 1904, Coca-Cola was one of the most-recognized brand names in America.

However, the inclusion of cocaine caused problems with temperance movement leaders and medical professionals. The company reduced the amount of cocaine in its beverage but could not remove it entirely, since their trademark rested on the fact that it was part of the beverage. In 1913, the company came up with a compromise: it tried to eliminate the active ingredient in cocaine by replacing it with "spent coca leaves," which are still used today for flavoring. It was not until 1929 that improvements in technology permitted the company to remove all of the cocaine.

Competition

Coca-Cola was enormously popular and many other druggists began to imitate its success. Pepsi-Cola, for instance, was invented in 1898 by Caleb Bradham, a pharmacist in New Bern, North Carolina, and Claude A. Hatcher, a pharmacist in Columbus, Georgia, launched "Chero-Cola" (later revised and renamed **Royal Crown Cola**) in 1905. Coca-Cola responded with lawsuits charging copyright infringements. The courts eventually concluded that the term ***cola*** was generic and could be used by other companies, but the term *Coca-Cola* was protected.

Bottling, Canning, and Packaging

In 1899, Coca-Cola assigned exclusive rights to bottle its beverages to a Tennessee company. By 1909 there were more than 400 Coca-Cola bottlers in America. The bottles, however, were similar to those of the company's rivals, so Coca-Cola had a competition and its unique 6½-ounce contoured bottle was released in 1916; this remained the company's standard serving size more than four decades. By the 1920s, there were more than 1,000 Coca-Cola bottlers, and more Coke was sold in bottles than at soda fountains. The six-bottle carton was designed in 1923, making it easier to buy. During the 1950s, the company began manufacturing different-sized bottles, and by 1955 Coke was sold in cans.

World War II greatly affected the soft drink industry. Pepsi-Cola's and Coca-Cola's operations throughout the world were disrupted by German and Japanese conquests. In the United States, **sugar** rationing was imposed early in 1942. Rationing drastically restricted the amount of soft drinks that Pepsi-Cola could produce. The Coca-Cola Company, however, received contracts from the U.S. government to supply America's military with soft drinks. After the war, Coca-Cola sales exploded as soldiers returned home.

Advertising and Promotion

Coca-Cola invested heavily in advertising and promotion since its beginning. Its **slogans** "The Pause that Refreshes," "I'd Like to Buy the World a Coke," "Coke Is It," and "Things Go Better with Coke" were widely heard and remembered. In the 1970s, a song from a Coca-Cola commercial called "I'd Like to Teach the World to Sing" became a popular hit single, but there is no evidence that it did anything to increase sales of the soft drink. *Advertising Age* rated Coke's "It's the Real Thing," which first aired in 1973, as one of the best advertising campaigns of the twentieth century.

The Coca-Cola Company has historically targeted children and youth in its advertising and promotional activities. The Coca-Cola Foundation gives scholarships to youth and, to reach children outside of school, the company paid Boys & Girls Clubs of America $60 million over 10 years for exclusive marketing rights in more its 2,000 clubs.

Product Diversification and Acquisition

Beginning in the 1960s, the Coca-Cola Company began introducing new brands, including Sprite, Fanta, Fresca, Tab, Mr. Pibb, Mello Yello, Diet Coke, Cherry Coke, and many more. Perhaps the most famous new Coca-Cola brand was New Coke. During the 1980s, Pepsi-Cola, a sweeter drink, ran advertisements called "The Pepsi Challenge" on **television**, reporting that in double-blind taste tests people preferred Pepsi over Coke. In 1985, the Coca-Cola Company decided to change its formula and introduce a sweeter New Coke, which had been preferred in double-blind taste tests over both Pepsi and the old

Coke. The company supported its introduction with a massive advertising campaign. Many Coca-Cola drinkers were outraged at the change, and within months Classic Coke was back on the market. When purchases of New Coke dwindled; it was withdrawn from most markets.

In 2005, the Coca-Cola Company introduced Diet Coke sweetened with the artificial sweetener sucralose (Splenda) and released Coca-Cola Zero, sweetened partly with a blend of aspartame and acesulfame potassium.

Globalization

In 1909, Coca-Cola began exporting its syrup to the United Kingdom. Beginning in the 1920s, bottling plants were opened in France, Guatemala, Honduras, Mexico, Belgium, Italy, and South Africa, and by the beginning of World War II Coca-Cola was bottled in 44 countries. During World War II, German bottlers of Coca-Cola were unable to acquire the syrup; they invented Fanta, which, after the war, was later released as a beverage in the United States. During the war, U.S. armed forces established Coca-Cola bottling operations in other countries and after the war many of these plants were converted to civilian production, thus enhancing Coca-Cola's international position.

After the fall of the Berlin Wall in 1989, the Coca-Cola Company began to invest heavily in Eastern Europe. In China, **McDonald's** standard fare, for example, could not be absorbed into preexisting cuisines of East Asia. But Coca-Cola was relatively neutral import, and today it is the favorite drink of Chinese children. As the twentieth century closed, Coca-Cola had begun to construct many new bottling facilities in Africa. Today, Coca-Cola is sold in more than 200 countries and territories.

Coca-ization

Today, the Coca-Cola Company manufactures scores of brands around the world to meet consumer preferences. The Coca-Cola drink has a high degree of identification with the United States itself and is considered an American brand. Coke is less popular in some places, such as India (due to suspicions regarding the health standards of the drink) and in Arab countries (due to disapproval of U.S. foreign policy in Israel and elsewhere). However, a clone, Mecca Cola, has become a hit in the Middle East in the past few years.

Today

Today, Coca-Cola Company is the largest soft drink company in the world. It accounts for about 44 percent of the market in the United States and the company spends about $3 billion on advertising annually. Its annual sales are estimated at one billion servings, which are sold in more than two million stores, 500,000 restaurants, and 1.4 million vending machines. Coca-Cola is emblematic of Americana as well as being one of the most widely known brands in the world.

SUGGESTED READING: Frederick Allen, *Secret Formula: How Brilliant Marketing and Relentless Salesmanship Made Coca-Cola the Best-known Product in the World* (New York: HarperBusiness, 1994); David Greising, *I'd Like the World to Buy a Coke: The Life and Leadership of Roberto Goizueta* (New York: John Wiley & Sons, 1998); Roger Enrico and Jesse Kornbluth, *The Other Guy Blinked: How Pepsi Won the Cola Wars* (New York: Bantam, 1986); Constance L. Hays, *The Real Thing: Truth and Power at the Coca-Cola Company* (New York: Random House,

2005); E. J. Kahn, Jr., *The Big Drink: The Story of Coca-Cola* (New York: Random House, 1960); J. C. Louis and Harvey Yazijian, *The Cola Wars: The Story of the Global Corporate Battle between the Coca-Cola Company and PepsiCo* (New York: Everest House, 1980); Milward W. Martin, *Twelve Full Ounces*, 2nd ed. (New York: Holt, Rinehart and Winston, 1969); Mark Pendergrast, *For God, Country and Coca-Cola* (New York: Scribner's, 1993); Allan Petretti, *Warman's Coca-Cola Collectibles: Identification and Price Guide* (Iola, WI: KP Books, 2006); Coca-Cola Web site: www.coca-cola.com; World of Coca-Cola Web site: www.woccatlanta.com; Biedenharn Candy Company Museum of Coca-Cola Memorabilia Web site: www.travelsphere.com/MS/601/e_tou/main.html

Cola Colas are flavored with the kola nut—the bitter fruit of the kola tree (*Cola vera, Cola acuminata, Cola nitida*), which is native to Central and West Africa, where natives eat it and use it as a medicinal for pain. It is a stimulant and contains a high amount of **caffeine**. The kola nut was introduced into West Indies and Brazil through the slave trade and was imported into the United States, where it was used as a stimulant for slaves. The first cola **beverage** was invented in 1881. Five years later, John S. Pemberton, a pharmacist, invented **Coca-Cola** in Atlanta, Georgia. Another pharmacist, Caleb Bradham, invented Pepsi-Cola in 1898. **Royal Crown Cola** was created in Columbus, Georgia, in 1905. Royal Crown Cola introduced the first diet cola—Diet Rite Cola—in 1958. The Coca-Cola Company introduced Tab, a cola diet beverage, in 1963. Coca-Cola and Pepsi-Cola came out with their own diet versions in 1982. Since then, cola manufacturers have greatly increased their cola lines, including manufacturing caffeine-free colas and adding flavorings into their regular products, including cherry, lemon, lime, and vanilla. Cola drinks are the most important component of the soft drink industry.

SUGGESTED READING: E. J. Kahn, Jr., *The Big Drink: The Story of Coca-Cola* (New York: Random House, 1960); J. C. Louis and Harvey Yazijian, *The Cola Wars: The Story of the Global Corporate Battle between the Coca-Cola Company and PepsiCo* (New York: Everest House, 1980); Milward W. Martin, *Twelve Full Ounces*, 2nd ed. (New York: Holt, Rinehart and Winston, 1969); Mark Pendergrast, *For God, Country and Coca-Cola* (New York: Scribner's, 1993); Gyvel Young-Witzel and Michael Karl Witzel, *The Sparkling Story of Coca-Cola: An Entertaining History Including Collectibles, Coke Lore, and Calendar Girls* (Stillwater, MN: Voyageur Press, 2002).

Coke vs. Pepsi. © Kelly Fitzsimmons

Cola Wars Coca-Cola and its competitors have been at war for almost a century. For the first half of the century, **Coca-Cola** dominated the soft drink world. Coca-Cola challenged other manufacturers in court and, when this failed, the company did its best to undercut competition. Throughout the twentieth century, Coke's main rival was Pepsi-Cola, which began to slowly gain ground beginning in the 1950s.

In the 1970s, Pepsi-Cola's market share in Dallas, Texas, was a dismal 4 percent—far behind **Dr Pepper** and Coca-Cola. To find out why, Pepsi ran a series of double-blind taste tests comparing how people responded to the different soft drinks. Much to their surprise, the majority of testers, even die-hard Coke drinkers, preferred Pepsi. Pepsi launched a series of commercials called The Pepsi Challenge, showing Coke consumers stating in a blind taste test that they preferred Pepsi. This launched the so-called cola wars. Coca-Cola sales declined, so the company responded with an advertisement that compared the Pepsi challenge to two chimpanzees deciding which tennis ball was furrier. Other soft drink companies became involved: **7-Up**, for instance, came up with a campaign that positioned it as the Uncola.

Coca-Cola launched another **advertising** campaign in 1981 with the slogan "Coke Is It." However, Coca-Cola sales continued to decline and the company's own double-blind taste tests confirmed that most people preferred the sweeter taste of Pepsi to Coke. Company executives concluded that they needed to change the formula for Coca-Cola and in 1985 the company introduced a sweeter New Coke, which had been preferred in double-blind taste tests over both Pepsi and the old Coke. The company supported its introduction with a massive advertising campaign. Many Coca-Cola drinkers were outraged at the change and within months Classic Coke was back on the market. Sales of New Coke dwindled and it was no longer marketed nationally by the 1990s.

Since the 1980s, the term *cola war* has been applied to competition between Pepsi and Coke companies. It has played out globally as each company tries to expand its markets abroad, and it plays out locally in schools, where each company has tried to sign exclusive advertising and sales contract with local **school** districts.

SUGGESTED READING: Roger Enrico and Jesse Kornbluth, *The Other Guy Blinked: How Pepsi Won the Cola Wars* (New York: Bantam, 1986); J. C. Louis and Harvey Yazijian, *The Cola Wars: The Story of the Global Corporate Battle between the Coca-Cola Company and PepsiCo* (New York: Everest House, 1980).

Collectibles and Americana For almost a century, **snack food** and **fast food** manufacturers have given away or sold at low cost a vast array of merchandise, including coloring books, watches, games, merchandise, and toys. Perhaps the first snack food to do so was the **Cracker Jack** manufacturer, which placed coupons in each box of Cracker Jack beginning in 1910. Coupons could be redeemed for over 300 "varieties of handsome and useful articles, such as Watches, Jewelry, Silverware, Sporting Goods, Toys, Games, Sewing Machines, and many other useful Household articles." Beginning in 1912, the company did away with the coupons and placed toys directly in every package. Cracker Jack sales exploded.

Other **junk food** companies noted Cracker Jack's success and began issuing a wide array of merchandise, from coloring books to games and toys. Children collected the merchandise and ephemera. It was not until after World War II that the collecting habit matured. During the 1960s, there were systematic attempts to classify and catalogue collectibles for specific companies or specific industries. The first book written on junk food collectibles was Shelly and Helen Goldstein's *Coca-Cola Collectibles* (1971), and many similar books have been subsequently published. Allan Petretti, for example, has authored or co-authored more than a dozen books related to **Coca-Cola** collectibles. Coca-Cola collectibles have also been saved in museums, such as the Biedenharn Candy Company Museum of Coca-Cola Memorabilia and the World of Coca-Cola in Atlanta. In addition, several Coca-Cola collectors' organizations have been established, such as Coca-Cola Collectors Club (founded in 1974) and the Cavanagh's Coca-Cola Collectors' Society (established in 1993). Fewer books have been written on Pepsi-Cola collectibles, but Bob Stoddard published two: *Pepsi: 100 Years* (1999) and *The Encyclopedia of Pepsi-Cola Collectibles* (2002). The **Dr Pepper** Museum had gathered extensive ephemera related to that soft drink.

The first Cracker Jack collectible book was James D. Russo's *Cracker Jack Collecting for Fun and Profit* (1976). It was followed by Alex Jaramillo's *Cracker Jack Prizes*, Ravi Piña's *Cracker Jack Collectibles*, and Larry White's *Cracker Jack Toys*. In 1987, a permanent Cracker Jack exhibit at the Ohio Center of Science and Industry in Columbus was opened with 10,000 Cracker Jack toys and other memorabilia. In 1993, the Cracker Jack Collectors Association, which publishes a newsletter, the *Prize Insider*, was formed; it conducts annual meetings for those who collect Cracker Jack memorabilia.

Collectors of Planters Peanuts ephemera have joined in Peanut Pals, the Associated Collectors of Planters Peanut Memorabilia, founded in 1978. This group publishes *Peanut Papers for Peanut Pals* and currently has more than 800 members. The first listing of Planters Peanuts ephemera was published in 1978 by Richard D. Reddock. This was followed by two more comprehensive volumes by Jan Lindenberger and Joyce Spontak in 1995.

During the 1990s, books on **McDonald's** collectibles began to be published, such as Meredith Williams's *Tomart's Price Guide to McDonald's Happy Meal Collectibles* (1992), Terry and Joyce Losonsky's *McDonald's Happy Meal Toys Around the World* (1995), and Gary Henriques and Audre DuVall's *McDonald's Collectibles* (2002). While less attention has been paid to other fast food chains, many of the ephemera and collectibles have been catalogued in works such as Elizabeth A. Stephan's, *Ultimate Price Guide to Fast Food Collectibles* (1999).

In addition to focus on specific companies, there are many collectors of particular categories related to junk food. Ice Screamers, founded in 1982, collect **ice cream** parlor and **soda fountain** memorabilia. The Candy Container Collectors of America, organized in 1984, promotes, as the name suggests, candy container collecting. Collectors' societies typically have newsletters and annual conventions.

With the Internet, collecting junk food and fast food ephemera has become easier. Specifically, E-Bay and other online auctions have greatly improved the ease of locating and selling collectibles.

SUGGESTED READING: Shelly Goldstein and Helen Goldstein, *Coca-Cola Collectibles, with Current Prices and Photographs in Full Color* (Paducah, KY: Collector Books, 1991); Gary Henriques and Audre DuVall, *McDonald's Collectibles,* 2nd ed. (Paducah, KY: Collector Books, 2001); Jan Lindenberger with Joyce Spontak, *Planters Peanut Collectibles Since 1961* (Atglen, PA: Schiffer Publishing, 1995); Jan Lindenberger with Joyce Spontak, *Planters Peanut Collectibles 1906–1961,* 2nd ed. (Atglen, PA: Schiffer Publishing, 1999); Terry Losonsky and Joyce Losonsky, *McDonald's Happy Meal Toys Around the World* (Atglen, PA: Schiffer Publishing, 1995); Joyce Losonsky and Terry Losonsky, *McDonald's Pre-Happy Meal Toys from the Fifties, Sixties, and Seventies* (Atglen, PA: Schiffer Publishing, 1998); Ravi Piña, *Cracker Jack Collectibles with Price Guide* (Atglen, PA: Schiffer Publishing, 1995); Allan Petretti, *Warman's Coca-Cola Collectibles: Identification and Price Guide* (Iola, WI: KP Books, 2006); Robert J. Sodaro with Alex G. Malloy, *Kiddie Meal Collectibles* (Iola, WI: Krause Publications, 2001); Elizabeth A. Stephan, ed., *Ultimate Price Guide to Fast Food Collectibles* (Iola, WI: Krause Publications, 1999); Bob Stoddard, *Pepsi: 100 Years* (Los Angeles, CA: General Publishing Group, 1999); Bob Stoddard, *The Encyclopedia of Pepsi-Cola Collectibles* (Iola, WI: Krause Publications, 2002); Gyvel Young-

Witzel and Michael Karl Witzel, *The Sparkling Story of Coca-Cola: An Entertaining History Including Collectibles, Coke Lore, and Calendar Girls* (Stillwater, MN: Voyageur Press, 2002); Meredith Williams, *Tomart's Price Guide to McDonald's Happy Meal Collectibles.* Revised and updated. (Dayton, OH: Tomart Publications, 1995); Cavanagh's Coca-Cola Collectors' Society Web site: www.cavanaghgrp.com/ccccs; Coca-Cola Collectors Club Web site: www.cocacola-club.org; Cracker Jack Collectors Association Web site: www.tias.com/mags/cjca; Ice Screamers Web site: www.icescreamers.com; Peanut Pals Web site: www.peanutpals.org; Candy Container Collectors of America Web site: www.candycontainer.org; Dr Pepper Museum Web site: www.drpeppermuseum.com; Biedenharn Candy Company Museum of Coca-Cola Memorabilia Web site: www.travelsphere.com/MS/601/e_tou/main.html; World of Coca-Cola Web site: www.woccatlanta.com

Condiments The term *condiment* originally meant pickled or preserved foods. Today, it is broadly applied to a variety of substances that enhance, intensify, or alter the flavor of other foods. Condiments enhance flavor and often turn bland or unsatisfying foods into palatable and pleasurable eating experiences.

Condiments have been used by Americans since colonial times, but they changed over time. Initially, cost was a major limiting factor: only the middle and upper classes could afford many condiments and the ones that were used were simple ones—**salt**, pepper, butter, jams, jellies, mustard, syrup, **sugar**, or molasses. During the nineteenth century, table condiments such as **ketchup** and mayonnaise became common.

In the twentieth century, use of American condiments expanded, mainly due to the decrease in cost. The downside of the widespread dissemination of certain condiments has been standardization and the loss of diversity. This has been offset by the infusion of new condiments, occasionally based on immigrant food traditions, such as salsa or guacamole. Gradually, ethnic condiments became part of the culinary mainstream. American condiments have greatly influenced the world as many have been transported into other cuisines through American **fast food** establishments.

Condiments usually appear on the table and are intended for individual use by the diner. They fall into several nonexclusive categories: salt, which is used extensively in fast food and in many **junk foods** and **beverages**; spices, such as red pepper, used on **pizza**; bread spreads, such as butter (or, more likely, butter substitutes), jellies, jams, honey, and syrups used on fast food breakfasts; table sauces such as ketchup, mayonnaise, and mustard (which are generally available at **hamburger** and **sandwich** fast food restaurants); vegetables such as pickles, onions, tomatoes, and lettuce generally available at fast food chains); beverage sweeteners and flavorings, such as sugar; salad dressings such as vinegar and oil, and ranch dressing (available for fast food salads); **dips**, such as French onion dip, used for chips; and ethnic condiments such as salsa or hot sauce (used in Mexican and other fast foods as well as accompaniment for chips).

SUGGESTED READING: Carol Ann Rinzler, *The New Complete Book of Herbs, Spices, and Condiments: A Nutritional, Medical and Culinary Guide* (New York: Checkmark Books/Facts on File, 2001); Andrew F. Smith, *Pure Ketchup: The History of America's National Condiment* (Columbia, SC: The University of South Carolina Press, 1996).

Conformity Observers have many criticisms of **fast food** and **junk food**; one is that they promote homogenization of food. Foods produced en mass create low-priced goods which large food processors are able to purchase in bulk, thus reducing their costs. Large firms are also able to purchase large, automated equipment that reduces labor expenses, and they are able to advertise their products nationally. Small or regional producers are not able to compete against these forces.

In the early 1970s, the farm activist Jim Hightower warned of "the **McDonaldization** of America." According to Hightower, fast food **chains** threatened small businesses. He also believed that the fast food industry had a homogenizing influence on American life because central purchasing departments of large restaurant chains demand standardized products. These chains have an unprecedented degree of power over the nation's food supply. This has created uniformity: identical stores are constructed throughout the country and they serve the same products. Due to fast food chains, Americans consume much more **chicken** and beef today than 30 years ago, mainly because fast food chains serve those two meats. Soft drinks, iceberg lettuce, and **ketchup** became culinary mainstays and soon ranked among the most-often-consumed foods in the nation. Traditional American favorites have faded into the background.

Likewise, fast food operations have promoted conformity among their employees, who wear **uniforms** and commonly provide services in the same manner. An estimated 20 percent of all Americans have worked in a fast food chains; this has had a major influence upon American life.

Finally, Americans are indoctrinated from an early age to love junk food and fast food through **advertising** on children's **television** and through many other mechanisms.

SUGGESTED READING: Jim Hightower, *Eat Your Heart Out: Food Profiteering in America* (New York: Crown Publishers, 1975).

Consumerism Many observers have commented on the materialistic values of contemporary American society. Consumerism is the tendency to identify strongly with products or services, especially those with brand names. **Fast food** and **junk food** have contributed to rampant consumerism by promoting their products through massive **advertising** and promotional gimmicks targeted particularly at children. Through advertising, corporations encourage youth to purchase and value their goods. Billions of dollars are expended annually to create a relationship between children and specific products. Some observers believe that consumer relationships with products or brand names are substitutes for healthy human relationships.

Critics maintain that consumerism related to fast food and junk food is destroying the **environment** and the health of the world. "Overcoming consumerism" is a growing philosophy that embodies active resistance to consumerism.

SUGGESTED READING: George Ritzer, ed., *McDonaldization: The Reader*. 2nd ed. (Thousand Oaks, CA: Pine Forge Press, 2006).

Controversies **Fast food** purveyors and **junk food** manufacturers have been involved in a series of controversies since the early twentieth century. The general categories of controversies include health matters, such as those concerned with **caffeine**, **diabetes**, **fat**, **nutrition**, **obesity**, **salt**, and **sugar**; legal matters, such as **McLibel** and **lawsuits**; **foodborne illnesses**, such as caused by ***Escherichia coli*** and **salmonella**; employee relations, such as **anti-unionization** and **exploitation** of workers; and **advertising**, particularly that targets children and youth. Fast food purveyors have also been the target of national and international **boycotts** and **violence** due to their policies as well as the foreign policies of the United States.

SUGGESTED READING: Kelly D. Brownell and Katherine Battle Horgen, *Food Fight: The Inside Story of the Food Industry, America's Obesity Crisis, and What We Can Do about It* (Chicago: Contemporary Books, 2004); Stanley A. Feldman and Vincent Marks, eds., *Panic Nation: Unpicking the Myths We're Told about Food and Health* (London: Blake, 2005); Eric Schlosser, *Fast Food Nation: The Dark Side of the All-American Meal* (New York: Houghton Mifflin Company, 2001).

Convenience Foods/Drinks Convenience foods consist of packaged dishes or foods that can be prepared quickly and easily. While convenience foods, such as canned soup, existed in nineteenth century, their real growth occurred in the twentieth century. During this time, improvements in canning, bottling, freezing, and **packaging** permitted the price of convenience foods to decline. Simultaneously, disposable income increased, particularly among the middle class, making it possible for many Americans to afford the new products emerging from food manufacturers. Simultaneously, **employment** opportunities increased for women, and those who took advantage of these opportunities had less time to prepare food in the home. At the same time, new technologies, such as refrigerators, electric equipment, and microwaves, became affordable, making it easier to store and prepare convenience food. Finally, an **advertising** revolution, particularly through **television**, made it possible for convenience foods to be sold nationally.

Early convenience foods included **breakfast cereals**, cocoa mixes, **Jell-O**, **Kool-Aid**, and bottled soft drinks as well as all **snack foods**, such as **Cracker Jack**, **Hersheys Chocolate Bars**, and Fritos. Ready-to-eat foods could be consumed on the spot. The convenience revolution extended to more substantial foods when Clarence Birdseye, a Gloucester, Massachusetts, businessman, developed efficient methods of freezing foods during the 1920s. His most important addition was the use of cellophane, which made the contents more appetizing when thawed. Frozen foods made little headway with the American population until after World War II, when grocery stores installed large freezers and the freezer sections of home refrigerators were enlarged.

During the late 1940s, several new convenience foods were launched. The Pillsbury Company introduced a prepackaged pie crust mix, and many other food processors marketed cake and other mixes. Minute Maid released frozen orange juice, Sara Lee introduced frozen cakes, Quaker Oats launched frozen waffles, C. A. Swanson and Company produced frozen **chicken** and turkey pies, and **General Foods** developed **Tang**.

None of these successes prepared America for the revolution launched by Swanson, when it decided to produce a complete frozen meal in a tray in 1952. All customers had to do was heat up the tray, and a complete meal was ready within minutes. Part of its success was the name it gave its new product, the TV dinner. It was so successful that by 1955 Swanson was selling 13 million frozen dinners annually. Based on this phenomenal success, virtually every other food manufacturer in America hopped on the convenience food bandwagon and began producing foods that could be easily prepared in a short time.

The wedding of the microwave and frozen food was the next major leap forward. The microwave made it possible for frozen foods to be cooked in minutes, which was particularly useful in restaurants. However, food processors needed to change their products for microwave use by reducing the moisture content of food and replacing metal foil (which blocked microwaves and damaged ovens) with other materials. At first, the market was not big enough to encourage food processors to cater to the needs of microwave oven users. This had changed by the 1970s, by which time more than 10 percent of all American homes possessed microwave ovens.

Eating at a lunch counter in a drugstore or in a diner was both convenient and economical for many workers and shoppers. The **fast food** revolution was spurred on by the American drive for convenience and speed. Rather than prepare food easily and quickly at home, all customers had to do was visit a fast food outlet and food would be available almost immediately. What was also good about fast food was that there were no dishes or pots to clean up afterwards.

During the late twentieth century, the convenience revolution hit restaurants. Rather than prepare food from scratch, many restaurants were supplied by central commissaries which froze food. All restaurants had to do was microwave it when customers ordered it.

SUGGESTED READING: Carol Curtis, *New Convenience Foods* (Norwalk, CT: Business Communications Company, 1992); Harvey Levenstein, *Paradox of Plenty: A Social History of Eating in Modern America* (New York: Oxford University Press, 1993).

Cookies and Crackers Cookies are small, usually flat, sweet wafers; crackers are similarly shaped but are usually unsweetened or semisweet. Manufacturing crackers was among the first food industries in America. During the eighteenth century, cheap, hard crackers called ship's bread or ship's biscuits (and later, hardtack) were widely manufactured for use on ships and for those migrating westward. These large, sturdy crackers, made only of flour and water, kept for a very long time. One of the earliest branded foods was Bent's water-crackers, which were initially manufactured in 1801 by Joshua Bent, a ship's bread baker in Milton, Massachusetts. It is still manufactured today.

Crackers were packed in barrels and sold to grocery stores and restaurants. Recipes for simple crackers appeared in early American cookbooks and were little more than baked flour and water; they did not use fermented dough. By the 1840s, three major cracker varieties that were made with shortening were introduced—the soda cracker, the butter cracker, and the round sugar-biscuit. During the 1850s, a new product—the graham cracker—was probably first manufactured by Russell Thacher Trall, a follower of Sylvester Graham. **Graham crackers** were made with graham flour (coarsely milled, unbolted whole wheat flour) and were intended for use by those following Sylvester Graham's dietary regimen. Graham crackers made commercially today include **sugar** and other ingredients that Sylvester Graham would not have approved.

During the Civil War, the Union army and navy were supplied with hardtack. To meet the greatly increased demand, cracker bakers constructed continuous-fired, revolving-reel ovens, which greatly increased output. They also installed mixing machines, dough brakes, rolling machines, and automatic dough cutters and stamps to cut the dough into various shapes. After the Civil War, however, sales of hardtack declined but crackers made with sugar became popular. Commercial production of crackers increased when compressed yeast became available in America during the late 1860s.

In the nineteenth century, crackers were generic products, sold from open barrels so that the crackers were exposed to air, dust, moisture, odors, and the depredations of flies and mice. The era of generic crackers ended in 1898 with the formation of the National Biscuit Company (NBC), forerunner of **Nabisco**. NBC had been formed by merger of several companies and at the time controlled about 70 percent of the American cracker industry. The new company introduced wrapping and packaging machines for their new brand-named product, Uneeda Biscuits. To promote it, they launched a major national **advertising** campaign, stressing its particular advantage: their crackers were sealed in a moisture-proof package that kept them dry, crisp, and unspoiled. In the first full year of their campaign, NBC sold 120 million packages of Uneeda Biscuits. Almost from the company's beginning, another cracker in the NBC product line was the Premium saltine, a square soda cracker. Nabisco released **Ritz Crackers** in 1934.

Henry D. Perky of Denver, Colorado, invented a machine to make biscuits in 1892. In 1901 he moved his company to Niagara Falls, New York. The following year he expanded his operation to include the production of a small wheat cracker he named Triscuits.

After World War II, the cracker industry expanded along with the rest of the **snack food** field. As Americans broadened their tastes, new technology made possible a greater variety of flavors and shapes. Crackers are now flavored with onion, herbs, or spices and topped with sesame or poppy seeds. No longer just rectangular or round, crackers may be triangular, oval, scalloped, or shaped like fish. In response to market demand, some crackers (including Saltines) are now made in low-sodium versions, and a few manufacturers have reduced the amount of hydrogenated **fat** in their products. Crackers are eaten with soups and chowders, softened in milk, and served as a snack food and for dipping.

Emergence of Cookies

The word *cookie* derives from the Dutch word *koeptje* (*koekje*), meaning small cake. It came to America with Dutch colonists who settled in New Amsterdam (later renamed New York). The term was adopted throughout the American colonies, while the term used in England is *biscuit*. Amelia Simmons, author of *American Cookery* (1796), is credited with publishing the first known cookie recipes, one of which was for Christmas cookies. American cookbooks have included numerous recipes for cookie (also called small cakes) ever since.

Commercial cookies had been manufactured by many companies during the nineteenth century, but their popularity soared in about 1900. The National Biscuit Company, also introduced another wheat product in honor of Sylvester Graham, called the Graham Cracker in 1898. It had little in common with what Sylvester Graham had originally advocated. In 1902, the company relaunched yet another cracker, Animal Biscuits, by changing its name to Barnum's Animals. Subsequently, thousands of other wheat-based cookies and crackers have been manufactured in the United States.

In 1910, the Loose-Wiles Biscuit Company of Kansas City, Kansas, using the brand name Sunshine Biscuits, introduced the Hydrox Biscuit Bonbons, which was later shortened to just Hydrox cookies. They were very popular. The success of Hydrox encouraged Nabisco to introduce **Oreo** cookies in 1912. Oreos became America's best-selling cookie, a position it has held ever since.

Selling cookies has been a traditional method of raising money for charities and nonprofit causes. Girl Scouts began selling cookies about 1917 to raise money, but it was not until 1922 that the national organization endorsed the idea. Beginning in 1934, the Girl Scouts sold commercially baked cookies. The following year, boxes were manufactured with the name **Girl Scout Cookies** on the outside, and in 1936 bakers were first licensed to make them. One of their leading licensed bakers is Little Brownie Bakers, a subsidiary **Keebler** Foods. Three varieties emerged in 1951—sandwich, shortbread, and thin mints. They have been an important source of income for the Girl Scouts ever since.

The most popular cookie in America is the **chocolate chip cookie**, which is attributed to Ruth Wakefield. Her Toll House Cookies, also called Chocolate Chip Cookies, originated about 1933. Making fresh chocolate chip and other cookies is at the center of commercial cookie chains, including **Famous Amos** (launched in 1975) and **Mrs. Fields** (1977).

Today, total annual cookie and cracker sales in the United States are estimated at $7 billion. By far, the largest commercial cookie manufacturer is **Nabisco**, maker of Oreo cookies and **Chips Ahoy!** The Kellogg subsidiary, Keebler Foods, maker of Cheez-It, Chips Delux, Famous Amos, Sesame Street Cookies, and Sunshine cookies is the second-largest producer of commercial cookies and crackers in America. Other cookie manufacturers include Parmalat, maker of Mother's Cookies, Delicious brand cookies, and Archway cookies; **Pepperidge Farm** cookies and crackers; and McKee Foods, maker of **Little Debbie** products. Private labels control only about 11 percent of the American commercial cookie market.

SUGGESTED READING: Biscuit and Cracker Handbook (Washington, D.C.: Biscuit Bakers Institute Department of the Biscuit and Cracker Manufacturers' Association, 1981); William Cahn, *Out of the Cracker Barrel* (New York: Simon and Schuster, 1969); *Crackers* (New York: Mintel International Group, 2003); Peter E. Ellis, ed., *Cookie & Cracker Manufacturing* (Washington, D.C.: Biscuit and Cracker Manufacturers' Association, 1990); Duncan J. R. Manley, *Technology of Biscuits, Crackers, and Cookies,* 3rd ed. (Boca Raton, FL: CRC Press/Woodhead Publishing, 2000); William G. Panschar, *Baking in America* (Evanston, IL: Northwestern University Press, 1956); Girl Scout Cookies Web site: www.girlscoutspc.org

Corn Chips The success of **potato chips** created a market for other commercial salty snacks. Corn chips originated as a Mexican snack—cut-up, fried, or hardened tortillas. Isadore J. Filler, a traveling salesman, ate tostados (hard tortillas with various toppings) in San Antonio, Texas, and thought they might have wide appeal as a **snack food**. In 1932, he conceived the idea of manufacturing a rectangular-shaped corn chip and applied for a trademark for Corn Chips, which he was granted.

At the same time that Filler trademarked corn chips, Elmer Doolin was also in San Antonio snacking on *friotes,* which were made from fried masa or corn flour. Doolin purportedly bought a recipe for friotes for $100. Doolin began manufacturing them under the name Frito Corn Chips, which was an immediate success. Sales expanded as far as St. Louis, Missouri. In 1945, Doolin met potato chip manufacturer, Herman Lay, who agreed to distribute Fritos. Fritos became popular nationwide.

Doolin died in 1959 and the company he created merged with Herman Lay's, creating **Frito-Lay**, Inc. which continued to grow and acquire other snack foods. In 1965, it was itself acquired by the Pepsi-Cola Company. The newly merged company launched many new snack foods. A triangular corn chip, **Doritos**, debuted in 1966 and almost overnight became America's second-most popular snack item.

By the end of the twentieth century, the corn chip industry was dominated by Frito-Lay, with the top sellers being Doritos and Tostitos. Fritos do not rank in the 20 top-selling corn chips today.

SUGGESTED READING: Andrew F. Smith, "Tacos, Enchiladas and Refried Beans: The Invention of Mexican-American Cookery," in Mary Wallace Kelsey and ZoeAnn Holmes, eds., *Cultural and Historical Aspects of Foods* (Corvallis, OR: Oregon State University, 1999), pp.183–203.

Corporate Concentration During the early twentieth century, thousands of companies manufactured **snack foods** and soft drinks. Since then, small manufacturers have given way to large, multinational corporations. Food produced en mass creates low-priced goods; large corporations are able to purchase in bulk, thus reducing their costs; they are able to purchase large, automated equipment that reduces labor expenses; and they are able to promote their products nationally. Small or regional producers are not able to compete against these forces.

In the soft drink industry, there were thousands of bottlers during the early twentieth century. Today, in the United States there are just three major manufacturers: the **Coca-Cola Company**, **PepsiCo**, and **Cadbury Schweppes**, which together control 90 percent of the carbonated **beverage** trade in this country.

Similarly, in the **fast food** industry, thousands of independent restaurants were launched since the 1920s. Many did not survive. Those that survived were systematically acquired by multinational corporations. During the 1960s and 1970s, larger corporations systematically purchased fast food **chains**. Burger Chef, for instance, was sold to General Foods in 1968; **Burger King** was purchased by Pillsbury; Ralston Purina bought **Jack in the Box** in 1970; international liquor and food powerhouse Heublein bought **Kentucky Fried Chicken**; United Brands purchased the A&W **drive-in** chain; Imasco acquired **Hardee's** in 1974; PepsiCo bought **Pizza Hut** in 1977 and **Taco Bell** a year later; and **Royal Crown** bought **Arby's**. By end of 1970s, most major chains belonged to larger corporate families. As a result of this concentration, fast food chains expanded at even faster rates with infusions of capital from their parent companies.

For most of the twentieth century, fast food franchises were owned by individuals who wanted to own their own business. Today, the cost of buying a franchise is prohibitive for most individuals. As a result, there has been a similar increase in concentration of **franchises**, where many franchise outlets are owned by companies and groups rather than individuals.

The importance of these mergers and acquisitions is multifold. On the positive side, the large food giants such as PepsiCo, **Yum! Brands**, ConAgra, **Nestlé**, and Cadbury Schweppes have the funds to invest in national distribution and marketing. They also have global systems that can guarantee widespread distribution. On the negative side, giant corporate structures often make decisions based almost entirely on profit margins and projected future growth. Brands of multinational corporations need to make a large profit. The **junk food** and fast food fields expanded largely due to individuals who made quick decisions and were willing to take risks. Likewise, in the past anyone with a good idea could easily test it out; this entrepreneurial spirit is now limited.

SUGGESTED READING: Eric Schlosser, *Fast Food Nation: The Dark Side of the All-American Meal* (New York: Houghton Mifflin Company, 2001).

Corporate Sponsorships and Programs in Schools From the beginning, **junk food** manufacturers have targeted youth in their print and **radio** promotions and **advertising**. It was not until after World War II that junk food and **fast food** corporations targeted youth in **schools**. These programs have been varied—soft drink and fast food companies such as **Coca-Cola**, **PepsiCo**, and **McDonald's** sponsor sports and other school programs and advertising programs in school, such as those on Channel One, which reaches 12,000 schools with eight million viewers. Studies have reported that almost 70 percent of the advertising on Channel One is for fast food and junk food.

At the forefront of corporate sponsorships in public elementary and secondary schools are fast food and junk food companies. Fast food and junk food corporations are selling their products in public elementary and secondary schools and are advertising their products through sponsorship arrangements. For more than two decades, soft drinks such as Coca-Cola and Pepsi-Cola have been sold on public school campuses, and many manufacturers have given schools large amounts of money for exclusive rights to sell their drinks to students. These sponsorships generate thousands of dollars for schools. These rights often include placing advertisements and banners in hallways, promotion over the public address system and at sporting and other events, and the dissemination of corporate educational materials in classrooms, which have often been produced with tax-deductible dollars. In ***Fast Food Nation*** (2001), Eric Schlosser reports on the rise of school districts seeking corporate sponsors. A brochure put out by a company that encourages corporations to make sponsorship deals with school districts proclaims, "Whether it's first-graders learning to read or teenagers shopping for their first car, we can guarantee an introduction of your product and your company to these students in the traditional setting of the classroom."

Fast food chains and soda manufacturers have also arranged sponsorships for schools and school districts that have included the placement of signs promoting their products on buses, in hallways, and at sporting venues. Other companies developed academic contests, such as **Pizza Hut**'s Book It! program. Students achieving reading targets are rewarded with a certificate for a Personal Pan Pizza at Pizza Hut. Many corporations give scholarships to seniors in high school who plan to attend college.

Many corporations have also developed educational materials intended to be used in classrooms. Coca-Cola, PepsiCo, and McDonald's, for instance, spend millions of dollars annually distributing sophisticated educational programs with videos featuring sports figures who encourage children to be active. Pop Secret uses **popcorn** kernels in its educational material. **Domino's Pizza**'s Encounter Math (Count on Domino's) materials are highly commercial, with activities involving **pizza** labeled as Domino's, and the company's logo appears on all materials and its name is often mentioned in the materials. **Mars, Inc.**'s Team **Snickers** with World Cup Soccer, 100% Smart Energy To Go is considered incomplete, biased, and commercial. The National Potato Board with the Snack Food Association's Count Your Chips program is considered advertisement for **potato chips**, not math materials. **Dunkin' Donuts**'s program, Grade A Donuts: Honoring Homework Stars offered **doughnuts** to those who successfully complete their homework. Critics do not believe that **carbohydrate**-filled doughnuts should be the reward for completing homework.

Some teaching units include nutritional information but none of it mentions the amount of **sugar**, **salt**, or **caffeine** in junk food and fast food. These teaching materials are intended to show that these companies are interested in health. By omission, they suggests that drinking soda and consuming fast food do not contribute to the national epidemic. These materials are promotions for their sponsors and their intent is to deflect attention from **obesity** and focus it on physical activity; these corporations are interested promoting their products through these materials. By providing the material for free, this also undercuts the distribution of nonpartisan material on **nutrition** provided by medical and governmental groups.

Advocates for corporate sponsorships state that this is one way to cover shortfalls in school districts' budgets. Others note that corporate sponsorships can offer more opportunities to students because businesses often possess expertise and equipment that schools just do not have. Critics say such corporate involvement sends mixed messages to students about nutrition. When Sen. Patrick Leahy introduced a bill into Congress in 2001 giving the **U.S. Department of Agriculture (USDA)** more authority to restrict sales of junk food in schools, he said, "Schools teach kids all about the four food groups and the importance of a balanced diet, yet many schools are not only allowing but encouraging kids to fill up on **sodas** and empty-calorie snacks." The **Center for Science in the Public Interest (CSPI)** has also strongly opposes these corporate arrangements.

SUGGESTED READING: Kelly D. Brownell and Katherine Battle Horgen, *Food Fight: The Inside Story of the Food Industry, America's Obesity Crisis, and What We Can Do about It* (Chicago: Contemporary Books, 2004); Consumers Union Education Services, *Captive Kids: A Report on Commercial Pressures on Kids at School* (Yonkers, NY: Consumers Union, 1998); Sheila Harty, *Hucksters in the Classroom: A Review of Industry Propaganda in Schools* (Washington, D.C.: Center for Study of Responsive Law, 1979); Eric Schlosser, *Fast Food Nation: The Dark Side of the All-American Meal* (New York: Houghton Mifflin Company, 2001); Mary Story and Simone French, "Food Advertising and Marketing Directed at Children and Adolescents in the US," *International Journal of Behavioral Nutrition and Physical Activity,* 1 (2004); Pizza Hut's Book It! program Web site: www.bookitprogram.com

Cracker Jack During the 1870s, German immigrants Frederick and Louis Rueckheim sold popcorn on the streets of Chicago. They began to experiment with combining popcorn with several other products. When the World's Columbian Exposition opened in Chicago in 1893, they sold a confection composed of **popcorn**, molasses, and peanuts, which they prepared in a small factory. After the Exposition, orders for the confection increased. The Ruckheims increased production, repackaged it so that it would stay fresh, named it Cracker Jack, and promoted it nationwide.

Cracker Jack was soon sold in snack bars, at circuses and fairs, and sporting events. In 1908, the lyricist Jack Norworth and composer Albert von Tilzer immortalized Cracker Jack in their song "Take Me Out to the Ball Game," with the lyrics:

> Buy me some peanuts and cracker-jack—
> I don't care if I never get back.

Throughout the early twentieth century, the Cracker Jack Company expanded, opening operations in Canada and the United Kingdom. By 1913, Cracker Jack was the world's best-selling commercial confection. A major reason for its longevity was extensive national **advertising**, specifically focused on children. In 1912, a small toy was included in every package. The corporate icon, a little sailor boy and his dog, were first used in advertisements in 1916 and three years later they appeared on the Cracker Jack box. According to legend, the boy and dog were based on a picture of Frederick Rueckheim's grandson, Robert, with his dog Bingo. Robert died of pneumonia shortly after the package was introduced.

In 1970, Cracker Jack was enjoyed in 24,689,000 homes—41 percent of all American households. Then other companies began manufacturing clones and Cracker Jack sales declined. By the 1990s, Cracker Jack ranked behind its competitors in sales. In 1997, Cracker Jack was sold to **Frito-Lay**, Inc., a subsidiary of **PepsiCo**.

SUGGESTED READING: Cracker Jack Web site: www.crackerjack.com; Ravi Piña, *Cracker Jack Collectibles with Price Guide* (Atglen, PA: Schiffer Publishing, 1995); Andrew F. Smith, *Popped Culture: A Social History of Popcorn in America* (Columbia, SC: University of South Carolina Press, 1999).

Crime Fast food operations have suffered serious crime problems since their beginning in the 1920s. **White Castle**, the first **fast food chain**, built its outlets in inner cities near transportation hubs and its major customer target was workmen from nearby industries. To reach the night shift, White Castle outlets were generally open late at night. As inner cities deteriorated during the 1950s, crime, **violence**, and vagrancy increasingly became problems for White Castle. Outlets that were open late were frequent targets for robbery because they were the only retail business open at those hours. White Castle outlets also became havens for homeless people and prostitutes; many used White Castle restrooms to bathe. White Castle invested heavily in security measures and began closing establishments early. One reason why many post–World War II fast food chains moved to the suburbs was due to the crime, violence and vagrancy of plaguing inner-city fast food establishments. However, during the 1960s this policy was reversed and many fast food chains began opening outlets in inner cities, as suburbs became saturated with fast food outlets.

Fast food restaurants have been more attractive to armed robbers than other retail businesses open late at night. Convenience stores and gas stations, for example, increasingly rely on credit, whereas most fast food operations rely on cash, which means that many outlets have thousands of dollars on the premises. In addition, many fast food restaurants are near off-ramps and **drive-thru** windows permit an easy getaway.

Particularly vulnerable have been employees who deliver fast food to homes. On average, four to five fast-food workers are killed every month on the job, usually during the course of a robbery. In 1998, more restaurant workers than policemen were murdered on the job.

In addition, fast food employees are responsible for inside theft. In fact, no other industry is robbed so frequently by its own employees as are fast food chains. The combination of low pay, high turnover, and ample cash has made fast food outlets ideal for employee theft.

In 1996, the **Occupational Safety and Health Administration (OSHA)** proposed guidelines for preventing violence at restaurants that do business at night. The National Restaurant Association opposed those OSHA guidelines on retail violence, as did the National Association of Convenience Stores. Companies were afraid that employees would use the guidelines in **lawsuits** against companies where violence occurred and they did not want OSHA to impose fines or compel security measures.

Fast food chains have reduced violence by installing security measures, including video cameras, panic buttons, drop-safes, burglar alarms, and additional lighting, but they remain vulnerable. In May, 2000, five employees at **Wendy's** in Queens, New York, were murdered. One of the murderers had previously worked there.

To discourage robbery, some fast food chains now accept credit cards, which limits the amount of cash on hand. Other chains have limited their hours and installed bulletproof glass for drive-thru windows.

SUGGESTED READING: OSHA Web site: "Teen Worker Safety in Restaurants," www.osha.gov/sltc/restaurants/serving.html

D

Dairy Queen John F. McCullough began selling **ice cream** in 1927. A few years later, he and his son, H. A. "Alex" McCullough, founded the Homemade Ice Cream Company in Green River, Illinois. Ice cream is generally served at 5 degrees F, but John McCullough believed that it would be more flavorful if it were served at a higher temperature, as cold temperatures numbed the taste buds. The McCulloughs began experimenting with what would later be called soft-serve ice cream. They found that it tasted best when it contained about 6 percent butterfat and when it was served at 18 degrees F. At this temperature, it still held its shape. In 1938, they believed that they had found a winning, flavorful combination, so they asked a friend to test-market it with his customers. It was a big hit. Before the McCulloughs could commercialize it they needed a machine that could make large quantities of the soft-serve ice cream. They approached manufacturers, but none was interested in designing or producing it.

The McCulloughs then heard about Harry M. Oltz, a **hamburger** stand proprietor in Hammond, Indiana, who claimed to have invented a continuous freezer that made it possible to serve ice cream at 20 degrees F. The McCulloughs met with Oltz and gained manufacturing rights to his machine, which Alex McCullough perfected. F. J. McCullough improved the mix and acquired a manufacturer. They named their new product Dairy Queen, as they believed that it would be the queen of the dairy industry. In June 1940 Sherb Noble, an ice cream store owner in Kankakee, Illinois, acquired a **franchise** for the soft-serve product and opened his first outlet in Joliet, Illinois; he named the store after his new ice cream, Dairy Queen. Noble opened additional outlets, and by the time World War II broke out in 1941 there were 10 Dairy Queen outlets.

The McCulloughs did not franchise Dairy Queens in the same way that **fast food** companies franchised their operations. They informally licensed operators, for cash, to control territories and did not include royalties as part of the arrangement. Operators purchased the continuous freezers and the mix from them and displayed the Dairy Queen logo, and that was about it. The parent company did not set operating standards and did not offer business support to franchisees, which meant that there was considerable variation among outlets.

The World War II halted expansion as materials for making the continuous freezer were needed for the war effort. After the war, the McCulloughs sold 50 percent of Dairy Queen to Harry Axene, who aggressively pushed the franchising. Axene charged franchisees a small up-front fee, along with royalties on all Dairy Queen ice cream that was sold. Dairy Queen expanded quickly from 17 outlets in 1946 to 2,600 in 1955, most of which were closed during the winter months. Each franchise was independently owned, which led to its motto "Nationally Known, Locally Owned." The company opened its first franchise outside the United States in Saskatchewan, Canada (1953), Japan (1972), the Middle East (1979), and Mexico (1991).

The changes that Axene instituted did not solve Dairy Queen's corporate structure problems. To resolve these, franchisees formed the Dairy Queen National Trade Association (later renamed International Dairy Queen) in 1948. It bought back many territories from franchisees and launched a national training school for operators. One person who attended the first meeting of the association was **Ray Kroc**, who at the time sold Multimixers, which made multiple **milk shakes** simultaneously, to Dairy Queens operators. Kroc later launched the national franchise operation for **McDonald's**.

The Dairy Queen National Trade Association expanded the menu to include malts and milk shakes (1948) and banana splits (1953). Many Dairy Queen outlets also served more substantial food, so in 1958 its Brazier food line, consisting of broiled hamburgers and **hot dogs**, was launched. Its most successful product was the Blizzard, a blend of soft-serve ice cream, crushed **cookies**, and **candy**. It was test-marketed in 1984 and was officially introduced in 1985. Subsequently, the company has regularly added new items to its menu.

The 1960s saw the introduction of a new Dairy Queen building prototype, called the Country Fresh design; franchisees were encouraged to upgrade old buildings or build new ones. Dairy Queen's success is attributed to the view that its basic product, soft-serve ice cream, is good-quality and it has a special taste that is remembered. The company targeted America's small towns; it was the only national chain to do so, with the exception of **A&W Root Beer**.

Dairy Queen has continued to expand and diversify; it has purchased Karmelkorn Shoppes, Inc. and Orange Julius of America. These additions brought the company into urban areas. In January, 1998, International Dairy Queen, Inc. and its subsidiary companies were purchased by Warren E. Buffett's investment group, Berkshire Hathaway Inc., which also owns See's Candies. In 2004, Dairy Queen opened its first outlet in the Middle East in Bahrain. As of 2005, Dairy Queen had more than 5,900 restaurants, mainly in the United States, Canada, and 20 other countries.

SUGGESTED READING: Anne Cooper Funderburg, *Chocolate, Strawberry, and Vanilla: A History of American Ice Cream* (Bowling Green, OH: Bowling Green State University Popular Press, 1995); Anne Cooper Funderburg, *Sundae Best: A History of Soda Fountains* (Bowling Green, OH: Bowling Green State University Popular Press, 2002); John A. Jakle and Keith A. Sculle, *Fast Food: Roadside Restaurants in the Automobile Age* (Baltimore: Johns Hopkins University Press, 1999); Philip Langdon, *Orange Roofs, Golden Arches: The Architecture of American Chain Restaurants* (New York: Knopf, 1986); Caroline Hall Otis, *The Cone with the Curl on Top: Celebrating Fifty Years 1940–1990* (Minneapolis, MN: International Dairy Queen, 1990).

Deep-fried Mars Bars and Twinkies Deep-fried **junk food** appears to have originated in Scotland. Deep-fried Mars bars reportedly were invented in Glasgow or Stonehaven in 1995. Others claim the original source was the Bervie Chipper in nearby Inverbervie. Whatever the source, it was widely copied in Scotland's fish-and-chip shops, and some shops reportedly sold as many as 200 a week.

Twinkies may have been invented by a Chicago bakery, but it took English-born Christopher Sells to invent Deep-Fried Twinkies. Sells operated the Park Slope Chip Shop, a British fish-and-chip restaurant in Brooklyn, New York. They are now served in many locations. To prepare them, Twinkies are taken from their package and placed in the freezer. When needed, they are dipped in tempura batter and deep-fried for about two minutes. They are sprinkled with sugar and typically served with vanilla **ice cream** or **chocolate** sauce. They contain about 425 calories. Other deep-fried junk foods sold in America include deep-fried Snickers, 3 Musketeers, and Milky Way **candy** bars.

SUGGESTED READING: BBC Web site: http://news.bbc.co.uk/2/hi/uk_news/Scotland/4103415.stm; *The Twinkies Cookbook: An Inventive and Unexpected Recipe Collection* (Berkeley: Ten Speed Press, 2006).

Del Taco In 1964 Ed Hackbarth, a former manager of a Mexican **fast food** restaurant, and David Jameson founded Del Taco in Barstow, California. The first Del Taco restaurant was a success and the company spread throughout southern California. Its second outlet opened in Corona, California. In 1966, Red-E-Foods Systems, Inc. was created to manage **franchising** operations. Six years later, Red-E-Foods Systems changed its name to Del Taco, Inc. By 1978, Del Taco had 100 outlets and was rapidly growing. In 1975, Hackbarth and Jameson sold the company to an independent management firm. Del Taco and Naugules, another Mexican-American fast food chain, merged in 1988. The Del Taco menu features tacos, burritos, quesadillas, **nachos**, cheeseburgers, shakes, sodas and breakfast burritos. Today, Del Taco is the second-largest Mexican-American fast food chain. It is a privately held company headquartered in Lake Forest, California.

SUGGESTED READING: Del Taco Web site: www.deltaco.com

Diabetes Diabetes mellitus is a chronic disease involving the body's inability to use glucose, which is absorbed by cells according to need. The agent that controls this process is the hormone insulin. In Type 1 diabetes, the pancreas fails to produce insulin. Type 2 diabetes, which is more common, is caused by the failure of cells to respond to insulin. Type 2 diabetes can be caused by heredity but it is generally believed that the major cause is diet. Insulin levels normally rise after eating and then decline. In Western diets which often include snacking on processed foods, **junk food**, and soft drinks filled with sugar, insulin remains high throughout the day and this causes metabolic problems, including the development of insulin resistance in cells, which is type 2 diabetes. Type 2 diabetes is highly linked with **obesity**, which is also associated with high blood pressure, heart diseases, some cancers, and many more medical problems. An estimated 2.6 percent of the Americans are known to have diabetes, but a similar number likely have it but are undiagnosed. More than 600,000 new cases of diabetes are diagnosed each year. According to the Center for Disease Control (CDC), in 2001, 71,372 deaths were attributed to diabetes. In addition diabetes is a significant contributing factor to many of the 320,000 individuals with diabetes who die each year.

SUGGESTED READING: Walter Gratzer, *Terrors of the Table: The Curious History of Nutrition* (New York: Oxford University Press, 2005).

Diet Soda In 1904, a Russian immigrant, Hyman Kirsch, founded a soft drink business in New York City. Later, as vice president of the Jewish Sanitarium for Chronic Disease,

Tab cola. © Kelly Fitzsimmons

he decided to develop a sugar-free soft drink for the institution's diabetic and cardiovascular patients. Using the artificial sweetener calcium cyclamate, he created the first diet beverage. In 1952, Kirsch Beverages began marketing No-Cal (no calorie) **ginger ale** and **root beer**. Their sales were moderate but the idea encouraged others to produce diet beverages.

In 1958 Diet Rite Cola was introduced by the **Royal Crown Cola** Company. By 1963, a study concluded that 28 percent of Americans were dieting. In 1963, the **Coca-Cola** Company introduced Tab, a diet cola drink. The name was a play on words that derived from people "keeping tabs on their weight." It sold well and, in 1967, the company released Fresca, a no-calorie, grapefruit-flavored soda. In 1970, Dr Pepper/Seven Up, Inc. released sugar-free **7-Up**, which was renamed Diet 7-Up in 1979.

Sales of diet drinks took off in the late 1970s. The main reason for this was the attacks on **sugar** by nutritionists, who proclaimed that sugar caused many illnesses, including **diabetes**, heart disease, and **obesity**. By 1980, diet drinks claimed about 20 percent of the soda market. In 1982 Coca-Cola and **PepsiCo** both released diet colas: Diet Coke and Diet Pepsi, respectively. These were supported by vast advertising campaigns. Sales of diet colas greatly reduced the sales of Tab, which is now available only in some localities. By the late 1980s, a variety of diet drinks were sold on the markets. Diet **Mountain Dew**, for instance, made its debut in 1988.

One major shift concerning diet cola beverages has been the diversification of diet products. The Coca-Cola Company came out with caffeine-free Diet Coke in 1983. It launched Diet Cherry Coke in 1985 and Lemon Coke in 2001. In response, PepsiCo marketed a lemon-flavored drink, Diet Pepsi Twist, in 2001. Recently, both PepsiCo and the Coca-Cola Company have introduced new diet cola flavors, including lime and vanilla. To liven up sales of Fresca, the Coca-Cola Company has recently released Sparkling Peach Citrus Fresca and Sparkling Black Cherry Fresca.

Early diet sodas used artificial sweeteners called cyclamates. Cyclamates were banned by the U.S. Food and Drug Administration (FDA) in 1970. Cyclamates were generally replaced by saccharin. In 1977, a Canadian study confirmed that sacchrin caused cancer in test animals and the FDA placed a moratorium on its use. That ban was lifted in 1991, but by that time diet soda production had shifted to using aspartame (marketed under the names NutraSweet and Equal), a sweetener discovered in 1965 and authorized to enter the market in 1974. Numerous allegations have been made against aspartame, none of which has been conclusively proven. Recently, other sweeteners, such as sucralose (marketed as Splenda), have come into increased use. For instance, in 2005, the Coca-Cola Company introduced Diet Coke sweetened with Splenda, the same sweetener in Diet Pepsi. The company also and released Coca-Cola Zero, partly sweetened with a blend of aspartame and acesulfame potassium.

The long-term health risks, if any, of artificial sweeteners are unclear. In addition to the sweeteners used, there are concerns with **salt** and **caffeine**, which are common in many diet drinks. Others assert that the phosphoric acid component of many diet soft drinks may be deleterious to bone health in both men and women. Nevertheless, the popularity of diet sodas has dramatically increased. These drinks emphasize taste without calories.

SUGGESTED READING: Paula M. Kalamaras and Paul T. Kraly, *Sugar and Sweeteners: Trends and Developments in Foods and Beverages* (Norwalk, CT: Business Communications Co., 2003); Harvey Levenstein, *Paradox of Plenty: A Social History of Eating in Modern America* (New York: Oxford University Press, 1993): Tim Richardson, *Sweets: A History of Candy* (New York: Bloomsbury, 2002).

Dieting Dieting—a regimen of eating and drinking designed to lose weight—has been part of American life for almost 200 years. During the early nineteenth century, some medical professionals believed that gluttony led to indigestion, which in turn led to illness. But this was a minority view; at that time, corpulence was not considered either unappealing or unhealthful. This began to change in the late nineteenth century, when fashion magazines and women's clothing manufacturers began to promote thinness as a social value. By the 1890s, weight-loss products, with ingredients such as laxatives, purgatives, and Epsom salts, began to be marketed.

At the same time, Wilbur O. Atwater, an American agricultural chemist, began measuring the caloric values of food, which became the building blocks of many subsequent diets. Russell Chittenden, a chemist at Yale University, linked the idea of calories to the amount of energy burned during exercise. A Los Angeles physician, Dr. Lulu Hunt Peters, built on these two ideas in his *Diet and Health, with Key to the Calories* (1917), which advocated calorie counting as a method of weight reduction. This principle has also been part of many subsequent diets.

In the 1930s, a variety of diets became popular. "Dr. Stoll's Diet-Aid, the Natural Reducing Food," was a liquid diet consisting of a teaspoon of milk **chocolate**, starch, whole wheat, and bran in one cup of water. It was to be consumed at breakfast and lunch. It was promoted through beauty parlors. Since then, numerous diet drinks have been offered, including Metrecal (1959) and Slim-Fast (1977).

Another 1930s diet was proposed by William H. Hay, who believed that starches, proteins, and fruits should be consumed separately. His diet called for a few select vegetables, protein sources, and grapefruits, which Hay claimed had a special fat-burning enzyme. The grapefruit diet reemerged in the 1970s, when it was based on the unproven idea that the fruit's low glycemic index helped the body's metabolism burn fat. It was rejected by nutritionists as a crash diet, which deprived the body of essential nutrients.

After World War II, individual stories of weight loss were published in women's magazines. Alternatively, it became commonplace to believe that individuals who were unable to control their weight lacked discipline or self-control. Being overweight became a sign of moral or psychological weakness.

Entrepreneurs cashed in on these views toward **fat**. In 1951, Tasti-Diet, the first diet food line, was launched by Tillie Lewis, who sweetened her food products with saccharin. Likewise, the physical fitness guru Jack LaLanne went on television to promote weight loss through exercise; he generated additional profits through sales of exercise equipment, vitamins, diet foods, and books. Others, such as Richard Simmons, have followed LaLanne's example.

Borrowing a technique from Alcoholics Anonymous, Jean Nidetch, a housewife from Queens, New York, started a self-help peer group to help her lose weight. Albert Lippert and his wife, Felice (who lost 50 pounds), were members of the group. In 1963 Nidetch and the Lipperts started Weight Watchers. Other weight-loss programs, such as Weight Losers Institute (1968), NutriSystem Weight Loss (1971), and Jenny Craig (1982), followed the Weight Watchers example.

Do-it-yourself diets also proliferated. Robert C. Atkins's *Dr. Atkins' Diet Revolution* (1972) and Herman Tarnower's *The Complete Scarsdale Medical Diet* (1978) were based on the theory that too many carbohydrates prevent the body from burning fat; hence, dieters could and should consume protein in unrestricted quantities, while pasta, bread, and foods with **sugar** were eliminated. High-protein diets, such as Barry Sears's *The Zone* (1995) and Michael R. Eades's *Protein Power* (1996), are variations on Atkins's theme. Sears permits low-carbohydrate vegetables, such as broccoli and green beans, and fruit. Eades avoids most fruit. Critics proclaimed that these diets included too much saturated fat and cholesterol, which can increase the risk of heart disease. In 1979, Nathan Pritikin proposed in his *Pritikin Program for Diet and Exercise* (1979) a very-low-fat diet combined with exercise. Like Pritikin, Dean Ornish's book *Eat More, Weigh Less* (1993) proposed reducing fat intake down to less than 10 percent of calorie intake, along with exercise and meditation.

In 2002, Gary Taubes's article, "What If It's All Been a Big Fat Lie?" in the *New York Times Magazine* questioned the view that fat consumption is the main reason why Americans were overweight, and it pointed to the consumption of carbohydrates as a major culprit. His article gave new life to the Atkins diet. Critics pointed out that calories did matter in dieting, since fat contains twice the calories of either protein or carbohydrates. Just as interest in the Atkins diet began to wane, Miami cardiologist Arthur Agatston recommended reducing carbohydrates (bread, rice, pastas, and fruits) and increasing high-fiber foods, lean proteins, and healthy fats. His book, *The South Beach Diet: The Delicious, Doctor-Designed, Foolproof Plan for Fast and Healthy Weight Loss* (2003), was a best-seller and his diet plan swept the nation.

To support weight-loss programs and do-it-yourself diets, food manufacturers have produced tens of thousands of weight-loss products. In 1969, Weight Watchers introduced frozen low-calorie dinners. NutriSystem and Jenny Craig followed with a complete line of prepackaged foods with the correct portion sizes and the proper nutrition for participants. In addition to diet products, in the 1970s hospitals began offering liquid diets to obese patients. Commercial spin-offs included Stouffer's Lean Cuisine and Heinz's Weight-Watchers line. Slim-Fast and Nestlé's Sweet Success replace two meals with convenient, 200-calorie, nutritionally balanced shakes made from skim milk. Thousands of food products that purport to be diet foods are now on the market. An estimated 50 percent of all food products on the market include such labels as diet, low calorie, "reduced fat," or no fat. Even premium **ice cream** manufacturer **Häagen-Dazs** introduced low-fat ice cream. Lay's produced Baked Potato Chips and Pringles offered a fat-free version, while **Frito-Lay** introduced its Wow! line of low-fat chips. **Fast food** purveyors also developed low-fat foods. Not all commercial low-fat or low-calorie foods have been successful, however. **McDonald's**, for example, tried a low-fat burger, called the McLean, which was discontinued due to lack of interest by customers. Salads, carrot sticks, and other similar products were more successful.

In addition to diets and diet foods, drugs have been regularly promoted for weight loss. Phenylpropanolamine (PPA) was used in a variety of over-the-counter drugs, such as Dexatrim. In 1993, fen-phen, a combination of two diet drugs, fenfluramine and phentermine, appeared. It was proven to cause heart valve problems; the manufacturer withdrew it from the market in 1997. Ephedrine-based herbal supplements have become popular. Olestra (under the trade name Olean), a fat molecule that was too big to be digested, was introduced in 1994, only to be withdrawn a few years later.

Most diets did work in the short run but, long-term, most dieters gain their weight back. There are many reasons for this. Some diets worked because of water loss in the first few days of the diet. Most diets are based on the drastic reduction of calories. A normal-sized person has between 30 and 35 billion fat cells. When a person gains weight, these fat cells increase in size and later in number. When a person starts losing weight, the cells decrease in size but the number of fat cells stays the same. When the body is starved of calories, the metabolism slows down to conserve energy and weight loss stops. The body compensates for decreased caloric intake by lowering energy expenditure, which is why it is easier to lose weight at the beginning of a diet and less so as the diet continues. When dieters go off their regimen, their metabolisms are still working at a high efficiency and consequently continue to store carbohydrates to make up for the loss of weight.

Many diets deprive bodies of essential nutrients and they may trigger overeating, making it more difficult to lose weight in the long run. There is not much evidence that sustained weight loss is possible for most people through fad diets, while there is some evidence that repeatedly trying to lose weight can cause harm.

Today, dieting is ubiquitous in United States. According to the PBS film *Diet Wars*, the American diet industry generates $40 billion in overall revenue, and is projected to increase substantially in the near future. Despite extensive dieting, diet programs, diet books, and diet products, Americans have continued to gain weight. According to the U.S. Surgeon General, 6 out of 10 people in the United States are overweight. As a result, it is believed that **obesity** will soon lead to 300,000 premature deaths, and financial costs for healthcare and lost wages are estimated at $117 billion.

SUGGESTED READING: Paul Campos, *The Obesity Myth: Why America's Obsession with Weight is Hazardous to Your Health* (New York: Gotham Books, 2004); Chris Chase, *The Great American Waistline: Putting It on and Taking It Off* (New York: Coward, McCann & Geoghegan, 1981); Laura Fraser, *Losing It: America's Obsession with Weight and the Industry That Feeds on It* (New York: Dutton, 1997); J. Eric Oliver, *Fat Politics: The Real Story Behind America's Obesity Epidemic* (New York: Oxford University Press, 2005); Hillel Schwartz, *Never Satisfied: A Cultural History of Diets, Fantasies and Fat* (New York: The Free Press, 1986).

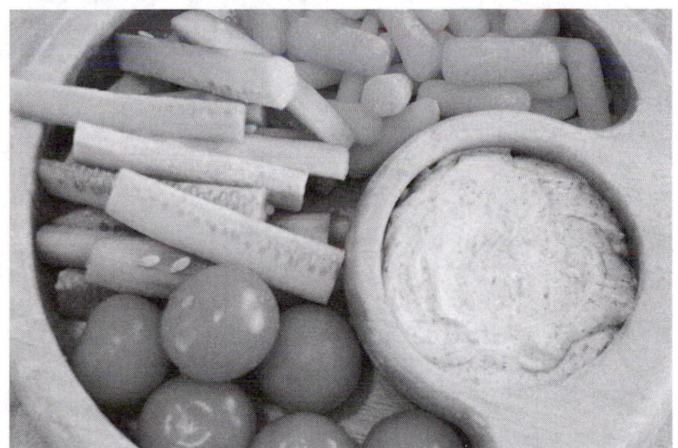
Dip. © Kelly Fitzsimmons

Dips Humankind has been dipping solid food into semiliquid complements for thousands of years, but it was not until the second half of the twentieth century that commercial dips emerged as an important category of food.

Credit for this shift goes to the Thomas J. Lipton Company, which mounted a massive promotional campaign in the 1950s featuring dips made from its dried onion soup mix combined with sour cream or cream cheese. While the Lipton dips could be served with many foods, such as carrot and celery sticks, the major host foods were salty **potato chips** and **corn chips**, which were also extensively marketed during the 1950s. Within six months, sales of Lipton soup mix skyrocketed.

Many successful commercial dips have been based on strong flavors. For example, by far the single most successful dips have been based on Mexican culinary heritage, such as chili, guacamole, and salsa. During the 1930s, Calavo, the California association of avocado growers, began dissemination of instructions for making guacamole. After World War II, potato chips and corn chips were recommended as guacamole dippers, But guacamole did not become a prominent dip until the commercial production of larger and thicker corn chips in the 1960s and the adoption of this combination in Mexican-style restaurants in the United States. In the 1960s, Calavo produced the first commercial guacamole, which was subsequently sold to restaurants and grocery stores.

Another dip originating in Mexican culinary traditions was salsa, generally composed of chili peppers, tomatoes, and flavorings. Salsas are diverse and traditionally were usually intended as condiments for other foods, such as tacos and enchiladas. Their use as a dip was championed by Mexican restaurants in the United States, which served salsa as a dip with tortilla chips; soon the combination became an American staple.

The first known manufacturer of bottled salsa was Pace Foods of San Antonio, Texas. Its owner, Dave Pace, experimented with bottling salsa in 1947 and finally succeeded in getting the formula correct the following year. His success encouraged other manufacturers to produce salsa, including Old El Paso and Ortega. The salsa market exploded during the 1980s and continued to increase during the following decade. During the 1990s, salsa briefly outsold ketchup, which shook up the condiment world.

Today, hundreds of commercial dips are available in **supermarkets**. The major host foods for the dips remain corn and potato chips. In addition, dips and sauces, such as guacamole and salsa, are now given away in many fast food outlets, including **Taco Bell**.

SUGGESTED READING: Carol W. Costenbader, *The Well-Stocked Pantry; Mustards, Ketchups & Vinegars; Dips & Dressing, Sauces & Oils* (Pownal, VT: Storey Communications, Inc., 1996); Judith Dunham and Jane Horn, *Dips, Salsas & Spreads* (San Francisco: Collins, 1996); Christine France, *The Complete Book of Sauces Salsas, Dips, Relishes, Marinades & Dressings* (New York: Lorenz Books, 2001).

Disclosure Fast food franchisers sign contracts with franchisees. These agreements include complicated provisions requiring franchisees to buy only from approved suppliers and permitting franchisers to take payments from these suppliers. Agreements may give franchisers the right to evict a franchisee without giving cause or paying compensation. They may also require a franchisee to waive legal rights to file complaints under state law; to sell the restaurant only to a buyer approved by the chain; and to accept termination of the contract for any reason offered by the **chain**. To make certain that franchisees understand these contracts, the Federal Trade Commission requires **fast food**

chains to provide lengthy disclosure statements that spell out the rules governing franchisor–franchisee relations. These statements are often hundreds of pages long. One the franchisees sign the forms, they are on their own.

In the **junk food** world, companies, such as Mars, Inc., required senior executives to sign nondisclosure statements. In these, the executives agree not to disclose anything about the operations of the company. This protects the company's trade secrets and makes it difficult for anyone to gain information about the company.

SUGGESTED READING: Joël Glenn Brenner, *The Emperors of Chocolate: Inside the Secret World of Hershey and Mars* (New York: Broadway Books, 2000); Eric Schlosser, *Fast Food Nation: The Dark Side of the All-American Meal* (New York: Houghton Mifflin Company, 2001).

Discrimination Historically, **fast food chains** discriminated against minorities and women in their hiring practices. Prominent leaders of the fast food industry were white males. When they selected subordinates and managers for their outlets, these, too, were mainly white males. **White Castle** was largely an inner-city fast food chain and many of its outlets served minorities. As the civil rights movement gained momentum in the United States in the early 1960s, White Castle and other fast food chains reversed these policies. In 1963, White Castle actively sought African-American workers and managers. As **McDonald's** began to expand into inner cities in the 1960s, it also actively recruited African-Americans employees and managers. In 2000, some African-American leaders were ready to boycott Burger King due to problems that the company had with African-American franchisees in Detroit; the boycott did not materialize.

Both White Castle and McDonald's also had policies of hiring only males. As the women's rights movement picked up speed in the 1960s, both companies removed this restriction and began to seek female workers and managers.

Another concern was raised by researchers who examined television programs geared toward African-Americans. Vani R. Henderson and Bridget Kelly's research showed that the commercials shown during these programs contained many more advertisements for fast food and **junk food** than did program targeted at other marketing segments. Because additional research has demonstrated that African-American children watch more television, observers consider this a contributor to **obesity** and eating unhealthy diets among minorities.

A very different concern with discrimination relates to the critics of fast food. Because customers of fast food establishments tend to be those with limited incomes, many of whom are minorities, some critics believe that attacks on fast food are just another mechanism for the upper class to put down the lower class and minorities

SUGGESTED READING: Vani R. Henderson and Bridget Kelly, "Food Advertising in the Age of Obesity: Content Analysis of Food Advertising on General Market and African American Television," *Journal of Nutrition Education & Behavior*, 37 July/Aug. 2005, 191–196; (David Gerard Hogan, *Selling 'em by the Sack: White Castle and the Creation of American Food* (New York: New York University Press, 1997); Eric Schlosser, *Fast Food Nation: The Dark Side of the All-American Meal* (New York: Houghton Mifflin Company, 2001).

Domino's Pizza In 1961, brothers Thomas S. and James Monaghan purchased Dominick's, a **pizza** store in Ypilanti, Michigan. Eight months later, James traded his share to his brother for a used Volkswagen car. In 1965, Tom renamed the business Domino's Pizza and he sold his first **franchise** within a few years. The company expanded and in 1978 the 200th Domino's franchise opened.

Domino's introduced many innovations into the pizza industry. One was home delivery, which had not been possible with other fast foods, such as **hamburgers**, because they become soggy after preparation. Pizza flavors blend after preparation and therefore lent themselves to home delivery. Another innovation by Domino's was its Heat Wave, which is a bag that keeps the pizza hot during delivery. When **Pizza Hut** was forced to follow Domino's lead and begin home delivery to remain competitive, Domino's then guaranteed that the delivery of their pizza would take less than 30 minutes or the customer received the order for free. Many Domino's outlets were located in towns with military installations or colleges. One of the company's most difficult confrontations was a 1967 lawsuit brought against Domino's by Amstar, owner of Domino Sugar, for infringement on their trademarked name Domino's. The lawsuit was settled out of court.

Domino's began to expand internationally during the 1980s, opening outlets in Canada, Australia (1983), and the United Kingdom (1985). The company continued to expand abroad and has localized many of its products. In Japan, for instance, the company's best seller is a pizza with mayonnaise, potatoes, and ham or bacon. In Hong Kong, it is its pizza with Cajun spices with small marinated cubes of meat. By 2006, the company had expanded even more and currently has over 8,000 outlets, 5,000 in the United States and 3,000 in 50 other countries. Domino's, headquartered in Ann Arbor, Michigan, is the second-largest pizza chain after Pizza Hut.

SUGGESTED READING: John A. Jakle and Keith A. Sculle, *Fast Food: Roadside Restaurants in the Automobile Age* (Baltimore: Johns Hopkins University Press, 1999); Tom Monaghan, with Robert Anderson, *Pizza Tiger* (New York: Random House, 1986).

Doritos Arch West, an executive vice president of **Frito-Lay**, Inc., is credited with inventing the triangular corn chips called Doritos, which means "little bits of gold" in Spanish. The name was likely also selected because it rhymed with **Cheetos**, another popular snack food manufactured by Frito-Lay. Doritos brand tortilla chips were released in 1966, the first tortilla chip launched nationally. They quickly became the most popular snack chip in the United States. Frito-Lay has expanded the Doritos product line to include a wide variety of flavors, including Nacho Cheesier, Salsa, Black Pepper Jack, Guacamole! Taco, and Natural White **Nacho** Cheese Tortilla Chips, to name a few. The Frito-Lay company has eliminated trans **fats** (which raise LDL cholesterol and increase the risk of heart disease) from Doritos. Today, Doritos can be purchased in 20 countries and its international retail sales exceed $250 million per year.

SUGGESTED READING: Andrew F. Smith, "Tacos, Enchiladas and Refried Beans: The Invention of Mexican-American Cookery," in Mary Wallace Kelsey and ZoeAnn Holmes, eds., *Cultural and Historical Aspects of Foods* (Corvallis, OR: Oregon State University, 1999), 183–203; Doritos Web site: www.doritos.com

Doughnuts Doughnuts were probably of German origin. Early Dutch settlers in New Amsterdam (later renamed New York) called them *olykoeks*. They were popular in colonial America but were mainly constructed in solid shapes. They were literally nuts of dough.

Doughnuts with holes in the center were not common until the end of the nineteenth century. Purportedly, the hole was developed by the Pennsylvania Dutch because it made for easier dunking in coffee. Others maintain that the shape made for better frying. During World War I, the Salvation Army served doughnuts to soldiers and since 1938 has celebrated Donut Day in Chicago (June 4–5) in honor of their work during that war.

The sale of commercial doughnuts greatly expanded after World War II. Doughnut retailing lends itself to franchising because the equipment is not too expensive. The trend toward healthier foods caused doughnut sales across most of United States to decline beginning in the 1980s. However, doughnut sales did not decline in Canada, where Tim Horton's restaurant **chain** complemented doughnuts with **sandwiches** and other light fare to capture much of Canada's **fast food** business. In 1995, Horton's was bought by **Wendy's**, which began to co-brand with the Canadian company.

About 80 percent of doughnut business is take-out, and 80 percent of doughnuts are sold before noon. Major doughnut franchisers include **Dunkin' Donuts**, **Krispy Kreme**, and **Winchell's**. Dunkin' Donuts alone sells an estimated 6.4 million doughnuts per day (2.3 billion per year). Krispy Kreme doughnuts are the best-selling doughnut in grocery stores, followed by those manufactured by Entenmann's and Dolly Madison.

SUGGESTED READING: John A. Jakle and Keith A. Sculle, *Fast Food: Roadside Restaurants in the Automobile Age* (Baltimore: Johns Hopkins University Press, 1999); Peter Rose, *The Sensible Cook: Dutch Foodways in the Old and the New World* (Syracuse, NY: Syracuse University Press, 1989).

Dove Bar A Greek immigrant, Leo Stefanos, opened a **candy** business on the South Side of Chicago called the Dove Candy Shop. In 1956, he dipped **ice cream** into thick, hot **chocolate**, and the Dove Bar was born. Its fame spread beyond Chicago during the 1970s and became widely popular in the 1980s. In 1985, **Mars, Inc.** acquired the Dove Bar and the following year began to market the brand nationally. The Dove bar became known for its richness; each bar contains 320 calories and 13 grams of fat. In 1990, Mars began to extend the line of Dove confections, releasing Dove Chocolates and, two years later, Dark Chocolate and Milk Chocolate Dove Bars. In addition, the Dove brand includes seasonal candy and bagged chocolates. Dove confections are sold in 30 countries today.

SUGGESTED READING: Joël Glenn Brenner, *The Emperors of Chocolate: Inside the Secret World of Hershey and Mars* (New York: Broadway Books, 2000); Mike Stefanos, "Sweet Success—Dove Bar's Mike Stefanos Reflects on Warm Family Memories," *Greek Circle* (Summer 2002); Dove Bar Web site: www.dovechocolate.com

Dr Pepper Toward the end of the nineteenth century, Charles Alderton was employed at Morrison's Old Corner Drug Store in Waco, Texas, where carbonated beverages were served at a soda fountain. Alderton experimented with different formulas, many of which became popular. The owner of the store, Wade Morrison, is credited with naming one of the soft drinks Dr. Pepper in 1885. A number of different stories have circulated as to why the drink was named Dr. Pepper, a common one being that Morrison named it after Charles T. Pepper, a Confederate surgeon.

One person who liked Dr. Pepper was Robert S. Lazenby, who owned The Circle A Ginger Ale Company in Waco. In 1891, Lazenby went into business with Morrison and formed the Artesian Manufacturing & Bottling Company. One of their products was a black cherry-flavored soft drink that they called Dr. Pepper's Pho-Ferrates. It quickly became a favorite in the Southwest. In 1904, it was marketed at the St. Louis Exposition. The first located advertisement to employ Dr. Pepper's first slogan ("Vim, Vigor, and Vitality") and its **mascot** (a lion) appeared in Waco in 1906. This beverage was a tremendous success and the company's name was changed to the Dr. Pepper Company. Subsequently, the period was removed from the Dr Pepper name.

During the twentieth century, the company used several slogans for Dr Pepper, including "King of Beverages." An image of a doctor with monocle and top hat, called Old Doc, became the beverage's logo during the 1930s. After World War II, the company described Dr Pepper as "the most misunderstood soft drink," and then in the 1970s it was called "the most original soft drink ever in the whole wide world." In 1977, Dr Pepper advertising was marked by the famous "Be a Pepper" campaign, and later "Be You."

Lazenby moved the company from Waco to Dallas in 1923. The Dr Pepper Company is one of the oldest manufacturers of soft drink concentrates and syrups in America. It merged with **7-Up** in 1986. In turn, Dr Pepper/ Seven Up, Inc. was acquired by **Cadbury Schweppes** in 1995. Today, the Dr Pepper brand is part of Cadbury Schweppes Americas Beverages (CSAB), located in Plano, Texas. There is a Dr Pepper Museum and Free Enterprise Institute in Waco, Texas.

SUGGESTED READING: Harry E. Ellis, *Dr Pepper: King of Beverages* (Dallas, TX: Dr Pepper Company, Dallas, 1979); Harry E. Ellis, *Dr Pepper: King of Beverages Centennial Edition* (Dallas, TX: Dr Pepper Company, Dallas, 1986); Anne Cooper Funderburg, *Sundae Best: A History of Soda Fountains* (Bowling Green, OH: Bowling Green State University Popular Press, 2002); Jeffrey L. Rodengen, *The Legend of Dr. Pepper/Seven-up* (Ft. Lauderdale, FL: Write Stuff Syndicate, 1995); Dr Pepper Web site: www.drpepper.com; Dr Pepper Museum Web site: www.drpeppermuseum.com

Dreyer's/Edy's Ice Cream In 1921, William Dreyer opened an ice creamery in Visalia, California. He moved his operation to Oakland, California, where he met Joseph Edy, a **candy** maker. In 1929, the company invented Rocky Road **ice cream**, which remains one of America's favorite ice creams. In 1947, Edy and Dreyer dissolved their business partnership and the company was purchased in 1977 by T. Gary Rogers and W. F. Cronk, who increased the distribution of Dreyer's Grand Ice Cream. In 2003, the company merged with **Nestlé** Ice Cream Company to form Dreyer's Grand Ice Cream Holdings, Inc. It markets many ice cream brands, including **Drumstick**, Nestlé, **Push-Ups**, **Häagen-Dazs**, and many others.

SUGGESTED READING: Dreyer's Web site: www.dreyers.com

Drive-ins Inexpensive automobiles flooded America after World War I. By 1920 there were 9.2 million cars, trucks, and buses in the United States. It was only a matter of time before someone created a restaurant specifically designed so customers could eat in their cars.

Two restaurants **chains** claim to have opened the first drive-ins. The one usually credited is the Pig Stand, launched by J. G. Kirby, a Dallas, Texas **candy** and tobacco wholesaler, who opened a barbecue **sandwich** outlet in 1921 on Dallas–Ft. Worth Highway; a second one opened in Dallas three years later. The chain then expanded to other Texas cities, Oklahoma, Louisiana, Mississippi, Florida, New York, and California. Pig Stands came to Los Angeles in 1927. Kirby's restaurants were rectangular drive-ins, permitting cars to park facing toward the building. On the exterior were large signs saying "Eat a Pig Sandwich" and the main item on the menus was barbecue sandwiches. In 1931, one of the restaurants in Texas installed a canvas canopy, which offered protection from rain and provided shade. Other restaurants created permanent structures made of metal, and a new dimension was added to drive-in architecture.

The other restaurant chain that claims to have been the first drive-in is **A&W Root Beer**, launched by Roy Allen in Lodi, California, in 1919. This stand was not a drive-in but, shortly thereafter, Allen opened additional units in Sacramento, at least one of which was reportedly a drive-in. A&W initially sold just **root beer** but they expanded their menu over the years.

Both Kirby and Allen constructed parking lots at their stands, mainly dirt affairs. Later drive-ins constructed canopies over the cars so that customers could have protection from rain and sun. Eating in the car was novel at the time, but it was also convenient, particularly for families with small children. Also, eating in cars was more relaxed, which was appreciated by customers who wanted privacy not easily available in a walk-in restaurant. **Carhops** went out to the cars, picked up orders, and delivered the food to the cars, where customers ate their food. In addition, carhops provided entertainment. They were usually festooned in unusual costumes and they frequently engaged in outlandish activities. As carhops, usually female, frequently did not receive wages but were paid just with tips, they were usually extremely friendly to customers, especially to males.

Drive-ins quickly multiplied throughout the United States. In the northern and eastern states they were usually seasonal phenomena, closing at the end of every summer. It was just too cold to eat in cars during the winter. In the South, Southwest, and in southern California, however, drive-ins operated year-round and in these regions drive-ins reached the pinnacle of success. One problem faced by all drive-ins was how to be spotted by motorists who were speeding by on highways. The solution was to design gaudy buildings to advertise the drive-in. Many had large signs and flashing neon lights.

White Castle and its clones were built on a different model. White Castles were mainly located in inner cities and management targeted walk-in workers. They were based on self-service, where customers ordered their food at a window or counter. Some White Castles built parking lots or were built near parking facilities, but mainly customers ate their food indoors or took their food to a different location.

The heyday of the drive-ins was the 1930s and 1940s, but after their novelty wore off no one considered their gaudy and flimsy architecture attractive. Planning commissions began to regulate their construction and municipalities began to restrict operations of drive-ins, which had become hangouts for teenagers, resulting in rowdiness and excessive litter.

Perhaps the most important reason for the decline of drive-ins had to do with the owners of a restaurant in southern California, Richard and Maurice McDonald. In 1940, the brothers constructed a drive-in with carhops in San Bernardino, California. It worked moderately well, but after World War II, their expenses went up, mainly due to wages paid to employees. They also had difficulty getting good workers and they believed that carhops were more interested in socializing with customers than in selling **hamburgers**. So the brothers designed a new, self-service restaurant without carhops and an extremely efficient assembly line operation inside. They pared down their menu to increase the speed of meeting customers' orders and began experimenting with labor-saving technology. As a result they significantly lowered their expenses and passed these savings on to their customers. The result, **McDonald's** hamburgers, was copied by many others. Drive-ins could not compete with these new fast food, self-serve, low-cost chains, and most drive-ins closed. Today, a few drive-ins remain, primarily in small towns. Only one national fast food chain, **Sonic**, has attempted to keep carhops, mainly for nostalgic reasons.

SUGGESTED READING: Anne Cooper Funderburg, *Sundae Best: A History of Soda Fountains* (Bowling Green, OH: Bowling Green State University Popular Press, 2002); Jim Heimann, *Car Hops and Curb Service: A History of American Drive-In Restaurants, 1920–1960* (San Francisco: Chronicle Books, 1996); Philip Langdon, *Orange Roofs, Golden Arches: The Architecture of American Chain Restaurants* (New York: Knopf, 1986); Lawrence Winchell, ed., *Drive-In Management Guidebook* (New York: Harcourt Brace, 1968); Michael Karl Witzel, *The American Drive-in* (Osceola, WI: Motorbooks International, 1994).

Drive-thrus Take-out operations had existed in delicatessens since the late nineteenth century. By definition, drive-thrus needed **automobiles**, which were not common until after World War I. Some claim that Roy Allen, founder of **A&W Root Beer**, constructed the first drive-thru so in 1921. Others claim that the first drive-thru window was created in 1931 by the Pig Stand Number 21 restaurant in Los Angeles, California, which created a small window where customers ordered and received their food. In these early versions, customers would drive up to the window, get out of their cars and place their order at the window.

In-N-Out Burger installed a two-way speaker box for customers to order at its first outlet in Baldwin Park, California in 1948. This sped up ordering and fulfilling the orders. It has been a feature of In-N-Out Burger outlets ever since. A recent innovation has been the use of mobile employees when the lines are particularly long. Employees take orders from the cars in line on a handheld communicator, which sends the order directly to the kitchen, thus speeding up the ordering process.

During the 1950s, **Jack in the Box** and **Burger King** both experimented with drive-thrus similar to that of the In-N-Out Burger system. Burger King assigned a separate staff to run their drive-thru operations. These efforts were unsuccessful and were discontinued. John Galardi, founder of **Wienerschnitzel** in 1961, constructed A-frames with an automobile-sized hole in the center of the building. Signs had to be placed strategically around outlets directing customers where to steer their cars to order their food. **Del Taco** constructed a drive-thru window in its second outlet in 1961, and continued doing so as it built additional outlets. These were moderately successful.

Wendy's, founded in 1969, incorporated drive-thru windows beginning in 1971. Within 10 years, Wendy's had more than 1,800 outlets, and many observers credit drive-thrus as one of the reasons for this phenomenal success. Drive-thru windows had many advantages, including the fact that Wendy's saved on space in its parking lots and indoor eating areas, as drive-thru customers normally drove off and ate their order elsewhere. Other **chains** saw Wendy's success and immediately began tearing down walls to construct drive-thru windows in their outlets. Tests demonstrated that drive-thru windows actually increased sales. By 1976, most national **fast food** chains had drive-thru windows. Some constructed double

Drive-thru menu. © Kelly Fitzsimmons

drive-thrus, with two traffic lanes, to speed up delivery of orders. Menu boards and microphones were installed to further speed up operations.

McDonald's constructed its first drive-thru window in 1975; it was so successful that the company encouraged all of its outlets to install them. By 1981, 51 percent of McDonald's sales were through the chain's drive-thru windows. Other chains had similar results.

While it may have been unsafe, many drive-thru customers ate while driving. This induced car manufacturers to equip front seats with cup-holders to facilitate dashboard dining. Drive-thru windows featured food that could be held in one hand, such that drivers could eat and drive simultaneously. This favored **hamburger** fast food operations. Hamburgers could be more easily consumed than fried chicken, for example. **Taco Bell** developed a soft tortilla that would not crumble when drivers bit into it; **Kentucky Fried Chicken** launched a **chicken** pita sandwich that could easily be held in the driver's hand and did not drip all over. Hamburger chains began to develop more foods that could be easily consumed in cars. In 1979, McDonald's introduced its **Chicken McNuggets**, which were intentionally constructed so that they could easily be consumed by drivers. Other fast food operations followed McDonald's lead, and similar foods that could easily be handled by drivers were rolled out. By early 2000s, drive-thrus were common throughout the United States and today usually account for more than half of the sales of fast food establishments. At Burger King, drive-thru sales amount to 68 percent of total sales.

When fast food chains open outlets in other countries, the architecture must frequently be modified to meet local conditions. The most unusual modification to date is Sweden's McSki, which provides ski-thru service so that skiers "can ski up to the counter and order their favorite McDonald's **sandwich** without missing a beat on the slopes."

SUGGESTED READING: John A. Jakle and Keith A. Sculle, *Fast Food: Roadside Restaurants in the Automobile Age* (Baltimore: Johns Hopkins University Press, 1999); Philip Langdon, *Orange Roofs, Golden Arches: The Architecture of American Chain Restaurants* (New York: Knopf, 1986); A&W Root Beer Web site: www.awrootbeer.com/hist_hist.htm; In-N-Out Burger Web site: www.in-n-out.com

Drumsticks During the 1920s, **ice cream** novelties such as the **Eskimo Pie** and the **Good Humor** bar encouraged others food manufacturers to develop new products. J. T. "Stubby" Parker of Ft. Worth, Texas, was the manager of the Pangburn Candy and Ice Cream Company. In 1930 he figured out how to package a sugar cone filled with ice cream, topped with **chocolate** and **nuts**. He named it a Drumstick because it looked like a **fried chicken** leg. In 1931, he formed the Frozen Drumstick Company to commercially manufacture his new product. In 1962, the company was merged to create Big Drum, Inc., a publicly traded company. In the early 1990's, Big Drum was acquired by **Nestlé**.

SUGGESTED READING: Anne Cooper Funderburg, *Chocolate, Strawberry, and Vanilla: A History of American Ice Cream* (Bowling Green, OH: Bowling Green State University Popular Press, 1995).

Dunkin' Donuts William Rosenberg dropped out of school at the age of 14 and engaged in various employments. In 1946, Rosenberg founded Industrial Luncheon Services in suburban Boston. The company sold coffee, **sandwiches**, and baked goods from trucks to workers Within three years, his company was operating 140 trucks. In 1948, he saw that doughnuts were in high demand, and he opened a small **doughnut** shop called the Open Kettle in Quincy, Massachusetts. Two years later, he renamed it

Dunkin' Donuts. © Kelly Fitzsimmons

Dunkin' Donuts. Rosenberg developed a distinctive logo initially for take-out packaging. In 1955, he sold his first **franchise** and the franchise operations quickly expanded. In 1966 he opened the Dunkin' Donuts University to help franchisers run their shops. In 1968, there were 334 outlets; by 1986, there were 6,900. In 1970, the company opened its first overseas outlet, in Japan. The company began to advertise on **television** in 1978. In 1983 they had incredible success with the release of a commercial of Fred the Baker (played by Michael Vale) saying "Time to make the donuts." This was honored by the Television Bureau of Advertising as one of the five best commercials from the 1980s.

The company has regularly developed its menu and it has often advertised its products with humor. Its Munchkins, according to the company's commercials, were the holes from the middle of traditional doughnuts. In 1996, the company began selling freshly baked bagels. In 2002, it introduced espressos, lattés, and cappuccinos.

Dunkin' Donuts bought Mister Donut, the nation's second-largest doughnut chain. In 1990, Dunkin' Donuts was acquired by the French-based multinational corporation Allied Lyons, which in turn was acquired by another French corporation, Pernod Ricard. Pernod Ricard combined Dunkin' Donuts, **Baskin-Robbins**, and Togo's Sandwiches to form a subsidiary, Dunkin' Brands. In 2006, Pernod Ricard sold Dunkin' Brands to a group of American equity investors. There are now more than 5,500 Dunkin' Donuts outlets in 30 nations. The company sells an estimated 6.4 million doughnuts per day, totaling 2.3 billion per year.

SUGGESTED READING: John A. Jakle and Keith A. Sculle, *Fast Food: Roadside Restaurants in the Automobile Age* (Baltimore: Johns Hopkins University Press, 1999); Dunkin' Donuts Web site: www.dunkindonuts.com

E

Easter Candy Fertility symbols employed in pagan celebrations of spring—bunnies, eggs, and chicks—were absorbed into Christian celebrations of Easter. Giving Easter eggs to poor children was a tradition that began in Medieval Europe. The American tradition of hiding and hunting for Easter eggs may have derived from a similar tradition in Austria.

Easter **candy** is a relatively recent addition to Easter traditions. It likely originated in Eastern Europe. The first located reference to **chocolate** Easter eggs is dated 1820 in Italy. In England, candy Easter eggs may have been inspired by the mid-nineteenth Christmas celebration, which included Christmas **cookies** and candies. In the United States, children's Easter baskets were traditionally filled with boiled eggs dyed with various colors, and other foods. During the 1930s, Easter candies, such as **jelly beans** and chocolate Easter bunnies, became part of the Easter basket tradition.

One early maker of Easter candies was the Rodda Candy Company of Bethlehem, Pennsylvania. It manufactured jelly beans and marshmallow figures. The **Just Born** Company acquired the Rodda Candy Company in 1953. They focused on the three-dimensional marshmallow Easter chicks called Peeps. At the time, Peeps were handmade by a group of women in the back of the factory. Just Born mechanized Peep production and in 1954, began to bring Peeps to consumers on a mass scale. Another manufacturer of Easter candies is Palmer Chocolates, which sells Easter treats such as giant bunnies and hollow eggs.

According to the **National Confectioners Association**, which has strongly supported the tradition of giving candy at holidays, Easter is second only to **Halloween** as the most important candy-consuming holiday in America. Annually, Americans purchase almost $2 billion in Easter candies, including 90 million chocolate Easter bunnies, 16 billion jelly beans, and 700 million marshmallow Peeps.

Easter candy. © Kelly Fitzsimmons

Suggested Reading: Tim Richardson, *Sweets: A History of Candy* (New York: Bloomsbury, 2002); Jack Santino, *New Old-Fashioned Ways: Holidays and Popular Culture* (Knoxville, TN: The University of Tennessee Press, 1996).

Efficiency Henry Ford hoped to sell inexpensive cars and make a profit by increasing the volume of his sales. He installed assembly lines to make Model T **automobiles**. While the tasks were repetitive and boring on the assembly line, Ford paid workers a comparatively decent wage for the time and he stressed a lifelong commitment to his company. In many respects, **White Castle**, attempted to use Ford's principles to make and sell inexpensive **hamburgers** and make a profit by increasing the volume of its sales. Like Ford, White Castle set up a fund for employee medical expenses and developed a profit-sharing system with cash bonuses.

Efficiency was an important part of **McDonald's** model, which was called the Speedee Service System. Richard and Maurice McDonald carefully eliminated all unnecessary steps in the making and packing of hamburgers, **French fries**, and beverages. They acquired the best equipment and designed their kitchens for maximum efficiency. However, the model developed by the brothers diverged when it came to employees. McDonald's employees were paid minimum wage with no benefits. The system that the brothers developed was been refined by fast food chains during the subsequent 50 years.

The application of efficiency to food has dramatically changed what Americans eat and how Americans live. Most **fast food chains** and many full-service restaurants use frozen foods—hamburger patties, **chickens**, taco meat, buns, and potatoes. Some chains actually use conveyor belts and assembly lines to ensure standardization. Employees dress alike and they are trained to greet customers in the same specific way. The kitchens are filled with buzzers and flashing lights that tell employees what to do. Computerized cash registers issue their own commands.

Fast food companies can request anything they want from suppliers. Because fast food chains are extremely large, they can bargain for lower prices. To meet their contracts with fast food chains, suppliers have reduced wages, and critics say suppliers have reduced safety and health standards as well.

George Ritzer, author of *The McDonaldization of Society* (1996), has argued that the fast food industry has promoted efficiency over other important human values. According to Ritzer, the fast food industry's striving toward efficiency has homogenized American life and, due to the globalization of fast food, the industry is now homogenizing other cultures around the world.

SUGGESTED READING: Robert Kanigek, *The One Best Way: Frederick Winslow Taylor and the Enigma of Efficiency* (New York: Viking, 1997); George Ritzer, ed., McDonaldization: the Reader. 2nd ed. (Thousand Oaks, CA: Pine Forge Press, 2006); Eric Schlosser, *Fast Food Nation: The Dark Side of the All-American Meal* (New York: Houghton Mifflin Company, 2001).

Egg Fast Food Early **fast food chains** were often open 24 hours a day. Their menu did not include egg dishes, so breakfast tended to be coffee and pie or some other sweet. During World War II, meat was rationed and fast food chains looked around for alternative foods to serve. Bruce LaPlante, a **White Castle** manager in the St. Louis area, created a fried egg **sandwich**. The egg was fried in a metal ring and it was served on a bun like a **hamburger**. It was not popular and as soon as meat restrictions ended, the fried egg sandwich was discontinued.

Post–World War II fast food establishments did not start serving breakfast until the 1970s. Most managers worked late into the evening and were not interested in opening early in the morning. In addition, most customers were not interested in hamburgers or fries for breakfast, so entirely new menus needed to be developed. Yet from an economic point of view, it was inefficient not to use facilities that could otherwise be producing income. The facilities were available and breakfast foods would not compete with the regular menu items.

This changed in 1970 when Jim Delligati, an early **McDonald's** franchisee in Pittsburgh, began serving a simple breakfast menu, which included coffee, **doughnuts**, and sweet rolls. In the following year he expanded the menu to include pancakes and sausage. The advantage of the breakfast menu was that it generated a totally new market and the items served did not compete with the traditional menu that McDonald's served at lunch and dinner.

About the same time, **Jack in the Box** began serving an Eggs Benedict sandwich. In 1971, Herb Peterson, a McDonald's operator in Santa Barbara, California, modified the Eggs Benedict sandwich and ended up with the Egg McMuffin, a grilled egg in an English muffin with Canadian bacon. Simultaneously, Delligati had developed a complete breakfast line, including scrambled eggs. By 1976, McDonald's also had a complete breakfast menu, which was served nationwide. The company continued to add to its breakfast menu with such items as the Breakfast Burrito (with scrambled eggs). In other countries McDonald's has also offered egg sandwiches, such as McHuevo (poached egg in buns) in Uruguay. Other chains developed egg dishes, such as **Burger King**'s Croissan'wich. Virtually all fast food chains have now incorporated breakfast items with eggs.

SUGGESTED READING: David Gerard Hogan, *Selling 'em by the Sack: White Castle and the Creation of American Food* (New York: New York University Press, 1997); John F. Love, *McDonald's: Behind the Arches*, revised ed. (New York: Bantam Books, 1995).

Elderly **Fast food chains** hired mainly teenage males until the 1960s, when anti-discrimination laws required them to hire women. Because the baby-boom generation coincided with the rapid growth of fast food chains, there was an excess pool of potential employees. By the 1970s, fast food chains began to feel the pinch for employees. There were many more fast food outlets and there were fewer teenagers who were willing to work for little pay there. Fast food companies began seeking nontraditional workers, and one group was the elderly. The elderly tended to be more stable in their work patterns and therefore stayed longer than did baby-boom employees who moved on to better employment.

The elderly have been attracted to fast food chains as customers because they are convenient and inexpensive. However, the elderly are also extremely vulnerable to food-borne pathogens, such as ***Escherichia coli*** and ***salmonella***, which are becoming more common in fast food restaurants.

SUGGESTED READING: Eric Schlosser, *Fast Food Nation: The Dark Side of the All-American Meal* (New York: Houghton Mifflin Company, 2001).

Employment Early snack food manufacturers and fast food chains were highly dependent upon their employees. **Milton S. Hershey**, founder of the **Hershey Company**, recognized their importance and created an ideal community that offered employees parks, pools, and other amenities. He also offered insurance programs and a retirement plan decades before it became common to do so in America.

Likewise, **White Castle**, the first **fast food chain**, set up a medical expense fund for the company's employees and their families. The company also set up profit-sharing systems with cash bonuses. When the company began competing with other fast food chains that did not offer such benefits to their employees and were consequently able to undersell White Castle, these programs were curtailed.

Today, three fast food corporations—**Burger King**, **McDonald's**, and **Yum! Brands** (which manages **Kentucky Fried Chicken**, **Pizza Hut**, **Taco Bell**, **Long John Silver's**, and **A&W** Restaurants)—employ about four million people worldwide and operate 120,000 restaurants. The industry is a major employer in America and its labor practices have been frequently criticized. The fundamental key to success of the fast food industry has been cheap labor and, on the whole, the industry pays minimum wage to the majority of its workers. Fast food chains have intentionally tried to keep unions out. They have consistently lobbied against increasing the minimum wage and have proposed eliminating minimum wages for teenagers. Over the past 50 years, these policies have enabled prices to remain low for fast food operations but have caused the industry's chronically high employee turnover rate.

Initially, McDonald's and other fast food chains sought teenagers for the bulk of their workers. For most teenagers, it was their first job and they were willing to work for minimum wage. In return, the industry taught teenagers basic job skills, such as getting to work on time, obedience, and how to improve their personal hygiene. The postwar growth in the fast food industry coincided with baby boomers coming of age. It was enhanced further during the 1960s, when the industry broadened employment opportunities for women and minorities.

But even this enlarged pool began to shrink as the baby-boom generation passed out of its teenage years. The fast food industry then shifted to nontraditional workers, such as the elderly, recent immigrants, and the handicapped. Because little training is required for most fast food functions, this has worked out well.

In the United States, wages are set by fast food managers based upon local labor conditions, but the vast majority of employees have marginal social status, receive minimum wage, and do not receive benefits. Most are part-time workers and few are permitted to work overtime. Fast food chains reward managers who keep labor costs low. Taco Bell managers, for instance, have been paid bonuses based on the reduction of labor costs. This has sometimes led to abuse, such as employees being required to work off the clock so they would not be paid overtime rates.

Companies have responded to these issues by proclaiming that the fast food jobs are ideal first jobs and that they are perfect for anyone who wants just part-time work. Companies also point to the fact that they hire the elderly, the newly arrived immigrants, and the handicapped.

The exception has been the labor policies of **In-N-Out Burger**, a small, regional hamburger chain in California, Nevada, and Arizona. It pays its employees significantly more than mandated minimum wages and offers workers a benefits package that includes dental, medical, vision, and life insurance. As a result, In-N-Out enjoys lower employee turnover than do other fast food chains.

The influence of fast food employment on the nation is clear: McDonald's alone hires one million new workers every year, more than any other American business, and one in every eight Americans has worked at McDonald's at some point in their lives.

SUGGESTED READING: Eric Schlosser, *Fast Food Nation: The Dark Side of the All-American Meal* (New York: Houghton Mifflin Company, 2001); Jennifer Parker Talwar, *Fast Food, Fast Track: Immigrants, Big Business, and the American Dream* (Boulder, CO: Westview Press, 2002); Stuart Tannock, *Youth at Work: the Unionized Fast-food and Grocery Workplace* (Philadelphia: Temple University Press, 2001); In-N-Out Burger Web site: www.in-n-out.com

Entrepreneurs The early **snack food** and **junk food** creators were individuals with dreams who, usually after many failures, succeeded in carrying them out. Once these businesses were launched, other people with different skills were needed to convert these ideas into expanding and financially viable enterprises. **Frank Mars** had failed numerous times before he finally launched **Mars, Inc. Milton S. Hershey** had failed at several businesses before he finally succeeded with a **caramel** company. He could have rested on this success but he decided to sell the caramel company and invest his time and energy in building the **Hershey Company**. Milton Hershey turned over his business to William Murrie, who managed the **chocolate** empire and guided it through the early years of the twentieth century.

A similar pattern occurred in the **fast food** industry. Walter Anderson, who had had many previous jobs, launched **White Castle** but it was Billy Ingram, a real estate agent, who figured out how to convert Anderson's good idea into a major commercial success. **Harland Sanders** figured out a good way to make fried chicken. When his restaurant business failed he hit the road, selling his secret for a percentage of sale profits. He sold many **Kentucky Fried Chicken franchises** but it was John Y. Brown and Jack Massy who converted the collection of franchises into a national **chain. McDonald's** took a similar path. Richard and Maurice McDonald, who really wanted to be in the movie industry, launched their Speedee Service System in 1948 but they lacked the organizational skill and the drive to take their idea national. **Ray Kroc** converted the brothers' ideas into the corporation that has dazzled America and the world ever since. Similar patterns occurred with **Burger King**, which was created by Keith Cramer but was converted from a local Florida fast food chain into a national enterprise by two franchisers, James McLamore and David R. Edgerton. McLamore and Edgerton sold the business to the Pillsbury Company, which converted it into an international operation.

This combination of the hard-working, risk-taking idea person coupled with the organizational skills, know-how, and promotional capacities of managers was the real story behind the emergence of the fast food industry. Entrepreneurs located or created a good, marketable idea and proved that it could be a success. Corporate leaders with organizational and financial skills converted good ideas into major national and international chains.

SUGGESTED READING: Wally Amos with Leroy Robinson, *The Famous Amos Story: The Face That Launched a Thousand Chips* (Garden City, NY: Doubleday, 1983); Tony Conza, *Success: It's a Beautiful Thing: Lessons on Life and Business from the Founder of Blimpie International* (New York: Wiley, 2000); Billy Ingram, *All This from a 5-cent Hamburger! The Story of the White Castle System* (New York: Newcomen Society in North America, 1964); Carl Karcher and B. Carolyn Knight, *Never Stop Dreaming: The Story of Carl Karcher Enterprises* (San Marcos, CA: Robert Erdmann Publishing, 1991); Ray Kroc, with Robert Anderson, *Grinding It Out: The Making of McDonald's* (Chicago: Henry Regnery Company, 1977); James W. McLamore, *The Burger King: Jim McLamore and the Building of an Empire* (New York: McGraw-Hill, 1998); Tom Monaghan, with Robert Anderson, *Pizza Tiger* (New York: Random House, 1986); Orville Redenbacher, *Orville Redenbacher's Popcorn Book* (New York: St. Martin's Press, 1984); Harland Sanders, *Life as I Have Known It Has*

Been Finger Lickin' Good (Carol Stream, IL: Creation House, 1974); R. David Thomas, *Dave's Way: A New Approach to Old-fashioned Success* (New York: G. P. Putnam's Sons, 1991).

Environment Critics have charged **fast food chains** with contributing to a number of environmental problems, such as pollution from plastic containers that fast food is served in, producing extensive waste that fills up land fills, and the destruction of rain forests of Central and South America. Fast food companies do generate large amounts of waste—cups, paper, and cardboard packaging. The total waste produced by fast food chains is estimated at less than 1 percent of land fill content.

McDonald's, one of the world's largest fast food chains, has responded to these charges in positive ways. Environmentalists charged that McDonald's was contributing to pollution through the boxes that its hamburgers were served in. The boxes were made from polystyrene, which is nonbiodegradable. McDonald's switched from plastic to paper boxes. For this, McDonald's received extensive positive media coverage. McDonald's sought advice from environment groups about how to make its operation more environmentally friendly. As a result, the company began using recycled paper and made major contributions to environmental groups, such as the Environmental Defense Fund. In addition, McDonald's has reduced the amount of electricity it uses and has eliminated some packaging.

Both fast food chains and **chocolate** companies have been charged with destroying the rain forests. For fast food producers, chains buy beef from many suppliers, some of which operate in countries with rainforests. Environmentalists claim that the large purchases of beef by fast food companies encourage ranchers to burn down rainforests to create feedlots for beef. Although fast food companies have made attempts to shift beef-buying from countries with rainforests, most companies do not operate ranches or meat-packing facilities. Many environmentalists believe that fast food companies should be held responsible for the actions of their suppliers. Likewise, cocoa producers have been accused of destroying rain forests, particularly in the Ivory Coast, Indonesia, and Brazil, through the purchase of cocoa from suppliers who destroy rainforests to build their plantations.

SUGGESTED READING: Jackie Prince, *Launching a New Business Ethic: The Environment as a Standard Operating Procedure at McDonald's and at Other Companies* (Washington, D.C.: Environmental Defense Fund, 1991); Eric Schlosser, *Fast Food Nation: The Dark Side of the All-American Meal* (New York: Houghton Mifflin Company, 2001).

Escherichia coli *Escherichia coli* is a strain of bacteria present in the intestinal tracts of humans and some animals. When ingested, it can be pathogenic and, hence, is a threat to food safety. In 1982, *E. coli* 0157:H7 was first isolated in cattle. It is a virulent and potentially lethal foodborne pathogen that may have been in the food system for decades before it was discovered. In an estimated 4 percent of cases, *E. coli* 0157:H7 produces shiga toxin that attacks the lining of the intestine and enters the bloodstream, causing hemolytic uremic syndrome (HUS), which can lead to kidney failure, anemia, internal bleeding, and other complications, including death. To be infected, one only need ingest as few as five organisms, which could be in a microscopically small piece of uncooked hamburger. People remain contagious for about two weeks. From infected persons, *E. coli* is shed in stool; it can be spread from person to person through poor hygiene.

Cattle infected with *E. coli* 0157:H7 can appear healthy for years and show few signs of illness. Foods tainted by this pathogen have most likely come in contact with an infected animal's stomach contents or its manure. Huge feedlots, slaughterhouses, and **hamburger** grinders have dispersed this pathogen into the nation's food supply.

In 1993, **Jack in the Box** suffered an outbreak of *E. coli* 0157:H7. About 10 percent of those afflicted did not eat a contaminated hamburger but were infected by someone who did. Since then, it is estimated that approximately 500,000 Americans have been made ill by *E. coli* 0157:H7. Of these, thousands have been hospitalized and hundreds have died.

To date, antibiotics have proven ineffective in treating *E. coli*-related illnesses. It is resistant to salt, acid, and chlorine; it can live in fresh or seawater; it can withstand freezing and high temperatures (up to 160 degrees F). The only known methods to prevent it from entering into the food supply chain are improved testing and cooking beef (hamburger) and **chicken** to temperatures higher than 160 degrees F.

SUGGESTED READING: Eric Schlosser, *Fast Food Nation: The Dark Side of the All-American Meal* (New York: Houghton Mifflin Company, 2001).

Eskimo Pie In 1919, Christian Kent Nelson, an immigrant from Denmark, taught at a high school in Onawa, Iowa. With a partner, he opened the Nelson-Mustard Cream Company, a confectionary store that also sold **ice cream**. He experimented with various confections and in 1920 came up with a **chocolate**-covered ice cream bar. Nelson patented his invention, which he named the I-Scream Bar. He also created a jingle: "I scream, you scream, we all scream for ice cream." His ice cream bar sold well at his store but he had no distribution beyond Onawa.

In 1921, Nelson met Russell Stover, who managed an ice cream plant in Omaha, Nebraska and the two signed a partnership agreement to license other companies to manufacture Nelson's ice cream bar for a fee plus a royalty on each bar sold. The name of the product was changed to Eskimo Pie. It was an immediate success. By the spring of 1922, one million Eskimo Pies were sold daily. Despite the sales, licensees failed to pay their fees and clones popped up around the country. The company became mired in litigation, some of which related to Nelson's original invention of the chocolate-covered ice cream bar. Stover became discouraged and moved to Denver, Colorado, where he opened the Russell Stover Candy Store.

By the end of 1923, the Eskimo Pie Corporation was near bankruptcy and the following year, it was sold to the United States Foil Company (later renamed Reynolds Aluminum), which had supplied the foil for the Eskimo Pie wrapper. By the late 1920s, Eskimo Pies were sold by street vendors. In 1927, it was the first ice cream to be sold in a **vending machine**.

The courts eventually held that Nelson's initial patent was invalid because ice cream had long been dipped in chocolate. By the time the ruling was made, Eskimo Pie was already a household word and sales of the Eskimo Pie increased throughout the 1920s. The ruling did permit the manufacturing of clones, albeit with different names. One such clone was developed by the Isaly family of Youngstown and Pittsburgh, Pennsylvania, who introduced the **Klondike Bar** in 1922.

In 1930, the Eskimo Pie Corporation was one of the first ice cream companies to begin selling its ice cream to grocery stores. Because grocery stores did not have freezers at the time, the company manufactured round vacuum jars refrigerated with frozen carbon dioxide. They then made containers for their ice cream to fit into the jars. Likewise, they made small vacuum jars for shoppers, most of whom also did not have freezers. Shoppers paid a deposit on the jars to make sure they were returned.

Sales of the Eskimo Pie declined during the Depression but increased during World War II, when they were distributed under government contract to the U.S. armed forces. In 1992, the Eskimo Pie Corporation became independent of Reynolds Aluminum but was later acquired by **Blue Bell** Creamery.

SUGGESTED READING: Anne Cooper Funderburg, *Chocolate, Strawberry, and Vanilla: A History of American Ice Cream* (Bowling Green, OH: Bowling Green State University Popular Press, 1995); John A. Jakle and Keith A. Sculle, *Fast Food: Roadside Restaurants in the Automobile Age* (Baltimore: Johns Hopkins University Press, 1999); National Museum of American History's Web site for Eskimo Pie: americanhistory.si.edu/archives/d8553.htm

Exploitation **Fast food chains** have been financially successful in part due to the low wages paid to their workers. Critics have attacked fast food chains for exploitation of their workers, many of whom are young teenagers and minorities. Workers at most fast food restaurants receive extremely low wages—often just minimum wage. Fast food companies have regularly lobbied Congress to exempt youth from minimum wages. Workers have little chance for advancement, no health insurance, and no paid vacation or other benefits. Workers are scheduled as needed and they can easily be fired. In addition, some managers of fast food chains are financially rewarded for keeping wages low. To keep wages low, managers prevent employees from working overtime. This has occasionally led to abuses, such as workers being required to work off the clock to retain their jobs.

Some restaurant leaders have begun to challenge these employment practices. James C. Doherty, the publisher of *Nation's Restaurant News,* has encouraged fast food chains to increase employee wages to attract better and more loyal workers, mainly because of the tremendous turnover of employees.

Exploitation also occurs with fast food suppliers, who are pressured into lowering the costs of their products. This has meant that meatpackers have begun hiring immigrant laborers who work long hours for low pay. An even more serious charge of exploitation related to suppliers has been made against **chocolate** companies. Major cocoa growing areas in Africa, such as the Ivory Coast, have been reportedly using kidnapped children as slaves to work their plantations. This issue has been raised for almost a century, and studies and reports have confirmed the existence of slavery on cocoa plantations in Africa.

SUGGESTED READING: Tim Richardson, *Sweets: A History of Candy* (New York: Bloomsbury, 2002). Eric Schlosser, *Fast Food Nation: The Dark Side of the All-American Meal* (New York: Houghton Mifflin Company, 2001); Stuart Tannock, *Youth at Work: The Unionized Fast-food and Grocery Workplace* (Philadelphia: Temple University Press, 2001).

Exposés Prior to the passage of the Pure Food and Drug Act in 1906, there were no national pure food laws. Many food manufacturers adulterated their goods with unsafe contents. This led to the a group of reformers, called muckrakers, who exposed the conditions in food processing plants and the horrors of adulteration. The most famous muckraker was Upton Sinclair, whose novel, *The Jungle,* exposed the appalling conditions in the meatpacking industry in Chicago. The publication of this book contributed to the passage of the Pure Food and Drug Act.

Despite laws against adulteration and contamination, problems continued and several exposés of the food industry were published during the 1930s. Frederick Schlink and

Arthur Kallet, for instance, published *100,000,000 Guinea Pigs: Dangers in Everyday Foods, Drugs, and Cosmetics* in 1932, exposing practices of the nation's food manufacturers.

Exposés have continued to be published, the most recent of which are Eric Schlosser's ***Fast Food Nation****: The Dark Side of the All-American Meal* (2001) and Danielle Nierenberg's *Happier Meals: Rethinking the Global Meat Industry* (2005). In a well-researched and thoughtful ways, both books condemn many of the practices currently followed in the fast food industry. *Fast Food Nation* has been on the *New York Times* best-seller list for years, an unusual success for any nonfiction book; the book was converted into a movie. What influence these books and movies will have on the fast food industry remains unclear.

SUGGESTED READING: Frederick Schlink and Arthur Kallet, *100,000,000 Guinea Pigs: Dangers in Everyday Foods, Drugs, and* Cosmetics (New York, The Vanguard Press, 1932); Danielle Nierenberg, *Happier Meals: Rethinking the Global Meat Industry* (Washington, D.C.: Worldwatch Institute, 2005); Eric Schlosser, *Fast Food Nation: The Dark Side of the All-American Meal* (New York: Houghton Mifflin Company, 2001); Upton Sinclair, *The Jungle* (Belmont, CA: Wadsworth, 2004).

Extruded Snacks The process of extruding was invented accidentally during the 1930s by Edward Wilson, a machine operator at the Flakall Company, which made corn-based feed for livestock. While experimenting with animal feed, he noticed that when moistened corn kernels are heated and forced through an extruder, they puffed up when they hit cool air. Wilson deep-fried the extruded products, added salt, and ate them. He offered them to other people, who also liked them. The result was a commercial product called Korn Kurls. Their manufacture was discontinued during World War II due to restrictions on nonessential foods, but after the war Korn Kurls were reintroduced by the Adams Corporation. They became popular during the 1950s. Since then, numerous extruded snack foods have become very popular, such as Cheese Puffs and **Cheetos**.

SUGGESTED READING: Samuel A. Matz, *Snack Food Technology* 3rd ed. (New York: AVI Van Nostrand Reinhold, 1993).

F

Factory Farming In 1920, 6.45 million farms operated in the United States. By 2004, the number of American farms had declined to 2.1 million. The main reason for the decline in family farms has been the rise of the factory farm (also called concentrated animal feeding operations), which dominate American agriculture today.

Factory farms are usually owned by large corporations. They are designed to bring food to the market as quickly and cheaply as possible. Factory farms that concentrate on meat production are intensive operations with thousands (in some cases, millions) of **chickens**, cows, pigs, or turkeys, which are usually confined in cages or buildings. These farms tend to make extensive use of antibiotics to prevent disease and use chemicals and hormones to promote faster growth. Many factory farms use lagoons to store massive amounts of raw manure and waste.

Factory farms have been criticized for a variety of reasons. It is claimed that large, centralized factory farms cause damage to the **environment** and destroy local communities throughout the world. As factory farms have spread around the world, this system has proven to be particularly harmful to communities in the developing world. In addition, the high concentration of animals, and the conditions in which they live on some factory farms, weaken their immune systems and create unsanitary conditions. This encourages the spread of diseases, such as avian flu and **mad cow disease**. The overuse of antibiotics has undermined the use of these medicines on humans. Critics believe that factory farms are contributing to the loss of diversity in gene pools because they focus on higher-producing industrial breeds. This has led to the loss of many indigenous breeds.

Critics have called for the passage of legislation to protect independent farmers and control the growth of factory farms. Advocates have argued that factory farms produce more food for less money.

SUGGESTED READING: Jim Hightower, *Eat Your Heart Out: Food Profiteering in America* (New York: Crown Publishers, [1975]); Danielle Nierenberg, *Happier Meals: Rethinking the Global Meat Industry* (Washington, D.C.: WorldWatch Institute, 2005).

Fair Food Commercial **snack foods** and some **fast foods** were popularized at fairs, circuses, and amusement parks. The first successful world exposition held in the United States was the Philadelphia's Centennial Exposition held in 1876. James W. Tufts and Charles Lippincott constructed a building there with a 30-foot **soda fountain** and dozens of soda dispensers ready to refresh thirsty fairgoers. They paid $20,000 for the soda concession, plus $2 per day royalty for each soda dispenser. This totaled an estimated $52,000—an astronomical sum in 1876. But it was a worthy investment: Temperance supporters had banned the sale of hard liquor at the Centennial Exposition and the summer of 1876 was an extremely hot one. The counters were crowded throughout the Exposition. After it closed, Tufts and Lippincott made a fortune selling soda fountains to drugstores around the nation. Along with the soda fountains came serving counters, which soon became social gathering places in towns throughout America.

The Centennial Exposition also popularized **popcorn** and peanuts. Both had been sold on the streets of American cities and in trains since early in the nineteenth century, and both were sold by vendors at the Exposition. Red-and-white popcorn balls were offered at a booth in Machinery Hall, and it was crowded all day. I. L. Baker, who sponsored the exhibit, had paid the steep price of $8,000 for the exclusive popcorn concession throughout the grounds. Baker set up several of his "curious and attractive furnaces and selling-booths" and sold popcorn for five cents a bag.

The 1893, the Columbian Exposition in Chicago dramatically influenced the **junk food** world. First, the Exposition opened, F. W. Rueckheim & Brother offered an unnamed confection consisting of popcorn, peanuts, and molasses to the crowds flocking to the exhibits. Frederick Rueckheim later commented that no matter how carefully they tried to plan, orders always exceeded production. After the Exposition, they solve production and packaging problems and named their new confection **Cracker Jack**. Beginning in 1896, they advertised and promoted it nationally; it was America's most popular confection by the early twentieth century. It was served at baseball games and thus wound up in the 1908 song by lyricist Jack Norworth and composer Albert von Tilzer, "Take Me Out to the Ball Game."

Yet another significant connection made at the Columbian Exposition has influenced American snack food ever since. **Milton S. Hershey**, then a caramel maker from Lancaster, Pennsylvania, visited the fair. He was intrigued with Johann Martin Lehmann's display of **chocolate**-making equipment from Dresden, Germany, and he bought the machinery and had it shipped to Lancaster when the Exposition closed. In 1894, he launched the **Hershey Chocolate Company** and by 1900 he was manufacturing **Hershey chocolate bars**, the first chocolate candy manufactured in America.

The 1904, St. Louis Louisiana Purchase Exposition is credited with popularizing cotton candy or candy floss. It was initially made from caramelized sugar twisted with a fork. In 1896, Thomas Patton invented a machine that liquefied **sugar** and forced it through small holes in a spinning machine. It was then collected on a stick or paper cone. Vendors at the St. Louis Exposition also popularized **hot dogs** and **ice cream** cones.

More recently, state fairs have continued to play an important role in promoting new junk foods. **Nachos**, for instance, were popularized at the 1964 Texas State Fair and were disseminated throughout the United States during the late 1960s and 1970s. During the past 20 years, stick food—hot dogs on a stick, Frito pies, frozen Mars bars, and dozens of other snack foods—have made their appearance in state fairs.

SUGGESTED READING: Tim Richardson, *Sweets: A History of Candy* (New York: Bloomsbury, 2002); Andrew F. Smith, *Peanuts: The Illustrious History of the Goober Pea* (Urbana, IL: University of Illinois Press, 2002).

Famous Amos In 1975, Wally Amos, a talent agent with the William Morris Agency, opened the Amos Chocolate Cookie Company on Hollywood's Sunset Boulevard, Los Angeles. He called his brand Famous Amos and his store was the nation's first gourmet **chocolate chip cookie** store. The recipe for his chocolate chip cookie was a variation of **Nestlé**'s toll house cookie, but Amos had plenty of big-name contacts from his talent agency days who helped him promote his store and his products. Bloomingdale's, the department store, began selling his **cookies** and the *New York Times* published an article about them in 1975.

Wally Amos, of Famous Amos Cookies. Courtesy of Photofest

Famous Amos was famous enough that Wally Amos could publish his memoirs, *Famous Amos Story: The Face That Launched a Thousand Chips* (1983), that described his great success. However, despite his fame, the company floundered and in 1984 controlling interest in it was acquired by Bass Brothers Enterprises. Wally Amos gave up the right to his name and became an employee of the company. Bass Brothers sold it to Baer Group and in it was sold to a venture capital firm, the Shansby Group in San Francisco. These changes left Amos without any equity in the firm. In 1992, he then began making baked goods, including muffins, under the brand name Uncle Noname. In 1994, Wally Amos complained of his problems in yet another book, *The Man with No Name*. In 1999, the name of the company was changed to Uncle Wally's, Inc.

The President Baking Company acquired Famous Amos in 1992 and six years later the company was sold to the Keebler Company, which in turn was acquired by Kellogg's in 2001. Despite the corporate changes, Famous Amos cookies are selling well; its revenues are reported at about $100 million per year.

SUGGESTED READING: Wally Amos with Leroy Robinson, *The Famous Amos Story: The Face That Launched a Thousand Chips* (Garden City, NY: Doubleday, 1983); Wally Amos with Camilla Denton, *The Man with No Name: Turn Lemons into Lemonade* (Lower Lake, CA: Aslan Pub., 1994); the Famous Amos Web site: www.famous-amos.com

Fast Food **White Castle** is considered to be the first **fast food** operation. Its major product was **hamburgers**, which had been sold as a **sandwich** by **street vendors** since the 1890s, but hamburgers were not a particularly popular food when White Castle opened in the 1920s. In fact, many Americans were leery of them. Because hamburgers consisted of ground beef, it was easy to adulterate them and many Americans were concerned with the sanitary conditions at hamburger stands. White Castle convinced Americans that its products were pure and thus tapped into the American concern with hygiene. White Castle also proved that hamburgers could be inexpensive, good-tasting, and quickly prepared. This success plowed the ground for other hamburger **chains**, such as **White Tower**, White Huts, Little Kastle, Royal Castle, and many others.

Other chains emerged during the 1920s, such as **A&W Root Beer** and **Nathan's Famous**; the latter was launched as a **hot dog** stand on Coney Island, New York, in 1915. Many small, regional chains developed during the 1920s. When the Depression hit in the 1930s, fast food not only survived but thrived. Thousands of fast food outlets dotted the urban landscape and the nation's highways, selling hundreds of thousands of low-cost hamburgers annually. Most were based on **franchising**, wherein local entrepreneurs usually paid a fee to and bought goods or equipment from franchisor. In turn, franchisees gained visibility though the promotional activities carried out by the franchisor, and they benefited from the consistency of the products and the methods of preparing them.

The early success of fast food can be directly linked to **automobiles**, which became common during the 1920s. Travelers needed places to eat, and fast food was offered through chains. Travelers were familiar with chains: they offered low-cost food, quick service, and chain outlets were easily and conveniently accessible on highways. The years during World War II were difficult for fast food operators because meat was rationed and many employees went into the military. Fast food chains barely survived by developing new products, such as **French fries** and egg sandwiches.

A robust self-confidence emerged in America after World War II that encouraged entrepreneurs to try new ideas. The construction of the new interstate highway system created a need to satisfy popular expectations for reliable roadside food. The highway system encouraged the growth of suburban communities, which had no established culinary infrastructure. Fast food restaurants jumped in to meet this need. Fast food chains initially catered to automobile owners in suburbia. The baby boom after World War II encouraged middle class families to purchase homes, and families meant young children and parents who preferred low-cost food. Also, the notion of fast food reflected American culture in which speed and **efficiency** were highly prized. As a result, many fast food operations emerged during the 1940s and 1950s. **Ice cream** chains were the first to develop. **Dairy Queen** (1940) and **Baskin-Robbins** (1948) expanded rapidly during their early years. The nation's first **doughnut** chains emerged at about the same time. **Dunkin' Donuts** in Quincy, Massachusetts, and **Winchell's Donut House** in Los Angeles both started in 1948. **Chicken**-based fast food chains began during the early 1950s. **Kentucky Fried Chicken**'s first franchise was established in Utah in 1952, the same year that **Church's Chicken** was launched in San Antonio, Texas. But it was the hamburger chains that dominated the fast food industry in America. **Jack in the Box** (1950) was launched in San Diego, **Burger King** (1954) was launched in Miami, and **Wendy's** (1969) started in Columbus, Ohio.

The most important fast food chain was **McDonald's**, which was launched in San Bernardino, California, in the 1940s, but it did not take shape until 1954. Founded by Richard and Maurice McDonald, it was greeted with wonder by the public. Its golden arches were modern; its facilities were bright and clean; its service was fast; and its food was inexpensive. Like White Castles, McDonald's were lined with white tiles to emphasize cleanliness and, like drive-ins, McDonald's architecture outlandish (but eye-catching) golden arches. The front of each store was glassed-in, putting food preparation into a fishbowl so the customers could see food the sanitary conditions of food preparation.

Ethnic fast food (specifically **pizza**) also matured during this time. **Shakey's** (1954) was started in Sacramento, California, **Pizza Hut** (1958) was launched in Wichita,

Kansas, and three years later **Domino's** was created in Ypsilanti, Michigan. Mexican-like fast food emerged later, with **Taco Bell** (1962).

As competition grew, so did the need for **advertising** and promotion. Fast food chains spent millions on **television** advertising, much of it targeted to youth. As competition grew, so did the need for innovation. Fast food chains adapted to the changing needs of the buying public. While a limited menu, low-cost food, and eating in the car were important components of the early chains, each of these elements changed during this period. The appeal of eating in the car declined, especially in cold winters or hot summers, And fast food operations opened indoor dining facilities. Menus became more complex as new items were tested and incorporated if successful. Many new items, such as Burger King's Whopper, were more expensive but they attracted a wide following, and other chains began to develop more costly items. McDonald's began serving chicken; Burger King offered croissants; and the pizza chains began serving hot and cold sandwiches and pasta dishes.

Globalization

Fast food establishments in the United States were built on the notion of standardization—every restaurant was the same, as were menus and procedures. Fast food customers behaved in certain ways: they stood in line, paid in advance, picked up their own utensils and napkins, ate quickly, cleaned up after themselves, and left promptly, thereby making room for others. While these assumptions are understood in the United States, they are not necessarily understood in other countries. Russian and Chinese customers, for example, needed guidance when McDonald's opened in Moscow and Beijing, respectively. They were unprepared to be smiled at by employees and they had no idea what was inside a hamburger or how it should be eaten. The vast majority of McDonald's customers accepted the queue, which was not a common practice in many other countries. The physical setting of fast food restaurants encourages discipline, and customers and employees are standing, which establishes an egalitarian relationship.

Problems

Fast food operations were started by individual entrepreneurs who had ideas and were willing to experiment. Once good ideas were launched, entrepreneurs sold out to organizers and managers who took fast food operations into larger arenas. During the 1960s and 1970, large corporations began to purchase chains. The Pillsbury Company bought Burger King, the Heublein Company bought Kentucky Fried Chicken, **PepsiCo** bought Taco Bell and Pizza Hut, and **Royal Crown** bought **Arby's**. Many fast food chains subsequently were sold to investor groups or have been spun off into large restaurant conglomerates, such as **Yum! Brands**.

Franchisers initially managed a single outlet. Today, most franchisees are large groups which manage numerous outlets. It is very difficult for an individual to acquire a franchise from many large fast food chains.

There have been many criticisms of the fast food industry, including health-related concerns about consumption of so much **fat**, calories, and **salt**. As a result, many chains developed lighter entrees such as fish, salads, and salad bars. Other critics have been concerned with the **exploitation** of workers, who are paid minimum wages without benefits. Still others proclaim that the fast food industry culture is creating a homogeneous diet among Americans. Soft drinks, hamburgers, fries, iceberg lettuce, fried chicken, and ketchup have become mainstays of America's diet as traditional foods or foods not easily converted into fast foods have faded.

The fast food industry has also been criticized for targeting children. Since the 1950s, fast food chains have targeted a large proportion of their advertising dollars on children. Fast food chains hand out coloring books or pages, entice children with brightly colored Happy Meals and **mascots**, give or sell inexpensive toys and other merchandise, offer playgrounds, and have **tie-ins** with children's movies. In addition, fast food and junk food companies now advertise and promote their foods in schools. The American **School** Food Service Association estimates that 30 percent of public high schools offer branded fast food for sale in their cafeterias or vending machines.

As fast food chains have moved abroad, a number of additional criticisms have been raised, such as the homogenization or Americanization of the culinary world, the loss of food-supply genetic diversity, the vast waste generated by fast food establishments, and the destruction of the rainforests.

Despite these concerns, fast food operations have continued to expand in the United States and worldwide. According to the National Restaurant Association, fast food restaurants generated an estimated $134 billion in sales during 2005 in America. The largest growth, however, has been abroad. McDonald's, for instance, now has more operations in other countries than it does in the United States.

SUGGESTED READING: Myrna Chandler Goldstein and Mark A Goldstein, *Controversies in Food and Nutrition* (Westport, CT: Greenwood Press, 2002); Robert L. Emerson, *The New Economics of Fast Food* (New York: Van Nostrand Reinhold, 1990); Robert L. Emerson, *Fast Food: The Endless Shakeout* (New York: Lebhar-Friedman Books, 1979); Michael F. Jacobson and Sarah Fritschner. *Fast-Food Guide*, 2nd ed. (New York: Workman Publishing, 1991); Harvey Levenstein, *Paradox of Plenty: A Social History of Eating in Modern America* (New York: Oxford University Press, 1993); Stan Luxenberg, *Roadside Empires: How the Chains Franchised America* (New York: Viking, 1985); Sidney Mintz, "Afterward," in James L. Watson, ed., *Golden Arches East: McDonald's in East Asia* (Stanford, CA: Stanford University Press, 1997); Lila Perl, *Junk Food, Fast Food, Health Food What America Eats and Why* (New York: Houghton Mifflin/Clarion Books, 1980); Eric Schlosser, *Fast Food Nation: The Dark Side of the All-American Meal* (New York: Houghton Mifflin Company, 2001); Eric Schlosser and Charles Wilson, *Chew On This: Everything You Don't Want to Know about Fast Food* (Boston: Houghton Mifflin, 2006); Tina Volpe, *The Fast Food Craze: Wreaking Havoc on Our Bodies and Our Animals* (Kagel Canyon, CA: Canyon Publishing, 2005).

Fast Food and Snack Food Associations Since the late nineteenth century, American businesses have joined together to form associations to lobby governmental bodies, to identify, research and, where appropriate, resolve industry-wide issues, and to promote their industries to the American public. Within the snack food and fast food worlds, there are dozens of such organizations. The most prominent are the National Confectioners Association (founded in 1884), the Snack Food Association (1937), the American Beverage Association (1919), the **Sugar** Association (1943), and the National Restaurant Association (1919), which represents 900,000 restaurants. In addition, these businesses have joined together to form associations, such as the American Council for Fitness and Nutrition (ACFN), which promotes physical fitness and opposes creating national standards for **school** food.

SUGGESTED READING: American Beverage Association Web site: www.ameribev.org; American Council for Fitness and Nutrition Web site: www.acfn.org; National Confectioners Association Web site: www.ecandy.com; National Restaurant Association Web site: www.restaurant.org; Snack Food Association Web site: www.sfa.org; Sugar Association Web site: www.sugar.org

Fast Food Nation In 2001, the journalist Eric Schlosser released his exposé *Fast Food Nation: The Dark Side of the All-American Meal,* and it remained a best-seller for years afterward. It told the story of the **fast food** industry, from its meager beginnings in post-World War II suburban southern California to its rise to global prominence. He exposed the problems the industry has caused, such as those connected with potato growing, to French fries, union-busting and unsanitary practices in the **meatpacking industry** that supplies fast food operations. Schlosser chronicled how the fast food industry has shaped the American diet and economy. He reported that fast food companies have targeted youth: fast food corporations run advertisements in **school** on Channel One, the commercial television network viewed by an estimated 8 million students daily. He reported that a school district in Colorado Springs, Colorado, placed advertisements for **Burger King** in its hallways and on the sides of its school buses.

A film based on *Fast Food Nation* was under development in 2006.

SUGGESTED READING: Eric Schlosser, *Fast Food Nation: The Dark Side of the All-American Meal* (New York: Houghton Mifflin Company, 2001); Eric Schlosser and Charles Wilson, *Chew On This: Everything You Don't Want to Know about Fast Food* (Boston: Houghton Mifflin, 2006).

Fats Dietary fats can be saturated, unsaturated, polyunsaturated, monounsaturated, and partially hydrogenated. In the United States, saturated fat is mainly found in dairy products, meat, poultry, and vegetable shortenings such as coconut oil, palm oil, and palm kernel oil. Saturated fat can raise blood **cholesterol** levels, while unsaturated fat does not. Polyunsaturated fats are contained in corn oil, cottonseed oil, safflower oil, soybean oil, and sunflower oil as well as certain fish oils, margarines, mayonnaise, almonds, and pecans. Monounsaturated fat is found in poultry, shortening, meat, dairy products, and olive and canola oils. Partially hydrogenated vegetable oils are harder and more stable; manufacturers mix them with hydrogen, which increases amount of saturated fat and creates trans fat, which raises blood cholesterol.

Fats are important components of most **fast food** and of many **junk foods**. **Burger King**'s Double Whopper with cheese, for instance, contains 780 calories, of which 420 come from fat, and 47 of these are saturated. **Kentucky Fried Chicken**'s Chunky Chicken Pot Pie contains 770 calories, of which 378 come from fat, and 42 of these are saturated. **McDonald's** Big Mac contains 560 calories, 130 of which come from fat, and 34 of these are saturated.

SUGGESTED READING: Susan Allport, *The Queen of Fats: Why Omega-3s Were Removed from the Western Diet and What We Can Do to Replace Them* (Berkeley, CA: University of California Press, 2006); Walter Gratzer, *Terrors of the Table: The Curious History of Nutrition* (New York: Oxford University Press, 2005); Michael F. Jacobson and Bruce Maxwell, *What Are We Feeding Our Kids?* (New York: Workman Publishing, 1994).

Film Films have greatly influenced **snack food** and **fast food** in America. Because food is an important part of life, it is often a central theme in films. In addition, the movie industry has had a lengthy and financially lucrative relationship with **junk food** and fast food chains. The earliest relationship was the selling of junk food in **theaters**. Early movie theaters did not sell food of any kind because they had expensive carpets in their lobbies

Mels drive-in from *American Grafitti* (1973), directed by George Lucas. MCA/Universal Pictures/Photofest

and walkways. Theater operators were not interested in having their expensive carpets soiled by spilled popped kernels, soda pop, and other confections. The cost of cleaning up **popcorn**, **gum**, **candy** wrappers, and **soda** containers was not worth the income generated by the sale of junk food.

Theater owners shifted their perspectives dramatically during the Depression, however, when they were required to lower their ticket prices to attract customers. Once theater owners discovered that they could make a substantial profit on selling junk foods and beverages, they began promoting and advertising their concession stands and the foods they sold. Today, many theaters make more profit from their concession stand sales than they do from their ticket fees.

Beginning in 1949, snack foods began appearing on-screen in films. For example, in *White Heat,* a 1949 thriller, Buddy Gorman plays a popcorn vendor. *Good Humor Man,* starring Jack Carson, featured a man selling **Good Humor** ice cream. A **McDonald's** restaurant appeared in Woody Allen's 1973 movie, *Sleeper.* When these movies were released, Good Humor **ice cream**, McDonald's **hamburgers**, and **popcorn** received extensive visibility. This led to a different arrangement between movies and junk food and fast food companies.

The George Lucas film, *American Graffiti,* centered around Mels **drive-in**, which was a restaurant chain founded in 1947 by Mel Weiss and Harold Dobbs in San Francisco. When Lucas was looking for a location to shoot part of the film, they used an old Mel's Drive-In that was scheduled for destruction. The movie portrayed America in the early 1960s, and the drive-in was complete with **carhops** on roller skates.

In addition to reflecting American life, films have been used to sell junk and fast food as well as soft drinks through placements of products in the film, such as for Reese's Pieces and **PEZ** in *ET, The Extra-Terrestrial.* In 1990, **Domino's** pizza appeared as a product placement in the blockbuster movie *Teenage Mutant Ninja Turtles.*

In addition, movie producers have developed tie-ins with fast food, soft drink, and junk food companies, including **McDonald's**, **Burger King**, **Coca-Cola**, and the **Hershey Company**. Until recently, for instance, Disney had a close connections with McDonald's. Figures related to Disney films were sold at McDonald's or included as promotional items in Happy Meals.

In 2004, yet another relationship between film and fast food came to fore: the use of a documentary film to attack the fast food industry. Morgan Spurlock's film *Super Size Me* generated bad publicity for McDonald's throughout the world. Spurlock converted the movie into a book in 2005. The reverse is underway with Eric Schlosser's book, *Fast Food Nation* (2001), which is now being made into a movie. In 2005, *The Future of Food,* a polemic against genetically modified foods, demonstrated yet another dimension of film's relationship with food.

SUGGESTED READING: Eric Schlosser, *Fast Food Nation: The Dark Side of the All-American Meal* (New York: Houghton Mifflin Company, 2001); Morgan Spurlock, *Don't Eat this Book: Fast Food and the Supersizing of America* (New York: G. P. Putnam's Sons, 2005).

Fish and Chips The combination of battered and fried fish with chips (the latter also known as French fries) originated in the United Kingdom in the mid-nineteenth century. Charles Dickens mentioned a "fried fish warehouse" in his novel *Oliver Twist* (1829). Joseph Malin is credited with opening the first combined fish and chip shop in London in the 1860s. Malin's has survived and its recipe for fish and chips is reportedly used by **Arthur Treacher's** fish and chip chain in the United States.

Cod is the most common fish used in this dish but pollock, haddock plaice, skate, and rock salmon are also used. Historically, fish and chips were wrapped in white paper and an outer layer of newspapers. Newspapers are no longer used due to health concerns of the ink rubbing off on to hands and food. Fish and chips are commonly served with vinegar Fish and potatoes were two of the few foods not rationed during World War II. In the United Kingdom, there are an estimated 8,000 fish and chip shops and the combination is considered the United Kingdom's national dish.

Fish and chips are also popular in Australia, Canada, Ireland, New Zealand, and South Africa, and are also becoming increasingly popular in the United States. Arthur Treacher's Fish & Chips **fast food chain** was incorporated in 1969. Other American fast food chains that sell fish and chips include Cerdic's Fish and Chips, **Long John Silver's**, H. Salt Fish and Chips, and Ivar's in the Pacific Northwest. In addition, independent fish and chip shops have opened up in the United States, such as the Chip Shop in Brooklyn, New York.

SUGGESTED READING: John K. Walton, *Fish & Chips and the British Working Class 1870–1940* (London: Leicester University Press, 1992).

Fish as Fast Food Although fish has been consumed as a **fast food** in the United Kingdom since the mid-nineteenth century, it came late to America's fast food world. During World War II, meat was rationed in the United States and fast food **chains** scrambled for a substitute. **White Castle** produced a fish **sandwich** but it was not successful. After the war, fast food fish was introduced into Catholic areas of Chicago, New York, St. Louis, and other cities, where it was expected to bolster sales on Friday and during Lent, when Catholics could not eat meat. It had moderate sales.

McDonald's introduced Fillet-O-Fish in 1962 and other fast food chains developed similar dishes. McDonald's in other countries have had more success with fast food fish. For instance, McDonald's in Norway offer a salmon fillet sandwich called the McLak. In addition, several fast food chains sell **fish and chips** as part of their core menu, such as **Arthur Treacher's** and **Long John Silver's**.

SUGGESTED READING: David Gerard Hogan, *Selling 'em by the Sack: White Castle and the Creation of American Food* (New York: New York University Press, 1997); John K. Walton, *Fish & Chips and the British Working Class 1870–1940* (London: Leicester University Press, 1992).

Food Pyramid In 1992, the **U.S. Department of Agriculture** (USDA) developed a Food Guide Pyramid which recommended a hierarchal—and therefore controversial—dietary pattern based on breads, cereals, rice, pasta, dairy products, and fruits and vegetables. It also recommended that high-fat processed meats be limited and that only two to three servings of meat, poultry, fish, beans, eggs, and nuts be consumed daily. These recommendations were based on four major studies conducted during the 1980s that identified the need to restrict **fat**, particularly saturated fat. Because the Pyramid was hierarchal, many food companies felt threatened and applied pressure to change the recommendation. A revised food pyramid was eventually released.

In 1994, the Center for Nutrition Policy and Promotion, a part of the USDA, was established to improve American nutrition. It began working on a replacement for the controversial Food Pyramid. In 2005, the center unveiled its new food pyramid, now called MyPyramid, which was based on the Dietary Guidelines for Americans 2005. The new pyramid was, in fact, 12 individualized pyramids based upon age, sex, and physical activity. Critics have considered MyPyramid needlessly confusing and some claim that the revised 2005 Dietary Guidelines were based more on lobbying efforts of the food industry rather than upon scientific research.

SUGGESTED READING: Marion Nestle, *Food Politics: How the Food Industry Influences Nutrition and Health* (Berkeley, CA: University of California Press, 2002); Center for Nutrition Policy and Promotion Web site: www.cnpp.usda.gov; MyPyramid Web site: mypyramid.gov; Dietary Guidelines for Americans 2005 Web site: www.health.gov/dietaryguidelines

Foodborne Illnesses In 2001, the Centers for Disease Control (CDC) has estimated that food-related illnesses caused 76 million incidents annually. Of these, each year an estimated 325,000 Americans are hospitalized and 5,000 die. Those mainly at risk are children, the elderly, and people with impaired immune systems.

Many people who suffer from food poisoning are not aware of the cause. Symptoms may take a week or longer to appear, and victims frequently incorrectly attribute the distress and discomfort to the stomach flu. It is not until victims' affliction becomes acute that tests are taken to determine the real cause. For those at risk, this is frequently too late and the consequences can be deadly.

The recent increase in foodborne illnesses has many causes. Fifty years ago, a main cause was the improper handling or storage of food. This caused health problems for a limited number of people. Due to increased industrialization and centralization of America's food system, however, a problem anywhere in the system can affect large numbers of people. Eric Schlosser's ***Fast Food Nation*** (2001) has pointed to one cause for this increase in foodborne illnesses: the vast expansion of the **meatpacking industry** due to increased demand from the **fast food** industry. Schlosser estimates that there are roughly 100,000 Americans, mainly children and the elderly, who are annually sickened by ***Escherichia coli*** bacteria. Indeed, according to Schlosser, outbreaks of the potentially deadly *E. coli* 0157:H7 have occurred recently that have been traced to meat processors' operations, just as ***Salmonella*** has increasingly been traced to poultry processing plants. In one study cited by Schlosser, 7.5 percent of the samples taken at processing plants were contaminated with *Salmonella;* 11.7 percent were contaminated with *Listeria monocytogenes* (of which one in five cases proves fatal), 30 percent with *Staphylococcus aureus,* and 53 percent with *Clostridium perfringens*; 78.6 percent of ground beef contained fecal matter.

On the other hand, the Food Safety and Inspection System (FSIS), the public health agency in the USDA, has tested more than 26,000 samples of ground beef since 1996. Of these, only 25 tested positive for *E. coli* and none of these samples were associated with any outbreak of illness. Even if food safety problems in the meatpacking industry were somehow solved tomorrow, foodborne illnesses would likely still increase. The Government Accounting Office has estimated that 85 percent of foodborne illnesses comes from fruits, vegetables, seafood, and cheeses—not meat or poultry.

Schlosser also raises concerns about the **fat** and nutritional content of the food served in fast food establishments. High **cholesterol** can cause health problems, and consuming vast quantities of fast food contributes to **obesity**. However, for most Americans an occasional trip to **McDonald's** is not hazardous to health. It just depends on the rest of one's diet. Popular images to the contrary, fast food establishments have a positive record of cleanliness when compared with other restaurants, and particularly when compared with home kitchens.

In fact, food safety experts have concluded that the home is the number one place where foodborne illnesses originate. Indeed, most home kitchens would not pass food inspections that public facilities regularly pass with flying colors. Most cases of illnesses caused by *E. coli* and *Salmonella*, even those originating at meat and poultry packers, could have been averted if homemakers had followed basic health procedures—proper storage of meat and poultry, washing hands frequently, prompt disinfection of all areas touched by raw meat or poultry, and cooking long enough at a high enough temperature.

SUGGESTED READING: Danielle A. Brands, *Salmonella* (Philadelphia: Chelsea House Publishers, 2005); Eric Schlosser, *Fast Food Nation: The Dark Side of the All-American Meal* (New York: Houghton Mifflin Company, 2001); Murray Waldman and Marjorie Lamb, *Dying for a Hamburger: Modern Meat Processing and the Epidemic of Alzheimer's Disease* (New York: Thomas Dune Books/ St. Martin's Press, 2005).

Fortune Cookies Chinese restaurants have been common in California since the mid-nineteenth century, but it was not the Chinese community that created the fortune cookie. A Los Angeles preacher, Baker David Jung, is credited with doing so around 1916. His fortune cookies enclosed strips of paper bearing Biblical passages. He later launched the Hong Kong Noodle Company, which produced cookies with sayings purported to be ancient Chinese aphorisms. Fortune cookies were later adopted in Chinese restaurants all over the country.

SUGGESTED READING: Andrew F. Smith, ed., *Oxford Companion to Food and Drink in America* (New York: Oxford University Press, forthcoming).

Fosters Freeze In 1946, George Foster launched Fosters Freeze in Inglewood, California. It specialized in soft serve **ice cream**, **milk shakes**, and other desserts. The **chain** later expanded its offerings to include **hamburgers**, **chicken**, fish, and other **fast foods**. The Fosters Freeze outlet in Hawthorne, California, is reportedly the hamburger joint where Denny Wilson of the Beach Boys saw the girl in the Thunderbird in his song, "Fun, Fun, Fun." As of 2005, Fosters Old Fashion Freeze maintained about 100 outlets, all in California. In addition, Fosters co-branded with **El Pollo Loco** so that Fosters Freeze desserts are now sold in many El Pollo Loco outlets.

SUGGESTED READING: John A. Jakle and Keith A. Sculle, *Fast Food: Roadside Restaurants in the Automobile Age* (Baltimore: Johns Hopkins University Press, 1999); Fosters Freeze Web site: www.fostersfreeze.com

Franchising The system of franchising began in the United States during the mid-nineteenth century and has evolved over the following century and a half. The main reason for franchising started with manufacturers who wanted to expand retail operations without expending their own capital, and franchisees who wanted to start their own business without risking everything on a new venture. The Singer Sewing Machine Company, for instance, licensed individuals to sell its products in communities across America. General Motors (GM) followed a similar path in 1898. Lacking the money to hire salesmen in every city of the United States to sell its automobiles, GM sold franchises to potential car dealers, who then acquired the buildings and hired the salesmen who sold GM automobiles. Many manufacturers and service providers, such as hotels, soft drink companies, retail companies, and oil companies developed similar franchising systems.

The **beverage** industry began to franchise its operations during the late nineteenth century. The **Coca-Cola Company**, for instance, began franchising bottlers in 1894. By 1921, the company had more than 2,000 bottlers throughout the nation. A very different type of franchise operation was begun by **A&W Root Beer**, which franchised its first outlet in 1924. A&W sold territorial franchises in which a franchisee was given a vast territory, such as a major city, a state, or a group of states. They then could franchise others in a pyramid scheme. While A&W root beer quickly achieved national prominence, the system of territorial franchises had serious problems. For example, one A&W franchisee, J. Willard Marriott, bought the franchise for Washington, D.C. in 1927. Within a year, Marriot converted his A&W Root Beer stands to Hot Shoppes, which sold barbecue sandwiches. This was not a great success but he went on to create one of America's largest hotel **chains**, Marriott Corporation, which later created the franchise fast food chain, **Roy Rogers**.

Billy Ingram, owner of the first **hamburger fast food** chain, **White Castle**, refused to franchise his operation. Ingram built new outlets only when he had the funds to do so, refusing to borrow money or franchise his operation to others. He had good reasons for refusing to franchise. In the 1920s, many franchisers did not control their franchisees. For instance, A&W Root Beer stands were all different: there were no common architectural structures at early A&W stands, and no common menus. All that franchises had in common was A&W root beer and a logo. Ingram was also concerned with the quality of service among franchisees. His view was that it was crucial to maintain control of service and image and, hence, he opposed franchising. As a result, White Castle was slow to develop nationally. The advantage was that Ingram controlled all aspects of White Castle's operations, including its **architecture** (which was designed for instant visibility), its suppliers, its menu and the way its foods were served. On the other hand, **White Tower**, a White Castle clone, had no problem with franchising its operation and its franchisees. As a result, White Tower expanded rapidly during the late 1920s and 1930s.

Two other restaurant chains did successfully franchise their operations before World War II. The first was the Pig Stand restaurant, which was launched by J. G. Kirby, a Dallas candy and tobacco wholesaler, who built the first **drive-in** restaurant on Dallas–Ft. Worth Highway in September, 1921. The second Pig Stand drive-in that was opened in Dallas in 1924 was a franchise outlet. The Pig Stands expanded throughout the southwestern United States and achieved their most visible success in Los Angeles during the 1930s. The second restaurant franchise chain was launched by Howard Johnson, who bought a drugstore with a **soda fountain** in 1925 and invented his own 28 flavors of **ice cream**, which were extremely successful. He began setting up ice cream stands that proved very popular during the summer. In 1935, he his first roadside coffee shop opened; within six years, there were 150. Howard Johnson's coffee shops had similar orange-roofed buildings and served a common **menu**—sodas, shakes, and sundaes—and they all featured his ice cream. He later added **hot dogs**, hamburgers, **chicken**, steaks, and clams to his menu. The company retained 50 percent ownership of each new franchise and Johnson required franchisees to buy food products exclusively from him. This maintained the quality of the food, which was crucial for the success of the chain. During the 1950s, the company expanded to include hotels. The fast food industry followed the same franchising system as did Howard Johnson's. When the fast food franchises began taking business away from Howard Johnson's, the company launched Ho Jo Jr's. but its service was too slow and its menu was too large. Fast food operations did create the franchise path that other fast food operations followed.

Following World War II, fast food franchising took off. This was fueled in part by former soldiers returning from the war who were looking for investment opportunities. Franchises initially catered to the rapidly growing suburbs. They spread to every small town in America. **Dairy Queen** was one of the earliest success stories. Harry Axene had begun franchising soft-serve ice cream parlors after World War II. At that time, the complete cost of launching a Dairy Queen was $30,000, and most of these franchisees were closed during the winter. By the time Axene left the business in 1948, there were 2,500 outlets. Its success triggered a revolution in food franchising. Other franchise chains quickly followed. **Dunkin' Donuts**, **Baskin-Robbins**, **Chicken Delight**, **Burger King**, **Jack in the Box**, and **Kentucky Fried Chicken** all began franchising in the early 1950s.

Richard and Maurice McDonald began franchising **McDonald's** in 1952. They advertised in national restaurant trade magazines and quickly acquired 21 franchisees, mainly in southern California. **Ray Kroc** saw the advertisements, visited the McDonald brothers, and was impressed with what he saw. In 1954 he signed an agreement to franchise McDonald's operations nationally. In 1955, Kroc sold his first franchise to himself and opened an outlet in Des Plaines, Illinois. Kroc also began selling franchises to members of his country club, but quickly concluded that he needed a different type of franchisee. What was needed were people who wanted to operate their own restaurants. Kroc's general avoidance of territorial franchises (which relinquished control over large geographic areas) was a reason for McDonald's early success.

At the time, other chains demanded large franchise fees and sold off rights to entire territories and earned money by selling supplies directly to their franchisees. Kroc kept the initial franchise fee very low, at $950. Kroc's business partner, Harry J. Sonneborn (who had developed his franchising expertise as a **Tastee-Freez** executive), created the mechanism for financial control of franchises. McDonald's purchased or leased the property for most of its American franchises; the property was then leased to franchisees at a hefty profit. If franchisees refused to obey the franchise contract, McDonald's could evict them. This control greatly assisted the growth of McDonald's.

Franchising was also boosted when federal loans became available from the Small Business Administration (SBA). This made it possible for potential franchisees to launch their business with federal funds. Between 1967 and 1979, the SBA guaranteed 18,000 franchise loans, many of which were to fast food franchises, 10 percent of which ended in default.

The relationship between franchiser and franchisee evolved into a lengthy contractual relationship. The franchiser often developed business plans for franchisee, created specific building requirements, supplied expertise, equipment, and supplies, and engaged in **advertising** that increased sales of the product. The franchiser imposed strict policies and procedures upon franchisees. Franchisers made money on selling licenses to distributors and they also received a portion of the profits when the products or services were sold. Because franchisees were often small investors who lacked proper credentials to acquire loans from banks who were not eager to invest in new business, the franchisers often purchased or leased property to build the franchises and sometimes put up a portion of the funds necessary to launch the operation.

The legal basis for franchising remains subject to judicial reinterpretation. Decisions involving **Carvel Corporation** held that the trademark was a central element in the legal structure of a franchise agreement and therefore franchisers could require the purchase of equipment from the parent company or from suppliers it specified. Litigation involving the Chicken Delight Company, on the other hand, concluded that the trademark was separate from quality of the food and therefore was not included in franchise agreements. In 1980 court rulings recognized business-format franchising as distinct type of business arrangement, separate from product franchising.

Unscrupulous promoters have been attracted to restaurant franchising. Franchise schemes abounded during the 1960s, and many verged on fraud. One serious abuse was the pyramiding of territorial licenses, wherein a licensee holding a franchise for a broad geographical area sublicensed his or her rights to others, who in turn sold them to still others. All along, licensors had no real intention of operationally supporting franchisees; they just wanted the initial fees. Congress stepped in during the 1960s and began to pass legislation regulating franchising. The Federal Trade Commission now requires that franchisers provide lengthy **disclosure** statements for franchisees. Contracts often require franchisees to waive legal rights to file complaints. They also often require franchisees to buy only from approved suppliers, regardless of the price, and franchisees must sell the restaurant only to a buyer approved by the parent company. Franchisees must accept termination of the contract for any reason determined by the parent company. Once the contract is signed, franchisees are on their own. Franchisees must obey corporate directives, whether or not they were spelled out in the contract. Some franchisers can open a competing franchisee next door or evict a franchisee without giving cause or paying compensation.

When the Jack in the Box chain was having financial problems in the 1980s, the parent company, Ralston Purina, terminated the contracts of 642 franchisees and gave them 30 days to move out of their outlets. Chains have frequently ended up in court regarding the rights of franchisers. **Subway**, for instance, has been involved in more legal disputes than any other chain. Subway has relied on what it calls development agents to sell new franchisees. The income of the agents depends upon the number of franchises they sell; agents who fail to meet a quota are required to pay the company. A large percentage of the franchisees have therefore been immigrants, who end up working many hours just to pay their expenses.

When profits roll in, both franchisers and franchisees are happy; when things go wrong, the franchisers usually come out ahead. Fast food is now considered a mature business in the United States. For most fast food chains the American market is saturated. Franchisers sometimes place new franchisees close to existing franchises, which is called encroachment. Sales and profits decline when new franchises open near existing outlets. Another problem relates to product sourcing, where franchisers require franchisees to purchase products only from them or their designated suppliers, often at inflated prices.

Many chain franchisees have formed organizations to protect themselves. For example, A&W franchisees formed the National A&W Franchisees Association (NAWFA). This franchise association had a voice in the development of their contract with the parent company. The 1970 contract featured a revised royalty agreement and also permitted franchisees to purchase concentrates, food items, paper goods, and glass mugs from alternate sources. Groups similar to NAWFA, although generally less powerful, have been formed by franchisees with other chains. McDonald's franchisees, for instance, created Consortium Members, Inc., and the **Popeyes** Independent Franchise Association (PIFA) was formed in 1991.

Typical contracts today call for the franchiser to assist with site selection, furnishings, training, promotions, operating instructions, record keeping, and accounting systems, as well as building designs and equipment layouts. These are covered by license fees and assessments to support chain advertising.

SUGGESTED READING: Peter M. Birkeland, *Franchising Dreams: The Lure of Entrepreneurship in America* (Chicago: University of Chicago Press, 2002); Thomas S. Dicke, *Franchising in America: The Development of a Business Method, 1840–1980* (Chapel Hill, NC: University of North Carolina Press, 1992); John A. Jakle and Keith A. Sculle, *Fast Food: Roadside Restaurants in the Automobile Age* (Baltimore: Johns Hopkins University Press, 1999); Stan Luxenberg, *Roadside Empires: How the Chains Franchised America* (New York: Viking, 1985); Ronald L. McDonald, *Ronald McDonald's Franchise Buyers Guide: How to Buy a Fast Food Franchise* (Philadelphia: Xlibris, 2003); H. G. Parsa and Francis A. Kwansa, eds., *Quick Service Restaurants, Franchising, and Multi-unit Chain Management* (New York: Haworth Hospitality Press, 2002); R. David Thomas and Michael Seid, *Franchising for Dummies* (Foster City, CA: IDG Books Worldwide, 2000); A&W Web site: www.awrestaurants.com/about/service.htm; National A&W Franchise Association Web site: www.nawfa.com

French Fries Deep-frying is a cooking technique that was developed in France during the late eighteenth century. Many types of foods can be deep-fried, including potatoes. In the United States, potatoes were fried in lard during the nineteenth century. By the 1870s, fried potatoes were standardized into particular shapes and sizes—those that were round and extremely thin became **potato chips**; those that were long and rectangular became French fried potatoes, which was shortened to French fries by 1918.

McDonald's French fries. © Kelly Fitzsimmons

By the early twentieth century, French fries were occasionally served in cafés, diners, roadside eateries, and fast food outlets. Their advantage was that they could be eaten without utensils and could easily be eaten in a car. In many ways, they fit right in with fast foods but they were marginally successful at first because they required considerable effort to prepare. Potatoes had to be peeled and cut several times a day, depending upon demand. The frying substance, initially lard, had to be kept at a constant temperature between 340 and 370 degrees F. French fries could only be heated for a specific amount of time: too much time and they burned, too little time and they tasted raw. French fries had to be served when hot, or they ended up soggy and limp. To properly prepare them and maintain safety, employees needed to be properly trained. During the 1930s, accidents convinced many **fast food** operators and managers that French fries just weren't worth the trouble.

During World War II, meat was rationed and became scarce. Fast food **hamburger** stands sought alternatives, and potatoes were not rationed, were abundant, and were low-cost. During the war, French fries became a staple on the menus of many restaurants. When rationing ended after the war, the demand for French fries increased. The combination of hamburgers and French fries was a continuation of "meat and potatoes" that had been at the core of American food since the eighteenth century.

Some chains, such **White Castle**, stopped making French fries due to the danger to their workers. However, when new, safer fryers were introduced in the 1950s, French fries became a fixture in the fast food industry. By the 1970s, fryers included automatic timers and lifts that produced good French fries with much less risk for employees.

In the United States, the most common condiments consumed with French fries are **salt** and **ketchup**. Recently, Belgian fries have appeared, the idea having been purportedly imported from Belgium. They are larger than typical. French fries and are served with mayonnaise. Chips (as in fish and chips) are what French fries are called in the United Kingdom and many other English-speaking countries; they are frequently served with malt vinegar and tartar sauce. Other dips for French fries include peanut sauce, chili sauce, and gravy.

French fries have been a flagship product at the **McDonald's** restaurant **chain** because they are more profitable than hamburgers. The founders of the chain, Richard and Maurice McDonald, believed that their French fries were one of the important reasons for their success. They perfected the way fries were made and promoted the combination of hamburgers and fires. The brothers used Russet Burbank potatoes, which were peeled daily and thinly sliced. They were cooked in special fryers that produced a crispy texture that became the hallmark of McDonald's fries. As the chain began to grow in the 1960s, dozens of different suppliers were contracted, and the diversity of suppliers meant that the uniformity of McDonald's French fries declined. **Ray Kroc**, who acquired the McDonald's operation from the brothers, began looking for better ways to prepare and distribute their French fries.

French fries had been commercially frozen since 1946, but the problem was that their flavor disappeared when they were fried. Idaho potato grower J. R. Simplot started producing frozen French fries in 1953 but sales were disappointing. The fries had to be deep-fried, which was difficult to do in the home, so Simplot looked for fast food chains that might be interested in the labor-saving benefits of his frozen fries. Simplot met Kroc in 1965 and the French fry world has never been the same since. Working with the Simplot Potato Company, McDonald's researchers devised ways of freezing raw fries and retaining their good qualities. To maintain the taste, McDonald's and other fast food companies fried their fries in a mixture of 7 percent soy oil and 93 percent beef tallow. Other chains emulated this process.

In 1989, it was revealed that the company used beef tallow in making its French fries and **vegetarians** complained that the company had not informed customers that the fries were prepared using an animal product. In addition, a number of nutritionists complained about the amount of cholesterol in the fries. In 1990, with considerable fanfare, McDonald's announced that they had switched to vegetable oil with "added natural flavorings." When it was disclosed that the flavorings included small amounts of beef tallow, Hindu vegetarian customers in Bombay, India, ransacked a McDonald's restaurant and smeared cow dung on a statue of **Ronald McDonald**. The company denied that any beef product had ever been used in its restaurants in India. In the United States, 12 vegetarians sued McDonald's for falsely claiming that the fries were vegetarian, a claim that the company denied making. McDonald's eventually settled out of court, agreeing to post an apology on the company's Web site and to pay $10 million to vegetarian organizations and to the 12 individuals involved in the suit.

French fries have been criticized for their levels of **cholesterol**, trans fat, salt, and their lack of essential nutrients. This is a special problem for children and teenagers. Approximately one-quarter of the vegetable products consumed by children are in the form of potato chips and French fries. This increases to about one-third of the vegetable servings consumed by teenagers.

McDonald's continued to innovate the way its French fries are prepared. It was the first fast food company to use computers that automatically adjust cooking times and temperatures. It created a rapid frying system for frozen potatoes that pared down the delivery time by 30 to 40 seconds. While this may not seem to be a lot of time, when millions of customers order fries, the time saved easily covers the cost of the equipment. Eric Schlosser, author of ***Fast Food Nation*** (2001), has pointed out that the special taste of McDonald's French fries does not derive from the type of potatoes, the technology the processes them, or other restaurant equipment that fries them. Other chains buy from the same sources and use similar equipment. What gives McDonald's fries their unique taste today is the chemical flavorings that are added to the oil.

During the past 50 years, the size of French fry portions has steadily increased. Initially, McDonald's only offered a large, 2-ounce size. Today, the former large size of a French fry order is now the small size and the new large size weighs in at 6 ounces. At one time, McDonald's supersized its fries to 8-ounce portions but, due to pressure from the documentary film *Super Size Me*, released in 2004, McDonald's discontinued this size. Other fast food chains continue to serve 8-ounce fries.

Today, French fries are the single most popular fast food in America. As a result, annual sales of frozen French fries have grown dramatically over the past 50 years. In 1970, frozen French fries surpassed regular potato sales in the United States. Since then, the sales of frozen French fries have continued to skyrocket. By 2000, annual sales of frozen French fries worldwide grew to more than $1.9 billion. Some unusual types of French fries have recently been released by Ore-Ida, owned by the H.J. Heinz Company: Funky Fries comes in five varieties, including Cinna-Stiks (with cinnamon and sugar), Cocoa Crispers (with chocolate), and Kool Blue (with a blue color). In 2004, Americans consumed 7.5 billion pounds of frozen French fries, 90 percent of which were sold by foodservice outlets.

One exception to the trend toward frozen fries is that of **In-N-Out Burger**. Depending on the season, the company uses Kennebec or Russet potatoes. Each potato is sliced by hand shortly before it is placed in the deep fryer. The company uses cottonseed oil. Its "secret menu" offers a variety of different types of fries. Animal Fries, for instance, include cheese and grilled onions; Fries Well-Done are fried longer, making them crisper; and Cheese Fries have cheese melted on top.

As fast food chains moved abroad, so did production of frozen French fries. Russet Burbank potatoes are grown for making French fries in many countries today. As of 2004, the United States remains the world's largest producer of frozen French fries, the Netherlands now ranks second, and Canada third.

French fries have also become entangled in international politics. When France refused to join the American-led coalition against Iraq in 2003, some Congressional Republicans urged that the term French fries be changed to liberty fries, but this name change never caught on.

SUGGESTED READING: Karen Hess, "The Origin of French Fries," *Petits Propos Culinaires #68* (November 2001): 39–48; Stan Luxenberg, *Roadside Empires: How the Chains Franchised America* (New York: Viking, 1985); Elizabeth Rozin, *The Primal Cheeseburger: A Generous Helping of Food History Served Up on a Bun* (New York: Penguin Books, 1994); Eric Schlosser, *Fast Food Nation: The Dark Side of the All-American Meal* (New York: Houghton Mifflin Company, 2001); In-N-Out Burger Web site: www.in-n-out.com

Fried Chicken Fried chicken has been a Southern delicacy for decades. It takes considerable time to fry chicken, and the problem for fast food operators was that it had to be fried before customers arrived at restaurants. If too much was cooked, it would be wasted; if too little, restaurants would lose sales. **Harland Sanders** solved this problem through the use of a pressure cooker. It greatly shortened the time of preparation, making it possible to prepare smaller quantities of fried chicken ahead of time and additional orders as they came in. This method, along with his secret combination of herbs and spices, was the basis for **Kentucky Fried Chicken**. Other chains used the same equipment and slight variations on the methods he devised.

SUGGESTED READING: Harland Sanders, *Life as I Have Known It Has Been Finger Lickin' Good* (Carol Stream, IL: Creation House, 1974).

Frito Bandito The **Frito-Lay** company became very creative in its **advertising** during the 1960s. The Frito Bandito was one of its cartoon characters used to promote **Frito-Lay Corn Chips**. The Frito Bandito was a stereotypical Mexican bandit who stole Fritos from everyone. It was created by Tex Avery, who had also created the Bugs Bunny and Daffy Duck cartoon characters. The Bandito's voice was done by Mel Blanc, who was also the voice for Bugs Bunny and Daffy Duck. The Frito Bandito advertisements first appeared in 1967. Although many Mexican-Americans approved of the caricature, a vocal minority did not. A lawsuit against Frito-Lay was launched and the company eventually withdrew the Frito Bandito from its advertising.

SUGGESTED READING: Andrew F. Smith, "Tacos, Enchiladas and Refried Beans: The Invention of Mexican-American Cookery," in Mary Wallace Kelsey and ZoeAnn Holmes, eds., *Cultural and Historical Aspects of Foods* (Corvallis, OR: Oregon State University, 1999, 183–203).

Frito-Lay Herman W. Lay of Nashville, Tennessee, was a salesman for Sunshine Biscuits, which were manufactured by the Loose-Wiles Biscuit Company in Kansas City, Kansas.

During the Depression, he lost his job. In 1932, he was hired by Barrett Foods, an Atlanta snack food firm, to sell peanut butter **sandwiches** in southern Kentucky and Tennessee. He was an aggressive businessman and began acquiring distributorships. When Barrett's founder died in 1937, Lay bought the company, which included plants in Atlanta and Memphis. **Popcorn**, manufactured in Nashville, was the first product to have the Lay's brand name.

Lay's company began manufacturing **potato chips** in 1938. During World War II, the sale of potato chips increased in part because of the lack of competitive snack foods that contained **sugar** and **chocolate** due to rationing. By the end of the war, Lay's had become a major regional producer of snack foods. After the war, Lay automated his potato chip manufacturing business and diversified its products. In 1945, Lay met Elmer Doolin, who manufactured Frito **Corn Chips** in San Antonio. Doolin **franchised** Herman Lay to distribute Fritos. The two companies cooperated on other products. For instance, **Cheetos** were invented by the Frito Company and were marketed by Lay in 1948. In 1958, Lay acquired the rights to the new type of potato chip, called Ruffles, which was a thick chip with ridges made especially for dipping.

Doolin died in 1959 and two years later his company merged with Lay's, creating Frito-Lay, Inc., with headquarters in Dallas. The merged company continued to grow. Six years later, it merged with the Pepsi Cola Company, creating **PepsiCo**. By the end of the 1960s, Frito-Lay was the dominant company in the snack world.

Frito-Lay continued to innovate and develop new products. In 1966 it released **Doritos**, which became popular nationwide. Beginning in 1980, the company introduced cheese-flavored snacks, such as Puffed Balls. In 1988 Frito-Lay introduced Cheetos Cheddar Cheese Flavored Popcorn and launched a major promotion campaign starring Chester Cheetah, a cartoon character targeted at children and young adults. Rold Gold brand **pretzels** were introduced in 1989 and were subsequently promoted by *Seinfeld* **television** star Jason Alexander, who appeared as Pretzel Boy. Basketball stars Kareem Abdul-Jabbar and Larry Bird advertised a new reformulation of Lay's potato chips in 1992, and the slogan "Too Good to Eat Just One" was launched. In 1993, Doritos Thins brand tortilla chips were introduced nationally with Chevy Chase as the celebrity spokesman. As Americans became concerned with **obesity**, in 1966 the company introduced baked potato chips with fewer calories.

Frito-Lay has acquired other food companies, such Grandma's brand cookies in 1980 and **Cracker Jack** in 1997. Frito-Lay is now the largest snack food conglomerate in the world.

SUGGESTED READING: Keith J. Guenther, "The Development of the Mexican-American Cuisine," in Alan Davidson, ed., *Oxford Symposium 1981: National & Regional Styles of Cookery: Proceedings* (London: Prospect Books, 1981); Andrew F. Smith, "Tacos, Enchiladas and Refried Beans: The Invention of Mexican-American Cookery," in Mary Wallace Kelsey and ZoeAnn Holmes, eds., *Cultural and Historical Aspects of Foods* (Corvallis, OR: Oregon State University, 1999, 183–203).

Frito-Lay Corn Chips In the early 1930s, Elmer Doolin, an unemployed salesman, bought a 5 cent bag of corn chips in San Antonio. They were called *friotes*—cut-up, hardened tortilla shells made from fried masa (corn flour). Doolin claims to have purchased the recipe from a cook who made them but, if so, the person has not been identified. In 1932, Doolin began manufacturing Fritos in his kitchen. He was successful in selling them and he quickly opened a factory in San Antonio, Texas, to increase production.

Fritos were the first commercial corn chips. His sales expanded as far as St. Louis. In 1945, Doolin licensed **Herman W. Lay**, the **potato chip** manufacturer, to manufacture and sell Fritos in the Southeast. In 1949 this license was expanded nationwide. Fritos were also introduced to other nations, and by 1962, Fritos were sold in 48 countries.

The main target of Frito promotions was children. The cartoon character, The Frito Kid, appeared 1953, which was used until 1967. In 1958, the slogan "Munch a Bunch of Fritos" was introduced. At about this same time the "Frito pie" gained currency. This homespun favorite was made by pouring a portion of hot chili into a partially opened bag of Fritos, then topping this with grated cheese, and optionally chopped onions. Today, Frito pie gourmets make them in a dish, not in the bag.

The **Frito Bandito** character was launched in 1967, but it was discontinued two years later due to pressure from the Mexican-American community. A cartoon character, W. C. Fritos, whose slogan was "Greetings, my little Chip-adees," appeared in 1969. It was a take-off of a favorite saying associated with the famous actor W. C. Fields: "Greetings, my little chickadees." In 1991, "Munch a Bunch a Fritos Brand Corn Chips Right Now!", a modification of the 1958 slogan, was reintroduced and the packaging was redesigned, adding brighter colors and a revised logo. Today, Fritos rank among the top 10 salty snacks in the United States.

SUGGESTED READING: Andrew F. Smith, "Tacos, Enchiladas and Refried Beans: The Invention of Mexican-American Cookery," in Mary Wallace Kelsey and ZoeAnn Holmes, eds., *Cultural and Historical Aspects of Foods* (Corvallis, OR: Oregon State University, 1999, 183–203); the Frito-Lay Web site: www.fritolay.com

Frozen Pizza Pizza became popular in America during the late 1950s. In the early 1960s, frozen pizza was introduced and pizza became the most popular of all frozen foods. Precisely who was the first to develop a commercial frozen pizza is unknown. Rose Totino of Totino's Italian Kitchen in Minneapolis, Minnesota, claims to have done so in 1962. By the late 1960s, Totino's was the top-selling frozen pizza. The Pillsbury Company bought the company in 1975.

Joseph, Ronald, Frances, and Joan Simek, who owned the Tombstone bar, a small country tavern across the street from a cemetery in Medford, Wisconsin, also claimed to have produced frozen pizza in 1962. **Kraft Foods** bought the **Tombstone Pizza** enterprise in 1990s and, after a major promotional campaign, it quickly became the top seller of frozen pizza in supermarkets.

In 1975, the Schwan Food Company introduced frozen Red Baron Pizza. When Kraft Foods introduced DiGiorno's pizza, Schwan introduced Freschetta frozen pizza. As of 2005, the best-selling frozen pizza brand was DiGiorno, followed by Tombstone, Red Baron, and Freschetta. Americans eat an estimated 1.8 billion slices of frozen pizza annually. Total annual sales of frozen pizza is about $2.4 billion out of an estimated $30 billion total pizza sales.

SUGGESTED READING: Kraft Food Web site: www.kraftfood.com; Schwan Food Company Web sit: www.theschwanfoodcompany.com

G

General Foods Corporation The Postum Company, maker of Post cereals, was launched in 1895 by Charles W. Post. During the 1920s, Postum went on a buying spree, acquiring such companies as Baker's chocolate, Maxwell House coffee, and **Jell-O**. Company management concluded that because the Postum was closely associated with cereal, the company needed another name to encompass these new subsidiaries. Thus, the General Foods Corporation was launched in 1929.

In 1953, General Foods Corporation acquired Perkins Products Company, maker of **Kool-Aid**. Four years later, the company invented **Tang** crystals, which was a Kool-Aid-like breakfast drink. In 1985, the General Foods Corporation was acquired by Philip Morris Companies, Inc. Four years later, General Foods was merged with Kraft to create Kraft General Foods. Ten years later, the merged company was renamed **Kraft Foods**, Inc.

SUGGESTED READING: James L. Ferguson, *General Foods Corporation: a Chronicle of Consumer Satisfaction* (New York: Newcomen Society of the United States, 1985).

General Mills In 1856, Cadwallader C. Washburn founded the Minneapolis Mill Company, which began to mill flour in 1866. The company concentrated on promoting its signature product, Gold Medal flour. In 1928, the Washburn Mills Company, soon to be renamed General Mills, introduced a **cereal**, Washburn's Gold Medal Whole Wheat Flakes. Its name was shortened to Wheaties. The cereal's first connection with sports was not until 1933, when the slogan "Wheaties—The Breakfast of Champions" emerged. During the 1950s, General Mills began marketing its cereal to children, and sugar-coated wheat cereals became the norm. General Mills introduced many new cereals, including Trix (1954), Lucky Charms (1963), and Honey Nut Cheerios (1979).

In addition to cereal, General Mills has also introduced many **snack foods** and **junk foods**, such as **Bugles** (1965) and Milk 'n Cereal Bars. In 2001, General Mills acquired the Pillsbury Company.

SUGGESTED READING: Scott Bruce and Bill Crawford, *Cerealizing America: The Unsweetened Story of American Breakfast Cereal* (Boston: Faber and Faber, 1995); General Mills Web site: www.generalmills.com

Genetically Modified Organisms (GMOs) Genetically modified organisms have been variously defined but, in general, a GMO is an organism whose genome has been modified by genetic engineering. Much of the food in the United States today contains GMOs. Europeans have been much more circumspect regarding the use of GMOs and the European Union and many countries have passed laws regulating or banning their use.

Opponents of GMOs have insisted that more research is needed before GMOs are used and many have expressed concern on the effects of GMOs on the environment and on humans. They have demonstrated against the Monsanto Company, one of the largest makers of GMOs. They have called GMOs Frankenfoods, a term that conveys derision and opposition to the use of GMOs. Proponents claim that there is no evidence of problems to date with GMOs, which have been used widely in the United States and other countries.

Because European **fast food** and **junk food** manufacturers largely buy from local farmers, they do not use genetically modified foods. Some fast food chains have tried to avoid public relations problems with GMOs. In 1999, **Burger King** outlets in Portugal banned the use of any GMOs in their food. In the United States, **McDonald's** Corporation has banned the use of GMOs in potatoes.

SUGGESTED READING: Myrna Chandler Goldstein and Mark A Goldstein, *Controversies in Food and Nutrition* (Westport, CT: Greenwood Press, 2002).

Ginger Ale Ginger beer was a low-alcohol drink that was popular in England and America during the eighteenth century. Fermentation created the carbonation. Ginger ale was a lighter, nonalcoholic **beverage** that was common in England, Ireland, and America in the early nineteenth century. Ginger beer and ginger ale were put into stoneware bottles, which were corked and wired to withstand the pressure that built up inside due to the carbonation. Irish immigrants brought the recipe for ginger ale to Canada and the United States, where recipes for it were published beginning in 1863. In 1866, James Vernor, a Detroit pharmacist, introduced **Vernor's Ginger Ale**, which is considered the first commercial carbonated soft drink.

In 1952, the first **diet soda**, No-Cal Ginger Ale, was sold by Kirsch Beverages in New York. Today, ginger ale is manufactured by several companies, including **Cadbury Schweppes**, Vernor's, **Royal Crown**, and the Seagram Beverage Company. Ginger ale is frequently used as a mixer for alcoholic beverages and some nonalcoholic drinks made with **ice cream**.

SUGGESTED READING: Donald Yates and Elizabeth Yates, eds., *American Stone Ginger Beer & Root Beer Heritage, 1790 to 1920; Written by Numerous Authors and Historians* (Homerville, OH: Donald Yates Publishers, 2003); Cadbury Schweppes Web site: www.dpsu.com/canada_dry.html

Girl Scout Cookies Girl Scouts began selling homemade **cookies** by 1917. This was intended to give girls experience making and selling cookies as well as to generate funds for Girl Scout activities. Five years later, Florence E. Neil, a local Girl Scout director in Chicago, Illinois, published the first Girl Scout cookie recipe in *The American Girl* magazine. At first, Girl Scout cookies were packed in wax paper bags and sold door-to-door, or they were sold by parents through their businesses. By the 1930s, Girl Scout councils were selling commercially baked cookies. In 1936, the national Girl Scout organization began licensing commercial bakers to produce cookies. The following year, many Girl Scout councils sponsored cookie sales.

During World War II, the Girl Scouts discontinued selling cookies due to rationing of flour, **chocolate**, **sugar**, and butter, but after the war, cookie sales resumed. In the 1950s, Girl

Scout cookies were sold in three main varieties: sandwich (vanilla- and chocolate-filled), shortbread (also called Trefoils), and chocolate mints (also called Thin Mints). In 1960s, sales of Girl Scout cookies increased greatly and additional varieties became available, including peanut butter sandwich cookies (also called Do-si-dos or Savannahs) and Samoas (also called Caramel deLites).

Concerns for the nutritional content of Girl Scout cookies became an important issue during the 1990s. As a result, new low-**fat** and sugar-free cookies became part of the selections. In the 2000s, Girl Scout cookies were criticized for their trans fats, and the Girl Scouts of the USA has strongly encouraged bakers to manufacture cookies without trans fats. As of 2005, annual sales of Girl Scout cookies are estimated to be $400 million; the best-selling variety is Thin Mints.

SUGGESTED READING: Mary Degenhardt and Judith Kirsch, *Girl Scout Collector's Guide: A History of Uniforms, Insignia, Publications, and Memorabilia* (Lubbock, TX: Texas Tech University Press, 2005); Girl Scout cookie Web site: www.girlscoutcookiesabc.com

Globalization The term *globalization* describes the increased mobility of goods, services, and capital across national boundries. Although globalization is not a new development, its pace has greatly increased due to jet planes and the advent of new technologies, especially telecommunications and the rise of the Internet.

Over the past century, **junk food** manufacturers expanded their sales and manufacturing operations into other countries. America's first commercial junk food, **Cracker Jack**, for instance, was introduced into the United Kingdom in 1897 and into Canada in 1901. Planters Peanuts opened its first international facility in Canada and the United Kingdom during the Depression, and **Forrest Mars**, son of the founder of **Mars, Inc.**, set up a factory in the United Kingdom in the 1930s. Mars quickly expanded to other countries. Today, Mars sells about 15 percent of the all commercial **candy** in the world.

Soda manufacturers followed a similar pattern. **Coca-Cola** was exported to the United Kingdom in 1909 and the company quickly expanded to other countries. Soft drinks were largely an American invention, and there were no equivalent beverages in other countries. Hence, they were more readily accepted.

In the United States, **fast food** is now considered a mature industry. Because it has grown more competitive and the profits per outlet have declined, major fast food chains have looked to other countries for growth. Hence, fast-food **franchises** are visible manifestations of globalization, which means that they are often targeted by those upset with globalization or with American policies. For example, radical French farmer José Bové destroyed a **McDonald's** under construction in France, and demonstrators often ransack or destroy fast food outlets around the world as a protest against American policies or fast food. To avoid these problems, fast food **chains** have done their best to localize their operations. Most fast food chains are run and operated by locals. Chains purchase a high percentage of the basic ingredients in the local country, buying from local farmers; and they import only necessities.

Overseas fast food chain menus also try to fit in with the local culture. **Hamburgers**, for instance, are not served in India out of respect for Hindu religious beliefs. Beer is served in McDonald's in Germany and wine is served in France. Specialty items that appeal to local tastes have developed. In addition, fast food chains support local charities and participate in local customs.

Globalization has been reflected in a number of economic agreements, most of which have affected American fast food and junk food operations. For instance, the North American Free Trade Agreement (NAFTA) economically binds the United States, Canada, and Mexico. This agreement makes it possible for American junk foods to be manufactured in Mexico. Besides lower labor costs in Mexico, **sugar** (a major ingredient in junk foods) is also less expensive because the United States has high federal price supports to protect domestic sugarbeet growers. Mexico has no such price supports and the price of sugar in Mexico is about half that of the United States. In addition, many fast food facilities have been established in Mexico. Guacamole, for instance, is made in Mexico and shipped to the United States for sale in fast food chains.

Globalization, of course, works both ways. Large European food giants have purchased fast food and junk food operations in the United States. **Unilever**, an Anglo-Dutch company, owns **Ben & Jerry's** and **Breyer's** as well as **Dove** and **Klondike** ice cream bars. The Swiss multinational **Nestlé**, for example, sells many confections, such as Nestlé's Crunch, in the United States, and it owns many brands, such as **Butterfinger** and **Baby Ruth** bars, that originated in the United States. The British multinational **Cadbury Schweppes** is America's third-largest **soda** manufacturer. In addition, American corporations are licensed to sell confections that originated in other countries. The **Hershey Company**, for instance, sells Kit-Kat bars—which originated in England—in the United States. The only foreign fast food company that successfully entered the United States was **El Pollo Loco**, which was subsequently purchased by American investors. But firms that originated in the United States have been acquired by foreign companies. For instance, **Dunkin' Donuts** and **Baskin-Robbins** were both owned by the French conglomerate Pernod Ricard.

Opponents to globalization of fast food and junk foods have many concerns. Leaders of Labor unions point out that globalization has contributed to outsourcing of American jobs to other countries. Others believe that "fair trade" often means American economic dominance of other countries. Indeed, American fast food chains have achieved substantial international economic dominance. Through this dominance, fast food chains have influenced culinary practices and tastes worldwide. This success has led to yet another concern—that fast food is destroying local culinary values and replacing local traditions with unhealthy food. The rapid expansion of American fast food has, in fact, led to the rejection of traditional local street foods, often due to fear of food poisoning, adulteration, and unsanitary conditions. Thus, critics believe that globalization has contributed to global homogenization or Americanization of culinary life. Finally, some analysts blame American the fast food ethic for the growing global **obesity** crisis on the expansion of American fast food chains.

SUGGESTED READING: Alessandro Bonanno et al., eds., *From Columbus to ConAgra: The Globalization of Agriculture and Food* (Lawrence, KS: University Press of Kansas, 1994); José Bové, François Dufour and Gilles Luneau, *The World Is Not for Sale: Farmers Against Junk Food* (New York: Verso, 2001); Deborah Brandt, ed., *Women Working the NAFTA Food Chain: Women, Food & Globalization* (Toronto: Second Story Press, 1999); C. Hawkes, "Marketing Practices of Fast Food and Soft Drinks Multinationals: A Review," *Globalization, Diets, and Noncommunicable Diseases* (Geneva: World Health Organization, 2002); Francoise Gollain, "Anti-globalisation Movements: Making and Reversing History," *Environmental Politics* 11 (Autumn 2002): 164–167; Jerry Mander and Edward Goldsmith, eds., *The Case Against the Global Economy: and for a Turn Toward the Local* (San Francisco: Sierra Club Books, 1996); Drew Eliot Ross, "Topography of Taste: Globalization,

Cultural Politics, and the Making of California Cuisine," Ph.D. dissertation (Madison, WI: University of Wisconsin-Madison, 1999).

Goldfish In 1962, **Pepperidge Farm**, a subsidiary of the Campbells Soup Company, began manufacturing Goldfish, a small orange-colored, cheese-flavored cracker shaped like a fish. It became an instant sensation. Although it was not fat-free, it was baked rather than fried.

Goldfish. © Kelly Fitzsimmons

Others tried to duplicate Goldfish. In the late 1990's, **Nabisco** reported that it intended to manufacture CatDog crackers, an orange-colored cheese snack shaped like fish, bones, and a CatDog cartoon character. These crackers would be sold in a box that would be decorated with the cartoon character and the other shapes as background. Pepperidge Farm sued Nabisco for trademark infringement based on the dilution law, which is intended to prevent the diminution of trademarks. Pepperidge Farm won the case in 1999; Nabisco appealed the decision but Pepperidge Farm won on appeal.

When trans **fats** became a concern, Pepperidge Farm began producing its Goldfish without trans fats by 2004. Today, about one half of all U.S. households with children under 18 purchase Goldfish products annually. More than 85 billion Goldfish crackers are consumed each year, which means that Pepperidge Farm manufactures 3,000 Goldfish every second. Because Goldfish have been a very successful product, Pepperidge Farm has expanded the product line to include other products, such as Nacho-Flavored Goldfish.

SUGGESTED READING: Goldfish Web site: www.pfgoldfish.com/flash.asp

Good & Plenty First produced by the Quaker City Confectionery Company in Philadelphia in 1893, Good & Plenty, small candy-coated licorice pieces, is reportedly the oldest brand-named **candy** in the United States, although the name was not trademarked until 1928. Good & Plenty became part of American culture when it was advertised nationally beginning in 1950. Its television promotions, such as the song "Choo Choo Charlie," became favorites among youth. Good & Plenty brand was eventually purchased by the **Hershey Company**.

SUGGESTED READING: Ray Broekel, *The Chocolate Chronicles* (Lombard, IL: Wallace-Homestead Book Company, 1985); Tim Richardson, *Sweets: A History of Candy* (New York: Bloomsbury, 2002); Good & Plenty brand Web site: www.hersheys.com

Good Humor In 1910, **candy** maker Harry Burt of Youngstown, Ohio, introduced the Good Humor Sucker. His reason for selecting the name was that he believed that bodily humors determined one's disposition. Burt also manufactured **ice cream** which he deliver by car.

When the **Eskimo Pie** became a national sensation in 1921, Burt began experimenting with **chocolate**-dipped ice cream. After some experimentation, he came up with a good-tasting product into which he stuck a wooden stick to make it less messy to eat. The result was the Good Humor Ice Cream Sucker. Burt applied for two patents, but he did not wait until the applications were approved. He immediately began selling his ice cream bars packed in ice in trucks, which drove around Youngstown with bells clanging to announce their presence.

When Harry Burt died, the company was sold to a group of Cleveland businessmen in 1926. They created the Good Humor Corporation of America and began **franchising** the operation. The financiers needed funds to expand, so they approached the New York financier Michael J. Meehan. He liked the company and acquired it.

For decades, Good Humor men dressed in clean, white uniforms drove ice cream trucks around the streets of America's cities. They worked on commission and many did well during the summer. They became such an important component of American culture that they appeared in magazines, comics, and radio programs. The movie *The Good Humor Man* (1950), starring Jack Carson, popularized the company and the Good Humor bar. The company discontinued selling its ice cream from trucks in 1976, although some private contractors continued driving Good Humor trucks after this date. The Meehan family sold the company to Thomas J. Lipton, Inc., in 1961. Today, the brand today is part of **Unilever**, an Anglo-Dutch company.

SUGGESTED READING: Anne Cooper Funderburg, *Chocolate, Strawberry, and Vanilla: A History of American Ice Cream* (Bowling Green, OH: Bowling Green State University Popular Press, 1995).

Graham Crackers During the late 1820s and early 1830s, Sylvester Graham (1795–1851) launched America's first culinary revolution by stressing the importance of coarsely milled, unbolted whole-wheat flour. Recipes for so-called Graham crackers made from this flour appeared in cookbooks during the nineteenth century. Russell Thacher Trall, one of Graham's disciples, began manufacturing Graham flour. The National Biscuit Company (subsequently renamed **Nabisco**) was the first national manufacturer of Graham Crackers. Today, most commercial products called graham crackers are made with white flour, **sugar**, preservatives, and other ingredients that Sylvester Graham would not have approved of. Commercial graham crackers are an ingredient in S'Mores, a homemade confection made with **chocolate** and marshmallows, also products Graham would not have approved of.

SUGGESTED READING: William Cahn, *Out of the Cracker Barrel* (New York: Simon and Schuster, 1969); *Crackers* (New York: Mintel International Group, 2003).

Gross-out Candy Children seem to love candies with extreme flavors and unusual names that conjure crude or naughty images. Unusual candies, such as wax lips, were manufactured during the nineteenth century. During the 1920s, these expanded to include **chocolate**-covered onions and cheese, were produced in the 1920s. Cinnamon-flavored Redhots were manufactured by the Ferrara Pan Candy Company during the 1950s, **Just Born** produced Hot Tamales in 1950, and Ferrara Pan Candy Company came out with really hot Atomic Fireballs in 1954 and the very sour Lemonheads in 1962.

Three unusual candies were hallmarks of the 1970s. **General Foods** developed Pop Rocks (hard candy with air pockets that contained carbonation that gave a crackling sensation when they melted in the mouth) in 1956 but they were not released until 1975. They were taken off the market because of rumors that the candy exploded. Other unusual candies of the era included Zotz, which was a very tart hard candy that fizzed in the mouth, and orange and strawberry Space Dust, which was a crackling candy.

These are all mild when compared with the gross-out candy of the twenty-first century. In 2001, the Jelly Belly Company released Bertie Bott's Every Flavour Beans in association with J. K. Rowling's Harry Potter books and movies. Flavors include Rotten Egg, Vomit, and Earthworm. The Danish candy company Dracco sells candy-pooping dogs, scorpion lollipops, and candy tongue tattoos. Fear Factor candy, based on the television series, includes crunchy worm larvae, slimy octopi, and frogs' legs served with a blood-red candy sauce. According to candy manufacturers, gross-out candy is one the fastest-growing segment of the candy market.

SUGGESTED READING: Kim Severson, "Gross-out Factor Could Boost Crude Candy Sales," *New York Times*, July 13, 2005.

Gross-out flavors including dirt, earwax, and rotten egg. © Kelly Fitzsimmons

Gum People have been chewing gum-like wax, resin, and latex for thousands of years. American Indians introduced American colonists to chewing resin from spruce trees. By the mid-nineteenth century, sweetened paraffin was commonly chewed in America. Modern commercial chewing gum got its start with Thomas Adams of New York. In 1869, Adams met the Mexican general Antonio de Santa Ana, the president of Mexico who as military commander led the Mexican forces at the Alamo during the Texan war for independence in 1836. More than 30 years later, Santa Ana was living in Staten Island, New York, and needed money to fund another revolution in Mexico. Santa Ana had discovered chicle—a latex from the sapodilla tree—when he visited the Yucatan peninsula in 1867. People in the Yucatan had been chewing it since prehistoric times. Santa Ana believed that there should be some commercial use for it that would help generate money for his cause.

Adams rose to the challenge and imported a ton of chicle into the United States from the Yucatan. He tried to make rubber, toys, and other products but was unsuccessful. Finally, he hit on chewing it, just like the people in the Yucatan had been doing for millennia. At that time Americans chewed a flavored paraffin-based gum called White Mountain. Adams's first gum without added flavoring was mass-produced in 1871. It was wrapped in tissue and sold as a penny stick. Adams introduced flavored gums beginning in 1884 and gum balls were sold in vending machines by 1888.

Other manufacturers began producing gum. John Colgan manufactured Taffy Tolu Chewing Gum by 1879. To improve digestion, Dr. Edward Beeman marketed pepsin gum in 1891. Thomas Wrigley, Jr. launched Wrigley's Spearmint and Juicy Fruit gums in 1893. In 1899, a dentist named Franklin V. Canning introduced Dentyne Gum and Chiclets, both of which were later acquired by the American Chicle Company.

Bubble gum was invented in 1928 by Walter E. Diemer, an accountant for the Fleur Chewing Gum Company in Philadelphia. He experimented with different ways of making gum and finally found one that stretched more easily and was less sticky. It was marketed by Fleur as Double Bubble gum. The rights to this gum were bought by Marvel Entertainment Group, who packaged it with trading cards until the late 1980s. In 1988, the rights for Double Bubble gum were sold to Concord Confections, which manufactured bubble gum balls.

The Topps Gum company, which started in Brooklyn, New York, in 1939, began marketing Bazooka Bubble Gum after World War II. Bazooka Bubble Gum, along with Bazooka Joe comics, quickly became the best-selling gum in America. In 1953, the company began placing baseball cards in each package of gum. Topps's most wacky gum was its 1985 Garbage Pail Kids (a satire on Cabbage Patch Kids), which came with trading cards.

Sugarless gums were produced in the 1950s but their basic sweeteners were cyclamates, which was banned by the U.S. Food and Drug Administration (FDA) in 1972. Aspartame became the main sweetener for sugar-free gums.

Wrigley was the first American gum manufacturer to begin selling his products abroad. Today, chewing gum is manufactured and sold throughout the world; India, China, and Eastern Europe are rapidly expanding their manufacture and consumption of gum. As of 2004, gum comprised about 25 percent of the total candy sales in the United States.

SUGGESTED READING: Brendan C. Boyd and Fred C. Harris, *The Great American Baseball Card Flipping, Trading, and Bubble Gum Book* (New York: Ticknor & Fields, 1991); Robert Hendrickson, *The Great American Chewing Gum Book* (Radnor, PA: Chilton Book Co., 1976); Michael R. Redclift, *Chewing Gum: The Fortunes of Taste* (New York: Routledge, 2004); Tim Richardson, *Sweets: A History of Candy* (New York: Bloomsbury, 2002).

Gummi/Gummy Candy See **Chewy Candy**

H

Häagen-Dazs In the 1930s, Reuben Mattus, an immigrant from Poland who sold fruit ices and **ice cream** pops from a horse-drawn cart in the Bronx, New York, began manufacturing ice cream and distributing it to grocery stores. His business prospered through the Depression and World War II. By the 1950s, large ice cream makers such as **Breyers** and Bordens undersold small producers, and supermarkets switched to the national brands. Mattus believed that large manufacturers had opened up a niche for premium ice cream, hoping that there would be customers who would be willing to pay more for it. He also decided to use only natural ingredients without preservatives or additives.

In 1960, he formed a company of his own that targeted those interested in premium ice cream. His wife came up with the name Häagen-Dazs. It conveyed visions of Denmark, which he believed had a positive image in the United States. He started with three flavors, vanilla, chocolate, and coffee, that he sold to small shops in Manhattan, and then expanded throughout the East Coast, and finally expanded nationally. He increased the number of flavors and decided to open up his own retail outlets in 1976. Mattus sold the company to The Pillsbury Company in 1983. Since then, Häagen-Dazs has expanded its product lines. It introduced an ice cream bar in 1986, frozen yogurt in 1991, and sorbet in 1993. In 2005, Häagen-Dazs was sold in 54 countries.

The Häagen-Dazs brand was a success, and others imitated Mattus. One such clone was Frusen Glaje, which had originated with Richie Smith, an ice cream manufacturer who also distributed Dolly Madison ice cream.

SUGGESTED READING: Anne Cooper Funderburg, *Chocolate, Strawberry, and Vanilla: A History of American Ice Cream* (Bowling Green, OH: Bowling Green State University Popular Press, 1995); Häagen-Dazs Web site: www.haagen-dazs.com

Halloween Halloween is observed on the night of October 31, when an estimated 41 million children dress in costumes and go house-to-house requesting **candy**, usually by yelling "trick or treat." Historically, candy became part of this American celebration during the 1930s and became a truly significant aspect after World War II. Initially, treats included candy corn ("chicken feed"), **caramel** candied apples, and **popcorn** balls. The practice or giving out homemade treats declined after 1967 when reports circulated of pins and razor blades in apples and other adulterated candies that had been passed out to children. A few reports were authenticated; others were hoaxes.

Whatever the risk, most parents threw out candy that children collected that was not commercially produced and wrapped.

Candy manufacturers have greatly encouraged the practice of giving out candy. According to the **National Confectioners Association**, which has strongly supported the tradition of giving candy on Halloween, more than $2 billion of candy is sold at Halloween, more than is sold at any other holiday. Halloween is also celebrated in other countries, including Mexico, the United Kingdom, Australia, and Canada, in a similar manner as it is in the United States.

SUGGESTED READING: Lisa Morton, *The Halloween Encyclopedia* (Jefferson, NC: McFarland, 2003); Nicholas Rogers, *Halloween: From Pagan Ritual to Party Night* (New York: Oxford University Press, 2002); Jack Santino, ed., *Halloween and Other Festivals of Death and Life* (Knoxville, TN: The University of Tennessee Press, 1994); Jack Santino, *New Old-Fashioned Ways; Holidays and Popular Culture* (Knoxville, TN: The University of Tennessee Press, 1996).

Hamburgers People have been scraping and shredding beef for millennia, but it was not until the invention of the meat grinder in the mid-nineteenth century that ground meat became a common food. Ground beef had the advantage of combining meat, **fat**, and organs into a palatable concoction. Ground meat was easier to consume, and this made a difference during a time when dentistry was in its infancy and many people lacked teeth. Finally, ground hamburger could be extended with flour, rice, or oats, thus resulting a larger quantity of food for those on a budget. The disadvantage of ground meat was that virtually anything could be added to the mix, including adulterants, food colorings, and other obnoxious contents.

In the nineteenth century, Hamburg Steak and Beef Steak were commonly served in fancy restaurants. These terms originally meant a particular cut of beef. By the 1870s, both terms had come to mean ground beef. It was popularized as a health food by an American doctor named James H. Salisbury, who believed that the stomach was a " meat-eating machine." He encouraged the consumption of broiled lean beef made into cakes. He reported that it should be served on a plate and could be seasoned with butter, pepper, **salt**, Worcestershire sauce, mustard, horseradish, or lemon juice. This was called Salisbury Steak by 1897, but this name did not become popular until World War I when German-sounding words, such as Hamburg Steak, were replaced with more patriotic alternatives.

Ground raw beef was used in making **sandwiches** by the 1870s and recipes for raw hamburger sandwiches frequently appeared in cookbooks of that period. Hamburger sandwiches were first popularized by pushcart **street vendors** in the late nineteenth century. Numerous claims have been made about the individual who made the first hamburger sandwiches. The first located printed reference to them appeared in the *Los Angeles Times* in 1894, but it is likely that other vendors were selling them in other places by that date. Hamburger sandwiches may have been served at the Louisiana Purchase Exposition in St. Louis in 1904. Later observers claimed that the vendor was Fletcher Davis of Athens, Texas, but this is far from settled.

The reputation of ground meat in general, and hamburger in particular, dipped after the early twentieth century when muckracking journalists, such as Upton Sinclair (author of *The Jungle* [1906]), exposed the horrific practices of the **meatpacking industry**. From the beginning, hamburgers were condemned as unhealthy. Fastidious consumers avoided them, mainly because they were concerned with the contents of the ground meat and the cleanliness of the manufacturing and serving establishments. Arthur Kallett's *100,000,000*

Guinea Pigs (1933) condemned hamburger for containing preservatives, which, he claimed, were used to restore the color of the ground beef and also to destroy odor of spoilage. As commercial hamburger was ground, it could include virtually anything—not just beef and fat, but also lungs, lips, and other organs as well as nonbeef adulterations.

One early twentieth-century hamburger sandwich vendor was a short-order cook named J. Walter Anderson of Wichita, Kansas. In 1916, Anderson opened up his own stand and sold hamburgers for 5 cents apiece to attract working-class Americans. Aware of the negative reputation of hamburgers, Anderson had fresh beef delivered twice a day to his outlets, which he constructed so that customers could watch his employees preparing hamburgers. In 1921, he went into business with Edgar Waldo "Billy" Ingram. Ingram architecturally repackaged Anderson's hamburger stands into castles and named the operation **White Castle**. White Castle imitators sprang up around the United States, such as **White Tower**. Within a decade, the hamburger had changed from a fad into a common food served in **drive-ins** throughout America.

In 1931, Popeye's Thimble Theatre, a movie series, featured a cartoon character named character J. Wellington **Wimpy**, who in 1931 became known for the phrase "I would gladly pay you tomorrow for a hamburger today." Three years later, Ed Gold launched Wimpy Grills, featuring the 10-cent Wimpy burger. Wimpy Grills was the first fast food corporation to expand abroad. Another tough competitor was Bob Wian, who founded Bob's **Big Boy** in 1936. He featured an upscale double-patty burger and **franchised** his operation, which quickly spread to other regions of the country. By the 1930s, virtually every medium-sized city in America had **fast food** hamburgers, and many drive-ins, roadside stands, diners, and coffee shops served hamburgers.

Despite these commercial successes, fast food hamburgers did not immediately become a significant part of the American foodscape. Before World War II, pork was the most popular meat in the United States. After the war, rising incomes, falling cattle prices, and the growth of the fast food industry pushed American consumption of beef higher than that of pork, and the popularity of the hamburger soared.

Several entrepreneurs contributed to this change. The most important were Richard and Maurice McDonald, who designed a new type of hamburger fast food stand. Its Speedee Service System incorporated assembly-line efficiency into a commercial kitchen. They also reduced their expenses by eliminating waitresses, thereby permitting them to sell hamburgers at a lower price. They hoped that the lower price would increase the number of customers, and the greater volume would lead to higher profits. They also decided to concentrate on selling a few items (limited **menu**).

In 1948, the McDonald brothers opened an octagonal-shaped hamburger stand in San Bernardino, California. The initial **McDonald's** operation did not include indoor tables, and thus encouraged customers to order their food at a window and eat in their cars. At first they sold only hamburgers, cheeseburgers, **French fries**, and **beverages**. These efforts to streamline and mass-produce hamburgers paid off. In 1951, they grossed $275,000.

Despite their success, the McDonald brothers concluded that they needed a new architectural design for their restaurant. Richard came up with the idea of constructing golden arches right through the roof, which sloped upward toward the front. The McDonald brothers also decided to franchise their operation. Franchising permitted others to build McDonald's drive-ins throughout the nation, based upon the design developed in San Bernardino. Those receiving franchises paid the McDonald brothers a fee and a percentage of their sales. In 1953, newly designed franchises opened in Phoenix, Arizona, and Downey, California.

At this time, McDonald's was just one of several regional hamburger **chains**. In San Diego, **Jack in the Box** was launched in 1951 and sported the first **drive-thru** service. In Miami, Insta-**Burger King** was launched in 1954. Dave Thomas opened his first **Wendy's** restaurant in 1962 in Columbus, Ohio.

In 1954, **Ray Kroc**, a salesman who sold Multimixers, visited the McDonald's operation. He was so impressed that he arranged with the McDonald brothers to sell franchises. Kroc opened his own McDonald's restaurant in Des Plaines, Illinois, and streamlined the operation even further. By the end of 1957, there were 37 McDonald's; by 1959, the total had reached over 100. By 1961, Kroc had bought out the McDonald brothers and expanded his operation throughout America. Kroc's success encouraged the growth of other fast food chains, and those chains adopted McDonald's methods. Likewise, McDonald's adopted the successful components of other fast food establishments. To compete with upscale hamburgers, McDonald's developed new products, such as the Big Mac with its two beef patties.

A basic hamburger consists of a ground hamburger patty inside two pieces of bread or a bun with **condiments**. The common condiments include salt, pepper, mustard, mayonnaise, pickle relish, and **ketchup**. Less-common condiments include ranch dressing, salsa, soy sauce, and barbecue sauce. Commercial hamburger producers frequently include a so-called secret sauce, which usually consists of some special combination of the above condiments, plus flavorings. American cheese is frequently added to make a cheeseburger, but other cheeses include blue cheese, Swiss cheese, and cheddar cheese. Bacon is added to make a bacon burger. Add chili and it becomes a chili burger. **Pizza** burgers are made with pizza sauce and mozzarella cheese. Common additives include vegetables such as iceberg lettuce, raw or fried onions, tomatoes, and pickles. Hundreds of other combinations have been conceived, such as ones with beans, mushrooms, guacamole, olives, chili peppers and sauerkraut. Hamburgers are commonly served on buns, particularly ones that are sesame-seeded, but they have also been served on muffins and pita bread; taco burgers are made with tortillas.

Hamburgers can be prepared in a variety of ways; the most common are frying and broiling. Microwaving hamburgers is becoming increasingly common, particularly with frozen hamburgers. In addition to hamburgers made from beef, they have also been made with **chicken**, fish, pork, lamb, and eggs. In 1993, Max Shondor introduced Boca Burger, a soy-based burger. Today, veggie burgers are frequently made from soy-based products and are sold in fast food chains as well as in the frozen food sections of supermarkets. For those concerned about weight, low-calorie burgers are also sold, usually made from very lean beef.

Side dishes for the hamburger have varied over the years, but since World War II, the main one had been French fries of various shapes and sizes. Recently, **onion rings** and other fried vegetables have become alternatives. Hamburgers are frequently consumed with **sodas**, particularly **colas**, **root beers**, orange- and lemon-flavored drinks, and shakes, including chocolate, strawberry, and vanilla.

The appeal of the hamburger was that it was inexpensive, convenient, versatile, filling, and in many circles even trendy. Hamburgers were generally inexpensive compared to other common foods. For travelers, hamburger chains provided uniformity—when travelers visited new city, hamburger chains offered something familiar.The hamburger is America's national sandwich. The large national franchise chains of MacDonald's and Burger King have thousands of domestic outlets. Hamburger establishments caught on quickly in other countries and today there are few countries without an American fast food restaurant; these foreign establishments are expanding at a fast clip. In 1988, McDonald's had 2,600 locations abroad and by 1994 had expanded to more than 4,500 restaurants in 73 other countries. Today, there are more than 30,000 McDonald's restaurants in about 120 countries. There are more than 1,000 McDonald's outlets in Japan alone; the most popular restaurant in Japan, measured by volume of customers, is McDonald's.

There are many reasons for the success of fast food chains in other countries. Most chains have adapted to foreign cultures, including revising the contents of hamburgers. Other factors contributing to this success abroad are cleanliness, a family atmosphere, clean public restrooms, and air-conditioning in addition to efficient service to customers. When coupled with the expansion of the other fast food hamburger franchises, the hamburger is now the icon of American food.

Despite the rapid success of fast food and soft drink enterprises throughout the world, there has been heated criticism of their affects upon local cultures and businesses. Serious nutritional, environmental, and cultural questions about fast food remain. As the homogenization of food choices continues worldwide, some consider the rapid expansion of fast food chains as examples of insidious American imperialism that is destroying local cultures and culinary values. McDonald's success abroad has cause deep resentment by others who see the company as a symbol for the United States, and who believe that McDonald's expansion threatens local culinary traditions.

SUGGESTED READING: Gyula Décasy, *Hamburger for America and the World: A Handbook of the Transworld Hamburger Culture* Volume 3 of the Transworld Identity Series (Bloomington, IN: EUROPA, European Research Association, 1984); David Gerard Hogan, *Selling 'em by the Sack: White Castle and the Creation of American Food* (New York: New York University Press, 1997); Philip Langdon, *Orange Roofs, Golden Arches: The Architecture of American Chain Restaurants* (New York: Knopf, 1986); Harvey Levenstein, *Paradox of Plenty: A Social History of Eating in Modern America* (New York: Oxford University Press, 1993); Eric Schlosser, *Fast Food Nation: The Dark Side of the All-American Meal* (New York: Houghton Mifflin Company, 2001); Murray Waldman and Marjorie Lamb, *Dying for a Hamburger: Modern Meat Processing and the Epidemic of Alzheimer's Disease* (New York: Thomas Dune Books/St. Martin's Press, 2005).

Happy Meal In 1973, Burger Chef, a small, regional **hamburger chain**, began offering a kids' meal promotion. The kids' meal was a success but the chain failed. The success of Burger Chef's kids' meal encouraged **McDonald's** to launch its brightly colored Happy Meals in 1978. It offered kid-sized portions, along with toys. As these children matured and continued to frequent McDonald's long after they stopped buying Happy Meals, McDonald's learned the importance of gaining brand loyalty

Happy Meal containers. © Kelly Fitzsimmons

from small children. In 2001, McDonald's added Mighty Kids Meals to its menus. These target children 8 to 10 years old.

McDonald's has scored several major promotional successes based on toys in Happy Meals. In 1997, McDonald's included a Teenie Beanie Baby in Happy Meals; customers waited in long lines to acquire their Happy Meals with Teenie Beanie Babies inside. This campaign is considered one of the most successful promotions in the history of **advertising**. Before the promotion, McDonald's sold 10 million Happy Meals per month but during the promotion, Happy Meal sales increased to 100 million per month. In 2006, McDonald's offered characters from the new Walt Disney Pictures/ Walden Media film *The Chronicles of Narnia: The Lion, The Witch and The Wardrobe* in McDonald's Happy Meals and Mighty Kids Meals. Despite tremendous success, in May 2006 Disney broke off its relationship with McDonald's citing concerns with the healthfulness of **fast food**.

SUGGESTED READING: Terry Losonsky and Joyce Losonsky, *McDonald's Happy Meal Toys around the World* (Atglen, PA: Schiffer Publishing, Ltd., 1995); Meredith Williams, *Tomart's Price Guide to McDonald's Happy Meal Collectibles* (Revised and updated) (Dayton, OH: Tomart Publications, 1995).

Hard Candy Hard candies consist of crystalized **sugar** with colorings and flavorings. They are typically made by boiling water, sugar (or treacle), and other ingredients, then pouring the contents into a mold. When dry, the candies are removed. **Lollipops** were made by dipping sticks into spun sugar. Today, manufacturers use pans and steam-pressure cookers that control and speed up the process.

During the late nineteenth century, hard candies were typically retailed generically as penny candy, sold loose in jars by grocers and later through **vending machines** and kiosks on the street and at movie theaters. Hard candy remains an important part of the candy industry today. Common hard candies include lemon and gum drops, lollipops, suckers, candy canes, and jawbreakers. Major producers of hard candy include the **New England Confection Company**, which began making NECCO Wafers in 1912, the Tootsie Roll Company, which makes Tootsie Pops (a hard candy shell with a chewy chocolate center), and the Ferrara Pan Candy Company, which makes numerous types of candy, such as Lemonheads and Atomic Fireballs.

SUGGESTED READING: Louis Untermeyer, *A Century of Candymaking 1847–1947: The Story of the Origin and Growth of New England Confectionery Company* (Boston: The Barta Press, 1947).

Hardee's Wilbur Hardee in Greenville, North Carolina, launched Hardee's restaurant in 1960. It featured 15-cent charbroiled **hamburgers**, soft drinks, **French fries**, and **milk shakes**. In 1961, J. Leonard Rawls and James Carson Gardner bought out Wilbur Hardee. They took out advertisements and quickly expanded their operations, particularly in small towns. Fourteen years later, Hardee's had more than 900 outlets. It employed modular buildings, which reportedly took only six hours to construct. At first, these outlets were red-and-white-striped like **McDonald's**, but later the company shifted to a brown-and-orange color scheme similar to **Burger King**'s. The company also purchased suppliers, including makers of bakery goods, seafood, and frozen hamburger patties. Hardee's was one of the first fast food **chains** to sell its stock on the open market. In 1977, Imasco, the Canadian tobacco, food, and retail conglomerate began purchasing stock, and in 1980 it took control of Hardee's, which by then had 2,141 outlets in North America. The company expanded to Central America and the Middle East, and absorbed many Burger Chef restaurants when that chain folded. In 1990, Hardee's purchased the **Roy Rogers** chain, and closed unprofitable outlets. In turn, Hardee's was acquired by **Carl's Jr.** in 1997.

SUGGESTED READING: John A. Jakle and Keith A. Sculle, *Fast Food: Roadside Restaurants in the Automobile Age* (Baltimore: Johns Hopkins University Press, 1999); Hardee's Web site: www.bneinc.com/hardeeshistory.htm

Health Concerns Beginning in the 1970s, criticism of **fast food** spread throughout the country. The concerns focused on the overload of **fat**, **cholesterol**, and calories coupled with the lack of vitamins, minerals, and fiber. The *New England Journal of Medicine* published a study in 1989 reporting on the massive amounts of fat contained in typical fast foods, such **hamburgers** and **French fries**. Sensitive to criticism, chains made numerous shifts in their preparation procedures. **McDonald's**, for instance, switched from animal to mainly vegetable oil and added more nutritious items, such as salads, to its menus.

Many fast food chains have rushed to offer more nutritious items in their traditional menus. **Carl's Jr.**, for instance, began offering a salad bar in the 1970s. Most fast food chains now offer ready-made salads or traditional offerings with greatly reduced fat and calories. In 1987, McDonald's introduced a mixed-green salad and, in 1991, the McLean Burger. Customers were not excited about these healthier alternatives and the McLean was eventually dropped from the menu.

In 1994, Congress passed the Nutrition Labeling and Education Act (NLEA), which required food producers to label packages with nutritional information, such as the amount of calories, fat grams, cholesterol, sodium, carbohydrates, protein, vitamins, and mineral content per serving of the product.

Consuming **snacks**, fast food and soft drinks to excess can be harmful, particularly for young children whose **junk food** consumption competes with a balanced diet necessary for growth and good health. Regular consumers of junk food have lower intakes of nutritious foods necessary for a well-balanced diet. The consumption of fast food and junk food has paralleled the rise in **obesity** in America and the rise in type 2 **diabetes**. The increasing obesity among America's youth is of great concern.

In addition, health concerns have been raised regarding the conditions under which food (particularly meats) is processed by suppliers or prepared by workers in fast food outlets. **Diseases** that often spread through fast food chains include ***salmonella***, ***Escherichia coli*** infections, and **mad cow disease**.

SUGGESTED READING: Walter Gratzer, *Terrors of the Table: The Curious History of Nutrition* (New York: Oxford University Press, 2005).

Hershey, Milton S. Milton Snavely Hershey (1857–1945) was born in Derry Township, Pennsylvania. His formal education ended in the fourth grade. He became an apprentice to Joseph R. Royer, a well-known **candy** maker in Lancaster, Pennsylvania. In 1876, Hershey opened a taffy shop in Philadelphia, which failed six years later. He then moved to Denver, Colorado and began working with a **caramel** manufacturer. Hershey moved on to Chicago in 1883, then to New Orleans, and later to New York City, but failed to launch candy businesses in each location. In 1886 Hershey returned to Pennsylvania, where he opened the Lancaster Caramel Company, which became a tremendous success.

In 1893, Hershey visited Chicago's Columbian Exposition, where he found the exhibit of a German supplier of **chocolate**-making equipment. He purchased the equipment and had it shipped to Pennsylvania after the Exposition closed. Hershey hired chocolate makers and launched the Hershey Chocolate Company. In 1900, he sold the caramel company to the American Caramel Company for $1 million but retained his chocolate company. Hershey manufactured chocolates and in about 1900 came out with his chocolate bar, but he continued to experiment with the formula for several years. In 1903, he broke ground for a new factory in Derry Township, which he named Hershey. Around the community, he built what was considered at the time to be an ideal community with homes for his employees, churches, a park, pools, a community building, and many other amenities. To his workers, he offered insurance benefits and a retirement plan.

The Hershey Chocolate Company thrived and Milton and his wife Catherine became very wealthy. Because they were childless, they decided in 1909 to establish the Milton Hershey Industrial **School**, an educational institution for orphaned boys, in Hershey, Pennsylvania. After his wife's death in 1918, he donated most of his fortune to a trust for the school.

SUGGESTED READING: John F. Halbleib, *Milton S. Hershey* ([Hershey, Pa.?]: J. F. Halbleib, [2004]); Jane Sutcliffe, *Milton Hershey* (Minneapolis, MN: Lerner Publications, 2004); Joseph Richard Snavely, *An Intimate Story of Milton S. Hershey* (Hershey, PA: np, 1957).

Hershey Company The Hershey Chocolate Company was launched by **Milton S. Hershey** in 1894. Hershey was manufacturer of **caramel** candies in Lancaster, Pennsylvania. In 1983, he visited Chicago's Columbian Exposition and was interested in the exhibit Walter M. Lowney, a Boston **chocolate** maker, but he was fascinated in the chocolate-making machinery exhibited by Lehmann and Company of Dresden, Germany. Hershey bought the Lehmann machinery. When the exhibition closed, he had it shipped to Lancaster. Hershey hired two chocolate makers from Baker's chocolate and began manufacturing chocolate candies. Prior to this, all American chocolate candies were made by hand. The Hershey Chocolate Company, a small subsidiary of Hershey's caramel business, initially produced breakfast cocoa, sweet chocolate, baking chocolate, and a variety of small chocolate candies such as Chocolate Cigars and Chocolate Cigarettes, Chocolate Blossoms, and Sweet Peas.

In 1898, two other major manufacturers of a caramels—Breisch-Hine Company of Philadelphia and the P. C. Wiest Company of York, Pennsylvania—merged to form the American Caramel Company. They wanted Hershey to join their monopoly. When he refused, they offered him $1 million for the Lancaster Caramel Company. Hershey accepted in 1900 and refocused his energies on his chocolate company, which was excluded from the sale.

Initially, Hershey did not try to manufacture milk chocolate, which was difficult to make. He experimented with the process and created a **secret formula** for processing the milk. In 1900, he began manufacturing milk chocolate candies while he continued to revise formula, which he continued to perfect through 1905. In 1900, Hershey also manufactured the **Hershey's Chocolate Bar**.

In 1903, Hershey moved his operation to Derry Church, Pennsylvania, near where he was born, and began to construct the largest chocolate manufacturing plant in the world. Surrounding the factory he constructed an ideal town, complete with churches, pools, a park, a community building, and a school for orphans. He also offered his employees insurance programs and a retirement plan decades before it became common to do so. In 1908, Hershey stepped down as president of the company and selected William Murrie to succeed him. Murrie was Hershey's closest friend and he continued to serve as president of the company until 1947.

The company continued to innovate and produce new products, but it pared down its product line to concentrate on particular milk chocolate products, such as Hershey's Kisses, which were released in 1907. They were so successful that other companies duplicated their design and packaging. The company added plumes in 1921 as a means of identifying Hershey's Kisses from the clones manufactured by others. In 1925, Hershey began manufacturing a chocolate-peanut-based confection christened Mr. Goodbar. Hershey initially used peanuts as an ingredient in its Krackel bar, but the peanuts were discontinued in 1940.

Because Hershey products were mass-produced, the company could undersell its competitors who continued to make handmade chocolate candies. Hershey faced the problem of how to distribute his new confections. Traditionally, expensive chocolates were distributed through specialty stores. Hershey had a better idea. He wanted to sell them through kiosks on streets and in train stations, **soda fountains**, drugstores, diners, and **vending machines**, as well as in grocery stores and newsstands. To support this ambitious distribution system, Hershey began a massive promotional campaign in magazines, and later through radio and television.

When Hershey's factory had become the largest maker of chocolate in the world, the company supplied chocolate to its competitors, such as the H. B. Reese Candy Company, makers of the **Reese's Peanut Butter Cup**, and **Mars, Inc.** Whenever Americans ate chocolate from the 1920s to the 1960s, it was likely that regardless of the brand name on the package, the chocolate was manufactured by Hershey.

While Hershey's was a successful company from the start, it received a major boost during World War I when its chocolates were given to American soldiers fighting in Europe. Many soldiers had never eaten a chocolate bar before, and when they returned after the war, the demand for Hershey's products greatly increased.

During the Depression, Hershey's profits fell but the company survived due to a steeper drop in **sugar** and chocolate prices. The company had always considered itself to be benevolent, so its leadership was surprised when 600 workers went on strike in 1937, demanding union representation. Eventually, the Hershey Chocolate Corporation signed an agreement with American Federation of Labor through the Bakery and Confectionery Workers International Union; thus, Hershey's became one of the first **junk food** companies to unionize.

During the 1930s, the Hershey Company continued to release new products. Its 5th Avenue bar was launched in 1936 and in the following year Hershey bought the rights to the Kit Kat bar from the British firm **Rowntree's of York**. Hershey engineers could not figure out how to manufacture it, so Rowntree's had to send its engineers to the United States to help set up the manufacturing process.

During World War II, nonessential manufacturing unrelated to the war effort was discontinued. Chocolate was in short supply because cocoa all had to be imported into the United States from Africa or South America. Since shipping was limited due to the war, chocolate virtually disappeared from civilian use until after the war. The Hershey Chocolate Company lobbied for the continuation of chocolate manufacturing, claiming that it was good for the morale of the American armed forces.

Globalization

During its early years, the Hershey Company completely ignored the international market. This gave its European and American competition an edge in globalization, and the Hershey Company never recovered. During World War II, Hershey's candy bars were again given to American military forces and, though the soldiers, Hershey products were introduced abroad. Unlike other American products, such as **Coca-Cola**, Hershey's chocolates were generally unsuccessful in developing markets in other countries. Europeans simply preferred the flavor of chocolates made or distributed in their countries, such as those produced by **Cadbury**, **Nestlé**, Rowntree's, and **Toblerone**. Recently, the Hershey Company has expanded it global presence through increased sales and acquisitions. Today the company has operations in 90 countries around the world, and is particularly strong in Canada and Mexico due to the North American Free Trade Agreement (NAFTA).

Advertising and Promotion

During the 1960s, the price of chocolate increased, which meant that the company decreased the size of its chocolate bar so that it could retain its 5 cent price. By 1968, the Hershey chocolate bar was about one-half of its original size. Candy bars manufactured by other companies had much less chocolate in them, and consequently the increase in the price of chocolate did not affect them in the same way that it did Hershey. In 1969, the company increased the price of its chocolate bar to a dime, and during the following years the company began a massive advertising campaign on behalf of its products.

Acquisitions and New Products

During the 1920s, H. B. Reese, a former Hershey employee, founded a candy company, which made Reese's Peanut Butter Cups. After Reese's death, the company had financial difficulties in 1963, and the company sold out to Hershey, which began national distribution of Reese's Peanut Butter Cups. After 1970, Hershey began massive promotional campaign on its behalf. It also extended the product line with new candies, such as Reese's Crunch Cookie Cups, Reese's NutRageous, and Reese's Pieces, which received great visibility in the film *ET, The Extra-Terrestrial.* In 2002, Hershey packed Reese's and Kit Kat bites into plastic cups at the request of the **7-Eleven** convenience store chain. These containers fit into car cups-holders and could be consumed by drivers while the car was underway.

In 1977 Hershey acquired Y & S Candies, makers of **Twizzlers**. In 1988 Hershey purchased **Peter Paul** brands—**Mounds**, Almond Joy, and Peppermint Patties. In 1996 Hershey bought Leaf North America, maker of **Good & Plenty**, Jolly Rancher, Whoppers, Milk Duds and PayDay. In 2000, the company acquired the Bubble Yum! brand. Two years later, it purchased Henry Heide, Inc., maker of Juicyfruits and Wunderbeans, which it in turn was sold to Farley's & Sathers Candy Co., Inc. In addition to acquisitions, Hershey's has continued to release new products, such as Skor, Cookie 'n' Mint bars, Hugs, Sweet Escapes, Ice Breakers chewing gum and mints, and Snack Barz. Hershey's remains the largest chocolate manufacturer in the United States.

SUGGESTED READING: Joël Glenn Brenner, *The Emperors of Chocolate: Inside the Secret World of Hershey and Mars* (New York: Broadway Books, 2000); Andrew F. Smith, *Peanuts: The Illustrious*

History of the Goober Pea (Urbana, IL: University of Illinois Press, 2002); Hershey Company Web site: www.thehersheycompany.com

Hershey's bars. © Kelly Fitzsimmons

Hershey's Chocolate Bar **Milton S. Hershey**, a manufacturer of **caramels** in Lancaster, Pennsylvania, attended Chicago's Columbian Exposition in 1893. There, for the first time, he saw machinery that manufactured **chocolate**. He was particularly impressed with equipment made by J. M. Lehmann of Dresden, Germany. He purchased the equipment on the spot and had it shipped directly to his caramel plant when the Exposition closed. In 1894, Hershey launched the Hershey Chocolate Company. He hired two chocolate makers from Walter Baker's mills and began manufacturing chocolates. In 1900, Hershey sold his caramel company and began manufacturing many chocolate products, including a milk chocolate bar. It took several years to perfect this recipe and it was not trademarked until 1906. He first manufactured his chocolate bar with almonds in 1908. Hershey set the price for his chocolate bars at 5 cents. It was the world's first chocolate bar and it became the company's flagship product. Over the years, prices for the bar's ingredients have fluctuated and the size of the chocolate bar was modified to maintain the price. When chocolate prices skyrocketed in the 1960s, Hershey's finally had to change the price of its chocolate bar.

During World War II, special Hershey chocolate bars were given to the U.S. armed forces as part of Ration D. It weighed four ounces and could withstand extreme heat. Special versions were manufactured for use in the tropics. During the war, the company manufactured more than 3 billion bars. Advanced versions of this bar were made by Hershey for Operation Desert Shield and Operation Desert Storm.

The **Hershey Company** states that it makes its chocolate bar with the same recipe developed by Milton Hershey, although the size has decreased and price of the bar has increased over the years. In 1971, the company introduced a Hershey's Special Dark chocolate bar. This was followed six years later with the Golden Almond chocolate bar and the Symphony milk chocolate bar with almonds and toffee chips in 1989.

SUGGESTED READING: Joël Glenn Brenner, *The Emperors of Chocolate: Inside the Secret World of Hershey and Mars* (New York: Broadway Books, 2000); Ray Broekel, *The Great America Candy Bar Book* (New York: Houghton Mifflin Company, 1982); Ray Broekel, *The Chocolate Chronicles* (Lombard, IL: Wallace-Homestead Book Company, 1985); Hershey's Web site: www.hersheys.com

Hires Root Beer **Root beer** was a common beverage in America since at least the eighteenth century. It was made in various ways with roots and leaves of available plants. A Philadelphia pharmacist, Charles E. Hires, took his wife on a honeymoon in 1875 and found one recipe for "herb tea" in New Jersey. The formula reportedly contained at least eight different ingredients. When Hires returned to Philadelphia, he began to experiment with ingredients and finally produced Hires Rootbeer Household Extract, which was exhibited at the Centennial Exposition in Philadelphia in 1876.

Hires's root beer was nonalcoholic and was considered a health **beverage**. Hires's **advertising** campaign on behalf of his new beverage purportedly encouraged coal miners to switch from hard drinks to his root beer, which was advertised as "The National Temperance" drink and as "The Greatest Health-Giving Beverage in the World."

In 1884, Hires Root Beer advertisements appeared in *Harper's Weekly* and *Harper's Monthly Magazine.* Two years later Hires root beer was sold in bottles, but its advertising emphasized brewing a home extract. By the early 1890s, over three million packages of extract were sold annually, as were three million bottles. In 1936, the Charles E. Hires operations expanded and established branch plants in several cities. The following year, Hires died at Haverford, Pennsylvania, at age 83. In 1962, Crush International acquired the Charles E. Hires Company. It was not until 1983 that Hires discontinued selling root beer extract.

In 1980, Crush International, along with Hires Root Beer, was sold to Procter & Gamble, which sold it nine years later to **Cadbury Schweppes** Americas Beverages (CSAB), a subsidiary division of Cadbury Schweppes. Hires Root Beer, along with **Vernor's Ginger Ale**, are considered the oldest continuously marketed soft drinks in the United States.

SUGGESTED READING: L. A. Enkema, *Root Beer: How It Got Its Name; What It Is; How It Developed from a Home-brewed Beverage to Its Present Day Popularity* (Indianapolis, IN: Hurty-Peck & Co., 1952); Tom Morrison, *Root Beer Advertising: A Collector's Guide* (Atglen, PA: Schiffer Publishing, 1992); Tom Morrison, *More Root Beer Advertising and Collectibles* (Atglen, PA: Schiffer Publishing, 1997); Donald Yates and Elizabeth Yates, eds., *American Stone Ginger Beer & Root Beer Heritage, 1790 to 1920; Written by Numerous Authors and Historians* (Homerville, OH: Donald Yates Publishers, 2003); Hires Web site: www.dpsu.com/brands_hires_root_beer.html

Hollywood, Movie Tie-ins, and Celebrity Endorsements Since the 1970s, movie producers have approached **fast food** and **junk food** companies with offers to include their products in movies for a fee or in exchange for **advertising** and other promotions. The classic example was Universal Studios's approach to **Mars, Inc.** to use **M&M's** in its movie *ET, The Extra-Terrestrial.* Mars turned it down, and Universal then approached the **Hershey Company**, which produced Reese's Pieces. Universal and Hershey's came to an agreement in which Reese's Pieces were used in the movie and Hershey agreed to promote *ET* with $1 million worth of promotions. In turn, Hershey was granted rights to use the film to promote its own products. When the movie was released, sales of Reese's Pieces skyrocketed.

Product placements have been common elements in many movies. In 1982, the **Coca-Cola Company** purchased Columbia Pictures to provide publicity through Coke product placements in its films. (Coca-Cola later sold Columbia Pictures.) **McDonald's** appears in *Bye, Bye Love* (1995), *George of the Jungle* (1997), and *Clear and Present Danger* (1994). In the movie *Richie Rich* (1994), Macaulay Culkin playing Richie Rich has a McDonald's restaurant in his home. Product placements costs run between $50,000 and $100,000, depending upon the prominence of the placement. Film makers typically receive advertising estimated to be valued between $25 million and $45 million.

Product placement is but one relationship between movies and junk food and fast food. Movie placements have been so successful that they are now included in books, music videos, comic strips, and songs. Cooperative marketing relationships have developed which include the manufacturing of toys and other merchandise. Even more unusual relationships have been created. For instance, **Hostess** produced Hostess Turtle Pies prior to the release of the movie *Teenage Mutant Ninja Turtles II* (1991). The pies were advertised as "Fresh from the sewers to you!"

Relationships have progressed beyond film agreements. The Walt Disney Company, for example, agreed to a 10-year global marketing agreement with McDonald's Corporation. McDonald's promoted Disney's films; in return, McDonald's placed Disney toys in its **Happy Meals** and promote movie spin-off products, such as toys and lunch boxes. In May 2006 Disney broke off its relationship with McDonald's citing concerns with the healthfulness of fast food. In 2001 Disney and Coca-Cola signed an agreement to produce children's **beverages** using Disney characters. In the same year, Coca-Cola paid Warner Brothers an estimated $150 million for global marketing rights to the first Harry Potter movie. As a result, the **Center for Science in the Public Interest**, along with other organizations around the world, launched the "Save Harry" campaign to protest the use of a children's film to promote junk food.

In addition to movies, fast food and junk food have had close relationships with **television** programs. **Burger King**, for instance, has a relationship with Nickelodeon and McDonald's has one with the Fox Kids Network.

Hollywood and sports celebrities have appeared on commercials and endorsed fast food and soda companies. The comedian Bill Cosby has been a spokesperson for **Jell-O** since 1988. Halle Berry, Britney Spears, Barry Bostwick, and Beyoncé Knowles have all advertised Pepsi-Cola. Michael Jordan, Kobe Bryant, Donald Trump, Serena Williams, and Venus Williams have all promoted McDonald's. Shaquille O'Neal and B. B. King have advertised Burger King. The actor Jason Alexander has endorsed **Kentucky Fried Chicken**. Garth Brooks, the country music singer, has promoted **Dr Pepper**.

These relationships have generated millions of dollars from box office attendance, sales of soft drinks, fast food, and junk food, and sales of toys and merchandise.

SUGGESTED READING: Kelly D. Brownell and Katherine Battle Horgen, *Food Fight: The Inside Story of the Food Industry, America's Obesity Crisis, and What We Can Do about It* (Chicago: Contemporary Books, 2004); P. B. Gupta and S. J. Gould, "Consumers' Perceptions of the Ethics and Acceptability of Product Placement in Movies: Product Category and Individual Differences," *Journal of Current Issues and Research in Advertising* 19 (1997): 37–50; Save Harry campaign Web site: www.SaveHarry.com

Hostess In 1925, Continental Baking Company acquired the Taggart Baking Company, which made Wonder Bread and chocolate cup cakes. Continental wanted additional products to sell to grocers, and in 1927 it hit upon spongecakes used for making strawberry shortcake. Continental gave the brand name of Hostess to its new line of cake products.

While shortcakes were a good seller during the strawberry season, Continental sought products that could be sold year-round to grocers. One result was **Twinkies** in 1930, the most successful Hostess cake. Other products include Ding Dongs, Ho Ho's, Suzy Q's, Sno Balls, fruit pies, and other products. Continental advertised these products extensively and in the 1970s created cartoon characters for them, such as Twinkie the Kid, Happy Ho Ho, King Ding Dong, Captain Cupcake, and Fruit Pie the Magician.

In 1995, Interstate Bakeries Corporation, headquartered in Kansas City, Missouri, acquired Continental Baking Company. This made Interstate Bakeries Corporation the largest wholesale maker of cake in the United States. Interstate faltered during the early 2000s, when the Atkins and other low-carbohydrate **diets** became popular. In 2004,

Interstate Bakeries filed for bankruptcy protection under Chapter 11. As of 2006, the company continues to operate under the protection of the court.

SUGGESTED READING: Interstate Bakeries Web site: www.bakeryoutlets.com

Hot Dog Sausages have been made for hundreds of years in Europe, and European colonists brought the sausage making art to America. They were both a means of preserving meat as well as a good way to use the less-desirable parts of an animal carcass, including **fat**, muscle, and gristle. These were chopped up, salted and spiced, and then stuffed into intestinal casing. Sausages were easy to transport and store, and were relatively easy to eat. Because the contents were no longer recognizable, it was always possible for the unscrupulous to adulterate the sausage.

The hot dog—defined as a sausage on a bun—was clearly an American invention. The connection came after the Civil War and were associated with leisure-time activities, such as fairs and amusement parks. By 1867, Charles Feltman, a pushcart vendor on Coney Island (an amusement park near New York), was selling sausages on white rolls. They were a success and Feltman converted his cart into a large, formal restaurant eventually employing many waiters. One waiter was Nathan Handwerker, a Polish immigrant, who decided to launch his own hot dog stand in 1916. Handwerker sold his hot dogs at a lower price than did Feltman. Nathan's stand thrived and was converted into an East Coast **chain** of hot dog purveyors called Nathan's Famous.

Hot dogs spread quickly across the United States during the late nineteenth and early twentieth centuries. They were commonly sold in baseball stadiums and at other sporting events. In Chicago, hot dogs were made by a German immigrant named Oscar Mayer. He started out working in Chicago's stockyards, then joined his brother, a sausage maker and ham curer, in opening a small retail butcher shop in a German neighborhood on Chicago's Near North Side. The Mayers took the bold step of putting their own name on their products and began selling America's first brand-name meats. By 1924, Oscar Mayer offered its bacon sliced and wrapped; in 1929 the company used a yellow band to distinguish it from other brands; the Oscar Mayer Wienermobile began life as a traveling ambassador for their hot dogs in 1936.

In Los Angeles, hot dog vendors plied the street. Two brothers, Maurice and Richard McDonald, sold hot dogs in a stand near the Santa Anita racetrack in Arcadia. They also sold **hamburgers**; when they found that their customers wanted more hamburgers they stopped selling hot dogs and created **McDonald's** hamburgers. Another Los Angeles area fast food purveyor was John Galardi, who in 1961 launched **Wienerschnitzel**, the largest fast food hot dog chain in the world.

Typical hot dog **condiments** include **ketchup**, mustard, onions, and pickle relish. Other additions include cheese, chili, and sauerkraut. Geographgic regions have their own additions to hot dogs. In Chicago, for instance, hot dogs are served on a steamed poppy-seed bun with mustard, relish, chopped raw onion, pickle slices, pickled hot peppers, celery salt, and diced or wedged tomatoes. The required "side" is an order of **French fries** smothered with Cheddar cheese. The Maxwell Street–style hot dog is served on a plain bun with fried or grilled onions and mustard.

Hot dogs are sold year-round, but they are mostly consumed during the summer. According to the National Hot Dog and Sausage Council, Americans consume 155 million hot dogs on the Fourth of July and about 7 billion hot dogs during the summer.

SUGGESTED READING: Gerald Leonard Cohen, Barry Popik, and David Shulman, *Origin of the Term "Hot Dog"* (Rolla, MO: G. Cohen, 2004); John A. Jakle and Keith A. Sculle, *Fast Food: Roadside Restaurants in the Automobile Age* (Baltimore: Johns Hopkins University Press, 1999); National Hot Dog and Sausage Council Web site: www.hot-dog.org

Hyperactivity Hyperactivity is a persistent, severe pattern of excessive muscular activity characterized by higher-than-normal restlessness and movement. People who are hyperactive have difficulty sitting still and may talk incessantly. They may have difficulty focusing attention and may be impulsive. In children, hyperactivity is considered a problem more for schools and parents than it is for the affected child. There are many causes of medical hyperactivity, including attention deficit disorder (ADD), emotional problems, brain or central nervous system disorders, and hyperthyroidism.

In 1975, B. F. Feingold suggested in an article *Journal of Nursing* that there was a link between hyperactivity and artificial colorings and flavorings. Because food colorings and flavorings are common to most **candy**, many observers have concluded that confections cause hyperactivity. Ever since, it has remained a popular belief that children are prone to hyperactivity if they eat foods containing large amounts of **sugar**, such as candy and **soda**, artificial sweeteners, such as aspartame, or certain food colorings. Research on the relationship between sugar consumption and children's behavior is unproven, although there is some evidence that dyes can affect some sensitive children.

SUGGESTED READING: Ben F. Feingold, "Hyperkinesis and Learning Disabilities Linked to Artificial Food Flavors and Color," *The American Journal of Nursing* 75 (May 1975): 797–803; Michael F. Jacobson and Bruce Maxwell, *What Are We Feeding our Kids?* (New York: Workman Publishing, 1994).

I

Ice Cream Ice cream and ices were known in Europe from the late seventeenth century, but ice cream was not common in America until the end of the eighteenth century. George Washington bought an ice cream freezer in 1784 and Thomas Jefferson acquired an ice cream recipe in France. Ice cream parlors were common in New York by the 1790s. Many French and Italian emigrants came to the United States and opened ice cream parlors. One such parlor was opened by the Delmonico brothers in New York City. The brothers expanded their operation into America's most famous restaurant in the nineteenth century, Delmonico's.

In 1846, Nancy Johnson invented a hand-cranked ice cream freezer. Two years later, William Young patented the similar Johnson Patent Ice-Cream Freezer, which helped make large-scale ice cream production possible. Jacob Fussell, a Baltimore merchant, is credited as the first wholesaler of ice cream in 1851. Fussell partnered with J. M. Horton, who in 1864 launched the Horton Ice Cream Company in New York. Yet another ice cream equipment maker was the White Mountain Freezer Company of Laconia, New Hampshire. For a time, it was the largest manufacturer of ice cream machines in the world.

The three main ice cream flavors—**chocolate**, vanilla, and strawberry—were determined in the nineteenth century and have remained favorites ever since. Flavors proliferated during the nineteenth century with the addition of sauces and other additives. During the twentieth century, thousands of different types of ice cream have been offered.

Commercial production of ice cream did not begin until technological improvements in refrigeration made it possible to sell ice cream through drugstores, **soda fountains**, and grocery stores. Drugstores and soda fountains competed with saloons and bars, and therefore were championed by the temperance movement. Early ice cream producers included William Breyers, who established a diary store in Philadelphia in 1866, and the Brenham Creamery Company (1907), which was launched in Brenham, Texas. The latter changed its name to the **Blue Bell** Creameries, Inc. in 1930. However, it was not until after World War II, when self-serve freezer chests for grocery stores came into wide use and the freezer sections of home refrigerators increased in size and efficiency, that packaged ice cream became an important part of America's diet.

Meanwhile, ice cream served by vendors took a major step forward when Italo Marchiony, an Italian immigrant in New York City, patented an ice cream cone mold in 1903. The ice cream cone was popularized at the 1904 St. Louis Louisiana Purchase Exposition. Ice cream's popularity soared beginning about 1910. Prohibition accounted

Soft serve. © Getty Images/PhotoDisc

for much of this increase as soda fountains thrived in the 1920s. By 1925, 30 percent of the country's ice cream was sold in soda fountains.

Ice cream parlors multiplied during the twentieth century. Howard Johnson invented his own "28" flavors of ice cream and set up ice cream stands that proved very popular during the summer. In 1935, he created his first roadside coffee shop which featured his ice cream. Thomas Carvel launched his first ice cream parlor in 1934. Many ice cream parlor chains were launched after World War II, such as **Baskin-Robbins** in 1946. Sales of conventional ice cream soared to new heights, but in 1948 began to decline largely due to the introduction of soft-serve ice cream parlors and drive-ins, including **Dairy Queen**, which began in 1940 but did not begin its expansion until after World War II; Baskin-Robbins, which began in 1948; and **Tastee-Freez**, founded in Chicago in 1949.

Beginning in the 1920s, ice cream novelties such as the **Eskimo Pie**, the **Klondike** bar, and the **Good Humor** ice cream bar, were launched and these successes encouraged others to develop new products. J. T. "Stubby" Parker of Ft. Worth, Texas, invented the **Drumstick** in 1930. Ice cream **sandwiches**, consisting of a ice cream center and thin, cake-like pastries on the top and bottom, were made by the late 1890s. The **Carvel Corporation** produced the first commercial round ones in 1951.The **Dove** bar was invented in 1956. By the 1960s, ice cream bars were sold in vending machines.

By the 1950s, large ice cream makers, such as **Breyers**, undersold small producers and supermarkets switched to the national brands. To reduce the price of their ice cream, large manufacturers had opened up a niche for premium ice creams. **Häagen-Dazs** was released in 1960 and **Ben & Jerry's** premium ice cream was launched in 1978.

During the last 50 years, ice cream manufacturers and ice cream parlors have been acquired by large conglomerates. Farrell's is owned by the Marriot Corporation and the Tastee-Freez brand is part of Galardi Group, Inc., which also owns the hot dog chain **Wienerschnitzel. Nestlé**'s subsidiary, **Dreyer's** Grand Ice Cream Holdings, includes the following brands: Drumstick, **Push-Ups**, Häagen-Dazs, **Dreyer's/Edy's**, and many others. **Unilever** owns Gold Bond Ice Cream, makers of **Popsicle**, Good Humor, Dove, Klondike, and Breyers. Many other multinational corporations have extended their confection lines into ice cream. **Mars, Inc.**, purchased the Dove bar, for instance, introduced the **Snickers** Ice Cream bars in 1984. Mars, Inc., acquired the Dove Bars the following year, and Mars has subsequently extended the Dove Bar line.

By 1951, Breyers was the largest ice cream manufacture in America, a position it has held ever since. It is followed by Dreyer's/Edy's and Blue Bell Creameries, Inc. Despite the concentration of the ice cream industry, the largest category of ice cream makers in America today is private labels, generally sold at the local and regional levels.

SUGGESTED READING: Paul Dickson, *The Great American Ice Cream Book* (New York: Atheneum, 1973); Anne Cooper Funderburg, *Chocolate, Strawberry, and Vanilla: A History of*

American Ice Cream (Bowling Green, OH: Bowling Green State University Popular Press, 1995); Anne Cooper Funderburg, *Sundae Best: A History of Soda Fountains* (Bowling Green, OH: Bowling Green State University Popular Press, 2002); John A. Jakle and Keith A. Sculle, *Fast Food: Roadside Restaurants in the Automobile Age* (Baltimore: Johns Hopkins University Press, 1999); Pamela J. Vaccaro, *Beyond the Ice Cream Cone: The Whole Scoop on Food at the 1904 World's Fair* (St. Louis, MO: Enid Press, 2004).

Iconography See **Mascots**

Ilitch, Mike Mike Ilitch (1929–) was born in Macedonia, then part of Yugoslavia. He immigrated to the United States, where he hoped to be a baseball player and did play for the Detroit Tigers farm team. He married Marian Bayoff in 1955 and worked in various jobs, including as a door-to-door salesman and in the awning business. Mike Ilitch persuaded a local nightclub owner on Detroit's West Side to let him make **pizza** in a kitchen in the back. Sales were good. By 1959, the Ilitches had saved $10,000 and invested it in a small pizzeria, which his wife named **Little Caesar's Pizza** Treat. It was located in a strip mall restaurant in Garden City, Michigan. The company is famous for its **advertising** catchphrase, "Pizza! Pizza!" Today, Little Caesar's Pizza remains family-owned and operated. Little Caesar's ranks eleventh among restaurant **chains** in America and fourth in selling pizza.

His financial success in the pizza world, Ilitch bought a hockey team, the Detroit Red Wings, for $8 million in 1982 and a baseball team, the Detroit Tigers, for $85 million in 1992. Ilitchs also owns Olympia Entertainment, a film theater company, a development company, the Hockeytown Café, and other property in downtown Detroit. To manage these assets, Ilitch Holdings was established in 1999. The holding company's 2004 total combined revenues reportedly exceeded $1 billion. Ilitch family entities remain privately held. Until 2005, Mike Ilitch was included in *Forbes Magazine*'s list of the 400 wealthiest Americans.

SUGGESTED READING: Little Caesars Pizza Web site: www.littlecaesars.com

Injury Since the 1950s, fast food chains have mechanized their operations to such an extent that the conditions inside kitchens are as safe as possible. The most common workplace injuries are slips, falls, strains, and burns. However, many employees receive serious injuries due to **crime** at fast food restaurants. Every month in the United States, four to five employees are killed on the job and many more are injured, usually during the course of a robbery.

Another dimension relates to the injuries suffered by **fast food** suppliers. According to Eric Schlosser, author of ***Fast Food Nation*** (2001), an estimated 40,000 to 50,000 meatpackers are injured every year. These workers are mainly producing hamburger and chicken for fast food chains. Today, the **meatpacking industry** is one of the most dangerous jobs in America, with an injury rate several times higher than the national average.

SUGGESTED READING: Eric Schlosser, *Fast Food Nation: The Dark Side of the All-American Meal* (New York: Houghton Mifflin Company, 2001).

In-N-Out Burger In 1948, Harry and Esther Snyder launched their first In-N-Out Burger stand in Baldwin Park, California. It offered a simple menu of **hamburgers**, cheeseburgers, **French fries**, **sodas**, and **milk shakes.** From its inception, it was a **drive-thru** operation complete with a two-way speaker system. Unlike other **fast food chains**, the Snyders decided not to franchise their operation. This meant a slower growth pattern; their second outlet was opened in 1951. By the time Harry Snyder died in 1976, there were only 18 In-N-Out Burger outlets. Despite his death, the chain has remained in family hands and it has continued to prosper.

To train managers for its outlets, the company established In-N-Out University. The company pays its employees significantly more than mandated minimum wages, and it offers workers a benefits package that include dental, medical, vision, and life insurance. As a result, In-N-Out enjoys lower employee turnover than other fast food chains.

While the official menu has changed little since it inception, a secret **menu** does exist, which consists of special items and variations of items on the menu, all of which are listed on the company's Web site. These include "2x4," which means two meat patties and four slices of cheese; "animal style," wherein the meat is fried in mustard and served on a bun with condiments, and "protein style" in which the meat is wrapped in lettuce, not a bun. Shakes can be combined, as can sodas.

In-N-Out Burger maintains its own meatpacking facility and sends hamburger to its outlets several times a week. The outlets have no microwaves or freezers. To make French fries, potatoes are peeled every day. The shakes are made from **ice cream.** The family has declined offers to sell the chain, which has continued to thrive. Today it is headquartered in Irvine, California, and has 150 outlets in California, Nevada, and Arizona. Many outlets now have indoor seating. In 2004, the original In-N-Out Burger location was closed and it is anticipated that it will be made into the In-N-Out Museum.

SUGGESTED READING: Eric Schlosser, *Fast Food Nation: The Dark Side of the All-American Meal* (New York: Houghton Mifflin Company, 2001); In-N-Out Burger Web site: www.in-n-out.com

J

Jack in the Box In 1950, Jack in the Box was started by Robert O. Peterson in San Diego, California. In 1951, it was sold to the San Diego Commissary Company, which later changed its name to Foodmaker, Inc. Initially, Jack in the Box served a simple menu of **hamburgers**, **French fries**, and **milk shakes**. Although the company experimented with other products such as tacos and **sandwiches**, the hamburger has remained its centerpiece.

Franchises were sold mainly in southern California. The distinctive feature of its **architecture** was a two-story high sign with a clown face that appeared to have sprung from a box. Jack in the Box was one of the first **fast food chains** to systematically incorporate **drive-thru** windows in its outlets. In 1968, Foodmaker, Inc. became a wholly-owned subsidiary of Ralston Purina. At that time Jack in the Box maintained 870 units. In 1970s, the company began serving **breakfast**. The Breakfast Jack and the Eggs Benedict sandwich were introduced in 1971; other breakfast foods, such as omelets, were introduced in 1976.

Jack in the Box's advertisements in 1975, amidst the so-called burger war, ended with "Watch out, McDonald's!" By 1979, the company had expanded to 1,100 units. It reorganized in 1979 by dropping outlets and diversifying the menu; it was the first fast food chain to add salads. In a leveraged buyout, an investment group acquired Foodmaker, Inc. from Ralston Purina in 1985. The Jack in the Box chain has continued to grow, even though four customers died and over 1,000 people became sick from undercooked hamburgers infected with a lethal bacteria in 1993.

Foodmaker, Inc. changed its name to Jack in the Box, Inc. in 1999. As of 2005, Jack in the Box was the fifth-largest hamburger chain in America and had 1,670 outlets nationwide.

SUGGESTED READING: John A. Jakle and Keith A. Sculle, *Fast Food: Roadside Restaurants in the Automobile Age* (Baltimore: Johns Hopkins University Press, 1999).

Jell-O Charles B. Knox patented a formula for making flavored gelatin in 1890. Frank Woodward, owner of the Genesee Pure Food Company in LeRoy, New York, bought the formula. Purportedly, Woodward's wife came up with the name Jell-O, which was first used in 1900. The company launched a massive **advertising** campaign and, by 1902, Jell-O annual sales reached $250,000. Beginning in 1904, the company began issuing booklets of recipes for using Jell-O. Tens of thousands of these color cookbooklets were issued, and today they are collectors' items.

The company changed its name to the Jell-O Company in 1923. Two years later, it was acquired by the Postum Cereal Company (later renamed the **General Foods Corporation**). General Foods was merged with **Kraft Foods** in 1989.

Beginning in the 1950s, the Jell-O line was extended to include pudding, Gelatin Snacks, and Jell-O Pudding Pops. New flavors have been regularly added, such as champagne. Some of its major advertising slogans are "There's Always Room for Jell-O" and "America's Most Famous Dessert." In 1997, the Jell-O Museum opened in LeRoy, New York. Today, Jell-O is manufactured by Kraft Foods, Inc. in Dover, Delaware.

Jell-O is more than just an usual product. It is considered an important part of American history. In 1991, the Smithsonian's National Museum of American History held a conference that solely examined the importance of Jell-O in American history.

*SUGGESTED READING:*Carolyn Wyman, *Jell-O: A Biography; The History and Mystery of "America's Most Famous Dessert"* (San Diego, CA: Harcourt, 2001); the Jell-O Museum Web site: www.jellomuseum.com

Jelly Beans Jelly beans are small, bean-shaped sugar confections with a soft center and a hard outer coating. Typically, they come in different colors and with various associated fruit flavors. Historically, jelly beans may have derived from Turkish Delight, a confection composed of gelatin that has been boiled, cubed, and dusted with sugar.

The earliest print reference to jelly beans appears in an advertisement dated 1886 in Illinois, where they were touted as a Christmas candy. Newspaper advertisements for them regularly appear after that date. They were commonly sold in glass jars or in vending machines as **penny candy**. It was not until the 1930s that jelly beans were also marketed as an Easter candy due to their egg-like appearance.

One traditional jelly bean manufacturer was launched by Gustav Goelitz in 1869 when he opened an ice cream and candy story in Belleville, Illinois. The company, then known as Herman Goelitz Candy Company, made butter creams and purportedly invented candy corn in about 1900. In 1976, it began manufacturing gourmet Jelly Bellys that are naturally flavored. They make about 50 flavors, including pear, watermelon, root beer, and buttered popcorn, which is reportedly the most popular flavor. Due to the success of this product, the company was renamed the Jelly Belly Candy Company and today it is located in Fairfield, California. The company makes Bertie Bott's Every Flavour Beans, named after a product identified in the Harry Potter series of books by J. K. Rowling. The company also makes Sports Beans, which are intended to be consumed while exercising.

Another important jelly bean manufacturer was the Rodda Candy Company of Lancaster, Pennsylvania. It was acquired by **Just Born**, Inc. in 1953. In 1977, Just Born extended its jelly bean line to include Teenee Beanee Jelly Beans, which have been popular ever since.

Jelly beans went into politics when Ronald Reagan became governor of California in 1966. He liked jelly beans and always had a large glass jar filled with them on his desk in Sacramento. When he became president, he carried on the jelly bean tradition in the White House.

SUGGESTED READING: Ray Broekel, *The Great America Candy Bar Book* (Boston: Houghton Mifflin Company, 1982); Tim Richardson, *Sweets: A History of Candy* (New York: Bloomsbury, 2002); Jelly Belly Web site: www.jellybelly.com

Junior Mints Junior Mints are a **chocolate**-covered mint, a smaller version of the **York Peppermint Patty**. Junior Mints were launched in 1949 by the James O. Welch Company in Cambridge, Massachusetts. According to company lore, Welch named the confection after his favorite Broadway play, *Junior Miss*. The play became a *New Yorker* magazine series, a book of the same name written by Sally Benson published in 1947, and a **radio** show starring Shirley Temple. The **candy** became a favorite, particularly at movie theater snack bars. Junior Mints also received visibility when they appeared in an episode of *Seinfeld* (episode #417).

The James O. Welch Company was sold to **Nabisco**, which sold it to the Warner-Lambert Company, which sold it to **Tootsie Roll** Industries in 1993. Today, Tootsie Roll Industries daily produces over 15 million Junior Mints annually.

SUGGESTED READING: Ray Broekel, *The Great America Candy Bar Book* (Boston: Houghton Mifflin Company, 1982); Tim Richardson, *Sweets: A History of Candy* (New York: Bloomsbury, 2002); Junior Mints Web site: www.tootsie.com/junior.html

Junk Foods Junk foods are defined as those foods with little nutritional value but a high calorie, **fat**, **salt**, or **caffeine** content. Junk foods often eaten as snacks, **sodas**, or at **fast food** outlets. Junk foods include many breakfast **cereals**, **candies**, chips, **cookies**, **French fries**, **gums**, **hamburgers**, **hot dogs**, **ice cream**, sodas, and most sweet desserts. The term *junk food* was first used in the 1960s but was popularized during the following decade when the song "Junk Food Junkie" climbed to the top of the charts in 1976.

Historically, junk foods became an important part of the American diet beginning in the 1920s, but it was not until the vast increase in junk food consumption following World War II promoted by **television advertising** that American nutritionists became alarmed. Their concerns were threefold. First, the increase in consumption of the junk foods is associated with an increase in heart disease, high blood pressure, certain cancers, and other diseases. Many medical professionals believe that **diet** plays a critical role in these diseases, particularly a diet high in fats, salt, oils, and calories contained in many junk foods. Second, also correlated with the increased consumption of junk food has been the increase in **obesity** in the world, with 23 percent of Americans now considered obese. Recent studies have reported that the number of overweight individuals worldwide rivals those who are underweight (estimated at 800 million). Finally, as junk food consumption has increased, consumption of healthier foods such as milk, fruit, and vegetables has decreased; thus, many people are decreasing their intake of proper nutrients and increasing the risk of tooth decay.

Junk food manufacturers have targeted youth, resulting in a vast increase in sales. Some studies suggest that almost 80 percent of food commercials aired on Saturday morning kids' TV shows are for products of low nutritional value. Advertisements for high-sugar products form the majority.

Of particular concern to nutritionists is the fact that some junk foods are now advertised and sold in the nation's **schools**. Candy and soda are sold on campuses in **vending machines** and they are advertised in schools through Channel One and through corporate sponsorship agreements. Many groups have attempted to ban the sale and advertising of junk foods in schools. Others have promoted the notion that junk foods should be taxed and the monies be given to the schools to promote **nutrition** education and to offset the funds derived from the sale or advertising of junk food.

SUGGESTED READING: Ashima K. Kant, "Consumption of Energy-dense, Nutrient-poor Foods by Adult Americans: Nutritional and Health Implications. The Third National Health and Nutrition Examination Survey, 1988–1994," *American Journal of Clinical Nutrition,* 72 (October 2000): 929–936; Richard F. Heller and Rachael F. Heller, *Carbohydrate-addicted Kids: Help Your Child or Teen Break Free of Junk Food and Sugar Cravings—for Life!* (New York: HarperCollins, 1997); Michael F. Jacobson and Bruce Maxwell. *What Are We Feeding Our Kids?* (New York: Workman Publishing, 1994); Michael S. Lasky, *The Complete Junk Food Book* (New York: McGraw-Hill, 1977); Lila Perl, *Junk Food, Fast Food, Health Food: What America Eats and Why* (New York: Houghton Mifflin/Clarion Books, 1980); Judith S. Seixas, *Junk Food—What it Is, What it Does* (New York: Greenwillow Books, 1984); Eric Spitznagel, *Junk Food Companion: The Complete Guide To Eating Badly* (New York: Penguin Group, 1999).

Just Born Samuel Born, a Russian immigrant, arrived in New York in 1910. He invented the Born Sucker Machine, which automatically inserted sticks into lollipops, thereby revolutionizing the **lollipop** industry. In 1917, he opened a retail **candy** store in Brooklyn, New York. In 1923, Born started his own manufacturing company, which he named Just Born, Inc. In 1932, the company relocated to Bethlehem, Pennsylvania, and three years later it acquired the Maillard Corporation, which made hand-decorated **chocolates**, crystallized fruits, Venetian mints, jellies, and "the best bridge mix in the country," according to company advertisement.

Just Born, Inc. continually introduced new candies. **Mike and Ike** candies, for instance, were first manufactured in 1940. Hot Tamales, a spicy cinnamon candy, were introduced in 1950. In 1953, the company bought the Rodda Candy Company of Lancaster, Pennsylvania, which specialized in marshmallows and **jelly beans**. With this technology, Just Born was able to create Marshmallow Peeps. Sam Born's son joined the company in 1946 and helped to mechanize the marshmallow forming process. Today, Just Born produces more than 4.2 million Marshmallow Peeps each day. In 1977, the company expanded its jelly bean line to include Teenee Beanee Jelly Beans.

Just Born remains a family-owned candy manufacturer. It also makes Root-T-Toot, Cool Kids, and Zours. The company began exporting its products to Canada in the 1990s and now exports to 20 countries.

SUGGESTED READING: Tim Richardson, *Sweets: A History of Candy* (New York: Bloomsbury, 2002).

K

Karcher, Carl N. Carl N. Karcher (1917–) was born near Upper Sandusky, Ohio. His father was sharecropper and the family moved regularly. Karcher dropped out of school and worked long hours on the farm. An uncle in Anaheim, California offered him a job in 1936, and he accepted. When he arrived in southern California, he was amazed at the number of **hot dog** stands on many major street corners. He concluded that operating such a stand could be profitable. He borrowed $311 and purchased a hot dog cart. It was so successful that he bought a second one. By the end of World War II, he owned four. In January 1945, he purchased a restaurant, which he named Carl's Drive-In Barbecue. His business soared after the war.

During the 1950s, Karcher visited the **McDonald** brothers' restaurant in San Bernardino, California. His visit convinced him to open his own **fast food** restaurant. The first **Carl's Jr.** opened in 1956 and Karcher quickly opened many more outlets in California. Ten years later the company incorporated as Carl Karcher Enterprises, Inc. (CKE). In the 1980s, it went public and began selling **franchises** nationwide. In 1988, Karcher and family members were charged with insider trading; he agreed to a settlement. The 1990s were a difficult time for CKE and the company ended up in debt. At that time, Karcher proposed making a deal with Green Burrito, a Mexican restaurant chain in California. The CKE board opposed the deal and ousted Karcher in 1993. Nine months later, he engineered a takeover and had the Green Burrito plan adopted. The corporation turned around in 1997 and Karcher purchased **Hardee's**, making CKE the fourth-largest **hamburger chain** in the world.

SUGGESTED READING: Carl Karcher and B. Carolyn Knight, *Never Stop Dreaming: The Story of Carl Karcher Enterprises* (San Marcos, CA: Robert Erdmann Publishing, 1991); B. Carolyn Knight, *Making It Happen: The Story of Carl Karcher Enterprises* (Anaheim, CA: C. Karcher Enterprises, 1981); Eric Schlosser, *Fast Food Nation: The Dark Side of the All-American Meal* (New York: Houghton Mifflin Company, 2001).

Keebler Godfrey Keebler opened a neighborhood bakery in Philadelphia in 1853. By the beginning of the twentieth century, Keebler products were distributed regionally, and it slowly expanded its operations. By 1944, company consisted of 16 bakeries located from Philadelphia to Salt Lake City. In 1966, Keebler Company became the official corporate name and the brand name for all of its products, and Ernie Keebler and the Elves became company symbols and represented snacks baked in the Hollow Tree. The Keebler jingle was "Man, you never would believe where the Keebler Cookies come from. They're baked by little elves in a hollow tree. And what do you think makes these **cookies** so uncommon? They're baked in magic ovens, and there's no factory. Hey!" The Elves, known for making "uncommonly good" products in a "magic oven," are among the best-recognized **advertising** characters in America. In 1996, Keebler acquired the Sunshine brand, makers of Hydrox cookies. Keebler decided to change Hydrox's flavor and rename the cookie Keebler Droxies. Through its Little Brownie Bakers subsidiary, Keebler is also a leading licensed supplier of **Girl Scout cookies**. Keebler's brands include Cheez-It, Chips Deluxe, **Famous Amos**, Fudge Shoppe, Keebler, Plantation, Sunshine, and Town House. Keebler was acquired by the **Kellogg Company** in 2001. It is the second-largest cookie and cracker manufacturer in the United States.

SUGGESTED READING: Keebler Web site: www.kelloggs.com/keebler

Kellogg Company John Harvey Kellogg established the Battle Creek Toasted Corn Flake Company in 1906. He named his younger brother, Will K. Kellogg, president of the new company. John Harvey Kellogg was unwilling to advertise the company's products. The brothers clashed and Will Kellogg gained control. To enhance sales, Will added **sugar** and other additives to the **cereal**. In its first year, the company shipped 175,000 cases of corn flakes. Within a few years, Kellogg's Corn Flakes had become a household name and could be found in nearly every kitchen in the United States. Will Kellogg expanded operations into Canada and Australia in 1924, followed by Europe and Asia. The name of the company was changed in 1922 to the Will K. Kellogg Company, and was subsequently shortened to the Kellogg Company.

Kellogg's makes many products, including All-Bran (1916), Rice Krispies (1928), Sugar Pops (1950), and Frosted Flakes (1952). The Kellogg Company began producing **snack foods** based on their cereal line, such as Rice Krispies Treats (1995). In 2001, the Kellogg Company acquired the **Keebler** Company, makers of **Famous Amos cookies**, Cheez-It, and many other **junk foods**.

SUGGESTED READING: Scott Bruce and Bill Crawford, *Cerealizing America: The Unsweetened Story of American Breakfast Cereal* (Boston: Faber and Faber, 1995); Gerald Carson, *Cornflake Crusade* (New York: Rinehart & Company, Inc., 1957).

Kentucky Fried Chicken (KFC) Harland Sanders devised his formula for making **fried chicken** at his restaurant in Corbin, Kentucky. He continued to develop it and by the early 1950s he believed that he had a successful formula that could be **franchised**. He attended a foodservice seminar in Chicago, where he met Pete Harmon, who operated a **hamburger** restaurant in Salt Lake City. Harmon became the first franchisee for what would become Kentucky Fried Chicken (KFC). Sander's chicken was the most successful item on Harmon's **menu**—accounting for 50 percent of his entire sales—and he urged Sanders to sell his recipe and methods for frying it nationwide. When Sanders's own restaurant failed in 1955, he went on the road selling franchises. Lacking money to promote his company, he dressed in a distinctive white suit and a black string neck tie, which set off his white hair and white goatee (the Colonel Sanders image). He charged no fee, but franchisees paid him a few cents on each chicken sold. Franchisees were required to display KFC signs and his likeness. It was a good formula for commercial success. By 1963, Sanders had 600 restaurants under license, all of which sold his chicken but had little else in common.

In 1964, Sanders sold KFC to John Y. Brown and Jack Massey for about $2 million, plus an additional salary of $40,000 per year for life to act as a spokesperson for the company. Brown and Massy stopped licensing existing restaurants. In 1966, they required a uniform structure for every franchise. They changed their franchising agreement so that royalties were based on a percentage of sales and franchisees were required to purchase some goods and seasonings from the parent company. In addition, franchisees were charged an annual **advertising** fee, and the company launched a major promotional blitz which cultivated a family image. Brown and Massey quickly expanded franchises. By the late 1960s, its sales exceeded that of **McDonald's**. In 1970, KFC had more than 6,000 franchise agreements. It dominated the **fast food chicken** market and during the early 1970s became the nation's largest commercial foodservice operation.

KFC had an influence upon other fast food **chains**. **Dave Thomas** was a KFC regional manager who worked closely with Harland Sanders. Thomas used the $1 million he generated though KFC to launch his own fast food chain, **Wendy's**, in 1969. When KFC began opening outlets in New Orleans, Al Copeland was encouraged to launch his own chicken chain, which he called **Popeyes**. McDonald's saw the KFC sales figures and created **Chicken McNuggets** to compete in the chicken line. **Burger King** launched a similar product and KFC finally developed a similar product of its own to compete with McNuggets.

In 1971, Brown and Massey sold KFC to the Heublein Company for a reported $280 million. Heublein was purchased by R. J. Reynolds in 1982, which sold it to **PepsiCo** in 1986. Over the years, KFC lost its first-place position among commercial foodservice operations and it was in need of rejuvenation. Due to the public's deep concern with anything fried, the company changed its name from Kentucky Fried Chicken to just KFC, to eliminate the word fried from its name. However, it soon returned to its original name.

KFC began opening outlets in other countries, which have fared extremely well. KFC was the first American fast food chain in Japan. From its start in 1970, it was a joint venture with Mitsubishi Trading Company, which encouraged development of a local menu, such as *yaki-musubi* (grilled riceballs) and *yaki musubi* (toasted riceballs), that would appeal to the Japanese. KFC was one of the first fast food chains in China and today it is the most-recognized foreign brand in China. Today, KFC has outlets in 45 countries and has more restaurants outside the United States than within it.

PepsiCo used KFC and other restaurant chains as outlets for its for its soft drinks. Other large fast food chains, such as McDonald's, refused to dispense Pepsi beverages due to competition with the PepsiCo-owned restaurants. PepsiCo divested itself of KFC and other restaurant subsidiaries by creating Tricon Global Restaurants, later renamed **Yum! Brands**.

SUGGESTED READING: John A. Jakle and Keith A. Sculle, *Fast Food: Roadside Restaurants in the Automobile Age* (Baltimore: Johns Hopkins University Press, 1999); John Ed Pearce, *The Colonel: The Captivating Biography of the Dynamic Founder of a Fast-food Empire* (Garden City, NY: Doubleday, 1982); Harland Sanders, *Life as I Have Known It Has Been Finger Lickin' Good* (Carol Stream, IL: Creation House, 1974).

Ketchup The word *ketchup* derives from the Amoy dialect of Mandarin, and originally meant a pickled fish or fermented sauce. British colonists brought ketchup recipes to

North America and Americans continued to experiment with it, using a variety of additional main ingredients, including beans and apples. Tomato ketchup may have originated in America. It was widely used throughout the United States in the early nineteenth century.

Small quantities of tomato ketchup were bottled in the 1850s. After the Civil War, commercial production of ketchup rapidly increased. One commercial producer was the H.J. Heinz Company, which first sold tomato ketchup in 1873. At that time it was not among Heinz's important products. By 1890, Heinz hit upon the now world-famous combination of the keystone label, the neck band, the screw cap, and the octagonal-shaped ketchup bottle. This bottle has become a culinary icon throughout the world. Shortly after the turn of the century, the H.J. Heinz Company was the largest tomato ketchup producer and it remains so today.

Another ketchup manufacturer was the Del Monte Corporation of San Francisco, which began bottling ketchup by 1915. It rapidly expanded production during the 1940s. Yet another manufacturer was the Hunt Brothers Packing Company, which began producing ketchup during the 1930s. Today, Heinz, Del Monte, and Hunt's are the three largest ketchup producers in the world.

Initially, ketchup was used as a cooking ingredient for making savory pies, as an ingredient in sauces, and as a condiment for meat, poultry, and fish. In about 1900, ketchup became mainly a condiment with the invention of three major host foods: **hamburgers**, **hot dogs**, and **French fries**. Ketchup has expanded along with the ever-growing **fast food chains**, where it is dispensed in single-serve packets or in large plastic dispensers with push-pumps. Overall, Americans purchase ten billion ounces per year, averaging out to about three bottles per person. Worldwide, more than 840 million 14-ounce bottles of Heinz ketchup are sold annually.

By the end of the twentieth century, ketchup was used the world over. Mainly due to the expansion of fast food chains, ketchup expanded rapidly throughout Latin America, Europe, Australia, and East and Southeast Asia. Few other sauces or **condiments** have transcended local and national culinary traditions as has tomato ketchup. Some denounce it as an American culinary atrocity and others condemn it as a promoter of global homogenization. Others view it as the Esperanto of cuisine.

SUGGESTED READING: Andrew F. Smith, *Pure Ketchup: The History of America's National Condiment* (Columbia, SC: The University of South Carolina Press, 1996).

Klondike Bar The Klondike bar consists of a vanilla **ice cream** square encased in a layer of **chocolate** on the outside. It was invented in about 1922 by the Isaly family, who owned the Mansfield Pure Milk Company in Mansfield, Ohio. The bar is believed that it was named after the Klondike River in the Canadian Yukon territory that was made famous by the 1890s gold rush. The bar was initially made on a stick and included several different flavors. It was made by hand at the family's store near Youngstown, Ohio, and later by the Isaly Dairy Company of Pittsburgh, founded in 1931. In 1967, the company's operations were consolidated in Pittsburgh.

Until the 1970s, Klondike bars were sold only in Ohio, western Pennsylvania, and West Virginia. In 1972, the company was sold to a group of investors, and 5 years later the Clabir Corporation purchased it and expanded distribution to Philadelphia, Florida, New York, and New England. In 1982, the company began a national advertising campaign featuring the jingle, "What would you do for a Klondike Bar?" It quickly became America's best-selling novelty ice cream bar. In 1993, the Isaly Klondike Company was acquired by **Unilever** and it was folded into a subsidiary, which also sold **Good Humor** bars and **Breyers** ice cream.

SUGGESTED READING: Brian Butko, *Klondikes, Chipped Ham & Skyscraper Cones: The Story of Isaly's* (Mechanicsburg, PA: Stackpole Books, 2001); Klondike Web site: www.unileverusa.com/ourbrands/foods/klondike.asp

Kool-Aid Kool-Aid, a powdered fruit-flavored beverage, was created by Edwin Perkins, head of the Perkins Products Company of Hastings, Nebraska. The firm manufactured a wide array of products sold through mail order. In 1920, Perkins marketed his first soft drink concentrate, Fruit Smack, a bottled syrup intended to be combined with water and **sugar**. Fruit Smack was successful but the bottles were heavy, which increased mailing expenses, and the bottles often broke in transit, which upset customers and required the company to refund money. Inspired by the tremendous success of **Jell-O** dessert powder, Perkins designed a powdered **beverage** concentrate that could be sold in paper packets, thus reducing expenses. Customers were only required to combine the powder with water and sugar.

In 1927, the packets were first sold through the mail for 10 cents apiece. The original six flavors were cherry, grape, lemon-lime, orange, raspberry, and strawberry. As the sales of Kool-Aid increased, Perkins phased out the company's other products and focused on marketing Kool-Aid. Rather then just sell it by mail, Perkins began an aggressive campaign to sell Kool-Aid through grocery stores. By 1929, it was sold throughout the United States. During the Depression, Perkins lowered the price of Kool-Aid to a nickel a packet and launched a major national **advertising** campaign aimed at children. Perkins tried to expand his Kool-Aid product line with pie fillings and **ice cream** mixes, but they were never as successful as his powdered beverage. During World War II, sugar was rationed and the manufacture of Kool-Aid was limited, but after the war Kool-Aid sales took off, enjoying its heyday in the 1950s.

In 1953, Perkins sold his company to **General Foods**, which added additional flavors, such as **Root Beer** and Lemon, in 1955. Presweetened Kool-Aid was first marketed in 1964. In 1988, General Foods merged with **Kraft Foods**, which launched new product lines, such as Kool-Aid Slushies and ready-to-drink Kool-Aid Splash. When Kool-Aid celebrated its 75th anniversary in 2002, the Museum of Natural and Cultural History, in Hastings, Nebraska installed a permanent exhibition of the company's memorabilia and history.

For many Americans, Kool-Aid evokes images of childhood, innocent summer fun, and a cool refreshment. Its longtime advertising image, a smiling face drawn in the condensation on an icy pitcher of Kool-Aid, has become a national icon.

SUGGESTED READING: Hastings Museum of Natural and Cultural History's Web site: www.hastingsmuseum.org

Kraft Foods In 1903, a Canadian named James L. Kraft began wholesaling cheese in Chicago. His brothers joined him in the business and in 1914 J. L. Kraft & Bros. opened a cheese factory in Stockton, Illinois, and in the following years began producing processed cheese in tins. During World War I, the company acquired a contract to supply process cheese to the American armed forces.

The company rapidly expanded aborad, opening an office in London (1924) and Germany (1927). In 1928, the Kraft Cheese Company acquired the Phenix Cheese Corporation, makers of Philadelphia Brand cream cheese, and renamed the company Kraft-Phenix Cheese Corporation. The parent company changed its name to Kraft, Inc. in 1976.

In 1988, Kraft was acquired by Philip Morris Companies, Inc. The food products divisions of Philip Morris—**General Foods** and Kraft—were joined to become Kraft Foods, Inc., in 1995. In 2000, **Nabisco** Holdings were acquired by Philip Morris and its brands were also integrated into the Kraft Foods. Today Kraft Foods, Inc., now a division of Altrie, markets over 70 major brands, including DiGiorno Pizza, **Jell-O**, **Tang**, **Kool-Aid**, **Tombstone Pizza**, and the **chocolate** bar **Toblerone**.

SUGGESTED READING: Kraft Foods Web site: www.kraft.com

Krispy Kreme In 1937, Vernon Rudolph launched a **doughnut** shop, which became known as Krispy Kreme, in Winston-Salem, North Carolina. He sold doughnuts to local grocery stores and to customers through a window in his small factory. During the 1940s, Rudolph opened other outlets for his doughnuts, particularly in the Southeast. Rudolph died in 1973 and Beatrice Foods purchased the company in 1976. A small group of investors purchased the **chain** from Beatrice in 1982. Krispy Kreme rapidly expanded its operation, opening its first outlet in New York in 1996, California (1999), and Toronto (2001). Krispy Kreme also sells doughnuts through grocery stores. In 2005, they were the largest selling doughnut in this category.

SUGGESTED READING: Krispy Kreme Web site: www.krispykreme.com

Kroc, Ray Raymond Albert Kroc (1902–1984), who created the **fast food** empire of **McDonald's**, was born in Oak Park, Illinois. He held various jobs, including selling beans, sheet music, Florida real estate, and an instant beverage. He became a Lily Cup salesman and later sold restaurant supplies. These positions gave him a broad knowledge of **soda fountain** and restaurant operations. In 1938, he became an agent for the Multimixer, a machine that could make several **milk shakes** simultaneously. A few years later he purchased the company. After World War II, the company thrived by selling Multimixers to operators of **ice cream** chains such as **Dairy Queen**. When the Dairy Queen franchisees created a national trade association in 1948, Kroc attended their first meeting. Through his association with Dairy Queen franchisees Kroc learned how **franchising** worked and came to understand the many problems facing franchisees.

During the early 1950s, the sale of Multimixers began to slide and Kroc began looking for ways to increase sales. Most restaurants bought a single Multimixer, but Kroc noted that a small fast food restaurant in San Bernardino, California had bought several. When Kroc read advertisements and articles about Richard and Maurice McDonald's fast food operation, Kroc decided to pay them a visit. Kroc liked what he saw and he struck an agreement with the brothers to sell franchises nationally. Kroc opened his first McDonald's in Des Plaines, Illinois in 1955, the same year he launched McDonald's Systems, Inc.

Kroc's relationship with McDonald's brothers was stormy from the beginning. The brothers wanted to maintain the quality of the chain that bore their name, and therefore required that all McDonald's outlets be precisely the same as their own They were inflexible on this matter, and this meant that Kroc could not change or improve upon their model.

In 1961, Kroc borrowed $2.7 million and bought the company from the brothers. At the time it had 228 outlets. The McDonald brothers insisted on keeping their San Bernardino restaurant, which was renamed the Big M. Eventually Kroc opened a McDonald's restaurant across the street and ran the Big M out of business.

Kroc took McDonald's national, creating a fast food empire. To do this, Kroc developed a three-tiered business system composed of corporate managers, franchisees, and suppliers. He was a strong believer in KISS—"Keep it simple, Stupid." His goal was to simplify all activities in the restaurants and reduce the level of complexity and the range of responsibilities for each of his employees. His organizing concepts were "Quality, Service, Cleanliness, and Value."

In 1972, Ray Kroc gave an illegal personal contribution of $250,000 to the presidential reelection campaign of Richard Nixon. It was uncovered during the Watergate scandal in 1974. Although it was a personal contribution, it turned out to be a public relations disaster for McDonald's. Kroc retired from managing the company in 1977. When he died in 1984, there were more than 7,500 McDonald's outlets.

SUGGESTED READING: Anne Cooper Funderburg, *Sundae Best: A History of Soda Fountains* (Bowling Green, OH: Bowling Green State University Popular Press, 2002); Ray Kroc, with Robert Anderson, *Grinding It Out: The Making of McDonald's* (Chicago: Henry Regnery Company, 1977); Philip Langdon, *Orange Roofs, Golden Arches: The Architecture of American Chain Restaurants* (New York: Knopf, 1986).

L

Lawsuits The **snack food** and **fast food** industries have been rife with lawsuits. Some have been initiated by corporations against other corporations, particularly related to trademark infringement. **Pepperidge Farm**, makers of **Goldfish**, sued **Nabisco** for trademark infringement when the latter manufactured CatDog crackers, an orange-colored cheese snack, some of which were shaped like fish. Pepperidge Farms won. When **Mars** tried to launch a version of **M&Ms** peanuts that copied the coloring and styling of **Hershey's** Reese's Pieces, Hershey sued, claiming that Mars was trying to capitalize on Hershey's goodwill and investment in Reese's Pieces. Hershey's won.

Individuals and groups have filed numerous lawsuits against **junk food** and fast food companies. The most well-known was 81-year-old Stella Liebeck's suit against **McDonald's**. She had bought a cup of coffee at a McDonald's drive-in window in Albuquerque in 1992 and, when she removed the lid, the coffee spilled onto her lap, causing third-degree burns. Her suit, filed in state court in Albuquerque, claimed the coffee was "defective" because it was so hot. The jury awarded her $2.9 million and McDonald's decreased the temperature of its coffee.

In another famous case, reminiscent of the lawsuits against tobacco companies, in 2002 Samuel Hirsch sued McDonald's, **Wendy's**, **Kentucky Fried Chicken**, and **Burger King** for contributing to **obesity**. He believed fast food chains violated New York state's consumer fraud statutes by deliberately misleading consumers that their food was healthy and nutritious. The suit claimed that the fast food restaurants contributed to or caused obesity and subsequent health problems. A revised lawsuit alleged that McDonald's engaged in deceptive **advertising**, in part because it failed to adequately disclose additives and processing methods in its **Chicken McNuggets**, Filet-O-Fish, Chicken Sandwich, **French fries**, and **hamburgers**. More lawsuits are expected. To head them off, the industry engaged in a massive public relations campaign. In 2004, the National Restaurant Association led the effort to pass the Personal Responsibility in Food Consumption Act (H.R. 339) in Congress to exempt fast food chains from lawsuits related to obesity. It passed in the House, but was not voted on in the Senate.

Yet another lawsuit was instituted against McDonald's for falsely claiming that its French flies contained no animal fat. In fact, the frying oil contained beef tallow. The company paid out millions in damages to vegetarians and devout Hindus living in the United States.

Likewise, individuals have filed lawsuits against junk food companies. For instance, lawsuits have been initiated against **Frito-Lay**, Inc. for its inclusion of olestra (Olean) in some of its so-called light snack foods.

In an unusual case, a company filed suit against two individuals, Helen Steel and Dave Morris, who passed out leaflets in front of McDonald's outlets in London. McDonald's claimed that the leaflet had libeled them. Dubbed **McLibel**, the lawsuit ended up being the longest case in British history and was a tremendous public relations disaster for McDonald's.

Some lawsuits have been fraudulent. On March 22, 2005, Anna Ayala of San Jose, California, reported finding a human finger in her bowl of chili served at Wendy's. She hired a lawyer with the intention of suing Wendy's, but in the days following she decided not to do so. Wendy's hired private investigators, who found no evidence that the finger had any connection with the company. Wendy's claimed that the incident decreased sales by an estimated $2.5 million at Wendy's restaurants and offered a $100,000 reward for information leading to the finger's original owner. On April 22, Ayala was arrested, and a month later San Jose police reported that the finger, which had been lost in an industrial accident, was that of an acquaintance of Ayala's husband. In September, 2005, Ayala and her husband pled guilty to conspiring to file a false claim and attempted grand theft.

SUGGESTED READING: Fred Charatan, "Lawyers Poised to Sue US Junk Food Manufacturers," *British Medical Journal*, 324 (June 15, 2002), 1414; Kelly D. Brownell and Katherine Battle Horgen, *Food Fight: The Inside Story of the Food Industry, America's Obesity Crisis, and What We Can Do about It* (Chicago: Contemporary Books, 2004); John Vidal, *McLibel: Burger Culture on Trial* (New York: The New Press, 1997).

Licorice Historically, licorice (or liquorice) was made from about twenty species of glycyrrhiza, a small, leguminous shrub native to Europe, Asia, and the Americas. The wild American licorice, *Glycyrrhiza lepidota,* has not been commercialized, but European licorice (*Glycyrrhiza glabra*) was imported into America by English colonists. Licorice was one of the earliest confections sold in stores. The plant's long, thick roots and rhizomes contain an aromatic sweet liquid that tastes bitter due to other substances. Large quantities of **sugar** are mixed with licorice extract along with thickeners to give it a sweet, pliable texture. Historically, licorice was considered a medicine and was used to make comfits. In was also used as a flavoring and coloring in gingerbread, beers, and liquors.

Licorice was sold as **penny candy** in grocery stores, and it forms the base for **Good & Plenty**, first marketed in 1893. Twizzlers, another common licorice-flavored candy, were first made in 1929 by Y & S Candies, which originated as Young and Smylie in 1845. In 1870, the company adopted the trademark of Y & S. In 1904, Y & S merged with two other candy companies to create the National Licorice Company. Y & S Candies was acquired by the **Hershey Company** in 1977. Today, Twizzlers come in a variety of sizes, shapes, and flavors, including strawberry, cherry, and chocolate. Similar in appearance to Twizzlers are Red Vines, which are made by the American Licorice Company of Union City, California. Today, most licorice is mass-produced with synthetic ingredients.

SUGGESTED READING: Laura Mason, *Sugar-Plums and Sherbet: The Prehistory of Sweets* (Devon, UK: Prospect Books, 2004); Tim Richardson, *Sweets: A History of Candy* (New York: Bloomsbury, 2002); Hershey Company Web site: www.hersheys.com/twizzlers

LifeSavers Clarence Crane, a **chocolate** confectioner in Cleveland, Ohio, had a problem—the pure chocolate that he used in his shop melted during the hot summer months. He began experimentation on a hard **candy** that he could sell during warm weather. He saw a druggist using a hand-operated pill-making machine and concluded he could use a similar machine to make candies. In 1912, he had created a small, round mint candy with a hole in the middle. Because they resembled ships' floating life savers, he named them accordingly. Crane packaged his LifeSavers in cardboard boxes, but the boxes' glue seeped into the candy and grocers refused to stock them. In 1913, Crane sold the manufacturing rights to Edward Noble, owner of the Mint Products Company of New York. To solve the glue problem, Noble repackaged the mints and wrapped them in tinfoil wrappers and sold them for a nickel. Due to their previous experience, grocers still refused to stock them, so Noble sold them to bars where displays were installed next to the cash registers. The mint candy served as a lifesaver to those who frequented bars but did not want others to know they had been drinking. In 1915, the United Cigar Store **chain** placed the displays in their many stores, and LifeSavers became successful. They are considered the first impulse food item.

LifeSavers. © Kelly Fitzsimmons

LifeSavers were made by hand until 1919, when machinery was acquired to manufacture them en mass. Noble marketed them to drugstores, grocery stores, and other retail stores, encouraging proprietors to place them by the cash register. For 10 years, the company only made Pep-O-Mint LifeSavers; later, it added fruit-flavored ones without the holes. By 1929, the fruit-flavored ones acquired holes and, five years later, the five flavors were combined to form the Five Flavor LifeSavers Roll. LifeSavers were manufactured in Canada by 1920; by 1969, the company's plant in Hamilton, Ontario produced a score of different flavors and more than a billion LifeSavers annually. In 1956, LifeSavers Candies acquired Beech-Nut, makers of **gum** and baby food. LifeSaver Candies in turn was acquired by **Kraft Foods**, which in 2004 sold LifeSavers to the **Wrigley Company**.

SUGGESTED READING: Ray Broekel, *The Great America Candy Bar Book* (Boston: Houghton Mifflin Company, 1982); Thomas Hine, *The Total Package: The Evolution and Secret Meanings of Boxes, Bottles, Cans, and Tubes* (New York: Little, Brown and Company, 1995); Tim Richardson, *Sweets: A History of Candy* (New York: Bloomsbury, 2002).

Little Caesar's Pizza In the 1950s, **Mike Ilitch** began making **pizza** in the kitchen of a Detroit night club. At the time, pizza was a minor **fast food**. Ilitch's operation, however, proved so successful that in 1959 Mike and Marian Ilitch opened a pizza restaurant, called Little Caesars Pizza Treat, in a strip mall in Garden City, Michigan. From the beginning, the Little Caesar logo was part of the operation.

Little Caesar's Pizza's carry-out operation was one of the chain's claims to fame, because its promotion campaign offered two pizzas for the price of one. This was the basis for the Little Caesar mascot and his famous **advertising** line "Pizza! Pizza!" which the company trademarked. The company quickly expanded and by 1987 was operating throughout the United States and in parts of Canada. Little Caesar's remains a privately owned company. The company is the world's largest carry-out pizza **chain**. Little Caesar's ranks eleventh among restaurant chains in America.

SUGGESTED READING: Little Caesar's Web site: www.littlecaesars.com

Little Debbie According to tradition, the Little Debbie logo was inspired by a photo of the four-year-old granddaughter of O. D. McKee, the founder of McKee Foods. Pearl Mann, an Atlanta artist, did the original artwork for the Little Debbie brand, which made four-year-old Debbie look older. It was not until after the first cartons had been printed in 1960 that Debbie's parents found out that their daughter's name and likeness were used on McKee Food's Oatmeal Creme Pie.

By 1964, the company was manufacturing 14 different products, and all had Little Debbie's image. The best-selling Little Debbie products include Swiss Cake Rolls, Nutty Bars Wafer Bars, Oatmeal Creme Pies, and Fudge Brownies. The company also licenses Little Debbie-style Barbie Dolls and Little Debbie Hot Wheels car sets. McKee Foods Corporation is a privately held company headquartered in Collegedale, Tennessee. Little Debbie products are also sold in Canada and Mexico. As of 2005, Little Debbie cakes manufactured by McKee Foods were the best-selling cakes in America.

SUGGESTED READING: Little Debbie Web site: www.littledebbie.com

Lobbying Lobbying—the act of trying to influence a government official—has become a major activity of **fast food chains** and **junk food** manufacturers as well as advocacy groups and nonpartisan organizations.

The late nineteenth and twentieth century was a period of intense political ferment regarding food. Large corporations maintain their own lobbyists in Washington, D.C. or hire firms to represent their interests. Corporations also join associations, which also lobby for or against legislation.

Many makers of confections adulterated their products by including colorings and flavorings that were harmful for the consumer. The **National Confectioners Association** (NCA) was formed in 1884 to foster industry self-regulation and lobby against adulterants. The NCA lobbied for passage of state pure food laws and, with its support, legislation was passed in New York state in the late nineteenth century.

During World War II, the NCA lobbied to ensure that candy would be declared an "essential food," thus ensuring that at least some members of the association received **sugar** rations. The NCA maintains a full-time lobbyist who has weighed in on NCA issues such as excise taxes on confections, sugar and peanut price supports, nutritional labeling laws, and issues related to international trade.

Corporations also have established alliances that support particular positions, such as the recently created American Council on Fitness and Nutrition, which has lobbied against national standards for **school** food.

In addition to formal lobbyists, fast food and junk food manufacturers have also contributed to political campaigns. Such contributions have not always been legal. In 1972 **Ray Kroc**, founder of **McDonald's**, a secretly gave $250,000 to President Richard Nixon's reelection campaign, which was against the law. To avoid detection, he divided his contribution into smaller donations, which he gave to different Republican agencies. During the Watergate scandal, these contributions came to light. At the time, McDonald's and other fast food chains were lobbying Congress to pass the so-called McDonald's bill that would allow employers to pay 16- to 17-year-old employees less than minimum wage. It was believed that Kroc made his contribution to buy the Nixon's administration's support for the legislation. The legislation did not pass.

Similarly, many grassroots groups organized to support the passage of pure food and drug acts in state legislatures and at the federal level. This effort achieved success with the passage of the Pure Food and Drug Act in 1906. Today, nonprofit and advocacy groups have lobbied for many issues. The **Center for Science in the Public Interest (CSPI)**, for instance, has lobbied on matters related to food safety and **nutrition**.

SUGGESTED READING: Marion Nestle, *Food Politics: How the Food Industry Influences Nutrition and Health* (Berkeley, CA: University of California Press, 2002); Eric Schlosser, *Fast Food Nation: The Dark Side of the All-American Meal* (New York: Houghton Mifflin Company, 2001).

Locations As with other retail businesses, one of the most important decisions that must be made is the location for **fast food chain** outlets. Beginning with the first fast food chains, such as **White Castle** and its clone **White Tower**, site selection for outlets was crucial: they selected urban areas near mass transit stops (train, trolley, subway, or bus stops). As **automobiles** became more common during the 1920s, **drive-ins** began constructing their outlets along highways, intersections, and in places where property values permitted them to buy, rent, or lease inexpensive space for large parking lots.

Thomas Carvel, founder of the **Carvel Corporation**, thought that the best place for **ice cream** stores was on secondary highways with free-flowing traffic moving along at a slow speed (25 mph or less). The problem with major highways was that automobiles sped by too fast and drivers were unable to stop. Likewise, highways where traffic was frequently snarled were not ideal, because potential customers were more interested in getting through the congestion than stopping for an ice cream. There also had to be a large enough permanent population in an area so that the store could generate repeat customers. Carvel brought in "location engineers" when he was in doubt; they used counters to determine the number of cars and people who passed by a given location.

After World War II, when families began to flee inner cities and buy homes in the suburbs, new criteria for site locations were used. **Ray Kroc** of **McDonald's** was one of the first to recognize the importance of this shift. He refused to build outlets in major urban areas and he carefully selected sites in fast-growing suburban communities. The chain bought satellite photos, which they used to predict suburban sprawl and determine locations for their outlets. Kroc personally selected many of the early McDonald's locations, occasionally traveling by helicopter to select the best location for an outlet. While Kroc may have been able to accurately predict areas that would grow, his successors employed a computer software program called *Quintillion—A Geographic Information System* for projecting suburban growth and identifying good potential site locations. Other fast food chains, such as **Burger King**, have used similar systems to select their sites.

During the 1950s and 1960s, suburban locations made sense. These areas were rapidly growing, particularly with families, and McDonald's and other fast food chains had concluded that their real target was children. In addition, **crime** and civil unrest was endemic to many inner cities, while suburbs tended to have less crime. Finally, fast food outlets were oriented toward automobiles because the outlets had few indoor eating areas in them until the late 1960s. As soon as indoor eating areas became common, fast food chains reexamined their decision not to open outlets in urban areas. In the 1970s, McDonald's, Burger King, and other fast food chains reversed their long-held policy of staying out of urban areas. By the end of that decade virtually all national fast food chains were present in large cities.

Some chains have used different strategies. For instance, **A&W Root Beer**, **Hardee's**, and **Dairy Queen** have intentionally selected small towns as their preferred locations for outlets. Still others have selected particular venues as profitable. For instance, Orange Julius targeted shopping malls and **Cinnabon** targeted airports.

During the late twentieth century and early twenty-first century, a number of other changes have occurred. Due to the acquisition of many different restaurant chains by single owners, such as **Yum! Brands**, co-branding, multibranding, and bundling have become common. In these locations, a single site will feature two or more different types of noncompeting fast foods, such as **pizza**, **hamburgers**, and ice cream. In addition, several fast food establishments have begun co-branding with other businesses, such as K-Marts, Wal-Marts, and gas stations. For instance, **Blimpie** had co-branded with Texaco and many Texaco gas stations now have Blimpie restaurants.

The fast food industry is considered mature in the United States, and placements of new outlets has become more difficult. Most fast food companies, however, have been rapidly expanding in other countries and different location criteria have been needed for development in each nation.

SUGGESTED READING: Anne Cooper Funderburg, *Chocolate, Strawberry, and Vanilla: A History of American Ice Cream* (Bowling Green, OH: Bowling Green State University Popular Press, 1995); John A. Jakle and Keith A. Sculle, *Fast Food: Roadside Restaurants in the Automobile Age* (Baltimore: Johns Hopkins University Press, 1999); Eric Schlosser, *Fast Food Nation: The Dark Side of the All-American Meal* (New York: Houghton Mifflin Company, 2001).

Lollipops and Suckers Lollipops are a hard **candy** made mainly of **sugar** or treacle. They first appeared in England in the late eighteenth century. References to them appear in the works of Charles Dickens and they were popularized at the 1851 Great Exposition in London. When sticks were added by hand in the late nineteenth century, lollipops, also called suckers in the United States, became an important early commercial candy in America. An early manufacturer of lollipops was George Smith, owner of a confectionery business called the Bradley Smith Company in New Haven, Connecticut.

Samuel Born, a Russian immigrant, founded the **Just Born** Candy Company in New York. He is credited with inventing the Born Sucker Machine, which automatically inserted sticks into lollipops. This invention revolutionized the sucker industry. Many companies began producing stick candy with various names during the twentieth century. The Spangler Candy Company of Bryan, Ohio, for instance, manufactured suckers beginning in 1922. They manufactured Dum Dum suckers two years later. The James O. Welch Company introduced **caramel**-covered Sugar Daddies in 1926, followed by Sugar Babies in 1935. The latter two are manufactured today by **Tootsie Roll** Industries.

SUGGESTED READING: Tim Richardson, *Sweets: A History of Candy* (New York: Bloomsbury, 2002); Spangler Candy Company Web site: www.spanglercandy.com

Long John Silver's In 1969, Long John Silver's **Fish 'n' Chips** was launched by Jerrico, Inc. of Lexington, Kentucky. Its name was derived from a character in Robert Louis Stevenson's *Treasure Island.* Its first outlet proved successful and **franchising** began the following year. Its first restaurants were small and the **architecture** was intended to resemble a building from an early American fishing village.

Initially, Long John Silver's featured fried battered fish and grilled fish along with **French fries** and cole slaw. Its menu has evolved and now includes seafood, **chicken**, **sandwiches**, salads, and desserts.

In 1989, senior management and a New York investment firm acquired Jerrico and its subsidiaries in a leveraged buyout. Long John Silver's had difficult times and went bankrupt in 1998. The following year it was merged with **A&W Root Beer** to form Yorkshire Global Restaurants based in Lexington, Kentucky. Yorkshire Global Restaurants, in turn, was purchased by Tricon Global Restaurants (now **Yum! Brands**) in 2002. As of 2005, there were 1,200 Long John Silver's restaurants in the United States, 200 in multibranded restaurants, and 33 in other countries. It is the largest **fast food** fish **chain** in America.

SUGGESTED READING: John A. Jakle and Keith A. Sculle, *Fast Food: Roadside Restaurants in the Automobile Age* (Baltimore: Johns Hopkins University Press, 1999); Long John Silver's Web site: www.ljsilvers.com

M

M&M's During the 1930s, **Forrest Mars**, the son of the founder of **Mars, Inc.**, established a **chocolate** manufacturing company in Chicago along with Bruce Murrie, the son of the president of the **Hershey Company**. Because both of their last names started with M, they called their new company M&M. In 1940, they launched their first product, which they named M&M's Chocolate Candies. These were small, colorful, round, **candy**-covered chocolates. They were packaged in paper tubes, which made them easy to carry around.

Mars, Inc. tradition has it that the idea for M&M's was based on Forrest Mars's visit to Spain during the Spanish Civil War (1936–1937). He saw soldiers eating chocolate candies covered with a layer of hard **sugar**. It is more likely that Forrest Mars acquired the idea from Smarties, which are small, round, colorful, sugar-coated chocolates that had been introduced in England by **Rowntree's of York** in 1937. Smarties were packaged in paper tubes. Forrest Mars later claimed that he had encouraged Rowntree's to produce candy bars and Smarties, which could well have been true.

The original M&M colors were red, yellow, green, orange, brown, and violet. These have been changed over the years, with some colors added and others removed. M&M's candies were popularized during World War II, when they were included in soldiers' rations. In 1948, M&M's were packaged in brown plastic bags, and later the company introduced M&M Peanut Chocolate Candies, which were packaged in yellow plastic bags. After the war, the relationship between Mars and Murrie became strained, and in 1949 Forrest Mars bought out Murrie for $1 million. He subsequently changed the name of M&M to Food Manufacturers, Inc. and it later merged with Mars, Inc.

During the 1950s, Forrest launched a major **advertising** campaign in national newspapers and magazines, **radio** spots, and billboards. By 1949, annual sales had increased to $3 million. The **slogan** for M&M candies was an immediate success: "The milk chocolate that melts in your mouth, not in your hand." Cartoon characters, Mr. Plain and Mr. Peanut, went along with the advertisements in 1954. Another commercial featured M&M's jumping into pool of chocolate. The advertisement ran on **television**, on the *Howdy Doody Show* and the *Mickey Mouse Club*. By 1956, M&M sales topped $40 million, ranking them the most popular candy in America.

In 1976, the U.S. Food and Drug Administration released a study correlating cancer with red dye food coloring. Even though M&M's did not include this dye, Mars pulled

M&M's. © Kelly Fitzsimmons

the red candies to avoid consumer misperception. Ten years passed before Mars reintroduced red M&M's.

Over the years, the company has made many additions to the M&M's product line. It released Peanut Butter M&M's to compete with "Reese's Pieces," but their sales peaked in 1991. Other additions include Almond Chocolate Candies and MINIS Mega Tubes. In 2000, the name of plain M&M's was changed to M&M's Milk Chocolate Candies. Peanut M&M's are America's most popular confection and M&M's are also sold around the globe, generating annual revenue of more than $2 billion.

SUGGESTED READING: Joël Glenn Brenner, *The Emperors of Chocolate: Inside the Secret World of Hershey and Mars* (New York: Broadway Books, 2000); Mars Web site: www.mms.com; Janice Pottker, *Crisis in Candyland: Melting the Chocolate Shell of the Mars Family Empire* (Bethesda, MD: National Press Books, 1995); Gerry Schremp, *Kitchen Culture: Fifty Years of Food Fads, From Spam to Spa Cuisine* (New York: Pharos Books, 1991).

Mad Cow Disease Bovine spongiform encephalitis (BSE), commonly known as mad cow disease, is a fatal disease affecting the bovine central nervous system. BSE was first discovered in the United Kingdom in 1986, but it was thought that it could not be transmitted to humans. It infected cattle that had consumed a protein-rich diet of remnants of rendered carcasses and bones of sheep, cattle, pigs, horses, chickens, and dogs and cats from animal shelters. However, it is an infectious, degenerative disease that can be transmitted to humans, causing a illness similar to Creutzfeldt-Jakob disease (CJD), although the relationship between the two diseases remains unclear. An epidemic of BSE hit England, France, and Italy in the mid-1990s; 157 people are known to have been infected and all died. It is acquired by eating infected beef that has not been cooked long enough.

As of 2005, six BSE-infected cows have been identified in North America. There is no known cure and the only known solution is prevention—not feeding cattle the rendered meal obtained from butchered animals, and cooking beef properly.

SUGGESTED READING: Laurie Winn Carlson, *Cattle: An Informal Social History* (Chicago: Ivan R. Dee, 2001); Elizabeth Connor, *Internet Guide to Food Safety and Security* (New York: Haworth Information Press, 2005); Carmen Ferreiro, *Mad Cow Disease (Bovine Spongiform Encephalopathy)* (Philadelphia: Chelsea House Publishers, 2005); Walter Gratzer, *Terrors of the Table: The Curious History of Nutrition* (New York: Oxford University Press, 2005).

Marriott Corporation J. Willard Marriott opened an **A&W Root Beer** stand in 1927 in Washington, D.C. Two years later, he created the Marriott Corporation, which is better known for its hotel operations. The company also developed an extensive foodservice operation, serving institutions, **schools**, colleges, and universities. In 1967, it launched the **Roy Rogers chain**, makers of roast beef **sandwiches**. It purchased the Gino's chain in 1982 and converted 180 of its restaurants to the Roy Rogers brand. The company acquired the Howard Johnson chain in 1987 and launched Farrell's Ice Cream Parlours, and has owned or held limited franchise rights to **Big Boy**, **Popeyes**, **Dunkin' Donuts**, **Burger King**, **Dairy Queen**, Denny's, and **El Pollo Loco** chains. The Marriott Corporation split in two and the food service division became the Host Marriott Corporation in 1993.

SUGGESTED READING: John A. Jakle and Keith A. Sculle, *Fast Food: Roadside Restaurants in the Automobile Age* (Baltimore: Johns Hopkins University Press, 1999).

Mars, Forrest Forrest Edward Mars (1904–1999) was the son of **Frank Mars**, the founder of **Mars, Inc.**, and Frank's first wife Ethel. Forrest's parents divorced and he did not see his father again until 1922, when he began working with Frank at Mars, Inc. Forrest later claimed that he invented the **Milky Way** bar, which was launched in 1923.

After a quarrel, Frank Mars removed Forrest from Mars, Inc. in 1932. Forrest was given $50,000 and the foreign rights to the Milky Way. Forrest traveled to Europe, where he claimed to have learned the **chocolate** business in Switzerland by working in various chocolate companies, including those of Tobler and **Nestlé**. Forrest moved to England, where he consulted with **Rowntree's of York**, assisting that company in producing the Kit Kat bar 1935 and subsequently other **candy** bars. Rowntree's also began manufacturing Smarties, a small, round chocolate enclosed in candy. Forrest opened a factory in Slough, England, and began to manufacture a sweeter version of the Milky Way bar with a new name, the Mars bar. By 1939, Mars, Ltd. was ranked as Britain's third-largest candy manufacturer. Mars opened a factory in Brussels, hoping to sell Mars bars across Europe, but the outbreak of World War II ended these activities.

In the United States, Forrest Mars went into a limited partnership with Bruce Murrie, son of William Murrie, the president of the **Hershey Company**. Forrest Mars put up 80 percent of the capital and Murrie 20 percent, and Forrest was in charge of the company, which was named M&M Inc., for the first initial of their respective last names. As a result of the partnership, Hershey supplied M&M Inc. with all the chocolate they wanted. Hershey also supplied M&M, Inc. with equipment and technical advice. The new company introduced **M&M's** in 1940. Because **sugar** and chocolate were rationed during the war, Forrest bought a rice mill in 1942 and launched Uncle Ben's Rice. After the war, M&M launched print **advertisements** in national newspapers and magazines, **radio** spots, and billboards. In 1949, Forrest Mars bought out Bruce Murrie for $1 million. The company, M&M, Inc., was eventually renamed Food Manufacturers, Inc.

Now completely in charge of the company, Forrest Mars hired Ted Bates & Co., an advertising firm in Chicago, to help market the company's products. Bates came up with the slogan "Melts in your mouth, not in your hand," which was an instant success. The company added Peanut M&M's in 1954 and introduced the cartoon characters Mr. Plain and Mr. Peanut in the same year. Bates also developed a **television** commercial of M&M's jumping into pool of chocolate; the company's advertisements ran on the television *Howdy Doody Show* and the *Mickey Mouse Club*. By 1956, M&M's annual sales topped $40 million.

Forrest Mars had tried to gain control of Mars, Inc., after his father's death in 1934. For years, he was unsuccessful in this quest, but when Ethel Mars (Frank Mars's second wife) died in 1945 she gave 50 percent of her stock to Forrest. This gave him a position on the board of directors and an office at Mars, Inc. In 1950, Forrest tried to oust the leadership of Mars, Inc., but failed, and he was banned from the company. He was eventually given control of several seats on the company's board. In 1959, Forrest became chairman of Mars, Inc. and continued to acquire shares in the company. In 1964, Forrest Mars merged Food Manufacturers Inc. into Mars, Inc., which became the new corporation's name.

In 1965, Mars, Inc. discontinued buying chocolate from Hershey and Forrest began to expand the company. To prevent trade secrets from leaking out, Forrest Mars required that all senior executive sign nondisclosure agreements. When Forrest Mars died in 1999, he left a fortune worth $4 billion and he was ranked by *Forbes* magazine as the among the most wealthy Americans, as were his children. Mars, Inc. was one of the largest companies in the world.

SUGGESTED READING: Joël Glenn Brenner, *The Emperors of Chocolate: Inside the Secret World of Hershey and Mars* (New York: Broadway Books, 2000); Mars Web site: www.mms.com; Janice Pottker, *Crisis in Candyland: Melting the Chocolate Shell of the Mars Family Empire* (Bethesda, MD: National Press Books, 1995).

Mars, Frank The candy maker Frank Mars (1883–1934) was born in Minneapolis, Minnesota. His father was a gristmill operator in Philadelphia, who had moved to St. Paul. Shortly after his birth, Frank Mars contracted polio; he remained disabled throughout his life. Frank Mars mastered his mother's **candy** recipes and experimented on his own, creating new confections. He started a business of selling **penny candies**, which were usually manufactured on a small scale by women. By 1902, he was operating a wholesale candy firm in Minneapolis. That year, he married Ethel G. Kissack and their only son, **Forrest Mars**, was born in 1904.

Frank Mars and his wife barely survived financially. When their money ran out in 1910, his wife divorced him. Mars married another woman also named Ethel and moved to Tacoma, Washington, where he began making nougat. He was bankrupt within a year. He kept trying but his efforts failed, so in 1920 he skipped town (owing money) and returned to Minnesota.

Back in Minneapolis, Frank Mars founded a candy company, later named **Mars, Inc.**, which turned out to be a success. It was during this time that Frank Mars was reintroduced to his son, Forrest, whom he had not seen since his divorce from his first wife. In 1923, the company introduced the **Milky Way** bar, which received local distribution. In 1930, Mars introduced the **Snickers** bar, which quickly became the most popular candy bar in America, a position it has held ever since. Snickers was followed by **3 Musketeers** in 1932. Frank and Forrest Mars quarreled and Forrest was forced out of the company in 1932. Fifteen months later, Frank Mars died at age 51. He left Mars, Inc. to his wife.

SUGGESTED READING: Joël Glenn Brenner, *The Emperors of Chocolate: Inside the Secret World of Hershey and Mars* (New York: Broadway Books, 2000); Janice Pottker, *Crisis in Candyland: Melting the Chocolate Shell of the Mars Family Empire* (Bethesda, MD: National Press Books, 1995)Mars Web site: www.mms.com

Mars, Inc. In 1922, after almost 20 years of business failure, **Frank Mars** founded the Mar-O-Bar Company in Minneapolis. The company was named after one of its confections, a gooey combination of **caramel**, **nuts**, and **chocolate**. His estranged son,

Forrest Mars, joined him and they changed the name of the company to Mars, Inc. Within a year, the company was successfully selling butter creams. Frank Mars borrowed a technique developed at Minneapolis's Pendergast Candy Company to create a fluffy, chewy nougat center for its Fat Emma bar. In 1923, Mars, Inc. introduced the **Milky Way** bar, which was different from its competitors in that the malt-flavored nougat—a whipped filling made of egg whites and corn syrup—was encased in a solid chocolate covering to keep it fresh. In its first year on the market, the Milky Way brand had grossed $800,000.

In 1930, Frank Mars introduced the **Snickers** bar, a peanut-flavored nougat bar topped with nuts and caramel and coated with chocolate. It quickly became the most popular candy bar in America, a position it has held ever since. In 1932, Mars released the **3 Musketeers** bar. The company used so much chocolate that the **Hershey Company** ended up supplying it to Mars, a relationship the two companies maintained until 1965.

In 1932, Frank and Forrest Mars had a falling out. Forrest was given $50,000 and the foreign rights to Mars's products. In 1933, Forrest visited Switzerland, where he claimed to have learned chocolate manufacturing as a worker at the Jean Tobler factory, which produced the **Toblerone** chocolate bar, and at **Nestlé**'s factories. Mars then moved to England. At the time, England was saturated with sweets from Rowntree & Co. and Cadbury Brothers. Despite stiff competition, Mars set up a factory in Slough, England in 1932. Because he had no chocolate, he purchased it from **Cadbury**, a practice that was continued until the 1950s. Among that factory's first products was the Mars bar, which was a slightly sweeter version of the American Milky Way. Mars battled Cadbury and **Rowntree** for retail shelf space and it was only after the Mars bar became England's best-selling bar that this problem was resolved. By 1939, Mars, Ltd. was ranked as Britain's third-largest **candy** manufacturer.

In addition to his business in England, Forrest Mars also created a candy business in the United States where he teamed up with Bruce Murrie, son of William Murrie, the president of the Hershey Company. They named their company M&M for the first letter of each founder's last name. Due to Murrie's influence, M&M obtained as much chocolate as it needed from Hershey. The company also received technical assistance and the latest production equipment. The company's first product was a small chocolate confection that was covered by a hard sugar shell, which they named M&M's Chocolate Candies. In 1942, Forrest bought a rice mill and launched Uncle Ben's Rice. (Uncle Ben was evidently a real person, but the caricature on box was of a Chicago waiter.) After the war, the relationship between Mars and Murrie became strained, and in 1949 Mars bought out Murrie for $1 million and changed the name of his company to Food Manufacturers, Inc. Forrest launched a major **advertising** campaign in national newspapers and magazines, **radio** spots, and billboards. By 1949, annual sales had increased to $3 million.

Merger

When Frank Mars died in 1934, Forrest had tried to gain control of the company. Unfortunately for Forrest, Frank Mars had left company to his second wife, Ethel, and their daughter, Patricia. Ethel left management of company in the hands of her brother, William Kruppenbacher. In 1945, Ethel died and half of her stock passed to Forrest Mars, who was given a seat on the board of directors and an office at Mars, Inc.'s headquarters. When Forrest Mars tried, but failed, to oust Kruppenbacher, Forrest was banned from the company's grounds. In 1950, Kruppenbacher offered Forrest one-third of the seats on the board, which Forrest accepted. He pushed Mars to update its equipment. At that time, Mars still hand-wrapped its candy. New equipment was purchased from Germany and in 1953 Mars mechanized its process for making candy bars. This allowed for continuous-flow production, which reduced manufacturing time. Forrest Mars also pushed Mars, Inc. to expand abroad and globalized its operations. He introduced Snickers, Milky Way, and other products into other countries, and introduced successful European candies, such as Starburst Fruit Chews and the Twix bar, into the United States.

Mars was first candy company to date its products and remove them from distributors if they were not sold in time. Forrest pioneered use of computers on the production line to measure the consistency of his output; if a candy bar was defective, it was scrapped, and the scrap would be ground up for use in another candy bar. In 1959, Forrest became chairman of Mars, Inc. and in 1964 he merged the company with his Food Manufacturers, Inc. By agreement, the name of the merged company was Mars, Inc.

Mars, Inc. has continued to expand, both through acquisitions (such as its purchase of the **Dove Bar** brand in 1986) and by creating new products, not all of which were successful. Mars tried to launch a version of M&M's peanuts that copied the coloring and styling of Hershey's Reese's Pieces. But Hershey sued Mars, maintaining that Mars was capitalizing on Hershey's goodwill and investment in Reese's Pieces. The Hershey Company won.

Today, Mars, Inc. is a $20 billion operation with interests from Helsinki to Hong Kong. Mars controls 15 percent of the global candy market. Mars is four times larger than Hershey on a global basis, but Mars's leading market is in the United Kingdom, not in the United States.

SUGGESTED READING: Joël Glenn Brenner, *The Emperors of Chocolate: Inside the Secret World of Hershey and Mars* (New York: Broadway Books, 2000); Mars Web site: www.mms.com; Janice Pottker, *Crisis in Candyland: Melting the Chocolate Shell of the Mars Family Empire* (Bethesda, MD: National Press Books, 1995).

Mary Jane Candies In 1884, Charles N. Miller of Boston formed a small business making and selling homemade candy. In 1914, the company began manufacturing Mary Janes, a bite-sized, chewy molasses and peanut butter candy. Miller named it for a favorite aunt and on the candy wrappers appeared the likeness of a little girl. In 1989, the Charles N. Miller Company was sold to Stark Candy Company, which was itself acquired a year later by the **New England Confectionery Company** (NECCO). NECCO markets a wide range of Mary Jane products, including Mary Jane Tubs and Mary Jane Peanut Butter Kisses. Although still marketed, Mary Jane candies are nostalgia candies today.

SUGGESTED READING: New England Confectionery Company Web site: www.necco.com

Mascots, Logos, and Icons Most **fast food chains** and many **junk food** manufacturers have adopted mascots. Among the first food mascots was the **Big Boy**, a plump boy with red-and white-checked overalls with the words "Big Boy" spread across his chest. He carries a large, triple-decker hamburger, and 12-foot statues of the Big Boy are erected in front of each restaurant in the Big Boy chain.

Burger King developed a little Burger King attired in a royal robe and crown. It stopped using that mascot for a while, but revived it later. The chain regularly gives out paper crowns to children so that they, too, can be a king. **Little Caesar's Pizza** created a Little Caesar mascot. **McDonald's** first mascot was Speedee, a little chef with a **hamburger** head. This had to be changed because Alka Seltzer had already adopted a mascot named Speedy. McDonald's settled on **Ronald McDonald** and today about 96 percent of American children recognize him.

Ronald McDonald. © Kelly Fitzsimmons

Not all mascots and icons have been successful, however. **Taco Bell** initially had a sleepy Mexican wearing a sombrero. When **PepsiCo** acquired Taco Bell, it jettisoned the existing icon and replaced it with a mission bell. **Pizza Hut** had its Italian chef tossing dough but it was considered "too Italian" by PepsiCo, which had acquired the chain, and the company shifted to a red roof that symbolized the "hut" in Pizza Hut. **Frito-Lay**, Inc. launched the **Frito Bandito**, only to be charged with ethnic stereotyping; the symbol was soon shelved.

Unusual mascots have been developed by Taco Bell and **Kentucky Fried Chicken** (KFC). In the case of Taco Bell, a massive television advertising campaign starred a talking Mexican Chihuahua, who squealed "Yo Quiero Taco Bell!" In the case of KFC, the mascot was based on a real person, the founder of the chain, **Harland Sanders**. When he started franchising his chicken, he had no money to advertise, so he dressed in a white suit and black string tie and called himself a Colonel (he was, in fact, an honorary Colonel). His image graces KFC paperware, posters, advertisements, and commercials.

In the **snack food** world, in 1969 **Keebler** came up with Ernie Keebler and the Elves who bake snacks in the Hollow Tree in the fictional community of Sylvan Glen.

For **M&M's**, **Mars, Inc.** developed Mr. Peanut and Mr. Plain. Planters Peanuts developed its own **Mr. Peanut** and McKee Foods created **Little Debbie**.

SUGGESTED READING: Thomas Hine, *The Total Package: The Evolution and Secret Meanings of Boxes, Bottles, Cans, and Tubes* (New York: Little, Brown and Company, 1995).

McDonaldization The term *McDonaldization* was coined by Jim Hightower in his book *Eat Your Heart Out* (1975). Hightower was a farm activist who warned that **fast food** threatened independent businesses and family-owned farms. He believed that the practices of large fast food corporations, such as **McDonald's**, were creating a food economy dominated by giant corporations.

The term was picked up and popularized in academic circles by George Ritzer, whose book *The McDonaldization of Society* (1993) examined the social effects of McDonald's in the United States. McDonald's rigorously controlled the appearance of each of its outlets, as well as their menus, equipment, procedures, **advertising**, **suppliers**, and polices. McDonald's success had launched many imitators, not only in fast food industry but also throughout America's retail economy. Ritzer defined McDonaldization as "the principles by which the fast-food restaurant[s] are coming to dominate more and more sectors of

American society and of the world." The principles included efficiency, predictability, and control. According to Ritzer, McDonald's is "the irrationality of rationality." Like Hightower, Ritzer attacked the fast food industry for its homogenizing influence.

McDonald's and other fast food chains have been exported to the rest of the world, and the phenomenon has been studied by numerous individuals, including James L. Watson, whose *Golden Arches East: McDonald's in East Asia* (1997) examined the effects of McDonald's in East Asia. Subsequently, many other academic articles and books have been written on McDonaldization, such as *McDonaldization Revisited: Critical Essays on Consumer Culture* (1998), edited by Mark Alfino, John S. Caputo, and Robin Wynyard.

The term *McDonaldization* has spawned similar terms, such *Snickerization*, used to described the influence of **Mars, Inc.** in Russia after the fall of the Berlin Wall in 1989; *Coca-Colonisation*, which refers to American influence in other parts of the world, such as Europe and China; and *Wal-Martization*, reflecting the major influence that Wal-Mart has had upon the United States and the world. The collapse of Soviet Union led to an unprecedented *Americanization* of the world.

SUGGESTED READING: Mark Alfino, John S. Caputo, and Robin Wynyard, eds., *McDonaldization Revisited: Critical Essays on Consumer Culture* (Westport, CT: Greenwood Press, 1998); Jim Hightower, *Eat Your Heart Out: Food Profiteering in America* (New York: Crown Publishers, [1975]); George Ritzer, *The McDonaldization of Society* (Revised edition). (Thousand Oaks, CA: Pine Forge Press, 1996); George Ritzer, *The McDonaldization Thesis: Explorations and Extensions* (Thousand Oaks CA: Sage Publications, 1998); Barry Smart, ed. *Resisting McDonaldization* (Thousand Oaks, CA: Sage Publications, 1999); George Ritzer, ed., McDonaldization: the Reader. 2nd ed. (Thousand Oaks, CA: Pine Forge Press, 2006).

McDonald's In 1930, two New Hampshire brothers, Richard and Maurice McDonald, moved to Los Angeles, attracted by potential employment in the movie industry. They bought a small movie **theater**, but it was not successful. To make ends meet, in 1937 they opened an orange juice and **hot dog** stand near the Santa Anita racetrack in Arcadia, a suburb of Los Angeles. Their stand grew and they shifted from hot dogs to barbecue and **hamburgers**. In 1940, they opened the McDonald Brothers Burger Bar **Drive-in** on E Street in San Bernardino, California. It featured 20 female **carhops** picking up and delivering food. The brothers noted that 80 percent of their sales were hamburgers, so they dropped the barbecue (which also took too long to make). After World War II, they had to deal with a labor shortage; the economy was booming and many young men who had been in the service were now at college on the GI bill. As a result, the McDonald brothers often ended up with fry cooks and dishwashers who showed up for work drunk.

The brothers decided upon a radical change to reduce expenses and increase profits by increasing efficiency. A central feature of their operation was an industrial assembly line model popularized by Henry Ford, whose techniques had previously been adapted for use in food service by cafeterias, automats, railway dining cars, and at the Howard Johnson restaurant chain. The model included division of labor into simple tasks that could be performed with a minimum of training. This meant that their employees were essentially interchangeable and could easily be shifted from one task to another. The brothers redesigned the kitchen, making room for larger grills and labor-saving equipment. They created an efficient assembly line to make hamburgers and **French fries**. This assembly line model provided customers with fast, reliable, and inexpensive food; in return, customers were expected to stand in line and pick up their own food, eat quickly, clean up their own waste, and leave without delay, thereby making room for more customers.

The McDonald brothers were convinced that their target audience was families, so they tried to create an environment that would discourage loitering teenagers, who littered and broke or stole cups, glasses, plates, silverware, and trays. Therefore, they did away with the attractive female carhops, whom the brothers believed were more interested in socializing than in selling burgers. They also did away with the plates, glasses, and tableware, replacing them with disposable paper and plastic utensils.

To implement these ideas, the brothers closed their restaurant, installed larger grills and purchased Multimixers (which made many **milk shakes** at a time in metal containers; the contents would then be poured into paper cups). To speed this up, the brothers reduced the length of the machine's arm so that milk shakes could be made directly in 12-ounce paper cups, thus eliminating a process step. Eighty or more shakes were prepared in advance and placed in a refrigerated holding case, thus speeding up the process of fulfilling orders.

This model created a militarized production system that was geared toward teenaged male employees, who were responsible for simple tasks—some heated the hamburgers, others packaged the food or poured the soft drinks and shakes, and still other placed orders in paper bags.

This new model did away with indoor seating and greatly reduced the menu to a few low-cost items, including 15-cent hamburgers, 19-cent cheeseburgers, 10-cent fries, 20-cent shakes, and large and small **sodas**. The hamburger patties weighed only 1.5 ounces and all burgers came with the same **condiments**: **ketchup**, chopped onion, and two pickle slices. In this new self-service restaurant, customers placed their orders at a window and ate the food in their cars. All food was **packaged** in disposable paper wrappers and paper cups, so there was no breakage or loss due to theft.

The McDonald brothers' restaurant was octagon-shaped, which was not unusual for Los Angeles at that time. The "McDonald's New Self-Service System" got off to a rocky start when it was launched in 1948: customers honked their horns and expected carhops to come out and pick up their order. Eventually, they understood the new system and they were attracted by the low prices, fast service, and good hamburgers. The service was speedy: the McDonald brothers claimed that their employees could serve a customer who ordered everything that they had—hamburger, fries, and a **beverage**—in 20 seconds. Increased volume led to higher profits. By 1951, the brothers grossed $275,000, of which $100,000 was profit. Reports of their phenomenal success spread around the nation and *American Restaurant* ran a cover story on the "McDonald's New Self-Service System" in July 1952. The brothers believed that they were ready to **franchise** their operation, so they began **advertising** for franchisees.

As good as their new design was, the McDonalds believed that they could make an even more efficient operation by changing the layout. They also wanted a more distinctive **architectural design** to make it easier to spot from the road and to make their drive-in stand out from the hundreds of other similar **fast food** establishments. Their new model restaurant was constructed with a forward-sloping front; its walls were painted with red and white stripes. Richard McDonald came up with the idea for yellow "golden arches," which poked through the roof. Under the arches was white tile that implied cleanliness, and lots of glass that made food preparation visible to all.

Before their new restaurant was completed in San Bernardino, the McDonald brothers sold their first franchises based on their new design. Franchisees paid the McDonald brothers a relatively small fee plus a percentage of their sales. Unlike previous foodservice franchises, the brothers demanded that every franchise be constructed in the same way as their model and that each outlet would sell exactly the same food prepared in exactly the same way. Their new model had no indoor dining; customers were expected to eat in their cars. A couple of plastic chairs and cheap tables were provided outside for walk-up customers or for those who preferred to eat outside. This model gave McDonald's a significant advantage over other emerging fast food **chains**, for it promised consistency, predictability, and safety. However, it was not considered an advantage by potential franchisees at the time because it meant they could not use existing facilities—a criterion not required by other franchisers. By the end of 1953, the brothers had sold only 21 franchises, of which only 10 became operating units (two in Phoenix, Arizona and the rest in the Los Angeles area). Compared to other fast food chains, such as that of **Dairy Queen**, this was not a great success.

The McDonald's restaurant in San Bernardino attracted large crowds. Many subsequent fast food **entrepreneurs** visited the San Bernardino site. For instance, in 1952 Matthew Burns of Long Beach, California, invited his stepson, Keith G. Cramer (who owned a carhop restaurant in Daytona Beach, Florida), to fly out to California and visit McDonald's. The following year, Cramer opened his Insta-Burger King in Jacksonville, Florida, which evolved into **Burger King**. After a visit to McDonald's, restaurant owner **Carl Karcher** of Anaheim, California, decided to develop a fast food chain of his own; he named it **Carl's Jr.** Glen Bell of San Bernardino also studied the McDonald's operation and tried to develop something similar using Mexican-themed food instead of hamburgers. He eventually launched **Taco Bell**. James Collins, chairman of Collins Foods International, visited San Bernardino, took notes on the operation, and opened up a **Kentucky Fried Chicken** franchise based on the brother's design. Numerous others opened up McDonald clones, so that by 1954 many other fast food operations were underway in southern California.

Another visitor to San Bernardino was **Ray Kroc**, an owner of the Chicago company that sold Multimixers. Kroc had sold Multimixers to many fast food franchisees, including Dairy Queen and **Tastee-Freez**. This experience gave Kroc a deeper understanding of the fast food business and some knowledge of problems related to franchising. In the early 1950s, increased competition reduced the sales of Multimixers and Kroc needed new outlets. He saw advertisements for McDonald's and was surprised to find that the McDonald brothers had purchased eight of his company's Multimixers. In 1954, he visited the McDonald brothers and was astounded by the crowds ordering food.

Kroc saw the potential of the McDonald's operation. He met with the brothers and signed an agreement allowing him to sell McDonald's franchises nationwide. In the mid-1950s, franchising consisted mainly of assigning territories to franchisees for huge up-front fees. However, Kroc wanted to control the McDonald's operations. He avoided territorial franchises by selling one store franchise at a time, thereby controlling the number of stores a licensee could operate. He also required strict conformity to operating standards, equipment, **menus**, recipes, prices, trademarks, and architectural designs. In 1955, Kroc created McDonald's System, Inc. and sold himself the first franchise in Des Plaines, Illinois, which he opened in 1955. He intended it to be a model operation that would attract potential franchisees.

Meanwhile, Kroc hired Harry Sonneborn, who had worked for Tastee-Freez and had established its franchising operation. Sonneborn designed McDonald's Franchise Realty Corporation, which purchased land for McDonald's franchises and then rented the land to the franchisee. In this way, McDonald's became one of America largest landowners. The corporation made money off the rental agreements and, if a franchisee violated the agreement, McDonald's could evict them. Franchisees therefore did basically whatever the parent company wanted. In this way, Kroc controlled the franchise operations, ensuring uniformity, maintaining standards, and generating profits.

By the end of 1959, there were more than 100 McDonald's operations. The early success of McDonald's rested, in part, on the managers selected to oversee operations. Kroc's mantra was "Quality, Service, Cleanliness, and Value," which he tried to instill into every franchisee. Kroc also believed in training managers. He established Hamburger University, which offered a degree in Hamburgerology. The first class of 15 students graduated in February 1961. Since then, 65,000 managers have graduated from that institution.

Kroc had numerous disagreements with the McDonald brothers. The brothers required that Kroc follow their architectural and operational design exactly, but Kroc wanted to innovate. Kroc finally bought out them out for $2.7 million. The buyout included a provision that permitted the McDonald brothers to continue operating the original McDonald's outlet in San Bernardino. That building burned down and Kroc then proclaimed that his operation in Des Plaines was the first real McDonald's hamburger outlet. Today, it is a McDonald's museum.

A significant component of McDonald's success was the changing demographics in America. Previous fast food chains (e.g., **White Tower**, **White Castle**, and the **automats**) were in inner cities. McDonald's targeted suburban America, which had begun to rapidly grow after World War II. The suburbs were home to families with plenty of baby-boom children, and residents were dependent upon the **automobile**. McDonald's tied franchising to fast food, cars, and families. McDonald's did everything it could to prevent its outlets from becoming **teen hangouts**. Kroc expanded upon the policies established by the McDonald brothers by banning jukeboxes, vending machines, and telephones. He refused to hire female employees, until he was required to do so by law. Kroc encouraged franchisees to support local, family-oriented community activities.

Within a decade of his first encounter with the McDonald brothers, Ray Kroc revolutionized fast food service. By 1963, McDonald's was selling one million burgers a day, and this was only the beginning. The company began advertising nationally in 1966, the same year that McDonald's was first listed on the New York Stock Exchange. Kroc's model for success was emulated by virtually every new fast food local, regional, and national operation in America. McDonald's symbolized success and it generated huge profits. Kroc had originally envisioned 1,000 McDonald's operations in the United States; when he died in 1984 at the age of 81, there were 7,500 McDonald's outlets worldwide.

Promotion and Children

McDonald's national promotional campaigns have been a significant reason for its success. Its **slogans**, such as "You Deserve a Break Today" (which *Advertising Age* rated as the top advertising campaign in the twentieth century) and "Two All-Beef Patties, Special Sauce, Lettuce, Cheese, Pickles, Onions On a Sesame Seed Bun," became national hits. According to Eric Schlosser, author of ***Fast Food Nation*** (2001), McDonald's expends more on advertising and promotion than does any other food brand.

In the 1950s, few major companies in America targeted their advertising toward children. The conventional wisdom was that children did not have money (which was true); hence, they targeted adults who brought the children into stores. Kroc had targeted the middle class families with children in the suburbs, but learned that children had pester power; studies indicated that children determined where many families ate, and children did like fast food establishments. It was a place where they could chose what they wanted to eat. Kroc set out to make visits to its outlets "fun experiences" for children. and **Ronald McDonald** was selected as the company's national spokesperson in 1966.

The McDonald's outlet in Chula Vista, California (near San Diego), opened the first McDonaldland Park in 1972. In its two-day grand opening, 10,000 people came to visit. This proved to be such a success that McDonald's began opening bright-colored Playlands for children, complete with playgrounds and mythical characters. The company has also **tied-in** much of its marketing with major children's motion pictures. McDonald's **Happy Meals**, inaugurated in 1979, package the food with toys; as a result, McDonald's became the world's largest toy distributor. By 1980, the millions of dollars expended on child-oriented **television** advertising and local promotions had succeeded: 96 percent of American children recognized Ronald McDonald, second only to Santa Claus. As advertisers later pointed out, brand loyalty begins with children, and advertising targeted at children today is intended to create such loyalty for future payoffs.

Kroc's success encouraged the growth of other fast food chains, which readily adopted McDonald's methods. The competition also innovated, and McDonald's needed to keep up with them. In 1967, Burger King launched a newly designed restaurant with indoor seating. This challenged one of the basic tenets of McDonald's model, which stressed eating in the car. But by the 1960s, the novelty of eating in the car had worn off. It was also uncomfortable on hot and humid days, as well as on extremely cold during the winter. Indoor eating areas permitted year-round climate control and customers greatly appreciated Burger King's new model. McDonald's reciprocated by developing a new model with indoor seating, which it inaugurated in 1968.

Initially, McDonald's had intentionally not constructed outlets in major cities. With the newly designed stores, it was possible for McDonald's to do so, which they did beginning in 1972. Several chains developed **drive-thru** windows, including **Wendy's**, **Jack in the Box**, and Burger King; McDonald's began installing drive-thru windows in 1975. Today, drive-thru windows generate about 50 percent of McDonald's sales.

New Product Development

To keep ahead of the competition, McDonald's also regularly developed new products. It diversified its menu beginning in the 1960s. The Big Mac with its two patties originated with a Pittsburgh franchisee, who was trying to create a competitive product to Burger King's Big Whopper. It was released nationally in 1968. The Egg McMuffin debuted in 1973. By 1977, McDonald's were serving complete line of breakfast sandwiches and biscuits for eating on the run. Other innovations include the Quarter Pounder, the McBLT and the McLean Deluxe, a 90-percent fat-free hamburger, which failed. In 1983, McDonald's introduced **Chicken McNuggets** consisting of reconstituted chicken delivered frozen and then reheated before serving.

Globalization

McDonald's opened its first Canadian outlet in 1967. Its success convinced Kroc that McDonald's should aggressively expand to other countries. It has continued to expand abroad ever since. McDonald's opened its first Tokyo outlet in 1971, followed by Australia and European countries. By 1988, McDonald's had established itself as one of France's most popular fast food operations. By 1994, McDonald's maintained more than 4,500 restaurants in 73 foreign countries. Today, McDonald's has more than 30,000 restaurants in 121 countries. McDonald's operates more than 1,000 restaurants in Japan alone. The most popular restaurant in Japan, measured by volume of customers, is McDonald's. The world's largest McDonald's is operated near Red Square in Moscow, where a Big Mac lunch costs the equivalent of a week's paycheck for the average Russian. Yet, this McDonald's serves 40,000 people every day. McDonald's boasts more than 546 restaurants in China—one of which overlooks Tiananmen Square in Beijing. About one-fourth of McDonald's outlets outside the United States are owned by local franchisees.

McDonald's faced numerous problems when it expanded its American model abroad. In America, it was understood that customers would stand in line to place their order, which was not necessarily a tradition that existed in other countries. McDonald's model was based on customers paying before they received their food, which, of course, is quite the reverse in restaurants, even in the United States. Customers were also expected to eat quickly and leave so that other customers would have room to sit and eat. In other countries, eating is not necessarily a "fast" activity. Hence, McDonald's had to educate customers and it had to localize its operations.

When McDonald's opened outlets in new countries, most customers were unprepared for the experience. James L. Watson in his *Golden Arches East: McDonald's in East Asia* (1997) pointed out problems confronting McDonald's. McDonald's employees were trained to smile at customers, which was standard practice in the United States, but this raised suspicions in Moscow and China where it was not the custom for food service employees to smile. Most first-time customers had no idea of what a hamburger was or how it should be consumed. McDonald's had to expend resources to educate customers. In most countries, customers easily adapted to the McDonald's experience but in other countries, McDonald's changed its procedures to fit in with local customs. In Rio de Janeiro, Brazil, McDonald's hired waiters and served champagne along with its hamburgers. In Caracas, Venezuela, hostesses seat customers, take orders, and deliver meals. In Taiwan, Hong Kong, and Beijing customers are attracted to McDonald's because of its uniformity and egalitarian atmosphere. In Korea, employees seat customers at tables occupied by others. However, some of McDonald's traditional practices have been rejected in some countries. For instance, the assumption that customers will eat and leave quickly has been reversed in East Asia, where many consumers have concluded that the "fast" in fast food refers to delivery of food, not its consumption.

In addition to **efficiency** and reliability, McDonald's is also appreciated for its hygienic procedures and cleanliness. People in Asia with disposable income who can eat at McDonald's have now rejected street cuisine due to the fear of food poisoning, adulteration, and unsanitary conditions. McDonald's employees wear **uniforms** and are constantly cleaning the restaurants.

Problems and Issues

Despite this success, McDonald's and other large fast-food chains have faced numerous problems. The most serious problem identified by managers at McDonald's were rising labor costs, the high employee turnover rate, and the lack of reliable workers. Fast food is based on low salaries for employees. To keep salaries low, McDonald's and other fast food chains have intentionally engaged in **anti-union** activities. In addition, companies have consistently **lobbied** government and legislative agencies against increased minimum wages and worker benefits. A related problem is the high turnover rate for workers experienced at many McDonald's and other fast food chains. Some McDonald's outlets' turnover rates approach 300 percent per year. In part, this is caused by the low pay workers receive and the view (instilled by the company) that employment at McDonald's is mainly part-time so that the company does not have to pay employee benefits, overtime, or increase wages due to longevity of service. When McDonald's was growing quickly during the 1950s and 1960s, it had an almost inexhaustible supply of young workers due to lack of other opportunities for employment and the baby-boom teens who came of age at that time. Teenagers were more impressionable and more manageable than older workers. When the baby-boom bulge began to decline, McDonald's was obliged to seek nontraditional workers. The company shifted from its all-male workforce and began hiring women and teenaged girls as a result of federal antidiscrimination laws and its need for good employees. Then it began hiring recent immigrants, the elderly, and the handicapped. This has meant that more training and supervision are required. Another solution was to adopt more automation and touchscreen computerized cash registers that made counter-duty easier.

In part because of McDonald's success, the company has been criticized on a variety of issues and it has frequently responded positively to meet criticism. When the company was criticized in the 1960s for the lack of African American managers of its restaurants, McDonald's made an effort to recruit more African American franchisees. When it was charged with promoting **junk food**, the company began selling salads, reduced the **fat** content of its hamburgers, and changed the way it made its French fries.

McDonald's has been accused of causing harm to the **environment**, specifically for its use of polystyrene foam for its coffee cups and food containers for Big Macs and Quarter Pounders. Polystyrene is a plastic that is not easily biodegradable, and McDonald's was the world's largest purchaser of it. McDonald's responded by creating an alliance with the Environmental Defense Fund to make McDonald's more environmentally friendly. The company switched from polystyrene to paper products and it encouraged recycling. The Environmental Defense Fund has estimated that since 1989 McDonald's has eliminated 150,000 tons of waste by requiring its **suppliers** to use improved packaging. In addition, the company has purchased more than $4 billion of recycled materials for its own operations. As a result of its environmentally friendly programs, McDonald's has received a good deal of positive press coverage.

McDonald's has also been criticized for its influence upon its suppliers. The logic for this is simple: McDonald's is the largest purchaser of beef in the world and it has some responsibility for the practices of its suppliers. In the 1980s, for example, McDonald's was specifically charged with destroying the rainforests in Brazil because the company's suppliers in that country were reportedly burning down rainforests to create grazing land for cattle supplied to McDonald's. The company changed its suppliers (specifically refusing to purchase beef from Brazil) and has made substantial contributions to environmental groups to help save the environment. McDonald's has also been attacked for the inhumane conditions at feedlots and slaughterhouses of some of the company's meat suppliers. For example, Eric Schlosser's *Fast Food Nation: The Dark Side of the All-American Meal* (2001), maintains that as a result of practices followed at McDonald's and other fast food chains, **meatpacking** is the most dangerous job in the United States and that practices followed at meatpackers "facilitated the introduction of deadly pathogens, such as *E. coli* 0157:H7, into America's hamburger meat." When McDonald's finally required that its ground beef be certified as safe, the company's suppliers acquired the equipment necessary for better testing.

McDonald's has also been criticized for its major influence upon potato growers; the company's annual orders for French fries constitute 7.5 percent of America's entire potato crop. Potential concern for **genetically modified organisms** (GMOs) encouraged McDonald's to state that it would no longer purchase genetically altered potatoes in the

United States. Because McDonald's largely buys from local farmers, it does not use genetically modified foods in European markets due to restrictions imposed by European Union and national laws.

McDonald's has also been charged with causing adverse affects on local cultures and businesses around the world. McDonald's success abroad has caused deep resentment in people who see the company as a symbol for the United States and who believe that McDonald's expansion threatens local culinary traditions. In France, radical farmer José Bové demolished a McDonald's restaurant nearing completion, and similar actions have occurred in other European countries. McDonald's has pointed out that many of its foreign operations are locally owned and most products used in McDonald's are produced in the country where the restaurant is located.

Studying McDonald's has also become a hot academic topic, and many popular works have tried to dissect its success and examine the company's influence. Among the more famous studies are George Ritzer's *The McDonaldization of Society* (1993), which examined the social effects of McDonald's in the United States, and Benjamin Barber's *Jihad vs. McWorld* (1995), which used McDonald's as a global symbol for modernization. Dozens of other works have examined McDonald's worldwide impact.

In other countries, McDonald's is often viewed as an American symbol, and it has both gained and suffered as a consequence. McDonald's outlets have been trashed, bombed, and boycotted due to policies of the U. S. government. On the other hand, at other times and in other places McDonald's has been considered a modernizing force that has improved the local culinary conditions.

By the end of the twentieth century, one out of every eight American workers had at some time been employed by McDonald's. Studies proclaim that 96 percent of Americans have visited McDonald's at least once. McDonald's serves an estimated 22 million Americans every day and has expanded even more rapidly abroad. In 1994, McDonald's operating revenues from non-U.S. sales passed the 50 percent mark. McDonald's is one of the world's most famous brand names and the company has become an icon for efficient and successful business that is ingrained in popular culture throughout the world. McDonald's is the largest purchaser of beef, pork, and potatoes and the second-largest purchaser of chicken. It is one of the largest owners of retail estate in the world, and it earns the majority of its profits from collecting rent, not from selling food.

SUGGESTED READING: Benjamin R. Barber, *Jihad vs. McWorld* (New York: Times Books, 1995); Max Boas and Steve Chain, *Big Mac: The Unauthorized Story of McDonald's* (New York: Mentor Books, The New American Library, 1977); Laurence W. Cartensen, "The Burger Kingdom: Growth and Diffusion of McDonald's Restaurants in the United States, 1955–1978," in George O. Carney, ed., *Fast Food, Stock Cars, and Rock 'N' Roll: Place and Space in American Pop Culture* (Lanham, MD: Rowman & Littlefield Publishers, 1995); Marshall Fishwick, ed., *Ronald Revisited: The World of Ronald McDonald* (Bowling Green, OH: Bowling Green University Popular Press, 1983); Anne Cooper Funderburg, *Sundae Best: A History of Soda Fountains* (Bowling Green, OH: Bowling Green State University Popular Press, 2002); William Gould, *Business Portraits: McDonald's* (Lincolnwood, IL: VGM Career Horizons, 1996); Gary Henriques and Audre DuVall, *McDonald's Collectibles: Identification and Value Guide* (Paducah, KY: Collector Books, nd.); John A. Jakle and Keith A. Sculle, *Fast Food: Roadside Restaurants in the Automobile Age* (Baltimore: Johns Hopkins University Press, 1999); Ray Kroc, with Robert Anderson, *Grinding It Out: The Making of McDonald's* (Chicago: Henry Regnery Company, 1977); Terry Losonsky and Joyce Losonsky, *McDonald's Happy Meal Toys around the World* (Atglen, PA: Schiffer Publishing, 1995); Joyce Losonsky and Terry Losonsky, *McDonald's Pre-Happy Meal Toys from the Fifties, Sixties, and Seventies* (Atglen,

PA: Schiffer Publishing Ltd., 1998); John F. Love, *McDonald's: Behind the Arches* (Revised edition). (New York: Bantam Books, 1995); Jackie Prince, *Launching a New Business Ethic: the Environment as a Standard Operating Procedure at McDonald's and at Other Companies* (Washington, D.C.: Environmental Defense Fund, 1991); George Ritzer, *The McDonaldization of Society* (Newbury Park, CA: Pine Forge Press, 1993); George Ritzer, ed., McDonaldization: the Reader. 2nd ed. (Thousand Oaks, CA: Pine Forge Press, 2006); Tony Royle, *Working for McDonald's in Europe: The Unequal Struggle?* (New York: Routledge, 2001); Eric Schlosser, *Fast Food Nation: The Dark Side of the All-American Meal* (New York: Houghton Mifflin Company, 2001); James L. Watson, ed., *Golden Arches East: McDonald's in East Asia* (Stanford, CA: Stanford University Press, 1997); Meredith Williams, *Tomart's Price Guide to McDonald's Happy Meal Collectibles* (Revised and updated). (Dayton, OH: Tomart Publications, 1995); McDonald's Web site: www.mcdonalds.com

McLibel In 1986, the London chapter of Greenpeace, a small but active group of pacifists, anarchists, and **vegetarians**, targeted what it believed were the evils of McDonald's. It distributed a six-page leaflet titled "What's wrong with McDonald's? Everything you don't want to know," which accused the company of promoting poverty, selling unhealthy food, **exploiting** workers and children, torturing animals, and destroying the Amazon rainforests. It included such statements as "[McDonald's used] lethal poisons to destroy vast areas of Central American rainforests." Members of London's Greenpeace distributed the flyer for four years, often in front of McDonald's outlets. In 1989, McDonald's infiltrated Greenpeace by hiring detectives to determine who was responsible for the leaflet and its distribution. Based on this information, McDonald's issued writs against five members for distributing the leaflet, which the company claimed was libelous.

Libel laws in the United Kingdom require defendants to prove in court the truth of their statements. McDonald's had previously used British libel laws to silence its critics. During the 1980s, for example, it threatened to sue British publications and organizations, which prompted retractions and apologies from the press. The cost of losing a libel case (legal fees and damages) can be huge. Three of the accused Greenpeace activists appeared in court and apologized to McDonald's. The other two, Helen Steel and Dave Morris, decided to defend themselves. They were not given any legal help from the court, but they were assisted by the Haldane Society of Socialist Lawyers on a pro bono basis. This David-and-Goliath fight was dubbed McLibel. As news of it spread, the British media seized upon it and often the trial ended up as front-page news. Steel and Morris received help from a large numbers of volunteers, some of whom formed the McLibel Support Campaign to assist the defendants with research. The trial began in March 1994 and continued for three years, becoming the longest-running trial in British history.

It also was a public relations disaster for McDonald's, which was required to defend itself regarding its labor, marketing, **environmental**, **nutrition**, food safety, and animal welfare practices. Steel and Morris forced the company's top executives to testify for days. In the midst of the testimony, it came out that McDonald's had spied on the defendants before and after the company had sued them and that Scotland Yard had supplied information to McDonald's. The McSpotlight Web site covered the trial and McDonald's alleged worldwide abuses. E-mail and press releases were sent out and "Days of Action" were held around the world protesting McDonald's actions. The original leaflet was translated into 27 different languages and, since 1990, an estimated three million copies have been handed out.

In the final judgment, Morris and Steel were found to have libeled McDonald's and were fined £60,000. The judge stated that most of the Greenpeace charges were unproven but he did find that McDonald's had exploited children, endangered the health of its customers, paid workers extremely low wages, and opposed union activity. He also found that the company did bear responsibility for the cruelty inflicted upon animals by many of its suppliers.

Morris and Steel appealed the decision and sued Scotland Yard. On March 31, 1999, the Court of Appeals overruled parts of the original McLibel verdict, supporting the leaflet's assertion that eating McDonald's food can cause heart disease and that McDonald's employees were treated badly. The Court of Appeals reduced the damages to £40,000. Steel and Morris refused to pay and appealed the case to the British House of Lords, which refused to hear it. In 2000, Morris and Steel filed an appeal with the European Court of Human Rights, challenging the verdict and stating that the trial breached their right to a fair trial and their right to freedom of expression. In June 2004, the European Court of Human Rights declared their claim to be admissible and in February 2005, the court held that Steel's and Morris's rights of free expression had been violated because they had not been given legal aid and, therefore, had been denied a fair trial. The decision was nonbinding.

SUGGESTED READING: Eric Schlosser, *Fast Food Nation: The Dark Side of the All-American Meal* (New York: Houghton Mifflin Company, 2001); John Vidal, *McLibel: Burger Culture on Trial* (New York: The New Press, 1997); McSpotlight Web site: www.mcspotlight.org

Meatpacking Industry The first major **exposé** of the meatpacking industry was in the novel titled *The Jungle,* written by Upton Sinclair. It was released in 1906, a few months before Congress voted on the passage of the Pure Food and Drug Act. Many observers at the time believed that its publication helped ensure passage of the Act. The Act created the U.S. Food and Drug Administration (FDA), which has been charged with the task of ensuring that the nation's food supply (including meatpacking) is safe. Rules and regulations were established for meatpacking; inspectors examined meatpacking plants to ensure compliance. During the following 70 years, the meatpacking industry gradually improved and by the 1960s meatpackers were among the highest-paid industrial workers in the United States.

Beginning in the 1960s, however, the industry began to feel the brunt of the **fast food** revolution. Fast food operators mainly developed menus based on beef and **chicken**. Large **chains** pressured meatpackers for uniform products that tasted the same regardless of where they were produced. This fundamentally affected how cattle and chickens were raised, slaughtered, and processed. It also encouraged consolidation in the meatpacking industry, such that there are now only 13 major meatpackers in America.

The fast food chains were so large that they used their purchasing power to negotiate among meatpackers for the lowest possible price. To compete, meatpackers lowered wages, decreased training, and reduced safety requirements. They also had to increase the volume of meat processed. Therefore, lines that once processed 200 head of cattle per hour were sped up to handle 300 or 400 hundred per hour. Increased volume, even with decreased price, meant increased profits for meatpacking companies. It also meant installing new equipment that scraped bones for the maximum amount of meat. In scraping bones, small fragments of bone came off, as well as pieces of spinal columns, with their potential for spreading **mad cow disease**. Hygiene declined and injuries to workers increased. As a consequence, the meatpacking occupation became one of the most dangerous jobs in the United States. In addition, vast shifts in the amount of meat processed has meant that the industry has become more prone to the introduction of pathogens, such as ***Salmonella*** and ***E. coli*** 0157:H7, than in the past.

In 1982, the entire industry was deregulated by President Reagan. The unions that represented workers at meatpackers were busted and strikebreakers (mainly migrant workers from Mexico) were brought in to operate the slaughterhouses and meat processing facilities. Pressure from fast food chains for lower prices resulted in sharply lower costs for raising animals and a vast increase in the speed of the slaughtering and butchering. Today, the meatpacking industry has some of the lowest-paid jobs in America.

The meat industry has continually **lobbied** against regulations for food safety. The FDA cannot order meatpacking companies to remove contaminated meat from fast food kitchens or supermarket shelves. In addition, the meatpacking industry has supported so-called veggie laws, which forbid defaming agricultural products. For comments about beef that Oprah Winfrey made on her **television** show, she was sued by cattle ranchers in a Texas court. She won the case but the meatpacking industry proved that it has the ability to threaten critics with expensive lawsuits. The **Occupational Safety and Health Administration (OSHA)** is authorized to levy fines on noncompliant meatpackers, but the maximum fine for a human death is $70,000, which is not a great burden for meatpackers who are making millions of dollars a year. However, **McDonald's** is largest purchaser of beef and the company has the ability to influence meatpackers' practices. For example, when McDonald's demanded that its ground beef be certified to be free of lethal pathogens, meatpacker suppliers had to purchase microbial testing equipment.

SUGGESTED READING: Danielle Nierenberg, *Happier Meals: Rethinking the Global Meat Industry* (Washington, D.C.: Worldwatch Institute, 2005); Eric Schlosser, *Fast Food Nation: The Dark Side of the All-American Meal* (New York: Houghton Mifflin Company, 2001).

Memoirs Memoirs have been written by many **fast food** innovators. The first to do so was Billy Ingram, the promoter of **White Castle**, America's first fast food **chain**. His purpose in writing *All This from a 5-cent Hamburger! The Story of the White Castle System* (1964) was to set the historical record straight. By 1964, when the book was published, Billy Ingram was in the twilight of his life and his famed White Castle chain was only a bit player in the rapidly growing drama of the fast food business. Ingram tried to make the case that he had established the model for the industry, and indeed he had.

Many others in the fast food industry followed in Ingram's footsteps, not only as inheritors of his system for making **hamburgers** but also as writers (usually with collaborators) of their own memoirs. **Harland Sanders** had sold his **Kentucky Fried Chicken** business10 years previous to the release of his memoirs, *Life as I Have Known It Has Been Finger Lickin' Good* (1974). It was part inspirational—how someone without an education (he only finished sixth grade) could have made it to the pinnacle of business success in America, and his greatest success, the founding of KFC, was not achieved until after his 65th birthday. Sanders told his story in a humorous and engaging way.

Three years later, **Ray Kroc** published his memoirs, *Grinding It Out: The Making of McDonald's* (1977). It told of his early life and his relationship with Richard and Maurice McDonald. Kroc gloats over the fact that when the brothers finally agreed to sell McDonald's to Kroc they had insisted in keeping their original restaurant in San Bernardino,

California, but when he launched a McDonald's hamburger outlet across the street from the brothers' restaurant he ran them out of business. The book was collaboratively written by Robert Anderson, who would also collaborate on an autobiography with Tom Monaghan (the founder of **Pizza Hut**) titled *Pizza Tiger* (1986).

In most cases, autobiographies were promotion pieces written by others to **advertise** their businesses and settle old scores. Wally Amos, in collaboration with Leroy Robinson, published his *Famous Amos Story: The Face That Launched a Thousand Chips* (1983) while his business was floundering. In 1984 **Famous Amos** was taken over by investors and Wally Amos became an employee of the company. This did not work out, so he engaged in other businesses. To tell of these terrible experiences, he wrote another memoir, in collaboration with Camilla Denton, *The Man with No Name* (1994).

Chocolate chip mogul Debbi Fields (founder of **Mrs. Fields**) and the editors of Time-Life Books promoted business by writing two partly autobiographical books that were sold also as a cookbook: *Mrs. Fields Cookie Book: 100 Recipes from the Kitchen of Mrs. Fields.* This was so successful that she published a second cookbook after she had sold her business.

Dave Thomas, founder of **Wendy's**, published three books. His first two, *Dave's Way: A New Approach to Old-fashioned Success* (1991) and *Dave Says—Well Done! The Common Guy's Guide to Everyday Success* (1994), were partly autobiographical, partly instructive, and partly promotional for Wendy's. His third book, written in collaboration with Michael Seid, was *Franchising for Dummies* (2000) and was intended to offer advice for prospective franchises. Likewise, **Carl Karcher**, founder of **Carl's Jr**., published *Never Stop Dreaming: The Story of Carl Karcher Enterprises* (1991), which was mainly a promotional book for his business enterprise. It was written in collaboration with B. Carolyn Knight, who wrote another promotional book, *Making It Happen: The Story of Carl Karcher Enterprises,* which was published by the firm.

Three unusual memoirs were penned by "**Ronald McDonald**," the fictitious **mascot** for McDonald's. The first book, *The Complete Hamburger: The History of America's Favorite Sandwich* (1997) includes a history of the company along with a myth-filled history of the hamburger. The second book, *Ronald McDonald's Franchise Buyers Guide: How to Buy a Fast Food Franchise* (2003), was targeted at those interested in buying McDonald's franchises. The third book, *Ronald McDonald's International Burger Book* (2004), adopted an international slant for a company that generated more revenue from its outlets in other countries than it did in the United States.

Many more have been published: George Cohon's *To Russia with Fries* (1997) describes how he set up McDonald's in Russia after the Berlin Wall fell in 1989; James W. McLamore's *The Burger King: Jim McLamore and the Building of an Empire* (1998) was published posthumously, more than 30 years after he sold the company to the Pillsbury Company; and Tony Conza's *Success: It's a Beautiful Thing. Lessons on Life and Business from the Founder of Blimpie International* (2000) offers sage advice and lots of personal anecdotes.

Compared to the fast food world, few memoirs have been written by those who helped make the **junk food** world. An exception was **Orville Redenbacher**, who published his *Orville Redenbacher's Popcorn Book* (1984) 10 years after he sold his business to Hunt-Wesson. Other founders of the **snack food** industry, such as **Frank** and **Forrest Mars** and **Milton S. Hershey**, preferred anonymity.

SUGGESTED READING: Wally Amos with Leroy Robinson, *The Famous Amos Story: The Face That Launched a Thousand Chips* (Garden City, NY: Doubleday, 1983); Wally Amos with Camilla

Denton, *The Man with No Name: Turn Lemons into Lemonade* (Lower Lake, CA: Aslan Publishers, 1994); Tony Conza, *Success: It's a Beautiful Thing: Lessons on Life and Business from the Founder of Blimpie International* (New York: Wiley, 2000); George Cohon, *To Russia with Fries* (Toronto: McFarlane, 1997); Billy Ingram, *All This from a 5-cent Hamburger! The Story of the White Castle System* (New York: Newcomen Society in North America, 1964); Carl Karcher and B. Carolyn Knight, *Never Stop Dreaming: The Story of Carl Karcher Enterprises* (San Marcos, CA: Robert Erdmann Publishing, 1991); Ray Kroc with Robert Anderson, *Grinding It Out: The Making of McDonald's* (Chicago: Henry Regnery Company, 1977); Ronald L. McDonald, *The Complete Hamburger: The History of America's Favorite Sandwich* (Secaucus, NJ: Carol Publishing Group, 1997); Ronald L. McDonald, *Ronald McDonald's International Burger Book* (Tucson, AZ: Hats Off Books, 2004); Ronald L. McDonald, *Ronald McDonald's International Burger Book* (Tucson, AZ: Hats Off Books, 2004); James W. McLamore, *The Burger King: Jim McLamore and the Building of an Empire* (New York: McGraw-Hill, 1998); Tom Monaghan with Robert Anderson, *Pizza Tiger* (New York: Random House, 1986); Orville Redenbacher, *Orville Redenbacher's Popcorn Book* (New York: St. Martin's Press, 1984); Harland Sanders, *Life as I Have Known It Has Been Finger Lickin' Good* (Carol Stream, IL: Creation House, 1974); R. David Thomas, *Dave's Way: A New Approach to Old-fashioned Success* (New York: G. P. Putnam's Sons, 1991); R. David Thomas, *Dave Says—Well Done! The Common Guy's Guide to Everyday Success* (Grand Rapids, MI: Zondervan, 1994).

Menus **Fast food chains** initially offered no-frills menus. During the 1920s, **White Castle** and its clones served only **hamburgers**, coffee, **soda**, and pie. Hamburgers composed of fried ground beef in a bun were easy and fast to prepare, and required little space to store. A limited menu was easier to prepare, required limited skills, and meant that preparation and service could be sped up. In addition, simple menus made it easy for fast food chains to order food from suppliers. Large orders for beef, buns, and potatoes gave the fast food chain corporations the power to set quality standards and seek the lowest possible prices from **suppliers**.

During the 1930s, a few new items were tried but menus generally remained limited. This changed during World War II due to wartime restrictions, such as rationing of beef and **sugar**. Because there were no restrictions on eggs, White Castle tried to replace hamburgers with egg **sandwiches** but they were not successful. There was also no restriction on potatoes, so **French fries** became an important part of fast food menus, only to be discontinued after the war due to hazards associated with the deep-frying equipment at the time. When the equipment improved during the 1950s, French fries were again added to the menus.

During the 1950s, the **McDonald's** menu was also highly restricted: hamburgers, cheeseburgers, sodas, shakes, and French fries. Other fast food chains, such as **pizza** parlors, fried **chicken** establishments, and **hot dog** purveyors, had similarly limited their menus. **Burger King** broke out of the mold when it introduced the Whopper in 1956. Its success encouraged McDonald's to introduce Big Macs and Quarter Pounders.

During the 1960s, Burger King and McDonald's added large dining areas, and fast food chains began to expand their menus. Another innovation, **drive-thru** windows, required the addition of items that could easily be consumed in the car, such as **Chicken McNuggets**, Chicken Tenders, and Chicken Fingers. During the 1970s, fast food chains added **breakfast** items to their menus, such as McDonald's Egg McMuffin and Burger King's Croissant Breakfast Sandwiches, French Toast Sticks, and Cini-Minis.

In 1973, Burger Chef added children's food to its menu. The chain was not successful, but McDonald's introduced child-oriented **Happy Meals** in 1978; other fast food chains did likewise. Studies of children's menus at Burger King, **Kentucky Fried Chicken**, **Wendy's**, **Taco Bell**, and **Pizza Hut** demonstrated that children's menus exceeded dietary recommendations in fat and calories.

Other menu innovations included so-called value meals, consisting of a preselected combination of foods such as a hamburger, French fries, and a soda. Customers order by the value meal number; this encourages customers to purchase more than they might if they just selected individual items. It also makes it easier and less time-consuming for the order taker and makes it easier for the person assembling the orders. Value meals led to another menu innovation, **supersizing**, which included extremely large portions of specific items such as French fries and sodas, and their inclusion in meal combinations.

Beginning in the 1980s, some restaurant chains added ethnic touches to their menus (e.g., McDonald's added its Breakfast Burrito). When fast food came under attack for being a **junk food**, salads, salad bars, carrot sticks, fat-free bran muffins, and low-fat **milk shakes** were added to many menus.

An unusual menu variation has been developed by **In-N-Out Burger**. It has a very simple public menu consisting of hamburgers, fries, sodas, and milk shakes. It also offers what it calls secret menu options, which are listed on its Web site, with all sorts of special variations on the basic menu. For instance, a 2x4 hamburger consists of two meat patties and four slices of cheese; Animal Fries include cheese and grilled onions with the French fries; and a Neapolitan Shake is a combination of **chocolate**, vanilla, and strawberry.

The launching of fast food restaurants in other countries necessitated changing menus to exclude items that might offend local sensibilities (such as beef hamburgers in India) and to add items intended to attract locals. Thus, beer and frankfurters are served at McDonald's in Germany; wine is served in France; chilled yogurt drinks are offered in Turkey; and espresso coffee, pasta, and Mediterranean Salad are on the menu in Italy. In India, Veggie burgers, Chicken Maharaja, Pizza McPuff, and cold coffee are offered. Teriyaki McBurgers are on the menu in Japan, Taiwan, and Hong Kong, and Samurai Pork Burgers are served in Thailand. A burger with a fried egg, called the Kiwi Burger, is a big item in New Zealand, and grilled salmon sandwiches, called McLaks, are served in Norway. The McNifica, a hamburger sandwich with cheese, is on the menu in Argentina and the McPepper is sold in Singapore. Customers in Athens can order a Greek Mac made with pita bread, beef patties, and a yogurt sauce.

Not all menu innovations have proven successful. In 2002, the McDonald's outlets in Norway released the McAfrika Burger, which supposedly had a "taste of Africa." At the time, South Africa was in the midst of disasters—heavy floods, drought, and finally starvation. Protesters complained that McDonald's should not have been profiting from a name when there were millions of people starving.

During the past 50 years, fast food menus have shifted from being simple and inexpensive (catering mainly to families and the working class) to being highly complex and occasionally costly, depending on location.

SUGGESTED READING: Eric Schlosser, *Fast Food Nation The Dark Side of the All-American Meal* (New York: Houghton Mifflin Company, 2001); Eric Schlosser and Charles Wilson, *Chew On This: Everything You Don't Want to Know about Fast Food* (Boston: Houghton Mifflin, 2006).

Mexican Food Mexican food has been consumed in the United States ever since the American annexation of Texas in 1845 and the American conquest of California and the Southwest in 1848. Mexican food, such as tamales, enchiladas, beans, and later tacos, were frequently served by street vendors in cities of the Southwest. To make them more appealing to Anglo tastes, Mexican foods were adapted in America. The taco was the staple of Cal-Mex food. Mexican tacos are basically any food rolled, folded, or fried into tortillas that are consumed by hand. The various fillings for tacos include chili sauce, beef (shredded or ground), **chicken**, pork, chorizo or sausage, egg, tomato, cheese, lettuce, guacamole, onions, and refried beans. Mexican tacos are usually soft-shelled, unlike the U-shaped crisp fried tortillas served in many American Mexican restaurants and fast food outlets.

Although avocados were grown in Florida during the early twentieth century, it was in California that avocado cookery took off. After World War II, corn chips and **potato chips** were recommended as guacamole dippers, but were soon replaced by **corn chips**.

The *burrito*, literally meaning little burro or donkey in Spanish, became irreversibly linked to the tortilla-rolled packages. Burritos entered Mexican-American cuisine in the Southwest around the 1950s and went nationwide a decade later. Many so-called Mexican dishes were concocted to please the American palate. Leftover tortillas could easily be cut up and used to scoop up sauces, beans and other foods. **Nachos**, for instance, originated in a Mexican border restaurant catering to Americans. They quickly spread throughout Texas, where they were served at a concession stand at the Texas State Fair in Dallas in1964. Within two decades, nachos were served nationwide in stadiums, airports, and fast food establishments.

The success of corn chips can be attributed in part to the related popularity of salsas, which are generally composed of various combinations of chili peppers, tomatoes, herbs, and spices. Salsa has been around since the time of the Aztecs. The first known manufacturer of salsa was Pace Foods of San Antonio, Texas. Dave Pace experimented with bottling salsa in 1947 and finally succeeded in getting the formula right the following year. Pace's initial market was regional. Other salsa products were produced by Old El Paso and Ortega. During the 1970s, salsa sales skyrocketed and Pace became the largest producer of Mexican sauces. The fresh salsa market exploded during the 1980s and continued to increase during the following decade. By the 1990s, salsa outsold **ketchup** in the United States. Consumption of these quasi-Mexican products was abetted by the American mania for salty **snack food**. Fritos, potato chips, **Doritos**, and tortilla Chips spurred supermarket sales of salsa and spicy dips, which in turn created a core of consumers willing to try more authentic Mexican food.

Thus, another significant type of commercialization was the establishment of Mexican fast food. Several small fast food operators established multi-unit, **drive-in** outlets near Los Angeles. Small Mexican-American roadside restaurants were often called taco stands. The first Mexican fast food franchise was launched in Downey, California, in 1962 by Glen Bell. **Taco Bell** quickly expanded around Los Angeles. In 1978, Taco Bell sold out to **PepsiCo**. Taco Bell had numerous imitators did not stray too far from the traditional American palate. The historian Harvey Levenstein attributes its success to being "no more spicy or un-American tasting than hamburgers." Still, Taco Bell had to overcome vast distrust and prejudice among consumers against Mexican restaurants and to emphasize that these were *American* restaurants that happened to serve somewhat Mexican ethnic food; Taco Bell exchanged its symbol of a sleeping Mexican in a sombrero for an innocuous pastel-colored bell. In terms of profit and popularity, tacos and other Mexican foods pale in comparison to pizza and other Italian foods. Other regional chains include **Del Taco** (Barstow, California), Taco Time, (Eugene, Oregon), Taco John's (Wyoming), Taco Maker (Ogden, Utah), Taco Casa (Topeka, Kansas), Pepe's (Chicago), and Pedro's Fine Mexican Foods (Mississippi).

SUGGESTED READING: Donna R. Gabaccia, *We Are What We Eat: Ethnic Food and the Making of Americans* (Cambridge, MA: Harvard University Press, 1998); Keith J. Guenther, "The Development of the Mexican-American Cuisine," in Alan Davidson, ed., *Oxford Symposium 1981: National & Regional Styles of Cookery. Proceedings* (London: Prospect Books, 1981); Harvey Levenstein, *Paradox of Plenty; A Social History of Eating in Modern America* (New York: Oxford University Press, 1993); Richard Pillsbury, *No Foreign Food: The American Diet in Time and Place* (Boulder, CO: Westview Press, 1998); Andrew F. Smith, "Tacos, Enchiladas and Refried Beans: The Invention of Mexican-American Cookery," in Mary Wallace Kelsey and ZoeAnn Holmes, eds., *Cultural and Historical Aspects of Foods* (Corvallis, OR: Oregon State University, 1999, 183–203).

Mike and Ike Mike and Ike candies were first manufactured in 1940 by **Just Born**, Inc. of Bethlehem, Pennsylvania. The original Mike and Ike was a chewy, fruit-flavored **candy**. Early flavors included as Root-T-Toot (root beer–flavored) and Jack and Jill (licorice-flavored). In 1953, Just Born acquired the Rodda Candy Company, one of whose specialties was making **jelly beans**. With this technology, Just Born was able to create additional types of fruit-flavored Mike and Ike candies. During the late twentieth century, the company began manufacturing stronger flavors, such as their Tropical Fruits and Berry Fruits. These were followed by Tropical Typhoon, Berry Blast, and Tangy Twister. Unlike most other large candy companies, The Just Born company remains family-owned.

SUGGESTED READING: Tim Richardson, *Sweets: A History of Candy* (New York: Bloomsbury, 2002); Just Born Web site: www.justborn.com

Milk Duds Introduced in 1926 by the Halloway Company of Chicago, Milk Duds were small pieces of **caramel candy** covered with **chocolate**, packaged in a small cardboard box. They were supposed to be round but they ended up oval-shaped, hence their name—duds. Milk Duds were commonly sold in movie theaters and in grocery stores. The company was sold to Beatrice Foods Company in 1960, which was then merged with the D. L. Clark Company, makers of the Clark Bar. Today, Milk Duds are manufactured by the **New England Confectionery Company**.

SUGGESTED READING: Ray Broekel, *The Great America Candy Bar Book* (Boston: Houghton Mifflin Company, 1982); Tim Richardson, *Sweets: A History of Candy* (New York: Bloomsbury, 2002).

Milk Shakes, Malts, and Ice Cream Sodas Milk, flavorings, and **ice cream** were combined by the mid-nineteenth century. At the Franklin Institute of Philadelphia, the first ice cream **soda** is credited to Robert Green; he reportedly added ice cream to soda water in 1874.

Before the advent of high-speed blenders, thick milk shakes remained a novelty sold largely at **soda fountains**. The term *malted milk* was trademarked by William Horlick of Racine, Wisconsin. His product consisted of malted barley and wheat flour mixed with powdered milk.

With the invention of practical electric blenders by Hamilton Beach in 1911, milk shakes and similar drinks, such as malts, became popular, particularly during Prohibition. **Fast food** restaurants began selling milk shakes by the 1930s, but **White Castle** discontinued them when they concluded that they took too long to make and they ruined customers' appetites for **hamburgers**.

In the late 1930s, the invention of the Multimixer permitted several milk shakes to be made simultaneously. Salesman **Ray Kroc** was so impressed with the invention that he purchased the rights for the Multimixer in 1939. After World War II, it was sold to ice cream fast food chains such as **Tastee-Freez** and **Dairy Queen**. Due to stiff competition, sales declined in the early 1950s. At that time, Kroc noted that Richard and Maurice McDonald had purchased eight Multimixers. He decided to visit their new fast food restaurant in San Bernardino, California. Employees made 80 milk shakes before the fast food operation opened, and stored them in the freezer. When customers ordered milk shakes, more shakes were made. The result was that the brothers were selling 20,000 shakes a month. Just as important, Kroc saw hundreds of customers waiting in line to buy the hamburgers, **French fries**, and **beverages** and he was impressed. The visit ended with Kroc acquiring the rights to **franchise McDonald's** nationwide.

In the early 1950s, George Read invented a Miracle Insta Machines, which was an improved version of the Multimixer. Keith Cramer, a **drive-in** restaurateur from Daytona Beach, Florida, acquired the rights to this and another machine. Cramer launched Insta-Burger-King in 1952 in Jacksonville, Florida. The name of the company was subsequently shortened to **Burger King**.

Since the 1950s, milk shakes have been an integral part of most fast food operations, although some **chains** have created similar products, such as **Wendy's** Frosty, a combination of milk, **sugar**, cream, and flavorings. Other types of shakes were developed by other chains.

SUGGESTED READING: Anne Cooper Funderburg, *Sundae Best: A History of Soda Fountains* (Bowling Green, OH: Bowling Green State University Popular Press, 2002); John A. Jakle and Keith A. Sculle, *Fast Food: Roadside Restaurants in the Automobile Age* (Baltimore: Johns Hopkins University Press, 1999).

Milky Way In 1923, **Frank Mars** of Minneapolis introduced the Milky Way bar, which received local distribution. It consisted of a center of malt-flavored nougat (made with egg whites, corn syrup, and air) with a **chocolate** coating that kept the candy bar fresh. It was bigger than the other **candy** bars, such as **Hershey's Chocolate Bar**, then on the market. It was also less costly to make than the Hershey's bar because it had half as much chocolate, which was the most expensive ingredient. In 1924, Milky Way was marketed nationally and its sales topped $800,000 in its first year. Because Mars, Inc. did not have the technology to make chocolate, its chocolate was supplied by Hershey's. In 1935 Milky Way was advertised as "The sweet you can eat between meals."

Forrest Mars, Frank Mars's son who later became the head of **Mars, Inc.**, claimed that he gave the idea for the candy bar to his father. Today, Milky Way remains one of America's best-selling candy bars.

SUGGESTED READING: Joël Glenn Brenner, *The Emperors of Chocolate: Inside the Secret World of Hershey and Mars* (New York: Broadway Books, 2000); Ray Broekel, *The Great America Candy Bar Book* (Boston: Houghton Mifflin Company, 1982); Tim Richardson, *Sweets: A History of Candy* (New York: Bloomsbury, 2002).

Minimum Wage Historically, **fast food chains** have thrived because of their low costs, which are directly connected their low employee wages. While most chains give outlet managers the responsibility of setting wages depending upon local conditions, by and large most employees receive minimum wage. In the United States, minimum wages are set by the federal and state governments. In 2006, the federal minimum wage is $5.15 per hour. States may have higher minimum wages; New York state's minimum wage, for instance, is $6.15 per hour.

Minimum wage does not encourage workers to remain long, and most employees leave such jobs after a few months. The incredibly high turnover rate for most fast food chains is one of the reasons why James C. Doherty, the publisher of *Nation's Restaurant News*, has encouraged fast food chains to increase employee wages to attract better and more loyal workers. Minimum wages do not provide enough income for a worker to make an independent living. There is minimal opportunity for upward mobility and fast food employment is not respected socially. Nevertheless, the National Restaurant Association and the fast food chains have all opposed increases in minimum wage. Some corporations have **lobbied** for even lower youth minimum wages, which would exempt them from paying minimum wages for 16- and 17-year-olds. They have also lobbied for exemptions from minimum wages for workers from overseas. As it is, fast food chains pay minimum wage to a higher percentage of its workers than does any other industry in America.

SUGGESTED READING: David Gerard Hogan, *Selling 'em by the Sack: White Castle and the Creation of American Food* (New York: New York University Press, 1997); Eric Schlosser, *Fast Food Nation The Dark Side of the All-American Meal* (New York: Houghton Mifflin Company, 2001); Jennifer Parker Talwar, *Fast Food, Fast Track: Immigrants, Big Business, and the American Dream* (Cambridge, MA: Westview Press, 2002).

Monaghan, Tom **Pizza** king Thomas S. Monaghan (1937–) was born in Ann Arbor, Michigan, and spent much of his early life in a Catholic orphanage and foster homes. He worked as a **soda** jerk and barely graduated from high school. He joined the Marine Corps in 1956 and, when he left four years later, he enrolled in the University of Michigan. While still a student, he and his brother James bought a pizzeria called Dominick's Pizza in Ypsilanti, Michigan. His brother quit the partnership eight months later and Tom Monaghan changed the name of the restaurant to **Domino's Pizza**.

Monaghan visited New York pizzerias and spent 12 years blending sauces before he ended up with one combination that he liked. Domino's developed a **fast food** delivery system and the company rapidly expanded. Under Monagham's leadership, Domino's prospered and he became a wealthy man.

In 1983, Monaghan bought the Detroit Tigers, who won the World Series a year later. Monaghan ultimately sold the Tigers to his pizza competitor Mike Ilitch of **Little Caesar's Pizza**. In 1992 Monaghan, a conservative Catholic, supported efforts to ban abortion. Domino's Pizza was adversely affected by the position he took, and in 1998 Monaghan sold most of his interest in the company to a private investment group. He subsequently became chancellor of Ave Maria University.

SUGGESTED READING: Tom Monaghan with Robert Anderson, *Pizza Tiger* (New York: Random House, 1986).

Moon Pie In 1917, the Chattanooga Bakery released the Moon Pie, a small, round confection consisting of two **chocolate**-covered, wheat-based cakes with a marshmallow filling. Earl Mitchell, Sr. claimed to have invented it based on what coal miners said they wanted in a snack. The Moon Pie was so successful that by the late 1950s the Chattanooga Bakery was producing only Moon Pies. The company has extended the product line with Mini Moon Pies, Double and Single Deckers, and Fruit-Filled Moon Pies. Moon Pies are mainly consumed in the South but have become an American icon.

SUGGESTED READING: Ron Dickson with William M. Clark and others, *The Great American Moon Pie Handbook* (Atlanta: Peachtree Publishers, 1985); Moon Pie Web site: www.moonpie.com

Mounds Bar In 1922, the **Peter Paul Candy Company** of New Haven, Connecticut introduced the Mounds bar, consisting of **chocolate**-covered sweetened coconut. Each package included two bars. The company released the Almond Joy **candy** bar in 1946. It was similar to the Mounds bar except that each bar included two almonds.

The company's **advertising** campaign for Mounds and Almond Joy remains a classic. Its jingle "Sometimes you feel like a nut, sometimes you don't" was inducted into the Advertising Slogan Hall of Fame in 2002.

Cadbury USA acquired the Peter Paul Candy Company in 1978. Ten years later, the **Hershey Company** acquired the brand and extended its product line to include new flavors, such as Pina Colada, Key Lime, Milk Chocolate, and Passion Fruit varieties.

SUGGESTED READING: Joël Glenn Brenner, *The Emperors of Chocolate: Inside the Secret World of Hershey and Mars* (New York: Broadway Books, 2000); Hershey's Web site: www.hersheys.com; Tim Richardson, *Sweets: A History of Candy* (New York: Bloomsbury, 2002).

Mountain Dew This **soft drink** was developed over a period of years, beginning in the 1940s. Bill Bridgforth of Tri-City Beverage of Johnson City, Tennessee, was instrumental in creating its final formula in 1958. Mountain Dew was acquired by the Pepsi-Cola Company (now **PepsiCo**) in 1964. PepsiCo aggressively promoted Mountain Dew nationally during the late 1980s, and expanded the product line. Diet Mountain Dew made its debut in 1988 and in 2001, PepsiCo introduced Mountain Dew Code Red and Amp Energy Drink. A 1993 Mountain Dew commercial popularized the phrase, "Been there, done that." The **Coca-Cola Company** introduced Mello Yello to compete with Mountain Dew in 1979.

SUGGESTED READING: Mountain Dew Web site: www.mountaindew.com

Moxie In 1876, Augustin Thompson, an itinerant pharmacist, concocted Moxie Nerve Food in Lowell, Massachusetts. He began distributing the dark syrup and other patent medicines throughout New England. Thompson promoted Moxie as a cure for such ailments as "dullness of the brain" and baldness. He was so successful in his promotional efforts that by 1890 the word *moxie* entered the American language as a synonym for nerve, courage, and vigor.

As many aficionados admit, the taste for Moxie is acquired. Its main ingredient is gentian root, which gives the beverage its distinctive medicinal smell and taste. When soda was first added to Moxie is unclear.

Frank M. Archer started his career as a clerk at Moxie and worked his was up to its advertising executive. He was an innovator in the use of creative **advertising**. In 1904 he released a Moxie song at the St. Louis world's fair, one of the first food companies to do so. He reinvented Moxie's image after the passage of the Pure Food and Drug Act in 1906. The drink became "the distinctive beverage for those of discerning taste." The Moxie logo was printed on everything from cardboard fans to Tiffany lamps, and eight-foot-high Moxie bottles were pulled by horse-drawn wagons to promote the **beverage** at seaside amusement parks and in small towns across New England.

By 1920, Moxie's sales of 25 million cases a year was greater than **Coca-Cola**. In 1925, high **sugar** prices forced the company to cut back on its promotional efforts. Moxie sales declined while those of Coca-Cola increased. Baseball player Ted Williams promoted the beverage in the 1940s and 1950s, but sales continued to decline and the Moxie Company was eventually acquired by the Monarch Company of Atlanta.

Moxie. © Kelly Fitzsimmons

Several books and numerous articles have told and retold the Moxie story. Moxie has a loyal following in New England, especially in Maine, where a Moxie festival draws 25,000 people annually.

SUGGESTED READING: Q. David Bowers, *The Moxie Encyclopedia,* Vol. 1 (Vestal, NY: Vestal Press, 1985); Anne Cooper Funderburg, *Sundae Best: A History of Soda Fountains* (Bowling Green, OH: Bowling Green State University Popular Press, 2002); Frank N. Potter, *The Moxie Mystique* (Virginia Beach, VA: Donning Co., 1981); Frank N. Potter, *The Book of Moxie* (Paducah, KY: Collector Books 1987); Joseph A. Veilleux, *Moxie: Since 1884, an Acquired Taste* (Bloomington, IN: 1st Books, 2003).

Mr. Peanut Two Italian immigrants, Amedeo Obici and Mario Peruzzi, launched Planters Peanuts in 1906. Ten years later, their firm had thrived and the partners believed that they needed to promote their company nationally. As the story goes, Planters conducted a contest to help select a logo for the company, which offered $5 for the best design. The winner was a 14-year-old boy named Anthony Gentile, who submitted a drawing of "a little peanut person." With this image as a starting point, Planters hired a Chicago art firm, which commissioned a commercial artist named Andrew Wallach to draw several different caricatures. Planters selected the image of a peanut person with a top hat, monocle, cane, and the look of a raffish gentleman, which was subsequently dubbed Mr. Peanut. Despite the preceding story perpetuated by the company, similar peanut figures, complete with top hat, monocle, cane and gloves, had appeared in print years before, in an illustrated article in *Good Housekeeping* magazine.

Whatever the origin, Mr. Peanut was a solid **advertising** success aimed at America's youth. Planters applied for a trademark on it on March 12, 1917. Mr. Peanut made his debut in New England newspapers and on advertising posters in New York City subways. This was followed by a national advertising campaign in which Mr. Peanut appeared in the *Saturday Evening Post.* These were so successful that Planters increased its advertising budget for each succeeding year, spending hundreds of thousands of dollars on ads in the best newspapers and magazines in the country. In advertisements, Mr. Peanut proclaimed that peanuts were a perfect food for picnics and baseball games, and was an ideal ingredient in main dishes served at lunch and dinner.

The company used other media as well; they published a Mr. Peanut's Paint Book, and the company's print promotions moved from commonplace advertising to novel schemes that drew in readers. Such advertising paid off, and annual sales rose from $1 million in 1917 to $7 million five years later.

Since its origin, Mr. Peanut has been on virtually every Planters package, container, premium, and advertisement. As a result, the Mr. Peanut caricature has become one of the most familiar icons in advertising history. His likeness graces mugs, pencils, pens, and tote bags that are available by redeeming product wrappers. Planters has offered a variety of premium items with its products: glass jars, charm bracelets, clocks, metal tins, wristwatches, ashtrays, plastic whistles, and display figures with monocles that light up. At the beginning of the twenty-first century, Mr. Peanut is an American culinary icon known the world over.

SUGGESTED READING: Jan Lindenberger with Joyce Spontak, *Planters Peanut Collectibles since 1961* (Atglen, PA: Schiffer Publishing, 1995); Jan Lindenberger with Joyce Spontak, *Planters Peanut Collectibles 1906–1961*, 2nd ed. (Atglen, PA: Schiffer Publishing, 1999); Andrew F. Smith, *Peanuts: The Illustrious History of the Goober Pea* (Urbana, IL: University of Illinois Press, 2002).

Mrs. Fields Cookies In 1977, Debra "Debbi" Fields, a 20-year-old mother with no business experience, and her husband opened their first **cookie** store near Stanford University in Palo Alto, California. Mrs. Fields began **franchising** in 1990. In 1992 she teamed up with Time-Life Books to publish a cookbook on cookies. The following year, she sold Mrs. Fields Cookies to private investors in Utah. As of 2005, Mrs. Fields Cookies had more than 700 locations in 11 countries.

SUGGESTED READING: Debbi Fields and the editors of Time-Life Books, *Mrs. Fields Cookie Book: 100 Recipes from the Kitchen of Mrs. Fields* (Alexandria, VA: Time-Life Books, 1992); Debbi Fields and the editors of Time-Life Books, *Mrs. Fields Best Cookie Book Ever!* (Alexandria, VA: Time-Life Books, 1996); Mrs. Fields Web site: www.mrsfields.com

Music Music has been used to promote food products since at least the early twentieth century. In 1904, the soft drink **Moxie** released a song at the 1904 St. Louis world's fair, one of the first food companies to do so. As **radio** became an important vehicle for snack food promotion, songs and jingles were used by various manufacturers, such as the **Cracker Jack** Company.

Songs have also affected the adoption of foods. In 1953 a popular song, "That's Amore," sung by Dean Martin, included the lyric "When the moon hits your eye like a big pizza pie," which is believed to have helped popularize **pizza** in the United States. So important was **snack food** in the song "Junk Food Junkie" climbed to the top of the charts in 1976.

Fast food chains have historically piped music into their outlets to attract a particular audience. Currently, most fast food chains are interested in attracting parents, so the music usually comes from the soft-rock tunes of the 1960s through the 1980s.

Most fast food chains and **junk food** manufacturers have advertised extensively on radio and **television**, and many have developed jingles, some of which have become popular, such as **Pizza Hut**'s 1965 musical jingle, "Putt-Putt to Pizza Hut" or **Peter Paul**'s jingle for Mound's/Almond Joy candy bars, "Sometimes you feel like a nut, sometimes you don't," or **McDonald's** jingle for Big Macs, "Two all-beef patties, special sauce, lettuce, cheese, pickles, onions on a sesame seed bun." It originally aired in 1982 and was resuscitated in 2003.

Fast food chains have begun to produce and sell music videos. McDonald's, for instance, has its own line of music videos featuring McDonaldland characters; they sell for $3.49. In 2005, McDonald's tested digital-media kiosks that allow customers to burn custom CDs from a catalog of 70,000 hit songs.

SUGGESTED READING: John A. Jakle and Keith A. Sculle, *Fast Food: Roadside Restaurants in the Automobile Age* (Baltimore: Johns Hopkins University Press, 1999); Eric Schlosser, *Fast Food Nation: The Dark Side of the All-American Meal* (New York: Houghton Mifflin Company, 2001).

N

Nabisco In 1889, William Moore united six Eastern bakeries into the New York Biscuit Company. In 1890, Adolphus Green united 40 Midwestern bakeries under the name the American Biscuit & Manufacturing Company. In 1898, Moore and Green merged their two companies, along with the United States Baking Company, to form the National Biscuit Company (its corporate name did not change to Nabisco until 1971).

In 1898, Adolphus Green, the first president of the National Biscuit Company, launched a cracker with a new shape that was lighter and flakier than other crackers at the time. Green named it Uneeda Biscuit and packaged it with an inner-seal package that kept the biscuits fresh. The company then launched one of the first national **advertising** campaigns for a food product.

The company acquired other companies, including the Shredded Wheat Company, maker of Triscuits and Shredded Wheat cereal. During this time, the company was also busy developing new **cookies** and crackers, including Barnum's Animal Crackers, **Oreos**, **Ritz Crackers**, and Honey Maid **Graham Crackers**. During the 1920s, the company expanded rapidly, acquiring companies such as **Jell-O** (1925), and opening offices abroad, including Canada, Puerto Rico, France, and the United Kingdom.

In 1981, Nabisco merged with Standard Brands, maker of Planters Nuts, **LifeSaver** candies, and other successful businesses. Philip Morris Companies, Inc. acquired Nabisco in December 2000 and merged it with **Kraft Foods**, Inc.

SUGGESTED READING: William Cahn, *Out of the Cracker Barrel: the Nabisco Story, from Animal Crackers to Zuzus* (New York: Simon and Schuster, 1969); Bryan Burrough and John Helyar, *Barbarians at the Gate: The Fall of RJR Nabisco* (New York: HarperBusiness Essentials, 2003).

Nachos Nachos are tortilla triangles covered with melted cheese and jalapeño peppers. They are credited to Ignacio Anaya, a chef at the old Victory Club in Piedras Negras, Mexico, across the border from Eagle Pass, Texas. Anaya assembled nachos for some Eagle Pass ladies who stopped in during a shopping trip in the 1940s. Nachos were popularized at the 1964 Texas State Fair and were disseminated throughout the United States during the late 1960s and 1970s. Nacho-flavored **corn chips** and **potato chips** were soon on the market. Nachos were also the spearhead of a national interest in ethnic flavors that were soon applied to corn chips, including jalapeño, cheese, nacho cheese flavor, and other spicy seasonings. Ballpark nachos were first introduced into the Texas Rangers's

Arlington Stadium in 1975. Nacho flavoring became popular and some commercial tortilla chips were called nacho-flavored. For instance, the **Frito-Lay** company introduced Nacho Cheese Flavored **Doritos** in 1972. Today, nachos are widely sold in a variety of different outlets, including **fast food** restaurants, air ports, fairs, and movie **theaters**.

SUGGESTED READING: Andrew F Smith. "Tacos, Enchiladas and Refried Beans: The Invention of Mexican-American Cookery," in Mary Wallace Kelsey and ZoeAnn Holmes, eds., *Cultural and Historical Aspects of Foods*. (Corvallis: Oregon State University, 1999), 183–203.

Nathan's Famous In 1915, Nathan Handwerker, a Polish immigrant, answered a Help Wanted advertisement for Charles Feltman's restaurant in Coney Island, New York. Feltman originated the sausage in a bun concept, which he sold for a dime apiece. Handwerker worked at Feltman's for a year, and with $300 savings he opened a **hot dog** stand of his own a few blocks from Feltman's.

On a 12-foot grill Handwerker sold his take-out hot dogs for a nickel, thus undercutting Feltman. Handwerker installed signs with horns that sounded like fire-engine sirens. Tradition has it that he hired students to wear white coats (imitating doctors) to sit and eat at his stand, giving the impression that his low-cost hot dogs were healthy.

When the New York subway opened in the 1920s, Nathan's became extremely popular, but Coney Island faded after World War II. Feltman's closed in 1954. Nathan's survived by expanding its operation, opening outlets in other cities. Nathan's expanded rapidly during the 1980s when investors encouraged the growth of larger restaurants. They proved unsuccessful and the company downsized.

Nathan's Famous, Inc. has attempted to promote its operation in a variety of ways. In the 1980s, it published a series of hot dog cookbooks. More spectacular has been its sponsorship of a hot dog eating contest, which is conducted at its outlet on Coney Island every July 4th. In 2005, the winner, Takeru Kobayashi of Japan, consumed 49 Nathan's Famous hot dogs and buns in 12 minutes.

As of 2001, Nathan's consisted of 24 company-owned units and 380 franchised or licensed outlets. Nathan's branded products are also sold by more than 1,400 independent foodservice operators which have outlets at airports, hotels, sports arenas, convention centers, colleges, and convenience stores. In all, the company operates in 41 states and 17 foreign countries. Nathan's has also acquired the rights to co-brand with **Arthur Treacher's** Fish & Chips and it has acquired Kenny Rogers Roasters and Miami Subs.

SUGGESTED READING: Murray Handwerker, *Nathan's Famous Hot Dog Cookbook* (New York: Gramercy Publishing, 1983); Nathan's Web site: www.nathansfamous.com

National Confectioners Association In 1884, 69 confectionery manufacturing companies met in Chicago and formed the National Confectioners Association (NCA). At the time, due to a lack of hygiene, some confectioners adulterated their products with varnish, brick dust, lead, and insect parts to improve coloring. The NCA's goal was to foster industry self-regulation and lobby against adulterants. The NCA also encouraged its members to connect candy promotions to holidays, such as **Valentine's Day**, Christmas, Mother's Day, and **Halloween**. It has held annual meetings to address problems confronting the industry. Its 2005 All Candy Expo, held in Chicago, drew more than 17,000 participants. Today, the NCA has a membership of 700 **candy** manufacturers and suppliers. The NCA is affiliated with the Chocolate Manufacturers Association and the

World Cocoa Foundation. According to its Web site, the NCA "sponsors education programs, technical research, public relations, retailing practices, and statistical analyses." NCA is headquartered in Vienna, Virginia.

The NCA has also promoted the interests of its members by lobbing at all levels of government. It has been responsible for federal and state legislation prohibiting adulteration of confections. During World War II, the NCA successfully opposed government efforts to declare candy manufacturing a nonessential industry. In 1944, the NCA spent $21 million on magazine and other **advertising** proclaiming that candy gave the American military its energy. The NCA spends money on promotions which present confections as healthful foods, using the slogan "Eat Candy, the Energy Food."

Today, the NCA lobbies on matters of concern to the industry, favoring price supports for **sugar** and peanuts and the repeal of state taxation of candy, and opposing **nutrition** labeling. It has also weighed in on matters connected with international trade affecting the industry. Since 1968, the NCA and the Chocolate Manufacturers Association have stocked the U.S. Senate's Candy Desk so that candy is always available to senators. In addition, the NCA has joined with other **junk food** purveyors to create the American Council on Fitness and Nutrition, which encourages exercise and opposes the reduction of high-**fat**, high-sugar, low-nutrition junk foods. The Council has also lobbied against national standards for school food.

SUGGESTED READING: Joël Glenn Brenner, *The Emperors of Chocolate: Inside the Secret World of Hershey and Mars* (New York: Broadway Books, 2000); National Confectioners Association Web site: www.ecandy.com

Neighborhoods **Fast food chains** have selected specific neighborhoods for opening their outlets. For example, prior to World War II, **White Castle** intentionally selected inner-city sites, but after World War II **crime** increased in inner cities and the traditional customers of fast food establishments left those areas. Fast food outlets closed or deteriorated along with the neighborhoods they were in, and many critics blame fast food establishments for contributing to **urban blight**.

After World War II, fast food chains initially targeted suburbs as the best location for their outlets. At the time, fast food chains were mainly **drive-ins** and they needed space for parking lots, and space was easily available in fast-growing suburbs.

Fast food drive-ins, such as **McDonald's** and **Burger King**, in the 1950s did not have indoor dining space, making it more difficult for them to operate in inner cities. This changed in the 1960s when Burger King, and then McDonald's, began developing outlets with indoor dining areas, and moved full-speed into cities. Concern has been expressed that fast food chains run local restaurants out of businesses, thus homogenizing neighborhoods.

SUGGESTED READING: John A. Jakle and Keith A. Sculle, *Fast Food: Roadside Restaurants in the Automobile Age* (Baltimore: Johns Hopkins University Press, 1999).

Nestlé SA Headquartered in Vevey, Switzerland, Nestlé SA is one of the world's largest food and **beverage** companies. It was founded in 1866 by Henri Nestlé, a pharmacist who had developed an infant formula. By the early 1900s, the company was operating factories in the United States, the United Kingdom, Germany, and Spain. The company introduced Nestlé's Tollhouse Morsels in 1939. After World War II, Nestlé began to grow rapidly. It acquired Maggi seasonings and soups (1947), Crosse & Blackwell (1960), Libby's (1971), Stouffer's (1973), Carnation (1985), Ralston Purina (2002), Chef America (2002), and Dryer's (2002).

As of 2005, Nestlé's brands included **Drumstick**, **Push-Ups**, **Häagen-Dazs**, **Dreyer's/Edy's**, and many others. Its candy lines include Nestlé Crunch, Kit Kat, **Baby Ruth**, and **Butterfinger**.

SUGGESTED READING: Nestlé Web site: www.nestle.com; Friedhelm Schwarz (Maya Anyas, trans.), *Nestlé: The Secrets of Food, Trust, and Globalization* (Toronto: Key Porter Books, 2002).

NECCO landmark. © Kelly Fitzsimmons

New England Confectionery Company Begun in 1847, the New England Confectionery Company (NECCO) is the oldest continuously operating **candy** company in America. One of its earliest products was Conversation Hearts. NECCO renamed them Sweethearts in 1902, when they became associated with **Valentine's Day**. The company introduced a profit-sharing system for its workers in 1906 and a life insurance program in 1920. The famous NECCO wafers—hard disks of various-flavored and -colored candy—first appeared in 1912; they had previously been called Peerless Wafers. The Bolster Bar—peanut crunch covered with milk **chocolate**—was also manufactured by NECCO. The company introduced its Sky Bar in 1937 with a dramatic airplane skywriting campaign. NECCO has made a number of acquisitions: In 1990, it purchased the Stark Candy Company, which brought to NECCO the Peanut Butter Kiss, Salt Water Taffy, and **Mary Jane Candies**. It acquired the Clark Bar in 1999. Today, Sweethearts are the best-selling Valentine's Day candy in the United States.

SUGGESTED READING: Ray Broekel, *The Great America Candy Bar Book* (Boston: Houghton Mifflin Company, 1982); Tim Richardson, *Sweets: A History of Candy* (New York: Bloomsbury, 2002); Andrew F. Smith, *Peanuts: The Illustrious History of the Goober Pea* (Urbana, IL: University of Illinois Press, 2002); Louis Untermeyer, *A Century of Candymaking 1847–1947: The Story of the Origin and Growth of the New England Confectionery Company* (Boston: The Barta Press, 1947).

Newspapers Since the advent of commercial **snack food** in the late nineteenth century, manufacturers and retailers have used newspapers to **advertise** their products. Because most newspapers are generally distributed within a limited geographic region, advertisers are usually local retailers of products. Likewise, **fast food** outlets began advertising in newspapers beginning in the 1920s. Successful types of newspaper advertising include **coupons** that offer reduced prices for products.

Junk food and fast food companies have also worked hard to acquire space in the news sections of newspapers through press releases and by conducting unusual promotional activities.

SUGGESTED READING: John A. Jakle and Keith A. Sculle, *Fast Food: Roadside Restaurants in the Automobile Age* (Baltimore: Johns Hopkins University Press, 1999).

Nutrition For millennia, humans have been aware of the relationship between food and health. By 1840, chemists had classified food into three categories: **carbohydrates**, **fats**, and proteins. Carbohydrates, mainly **sugars** and starches, make up the bulk of our diet and constitute our chief source of energy. Dietary fats, now generally called lipids, include vegetable oil and animal fat. Lipids are highly concentrated sources of energy, furnishing more calories than either carbohydrates or proteins. Proteins are the major source of building material for the body; they repair and replace worn tissue.

During the twentieth century, vitamins were discovered, isolated, and identified. Today, 17 vitamins have been identified as essential, which means that the human body cannot synthesize them and they must be ingested for the body to function properly.

Minerals were also found to be essential for the proper functioning of the human body. Minerals act as catalysts in many biochemical reactions of the body and are also vital to the growth of bones, muscular contractions, digestion, and many other functions. Calcium, for instance, is essential for proper heart rhythm, iron for blood formation, and phosphorus for healthy bones and teeth. Some minerals, such as calcium, iron, and sulfur, are required in relatively large amounts whereas others, such as zinc, copper, iodine, and fluoride are required in smaller (trace) amounts. Today, 24 minerals, called micronutrients, have been identified as essential.

During the late twentieth and early twenty-first centuries, the major focus of nutrition has shifted from concern about which foods are required to avoid deficiencies and illness, to what foods and supplements may be consumed to promote health. Nutrition studies today are spread over the fields of medicine, biochemistry, physiology, behavioral and social sciences, as well as public health sciences.

Beginning in the 1970s, nutritionists began to attack **junk food** and **fast food**, which were linked with **diabetes**, heart disease, and **obesity**. Junk foods were vilified as containing empty calories. John Yudkin, a professor of nutrition at London University, attacked sugar in his *Pure, White and Deadly* (1972). The British Heart Foundation's attacks included "[S]aturated fat from red meat, biscuits, cakes, chips and dairy products can clog up your arteries and put strain on your heart." Many people prefer high-sugar and high-fat diets to healthier foods.

The **Center for Science in the Public Interest** has attacked soft drinks because of their calories and because consumers prefer **soda** instead of healthy, low-fat milk, fruit juice, or fruit—foods that contribute to reduction "of osteoporosis, cancer, or heart disease." Eating junk food filled people up and therefore they ate fewer healthier foods.

SUGGESTED READING: Carolyn D. Berdanier, et al., *Handbook of Nutrition and Food* (Boca Raton, FL: CRC Press, 2002); Myrna Chandler Goldstein and Mark A. Goldstein. *Controversies in Food and Nutrition* (Westport, CT: Greenwood Press, 2002); Babasaheb B. Desai, *Handbook of Nutrition and Diet* (New York: Marcel Dekker, 2000); Walter Gratzer, *Terrors of the Table: The Curious History of Nutrition* (New York: Oxford University Press, 2005); Autumn Libal, *Fats, Sugars, and Empty Calories: The Fast Food Habit* (Philadelphia: Mason Crest Publishers, 2005); Marion Nestle, *Food Politics: How the Food Industry Influences Nutrition and Health* (Berkeley, CA: University of California Press, 2002); "Junk Pack," *Nutrition Action Health Letter*, 32 (March 2005): 16; Jacqueline Yallop and Bill Campbell, "Junk Food," *Times Educational Supplement* (June 10, 2005): pp. F11–F14.

Nutritional Guidelines Various groups around the world have issued nutritional guidelines. Special guidelines have been issued for sports, the elderly, children, diabetics, babies, school meals, and so forth. For example, the Sloan-Kettering Cancer Center recommends a diet "low in fat (20 percent of daily calories from **fat**), high in fiber, and rich in fruits and vegetables (five to nine servings per day), which can encourage weight loss and may reduce the risk of some cancers, as well as other chronic diseases such as heart disease, **diabetes**, and hypertension."

In 1940, the National Academy of Sciences established a committee to advise the government on **nutrition**. It established standards for the armed forces and for the general population and offered Recommended Dietary Allowances (RDA) for energy, along with eight essential vitamins and minerals. During the war, the **U.S. Department of Agriculture** (USDA) developed food guides based on the availability of food during wartime food shortages. Its *National Wartime Nutrition Guide* promoted the Basic Seven, which were food categories to be consumed every day. This was modified after the war to the Basic Four, which stressed meat, eggs, poultry, and fish in one category. The other categories were milk, vegetables and fruits, and grain products. As new research demonstrated additional requirements, new guidelines were developed.

In the 1980s, the Department of Health and Human Services and the USDA developed the *Dietary Guidelines for Americans* and it is updated and re-released every five years. Based on the 1990 Guidelines, the USDA developed the **Food Pyramid**, which is a visual representation of the recommendations in *Guidelines*. The latest *Guidelines* were issued in June 2005. Simultaneously, MyPyramid was released by the USDA. The *Guidelines* provide authoritative advice about how good dietary habits promote health and reduce risk for major chronic diseases; this information is applicable to anyone older than two years of age. Among its recommendations are to "consume a variety of nutrient-dense foods and beverages within and among the basic food groups while choosing foods that limit the intake of saturated and trans fats, **cholesterol**, added **sugars**, **salt**, and alcohol." Regarding weight gain, the *Guidelines* recommend making "decreases in food and beverage calories and increase physical activity."

Two general problems have emerged with regard to guidelines. The first is that they change frequently. Several items that were highly recommended foods during the 1950s, for example, (including eggs, butter, and red meats) were later discouraged. The second is that nutritional guidelines released by countries differ greatly from each other, and even differ from the guidelines of neighboring countries.

SUGGESTED READING: Marion Nestle, *Food Politics: How the Food Industry Influences Nutrition and Health* (Berkeley, CA: University of California Press, 2002); Dietary Guidelines for Americans Web site: www.healthierus.gov/dietaryguidelines

Nuts Roasted chestnuts and other nuts have been sold on America's streets since colonial times. Nuts require little preparation and can be easily transported. They are relatively inexpensive and are generally nutritious. The most important nuts sold in America today are almonds, walnuts, and pecans, followed by chestnuts, pistachios, and Macadamias. All are grown extensively in California, with the exception of Macadamia nuts, which are grown mainly in Hawaii. In addition, cashews and Brazil nuts are imported. In the nineteenth century, nuts were roasted and salted, when necessary, by vendors and homemakers, but the commercial processes for salting nuts so that the **salt** remained on the nuts after packaging were not perfected until the early twentieth century.

Salted nuts have been commercially packaged and sold in the United States since the early twentieth century.

The most important snack nut, however, is technically a legume. The peanut originated in South America but was disseminated to Africa and Asia shortly after the arrival of Europeans in the New World. From Africa, peanuts were brought into North America in colonial times. Peanuts were relatively unimportant as a **snack food** until after the Civil War, when vendors began selling peanuts on city streets. One peanut vendor was Amedeo Obici, an Italian-born immigrant who lived in Wilkes-Barre, Pennsylvania. In 1906, Obici formed a partnership with another Italian immigrant to form the Planters' Peanut Company. Their products then went through a packaging revolution, permitting Planters to sell fresh peanuts to a larger clientele. Planters also emphasized **advertising** and marketing, and the company's mascot, **Mr. Peanut**, quickly became an American culinary icon. The company went from a small vendor operation to a national snack food company in less than two decades. In 2005, Planters was the best-selling nut brand in the United States.

While nuts and peanuts are healthy snacks compared with **junk foods** such as **candy** and **potato chips**, nuts are filled with fat, calories, and salt.

SUGGESTED READING: Andrew F. Smith, *Peanuts: The Illustrious History of the Goober Pea* (Urbana, IL: University of Illinois Press, 2002).

O

Obesity For the first time in history, the number of overweight people in the world rivals that of the underfed, according to a study by the WorldWatch Institute. In 2000, a 1999 United Nations study found the incidence of obesity to be increasing rapidly in developing countries. In China, the number of overweight people jumped from less than 10 percent to 15 percent of the population in just three years. In Brazil and Colombia, the obesity rate hovers around 40 percent of the population—a level comparable to many European countries. Even in sub-Saharan Africa, where most of the world's underfed live, there has been a rapid increase in obesity and overweight.

Nowhere is this problem more acute than in the United States, where the statistics are staggering. During the past 50 years, Americans have been gaining weight, such that today 61 percent of Americans are judged overweight. Obesity rates have risen from 12 percent to 20 percent of the population since 1991. An ominous statistic indicating that this may get worse is that the percentage of children and adolescents who are obese has doubled during the last 20 years. Today, 25 percent of American children are now classified as overweight. Obesity has been linked with high blood pressure, arthritis, infertility, heart disease, type 2 **diabetes**, strokes, birth defects, gallbladder disease, gout, impaired immune system, liver disease, and breast, prostate, and colon cancer. In addition to their increased risk for physical illness, obese people are victims of social discrimination. Fashion today lauds skinny models as the ideal body images and obesity is a stigmatized condition. Also, society holds the individual responsible for obesity and considers overweight individuals to lack control or have a moral defect. Psychologically, many overweight people believe the same and feel badly about themselves.

The Centers for Disease Control has estimated that 248,000 Americans die prematurely due to obesity; others believe that this figure is low and estimate that 400,000 people die prematurely due to obesity. Estimates for added health care expenses due to obesity vary, but they range between $80 billion to $250 billion annually. Obesity is considered the number-two cause of preventable death in the United States (the primary cause is smoking). Health officials from the Surgeon General to medical practitioners have identified obesity as a disease of epidemic proportions in the United States. In 1998, the World Health Organization used the word epidemic also to describe the global picture of obesity.

The rise in obesity is correlated with the rise in the **fast food** and **junk food** industries. Junk food manufacturers and fast food operators have been particularly targeted as responsible for the obesity epidemic. Both industries have made inexpensive high-caloric and high-fat foods widely available, and have promoted them through billions of dollars of **advertising**, much of which is targeted at children watching **television**. Numerous studies have linked obesity, poor **nutrition**, and the amount of time a person watches television.

Solutions for the obesity epidemic vary, but include **dieting**, exercising, behavioral modification, and drug treatments. For severe obesity, gastric bypass surgery has been recommended. This is a procedure that removes much of the stomach and creates a small stomach to which the small intestine is attached. With a smaller stomach, the patient will eat less and thus over time, weight will be decreased. Surgery is always a risk, and the long-term health effects of gastric bypass surgery are unknown.

Because obesity is extremely difficult to reverse, health professionals have concluded that prevention, rather than treatment, offers the best long-term solution. Of particular concern has been the increase in obesity of youth. Over the past three decades, the rate of obesity has more than doubled among preschool children and adolescents, and has tripled among all school-age children. Fast food chains and **snack food** purveyors have intentionally targeted youth through their advertising and promotional activities. Junk food **vending machines** have been installed in **schools** and fast food operators now control many school foodservice operations. Proposed solutions have included bans on the sale and promotion of junk food in schools, bans on junk food/fast food advertising on television targeted at youth, and a tax on junk foods.

Several senators have proposed national legislation to restrict marketing and sales of snack foods and **soda** in schools. In 2005, Sen. Edward M. Kennedy, for instance, introduced a bill titled the Prevention of Childhood Obesity Act. In support of the bill, Kennedy stated, "Prevention is the cornerstone of good health and long, productive lives for all Americans. Childhood obesity is preventable, but we have to work together to stop this worsening epidemic and protect our children's future."

SUGGESTED READING: Anne Scott Beller, *Fat & Thin: A Natural History of Obesity* (New York: Farrar, Straus and Giroux, 1977); Kelly Brownell and Derek Yach, "The Battle of the Bulge," *Foreign Policy* (November/December 2005), 27–28; Chria Chase, *The Great American Waistline: Putting It on and Taking It Off* (New York: Coward, McCann & Geoghegan, 1981); Greg Critser, *Fat Land: How Americans Became the Fattest People in the World* (New York: Houghton Mifflin Company, 2003); Gary Gardner, *Underfed and Overfed: The Global Epidemic of Malnutrition* (Washington, D.C.: WorldWatch, 2000); The American Obesity Association Web site: www.obesity.org

Occupational Safety and Health Administration (OSHA) The Occupational Safety and Health Administration (OSHA) was created in 1970 to ensure "so far as possible every working man and woman in the nation safe and healthful working conditions and to preserve our human resources." Since then, OSHA has examined workplaces related to **fast food** and its **suppliers** and has issued guidelines related to them. For instance, in 1996 OSHA issued *Guidelines for Workplace Violence*, but restaurants opposed them. A 1999 OSHA-funded study estimated that 12 percent of all violent **crimes** that took place in the workplace occurred at fast food restaurants. In fact, an estimated four to five employees—most of whom are teenagers—are murdered at fast food restaurants every month. This is mainly due to the late hours that many fast food outlets are open. In addition, the quantity of cash usually kept on hand in fast food restaurants and the minimal security that fast food chains have offered workers are also reasons for crime and **violence**

at fast food chains. Such studies and guidelines have drawn attention to this issue, and OSHA has issued a publication to help fast food restaurants decrease the opportunities for violence.

OSHA has also levied fines on meatpacking companies for safety violations. The maximum fine that OSHA can impose, however, for a workplace death is $70,000, which does not strike fear into companies whose firms earn billions of dollars annually. Advocates for better safety conditions in meatpacking operations have pushed for higher penalties, mandatory plant closures, and that those responsible should be charged with negligence.

SUGGESTED READING: Eric Schlosser, *Fast Food Nation: The Dark Side of the All-American Meal* (New York: Houghton Mifflin Company, 2001); OSHA Web site: www.osha.gov

Oh Henry! In 1914, George H. Williamson, a salesman for a **candy** broker in Chicago, opened his own candy store. He made candies in the kitchen in the back of the store. He doubled as salesman during the day and janitor at night. Sales grew steadily and Williamson observed what customers liked when they bought his candy. Based on this knowledge, he opened a second store, which was also successful. Rather than continue to make the candies by hand, he decided to manufacture them. In 1919, he closed both stores and began manufacturing the candies that his customers had preferred most. He soon had orders from jobbers in Illinois and surrounding states for one candy bar in particular, but he needed a catchy name for it. Several stories have circulated as to how he chose the name. One story was that the candy was named after a suitor who had pursued one of the girls in Williamson's shop. Every time the man came into the candy shop to flirt, the salesgirls would squeal, "Oh, Henry!"—or so goes the story. Another story was that Williamson liked the short stories of William Sydney Porter, whose pen name was O. Henry.

Williamson launched the Oh Henry! candy bar in 1920. It was originally a log-shaped bar with a fudge center surrounded by a **caramel** and peanut layer and coated in pure milk **chocolate**. The Oh Henry! sold for a dime—twice the going rate of the competition. Williamson knew that he would have to convince people to pay twice as much for his product. **Advertising** was the answer. He first advertised in newspapers in one city, then expanded to others. Oh Henry! ads appeared on posters in the same cities targeted by newspaper ads, and finally hit national women's magazines, describing how women cut Oh Henry! bars into dainty slices and served them for dessert at home. The result was that by 1923 Oh Henry! was the best-selling candy bar in America.

The Williamson Candy Company moved to a larger factory in 1925, where it manufactured 500,000 Oh Henry! candy bars every nine hours. The company issued a cookbook in 1926 titled *60 New Ways to Serve a Famous Candy,* in which the candy bar (sliced, diced, chopped, or melted) was used in salads, cakes, **cookies**, desserts, puddings and sauces, sweet breads and "tea dainties." It also included a recipe using Oh Henry! candy bars as a topping for sweet potatoes. By 1927, plants had been opened in Oakland and New York and millions of Oh Henry! bars were manufactured each day.

Even though **sugar** and chocolate were rationed during World War II, the production of Oh Henry candy bars set a new sales record in 1943, but more than half of the candy bars went to the armed forces. The Williamson Candy Company was eventually sold to Standard Brands, and then to **Nabisco**. In 1990, the candy bar was acquired by **Nestlé** USA. It remains one of America's most popular candy bars.

SUGGESTED READING: Ray Broekel, *The Great America Candy Bar Book* (Boston: Houghton Mifflin Company, 1982); Tim Richardson, *Sweets: A History of Candy* (New York: Bloomsbury, 2002); Andrew F. Smith, *Peanuts: The Illustrious History of the Goober Pea* (Urbana, IL: University of Illinois Press, 2002).

Onion Rings Onion rings are ring-shaped slices of onion that have been battered and deep-fried. Advocates claim that onion rings were invented by the Pig Stand restaurant chain in the 1920s. No primary source evidence has been produced to support this claim, and recipes for vegetables, including onions, fried in batter were present in American cookbooks well before the twentieth century. In 1955, frozen breaded onion rings were developed by Sam Quigley in Nebraska. In 1959, he began manufacturing frozen onion rings, and called his operation Sam's Onions. Other companies began manufacturing onion rings for home use and for **fast food** outlets.

Onion rings did not become popular fast food until the 1970s. In 1973, **Dairy Queen** began serving onion rings, followed by **Jack in the Box** in 1979. Today, **Burger King** also serves them, as does **A&W Root Beer**, **Carl's Jr.**, **Sonic**, and many other **chains**.

SUGGESTED READING: Whaoo Apetizers Web site: www.apetizer.com

Orange Crush California chemist Neil C. Ward experimented for four years before he came up with an orange **soda**. He partnered with Clayton J. Howell of Cleveland, Ohio, to market the new **beverage** in 1916. During World War I, **sugar** was difficult to acquire and the new beverage languished until the war ended in 1918. Ward and Howell named their company the Orange Crush Bottling Company and named their drink Ward's Orange Crush. It mainly consisted of sugar and carbonated water with a modicum of orange concentrate. The name was subsequently shortened to Orange Crush and it became extremely successful, in part because it was promoted as a health beverage at a time when medical professionals were touting vitamin C and encouraging everyone to drink orange juice. By 1924, Orange Crush had 1,200 bottlers in the United States and Canada. It subsequently expanded to Latin America and Europe. Ward became chairman of the Orange Crush Bottling Company in 1931.

During the 1920s and 1930s, Orange Crush dominated the market for orange soda. The company added citrus-flavored beverages, such as lemon and lime crush. In 1962, Crush International was acquired Charles E. Hires Co., maker of **Hires Root Beer**. In 1980, Crush International was sold to Procter & Gamble, who sold it in 1989 to **Cadbury Schweppes** Americas Beverages (CSAB).

SUGGESTED READING: David Gerard Hogan, *Selling 'em by the Sack: White Castle and the Creation of American Food* (New York: New York University Press, 1997).

Oreos In 1912, **Nabisco** introduced the Oreo cookie to compete with Hydrox Biscuit Bonbons, which had been released two years earlier. Oreos were a round cookie with white vanilla cream sandwiched between two black **chocolate sandwich** biscuits. It was one of the most successful **cookies** in American history.

In 1994, Nabisco introduced a lower-calorie version of Oreos. In 2000, Nabisco was acquired by **Kraft Foods**, Inc., which expanded the Oreo cookie line. In 2001, the company created extensions to the Oreo brand, including a version with chocolate filling and Mint 'n Creme Double Delight Oreos. It added different colors and flavors to mark special events and holidays. The company has also developed many new packages for Oreos, some of which, like Oreo Barz, are no longer cookies. In 2002, the **7-Eleven** convenience store chain worked with Nabisco to create plastic cups filled with Oreos. These containers fit into car cup-holders so that drivers could eat them while driving. Oreo cookies are America's best-selling cookies.

Oreos. © Kelly Fitzsimmons

SUGGESTED READING: Gary Ruskin and Juliet Schor, "Junk Food Nation: Who's to Blame for Childhood Obesity?" *Nation* (August 29, 2005).

P

Packaging Until the late nineteenth century, food was generally sold as generic commodities in barrels or sacks. The exceptions were a few specialty and luxury items. Baker's and Cadbury's **chocolates**, for example, had long been sold in boxes with tinfoil inner lining and the company's name printed on them.

The first general packaging revolution began in the United States during the 1870s. It was the flat-bottomed paper bag, which was initially used by grocers who scooped up the commodities and placed them in the bag. This became revolutionary when it was wed to the invention of the offset press in 1879 that permitted brands, logos, and other identifying marks to be printed on the bags. At the same time, the folding paper box began to be mass-marketed. With the cheap and rapid production of paper bags and boxes, retail life changed in America. Packing could include distinctive colors and shapes that set goods apart from others. Constant repetition helped consumers who had to make decisions about a vast array of commercial products. In addition, with a package the company could develop logos and visual designs that could attract customers.

The first commercial **snack foods**, such as **Cracker Jack** and Marshall's Potato Chips, were sold in barrels. As soon as the barrel was opened, however, the contents went stale, which lessened their appeal. The makers of Cracker Jack solved the packing problem, however; they acquired a patent for a type of wax paper from Germany and packed their product in wax paper bags. The bags were placed in box, which was covered with a waterproof outer seal. Consumer sales soared, thanks mainly to the **advertising** and the new packaging that kept the confection fresh. Other snack food manufacturers followed Cracker Jack's lead to develop packaging that kept freshness in and permitted them to advertise their product.

Shelled peanuts, like those in Cracker Jack, went stale unless they were packed in airtight containers. Planter's Peanuts initially sold shelled peanuts in glassine bags, but they were difficult to fill and transport and the cost of the glassine bag increased the selling price of their peanuts. So Planters, like most other peanut shellers and cleaners, sold peanuts in large tins. Planters placed glassine bags in the tin, and shopkeepers scooped out the peanuts for the customer and filled the glassine bags. This was complicated, so as the price of canning decreased, Planters Peanuts packaged many of its products in tin cans, which also made it possible for the company to advertise. The company placed the image of **Mr. Peanut** on virtually every package of peanuts manufactured after 1917.

The **potato chip** industry had a very difficult packaging problem to solve. In 1926, potato chip maker Laura Scudder of Monterey Park, California experimented with a new potato chip packing idea. She hand-packed the chips into waxed paper bags and her employees sealed the tops with a warm iron. This created an individual serving container that kept out moisture, but it was impossible to print on the outside of waxed paper. In 1933 the Dixie Wax Paper Company introduced the first preprintable waxed glassine bag, which made it possible for manufacturers to print brand names and other information on the outside of the bag. This mode of packaging promptly became the standard in the salty snack world.

Cellophane, which as invented in 1911, was commonly used in the United States by the 1930s. It protected food and permitted customers to actually see the food that they were purchasing. Cellophane encouraged impulse buying, where the allure of visible snacks encouraged customers to buy the product. This was particularly used by bakers for packaging **cookies**, pies and cakes.

Candy and chocolates have gone through numerous packaging changes. Until the late nineteenth century, candy fell into two categories: specialty chocolates, such as those made by Baker's and Cadbury's and were sold in boxes with printed brand names; and **penny candy**, which was generally a generic product sold individually from large glass containers in grocery stores and in **vending machines**. **Tootsie Rolls** were the first penny candy to be individually wrapped. Wrapping enables manufacturers to create brand names and logos, which in turn leads to advertising and promotion. Since the early twentieth century, candy packaging has diversified to include a variety of shapes and sizes.

Design of the packaging is vital for all food manufacturers. Research has demonstrated that customers initially recognize the color scheme on the package, then the logo, and finally the name of the product. **Wrigley's** gum and **Hershey's chocolate bar** wrappers are frequently cited as outstanding packaging—simple designs that are readily recognized by potential customers.

Soft Drink Packaging

In the soft drink world, packaging took a different direction. At first, soft drink manufacturers produced syrup or extract that was easily transported to drugstores and **soda fountains**, where the syrup and carbonated water were mixed just before serving. Bottling of soda **beverages** began in the mid-nineteenth century but the bottles broke easily and, due to the lack of airtight caps, they lost carbonation. This changed in 1892 when William Painter invented the crown bottle cap, which made it possible to easily seal bottles. Bottling of soft drinks was enhanced by improved glass bottles that could keep the carbon dioxide in and would not shatter during the manufacturing process. Another packaging innovation introduced by **Coca-Cola** in 1915 was the contoured bottle, which became one of the most recognized bottles in the world.

Beer was distributed in cans during the 1930s, but soft drinks built up greater pressure inside and the manufacture of stronger cans for soft drinks was not perfected until 1953. Royal Crown Cola was the first soft drink distributed in a can. Aluminum cans were first used in 1957. Five years later, pull-ring tabs were used on beer cans and later on soda cans. In 1965, soft drinks were dispensed from vending machines. By 1972, polyethylene terephthalate (PET) bottles were created.

Soft drink cans and bottles have been criticized because they are not biodegradable and take up considerable space in landfills. Recycling programs were begun against the wishes of many bottlers but, because relatively few people return the empties, most soft drink companies have come to consider the deposit for the bottles or cans to be a profit center. Likewise, PET bottles can be recycled into making other products, such as polyester carpets.

Recent Label Changes

Two recent changes in packaging have affected both snack foods and soft drink packaging. The first is the **nutrition** labels that are now required. The junk food manufacturers strongly opposed nutritional labeling, fearing that the lack of nutrition in most of their products would discourage customers for buying their products. Because most people do not read the labels, however, and many people who do are unable to easily understand the nutrition information, there is no evidence that sales have declined due to the addition of these labels. In fact, there is evidence that labeling has actually increased sales: the word *nutrition* on a package implies that the contents are healthy.

The second change in labeling has been the addition of bar codes, which began to be used during the 1960s. They permit easier, faster, and more accurate checkouts and, when combined with computers, permit an immediate feedback on sales of particular snack foods and soft drinks. Using this information, manufacturers can gain a great deal of information as to who is buying their products and how successful their product advertising and promotion is in particular areas.

Fast Food

In the **fast food** world, packaging has taken yet another path. **White Castle** came up with the idea that fast food was a packaged experience. Because most customers purchased food and ate it in their cars or took it off-site to consume, White Castle needed bags to transport the food. Paper cups, bags, and coverings were used. **McDonald's** has carefully constructed the containers for its **Happy Meals**, salads, and **Chicken McNuggets**. Its **French fry** containers have been carefully designed to suggest that the fries are packed to overflowing, giving the appearance of abundance. During the 1970s, McDonald's decided to use polystyrene foam for coffee cups and food containers for its Big Macs and Quarter Pounders. Since polystyrene is not easily biodegradable, environmental groups charged McDonald's with destroying the **environment**. McDonald's responded by withdrawing polystyrene and replacing it with paper. Other chains have similarly packaged their food. **Kentucky Fried Chicken**, for instance, has created its large paper bucket.

SUGGESTED READING: Jackie Prince, *Launching a New Business Ethic: the Environment as a Standard Operating Procedure at McDonald's and at Other Companies* (Washington, D.C.: Environmental Defense Fund, 1991); Gordon L. Robertson, *Food Packaging, Principles and Practice*, 2nd ed. (Boca Raton, FL: Taylor & Francis, 2005); Thomas Hine, *The Total Package: The Evolution and Secret Meanings of Boxes, Bottles, Cans, and Tubes* (New York: Little, Brown and Company, 1995); Tim Richardson, *Sweets: A History of Candy* (New York: Bloomsbury, 2002); Andrew F. Smith, *Peanuts: The Illustrious History of the Goober Pea* (Urbana, IL: University of Illinois Press, 2002).

Panda Express Entrepeneur Andrew Cheng, born in the Yangzhou region of China, immigrated to the United States in 1973. Ten years later, he launched Panda Express in Pasadena, California. It is the largest **fast food chain** based on Chinese food. Today, Panda Express has 800 outlets in the United States, eight in Japan, and five in Puerto Rico.

SUGGESTED READING: Panda Express Web site: www.pandaexpress.com

Patriotism **Snack foods** developed patriotic activities and themes during wartimes. During World War I, **candy** became an important component of military rations. The **Hershey Company**, for example, supplied the military with **chocolate** bars. Since peanuts were not rationed during the war, growing and consuming them (as opposed to rationed candy and chocolates) was viewed as patriotic. Stuart Judson's 1917 article in *The Forum*, titled "Peanuts and Patriotism," proclaimed that peanuts served valiantly in the war effort by conserving dairy products, substituting for meat, and feeding livestock.

When the United States entered the World War II, **Cracker Jack** discontinued putting toys in its packages. Toyless Cracker Jacks were distributed to soldiers, who complained about their absence, and soon prizes reappeared. Instead of the sophisticated whistles and miniature glass figures and animals that had delighted children previously, wartime prizes principally consisted of paper and tin gadgets, featuring patriotic symbols of pilots, commanders, aircraft, flags, and artillery. Perhaps the most unusual wartime prizes were paper propaganda cards, such as one with an effigy of a hanging Adolf Hitler.

During the war, many confection manufacturers lobbied the American government to guarantee that candy production would be considered essential war goods. They succeeded in their efforts and 70 percent of all candy manufactured in the United States during the war was sold to the military. Although **sugar** was rationed, candy production continued uninterrupted through the war, much of it going to soldiers. It was estimated that every American serviceman consumed 50 pounds of candy during the war. In addition to one billion chocolate bars that were made for the military, Hershey manufactured D rations and K rations for military use. D rations included a **Hershey's chocolate bar**, greatly revised so it would not melt in hot climates. **Mars, Inc.** also packed rations, which included **M&M's**. **Wrigley Company** produced K rations, each of which contained chewing **gum**. **Tootsie Rolls**, which were almost indestructible, were supplied in other rations. The **Frito-Lay** Company, as did other companies, experienced shortages, rationing, and loss of manpower. Throughout the war, Fritos were eaten by American armed forces.

To make sure that the American public was aware of the patriotic activities of candy makers during the war, in 1944 the National Confectioners Association (NCA) spent $21 million on **advertising** pointing out that candy "energized" the American military. Patriotic themes, such as the American flag, soldiers, and national symbols graced all of these promotions.

At the beginning of the war, soft drink manufacturers faced the possibility that they would be declared nonessential businesses. **Coca-Cola** immediately presented itself as a patriotic drink. It provided free drinks for American soldiers and published patriotic-themed advertisements in magazines. As a consequence, the military permitted Coca-Cola employees to set up bottling plants behind American lines to supply the soldiers with Coke.

Many patriotic themes and activities reemerged during the Iraq wars in 1991 and 2003. On Thanksgiving Day in 1990, Mars, Inc. gave a **Snickers** bar to every American soldier in the Middle East. When France refused to join the American-led coalition invading Iraq in 2003, some Congressional Republicans urged that the term **French fries** be changed to liberty fries in the Congressional dining room.

Some candy manufacturers today produce candy with particular patriotic themes. Tootsie Rolls, taffy, mints, and chocolate hearts have been encased in wrappings with the image of the American flag. Gummy army men, freedom rings, and airplanes are manufactured. Candy American flags are common. Special **jelly bean** bags consist of only beans colored red, white, and blue. Star-spangled **lollipops** are available on the Fourth of July, as are red, white, and blue Star Pops and Twisty Pops.

SUGGESTED READING: Joël Glenn Brenner, *The Emperors of Chocolate: Inside the Secret World of Hershey and Mars* (New York: Broadway Books, 2000); Andrew F. Smith, *Peanuts: The Illustrious History of the Goober Pea* (Urbana, IL: University of Illinois Press, 2002)

PayDay In 1932, the PayDay **candy** bar was invented by Frank Martoccio, founder of the F. A. Martoccio Company, and later head of Hollywood Brands, Inc. The PayDay bar consisted of peanuts, fudge, and **caramel**. Purportedly, it acquired its name because it was payday when the inventors tried to come up with a name. Hollywood Brands also made Butternut (1916), Zero (1920), and Milk Shake (1927) candy bars.

In 1967, the Martoccio family sold Hollywood Brands to Consolidated Foods Corporation, which sold it to Leaf, Inc. The North American confectionery division of Leaf, Inc. was acquired by the **Hershey Company**. Today, Payday candy bars are made by Hershey. Beginning in 2003, Hershey began extending the product line with the PayDay Honey Roasted Limited Edition Bar. Two years later, it introduced PayDay Pro, an energy bar with added vitamins and minerals.

SUGGESTED READING: Hershey Company Web site: www.hersheys.com

Penny Candy By the mid-nineteenth century, many factories in the United States produced candy, much of which sold for a penny. It was easily produced and it was sold loose from glass jars or tins in stores. Penny candy was later sold though **vending machines**. Common penny candies included **licorice**, hard candy, **lollipops**, ladyfingers, pillowcases, mint patties, jujubes, gum drops, wax candies, **jelly beans**, and marshmallows. The **Tootsie Roll** was the first penny candy to be wrapped in paper.

SUGGESTED READING: Joël Glenn Brenner, *The Emperors of Chocolate: Inside the Secret World of Hershey and Mars* (New York: Broadway Books, 2000).

Penny candy. © Kelly Fitzsimmons

Pepperidge Farm In 1937, Margaret Rudkin of Fairfield,

Connecticut, began a small business baking preservative-free, whole-wheat bread. She named her company Pepperidge Farm. After World War II, Rudkin began to expand production by opening a bakery in Norwalk, Connecticut. In addition to bread, the company manufactured dinner rolls, stuffing, and other products. Rudkin reached an agreement with Delacre Company in Brussels to produce its cookies in the United States. In 1955, Pepperidge Farm launched European-style cookies, such as Bordeaux, Geneva, and Brussels. Subsequently, the company acquired the Black Horse Pastry Company, and moved into the frozen food business.

In 1961, the Campbell Soup Company acquired Pepperidge Farm. The following year, the company produced **Goldfish** crackers. In 1963, the company published the *Margaret Rudkin Pepperidge Farm Cookbook*, which became the first cookbook to hit the *New York Times* bestseller list. Rudkin retired in 1966.

SUGGESTED READING: Pepperidge Farm Web site: www.pepperidgefarm.com

PepsiCo In the 1890s in New Bern, North Carolina, a pharmacist named Caleb D. Bradham experimented with extracts of coca leaves, kola nuts, and **sugar**. Bradham had purchased a pharmacy in 1893. At the drugstore's **soda fountain**, Bradham experimented with concocting soft drinks for his friends. One **beverage** based upon kola nut extract was first named Brad's Drink, but by August 28, 1898, he christened the new drink Pepsi-Cola. It was successful and its sales encouraged Bradham to incorporate the Pepsi-Cola Company in 1902. Bradham began to rapidly expand his sales. By 1907, the company had 40 bottling plants across the United States. By 1910, Bradham had franchised more than 300 bottlers in 24 states to produce Pepsi-Cola. But Bradham ran into financial problems and the company went into bankruptcy in 1922.

Pepsi-Cola was resurrected by a Wall Street broker, Roy C. Megarel. He controlled the company until 1931, when the company again went bankrupt. It was saved by Charles Guth, the president of the Loft Candy Company, which acquired Pepsi. The formula for Pepsi was changed at this time. The new formula eliminated pepsin, a digestive protease, as a major flavoring ingredient. By 1934, Pepsi-Cola turned the corner and began purchasing bottling operations throughout the United States. By 1939, Pepsi's net earnings had risen to over $5.5 million.

World War II greatly affected the soft drink industry. Pepsi-Cola's operations throughout the world were disrupted by German and Japanese conquests. In the United States, sugar rationing was imposed early in 1942. Rationing drastically restricted the amount of soft drinks that Pepsi-Cola could produce. After the war, the sugar restrictions were removed but Pepsi had a hard time competing with **Coca-Cola**, which had thrived during the war due to government contracts. By 1950, the Pepsi Company was almost forced to declare bankruptcy for a third time, when a highly successful **advertising** campaign came to the rescue. Throughout the 1950s, Pepsi continued to expand aggressively abroad, particularly into Latin America and Europe. In 1959, the leader of the Soviet Union, Nikita Khrushchev, and Vice President Richard Nixon were photographed drinking Pepsi at an American exhibit in Moscow. As a result, this was later dubbed the Kitchen Debate. (Later, Coca-Cola claimed that as a result Nixon was offered the presidency of a foreign division of Pepsi and he served as a lawyer for Pepsi while practicing in New York.)

During the 1960s, Pepsi introduced several new products, including **Mountain Dew** and Diet Pepsi. In 1965, Pepsi bought **Frito-Lay**, Inc. and renamed the new corporation PepsiCo. During the 1970s, PepsiCo acquired several fast food chains, including

Pizza Hut, Taco Bell, and **Kentucky Fried Chicken**. PepsiCo considered its **fast food chains** as important outlets for its soft drinks, because all of its chains sold Pepsi-Cola. However, other large fast food chains refused to handle PepsiCo beverages because of competition with Pepsi's fast food chains. In 1997, PepsiCo divested itself of its restaurant subsidiaries, creating a separate corporate entity now called **Yum! Brands**. PepsiCo maintains the largest ownership in Yum! Brands and all of these establishments continue to sell Pepsi beverages.

SUGGESTED READING: Anne Cooper Funderburg, *Sundae Best: A History of Soda Fountains* (Bowling Green, OH: Bowling Green State University Popular Press, 2002); Roger Enrico and Jesse Kornbluth, *The Other Guy Blinked: How Pepsi Won the Cola Wars* (New York: Bantam, 1986); J. C. Louis and Harvey Yazijian, *The Cola Wars: The Story of the Global Corporate Battle between the Coca-Cola Company and PepsiCo* (New York: Everest House, 1980); Bob Stoddard, *Pepsi: 100 Years* (Los Angeles, CA: General Publishing Group, 1999); Bob Stoddard, *The Encyclopedia of Pepsi-Cola Collectibles* (Iola, WI: Krause Publications, 2002).

Peter Paul Candy Company In 1919, Peter Paul Halajian and five Armenian associates founded the Peter Paul Candy Manufacturing Company in New Haven, Connecticut. One of their first products was a coconut and **chocolate** bar called **Mounds**, which was released in 1920. Following up this success was their Almond Joy, which was first manufactured in 1946. In 1972, Peter Paul acquired the York Cone Company, which made **York Peppermint Patties**, then a regional chocolate **candy**. Peter Paul expanded production and aggressively promoted it nationally, beginning in 1975. In 1978, **Cadbury** acquired the Peter Paul Candy Company. Ten years later, Cadbury sold the Mounds, Almond Joy, and York Peppermint Patties brands to the **Hershey Company**, which markets the brands today.

SUGGESTED READING: Tim Richardson, *Sweets: A History of Candy* (New York: Bloomsbury, 2002).

PEZ In 1927, the Austrian Eduard Haas introduced the Pfefferminze as a breath mint for smokers. It was composed of peppermint oil and **sugar**. When the **candy** was introduced into the United States, sales were dismal. In 1948, the first version of the PEZ dispenser was released; it was designed to look like a cigarette lighter. By 1952, the dispenser was improved and new images were incorporated into its design. It ejected candy from the heads of cartoon characters, such as those of Goofy or Popeye. PEZ was targeted at children and it was a hit.

PEZ Candy, Inc. is a private company based in Orange, Connecticut. Since 1960, McKeesport Candy Company of McKeesport, Pennsylvania, has been the distributor of PEZ dispensers. PEZ memorabilia are considered important collectibles, many of which are displayed at The Museum of PEZ Memorabilia in Burlingame, California. PEZ candies made a cameo appearance in the 1981 blockbuster movie, *ET, The Extra-Terrestrial.*

SUGGESTED READING: Joël Glenn Brenner, *The Emperors of Chocolate: Inside the Secret World of Hershey and Mars* (New York: Broadway Books, 2000); Richard Geary, *PEZ Collectibles*, 4th ed. (Atglen, PA: Schiffer Publishing, 2000); *PEZ: A Little Collectible Book* (Kansas City, MO: Andrews McMeel Publishing, 2002); Museum of PEZ Memorabilia Web site: www.spectrumnet.com/pez

Physicians Committee for Responsible Medicine Founded in 1985, the Physicians Committee for Responsible Medicine (PCRM) is a nonprofit organization supported by physicians and concerned citizens. Its president is Neal D. Barnard, author of *Turn Off the Fat Genes*; *Eat Right, Live Longer*; and *Food for Life*. PCRM's flagship publication is the quarterly magazine, *Good Medicine*. PCRM is an **animal rights** organization; it promotes **vegetarian** diets and opposes medical experimentation on animals. PCRM has supported **lawsuits** against **fast food** chains and **junk food** manufacturers. Film director Morgan Spurlock used Barnard's addiction theories in his movie *Super Size Me* (2004).

SUGGESTED READING: Physicians Committee for Responsible Medicine Web site: www.pcrm.org

Pizza Leavened and flattened breads with various toppings have been common in the Mediterranean region for hundreds, if not thousands, of years. Pizza can be traced to nineteenth-century Naples, Italy. It had a variety of toppings including tomato sauce and cheese. Pizza migrated to the United States late in the nineteenth century. The first known pizzeria in the United States was established by Italian bakers in New York about 1902. By the 1920s, pizza was a common food served in small outlets and at Italian festivals.

Pizza became an American mainstream food after World War II. It meshed well with casual dining and could easily be eaten in **automobiles** or around the **television** in the home. It was not negatively affected by delays between cooking and eating, which made it ideal for **drive-ins** and take-home places. The day's supply of pizza dough was rolled out in the morning and refrigerated in 10-inch pans, ready to be quickly topped and baked in the same pan when ordered. It drastically reduced labor costs and made the mealtime rush more manageable. This new method was a boon for **franchised chains**.

Pizza was distinctly different from other **fast foods**. Before the 1950s, pizza was considered a foreign food. A 1953 song sung by Dean Martin with the lyrics "When the moon hits your eye like a big pizza pie" helped popularize it. The first pizza franchises started in 1954 with the creation of **Shakey's Pizza** chain, which grew to more than 100 outlets by 1960. Most of Shakey's pizza was eaten in the restaurant. **Pizza Hut** was the first true fast food pizza chain. **Tom Monaghan** made it into the Fortune 500 with his **Domino's Pizza**, founded in 1960. **Frozen pizza** was introduced in the early 1960s. There are two claims to having been the first to sell commercially frozen pizza in 1962: **Tombstone Pizza** in Medford, Wisconsin, and Rose Totino of Totino's Italian Kitchen in Minneapolis.

There are many other makers of pizza, such as Red Baron Pizza, founded in 1979, Godfather's Pizza, founded in 1973 in Omaha, Nebraska, and Papa John's, founded in 1984 in Jeffersonville, Indiana. Today, Papa John's also has almost 3,000 outlets in 49 states and 20 countries. There are thousands of local and regional pizza parlors.

SUGGESTED READING: John A. Jakle and Keith A. Sculle, *Fast Food: Roadside Restaurants in the Automobile Age* (Baltimore: Johns Hopkins University Press, 1999); Ed Levine, *Pizza: A Slice of Heaven. The Ultimate Pizza Guide and Companion* (New York: Universe Publishing, 2005); Harvey Levenstein, *Paradox of Plenty: A Social History of Eating in Modern America* (New York: Oxford University Press, 1993); Food Franchise Web site: www.foodfranchise.com/pizzafranchise.asp; Godfather's Pizza Web site: www.godfathers.com

Pizza Hut Frank Carney, an 18-year-old student at the University of Wichita, read an article about **pizza** in the *Saturday Evening Post* and decided to open a pizza parlor in 1958. With his brother, Dan Carney, he opened a pizza parlor in Wichita, Kansas. They named it Pizza Hut because they believed that the small brick building they rented resembled a hut. Their main product was a small, thin, pan pizza with cheese, sausage, or pepperoni. Initially, it came in two sizes: small, which sold for 95 cents, and large, which sold for $1.50.

At the time there were other pizzerias in Wichita and in many other cities; these were mainly family-owned shops. Six months after the Carneys opened their first restaurant, the brothers opened a second one. Within a year there were six Pizza Hut outlets. The brothers began **franchising** Pizza Hut in 1959. Pizza Hut popularized pizza as a **fast food** in America.

In 1963, Pizza Hut designed a building style that was adopted for all restaurants throughout the **chain**. It had a large dining room with seating for 80 people, and an expanded menu was introduced. The company shifted to a thicker-crust pizza and added several additional types of pizzas, including Chicago pan-style pizza. About 50 percent of their operation was take-out. The company also began its first national **advertising** campaign with the jingle "Putt-Putt to Pizza Hut."

PepsiCo purchased Pizza Hut in 1977. Pizza Hut began a process to Americanize its image. Its initial logo—an Italian chef tossing a pizza—was changed to the red roof that symbolized their "hut." By 1990 Pizza Hut ranked fourth in sales among all chain restaurants.

In 1997, Pizza Hut was spun-off from PepsiCo into Tricon Global Restaurants, now **Yum! Brands, Inc.** As of 2005, the chain had more than 12,000 restaurants in 86 nations.

SUGGESTED READING: John A. Jakle and Keith A. Sculle, *Fast Food: Roadside Restaurants in the Automobile Age* (Baltimore: Johns Hopkins University Press, 1999); Philip Langdon, *Orange Roofs, Golden Arches: The Architecture of American Chain Restaurants* (New York: Knopf, 1986); Pizza Hut Web site: www.pizzahut.com

Politics of Junk Food Food-related matters have been political issues for more than a century. The **controversies** surrounding pure food were legion. Legislation promoting pure food was introduced into Congress for 30 years before the Pure Food and Drug Act was finally passed in 1906. This and other acts created an administrative structure to enforce the laws and prevent adulteration of food. This series of legislative acts created federal mechanisms to research food issues and, where necessary, take action against products or their ingredients which are determined to be a danger to health. Federal agencies also have the ability to spotlight serious food-related problems, such as **obesity** and **foodborne illnesses**.

Many federal laws and regulations affect the quality and price of foods Americans eat. Price supports for agricultural commodities, for instance, stabilize prices for farmers and consumers.

These decisions, however, are not made in a political vacuum. During the early part of twentieth century, food corporations formed associations, many of which had **lobbying** arms in Washington, D.C. When World War II broke out, **junk food** manufacturers pressed the federal government to declare their products essential for the war effort. Through lobbying, the **Coca-Cola Company** won the right to sell its **beverages** to the military. Other **soda** companies, such as **PepsiCo**, almost went out of business due to the rationing of **sugar** during the war.

During the war, **nutrition** standards were established to help Americans eat a balanced diet during a period of scarcity. Recommended Daily Allowances (RDAs) were set during the war and were regularly revised every five years based on subsequent research.

These nutritional recommendations were not controversial until 1992, when the USDA introduced the **Food Pyramid**. Unlike previous nutritional advice, this pyramid was hierarchical and was weighted in favor of **vegetarian** foods.

Food companies lobby the political system to convince Congress that their products promote health and should not be subject to restrictive regulations. To gain support for their positions, corporations contribute to congressional campaigns and lobby officials in federal agencies. They fund nutrition research, sponsor journals, and conduct conferences, and they support nutritional organizations that espouse their own views. Food company lobbyists often pressure political leaders to make compromises regarding nutritional recommendations.

In addition, food companies join trade associations. Many **fast food** and junk food businesses have formed alliances, such as American Council for Fitness and Nutrition (ACFN), which opposes creating national standards for **school** food. Fast food **chains**, such as **McDonald's**, have opposed increasing the minimum wage at both the federal and state levels. They have also encouraged the passage of legislation that would exempt teenagers under 18 from the minimum wage.

Food corporations also try to prevent **lawsuits** against them through passage of favorable federal legislation. When Samuel Hirsch sued McDonald's, **Wendy's**, **Kentucky Fried Chicken**, and **Burger King** for contributing to **obesity**, the fast food and junk food manufacturers and their associations began to lobby for the introduction and passage of the Personal Responsibility in Food Consumption Act (H.R. 339) in Congress that would exempt fast food chains from such lawsuits.

Nonprofit organizations, such as the **Center for Science in the Public Interest (CSPI)**, have attempted to counter the lobbying efforts of food manufacturers and they lobby Congress, support bills, and try to influence federal agencies. CSPI has presented studies and research supporting its position and has lobbied Americans to contact their representatives on matters before Congress.

SUGGESTED READING: Marianne Elisabeth Lien and Brigitte Nerlich, eds., *The Politics of Food* (New York: Berg, 2004); Marion Nestle, *Food Politics: How the Food Industry Influences Nutrition and Health* (Berkeley, CA: University of California Press, 2002); Marion Nestle, *Safe Food: Bacteria, Biotechnology, and Bioterrorism* (Berkeley, CA: University of California Press, 2003).

El Pollo Loco In 1975, El Pollo Loco ("the crazy chicken" in Spanish) began as a roadside chicken stand in Guasave on Mexico's Pacific Coast. The company expanded to northern Mexico and, in 1980, opened its first outlet in the United States in Los Angeles. The menu featured marinated chicken flame-grilled, which was popular across much of Latin America and with U.S. Latinos. El Pollo expanded its menu to include burritos, tacos, salads, and other products. In 1995, it launched a joint venture with **Fosters Freeze**, so that the latter's soft-serve **ice cream** desserts could be sold in many El Pollo Loco outlets.

In 1983, the El Pollo Loco chain was purchased by the Denny's restaurant chain, which in turn was bought by Flagstar (now Advantica Restaurant Group, Inc.) in 1987. In 1999, American Securities Capital Partners, a private equity investment firm, acquired El Pollo Loco, only to sell it in 2005 to Trimaran Capital Partners. As of 2005, the company had 330 outlets in Arizona, California, Illinois, Nevada, and Texas.

SUGGESTED READING: John A. Jakle and Keith A. Sculle, *Fast Food: Roadside Restaurants in the Automobile Age* (Baltimore: Johns Hopkins University Press, 1999); El Pollo Loco Web site: www.elpolloloco.com

Popcorn Popcorn appeared on the American culinary scene during the mid-nineteenth century after the invention of the wire-over-the-fire popper. This device made it possible to contain the popped corn in an enclosed space without have to chase after the kernels as they scattered around the cooking area. By the late nineteenth century, low-cost popcorn was America's favorite snack. **Cracker Jack**, a combination of popcorn, peanuts, and molasses, became America's first commercial **snack food** during the early twentieth century.

During World War I, popcorn became a patriotic snack food. It was not rationed during the war and it was not imported. The Depression did not hurt popcorn sales because it was a luxury that most Americans could afford. Movie **theaters** and World War II catapulted popcorn into the mainstream as **sugar**-based snacks vanished from grocer's shelves. The invention of the microwave oven and the release of hybrid kernels with tremendous popping volume created popcorn mania during the 1950s and 1960s.

Popcorn Mania

In 1988, the Wyandot Popcorn Company claimed that it had produced enough popcorn to fill the Empire State Building 30 times over. It issued videocassettes of the original 1933 version of King Kong and gave its personnel Popcorn Mania T-shirts. Mania was the appropriate word to describe what was then underway in the popcorn world. Magazines reinforced the upward spiral of popcorn mania. In 1984, *Reader's Digest* ran an article titled "Popcorn! It's No Flash in the Pan." The popularity of popcorn exploded for a variety of reasons, but particularly because of the booster-like efforts of **Orville Redenbacher** on behalf of gourmet popping corn and of the successful marriage of popcorn with microwave technology.

Health Issues

Popcorn is unquestionably nutritious. It consists of approximately 71 percent **carbohydrates**, 14 percent water, 10.5 percent protein, 3 percent **fat**, and small amounts of minerals. One cup of plain popcorn contains only 27 calories. Popcorn without additives does not contain the ingredients that other snack foods are criticized for—**salt**, sugar, and chemical additives. It has been highly recommended by the National Cancer Institute as a "a high-fiber food to choose more often." The Illinois division of the American Cancer Society praised popcorn as one of the "eleven things that don't cause cancer." The American Heart Association has recommended it as "low in saturated fat and fairly low in calories." The American Dental Association recommended sugar-free popcorn as a food that does not promote tooth decay but does remove tartar from teeth. These recommendations were all based on plain, hot-air popped popcorn without additives.

However, most people do not consume popcorn without oil and additives. The **Center for Science in the Public Interest** (CSPI) issued a warning in 1988 about the high fat content of most microwave and prepared popcorns. Their message was that most microwave popcorn makers (as well as ready-to-eat popcorn producers) loaded their products with high levels of salt, saturated fats, and artificial butter flavor consisting of hydrogenated oils, saturated fats, artificial colorings, flavorings, and other preservatives.

The first company to produce a low-fat, low-salt popcorn was Weight Watchers. A serving of Weight Watchers brand microwave popcorn contained 9 percent fat, 150 calories, and 8 milligrams sodium. Other manufacturers have followed suit. Redenbacher's Gourmet Light Microwave Popping Corn contained one-third less salt, one-third fewer calories, and two-thirds less fat than Redenbacher's regular popcorn. Other companies produced so-called light popcorn: Deli Express, Wise Foods, and the Boston Popcorn Company.

Despite these new products, the popcorn industry, swept up in a period of frenzied expansion, largely ignored the initial CSPI report. At the depths of the popcorn slump in 1994, CSPI again appalled popcorn lovers when it revealed that theater popcorn cooked in coconut oil was extraordinarily high in saturated fat. Saturated fat raises blood **cholesterol** and increases the risk of heart disease. Specifically, CSPI proclaimed that a tub of movie theater popcorn which had been popped in coconut oil without imitation butter contained 80 grams of fat—more than in six Big Macs. If imitation butter was added, fat was boosted to 130 grams (the same as in eight Big Macs).

The report shocked theater owners even more than the general public, because more than half of their revenues derived from their food concessions. Some movie chains switched to oils low in saturated fats. After the CSPI report was issued, AMC Entertainment Inc., one of the largest U.S. movie chains, and the Toronto-based Cineplex Odeon started popping with canola oil. The same-sized bucket of popcorn popped in canola oil had one-sixth the previous amount of saturated fat. "It's very positive press," said Dwight More, president of the Canola Council of Canada. His euphoria was short-lived, however. A week later scientists at Howard University reported that hydrogenated canola oil was full of trans fatty acids that clogged arteries even faster than butter.

Consolidation

Since World War II, the popcorn industry has consolidated. In 1963, the Cracker Jack Company was sold to Borden, Inc. Borden, based in New York City, embarked on an acquisition drive that resulted in the purchase of 23 companies during the 1980s. With the acquisition of Laura Scudder's snack food company and the Snacktime Company in Indianapolis, Borden became the number-two marketer of snack foods in the nation, behind **Frito-Lay**, a subsidiary of **PepsiCo**. Borden developed Cracker Jack Extra Fresh Gourmet Quality Popping Corn. In 1997, Borden sold Cracker Jack to Frito-Lay, which also marketed **Cheetos** Cheddar Cheese Flavored Popcorn and Smartfoods popcorn. By the 1980s, the Wyandot Popcorn Company had become the nation's second-largest processor of popcorn. It was acquired by Vogel Popcorn, which in turn was sold to ConAgra. ConAgra had previously purchased Orville Redenbacher's Gourmet Popping Corn during the mid 1970s, and it had acquired other snack food brands, such as Crunch N' Munch, a Cracker Jack competitor.

Globalization

Popcorn may be a mature industry in America, but it has begun to expand abroad. Canada consumes one-third of U.S. popcorn exports. Europeans consider popcorn a sweet snack, and most consume it in caramelized form. The Japanese have acquired a taste for snack food, and popcorn sales there have risen steadily. Popcorn consumption in the United Kingdom takes place mainly at movie theaters, carnivals, and (to a much lesser extent) at home. Many observers believe that there is a potentially explosive market for popcorn in the United Kingdom and other Western European countries. With the fall of the Soviet Empire and the end of the Cold War, popcorn processors began looking to Eastern Europe and Russia as emerging markets.

Popcorn is easily grown, inexpensive to buy, and accessible to most people. It is readily processed and almost effortlessly prepared for consumption. Minus the salt and the butter, popcorn is a healthy food.

SUGGESTED READING: Andrew F. Smith, *Popped Culture: A Social History of Popcorn in America* (Columbia, SC: University of South Carolina Press, 1999).

Popeyes In the early 1970s, Al Copeland owned a Tastee Donut franchise that had been started by his brother in New Orleans. Copeland decided to shift from **doughnuts** to **fast food** chicken when **Kentucky Fried Chicken** started opening outlets in New Orleans. He opened his own **chicken** outlet in 1972. He called it Chicken on the Run. It served traditional mild chicken and it was not successful. Copeland shifted to spicy fried chicken and renamed it Popeyes, supposedly after the Popeye Doyle a character in the then popular movie, *The French Connection*. His new fast food chicken operation was a success and Copeland began to **franchise** it. Its first franchise restaurant was located in Baton Rouge, Louisiana in 1976. By 1981, there were more than 300 Popeyes. He began to **advertise** Popeyes with slogans such as “Love that Chicken from Popeyes.” In 1987, consumers preferred Popeyes over Kentucky Fried Chicken in a blind taste test, which encouraged Copeland to employ the **slogan**: “America’s Fried Chicken Champ—The Spicy Taste That Can’t Be Beat.” Popeyes regularly added new products to its menu: buttermilk biscuits were added in 1985, Cajun Popcorn Shrimp was introduced four years later, and Cajun Crawfish in 1988.

Nine years later, Popeyes opened its 500th restaurant. Popeyes bought the **Church’s Chicken** restaurant chain in 1989. The Popeyes Independent Franchise Association (PIFA) was formed in 1991 with the mission to protect the interests of the franchisees. In the same year, Popeyes opened its first international restaurant in Kuala Lumpur, Malaysia and later opened an outlet in Schweinfurt, Germany. In 1993, America’s Favorite Chicken Company, now known as **AFC Enterprises, Inc.**, became the new parent company of Popeyes and Church’s. The brand’s headquarters moved to Atlanta. Popeyes developed new restaurants through conversions, mass merchandisers, convenience stores, and grocery stores, such as outlets in Kroger stores. The brand continued to grow internationally as it opened its 50th restaurant in Korea. In 1996, Popeyes opened its 1,000th restaurant worldwide. In 1998, Popeyes acquired 66 former **Hardee’s** restaurants and converted them into Popeyes restaurants.

In 1999, Popeyes opened the Cajun Kitchen in a Chicago suburb. Cajun Kitchen provided food associated with a traditional casual restaurant with the speed of a fast food restaurant. In the same year, the company opened the Popeyes Cajun Café intended for shopping malls, food courts, and other entertainment venues. In 2000, Popeyes achieved worldwide sales of approximately $1.2 billion. As of 2005, Popeyes has more than 1,800 restaurants in the United States and 27 international markets, including Puerto Rico, Japan, Germany, Korea, and the United Kingdom.

SUGGESTED READING: John A. Jakle and Keith A. Sculle, *Fast Food: Roadside Restaurants in the Automobile Age* (Baltimore: Johns Hopkins University Press, 1999); Popeyes Web site: www.popeyesgulfcoast.com/history.htm

Popsicle Street vendors sold Hokey-Pokies (frozen fruit juices) as early as 1870s in New York and other cities, but it was Frank Epperson, a lemonade salesman from Oakland, California, who began the commercial manufacture of them. Epsicles, as he first called them, were ice pops on wooden sticks in 1923. He trademarked the name, which was later changed to Popsicle. In 1925, Epperson sold the rights to the Joe Lowe Company of New York. By 1928, more than 60 million Popsicles were sold annually. Consolidated Foods Corporation acquired the company in 1965. Twenty-one years later, the Gold Bond Ice Cream Company of Green Bay, Wisconsin purchased Popsicle's American operations. In 1989, **Unilever** purchased Gold Bond. As of 2005, Unilever also owned **Good Humor**, **Dove**, **Klondike**, and **Breyers**.

SUGGESTED READING: Anne Cooper Funderburg, *Chocolate, Strawberry, and Vanilla: A History of American Ice Cream* (Bowling Green, OH: Bowling Green State University Popular Press, 1995).

Pop-Tarts. © Kelly Fitzsimmons

Pop-Tarts In 1960s, Post Cereals developed the process for making a breakfast food that could be heated in the toaster. They released their first product, Country Squares, to the public in 1963. The **Kellogg Company** immediately began a crash development program to counter Post Cereal's Country Squares. After six months of work, Kellogg's came up with a product that was initially called a Fruit Scone. The name was changed to Pop-Tart, which was a pun on the then popular Pop Art movement. Pop-Tarts have a sugary filling, which is sealed inside two layers of a pastry crust. They are thin enough to fit into normal toasters. Post Cereal's Country Squares failed to take off but Pop-Tarts sales were extremely successful when they were released in 1964.

As of 2005, Kellogg produced 32 flavors of Pop-Tarts. The most popular flavors are frosted strawberry and frosted brown sugar cinnamon. The Kellogg Company sells more than two billion Pop-Tarts annually. They are distributed mainly in the United States, the United Kingdom, and Canada.

SUGGESTED READING: Pop-Tart Web site: www.poptarts.com

Potato Chips According to popular tradition, in the 1850s, George Crum, chef of the Moon's Lake Lodge in Saratoga, New York, was the first person to fry thin slices of potatoes and serve them to customers. They were named Saratoga Potatoes. In fact, home-made recipes that called for fried shavings of raw potatoes had appeared in American cookery books since 1824. Recipes named Saratoga Potatoes and Potato Chips were first published during the 1870s.

Early commercial potato chips were not successful. They were mass-produced during the 1890s by a number of manufacturers, including John E. Marshall of Boston. They were sold in barrels to grocery stores. Proprietors dished out the chips into paper bags for customers, who warmed them in the home oven before serving. This cumbersome process produced stale chips, which limited sales. This **packaging** problem was not solved until the 1930s.

When World War II began, potato chips were initially declared a nonessential food, which meant that production would have stopped during the war. Manufacturers lobbied the War Production Board to change this designation. Their efforts succeeded. Potato chips increased in sales throughout the war. **Advertising** increased sales even more when the war ended.

The postwar period also saw the introduction of several new potato chip products. Long, narrow shoestring potatoes were sold in cans by the 1950s. Ruffles (stronger, ridged potato chips) were introduced in 1958. In the 1960s, Procter & Gamble introduced **Pringles**, much to the chagrin of the potato chip industry. **Frito-Lay**'s baked potato chips were produced in response to America's fixation with weight and health.

Potato chips in the school locker. © Getty Images/Brand X Pictures

Potato chips are commonly consumed around the world. In the United Kingdom, as in many other English-speaking countries, they are called crisps. Americans purchase $6 billion annually, which works out to about 17 pounds of potato chips and shoestring potatoes per person. An additional $6 billion are expended on potato chips in other countries.

SUGGESTED READING: William S. Fox and Mae G. Banner, "Social and Economic Contexts for Folklore Variants: The Case of Potato Chip Legends," *Western Folklore* 42 (May 1983): 114–126.

Powdered Mixes Powdered mixes, such as those to make hot and cold **chocolate beverages**, have been around since the mid-nineteenth century. Commercial powdered mixes, such as **Nestlé**'s Instant Chocolate and Ovaltine, were common in the United States by the early twentieth century. **Kool-Aid**, which was launched in 1927, dominated the children's beverage market throughout the 1930s and 1940s. Instant coffee was invented in 1901 but was not a commercial success until 1938, when Nescafe released its freeze-dried coffee. Instant tea was introduced in 1953, and Lipton's Instant Tea came out five years later. The diet craze spawned many powdered mixes, including Crystal Light and Country Time.

The powdered mixes industry received a jolt in 1957, when **General Foods** released **Tang**, a powdered orange flavored mix composed of sweeteners and artificial flavorings. All customers had to do was mix the powder with water for an easy-to-prepare breakfast drink. It became popular during the 1960s and 1970s. Today, Tang is the best-selling powdered mix. It is owned by **Kraft Foods** and is currently sold in 60 countries.

SUGGESTED READING: Michael Turback, *Hot Chocolate* (Berkeley, CA: Ten Speed Press, 2005); Tang Web site: www.kraft.com/archives/brands/brands_tang.html

Power and Energy Bars Brian and Jennifer Maxwell of Berkeley, California, founded PowerBar in 1986. It was intended to be used by longdistance runners to supply **carbohydrates** during endurance events. It was a success and other companies, such as Clif Bar, Inc. began to manufacture power bars in 1992. Gatorade manufactured its Energy Bar in 1999. During the early twenty-first century, the Atkins Advantage and the Atkins Endulge were successfully sold, as was the Zone Perfect. Today, hundreds of power bars (also known as snack bars, granola bars, food bars, **nutrition** bars, and cereal bars) are available for purchase at grocery stores. Power and energy bars are high in calories, most of which come from carbohydrates.

SUGGESTED READING: The U.S. Market for Food Bars (New York: Packaged Facts, 2003).

Pretzels Pretzels are glazed, salted biscuits shaped into long tubes that are often twisted into knots. The word derives from German, but the Dutch probably first introduced them into America. Homemade pretzels were sold during colonial times by **street vendors**. In 1861, the first commercial pretzel company was launched by Julius Sturgis in Lititz, Pennsylvania. These were twisted by hand and remained a regional product. The first automatic pretzel twisting machine was developed by the Reading Pretzel Machinery Company in 1933. Pretzels manufacturers remained concentrated in Pennsylvania and pretzels did not emerge as a national snack until the 1960s.

Pretzels are sold in two ways: the large, soft pretzel is perishable and must be sold as a fresh-baked item (usually by vendors) or as a frozen food; the smaller, crisp pretzel has a long shelf life and is sold in plastic barrels or bags. The two best-selling pretzel brands in 2004 were Frito-Lay's Rold Gold and Snyder's of Hanover.

SUGGESTED READING: Virginia K. Bartlett, *Pickles and Pretzels: Pennsylvania's World of Food* (Pittsburgh: University of Pittsburgh Press, 1980).

Pricing In the United States, the pricing for **fast food** and **junk food** has rapidly changed over the years. **White Castle**, the first fast food **chain**, initially targeted workmen and intentionally kept its prices low. Subsequent fast food chains have targeted different groups and consequently had different pricing patterns. **McDonald's**, **Jack in the Box**, **Kentucky Fried Chicken**, **Pizza Hut**, and **Burger King** started off targeting suburban families and their goal was to keep the price of the food down. Others targeted different groups. Bob's **Big Boy** launched a large **hamburger** that costs three times as much as the hamburgers offered by fast food chains. It worked. Big Boys sold and fast food chains got the picture. Burger King released the Whopper in 1957 at the price of 37 cents—more than twice as much as McDonald's burgers. And McDonald's responded with its Big Mac and Quarter Pounder. Eventually, most fast food chains began offering deluxe products with higher prices. As disposable income of suburban families increased, so did the offerings and prices of fast food operations. Likewise, junk foods, such as **penny candy**, were offered at low cost. As disposable income increased in the United States, prices for **potato chips**, **candy**, and **chocolate** bars, for example, have greatly increased. Part of the increase is related to supply; chocolate prices have increased over the years, while **sugar** prices have sharply declined.

The category with greatest price flexibility is **soda**. Because the cost of water and sugar is very low, great profits can be generated. The problem is that the competition can (and has) offered lower-priced soft drinks. Major soda companies—**Coca-Cola**, **PepsiCo**, and

Cadbury Schweppes—have responded by purchasing as many of their competitors as possible and by **advertising** their products extensively.

SUGGESTED READING: John A. Jakle and Keith A. Sculle, *Fast Food: Roadside Restaurants in the Automobile Age* (Baltimore: Johns Hopkins University Press, 1999). Eric Schlosser, *Fast Food Nation: The Dark Side of the All-American Meal* (New York: Houghton Mifflin Company, 2001).

Pringles In 1969, Procter & Gamble introduced Pringles Potato Chips, made from dehydrated and reconstituted potatoes. They were named after Pringle Street in Finneytown, Ohio. Unlike potato chips, Pringles are a uniform size and shape, making it possible to package them in a long tube. The potato chip industry went to court to prevent Procter & Gable from calling Pringles "potato chips." This was resolved in 1975, when the U.S. Food and Drug Administration defined Pringles as "potato chips made from dehydrated potatoes."

Pringles are one of Procter & Gamble's biggest brands and they are sold in more than 140 countries. Procter & Gamble has extended the Pringle product line to now include Sour Cream & Onion, Salt & Vinegar, and Hot & Spicy. In 1998, Fat-free Pringles, made with olestra, were introduced. The **Center for Science in the Public Interest** claimed that olestra disrupted some people's digestive tracts, but Proctor & Gamble argued the product posed no health threat. Nevertheless, the product was withdrawn from the market.

One reason for Pringles's success has been their extensive **advertising**. For instance, in 2005 Proctor & Gamble arranged a movie **tie-in** with *Star Wars Episode III—Revenge of the Sith*. Pringle cans featured special *Revenge of the Sith*-themed characters, such as Anakin Skywalker, Yoda, and Darth Vader.

SUGGESTED READING: Pringles Web site: www.pringles.com

Protests Protests against **junk food** and **fast food** have been growing since the 1970s for a variety of reasons. **Animal rights** and **vegetarian** activists have protested against the consumption of meat and meat products and the conditions at feedlots and slaughterhouses that supply meat to fast food operations. Leftists, anarchists, and nationalists have protested against **globalization** of fast food. **Environmentalists** have protested against the loss of rainforests due to activities of fast food **suppliers** and against the amount of waste needlessly generated by fast food chains and their suppliers.

Nutrition activists have protested about the empty calories as well as the high levels of **salt**, **fat**, and **sugar** present in most junk and fast foods. Recent concern has focused on the size of portions offered in fast food operations, particularly **supersized** meals. **Consumer** advocates and educators have protested against the targeting of children through **advertising** and sale of junk food and fast food in **schools**. Labor unions have protested the **anti-union** activities of fast food chains. Groups have engaged in **boycotts** against junk food manufacturers as well as fast food chains. Because fast food operations are often considered synonymous with the United States, people in other countries have protested against polices and actions of the U.S. government by destroying, trashing, and bombing fast food outlets.

Fast food chains and junk food manufacturers have responded to these protests in a variety of ways. **McDonald's** eliminated beef tallow and other beef products from its **French fry** oil, and **Burger King** placed signs in its outlets reporting that its French fries were made with beef products and to alert vegetarians as to the contents of its products. Fast food operations in other countries have intentionally localized their suppliers. The

McDonald's outlets in France buy 95 percent of the food they serve from local farmers and processors. All fast food chains have offered special foods and **beverages** appropriate to local sensibilities. For instance, McDonald's does not sell hamburgers in India, but does sell veggie burgers. When environmentalists attacked McDonald's for destruction of rainforests, the company shifted to suppliers in countries without rainforests.

Protests have also targeted fast food chains for political reasons. When the McDonald's outlets in Norway released the McAfrika Burger in August, 2002, protestors attacked the company for profiting from a name when there were millions of people starving in South Africa. (At the time, South Africa was in the midst of massive famine due to natural disasters—heavy floods, then drought.)

McDonald's has became a symbol of American prosperity and creativity. Simply due to the size, visibility and impact of fast and junk food operations around the world, fast food companies attract protesters. Many people believe that they threaten national cultures by shifting how, where, and what people eat.

SUGGESTED READING: José Bové, François Dufour and Gilles Luneau, *The World Is Not for Sale: Farmers Against Junk Food* (New York: Verso, 2001); McSpotlight Web site: www.mcspotlight.org

Push-ups During the 1980s, push-ups, also known as rocket pops, became popular. Push-ups were composed of many different ingredients, from **ice cream** to sherbet to yogurt. The mechanism varied by brand: some consisted of axles, wheels, and cylinders; others used just a stick in a tube. The consumer pushed up the bottom and licked the product at the top. Today, push-ups continue to be made by a number of companies, including **Nestlé**. Their new product line consists of vanilla-flavored sherbet with **chocolate**, strawberry, or **caramel**.

SUGGESTED READING: Anne Cooper Funderburg, *Chocolate, Strawberry, and Vanilla: A History of American Ice Cream* (Bowling Green, OH: Bowling Green State Univeristy Popular Press, 1995).

Q–R

Quiznos Sub In 1981, the first Quiznos Sub restaurant was opened Denver, Colorado. It featured toasted sub **sandwiches**, salads, soups, chips, and desserts. Rick Schaden ate at the restaurant and liked the sub sandwich so much that in 1987 he bought a franchise in Boulder, Colorado. He subsequently purchased additional **franchises**, and in 1991 he and his father bought the entire franchise operation, which then had 18 restaurants. Under Schaden's leadership, the **chain** expanded rapidly and by the year 2000 it reached more than 2,000 outlets. Four years later it topped 3,000 outlets in the United States and 15 other nations. In 2005, it ranked second in the sub sandwich category of **fast food** chains.

SUGGESTED READING: Quiznos Web site: www.quiznos.com

Radio Since the 1920s, **snack food** and **fast food** have been advertised on radio. From the manufacturers' standpoint, radio's immense power lay in its **advertising** potential and its relatively low cost. Products advertised on the radio sold. When radio programs became popular in the 1920s, food companies commissioned celebrities, such Jack Benny, to promote their products. Some of the earliest food companies to advertise effectively on radio were **cereal** makers. In 1926, **General Mills** (Wheaties) was the first advertiser to use a singing radio commercial. In 1933, Wheaties sponsored the program *Jack Armstrong, the All-American Boy* on the radio. The fast food chain **White Castle** began advertising on radio by the 1930s. Beginning in the 1950s, most fast food chains and **junk food** manufacturers advertised on radio. For instance, the **chocolate** drink Ovaltine sponsored the *Little Orphan Annie* and *Captain Midnight* radio programs.

Studies have indicated that Americans spend more time listening to the radio than watching **television**. Because radio advertising is low-cost compared with television advertising, it is frequently used by fast food chains at the local level. Radio advertising is particularly effective during commute times, when many people listen to the radios in their cars. It is estimated that food companies (mainly fast food) expend about 7 percent of their advertising budget on radio advertising.

SUGGESTED READING: David Gerard Hogan, *Selling 'em by the Sack: White Castle and the Creation of American Food* (New York: New York University Press, 1997); Andrew F. Smith, *Popped*

Culture: A Social History of Popcorn in America (Columbia, SC: University of South Carolina Press, 1999).

Orville Redenbacher. Courtesy of Photofest

Redenbacher, Orville Popcorn **entrepreneur** Orville Clarence Redenbacher (1907–1995) was born in Brazil, Indiana. He grew up on a farm and studied agronomy and genetics at Purdue University, where he conducted research on **popcorn** hybrids. Upon graduation in 1928, he was hired as a high school Vocational Agricultural Teacher, a position he held until 1929. He was then employed as an assistant county farm agent in Terre Haute, Indiana. When the senior agent moved to Indianapolis, Redenbacher took over his position and conducted a five-minute daily radio program beginning in 1930. He was the first county agricultural agent in the country to broadcast live from his office and the first to interview farmers in the field with a mobile unit.

In January 1940, Tony Hulman, owner of Indianapolis 500 racetrack, hired Redenbacher to manage his 12,000-acre farm in Princeton, Indiana, which produced seed for farmers. Redenbacher built a hybrid seed corn plant and began experimenting with popcorn hybrids. Under Redenbacher's management, Princeton Farms's operations grew by 50 percent.

While at Princeton Farms, Redenbacher met Charles Bowman, the manager of the Purdue Ag Alumni Seed Implement Association in Lafayette, Indiana. Redenbacher and Bowman went into partnership in 1951 and purchased the George F. Chester Seed Company at Boone Grove, Indiana. Popcorn was part of their hybrid field seed operation, and within a few years Redenbacher and Bowman became the world's largest supplier of hybrid popcorn seed. They also developed new hybrids. They reportedly crossed 30,000 popcorn hybrids to find the right mix. In 1965, their popcorn experimentation created a variety that expanded to nearly twice the size of existing commercial brands. It was fluffier and left few unpopped kernels. They called the new variety Red Bow after the first three letters in Redenbacher's and Bowman's last names. For five years Redenbacher tried to sell his new hybrid to the major processors. However, it cost more to harvest and its yields were smaller than traditional popcorn. Because popcorn was then considered a commodity, processors were not interested.

Redenbacher hawked his popcorn out of the back seat of his car to stores in northern Indiana. In 1970, Redenbacher quit producing popcorn seed for other processors and concentrated on selling Red Bow. Redenbacher and Bowman consulted a Chicago public relations firm that convinced them to change the name from Red Bow to Orville Redenbacher's Gourmet Popping Corn. Because its price was higher than that of other popcorn, consumers needed to be convinced that Redenbacher's popcorn was of a better quality than its competitors. The **advertising** tag "The World's Most Expensive Popcorn" emerged. Redenbacher and Bowman achieved regional success through word-of-mouth promotion and virtually no advertising, but they needed assistance to expand nationally.

In 1973, they teamed up with Blue Plate Foods, a subsidiary of Hunt-Wesson Foods based in Fullerton, California, to market their gourmet popcorn. This connection enabled national advertising and a widespread distribution system.

When Hunt-Wesson sold Blue Plate Foods in 1974, Redenbacher's gourmet popcorn was so successful that Hunt-Wesson kept the rights to it. In 1976, Orville Redenbacher's Gourmet Popping Corn business operations and property were sold to Hunt-Wesson, which launched a massive advertising campaign, starring Redenbacher himself, for their newly acquired product. He made hundreds of personal presentations a year and appeared in scores of **television** commercials. Redenbacher was one of America's most unlikely television stars, with his folksy image (bow tie, dark-framed spectacles, and Midwestern accent). The image worked. Consumers easily recognized the label adorned with Redenbacher's image. In 1984, he wrote *Orville Redenbacher's Popcorn Book*, which was mainly a promotion piece for his popcorn.

In 1990, Hunt-Wesson (along with the Redenbacher brand) was acquired by ConAgra Foods. Redenbacher's contract for television commercials was not renewed in 1994. While lounging in a whirlpool in his condominium in Coronado, California, Redenbacher suffered a heart attack and drowned in 1995.

After his death, *Time* magazine called Redenbacher "the Luther Burbank of popcorn." His gourmet popping corn stands as his shining legacy. Because his was one of the first foods called *gourmet*, it can be said that the naming of his popcorn launched a new category of foods and created gourmet sections in grocery stores.

SUGGESTED READING: Orville Redenbacher, *Orville Redenbacher's Popcorn Book* (New York: St. Martin's Press, 1984); Len Sherman, *Popcorn King: How Orville Redenbacher and His Popcorn Charmed America* (Arlington, TX: The Summit Publishing Group, 1996); Andrew F. Smith, *Popped Culture: A Social History of Popcorn in America* (Columbia, SC: University of South Carolina Press, 1999).

Reese's Peanut Butter Cups Harry Burnett Reese, a former employee of the **Hershey Company**, founded the H. B. Reese Candy Company in 1917. Reese experimented with molasses and coconut candies called Johnny Bars and Lizzie Bars. Reese moved his operation to Hershey, Pennsylvania, in 1923 and began purchasing **chocolate** from Hershey. In 1928 he came out with chocolate-covered peanut butter cups, which were packaged in five-pound boxes for sale in **candy** assortments. Ten years later, Reese marketed these cups separately for a penny apiece. These subsequently became known as Reese's Peanut Butter Cups, and they were extremely popular. Increased demand meant factory expansion, and Reese's became the second-largest buyer of chocolate in the United States. During World War II, difficulties in acquiring **sugar** and chocolate prompted Reese to discontinue his other lines to concentrate on the peanut butter cups, because

Reese's peanut butter cups. © Kelly Fitzsimmons

peanuts were not rationed during the war. After the war, the peanut candy market boomed. Reese's Peanut Butter Cup, distributed through wholesale jobbers, **vending machine** operators, and syndicated stores, gained popularity and the company constructed an even larger facility in 1957.

When Harry Reese died in 1956, the company went through a bitter battle for control among the six brothers who inherited it. With annual sales at $14 million, the company was acquired by Hershey Chocolate Company in 1963 for $23.3 million. Under the ownership of Hershey Chocolate Company, Reese's Peanut Butter Cups were sold nationally. The **advertising** slogan, "Two great tastes that taste great together," was developed by Ogilvie & Mather in 1970 for the Reese's Peanut Butter Cup. In 1976, Hershey expanded the product line by launching Reese's Crunchy Peanut Butter Cup, with a different flavor and a texture of chopped peanuts.

The remarkable success of the Reese's chocolate-peanut butter combination encouraged Hershey to test market a small peanut butter candy in 1979. While the product was under development, PB was its proposed name. Because **Mars, Inc.** already held the trademark on PB, Hershey decided on Reese's Pieces, which were released nationally in 1978. Within four years, they were so successful that a new production line was established in Stuart's Draft, Virginia. Mars, Inc. released Peanut Butter **M&M's** to counter Reese's Pieces. Their sales peaked in 1991 at $78 million, then dropped to $34 million in 1993. Mars purportedly then tried to relaunch the brand by copying the coloring and styling of Hershey's Reese's Pieces. This resulted in a **lawsuit**, with Hershey claiming that Mars was capitalizing on Hershey's goodwill and substantial investment in Reese's Pieces. Hershey won, and Mars changed the candy's appearance so that it looked less like Reese's Pieces.

In 1981, Hershey was approached by Universal Studios for assistance with making a new film. The main character in the film was a lovable alien, and the filmmakers wanted to have the children in the film lure the creature with a trail of candy. The producers had previously contacted Mars, Inc., requesting the use of M&M's, but Mars refused. So Universal turned to Hershey for permission to use Reese's Pieces, instead, and Hershey agreed. Reese's Pieces consequently received national visibility in *ET*, which was a blockbuster film. This was considered an inexpensive marketing triumph, and advertisers have tried to duplicate it ever since.

The Hershey Company has continued to expand its successful Reese's Peanut Butter Cup line by releasing White Chocolate Reese's Peanut Butter Cups in 2003. Reese's Peanut Butter Cups remain one of America's most popular candy bars.

SUGGESTED READING: Ray Broekel, *The Great America Candy Bar Book* (Boston: Houghton Mifflin Company, 1982); Tim Richardson, *Sweets: A History of Candy* (New York: Bloomsbury, 2002); Andrew F. Smith, *Peanuts: The Illustrious History of the Goober Pea* (Urbana, IL: University of Illinois Press, 2002); Hershey's Web site: www.hersheys.com/products/reese/index.html

Regional Fast Foods Major national chains dominate the American **fast food** world, but there are many local and regional operations that serve fast food **hamburgers**, **pizza**, and **chicken**, as well as various ethnic foods. Large regional hamburger chains include **Big Boy** and **In-N-Out Burger**. There are many others. Whataburger, founded in Corpus, Texas, in 1950, sells burgers, chicken, and salads, and mainly operates in Alabama, Arizona, Florida, Louisiana, New Mexico, Oklahoma, and Texas. Fatburger and Tommies Burgers mainly operate in southern California. Wolfe Burger sells the Big Bad Wolfe burger, mainly in Pasadena, California. Krystal, which started 1932, operates in southeastern states only, offering **breakfasts** and hamburgers. Blake's Lotta Burger has 75 locations in New Mexico. The Happy Chef has outlets in Iowa, Minnesota, South Dakota, and Wisconsin.

Many regional chains specialize in chicken. Bojangles, with its chicken and biscuits, has locations mainly in the South. Chester Fried Chicken was launched in Chester County, Pennsylvania, in 1974. By 2002, the Chester Fried Chicken brand was sold in more than 1,700 licensed locations throughout the country.

Most communities in the American Southwest have Mexican-American fast food outlets. Regional Mexican-American fast food restaurant chains include **El Pollo Loco** and **Del Taco**. There are many more: Taco Del Mar Mexican Food, launched in 1992, is headquartered in Seattle and has outlets in western and midwestern states. In 1959, Taco Time began in Eugene, Oregon, and today has more than 300 outlets. Taco John's started in 1969 and today operates in 27 states. Pepe's was launched in Chicago in 1967. Taco Maker was launched in Ogden, Utah in 1968.

American cities and most towns have at least one **pizza** parlor, and there are many regional chains. Boston Pizza was launched by a Greek immigrant in Edmonton, Canada, in 1964, and today it has 80 outlets, mainly in eastern Canada. In 1971, Jim Fox launched Fox's Pizza Den in Pitcairn, Pennsylvania. Vocelli Pizza, launched in 1988, has 100 outlets today.

Many American communities have Chinese fast food outlets. Chinese fast food chains include **Panda Express**, Manchu Wok, which started in Peterborough, Ontario, and today has 200 outlets, and Tasty Goody, which has eight locations in southern California, mainly in the area between Los Angeles and Riverside. Mr. Chau's Fast Food is in the San Francisco Bay/Silicon Valley area of California.

In addition to local chains, national and regional chains serve different foods in various regions. **McDonald's**, for instance, serves veggie burgers in New York. Regional chains serve regional favorites, such a barbecue or chicken fried steak in the South.

Commercial regional **snack foods** and soft drinks are quickly disappearing, but some have survived. **Moxie** soda, for instance, remains a favorite drink in New England. **Moon Pies** remain a favorite in Tennessee and the South, and TastyKakes are still made in Philadelphia.

SUGGESTED READING: John A. Jakle and Keith A. Sculle, *Fast Food: Roadside Restaurants in the Automobile Age* (Baltimore: Johns Hopkins University Press, 1999).

Ritz Crackers In November, 1934, the National Biscuit Company (later renamed **Nabisco**) test-marketed Ritz Crackers. They were so successful that the company released them nationally the following year. Their name, Ritz, originated with César Ritz, the Swiss hotelier who established luxury hotels in Europe and the United States. By 1920, the term *ritz-y* had commonly come to mean classy and glamorous. Ritz Crackers were released in the midst of the Depression, when few people could afford the luxuries of fancy foods. Ritz Crackers quickly became a staple American **junk food**. They were also exported to Europe, South America, and Australia, where they have maintained significant sales.

Ritz Crackers are usually consumed right out of the box. As appetizers, they have been used as a base for other foods, such as cheese and ham. Beginning in the 1930s, the National Biscuit Company began promoting the use of Ritz Crackers with **sugar** and spices to make mock apple pie, which had previously been made with soda crackers. Their recipe found its way into cookbooks by the 1960s. Crushed Ritz Crackers have also been used for toppings for many dishes, from casseroles to creamed corn.

Nabisco has continued to expand the Ritz product line, releasing smaller versions (Ritz Bits and Mini Ritz), a stick version (Ritz Sticks), and versions with different flavors, such as BBQ Chicken and Sweet Chilli & Sour Cream. Ritz Crackers were sold in boxes and, up to the 1970, were also sold in round tins. Today, they are also sold in bags.

SUGGESTED READING: Ritz Crackers Web site: www.kraft.com.au/nabisco/products_ritz.cfm

Ronald McDonald In 1960, Oscar Goldstein opened the first inner-city **McDonald's franchise** in Washington, D.C. to gain visibility for his new **fast food** outlet, Goldstein sponsored a local children's **television** program called *Bozo's Circus.* In the program, Willard Scott played Bozo dressed in a costume created by an **advertising** agency. It was a successful combination and Scott subsequently played Bozo at the grand openings of other local McDonald's outlets. Sales in Washington grew by a whopping 30 percent per year. In 1963, the Washington television station decided to drop *Bozo's Circus,* which lagged in ratings. The local McDonald's franchise decided to produce television commercials starring another clown. They debated what to name the clown and an advertising agency proposed Archie McDonald, which offered an allusion to McDonald's Golden Arches symbol. This was rejected because there was a sportscaster in the Washington area named Arch McDonald, so another name had to be found. Using a simple rhyme, Willard Scott came up with the name Ronald McDonald. Scott played Ronald McDonald in the first television commercials broadcast in October, 1963. It was the first commercial sponsored by a local McDonald's franchisee.

In 1965, the national McDonald's Corporation decided to sponsor the broadcast of the Macy's Thanksgiving Day Parade. They chose to feature Ronald McDonald but they fired Willard Scott because they wanted someone thinner to play the part. Coco, a Hungarian-speaking clown from the Barnum & Bailey Circus, was selected. (Willard Scott went on to become the weatherman on NBC's *Today Show.*) Previously, no **fast food** chain had advertised on national television, and it was a financial risk because McDonald's major sales were in the summertime, not in November. Likewise, Ronald McDonald appealed to children, who were not considered an important target of fast food promoters at the time. The Thanksgiving Day's commercials produced immediate nationwide results, which convinced McDonald's to expend more funds advertising on television, giving McDonald's an edge in the children's market.

Ronald McDonald became McDonald's official spokesman in 1966. He also became the centerpiece of a number of other advertising activities: his image appeared on television commercials and a vast array of products, including book covers, coloring books, comic books, cups, dolls, masks, Frisbees, games calendars, mugs, napkins, postcards, puppets records, toy parachutes, trains, and trucks, and the famous Flying Hamburger.

In addition, McDonald's Playlands in outlets featured Ronald McDonald and a cast of other mythical characters. While none of the other characters achieved the prominence of Ronald McDonald, the playlands strengthened McDonald's dominance in the children's fast food market. When McDonald's signed a contract to open 300 outlets at military bases, Ronald McDonald posed for pictures in front of an aircraft carrier. The first Ronald McDonald House, a residence located adjacent to a hospital to provide free or low-cost room and board for families with children requiring extended hospital care, was set up in Philadelphia in 1974. Since then, 200 more have been constructed in the United States and 11 in other countries. All are sponsored by local McDonald's operations. Ten years later, Ronald McDonald's Children Charities was founded in honor of **Ray Kroc**. Today it is one of the largest organizations financially devoted to the welfare of children.

"Ronald L. McDonald" has "authored" three books: *The Complete Hamburger: The History of America's Favorite Sandwich* (1997); *Ronald McDonald's Franchise Buyers Guide: How to Buy a Fast Food Franchise* (2003); and *Ronald McDonald's International Burger Book* (2004). Other books have used his name in their title, such as Marshall Fishwick's *Ronald Revisited: The World of Ronald McDonald* and *The Ronald McDonald House of NYC Cookbook* (1994).

As McDonald's expanded to other countries, so did Ronald McDonald. In some countries, adjustments were necessary. In Japan, for instance, the name was changed to Donald McDonald due to the difficulty of pronouncing the "r" in Ronald.

Because Ronald McDonald was a symbol of the company, it also has been a target for protestors who are upset with the company. In 2000, Hong Kong **protestors** dressed like Ronald McDonald carried signs that said that the company was **exploiting** workers in China due to alleged use of child laborers by McDonald's suppliers. When it became public in 2001 that McDonald's had used beef tallow in making its **French fries** in the United States, hundreds of enraged Hindus ransacked a McDonald's in Bombay and smeared cow dung on a statue of Ronald McDonald because they thought the same practice was followed in India.

Today, Ronald McDonald can be found in every McDonald's market, and he is among the most popular children's character in the world. He speaks in 25 languages, including Cantonese, Portuguese, Russian, and Hindi. Ninety-six percent of American children recognize Ronald McDonald, slightly less than the number who recognize Santa Claus. *Advertising Age* rated Ronald McDonald as the second-most-successful icon of the twentieth century. (Their number-one icon pick was the Marlboro Man.)

SUGGESTED READING: Marshall Fishwick, ed., *Ronald Revisited: The World of Ronald McDonald* (Bowling Green. OH: Bowling Green University Popular Press, 1983); Terry Losonsky and Joyce Losonsky, *McDonald's Happy Meal Toys around the World* (Atglen, PA: Schiffer Publishing, Ltd., 1995); Joyce Losonsky and Terry Losonsky, *McDonald's Pre-Happy Meal Toys from the Fifties, Sixties, and Seventies* (Atglen, PA: Schiffer Publishing Ltd., 1998); John F. Love, *McDonald's Behind the Arches* (Revised and updated) (New York: Bantam Books, 1995); Ronald L. McDonald, *The Complete Hamburger: The History of America's Favorite Sandwich* (Secaucus, NJ: Carol Publishing Group, 1997); Ronald L. McDonald, *Ronald McDonald's Franchise Buyers Guide: How to Buy a Fast Food Franchise* (Philadelphia, PA: Xlibris, 2003); Ronald L. McDonald, *Ronald McDonald's International Burger Book* (Tucson, AZ: Hats Off Books, 2004); McDonald's Web site: www.mcdonalds.com/corporate/index.html

Root Beer Root beer has been a commonly consumed **beverage** in America at least since the eighteenth century. It was made in various ways with roots, bark, flower buds, seeds, and leaves of plants such as wintergreen, sassafras, ginger, nutmeg, cinnamon, sarsaparilla, wild cherry, **licorice**, birch twigs, and vanilla. Usually, these are dried and converted into essential oils, which were then used to make the syrup. Each company maintained its proprietary **secret formula** for making root beer. Throughout the nineteenth century, root beer was a health beverage and was frequently made in the home. It was frequently served as a hot tea. By the 1840s, commercially root beer bottled in stoneware was sold in confectionery and general stores. Recipes for root beer appeared in cookbooks by the 1860s.

Precisely when root beer syrup was combined with carbonated water to form a cold soft drink is unclear. The earliest located record of commercial root beer production is about George Twitchell of Philadelphia, who manufactured a syrup for a root beer tonic that was intended to be combined with **soda** in 1850. Root beer was first mass-produced commercially by a Philadelphia pharmacist, Charles E. Hires. **Hires Root Beer** was one of America's most popular beverages during the late nineteenth and early twentieth century. In 1919, **A&W Root Beer** originated in Lodi, California. There are many regional root beers. Dad's Old-Fashioned Root Beer was launched in 1937. **Barq's Root Beer** was created in 1898 and remained a family-owned business based in Biloxi, Mississippi, until the company was purchased by the **Coca-Cola Company** in 1995. Due to this connection, it is today one of the nation's leading root beers.

SUGGESTED READING: L. A. Enkema, *Root Beer: How It Got Its Name; What It Is; How It Developed from a Home-brewed Beverage to Its Present Day Popularity* (Indianapolis, IN, Hurty-Peck & Co., 1952); Tom Morrison, *Root Beer Advertising: A Collector's Guide* (Atglen, PA: Schiffer Publishing,1992); Tom Morrison, *More Root Beer Advertising and Collectibles* (Atglen, PA: Schiffer Publishing, 1997); Donald Yates and Elizabeth Yates, eds., *American Stone Ginger Beer & Root Beer Heritage, 1790 to 1920; Written by Numerous Authors and Historians* (Homerville, OH: Donald Yates Publishers, 2003); Hires brand Web site: www.dpsu.com/brands_hires_root_beer.html

Rowntree's of York William Tuke and Sons of York, England, owners of a grocery business, began selling cocoa in 1785. In 1862, Henry Isaac Rowntree acquired the Tukes' cocoa business. In 1881, the company introduced Rowntree's Fruit Pastilles and in 1893 they released Rowntree's Fruit Gums. Four years later, Rowntree & Co was officially launched. The company was instrumental in creating what then were novel programs for employees, including a pension scheme, unemployment benefits, dining and other facilities, worker's councils, and annual paid holiday. Joseph Rowntree helped create the Industrial Welfare Society in 1919 and B. Seebohm Rowntree wrote a book on poverty, advocating higher pay for all workers.

During the early twentieth century, Rowntree introduced many new **chocolate** products, but none were as successful as those of its major competitor, **Cadbury**. In 1931, the company began an aggressive development program. One key to its success was the relationship between Rowntree and **Forrest Mars**, whose company, **Mars, Inc.** had successfully launched the Mars bar in England in 1933. Until then, combination bars had not been successful in England. One result of the collaboration was the Chocolate Crisp, which was launched in 1935. Two years later it was renamed Kit Kat bar. It was the company's most popular and successful chocolate **candy**. In the 1930s, the **Hershey Company** bought rights to manufacture the Kit Kat bars in America. Hershey's changed the formula because American taste in chocolate differed from that of the English.

Another likely result of the collaboration between Mars and Rowntree was Smarties, which were launched in 1937. They were a colorful sugar-coated chocolate confectionery packaged in a round tube, which remain popular today in the United Kingdom, South Africa, Canada, and Australia. It is believed that Forrest Mars developed his idea for **M&M's**, launched in 1940, from Smarties.

In 1988, **Nestlé SA** acquired Rowntree; subsequently, many new chocolate candies under the Rowntree brand have been introduced. The Kit Kat line, for instance, was extended to include Kit Kat Chunkies (1999) and Kit Kat Kubes (2003).

SUGGESTED READING: Tim Richardson, *Sweets: A History of Candy* (New York: Bloomsbury, 2002).

Roy Rogers In 1967, Roy Rogers, the famous **television** Western actor, agreed to permit the **Marriott Corporation** use his name on a **fast food** outlet **chain**. The Marriott executive in charge of the Roy Rogers chain was Jim Plamondon, Sr. The following year, the first Roy Rogers Western Roast Beef Sandwich restaurant was launched in Falls Church, Virginia. The chain quickly expanded the number of outlets through **franchising**. The company expanded its menu to include **chicken** and **hamburgers**.

In 1982, the Marriott Corporation bought Gino's, another fast food chain, and converted many of them into Roy Rogers outlets. Three years later, Marriott bought Howard Johnson's restaurants and converted some of them into Roy Rogers outlets. By 1990, Roy Rogers had 894 outlets. In that year Imasco, the parent company of **Hardee's**, purchased the Roy Rogers chain from Marriott. Hardee's converted 220 Roy Rogers outlets into Hardee's restaurants, but then reconverted them into Roy Rogers two years later. Other Roy Rogers outlets were sold to Boston Chicken (later renamed **Boston Market**), **Wendy's**, and **McDonald's**. Only 13 Roy Rogers franchisees survived, one of which was Plamondon Enterprises, Inc., which was controlled by Jim Plamondon's children. In 2002, Imasco sold the Roy Rogers trademark to Plamondon Enterprises, Inc., which then created a new company called Roy Rogers Franchise Company, Inc.

SUGGESTED READING: John A. Jakle and Keith A. Sculle, *Fast Food: Roadside Restaurants in the Automobile Age* (Baltimore: Johns Hopkins University Press, 1999); Roy Rogers Web site: www.royrogersrestaurants.com

Royal Crown Cola In 1905, Claud A. Hatcher, a pharmacist, launched the Union Bottling Works in the basement of his family's grocery store in Columbus, Georgia. Chero-Cola was the first of his Royal Crown line of beverages, and it was followed by **ginger ale** and strawberry- and **root beer**–flavored **sodas**. In 1912, Hatcher changed the name of the company to the Chero-Cola Company. The company struggled throughout World War I, when **sugar** was difficult to obtain, and it had financial difficulties during the early 1920s, but in 1924 it was strong enough to bring out a new line, called Nehi, of fruit-flavored sodas such as orange, grape, and root beer. By 1925, the Chero-Cola Company had 315 plants located primarily in the southern states. In 1928, Hatcher again changed the name of the company to the Nehi Corporation. Hatcher died in 1933 and his successor, H. R. Mott, streamlined operations, reformulated Chero-Cola, and shortened the brand name, Royal Crown Cola, to just RC. By 1940, the company's products were available in 47 of the 48 states. The company continued to expand and aggressively **advertised** in national publications, such as *Saturday Evening Post* and *Good Housekeeping.*

The Nehi Corporation was a major innovator in the soft drink world. In 1954, the company became the first to nationally distribute soft drinks in cans. Four years later, the company introduced the 16-ounce bottle, which contrasted favorably with **Coca-Cola**'s small, 8-ounce bottle. In 1958, the company released the first **diet** cola, called Diet Rite, on a local basis, and launched it nationally in 1962. At this time, the company changed its name from Nehi Corporation to the Royal Crown Company. In 1980, the company released RC 100, the first **caffeine**-free cola, and the first diet cherry cola, Diet Cherry RC.

In 1998, the company introduced RC Edge, the first maximum-power cola containing a synergistic blend of spices and caffeine. In 2000, the RC Cola brand was acquired by **Cadbury Schweppes** Americas Beverages, located in Plano, Texas.

SUGGESTED READING: Cadbury Schweppes Web site: www.dpsu.com/rc.html

Rules Many **fast food** restaurants have explicit rules, such as that patrons must wear shirts and shoes to enter, and only customers can use the restrooms. These and other rules are usually posted on public display in the outlets.

All fast food chains also have unwritten rules. In the United States, for instance, customers are expected to line up to order food. Customers expect rapid service. Employees are expected to smile. Customers usually take their own orders to the tables. Customers are expected to eat and leave promptly, thus permitting other customers to sit down. Customers are also expected to clean up their own messes. In other countries, these unwritten rules have led to confusion and some have been rejected. For instance, in East Asia, youth expect to spend considerable time in fast food chains, believing that the "fast food" refers to the delivery time and not the time expended eating the meals.

SUGGESTED READING: James L. Watson, ed. *Golden Arches East: McDonald's in East Asia* (Stanford, CA: Stanford University Press, 1997).

S

Salmonella *Salmonella* is a rod-shaped bacterium that takes its name from Daniel Salmon, an American veterinarian who discovered it in 1885. More than 2,200 varieties have been identified, but food poisonings are caused mainly by *Salmonella enteritidis* and *S. typhimurium*. *Salmonella* produces fever, abdominal pain, diarrhea, nausea, vomiting, and general weakness. The **U.S. Department of Agriculture (USDA)** estimates that *Salmonella* is present in 35 percent of turkeys, 11 percent of chickens, and 6 percent of ground beef. It can easily be spread to other foods by improper handling. The Centers for Disease Control estimates that salmonellosis causes about one-third of the 76 million **foodborne illnesses** each year and about 180 people die from *Salmonella* poisoning. Most people infected with it are unaware of the cause of their illness, placing the blame on the flu or some other ailment. Several *Salmonella* outbreaks have been traced to **fast food** outlets. *Salmonella* poisoning can be prevented by cooking meat to 165 degrees F, by proper handling of all food, and by preventing infected individuals from working around food.

SUGGESTED READING: Danielle A. Brands, *Salmonella* (Philadelphia: Chelsea House Publishers, 2005).

Salt Salt (sodium chloride) is essential to life and it is the most common **condiment** in America. Since colonial times, it was commonly used as a preservative and a seasoning on a wide range of foods. During the past 50 years, the consumption of salt in America has rapidly increased. Food manufacturers add salt to their processed food because it is cheap and makes their products taste better, and today Americans get almost 80 percent of their sodium from processed foods. In addition, salty **snack foods**, such as **potato chips** and **pretzels**, are consumed in increasing quantities in the United States.

Medical practitioners and health advocates have argued for decreased consumption of salt because excessive sodium intake has been associated with hypertension, stomach cancer, and other diseases. The **Center for Science in the Public Interest (CSPI)** has lobbied Congress to require food labeling on high-salt foods, and the U.S. Food and Drug Administration (FDA) launched a series of initiatives aimed at encouraging Americans to reduce their salt consumption. In 2005, CSPI urged Congress to create a new Division of Sodium Reduction. CSPI executive director Michael F. Jacobson proclaimed that "Excess sodium in the diet causes tens of thousands of preventable heart attacks and strokes each year. This salt assault is probably good for funeral directors and coffin makers, but it is a disaster for shoppers and restaurant patrons."

Elevated blood pressure or hypertension is a risk factor for heart attacks, strokes, and kidney failure. Cardiovascular events are a major cause of premature death and cost Americans billions of dollars every year in increased medical costs and lost productivity. Reducing blood pressure can reduce the risk of a heart attack or stroke. However, the connection between salt consumption and high blood pressure is not as clear as once thought. When healthy people consume excess salt, the human body maintains sodium by retaining more water until the kidneys excrete more salt. When body fluids cause swelling, there is a slight increase in blood pressure, which then declines.

How much sodium individuals need and how much they can tolerate vary enormously. The National Academy of Sciences recommends that Americans consume a minimum of 500 mg per day of sodium to maintain good health, but most Americans consume about 3,500 mg per day of sodium. The 2005 *Dietary Guidelines for Americans*, prepared jointly by the U.S. Department of Health and Human Services and the USDA, recommends that young adults consume less than 2,300 mg (approximately one teaspoon) of sodium per day. People with hypertension, African-Americans, and middle-aged and elderly people are advised to consume no more than 1,500 mg per day.

SUGGESTED READING: Stanley A. Feldman and Vincent Marks, eds., *Panic Nation: Unpicking the Myths We're Told about Food and Health* (London: Blake, 2005); Michael F. Jacobson with Jessica Emami and Stephanie Grasmick, *Salt Assault: Brand-Name Comparisons of Processed Foods* (Washington, D.C.: Center for Science in the Public Interest, 2005); Michael F. Jacobson, *Salt: The Forgotten Killer* (Washington, D.C.: Center for Science in the Public Interest, 2005); Walter Gratzer, *Terrors of the Table: The Curious History of Nutrition* (New York: Oxford University Press, 2005); Mark Kurlansky, *Salt: A World History* (New York: Walker and Company, 2002); Pierre Laszlo, *Salt: Grain of Life* (New York: Columbia University Press, 2001); Robert P. Multhauf, *Neptune's Gift: A History of Common Salt* (Baltimore: The Johns Hopkins University Press, 1978); Gary Taubes, "The (Political) Science of Salt," *Science* (August 14, 1998): 281, 897–906; *Dietary Guidelines for Americans* Web site: www.healthierus.gov/dietaryguidelines

Sanders, Harland Fried chicken entrepeneur Harland Sanders (1890–1980) was born in Henryville, Indiana. He left school when he completed the sixth grade, and for the next 25 years he worked at odd jobs, including farm hand, insurance salesman, railroad fireman, ferry operator, and tire salesman, and he served in the army. In 1929, he opened a service station on Route 25 in Corbin, Kentucky. At the time, the highway was a major thoroughfare from the Midwest to Atlanta and Florida, so his business thrived. He added a small lunch counter to serve home-cooked food to travelers. He expanded the counter into a restaurant, which was such a success that in 1936 the governor of Kentucky honored him with the title of honorary Colonel, and in 1939 Duncan Hines recognized it in his book *Adventures in Good Eating.*

In 1939, Sanders's restaurant burned down. He decided to rebuild it and he added a motel to his operation. His newly rebuilt restaurant seated 142 people. By then, Sanders had worked out a method for cooking **chicken** quickly in a pressure cooker and had developed a secret seasoning. Sanders claimed to have worked on the recipe for nine years before he perfected it. Convinced that he had made an important discovery that could be commercialized, he attended a seminar on food promotion in Chicago, where he met Pete Harmon, a **hamburger** restaurant operator from Salt Lake City. In 1952 Harmon used Sanders's recipe for chicken and his business boomed.

Meanwhile, Sanders's own restaurant in Corbin was not doing well. Mounting debts required the sale its at public auction in 1956. At the age of 65 Sanders hit the road, selling his secrets for making fried chicken to restaurateurs and the right to use the name **Kentucky Fried Chicken**. In exchange, franchisees paid him a 5-cent royalty on every chicken they sold. To gain visibility, Sanders dressed up like a Kentucky colonel, complete with a white suit, goatee, and black string tie. In the first two years he sold five franchises, but then the **franchising** business picked up steam. By 1964, when he sold his company to John Y. Brown and Jack Massey for $2 million, there were more than 600 Kentucky Fried Chicken franchises. He became a spokesman and goodwill ambassador for Kentucky Fried Chicken and Sanders's image became synonymous with the company. In 1974 he wrote a **memoir**; its title summed up his views: *Life as I Have Known It Has Been Finger-Lickin' Good.* Sanders died at the age of 90 in 1980.

SUGGESTED READING: David Gerard Hogan, *Selling 'em by the Sack: White Castle and the Creation of American Food* (New York: New York University Press, 1997); John A. Jakle and Keith A. Sculle, *Fast Food: Roadside Restaurants in the Automobile Age* (Baltimore: Johns Hopkins University Press, 1999); John Ed Pearce, *The Colonel: The Captivating Biography of the Dynamic Founder of a Fast-food Empire* (Garden City, NY: Doubleday, 1982); Harland Sanders, *Life as I Have Known It Has Been Finger Lickin' Good* (Carol Stream, IL: Creation House, 1974).

Sandwiches The Fourth Earl of Sandwich was probably not the first person to place food between two pieces of bread and consume it by holding it in his hand, but his doing so launched a culinary revolution. British immigrants introduced sandwiches into the United States, where they have thrived ever since. By the Civil War, sandwiches were extremely common. They were constructed of very thin slices of bread, day-old sponge cake, or small rolls cut in small, bite-sized squares or triangles. These dainty small pieces were used for luncheons, teas, supper, picnics, or the convenience of travelers. They were subsequently sold in fancy tea houses. For the working class, large rolls were often used to house diverse fillings. These substantial sandwiches were served at taverns and bars. Sandwich meat spreads started as a byproduct of the meat canning industry. They were composed of cuttings of minced ham, tongue, and seasonings. Sandwich **condiments** included shredded and leaf lettuce, **ketchup**, mayonnaise, and mustard as well as a variety of sliced and minced pickles. Other common sandwich condiments included spices, chopped and sliced onions, mushrooms, chili peppers, tomatoes, salad dressings, and many types of relishes.

Until the late nineteenth century, most sandwiches were served cold because bread could not easily contain the juices from hot meat or sausage. The solution was simple: use rolls or buns, but these were not considered delicate enough to be consumed easily in polite company. However, large, hot sandwiches were sold by vendors and in delicatessens and bars. Sandwiches based on sausages or ground meat, such as **hot dogs** and **hamburgers**, appeared in the late nineteenth century but did not become popular until the early twentieth century.

Commercial sandwiches took off in three different directions. Hamburgers were popularized by **White Castle**, **White Tower**, **McDonald's**, **Burger King**, and **Wendy's**. Hot dogs were popularized by **Wienerschnitzel** and **Nathan's Famous**. Roast beef sandwiches were popularized by **Arby's** and **Roy Rogers**, and large hoagies or submarine sandwiches have been popularized by **Subway**, **Blimpie**, and **Quiznos Sub**. Through the American military and American **fast food** establishments, the Anglo-American sandwich went global during the second part of the twentieth century. Sandwiches are now consumed in some form in almost every country in the world.

SUGGESTED READING: Becky Mercuri, *American Sandwich: Great Eats from All 50 States* (Layton, UT: Gibbs Smith, 2004).

Sbarro In 1959, Gennaro and Carmela Sbarro opened an Italian grocery store called Salumeria Italiana in Brooklyn, New York. They served homemade food and mozzarella, imported cheeses, sausages, and salamis. They expanded their ready-to-eat foods such as pastas, salads and sandwiches, but their best-selling product was **pizza.** Pizza by the slice was not a new concept in New York, but it was unique in other parts of the country. They focused on their pizza and opened additional locations in the New York City area and then throughout the Northeast. Unlike other **fast food** operations, Sbarro featured 35-foot, cafeteria-like counters at its outlets.

As of 2005, Sbarro operated 960 restaurants in 48 states and 26 countries, including the United Kingdom, Puerto Rico, Canada, Russia, and Israel. Sbarro is the largest shopping mall-based restaurant chain in the world, and has grown to include locations in airports, hospitals, travel plazas, movie **theaters**, toll road rest stops, universities, and train stations. Its corporate headquarters are in Melville, New York.

SUGGESTED READING: Sbarro Web site: www.sbarro-rus.com

Schools Public schools have been targeted by **fast food** and **junk food** manufacturers. About 12,000 schools show Primedia's Channel One, which features advertisements for junk and fast food such as **Coca-Cola**, Pepsi-Cola, **M&M's**, **Doritos**, **Hostess** cakes, **Mountain Dew**, and **Nestlé**'s Crunch.

Corporations sponsor school sports teams and sport contests, and schools permit corporations to **advertise** their products (in many cases, exclusively) on school grounds and at school events. It is estimated that 68 percent of the nation's schools now sell **soda** and junk food in **vending machines** on campus. These machines generate as much as $700 profit each month from some schools.

Fast food is served at primary and secondary schools. The American School Food Service Association estimates that 30 percent of public high schools offer branded fast food in their cafeterias. Sites for fast food restaurants are often intentionally selected near schools so that students will visit them for **breakfast**, lunch, and after school.

Many fast food and junk food corporations in America produce so-called educational materials for use in schools. These materials minimally advertise the company and its products, and often the content in the materials reflects corporate views on issues related to health. While the effectiveness of corporate materials has been questioned, there is no question that American youth are consuming increasing amounts of junk and fast food on and off campus.

Domino's-sponsored school award. © Kelly Fitzsimmons

The schools argue that they need the money. Some schools generate tens of thousands of dollars through **corporate sponsorships** and sales of products. Other schools have fought back and refused to sell or promote junk food and fast food. For example, the New York City Department of Education has banned the sale of non-nutritious soda and junk food in vending machines.

Local building commissions have sometimes refused to approved the construction of **McDonald's** near schools. Bills to require that schools stock their vending machines with healthy snacks and postpone soft drink sales until after lunch in the upper grades have been introduced into some state legislatures. In 2002, the Texas legislature restricted the sale of fast food in public schools. The Los Angeles Unified School District voted to ban the sale of soft drinks in schools during school hours, but permits them 30 minutes after school lets out and at sports and other events. In 2006 Connecticut banned the sale of soda and other sugary drinks in the state's public schools. Similar bans are under discussion in other states and school districts. In 2006, a bill was introduced into the Arizona legislature that would pay school districts $50,000 for forgoing junk food sales on campus. In May 2006, the major soft drink manufacturers agreed to remove sweet drinks from schools.

At the federal level, anti-junk food bills have also been introduced. In 2004, Sen. Tom Harkin introduced a bill titled "The Healthy Lifestyles and Prevention America Act," and in 2005 Sen. Ted Kennedy introduced a bill in Congress titled "The Prevention of Childhood Obesity Act." Both bills restrict the marketing of junk foods in schools and encourage improved nutritional education in schools.

SUGGESTED READING: Kelly D. Brownell and Katherine Battle Horgen, *Food Fight: The Inside Story of the Food Industry, America's Obesity Crisis, and What We Can Do about It* (Chicago: Contemporary Books, 2004); Consumers Union Education Services, *Captive Kids: A Report on Commercial Pressures on Kids at School* (Yonkers, NY: Consumers Union, 1998); Consumers Union Education Services, *Selling America's Kids: Commercial Pressures on Kids of the 90's* (Mount Vernon, NY: Consumers Union, 1990); John A. Jakle and Keith A. Sculle, *Fast Food: Roadside Restaurants in the Automobile Age* (Baltimore: Johns Hopkins University Press, 1999); Coleen McMurray, "Are Schools Havens for Junk Food Junkies?" *Gallup Poll Tuesday Briefing* (September 2003):103–104 J; Christina A. Samuels, "Lawmakers Pass Junk-Food Curbs," *Education Week* 24 (May 4, 2005):31; "Soda Ban Spreads in California," *Journal of Physical Education, Recreation & Dance* 73 (November/December 2002):9; "Texas Restricts Junk Food Sales in Schools," *Journal of Physical Education, Recreation & Dance* 73 (August 2002):18; Jacqueline Yallop and Bill Campbell, "Junk Food," *Times Educational Supplement* (Jun 10, 2005):F11–F14; Consumers Union Web site: www.consumersunion.org/other/sellingkids/index.htm

Schweppes In 1783, Jean Jacob Schweppes improved the process for manufacturing carbonated water and formed the Schweppes Company in Geneva, Switzerland. Shortly thereafter, he set up a factory in England for production of soda water and seltzers. In the aftermath of the French revolution in 1789, Schweppes moved his company to England. In 1870, the company began manufacturing Schweppes Tonic Water, which included quinine and **ginger ale**. Schweppes opened its first factory in America in 1884. Schweppes continued to expand its global operation, particularly after World War II. In 1969, Schweppes and **Cadbury** merged to form **Cadbury Schweppes**.

SUGGESTED READING: Cadbury Schweppes Web site: www.cadburyschweppes.com

Seasonal Candy Commercial seasonal candies have been sold at least since the mid-nineteenth century in America and Europe, when candy canes were mass-produced for

Christmas and Cadbury offered boxed chocolates for **Valentine's Day**. Sale of seasonal candy was strongly promoted by the **National Confectioners Association**. Today, seasonal candy has become a multibillion-dollar industry, with heavy sales at Christmas, **Chanukah**, **Easter**, Mother's Day, and Valentine's Day. **Patriotic candies** are also sold, particularly around the Fourth of July.

SUGGESTED READING: Tim Richardson, *Sweets: A History of Candy* (New York: Bloomsbury, 2002)

Secret Formulas Many **fast food** and **junk food** manufacturers have proudly announced that they have so-called secret ingredients in their products and secret ways of making their products. Part of the reason for the secret sauces and ingredients is to hype their products. In addition, the proclamations of secret ingredients discourages consumers from trying to make similar products in their home, thus depriving manufacturers of potential sales. Finally, there are secrets in every industry and companies do not want to give their competitors any hint of what goes into their successful products or product lines, since manufacturers try to duplicate the competition's products that are successful.

White Castle founder Walter Anderson proclaimed that White Castle's secret had been to flatten the meat into thin patties and then sear them on both sides "to seal in the natural juices." **Harland Sanders** figured out a way to cook **chicken** quickly in a pressure cooker and he developed a secret seasoning featuring a blend of 11 herbs and spices, which Sanders sold to franchisees. **McDonald's** claimed to have a secret sauce that made their **hamburgers** taste better. Today, McDonald's maintains its lead in **French fry** taste by adding secret ingredients to its flavorings.

The **chocolate** industry has been notorious for maintaining its secrets. **Nestlé**'s formula for making milk chocolate was a carefully guarded secret beginning in the nineteenth century. The secret formula for **Cadbury**'s chocolate is purportedly known only by six people and the formula itself is stored in a vault. Perhaps the longest-held secret in American chocolate manufacturing is how the **Hershey Company** processes the milk that gives their chocolate its flavor. **Mars, Inc.** is supposedly one of the most secretive companies in the world, requiring employees to sign nondisclosure statements that they will not impart any information about Mars to outsiders.

Soda manufacturers are also notoriously famous for their secret formulas. Roy Allen, who launched **A&W Root Beer**, reportedly purchased the formula for his root beer from a pharmacist in Arizona. To this day, its unique blend of herbs, spices, barks, and berries remains a proprietary secret. The **Coca-Cola Company** has long maintained the secret formula for making its beverages, and purportedly only a handful of people know it. It is claimed that the original copy of the formula is held in SunTrust Bank in Atlanta. When the company tried to change the formula in 1985 and introduce New Coke, it turned out to be a public relations disaster.

Today, it is relatively easy to analyze competitors' products. The real secrets generally remain in how products are manufactured and the technology that companies use to make them.

SUGGESTED READING: Joël Glenn Brenner, *The Emperors of Chocolate: Inside the Secret World of Hershey and Mars* (New York: Broadway Books, 2000); Frederick Allen, *Secret Formula: How Brilliant Marketing and Relentless Salesmanship Made Coca-Cola the Best-known Product in the*

World (New York: HarperBusiness, 1994); Mark Pendergrast, *For God, Country and Coca-Cola* (New York: Scribner's, 1993).

7-Eleven In 1927, Southland Ice Company in Dallas, Texas, began selling milk, eggs, and bread, and thereafter slowly expanded the packaged and canned items that its stores stocked. The company also began to increase its geographic reach, first in Texas, then in the United States, and finally throughout the world.

Southland Ice called these Tote'm stores, since customers toted away their purchases. In 1946, the company changed the name of the stores to 7-Eleven, which reflected its hours of operation, 7 A.M. to 11 P.M. The company did not change its corporate name to 7-Eleven until 1999.

Beginning in 1964, it began selling coffee to go. Two years later, 7-Elevens began selling **Slurpees**. Today, the company sells about 144 million Slurpees annually, the most favorite being **Coca-Cola** with cherry flavor.

The company began selling the 32-ounce Big Gulp in 1980. At that time it was the biggest cup on the market. Eight years later, 7-Eleven introduced the giant 64-ounce Double Gulp. It was the first retailer to introduce self-serve fountain drinks and today it sells almost 33 million gallons of fountain drinks per year. In 1988, 7-Eleven also began selling Big Bite **hot dogs**; today the chain sells 100 million hot dogs every year. In 1991, the company introduced its World Ovens pastries. Today, the company sells about 60 million fresh-baked doughnuts and pastries annually. The blueberry muffin is its best-selling pastry. As a bow to the growing concern about **obesity** in the 1990s, 7-Eleven introduced the Früt Cooler, which was a low-fat, smoothie-like beverage in 1999 and followed it up with sugar-free Slurpee drinks in 2002.

Today, 7-Eleven is the world's largest convenience store **chain** with more than 29,000 stores worldwide, 11,000 of which are in Japan. Other countries with large numbers of 7-Elevens include Taiwan (4,000), Thailand (3,206), and South Korea (1,209). Nearly 2 million consumers who visit a 7-Eleven store each day purchase immediately consumable foods, which makes 7-Eleven one of the world's largest purveyors of **fast food** and **junk food**. In 2000, 7-Eleven introduced **gummi candies** in a clear plastic cup, called the Candy Gulp. It fits nicely into car cup-holders and it promptly became the chain's best-selling candy. The company also worked with **Nabisco** to produce cups filled with Nabisco's **Chips Ahoy!** and Mini **Oreos**. Likewise, 7-Eleven worked with the **Hershey Company** to produce cups filled with Reese's Pieces and Kit Kat Bites, and worked with **Frito-Lay** to launch Go Snacks—plastic containers shaped like water bottles but filled with **Doritos**, **Cheetos**, and Fritos.

SUGGESTED READING: Ishikawa Akira, *The Success of 7-Eleven Japan: Discovering the Secrets of the World's Best-run Convenience Chain Stores* (River Edge, NJ: World Scientific Publishing, 1998); 7-Eleven Web site: www.7-eleven.com

7-Up In 1919 Charles Leiper Grigg of St. Louis, Missouri, was an advertising executive promoting Whistle, an orange **soda** manufactured by Vess Jones. After a dispute with Jones, Grigg went to work for the Warner Jenkinson Company, which developed flavoring agents for soft drinks. While there, he invented an orange-based soft drink called Howdy.

To promote his soft drink, Grigg, along with Edmund G. Ridgway, created the Howdy Company in St. Louis. Grigg's Howdy drink competed with many other sodas, such as **Orange Crush**, which then dominated the market. Grigg began experimenting with lemon-lime flavors. After two years of work, he came up with a beverage that blended seven different flavors; he introduced this Bib-Label Lithiated Lemon-Lime Soda in 1929. Shortly thereafter, the name was changed to 7-Up. Grigg created a winged logo.

It was the right time for the drink to be marketed. Prohibition ended a few years later and 7-Up was marketed as a mixer for alcoholic drinks. Sales were so successful that in 1936 Grigg changed the name of The Howdy Corporation to The Seven-Up Company. Within 10 years, 7-Up was the third-best-selling soft drink in the world. In 1967, The Seven-Up Company began an **advertising** campaign positioning the beverage as the "uncola," which greatly increased sales. Later it launched a campaign stressing the fact that it had no **caffeine**. This campaign was one reason why other soda companies began manufacturing decaffeinated drinks of their own.

The Seven-Up Company has regularly diversified its product line. In 1970, the company introduced sugar-free 7-Up (its name was changed to Diet 7-Up in 1979). The company introduced Cherry 7-Up and Diet Cherry 7-Up in early 1987. All three **diet** drinks received flavor enhancements in 2000.

In 1978, Philip Morris USA acquired the company, but it was sold again in 1986 when the company was merged with the **Dr Pepper** Company in 1986. In turn, Dr Pepper/Seven-Up Companies, Inc. was acquired by **Cadbury Schweppes** in 1995. The brand 7-Up is now part of Cadbury Schweppes Americas Beverages (CSAB), located in Plano, Texas. In 2006, the company removed several chemical additives and launched a major promotional campaign proclaiming that 7-Up was all natural. The **Center for Science in the Public Interest** threatened to take Cadbury Schweppes to court, claiming that one 7-Up ingredient, fructose, was not a natural ingredient.

SUGGESTED READING: Jeffrey L. Rodengen, *The Legend of Dr. Pepper/Seven-up* (Ft. Lauderdale, FL: Write Stuff Syndicate, 1995): 7-Up Web site: www.dpsu.com/seven_up.html

Shakey's Pizza In 1954, Sherwood Johnson and Ed Plummer opened the first Shakey's restaurant in Sacramento, California. "Shakey" derived from Johnson's nickname, which he received after suffering from malaria during World War II. The second Shakey's Pizza Parlor opened in Portland, Oregon, in 1956, and two years later Shakey's began **franchising** its restaurant. The chain spread to more than 272 outlets by 1967. The first franchise in Canada was established in 1968, and by 1975 outlets had reached Japan and the Philippines. Johnson was a banjo player and frequently played at his restaurants to entertain the customers. Johnson encouraged other franchisees to hire banjo players, and this became one of the chain's trademarks.

Shakey's was the first franchise **pizza chain**. It pioneered the concept of the chain pizza parlor and popularized pizza in the United States. It was not truly a fast food operation because most of its food was consumed inside in a restaurant and it had little carry-out and no home delivery. Due to stiff competition, in 1978 Shakey's shifted to buffets with pizza as an important adjunct.

Shakey Johnson retired in 1967 and sold his half of the company to Colorado Milling and Elevator Co., which acquired Plummer's half the following year. The company exchanged hands several times thereafter, and suffered as a result. In 2004, Shakey's was sold to Jacmar Companies of Alhambra, California. At that time, the chain had only 63 Shakey's restaurants in the United States and about 350 in the Philippines.

SUGGESTED READING: David Gerard Hogan, *Selling 'em by the Sack: White Castle and the Creation of American Food* (New York: New York University Press, 1997); Gerry Schremp, *Kitchen Culture: Fifty Years of Food Fads, from Spam to Spa Cuisine* (New York: Pharos Books, 1991).

The golden arches. © Kelly Fitzsimmons

Signage Since the 1920s, signage for **fast food** restaurants has been particularly important. **Automobiles** traveled quickly down highways and drivers and passengers could easily miss restaurants unless they were clearly marked with signs. Another means of visually attracting customers was through unusual **architecture**, such as upside-down **ice cream** cones, so that the building itself became a sign for a particular restaurant. **White Castle** was the first to recognize the importance of having all of its outlets similar in appearance so passersby would easily recognize them.

Other **chains**, such as **A&W Root Beer**, did not have a common architecture and hence relied on signs to convey the fact that they indeed sold A&W root beer. Likewise, **Kentucky Fried Chicken (KFC)** franchises at first did not have a common appearance. All that franchises were required to do was have put up an sign stating that they were a KFC restaurant and display a likeness of Colonel Sanders. Because small signs were hard to read from a passing automobile, large signs were the rule. At night, signs were difficult to read regardless of the size, so neon signs became common.

Many fast food signs were so large and outlandish that they alienated local residents who had to look at them regularly. President Lyndon B. Johnson successfully lobbied Congress to pass the Highway Beautification Act in 1965, which greatly restricted signs along highways paid for with federal funds. This and other local and state ordinances encouraged fast food chains to decrease the size and flamboyance of their signage as well as their building architecture.

SUGGESTED READING: Gerry Schremp, *Kitchen Culture: Fifty Years of Food Fads, from Spam to Spa Cuisine* (New York: Pharos Books, 1991).

Slogans and Jingles In the **junk food** and **fast food** world, slogans are usually short, striking phrases intended to encourage consumers to purchase products. Typically, slogans are used repeatedly in **advertising**. **Soda** manufacturers have used slogans since the late nineteenth century. **Dr Pepper** used "King of Beverages" and, more recently, "Be a Pepper!" **Mountain Dew** used the slogan "Get That Barefoot Feelin' Drinkin' Mountain Dew." Pepsi-Cola and **Coca-Cola** have had some of the most memorable slogans. Coca-Cola's slogans include "The Pause that Refreshes," "It's the Real Thing," "I'd Like to Buy the World a Coke," "Coke Is It," and "Things Go Better with Coke." Pepsi has countered with just as memorable slogans, such as "Come Alive! You're In the Pepsi Generation," and "Pepsi-Cola Hits the Spot," which *Advertising Age* rated as one of the most successful advertising campaigns of the twentieth century.

Snack food manufacturers have regularly used slogans in the advertising. **M&M's** has "The milk chocolate that melts in your mouth, not in your hand." The **Mounds** and Almond Joy jingle, "Sometimes You Feel Like a Nut, Sometimes You Don't," remains a classic. The National Confectioners Association slogan, "Eat Candy, the Energy Food," implies that anyone who needs energy should buy their members' products. Fritos popularized the slogan "Munch a Bunch of Fritos Corn Chips." Ruffles **potato chips** were popularized with the slogan "R-R-Ruffles Have R-Ridges" and Lay's potato chips with "Bet You Can't Just Eat One." **Dunkin' Donuts**'s commercial with "Fred the Baker," played by Michael Vale, first aired in 1983. His line, "Time to Make the Donuts," popularized Dunkin' Donuts.

Fast food chains have used slogans from the earliest days. **White Castle**'s slogan, "Buy 'em by the Sack," was copied by **White Tower**: "Take Home a Bagful." **Chicken Delight**'s slogan, "Don't Cook Tonight, Call Chicken Delight," was a popular refrain. **Kentucky Fried Chicken**'s "Finger-lickin' Good" has been used for decades. **Taco Bell**'s commercials starred a talking Chihuahua, who squealed "Yo Quiero Taco Bell!" **Burger King** jumped from one slogan to another, but their more popular ones include "Hold the pickles, hold the lettuce, special orders don't upset us, all we ask is that you let us serve it your way. Have it your way, have it your way at Burger King," "Battle of the Burgers" and "Aren't you Hungry for a Burger King Now?" **McDonald's** has also been extremely successful in their slogans, such as "Billions and Billions Served." Their most recent slogan, "I'm Lovin' It," was the company's first global advertising campaign. It was launched in Germany in 2003, using the slogan "Ich liebe dich" and then it was extended to other languages. Other McDonald's jingles, such as "Two all-beef patties, special sauce, lettuce, cheese, pickles, onions on a sesame seed bun" have been particularly popular. The company's "You Deserve a Break Today" jingle has been identified by *Advertising Age* as the most successful jingle of the twentieth century.

Perhaps the most famous fast food slogan was **Wendy's** "Where's the Beef?" which aired in 1984. It captured America's attention and was picked up by Democratic presidential candidate, Walter Mondale, as a criticism of Ronald Reagan's tenure as president. Recently, *Advertising Age* rated "Where's the Beef?" as one of the top ten slogans of the twentieth century.

Slogans have occasionally backfired. The McDonald's company penchant for prefixing its products with Mc, such as McNuggets, has encouraged others to use the Mc abbreviation for a range of less-enticing themes, such as McDollars, McGreedy, McCancer, McMurder, McProfits, McGarbage, and McCrap. The McSpotlight Web site is focused on anti-McDonald's issues.

SUGGESTED READING: Mary Cross, ed., *A Century of American Icons: 100 Products and Slogans from the 20th Century Consumer Culture* (Westport, CT: Greenwood Press, 2002); McSpotlight Web site: www.mcspotlight.org

Slow Food When the first **McDonald's** restaurant opened in Rome, Italy, in 1986 Carlo Petrini was deeply concerned. He believed that the industrialization of food was standardizing taste and leading to the loss of thousands of local and regional foods. In 1986, he launched the Slow Food movement in Barolo, Italy. Slow Food International was started in Paris three years later. Its international office is located in Bra, Italy. Its major publication is *Slow: The International Herald of Tastes; The Magazine of the Slow Food Movement.*

Today, Slow Food is active in 50 countries and has a worldwide membership of more than 80,000. Slow Food USA is a nonprofit education organization with 12,000 members, which is divided into 140 local "convivums." It is dedicated to preserving endangered foodways, celebrating local food traditions (such as dwindling animal breeds and heirloom varieties of fruits and vegetables) and promoting artisanal products. It advocates economic sustainability and biodiversity through educational events and public outreach programs.

SUGGESTED READING: Carlo Petrini, ed., with Ben Watson and the Slow Food Editors, *Slow Food; Collected Thoughts on Taste, Tradition, and the Honest Pleasures of Food* (White River Junction, VT: Chelsea Green Publishing Company, 2001); Carlo Petrini, *Slow Food: The Case for Taste* (New York: Columbia University Press, 2003); *Slow: The International Herald of Tastes; The Magazine of the Slow Food Movement.*

Slurpee Omar Knedlik, an operator of a Kansas **Dairy Queen**, placed bottled soft drinks in his freezer. The result was a slushy **beverage**. In 1959, Knedlik contacted the John E. Mitchell Company, a Dallas machinery manufacturer to construct a machine to make the slushy beverage. Mitchell experimented with automobile air conditioners to create a machine that would freeze carbonated soft drinks that could be served in a slushy form and could be consumed through a straw. Mitchell's machine reduced the temperature of soda to 28 degrees F.

The drink was not a huge success with retailers. However, **7-Eleven** tested the machines in 1965, and within two years they were installed in every 7-Eleven store. The name Slurpee was selected because it makes a slurping sound when it was consumed through the straw. The Slurpee product line has been regularly extended by 7-Eleven, using different flavors such as Slurpee Liquid-Filled Bubble Gum and the Slurpee Ice frozen treat. Today, the company sells about 144 million Slurpees annually, the favorite being **Coca-Cola** with cherry flavor.

The Slurpee machine inspired the frozen Margarita, which was invented in 1971 by Dallas restaurant owner Mariano Martinez.

SUGGESTED READING: Slurpee Web site: www.slurpee.com

Snack Foods Snacking—eating foods between meals—has always been a part of America's diet. Until the mid-nineteenth century, snacks mainly consisted of natural foods: fruit, such as apples, peaches, pears, and (when available) bananas and citrus; nuts, such as walnuts, chestnuts, and pecans; grain-based products, such as bakery desserts, biscuits, and **cookies**; and occasionally cheese. Even though it was a common to snack in nineteenth-century America, many medical practitioners spoke out against this practice as they believed that eating between meals promoted indigestion. Snacking also took away one's appetite for the upcoming meals, which had what medical practioners considered to be more nutritious and healthful food. Despite these concerns, **pretzels**, peanuts, **ice cream**, **candy**, **popcorn** and derivative products such as popcorn balls, were commonly sold at fairs, circuses, sporting contests, amusement parks, and other venues by the mid-nineteenth century. These were made and sold mainly by individuals in small kiosks, stands, or by vendors on the streets.

During the twentieth century, natural foods were replaced with commercially branded foods. For many people, snacking has become a continuous process indulged in at all times. Studies had demonstrated that almost 75 percent of Americans derive at least 20 percent of their calories from snacks. Snacking has replaced meals for many Americans. By the beginning of the twenty-first century, Americans annually consumed almost $22 billion of salted nuts, popcorn, **potato chips**, pretzels, **corn chips**, cheese snacks, and other salty snacks.

Commercial snack foods—foods manufactured and distributed over wide geographic areas—burst onto the American scene around the turn of the twentieth century. Some commercial snack foods were based on foods previously prepared in homes, restaurants, and by vendors, such potato chips, **gum**, taffy, and **chocolates**. In these cases, manufacturers had to convince the public that their commercial products were better than existing products. Whether or not these products were better, in many cases they were less expensive because they were usually mass-produced.

Other commercial snack foods had no antecedents, such as chocolate bars and soft drinks, and manufacturers struggled to attract potential consumers. Introductions of new snack foods therefore required extensive **advertising**. The first new commercial snack food was **Cracker Jack**, a combination of popcorn, peanuts, and molasses. It was formulated in Chicago and was marketed at the Chicago Columbian Exposition in 1893, and perfected in the years following. In 1896 it was advertised broadly in many cities in America. Subsequent snack foods thrived because of extensive advertising. Planter's Peanuts, founded in 1906 in Wilkes-Barre, Pennsylvania, became successful through promotion and the invention of the **Mr. Peanut** icon. **Baby Ruth** candy bars were dropped by parachute over the city of Pittsburgh to gain visibility.

From the early beginnings, snack foods rapidly charmed their way into American life. Many social conditions contributed to their success. The temperance movement and Prohibition, for instance, encouraged the creation of **soda fountains** as gathering places and distribution centers for soft drinks and ice cream. The rapid growth of grocery stores and **supermarkets** helped disseminate snack foods and sodas. The advent of advertising convinced Americans to buy these new products. This is particularly important with the invention of **radio** and **television**, which could easily and effectively be used to market their products. The ambition and drive of snack food moguls, such as **Milton S. Hershey**, built snack food and drink empires. The vast increase in disposable wealth in the United States during the twentieth century meant that most Americans could purchase snack foods, at least on occasion.

Commercial snack foods fall into two major categories. The most prominent is sweet snacks. America's craving for **sugar** blossomed after the Civil War. As sugar prices declined in the nineteenth century, candy manufacturers mass-produced candies that average Americans could afford. World War I brought attention to chocolate bars, when the U.S. Quartermaster Corps ordered 40-pound blocks of chocolate and sent them to the American soldiers in Europe. In the post–World War II era, sweets continued their relentless drive to stardom.

A second category of snacks are salty ones. America's first salty snacks were popcorn and peanuts. These products appealed to children and both were associated with children's holidays, especially Halloween and Christmas. During the late nineteenth century, potato chips were added to the salty snack list. Many factors contributed to the rise of salty snack foods in America; important ones were **packaging** and marketing revolutions. Prior to 1900, snack foods such as peanuts, popcorn, and potato chips were sold from barrels or large glass jars. Grocers scooped them and placed them in a twist of paper or a paper bag. Not only was this time-consuming but the snacks often went stale before they were sold. During the early twentieth century, manufacturers began experimenting with cans, wax paper, glassine, cellophane, and other packaging materials that made possible the sale of individual portions that could be easily examined by customers. The package also kept snacks fresh until the customer opened it. Other factors that contributed to the increase in consumption of salty snacks were the end of Prohibition in 1933 and food rationing during World War II. Bars reopened after Prohibition ended, and salty snacks were given free to customers to increase drink orders. The interest in salty snacks increased even more during World War II, because rationing caused a severe shortage of sugar, sweets, and chocolates, making many familiar candies unavailable. Salty snacks based on corn, potatoes, and peanuts were abundant during the war. Other salty snack foods include **extruded snacks**.

After World War II, the sale of sweet and salty snacks soared, greatly promoted by television advertising beginning in the 1950s. As the twentieth century progressed, the quantity and diversity of sweet and salty snack foods proliferated until every grocery store, kiosk, newspaper stand, and corner shop in America was heavily stocked with bags and packets of candies, chips, chocolates, crackers, pretzels, and much more. Thousands of snack foods have been manufactured in the United States. Collectively, these snack foods comprise a market niche generating billions of dollars of annual sales in 2004. While nutritionists complain about the consumption of snack foods, there is no sign that Americans are decreasing their consumption of them.

SUGGESTED READING: William S. Fox and Mae G. Banner, "Social and Economic Contexts for Folklore Variants: The Case of Potato Chip Legends," *Western Folklore* (May 1983) 42:114–126; Michael F. Jacobson and Bruce Maxwell, *What Are We Feeding Our Kids?* (New York: Workman Publishing, 1994); Samuel A. Matz, *Snack Food Technology*, 3rd ed. (New York: AVI Van Nostrand Reinhold, 1993); Andrew F. Smith, *Popped Culture: A Social History of Popcorn in America* (Columbia, SC: University of South Carolina Press, 1999); Andrew F. Smith, *Peanuts: The Illustrious History of the Goober Pea* (Urbana, IL: University of Illinois Press, 2002); Snack Food Association. *Fifty Years: A Foundation for the Future* (Alexandria, VA: Snack Food Association, 1987); "State of the Industry: For Your Eyes Only," *Snack Food & Wholesale Bakery* (June 2002): SI-1-SI71.

Snickers The Snickers candy bar built upon the success of earlier peanut and **chocolate** products, including the Goo Goo Cluster (1913), Goldenberg's Peanut Chews (1922), and Reese's Peanut Butter Cups (1928). Snickers was created in 1929 by **Frank Mars** and his family. It was first sold to the public the following year. Named for the Mars's horse, it was composed of peanut butter nougat, peanuts, and **caramel** encased in milk chocolate. The nougat was made by whipping egg whites until they were light and frothy. This was stabilized by **sugar** syrup, which was added along with flavoring ingredients. The caramel was made with milk, sugar, **fat**, and flavorings. Snickers were hand-wrapped until 1944, but thereafter were machine-wrapped.

Snickers quickly became the most popular **candy** bar in America, a position it has held ever since. The target of its **advertising** was children, and Snickers was a sponsor of the *Howdy Doody Show* on television from 1949 until 1952. Building upon the success, **Mars, Inc.** has introduced new types of Snickers: In 1984, for instance, it introduced the Snickers Ice Cream bars; it has also introduced Snickers Cruncher and Snickers Almond.

When the **Center for Science in the Public Interest** criticized **junk food** for having empty calories, consumption of many snack foods declined. Mars, Inc. responded with an advertising campaign that announced that "Snickers Really Satisfies." According to another advertisement, eating a Snickers bar relieves tension and helps a consumer enjoy life: "A Snickers a Day Helps You Work, Rest and Play." The company also used creative opportunities to promote its product. For instance, during the first Gulf War, frozen Snickers bars were sent to the American military. On Thanksgiving Day in 1990, Snickers bars were given to every American soldier in the Middle East.

Mars, Inc., has expanded its sales of Snickers abroad, and the candy bar is now sold throughout the world. In the United Kingdom, its name was changed to the Marathon Bar because "snickers" rhymed with knickers, a British colloquialism for women's panties. Recently, Mars, Inc., made the decision to use uniform names throughout the world for its confections, and the name Marathon Bar was changed to Snickers. Some customers have had such an attachment to the old name that they refuse to buy Snickers bars even though it was made in the same way as the old Marathon Bar, but in general the shift occurred without many problems. Snickers is very popular in other countries, particularly Russia and Eastern Europe, where it has been one of the best-selling candy bars. Snickers has remained America's best-selling chocolate bar for almost 70 years.

SUGGESTED READING: Joël Glenn Brenner, *The Emperors of Chocolate: Inside the Secret World of Hershey and Mars* (New York: Broadway Books, 2000); Ray Broekel, *The Great America Candy Bar Book* (Boston: Houghton Mifflin Company, 1982); Janice Pottker, *Crisis in Candyland: Melting the Chocolate Shell of the Mars Family Empire* (Bethesda, MD: National Press Books, 1995); Tim Richardson, *Sweets: A History of Candy* (New York: Bloomsbury, 2002); Andrew F. Smith, *Peanuts: The Illustrious History of the Goober Pea* (Urbana, IL: University of Illinois Press, 2002); Snickers Web site: www.snickers.com

Soda/Soft Drink Mineral waters have long been considered therapeutic, and water with carbon dioxide was considered to have medicinal attributes. European spas and resorts built at natural springs frequently included drinking bubbly mineral waters as part of their health regimens. During the eighteenth century, several scientists, including Joseph Priestly and Antoine-Laurent Lavoisier, are credited with the discovery that carbon dioxide was the source of the bubbles in natural springs, beer, and champagne. Priestly constructed an apparatus for manufacturing the gas, and reports of his invention were sent to the Earl of Sandwich (the same person credited with inventing the **sandwich**), who was then the Lord of the Admiralty. He requested that Priestly demonstrate his apparatus before the Royal College of Physicians. Priestly did so, and one person in the audience was Benjamin Franklin, the prominent American who lived in London at the time. Others constructed different systems for producing soda water. In 1783, Jean Jacob Schweppes improved a process for manufacturing carbonated water and formed the **Schweppes** Company in Geneva, Switzerland. During the French Revolution and its aftermath, Jacob Schweppes moved his operation to England, where his soda water was approved for medicinal use by the Royal family.

By 1800, manufacturers found they could produce the same bubbly water by placing a solution of sodium bicarbonate in water. Carbonated water, however, was generally made under high pressure with sulfuric acid. Operators could easily be burned by the acid and containers did explode. Apparatuses for making the water were patented beginning in 1810, but because of the complexity of the process and the medicinal use of the resulting product, they were only operated by trained technicians.

In 1819, Samuel Fahnestock, a Pennsylvanian, patented the first **soda fountain**, which looked like a beer keg. By 1824, soda fountains were in use, although they did not become commonplace until just before the Civil War. Because the apparatus was expensive and the resulting beverage was considered medicinal, soda water was generally dispensed only in drugstores.

It was a small step from soda water to flavored soda water. **Ginger ale** is usually credited with being the first carbonated commercial beverage. Commercial ginger ale appears to have been first marketed in 1866 by James Vernor, a Detroit pharmacist, who created **Vernor's Ginger Ale**.

Another early soft drink was **root beer**, which was made most commonly from the leaves, roots, and other parts of aromatic plants and trees. In its early years, root beer was also a health beverage. By the 1840s, many root beers were manufactured locally and they were sold in confectionery and general stores. Precisely when it was combined with carbonated water to form a cold soft drink is unclear. The first mass-produced root beer was manufactured in 1876 by a Philadelphia drugstore operator, Charles E. Hires. **Hires Root Beer** became extremely popular and was **advertised** at the Centennial Exposition held in Philadelphia in 1876. Alcoholic beverages had been banned at the exposition, and the summer proved to be extremely hot. Many fairgoers liked what they drank and demanded soda drinks when they returned home. Soda fountains, which sold combinations of **ice cream** and drinks composed of fruit syrups, **sugar**, and soda water, sprung up around the nation.

The first **cola**-flavored beverage was created in 1881. It may have stimulated John S. Pemberton of Atlanta, Georgia, to invent **Coca-Cola** in 1886. Its success did encourage others to develop cola beverages, including Caleb Bradham, who invented Pepsi-Cola in 1898. Chero-Cola, later reformulated and released as **Royal Crown Cola**, was created in Columbus, Georgia in 1905.

Many other soft drinks were manufactured during the late nineteenth and early twentieth centuries. **Moxie**, for instance, was introduced in 1884. **Dr Pepper** was invented in Waco, Texas, in about 1885. **Orange Crush** was first manufactured in Chicago in 1906. Charles Leiper Grigg created **7-Up** in 1929.

Early soft drinks were generally bottled in stoneware, which was much stronger than glass and would not explode like early glass bottles did due to the pressure of fermentation. It was much easier and cheaper to produced syrup or extract, which would be sold to drugstores where it would be combined with carbonated water. This began to change in 1892 when William Painter invented the crown bottle cap, which made it possible to easily and cheaply seal bottles. At the same time, bottling technology improved such that the new glass bottles could keep the carbon dioxide in and the bottles would not shatter during the manufacturing process. In 1919, there were more than 5,000 soda bottlers in the United States, and the industry was large enough so that it needed an organization to represent them. The result was the formation of the American Bottlers of Carbonated Beverages (later rename to the National Soft Drink Association).

Since their origin, soft drinks have gone through regular changes in the way they are dispensed and bottled. **Vending machines** dispensed soft drinks into paper cups by the 1920s. Bottled Coca-Cola was sold in vending machines after World War II. Iron cans were used in the 1950s and in 1957 aluminum cans were developed. Five years later, pull-ring tabs were first used on beer cans and later were used on soda cans. By 1965, canned soft drinks were dispensed in vending machines. In the same year, plastic bottles were used for soft drinks, but soda stored in plastic often exploded. In 1972, polyethylene terephthalate (PET) bottles were invented by Nathan Wyeth (brother of the artist Andrew Wyeth), who worked for DuPont Corp. Wyeth developed a stronger system of molding plastic, enabling DuPont to produce a lightweight, clear, and resilient bottle.

Diet soda was launched in 1952, when Kirsch Beverages began marketing No-Cal ginger ale and root beer. It was followed by many other diet sodas, including Royal Crown Company's Diet Rite Cola (1958), Tab (1963), and Diet 7-Up (1979). The Coca-Cola Company and Pepsi-Cola released their diet colas in 1982. In 1980, Royal Crown Company released its decaffeinated cola, RC 100, and other soda manufacturers followed with **caffeine**-free colas of their own. About the same time, soda companies began marketing decaffeinated sodas. As a backlash, in 1985 C. J. Rapp created Jolt Cola, and other similar sodas, such as Surge and Josta, came on the market with 30 percent to 60 percent more caffeine than either Coke and Pepsi.

There are many reasons why soft drinks have been so successful in America. The growth of the temperance movement encouraged soft drinks. Soft drinks were served in soda fountains, which competed with saloons and bars. Women's groups, such as the Women's Christian Temperance Union, supported soda fountains and the sale of soft drinks. Soft drinks greatly profited during Prohibition, when manufacturing and selling alcoholic beverages was illegal. It was also during the 1920s that **fast food** chains emerged and virtually all of them sold soft drinks. When Prohibition was repealed in 1933, soft drinks and fast food outlets were already well-established American institutions.

To sell more soda, the industry has greatly increased the size of soda containers. Serving size has increased from a standard 6½-ounce bottle to a 20-ounce bottle. At movie **theaters**, **7-Eleven** stores, and some fast food restaurants, the most popular size is now 64 ounces.

Beginning in the 1990s, soft drinks have been roundly condemned by many nutritionists. They have been called "liquid candy" and soft drinks are full of sugar, **salt**, and caffeine. Soft drink manufacturers spend billions of dollars on promotion and advertising. Marketing efforts are aimed at children through cartoons, movies, videos, **charities**, and amusement parks. In addition, soft drink companies sponsor contests, sweepstakes, games, and clubs via television, radio, magazines, and the Internet.

In ***Fast Food Nation*** (2001), Eric Schlosser reports that soft drink companies are increasingly making deals with public **schools** for exclusive sales rights on campus and for other promotional activities in schools. He states that a school district in Colorado Springs, Colorado, signed an $11-million deal with Coca-Cola that specifies annual sales quotas so that school administrators encourage students to drink Coke. He also reported that a high school in Beltsville, Maryland made nearly $100,000 in one year on a deal with a soft drink company. Some school districts, such as the New York Department of Education, have banned soda drinks from schools but other school districts respond by stating that they need the funds that **sponsorships** provide.

Soft drink manufacturers have spent as much as 25 percent of their entire revenues on advertising, much of it targeting youth. In 1998 the **Center for Science in the Public Interest's (CSPI)** study, *Liquid Candy*, reported that soft drink companies had targeted schools for their advertising and sales of their products. It also reported that soft drinks "provided more than one-third of all refined sugars in the diet." Soft drinks, according to CSPI, are the single greatest source of refined sugar, providing 9 percent of calories for boys and 8 percent for girls. CSPI states that at least 75 percent of teenage children drink soda every day.

Through advertising, soft drinks helped shape our lifestyles. When one quaffs a Coke or Pepsi, thirst-quenching is not the only matter at stake. Advertisements have associated soft drinks with new tastes and new status. Drinking the beverage makes the consumer feel young, sexy, strong, smart, cool, athletic, and fun-loving.

Advocates for limiting soda consumption have linked soda with tooth decay, delayed bone development, **obesity**, and **diabetes**. Diet sodas are not much better, because sugar substitutes also have potential risks. Aspartame, for instance, has been linked to a range of chronic disorders such as cramps, seizures, vertigo, and multiple sclerosis. There is particular concern with the amount of soft drinks consumed by children and youth. Soda companies have advertised extensively on children's television. With vending machines in schools, soft drinks are more accessible today than ever. If soda consumption means that youth are not drinking milk, then they may not be getting enough calcium and other vitamins and minerals.

High-fructose corn syrup, manufactured from corn starch, was widely introduced into food in the 1970s. During the last 10 years, federal subsidies to corn growers in the United States had amounted to $40 billion, so that corn syrup is cheaper than sugar. Today, most soft drink manufacturers use less-expensive sweeteners, such as fructose, rather than cane sugar for sweeteners.

The cost of soft drink production is low since water, carbon dioxide, sweeteners, colorings, and flavorings are inexpensive. The sales of soda are now more popular than coffee, tea and juice combined. According to the American Beverage Association, soft drink companies gross almost $93 billion in sales in the United States alone and the industry employees 211,000 people. Coca-Cola and **PepsiCo** sell more than 70 percent of the carbonated beverages in the world; Americans consume 52 gallons of soft drinks annually.

SUGGESTED READING: Michael F. Jacobson, *Liquid Candy: How Soft Drinks are Harming Americans' Health,* 2nd ed. (Washington, D.C.: Center for Science in the Public Interest, 2005); John J. Riley, *A History of the American Soft Drink Industry. Bottled Carbonated Beverages 1807–1957* (Washington, D.C.: American Bottlers of Carbonated Beverages, 1958); Eric Schlosser, *Fast Food Nation: The Dark Side of the All-American Meal* (New York: Houghton Mifflin Company, 2001); Jasper Guy Woodroof and G. Frank Phillips, *Beverages—Carbonated and Noncarbonated* (Revised ed.) (Westport, CT: AVI Publishing Co., 1981); Donald Yates and Elizabeth Yates, eds., *American Stone Ginger Beer & Root Beer Heritage, 1790 to 1920; Written by Numerous Authors and Historians* (Homerville, OH: Donald Yates Publishers, 2003); American Beverage Association Web site: www.ameribev.org

Soda Fountains Soda fountains, selling soda water in combination with other products, were an important part of American social life from the late nineteenth century to the mid-twentieth century. At first, the term *soda fountain* referred to the machine that produced carbonated water. The first patent for such a machine was granted to Samuel Fahnestock in 1819, and other patents followed. No evidence has surfaced that soda fountains were commonly used until just before the Civil War, when Gustavus D. Dows operated a marble soda fountain. He continued to improve his design and is considered the inventor of the soda fountain. It was not until after the Civil War that soda fountains, serving a variety of beverages composed of soda water and syrups, became common in drugstores. Many products under a variety of names, such as birch beer, pepsin, **ginger ale**, and sarsaparilla, were sold at soda fountains, as was **ice cream**, which required the construction of ice boxes to store it. Since customers consumed their sodas in the drugstores, stools and counters were constructed for serving these items.

Soda fountains rapidly proliferated. Beginning in the 1880s, many stores with soda fountains began to add light food, especially **sandwiches**. In 1883, James Tufts patented a soda fountain, which he called the Arctic. Tufts went on to become a major soda fountain manufacturer. In 1903, the soda fountain prototype emerged with its two units, a large, high-back section with a mirror or painting, and a low front section with stools for customers, permitting them to view their order being prepared. They mimicked fixtures common in bars and saloons at the time. They became an important social center, particularly in small towns, by the end of the nineteenth century, and as Prohibition was adopted in local counties and in states, soda fountains became important meeting places. It was from soda fountains that several of today's popular soft drinks emerged, including **Dr Pepper**, **Coca-Cola**, and Pepsi-Cola.

By 1908, there were an estimated 75,000 soda fountains in the United States. Operators began expanding their menus to include sandwiches, cakes, and other items, so that by 1912 many soda fountains had evolved into the luncheonette. When the 18th Amendment to the U.S. Constitution passed and the manufacture and sale of liquor became illegal, soda fountains were a major beneficiary. During the 1940s, soda fountains became places for teenagers to hang out. Soda fountains greatly declined in importance during the 1950s due to competition from bottled drinks and **fast food chains**.

SUGGESTED READING: Anne Cooper Funderburg, *Sundae Best: A History of Soda Fountains* (Bowling Green, OH: Bowling Green State University Popular Press, 2002); John A. Jakle and Keith A. Sculle, *Fast Food: Roadside Restaurants in the Automobile Age* (Baltimore: Johns Hopkins University Press, 1999); Philip Langdon, *Orange Roofs, Golden Arches: The Architecture of American Chain Restaurants* (New York: Knopf, 1986).

Sonic Troy Smith, opened a **root beer** and **hot dog** stand called the Top Hat Drive-In in Shawnee, Oklahoma. He installed a speaker system at his **drive-in** and used the slogan "Service with the Speed of Sound." He also hired **carhops** to deliver food directly to customers in their cars, and it became a success. In 1956, Smith franchised his first operation to Charlie Pappe of Woodward, Oklahoma, who acquired the **chain**. Pappe changed its name to Sonic Drive-In.

When Charlie Pappe unexpectedly died of a heart attack in 1967 at the age of 54, Sonic had 41 outlets, which expanded to 165 stores within six years. In 1973, the company was restructured into Sonic Systems of America, which was later changed to Sonic Industries. Ownership of the company shifted to its franchisees and it became a publicly traded company. By 1978, Sonic had expanded to more than 800 outlets in 13 Southern and Southwestern states.

Sonic confronted many problems in the early 1980s. Its profits fell and unprofitable outlets were closed. The chain survived mainly because its strength was in small towns, where real estate costs were lower and competition was less intense.

The first Sonic **television advertising** appeared in 1977. By 2000, Sonic's media spending approached $64 million. Sonic's "retro-future" logo was introduced and the entire system adopted a consistent new look and menu. With almost 3,000 Sonic Drive-Ins across the United States, Sonic is the only national **fast food** chain to retain carhops as an integral part of its operation.

SUGGESTED READING: Philip Langdon, *Orange Roofs, Golden Arches: The Architecture of American Chain Restaurants* (New York: Knopf, 1986); Sonic Web site: www.sonicdrivein.com

Sports Drinks Gatorade was formulated in 1965 by Robert Cade and Dana Shires of the University of Florida to solve a rehydration problem faced by football players. It is a noncarbonated drink consisting of water, electrolytes, and **carbohydrates**. It is believed that the beverage prevents heat stress and heat stroke during heavy workouts. Gatorade was used by the University of Florida football team in 1967, when the team won the Orange Bowl title. This gave the drink extensive national visibility and Gatorade began to be manufactured and sold in stores. Since 1986, barrels filled with Gatorade and ice have traditionally been emptied over the heads of coaches after wins.

Gatorade. © Kelly Fitzsimmons

Gatorade launched an industry focused on sports drinks. Powerade was launched in 1990 and it has been heavily promoted by the **Coca-Cola Company**. In 2001, Coca-Cola introduced new formulas in the Powerade line. **PepsiCo** created AllSport athletic drinks, which have been promoted as the "Official Sport Drink" of the top soccer leagues. Stokely-Van Camp, Inc. of Indianapolis, Indiana, secured the rights to Gatorade and marketed it nationally. In 1983, Stokely-Van Camp was acquired by Quaker Oats, which was acquired by PepsiCo in 2003.

While intended for athletes, sports beverages are more often consumed as a snack beverage. Most people lose few electrolytes during exercise. Sports drinks are high in **sugar** and calories. Consuming sports drinks while exercising can cause cramps and heat-related illnesses.

SUGGESTED READING: Darren Rovell, *First in Thirst: How Gatorade Turned the Science of Sweat into a Cultural Phenomenon* (New York: American Management Association, 2006).

Sports Sponsorships In 1928, **Coca-Cola** became the first sponsor of the International Olympic games; it has been an Olympics sponsor ever since. At the 1984 Olympics in Los Angeles, Coca-Cola was the second-leading advertiser, having spent $29 million on promotion. When the Olympics were hosted in Atlanta in 1996, the Coca-Cola Company spent $73 million on **advertising**. At the 2000 Olympics in Sydney, Australia, Coke spent an estimated $55 million on advertising. Pepsi-Cola cans were confiscated from spectators per the agreement with Coca-Cola. At the 2004 Olympic games in Athens, Greece, Coca-Cola spent $145 million on sponsorship and advertising. The Coca-Cola Company sponsors numerous athletic sports, including Major League Baseball, the National Basketball Association, the National Football League, and the National Hockey League. It has also sponsored collegiate and high school teams and contests. Other soft drink manufacturers have engaged in similar activities. **Dr Pepper** sponsors collegiate bowls and football title games.

Fast food chains have also found that sports sponsorships are an excellent venue for gaining visibility for their brands. National brands sponsor sporting events and franchises often support local events, such as local high school teams. **McDonald's** has sponsored high school basketball tournaments, such as the high school all-star games. It also has sponsored the National Basketball Association on four continents and sponsors the

International Olympics. **Pizza Hut**, **Taco Bell**, and **Kentucky Fried Chicken** have had contracts with the National Collegiate Athletic Association; **Wendy's** has sponsored the National Hockey League's All-Star Fan Balloting in the United States, while McDonald's sponsors the All-Star Fan Balloting in Canada. **Burger King** has supported youth programs such as President's Challenge Physical Activity and Fitness Awards Program. **Del Taco** had sponsored only the National Hockey League's Anaheim Mighty Ducks. Many fast food chains, **soda** manufacturers, and **junk food** makers also place advertisements in stadiums, on cars in **automobile** races, and on clothes that athletes wear. These advertisements are seen by those in attendance and then are viewed by those who watch the broadcast of the sporting event.

More important than the direct advertising message is the underlying one: dieting is not the answer to **obesity** and other health problems—a "healthy lifestyle" is. Sports sponsorships offer the mechanism for junk food, fast food, and sodas to be associated with exercise, athletics, and an active lifestyle.

SUGGESTED READING: Johnny K. Lee, "Marketing and Promotion at the Olympics," *The Sport Journal* 8 (Summer 2005); M. P. McAllister, "Sponsorship, Globalization, and the Summer Olympics," in Katherine Toland Frith, ed., *Undressing the Ad: Reading Culture in Advertising* (New York: Peter Lang, 1997); Eric Schlosser, *Fast Food Nation The Dark Side of the All-American Meal* (New York: Houghton Mifflin Company, 2001).

Street Vendors Vendors have sold food on the streets since the founding of American cities. The products sold by vendors have changed, as has their mode of operation. Among the first **snack foods** sold by vendors were **nuts**. Although many Americans ate fruit and other foods between meals, nuts needed to be roasted before they could be consumed. The advantage of nuts was that they were inexpensive, particularly when compared with other types of sweets or desserts.

Popcorn followed a similar path. Popcorn had to be processed either by popping or by conversion into popcorn balls and other confections before it could be sold. Vendors sold popcorn and other snacks at public gatherings by the 1840s. Street hawkers in Boston peddled popcorn balls by the wagonloads. One **entrepreneurial** seller, Daniel Fobes, decided to use maple syrup rather than the more costly molasses as the binder for popcorn balls. During the presidential election of 1848, he sold his product at political rallies for Zachary Taylor and Millard Fillmore. He expanded his business through a series of partnerships and an ever-increasing sale of **candy** products. The firm Fobes founded was one of the three constituents of the **New England Confectionery Company** (NECCO), which still survives.

Snacks vended at fairs, circuses, and expositions attracted crowds to their stands. By the 1890s, vendors prowled the streets with steam-driven wagons and many made an excellent living. In 1907, the *Chicago Tribune* reported that sympathy was wasted on vendors. While most people thought of a vendor "as an unfortunate individual, aged or decrepit, cut off from the legitimate lines of trade, and barely eking out a scanty living," the average vendor cleared about $150 per week, which was good pay in those days.

Vendors also frequented amusement parks. One such pushcart vendor was Charles Feltman, who sold sausages on white rolls at Coney Island, New York. He is credited with inventing the **hot dog**.

Another Chicago vendor was Frederick Rueckheim, who with his brother launched F. W. Rueckheim & Brother. They made all their confections by hand until 1884, when they shifted to steam-powered machinery. Like many other vendors, the Rueckheim brothers experimented with sugar-coated popcorn. They tested different sweeteners and tried a variety of combinations with marshmallows, nuts, and other products. They were satisfied with a new product that they introduced at Chicago's Columbian Exposition in 1893. It was a great success and three years later the brothers launched their new product, which they called **Cracker Jack**.

Mobile wagons became popular during the late nineteenth century. They created a new class of mobile street vendors who traversed America's streets for almost a half-century. As **automobiles** began to clog the streets of America, many cities passed laws licensing street vendors to prevent congestion. The result was that many vendors were required to move indoors. Vendors continue to sell their foods on the streets of New York City and in other major cities.

SUGGESTED READING: Andrew F. Smith, *Popped Culture: A Social History of Popcorn in America* (Columbia, SC: University of South Carolina Press, 1999); Andrew F. Smith, *Peanuts: The Illustrious History of the Goober Pea* (Urbana, IL: University of Illinois Press, 2002).

Subs/Grinders **Sandwiches** made with long Italian bread were developed in several different cities in the United States. In Philadelphia, **street vendors**, sold a variety of foods, including **ice cream**. They began serving their "anti-pasta" (from the Italian for "without pasta") such as sliced meats, salami, cheese, fish, and vegetables on a long, boat-shaped bread. They called the sandwich a hoagie. It was made from luncheon meats, lettuce, tomato, onion, cheese, and mayonnaise.

In New Orleans, Clovis Martin, owner of Martin Brothers Grocery, asked his cook to come up with a sandwich that would keep those "poor boys" who were unemployed during the Depression satisfied for an entire day but cost only a nickel. The result was the Po'Boy, a hefty cross-section of French bread stuffed with roast beef and cheese. Today, Po'Boys may contain a fried fish filet or thinly sliced roast beef or other cold cuts. If lettuce, tomatoes, and/or chopped cabbage was added, the sandwich is referred to as dressed. A variation is *La Mediatrice* ("The Peacemaker" in French), which stuffs fried oysters in the bread.

In Chicago, Italian beef sandwiches were sold by street vendors after World War I. It consisted of thin slices (shaved) of beef roasted in broth with garlic, oregano, and spices. Italian beef, along with mozzarella and green roasted peppers, was stuffed into Italian bread, which was then drenched with beef broth. This was called an Italian Beef Sandwich and it was an immediate hit in Chicago. It remains a hit, but today there are many different ways of making it. It can be bought on the streets through vendors or in most Italian restaurants in Chicago. Similar sandwiches developed in other cities across America.

The first **fast food chain** featuring these sandwiches was launched in 1964 by Tony Conza, Peter DeCarlo, and Angelo Baldassare in Hoboken, New Jersey. They called it **Blimpie**. The second sub sandwich chain was created in1965 by Frederick DeLuca and Dr. Peter Buck of Bridgeport, Connecticut, who called their chain **Subway**; it is the nation's largest sub chain today. **Quiznos Sub** restaurants were launched in 1981 and quickly surpassed other sandwich shops to become the second-largest sandwich chain.

SUGGESTED READING: Becky Mercuri, *American Sandwich: Great Eats from All 50 States* (Layton UT: GibbsSmith, 2004).

Subway In 1965, 17-year-old Frederick DeLuca of Bridgeport, Connecticut borrowed $1,000 from family friend Dr. Peter Buck and they opened Pete's Submarine Sandwiches restaurant in Milford, Connecticut. Their first shop floundered, but a second one was opened. It succeeded and the partners began expanding their operation. Its flagship product was the "sub" **sandwich** composed of a variety of cold cuts, including ham, turkey, and salad vegetables. They changed the name of the restaurant to Subway, although its corporate name is Doctor's Associates, Inc. DeLuca and Buck began **franchising** in 1974. Subway expanded its operation through development agents who sold Subway franchises—a system that has led to abuses and numerous lawsuits. The costs of setting up a Subway outlet, however, are comparatively low, as are the franchising fees. By 1979, Subway had 100 stores. A large number of franchisees are immigrants, who work long hours to make a success of their outlets.

Subway expanded its **menu** to include new creations, such as Sweet Onion Chicken Teriyaki and Southwest Chipotle Cheese Steak. In 1993, Subway began opening outlets in convenience stores, truck stops, and Wal-Marts. Subway increased its expansion abroad in the 1990s.

Subway's products are considered more healthful because the main products are not fried, as were most **hamburgers** and **chicken** sold at other fast food outlets. In 1999, Jared Fogle, an Indiana University student, claimed to have lost 245 pounds with a diet comprised mostly of Subway sandwiches and walking. He has become a spokesperson for Subway, promoting their healthy image. As of 2005, Subway is the largest sub chain in America and the second-largest fast food franchise in the world, with more than 24,000 locations in the United States and in 82 other countries.

SUGGESTED READING: John A. Jakle and Keith A. Sculle, *Fast Food: Roadside Restaurants in the Automobile Age* (Baltimore: Johns Hopkins University Press, 1999).

Suckers See **Lollipops and Suckers**

Sugars Sugars are simple **carbohydrates**, which are broken down by metabolic reactions to glucose. Glucose is an essential nutrient for the body and the brain, and its level needs to be constantly maintained.

The human preference for sweetness is inborn, and this preference likely contributed to early hominid survival. Historically, humans have sought sugar from many sources, including honey and fruit, but the plant with the highest concentration of sucrose is sugarcane, which contains up to 17 percent sucrose. Sugarcane likely originated in New Guinea but was cultivated in prehistoric times in Southeast Asia, India, and China. The word *sugar* derives from the Sanskrit *sarkara,* and it dates back at least 2,500 years. Sugarcane was cultivated in China at about the same time but, surprisingly, China did not develop sugar-based sweets, instead preferring maltose, an extract from sorghum.

In the ancient Mediterranean, the very small quantities of sugar that arrived from South Asia were mainly used for medicinal purposes. The process of extracting or refining sugar is complex and requires considerable technological expertise, which was probably first developed in Persia (today, Iran). Sugarcane cultivation did not reach the Mediterranean until the Middle Ages, when conquering Arabs brought it to southern Italy and Spain.

Christopher Columbus introduced sugarcane into the Caribbean but it did not become an important crop until the mid-seventeenth century, when Europeans figured out the complex process of making sugar, and also figured out how to make rum. Sugarcane thrived in the favorable climate and soil of the Caribbean. Along with sugarcane came slavery; estimates vary, but approximately 15 million Africans were brought into the New World, mainly to work in sugarcane fields. During this time, Europe's demand for sugar soared due to the simultaneous introductions of tea, coffee, and cocoa. Sugarcane cultivation began in North America in the middle of the eighteenth century, when it was planted in French-controlled New Orleans.

To make sugar, sugarcane must be crushed and the juice extracted. The juice is heated and, when cooled, some of it crystallizes: this is considered raw sugar. Left behind is a sweet residue called treacle or molasses, which could not be further refined by traditional methods. Its advantage was that it was much less expensive than white crystallized sugar. In colonial times, molasses was mainly used to make rum. The British passage of the Molasses Act and the Sugar Act, which imposed very unpopular taxes, contributed to the American Revolutionary War.

Molasses was also used as a sweetener, particularly for confections, such as molasses candy. America's first national commercial confection, **Cracker Jack**, was sweetened with molasses, but virtually all subsequent sweet snacks were made with sugar. As manufacturing processes became more efficient and the price of sugar declined in the mid-nineteenth century, the amount of sweeteners in American cookery ballooned.

Increasing demand for imported sugar contributed to the conquest of Puerto Rico and the Philippines during the Spanish-American War and led to the annexation of the Hawaiian Islands. These additions and increased access to sugar meant that during the period from 1880 to 1915, the per-capita consumption of sugar doubled and the use of molasses declined.

Sucrose is also produced from sugar beets but it requires a complicated process to extract, and the system to do this was not devised until the late eighteenth century. Production of sucrose from sugar beets is more expensive. In the United States, sugar beet farmers in Utah and other states have lobbied Congress to maintain price supports for their beet sugar, which means that Americans pay almost twice as much for sugar as do people outside the United States.

Sugar was easily transported and stored, and quickly became the major ingredient of **candy**. It was first used to make hard candy in the eighteenth century, then for making **penny candy** and **chocolates** during the nineteenth century. During the twentieth century, in addition to candy and other commercial confections, large quantities of sugar are consumed in many processed foods, baked goods (including cakes and **cookies**), and non-diet soft drinks.

Sucrose has no nutritional value (no minerals, vitamins, protein, or fiber) other than providing calories. Natural and refined sugar are identical, but natural sugars are usually accompanied by some vitamins and minerals, and fruit contains fiber and other healthy contents.

Concern with sugar consumption was voiced beginning in 1942 when the American Medical Association's (AMA) Council on Food and Nutrition stated that "[I]t would be in the interest of the public health for all practical means to be taken to limit consumption of sugar in any form in which it fails to be combined with significant proportions of other foods of high nutritive quality." The attack on sugar intensified during the 1970s when nutritionists proclaimed that sugar was a cause of many diseases, including **diabetes**, hyperactivity, heart disease, and **obesity**. This campaign started with John Yudkin's book *Pure, White and Deadly* (1972), which proclaimed that sugar consumption was linked with heart disease. Yudkin's ideas received extensive publicity in the United Kingdom and the United States, and many other writers joined his crusade against sugar. Studies purportedly demonstrated that rats became sugar-dependent, and when sugar was removed from their diet they suffered in a way that was similar to withdrawal from morphine or nicotine. One result of the sugar scare was the creation a great demand for diet foods, diet programs, and **diet sodas**, which blossomed during the 1970s and 1980s.

The only disease that has been directly tied to sugar consumption is dental caries. Refined sugar, however, is high in calories, and consumption of high levels of sugar is associated with obesity. The **Center for Science in the Public Interest (CSPI)** points out that consumption of products with high-sugar content with empty calories is frequently associated with the failure to consume other foods that are nutritious. The CSPI reports *Liquid Candy: How Soft Drinks are Harming Americans' Health* (2005) stated that if people fill up with **soda** and **junk food**, rather than consuming fruit juice or fruit, then they are "missing a chance to cut [their] risk of osteoporosis, cancer, or heart disease."

High-fructose corn syrup, manufactured from corn starch, was widely introduced into the beverage industry in the 1970s. Since the mid-1990s, federal subsidies to corn growers in the United States have amounted to $40 billion, so that corn syrup is now cheaper than sugar. Most carbonated **beverages** use less-expensive sweeteners, such as fructose, rather than cane sugar for sweeteners. Today, high-fructose corn syrups account for almost half the sweeteners used industrially in the United States, particularly in the beverage industry and in the confectionery industry. The **U.S. Department of Agriculture (USDA)** reports that each American consumes, on average, 152 pounds of sugar annually.

SUGGESTED READING: Kelly D. Brownell and Katherine Battle Horgen, *Food Fight: The Inside Story of the Food Industry, America's Obesity Crisis, and What We Can Do about It* (Chicago: Contemporary Books, 2004); William Duffy, *Sugar Blues* (New York: Warner Books, 1975); Michael F. Jacobson, *Liquid Candy: How Soft Drinks are Harming Americans' Health* (Washington, D.C.: Center for Science in the Public Interest, 2005); Peter MacInnis, *Bittersweet: The Story of Sugar* (Crows Nest, Australia: Allen & Unwin, 2002); Sidney W. Mintz, *Sweetness and Power: The Place of Sugar in Modern History* (New York: Elisabeth Sifton, Viking, 1985); Tim Richardson, *Sweets: A History of Candy* (New York: Bloomsbury, 2002); Wendy A. Woloson, *Refined Tastes: Sugar, Confectionery and Consumption in Nineteenth-Century America* (Baltimore: Johns Hopkins University Press, 2002); John Yudkin, *Pure, White and Deadly: The Problem of Sugar* (London: Davis-Poynter Ltd, 1972); Sugar Association Web site: www.sugar.org

Supermarkets The growth of supermarkets paralleled the growth of **fast food chains**. The term *supermarket* likely originated in southern California during the 1920s. Los Angeles was a sprawling metropolis highly dependent upon the **automobile**. Two chains—Ralph's Grocery Company and Alpha Beta Food Markets—constructed large stores that were organized into food departments. The major difference from other grocery stores of the time was size: typical supermarkets covered 5,000 square feet—10 times larger than grocery stores of the day. Because land was inexpensive in Los Angeles at that time, large parking lots could be constructed around the supermarkets.

Supermarket chains had advantages similar to those of large fast food chains. Their great strength lay in their enormous purchasing power. Buying wholesale reduced retail prices, and increased volume of sales meant increased profits. Also, centralized warehousing systems allowed supermarkets to get price concessions from manufacturers and save on distribution costs.

The success of the early supermarkets in southern California encouraged grocery store chains to close smaller stores and open supermarkets. In addition, independent grocers did not have access to capital, as did large chains, and they were unable to make the conversion; tens of thousands went out of business during the late 1930s and early 1940s.

The post–World War II growth of supermarkets was tremendous. Chain stores abandoned inner-city grocery stores and expanded into the suburbs with supermarkets. As a result, large chains increased their share of the nation's grocery business from 35 percent to 62 percent during the decade after the war. The variety of inventory grew with the number of supermarkets. In the 1940s, an average store carried 3,000 different items; by the late 1950s this had increased to 5,800. By the 1970s, supermarkets stocked more than 10,000 items. Because supermarkets made large profits on **junk foods**, these were stocked and sold extensively in supermarkets.

During the 1970s and 1980s, supermarket industry leaders became concerned as many Americans shunned their kitchens and began eating out at fast food chains. Supermarkets countered by expanding their offerings of ready-to-eat foods to take home, and some supermarkets constructed places for customers to eat their food in the stores. Supermarkets supply a large percentage of fast food and sell vast quantities of junk food.

SUGGESTED READING: Barbara E. Kahn and Leigh McAlister, *Grocery Revolution: The New Focus on the Consumer* (Reading, MA: Addison Wesley Longman, 1997); James M. Mayo, *The American Grocery Store: The Business Evolution of an Architectural Space* (Westport, CT: Greenwood Press, 1993); M. M. Zimmerman, *The Super Market: A Revolution in Distribution* (New York: McGraw-Hill Book Company, 1955).

Supersizing During the 1950s, the typical size for soft drinks contained about 8 ounces of **soda**; today, a small-sized **beverage** (when one can be found) is 12 ounces. A large-sized **cola** has graduated to 32 ounces with an estimated 310 calories, and the service station store at ARCO has stations has come out with The Beast, which weighs in at 88 ounces.

In the 1950s, **McDonald's** served only one size of **French fries**. In 1972, the company added a large size for its fries, but the large-sized fries of the late 1970s are the small size today. In 1994, McDonald's added Super Size Fries with 610 calories and 25 grams of **fat**. Supersized fries were three times the size of the 1950s French fries. The company also created supersized meals, which consisted of a **sandwich**, supersized French fries (7 ounces), and a supersized beverage (42 ounces). McDonald's signs encouraged customers to "Super Size It!" as did their employees, who were directed to ask customers if they wanted to supersize their order. Supersized meals were less expensive than ordering the three items separately, but even at this reduced price McDonald's made more profit on each supersized order.

Subsequently, the term *supersized* was used in many other retail establishments to mean the largest size. Other **fast food chains** created their own names for supersized portions. **Burger King**, for instance, created portions similar to McDonald's supersized ones, but called them King Size. Other fast food chains made similar offers. Supersizing was not limited to fast food outlets. **Junk food** manufacturers jumped onboard with large sizes of their own. For instance, **Frito-Lay** put out its Big Grab size.

Filmaker Morgan Spurlock after a McDonald's meal, from his 2004 documentary *Super Size Me*. Roadside Attractions/Photofest

Obesity and fast food became linked and supersized became a symbol of this relationship. The filmmaker Morgan Spurlock filmed his experiences eating three meals a day from McDonald's (supersized if offered) for 30 days and documented the effects on his body. According to the film, Spurlock gained 30 pounds and reported serious health problems at the end of the 30 days. The release of the film, *Super Size Me* (2004), generated bad publicity for McDonald's throughout the world. Prior to its release, McDonald's phased out supersizes from its meal options. Spurlock's film was nominated for a Oscar for Best Feature Documentary. He subsequently wrote a book, *Don't Eat This Book: Fast Food and the Supersizing of America* (2005), describing his experiences while making the movie and criticizing fast food restaurants and the food they serve.

SUGGESTED READING: Scott Ingram, *Want Fries With That? Obesity and the Supersizing of America* (New York: Franklin Watts, 2006); Morgan Spurlock, *Don't Eat This Book: Fast Food and the Supersizing of America* (New York: G.P. Putnam's Sons, 2005).

Suppliers Today, most **fast food chains** generally do not grow their own potatoes, raise their own cattle or **chickens**, or make their own buns. These are all acquired from suppliers. The size of chains such as **McDonald's** or **Kentucky Fried Chicken (KFC)** gives these companies purchasing power such that they influence which varieties of potatoes are grown and which animals are raised and how they are fed and processed. McDonald's is the largest purchaser of potatoes, beef, and pork in America and is second only to KFC in the purchasing of chickens. Fast food chains place massive orders for quantities of a specific variety of potato (Russet Burbank), for instance, and for specific breeds of cattle, pigs and chickens. This has led to dependence upon a limited number of varieties and breeds and has led to the near-extinction of some heritage potatoes and breeds of animals. As fast food chains have moved overseas, the companies have preferred to purchase from local suppliers, but these, too, must meet company standards. Thus, homogenization of foods has increased globally.

Because fast food chains order vast amounts of food, they acquire what they order at a greatly reduced price. As suppliers compete for fast food orders, they try to keep their costs down. Because a major cost is labor, many suppliers have sought immigrant employees who will work for lower wages. This has led to problems, particularly in slaughterhouses, as Eric Schlosser points out in ***Fast Food Nation*** (2001). Because fast food chains do not own suppliers, they maintain that they are not responsible for the behavior of their suppliers or for the effects their suppliers have upon the **environment**. This has particularly become a problem in developing countries, which often do not have protections for workers or proper working conditions.

Some fast food chains have begun to be concerned about the actions of their suppliers. McDonald's, for instance, formed an alliance with Environmental Defense Fund and announced that it would switch from plastic to paper packaging. In addition, McDonald's stopped purchasing beef from Brazil in order to prevent the destruction of the rainforests. In 2000. McDonald's said it would no longer accept **genetically modified (GMO)** potatoes and its suppliers had to change their potatoes. In response to protests by People for the Ethical Treatment of Animals (PETA), McDonald's imposed rules on its suppliers specifying how livestock should be raised and slaughtered, stressing the humane treatment of animals.

In 2004, PETA released a video taken at a chicken supplier for Kentucky Fried Chicken (KFC). As a result of the animal cruelty depicted in the film, Pilgrim's Pride fired several employees and began a workforce training programs to prevent animal cruelty in the future.

SUGGESTED READING: Eric Schlosser, *Fast Food Nation: The Dark Side of the All-American Meal* (New York: Houghton Mifflin Company, 2001).

Sweet Popcorn Throughout the first half of the twentieth century, **Cracker Jack** dominated the sweet **popcorn** field. In the 1950s, others began producing similar products. Howard Vair, a proprietor of a Detroit **candy** store, created Poppycock clusters, which were a combination of glazed popcorn and nuts. In 1960, Wander, a Swiss company bought the rights to Poppycock. In 1967, Wander launched Fiddle Faddle, a combination of perfectly popped popcorn mixed with caramel, butter toffee, Heath toffee bits, and honey nuts. Two years later, it launched Screaming Yellow Zonkers, a sweet popcorn without nuts. Wander was purchased by Sandoz, creating Sandoz-Wander. It changed its name to Lincoln Snacks, which was purchased in 2004 by Chicago-based Ubiquity Brands.

Meanwhile, American Home Products, owners of Jiffy Pop, launched Franklin's Crunch 'n Munch in 1966. It was eventually purchased by ConAgra, which shortened the product name to just Crunch 'n Munch.

By the end of the 1980s, Cracker Jack was still the leader in the sweet popcorn field in the United States, but it was losing market share to a pack of competitors. By the early 1990s, Crunch 'n Munch had toppled Cracker Jack as the nation's number-one ready-to-eat sweet popcorn confection. Fiddle Faddle is the number-three sweet popcorn.

SUGGESTED READING: Andrew F. Smith, *Popped Culture: A Social History of Popcorn in America* (Columbia, SC: University of South Carolina Press, 1999).

T

Taco Bell During the early 1950s, few Americans outside of California and the Southwest knew what a taco was. Today, Mexican-American food is one of America's fastest-growing cuisines in the United States. While there are many reasons for this upsurge, the Taco Bell **fast food chain** launched by Glen Bell played an important role in this national shift.

During World War II, Glen Bell had served in the Marines, working in foodservice. In 1948, Glen Bell operated a one-man **hamburger** and **hot dog** stand at San Bernardino, California. However, Bell preferred to eat Mexican take-out food. Taco stands dotted the southern California landscape, but none offered fast food and most had a poor reputation. Bell developed ways to improve the **efficiency** of preparing and serving Mexican food. At the time, taco shells were made by frying a soft tortilla for a few minutes. Bell invented a prefab hard taco shell that did not have to be fried, thus saving time on each order. Bell also developed procedures he believed would make for speedier service. As taco sales at his stand increased, he dropped hamburgers and focused on tacos.

With a partner, in 1954 Bell opened three Taco Tia outlets in San Bernardino—the same city where Richard and Maurice McDonald opened their revolutionary fast food establishment, **McDonald's**. Like the McDonald brothers, Bell opened more restaurants in the surrounding area, but when he wanted to expand to Los Angeles his partner refused. Bell sold out his interest in Taco Tia. In 1958, with new partners, Bell launched another chain, El Taco, in Long Beach, California.

Bell sold out to his new partners in 1961. He invested in and helped develop a new restaurant chain called Der **Wienerschnitzel**. In 1962, he opened his first Taco Bell in Downey, California. Bell targeted college students, traveling salesmen, and the military. The **menu** specialized in tacos, burritos, and a few other items. Bell opened three additional outlets, which generated $50,000 per year. In 1964, he began **franchising** his operation and soon eight additional outlets were launched in the Long Beach, Paramount, and Los Angeles areas. The resulting Taco Bell chain used the symbol of a Mexican man sleeping under a sombrero, and the chain's buildings had a California mission-style architecture. The company prospered and continued to grow.

In 1975, Glen Bell resigned as chairman of the company but retained a controlling interest in the company. By 1978, Taco Bell company had grown steadily for 16 years and had 868 restaurants. Both H.J. Heinz and **PepsiCo** wanted to purchase Taco Bell. PepsiCo won the bidding war, spending $130 million to acquire the chain. Management of the

PepsiCo subsidiary was placed in the hands of John Martin, who had previously worked for several fast food companies. He popularized Taco Bell's Mexican-style food nationally through heavy discounting and value meals, which combined foods and drinks for cost savings. By 1980, Taco Bell had 1,333 outlets and was rapidly expanding. One reason for the expansion was the continual introduction of new products, such as Fajitas, Wraps, Gorditas, and Chalupas.

While these names of Mexican foods might have been new to many Americans, their contents were not. Their components were similar to hamburgers—ground beef, cheese, tomatoes, lettuce, and sauce. The main difference was the tortilla, which most customers could easily understand as a substitute for the hamburger bun. Others who tried to imitate Taco Bell did not stray too far from this traditional American combination either.

Taco Bell learned from other fast food chains. Like other companies, most of its food is prepared outside and is assembled at the outlet. Its guacamole, for instance, is made at a factory in Mexico. The taco meat arrives frozen, ready for heating. Beans are dehydrated and employees just need to add water. Taco Bell also innovated by installing double **drive-thru** windows, which decreased waiting time for customers, increased the volume of sales, and increased profits.

Taco Bell has had both success and failure in its promotional efforts. For example, its original sleeping Mexican symbol was considered a negative stereotype by many Mexican-Americans, and was replaced with a mission bell when PepsiCo took over. Likewise, the **architecture** for the outlets had been a red-tiled mission style; PepsiCo changed it to a mainstream mansard style. These changes worked, and by 1990 there more than 3,500 Taco Bell outlets throughout the United States. In addition, the company licensed Taco Bell Home Originals dinner kits to **Kraft Foods** in 1996. These were sold in **supermarkets**. Taco Bell launched a major promotional drive with **television** commercials featuring a talking Chihuahua that squealed "Yo Quiero Taco Bell!"

Today, Taco Bell is the nation's leading Mexican-style quick-service restaurant chain, with more than $4.9 billion in systemwide sales. Annually, Taco Bell serves more than 55 million consumers each week in its 6,400 restaurants in the United States. In 1997, Taco Bell was spun off from PepsiCo and it is now a division of **Yum! Brands, Inc.**, which also owns **Kentucky Fried Chicken**, **Pizza Hut**, **Long John Silver's**, and **A&W** restaurants.

SUGGESTED READING: Debra Lee Baldwin, *Taco Titan: The Glen Bell Story* (Arlington, TX: Summit Publishing Group, 1999); John A. Jakle and Keith A. Sculle, *Fast Food: Roadside Restaurants in the Automobile Age* (Baltimore: Johns Hopkins University Press, 1999); Andrew F. Smith, "Tacos, Enchiladas and Refried Beans: The Invention of Mexican-American Cookery," in Mary Wallace Kelsey and ZoeAnn Holmes, eds., *Cultural and Historical Aspects of Foods* (Corvallis, OR: Oregon State University, 1999: 183–203); Taco Bell Web site: www.tacobell.com

Tang **General Foods Corporation** acquired the Perkins Products Company, maker of **Kool-Aid**, in 1953. It began experimenting with Kool-Aid and the company came up with a powdered orange-flavored breakfast drink that was fortified with vitamins. In 1958, this new product was released under the brand name Tang. It did not become popular until the National Aeronautic and Space Administration (NASA) popularized it on their Gemini space flights in 1965. Although it is full of **sugar**, it was touted as a health drink that could substitute for **soda**. Today, the brand is owned by **Kraft Foods**. In addition to North America, Tang is marketed throughout Latin America, Eastern Europe, China, and India.

SUGGESTED READING: Kraft Foods Web site: www.kraft.com

Tastee-Freez In 1950, Leo Maranz invented a small freezer to make soft-serve **ice cream**. He approached Harry Axene, who had helped launch the **Dairy Queen chain**. The two formed a new Chicago-based chain, which they named Tastee-Freez. The company sold its freezers at cost to franchisees and made its profit on the sale of ice cream mix. In addition to its soft-serve ice cream, Tastee-Freez introduced other foods, such as its Big Tee Burgers. By 1956, the chain had 1,500 outlets in the U.S.

One prominent early financial executive was Harry Sonneborn, who had gained a great deal of **franchising** experience while working with Tastee-Freez. In 1954, Sonneborn teamed up with **Ray Kroc**, and many consider him to be the cofounder of **McDonald's**.

In 1982, the DeNovo Corporation of Utica, Michigan, bought the Tastee-Freez brand and launched a program of store modernization. The majority of Tastee-Freez franchises serve a complete menu of **fast food**, including **breakfast**, lunch, and dinner. In 2003, Tastee-Freez became a part of Galardi Group, Inc. of Newport Beach, California, which also owns the **hot dog** chain **Wienerschnitzel**. It has about 95 outlets in 22 states nationwide and two in Panama. In addition, Tastee-Freez desserts are now served in many Wienerschnitzel outlets.

SUGGESTED READING: Anne Cooper Funderburg, *Chocolate, Strawberry, and Vanilla: A History of American Ice Cream* (Bowling Green, OH: Bowling Green State University Popular Press, 1995); John A. Jakle and Keith A. Sculle, *Fast Food: Roadside Restaurants in the Automobile Age* (Baltimore: Johns Hopkins University Press, 1999); Philip Langdon, *Orange Roofs, Golden Arches: The Architecture of American Chain Restaurants* (New York: Knopf, 1986); Tastee-Freez Web site: www.tastee-freez.com

Tater Tots Tater Tots is a registered trademark for a commercial form of deep-fried hash browns formed into small cakes and sold frozen. They are made from potato shreds, which are left over from **French fry** production. They were invented in 1953 by Golden and F. Nephi Grigg of the Ore-Ida (derived from abbreviations of Oregon and Idaho) Company, which is now a subsidiary of the H.J. Heinz Company. They first became available in stores in 1954.

In 2004, Tater Tots were popularized in the film *Napoleon Dynamite*. The Idaho state legislature was so pleased that it passed a resolution offering special praise for the movie. Today, in the United States Tater Tots are commonly found in school cafeterias and lunch counters, as well as in **supermarket** frozen food aisles. Today, Americans consume approximately 70 million pounds of Tater Tots per year. Heinz has extended the line to include other similar commercial products. The Ore-Ida Brand is the nation's leading marketer of frozen potatoes.

SUGGESTED READING: Ore-Ida Web site: www.oreida.com

Taxing Snack Food Concerned about the increasing health risks of **obesity** in the United States, some health advocates have proposed snack taxes to prevent obesity and to recover the costs of treating illness caused or exacerbated by obesity. California enacted a snack tax law in 1991 but it was repealed within a year because of administrative and bureaucratic problems. In 1994, E. K. Battle and Kelly Brownell proposed levying what they called a **fat** tax on **junk food** and **fast food** based on the specific food's contribution to obesity. Similarly, in an article in the *American Journal of Public Health* (2000) Michael Jacobson and Kelly Brownell argued for a small tax on soft drinks and fast foods.

Advocates argue that higher prices will change some consumers' diets in the same way that increased cigarette prices have discouraged smoking. The funds raised from such taxes could be devoted to educating youth about eating healthy food, cover costs of fitness programs (especially for youth), and help pay medical expenses related to obesity.

Others have proposed taxing people who are overweight. Advocates for this believe that overweight people are personally responsible for their weight due to their eating habits, and this ends up costing the nation billions of dollars for health care and in lost wages.

Fat taxes have been considered by several cities and states. Reports have been prepared on taxing junk and fast food by several states and the Economic Research Service at the **U.S. Department of Agriculture**. To date, no fat tax has been levied, although seven states have imposed special taxes or fees on soda drinks and 10 states exclude certain junk food from exemptions for taxes on food.

SUGGESTED READING: Kelly D. Brownell and Katherine Battle Horgen, *Food Fight: The Inside Story of the Food Industry, America's Obesity Crisis, and What We Can Do about It* (Chicago: Contemporary Books, 2004); Fred Kuchler, Abebayehu Tegene, and J. Michael Harris, *Taxing Snack Foods What to Expect for Diet and Tax Revenues* (Washington, D.C.: Economic Research Service, U.S. Dept. of Agriculture, 2004); Judith S. Lohman, *Taxes on Junk Food* (Hartford, CT: Connecticut General Assembly, Office of Legislative Research, 2002).

Teen Hangouts During the late nineteenth and early twentieth centuries, teenagers hung out at **soda fountains**, where **ice cream**, **sodas**, and light foods were served. With the development of **drive-ins** in the 1920s and with increased availability of **automobiles** at about the same time, youth began to congregate at drive-ins. Because many **carhops** were scantily clad females who worked mainly or exclusively for tips, young men frequently arrived in cars and flirted with the carhops.

Teenage boys did not purchase much food and they occupied space in the parking lot. Teenagers congregating at drive-ins were occasionally rowdy and this scared away many families who would have purchased food.

Two restaurateurs who were particularly upset with this were the brothers Richard and Maurice McDonald, owners of a drive-in in a Los Angeles suburb. Their solution was to eliminate the carhops and create a self-service restaurant and thus reduce the number of teenagers that would hang out. Customers bought the food at windows and returned to their cars before consuming it. To discourage flirting, **McDonald's** only hired male employees. McDonald's target audience was suburban families and they did not want teenagers at their establishments. Their new model worked precisely as planned, and virtually every **fast food chain** initially followed this example.

There were no indoor eating places at fast food establishments during the 1950s and early 1960s. This changed in 1967 when **Burger King** created an indoor dining area; McDonald's followed the following year with a new restaurant design that included indoor dining. Teen hangouts moved from drive-ins to malls, convenience stores, and video game parlors.

SUGGESTED READING: Philip Langdon, *Orange Roofs, Golden Arches: The Architecture of American Chain Restaurants* (New York: Knopf, 1986); John A. Jakle and Keith A. Sculle, *Fast Food: Roadside Restaurants in the Automobile Age* (Baltimore: Johns Hopkins University Press, 1999);

Harvey Levenstein, *Paradox of Plenty: A Social History of Eating in Modern America* (New York: Oxford University Press, 1993); Eric Schlosser, *Fast Food Nation: The Dark Side of the All-American Meal* (New York: Houghton Mifflin Company, 2001); Gerry Schremp, *Kitchen Culture: Fifty Years of Food Fads, From Spam to Spa Cuisine* (New York: Pharos Books, 1991).

Television Television technology had been perfected by the late 1930s, but monetary and technological demands during World War II stopped early experimentation. When the war ended, television burst on the scene but few Americans could afford to buy television sets, and the quality was poor.

In the 1950s, the price for televisions declined and disposable income of many Americans increased so that most middle class families could afford television sets. By 1956, 40 million television sets were in American homes. By the end of the decade, 86 percent of American homes possessed one. **Snack food** manufacturers were quick to understand the importance of this new medium. Beginning in the 1940s, snack food manufacturers began **advertising** on television. Many companies targeted children's television programs to sell their products.

Fast food chains were slow to take advantage of television advertising. This changed in 1960, when the **McDonald's franchise** in Washington, D.C. decided to sponsor a local children's television program called *Bozo's Circus*. Sales in Washington grew by a whopping 30 percent per year during the next four years. Previously, McDonald's franchisees had not developed television commercials. Using a simple rhyme, Willard Scott came up with the name **Ronald McDonald** for the company icon he portrayed in the first company television commercials broadcast in October, 1963.

The national McDonald's Corporation decided to sponsor the broadcast of the Macy's Thanksgiving Day Parade in 1965. Previously, fast food chains had not advertised on national television, and it was a risk because McDonald's major sales were in the summertime, not in November. The Thanksgiving Day's advertisement produced immediate nationwide results and this convinced McDonald's to expend more funds targeting children, giving McDonald's an edge in the children's market.

By 1970, hundreds of millions of dollars of corporate funds were expended on child-oriented television advertising. Television promotions had succeeded in making Ronald McDonald identifiable by fully 96 percent of American children, making him second only to Santa Claus.

SUGGESTED READING: Consumers Union Education Services, *Selling America's Kids: Commercial Pressures on Kids of the 90's* (Mount Vernon, NY: Consumers Union, 1990); Consumers Union Web site: www.consumersunion.org/other/sellingkids/index.htm; Michael F. Jacobson and Bruce Maxwell, *What Are We Feeding Our Kids?* (New York: Workman Publishing, 1994).

Theaters When motion pictures arrived in the early twentieth century, they drew huge audiences, which were prime targets for **snack food** sales, but theater owners refused to sell them. To some owners, vending concessions was an unnecessary nuisance or "beneath their dignity." In the rowdy burlesque days, hawkers went through the aisles with baskets, selling snack foods such as **Cracker Jack** and **popcorn**, which were tossed in the air or strewn on the floors. In addition, vendors were often slovenly dressed and did not always follow the most hygienic practices preferred by the middle classes who frequented movie theaters. These were not the images most theater owners wanted to cultivate for their upscale venues. Other owners considered the profits on concession sales to be negligible compared with the trouble and expense of cleaning up spilled popcorn and scattered boxes and sacks. Many movie theaters had carpeted their lobbies with valuable rugs to emulate the grand theater lobbies. Operators were not interested in having their expensive carpets destroyed by spilled **sodas** and other confections. Until the 1930s, most theater owners considered snacks to be a liability rather than an asset.

Theater owners shifted their perspectives dramatically during the Depression. Snacks, which cost 5 or 10 cents, were an affordable luxury for most Americans and movie theaters needed the profits to survive. At first, independent concessionaires leased lobby privileges in theaters. Vendors paid about a dollar a day for the right to sell snacks. Because many theaters did not have lobby space, operators leased space outside the theaters. This suited the vendors because they were able to sell both to movie patrons and passersby on the street.

However, when theater owners saw their customers entering the theater with snacks, they quickly saw the light. Independent movie theaters were the first to capitulate to the financial lure of snack food. By the mid-1930s, movie **chains** started to crumble, too. Popcorn was the main snack attraction. It sold so well because of its aroma—the same smell that some theater owners had reportedly despised earlier. The aroma was maximized during the popping process. As soon as popping machines were placed in the lobbies, business picked up. Popcorn and other confections were progressively introduced into more theaters as tales of snack bar-generated wealth circulated. These experiences and stories, whether or not accurate, convinced even more theater operators to examine the reality of snack food profits. To control expenses, the managers required concession stand operators to account for the boxes and sacks. The net weekly profit on some confections was about 70 percent.

In some small, independent theaters, concession stands paid the entire overhead. In other places it grossed more than admissions. Snack bar sales dramatically increased with movies aimed at children. The highest sales were counted during Abbott and Costello comedies, while the lowest were generated with horror films. As baby boomers grew up, so did their worship of movie stars. During the 1950s, Elvis Presley was the movie star who generated the highest snack bar sales. Bob Hope, a close second in 1958, triumphed the following year.

Movie theaters not only sold snacks in the lobbies; they also advertised them. At **drive-in** theaters, snack foods were even more important. In 1946, only about 300 drive-in movie theaters existed in America. By 1958, this had dramatically expanded to over 6,000. Because these theaters were designed from scratch, large cafeteria interiors were originally constructed to accommodate thousands of people during the 18-minute intermissions. Advertisements for snack foods appeared on-screen before the show began. The speaker in the car blared out, "At the snack bar now!" As sales increased though **advertising**, indoor theaters also advertised snack foods before the main feature was shown.

Likewise, when snacks appeared on-screen in films, sales at snack bars also increased. This gave product manufacturers and filmmakers the idea for product placements in movies. Product manufacturers paid filmmakers for the placement of their product in the film. The best example of product placement for a snack food was Reese's Pieces, which consequently received huge national visibility in the blockbuster film *ET, The Extra-Terrestrial* (1982).

SUGGESTED READING: Andrew F. Smith, *Popped Culture: A Social History of Popcorn in America* (Columbia, SC: University of South Carolina Press, 1999); Andrew F. Smith, *Peanuts: The Illustrious History of the Goober Pea* (Urbana, IL: University of Illinois Press, 2002).

Thomas, Dave **Wendy's** founder R. David Thomas (1932–2002) was born in Atlantic City, New Jersey. Six weeks later, he was adopted by Tex and Auleva Thomas of Kalamazoo, Michigan. At the age of 12, he was hired for a job at a barbecue restaurant in Knoxville, Tennessee. Four years later, he dropped out of high school to work at the Hobby House Restaurant in Fort Wayne, Indiana. After a stint in the army, he returned to Hobby House. In 1954, he married Lorraine Buskirk, and their daughter Melinda Lou was nicknamed Wendy. Thomas worked at many jobs, including one at **Arthur Treacher's fast food** restaurant. He became the operations manager for 300 regional **Kentucky Fried Chicken** (KFC) outlets and he met **Harland Sanders**, who was one of the greatest influences in his life, according to his 1991 autobiography, *Dave's Way.* In 1962, Thomas took over four failing KFC restaurants in Columbus, Ohio. He acquired additional KFC outlets but sold them back to the company in 1968. He used his profits to open the first Wendy's restaurant the following year. Thomas relinquished day-to-day control over Wendy's International in 1982, when he became senior chairman. In 1989, Thomas began appearing in Wendy's advertisements and he became an instant media star. In 1993, Thomas went back to school; he completed his GED three years later. Thomas wrote two inspirational books, *Dave's Way* (1991) and *Dave Says—Well Done!* (1994). From the profits he earned through Wendy's, he and his wife gave large sums to **charities**. He died in 2002 at age 69.

SUGGESTED READING: Steven J. Austin, "America's Favorite 'Hamburger Cook,'" *Mississippi 55 & Fine* (May–October, 1994: 4–7); R. David Thomas, *Dave's Way: A New Approach to Old-fashioned Success* (New York: G. P. Putnam's Sons, 1991); R. David Thomas, *Dave Says—Well Done! The Common Guy's Guide to Everyday Success* (Grand Rapids, MI: Zondervan, 1994).

3 Musketeers In 1932, **Mars, Inc.** introduced the 3 Musketeers Bar, which is a **chocolate**-flavored nougat covered with milk chocolate. Compared with the company's **Snickers** bar, 3 Musketeers is sweeter and has more chocolate flavor. The company claims that the chocolate bar was named after its original composition: three pieces and three flavors—vanilla, chocolate, and strawberry. When the price of strawberries rose, the company dropped them as an ingredient in the chocolate bar. At the time, Alexandre Dumas's novel *The Three Musketeers* was a children's favorite and Mars, Inc. has used musketeer characters from the book in its **advertising**.

The 3 Musketeers bar is one of the best-selling Mars products. It was so successful that the company has created a 3 Musketeers product line, including 3 Musketeers Chocolate Flavored Chews composed of **sugar**, corn syrup, processed cocoa powder, and other ingredients.

SUGGESTED READING: Joël Glenn Brenner, *The Emperors of Chocolate: Inside the Secret World of Hershey and Mars* (New York: Broadway Books, 2000); Ray Broekel, *The Great America Candy Bar Book* (Boston: Houghton Mifflin Company, 1982); Janice Pottker, *Crisis in Candyland: Melting the Chocolate Shell of the Mars Family Empire* (Bethesda, MD: National Press Books, 1995); Tim Richardson, *Sweets: A History of Candy* (New York: Bloomsbury, 2002); the 3 Musketeers Web site: www.3musketeers.com

Tie-ins Tie-ins are broadly defined as promotional campaigns that link two different media. Movie tie-ins began in the 1920s, particularly between movies and print media. Movie companies wanted free publicity for their films, hence they encouraged magazines and newspapers to print stories about the actors, actresses, or about how their films were made.

During the 1990s, the **fast food** industry began to take advantage of movie tie-ins. Tie-in campaigns typically include posters, **advertisements** on cups, bags, and containers, toys representing figures from the movie, and contests giving customers the ability to acquire tickets to special events or special showings of the film. The toys are given away or sometimes sold at low cost. Fast food **chains** still make a substantial profit on the sale of these toys, in addition to the sale of food items in the outlets. In 1997 **McDonald's**, for instance, made a deal for a tie-in with Disney's movie *Flubber.* The movie was not a great hit but the tie-in was considered a success, and fast food companies have been making deals with film studios ever since. Fast food chains have been particularly interested in films targeted at children. In 2005 alone, **Burger King** bought into LucasFilms and Twentieth Century's Fox's *Star Wars: Episode III—Revenge of the Sith* and Twentieth Century's Fox's *Fantastic Four*; McDonald's tied-in with Disney's *Herbie: Fully Loaded* and Miramax's *The Adventures of Shark Boy and Lava Girl*; and **Wendy's** went in with Warner Brothers' *Charlie and the Chocolate Factory.*

Tie-ins have also connected with other media. For instance, in 2004 McDonald's announced a huge global promotion arrangement with Sony Music, in which McDonald's gives away free music when customers buy their products.

SUGGESTED READING: Eric Schlosser, *Fast Food Nation: The Dark Side of the All-American Meal* (New York: Houghton Mifflin Company, 2001).

Toblerone bars. © Kelly Fitzsimmons

Toblerone In 1908, Theodore Tobler and his production manager, Emil Baumann, invented the Toblerone in Bern, Switzerland. It was an unusual triangular-shaped **chocolate** bar with almond and honey nougat. The name derives from Tobler (the name of the company and family) plus *torrone*, an Italian nougat specialty. In 1970, the Tobler Company merged with the Jacobs Suchard Company of Switzerland, which became one of the largest chocolate companies in the world. In 1990, **Kraft** General Foods International acquired Jacobs Suchard, including the Toblerone brand. Today, Toblerone is sold in 120 countries (more countries than any other Kraft brand).

SUGGESTED READING: Toblerone Web site: www.kraft.com/archives/brands/brands_toblerone.html

Tombstone Pizza In the early 1960s, Joseph, Ronald, Frances, and Joan Simek owned the Tombstone Bar, a small country tavern across the street from a cemetery in Medford, Wisconsin. In 1962, they began making small pizzas for their customers and expanded to making **frozen pizza** in a small factory next to their tavern for distribution to other bars and taverns. Demand was high, so they opened factories in Medford and Sussex, Wisconsin. **Kraft Foods** bought the operation from the Simek family in 1986. During the 1990s, Tombstone Pizza became America's top-ranked frozen pizza, which was partly due to **television** commercials. One particularly successful one aired in 1995, featuring an eighteenth-century French aristocrat who, for his last wish, asks for a Tombstone Pizza with cheese and pepperoni; a falling guillotine blade slices the pizza. In 2001, Kraft extended its Tombstone Pizza line with a Mexican-style pizza.

SUGGESTED READING: Kraft Foods Web site: www.kraftfoods.com

Tootsie Roll In the late nineteenth century, the word *tootsie* was slang for a girl or sweetheart. In 1896, Leo Hirshfield, an immigrant from Austria, opened a **candy** store in New York. One of his employees began making a small, log-shaped, chewy **chocolate caramel**. In 1905, Hirshfield named the candy after his daughter, Clara, who was nicknamed Tootsie, and began manufacturing them commercially. It was the first **penny candy** that was individually wrapped. The operation was named Sweets Company of America, and in 1917 it began **advertising** nationally. In 1931, the company introduced the Tootsie Pop, which had a hard candy shell with a soft center on a stick. During World War II, Tootsie Rolls were placed in soldiers' ration kits, mainly because the hard candy could survive various climatic conditions. After the war, the company targeted its advertising toward youth by sponsoring popular children's television shows such as *Howdy Doody*, *Rin Tin Tin*, and the cartoon show *Rocky & Bullwinkle*.

The company's name was changed to Tootsie Roll Industries, Inc. and the company began to expand its operations abroad, first into the Philippines and Southeast Asia, and later into Canada and Mexico. In 1991, Tootsie Roll Industries acquired the Charms Company, America's largest **lollipop** manufacturer and maker of Charms Blow Pop. Two years later, it acquired Warner-Lambert's **chocolate** and caramel division, which included **Junior Mints**, Sugar Daddy, Sugar Babies, and the Charleston Chew! Today, Tootsie Roll Industries is headquartered in Chicago.

SUGGESTED READING: Joël Glenn Brenner, *The Emperors of Chocolate: Inside the Secret World of Hershey and Mars* (New York: Broadway Books, 2000); Ray Broekel, *The Great America Candy Bar Book* (Boston: Houghton Mifflin Company, 1982); Tim Richardson, *Sweets: A History of Candy* (New York: Bloomsbury, 2002); Tootsie Roll Industries Web site: www.tootsie.com

Toys America's first commercial confection, **Cracker Jack**, targeted children from its earliest days. The problem was how to reach children at a time before **radio** and **television**. The company **advertised** in children's magazines but it needed something better. Beginning in 1910, it began inserting into every package of Cracker Jack a coupon that could be redeemed for 300 "varieties of handsome and useful articles, such as Watches, Jewelry, Silverware, Sporting Goods, Toys, Games, Sewing Machines and many other useful Household articles." Later, rather than expending time to fulfill the requests for coupon redemptions, the company took a radical step of including a children's toy in every package. This was so successful that within two years the company had inserted more than 500 different toys in boxes. These toys were certainly one reason why Cracker Jack became America's top commercial confection and, shortly thereafter, became popular in other nations, as well. More than 23 billion toys have been given out since 1912.

McDonald's was the first **fast food chain** to discover the importance of toys. During the 1970s, the company concluded that its major target audience was children. To reach this audience, McDonald's developed the **Happy Meal**, which was launched in

1979. It linked with manufacturers to produce low-cost toys, which were then given away with children's meals. McDonald's also distributed more expensive toys, which it sold at a discount. In 1997, McDonald's launched a promotion that included a Teenie Beanie Baby in its Happy Meals. Customers waited in long lines to acquire their Happy Meals with Teenie Beanie Babies inside. This campaign is considered one of the most successful promotions in the history of advertising. Before the promotion, McDonald's sold 10 million Happy Meals per month; during the promotion, Happy Meal sales increased to 100 million per month. It was so successful that McDonald's conducted a similar promotion the following year.

Toys are often related to movie **tie-ins**. For instance, in 2006 McDonald's offered characters from the new Walt Disney Pictures/Walden Media film *The Chronicles of Narnia: The Lion, The Witch and The Wardrobe* in Happy Meals and Mighty Kids Meals. Today, McDonald's is the nation's largest distributor of toys. Other fast food chains followed McDonald's lead.

Toys manufactured for **junk food**, fast food, and **soda** have become sought after as collectibles. Clubs have developed around them and many such toys are important sales items on the Internet.

SUGGESTED READING: Larry Dobrow, "It's All about the Toys," *Advertising Age* 76 (July 25, 2005: S14); Joyce Losonsky and Terry Losonsky, *McDonald's Pre-Happy Meal Toys from the Fifties, Sixties, and Seventies* (Atglen, PA: Schiffer Publishing, 1998); Terry Losonsky and Joyce Losonsky, *McDonald's Happy Meal Toys around the World* (Atglen, PA: Schiffer Publishing, 1995); Ravi Piña, *Cracker Jack Collectibles with Price Guide* (Atglen, PA: Schiffer Publishing, 1995); Eric Schlosser, *Fast Food Nation: The Dark Side of the All-American Meal* (New York: Houghton Mifflin Company, 2001); Bob Stoddard, *The Encyclopedia of Pepsi-Cola Collectibles* (Iola, WI: Krause Publications, 2002); Larry White, *Cracker Jack Toys: The Complete, Unofficial Guide for Collectors* (Atglen, PA: Schiffer Publishing, 1997).

Training A major problem confronting the **fast food** industry has been the rapid turnover of employees, most of whom last only a few weeks or months before quitting. Fast food **chains** have consistently tried to routinize their operations into a system of very simple rules, such as what activities employees should perform and how they should greet customers. Strict regimentation creates standardized products and ways of operating. Work is broken into tasks that can be performed by an average worker with a minimum of training. The products are produced in assembly-line fashion, following the industrial model popularized by Henry Ford's automobile assembly-line methods.

Fast food chains have consistently tried to automate their operations so there is little need to train employees. Kitchens are full of buzzers and flashing lights that tell employees what to do. Computerized cash registers issue their own directions. Hence, new employees require little training, and when they leave there is not a great loss.

Fast food chains have spent considerable time training managerial staff. **Ice cream** maker Thomas Carvel of the **Carvel Corporation** launched the Carvel College of Ice Cream Knowledge (affectionately known as the Sundae School) to help franchisees understand the business. **Ray Kroc**, the chairman of **McDonald's**, followed a similar path when he established Hamburger University in 1961. This is a managerial training center that trains managers how to deal with personnel issues, improve teamwork, and increase employee motivation. It promotes a common McDonald's culture. Those who complete the program receive a Degree in Hamburgerology. Later, **Burger King** established Whopper College started in 1963 in Miami.

The critic Eric Schlosser reported in ***Fast Food Nation*** (2001) that fast food chains obtain funds from federal job training programs even though the chains provide a minimum of training. He called for the elimination of these subsidies and tax breaks given to fast food chains.

SUGGESTED READING: John A. Jakle and Keith A. Sculle, *Fast Food: Roadside Restaurants in the Automobile Age* (Baltimore: Johns Hopkins University Press, 1999); Eric Schlosser, *Fast Food Nation: The Dark Side of the All-American Meal* (New York: Houghton Mifflin Company, 2001).

Tricon Global Restaurants See **Yum! Brands, Inc.**

Twinkies In the 1920s, the Continental Baking Company began making sponge cakes that were mainly used for making strawberry shortcake. At the time, strawberries were only in season during the summer, and hence their shortcakes were sold only during that time. The company sought ideas for products that could be produced so that the factory producing sponge cake could operate year-round. Jimmy Dewar, a Chicago bakery manager, came up with a banana creme-filled cake that could be sold year-round at the price of two for a nickel. Dewar claimed that he named the new product Twinkies after he saw an **advertisement** for the Twinkle Toe Shoe Company on a trip to St. Louis. Twinkies' popularity increased such that they became the best-selling snack cake in the United States after World War II.

During World War II, it was difficult to acquire imported bananas. The Continental Baking Company substituted a vanilla creme filling, which has been used in Twinkies ever since. During the 1950s, the company advertised Twinkies extensively, particularly on children's **television** programs such as the *Howdy Doody Show*, and Twinkies sales greatly increased.

Twinkies became a cultural icon. They have inspired a cartoon character (Twinkie the Kid) and have appeared in many movies, such as *Ghostbusters* (1984), *Grease* (1978), and *Sleepless in Seattle* (1993). Perhaps the most unusual cultural connection was with the so-called Twinkie Defense. At the 1979 trial of Daniel White, who admitted to the murders of San Francisco mayor George Moscone and supervisor Harvey Milk, White claimed that he should be absolved of his crime because of impaired mental capacity resulting from compulsive eating of too much **junk food**, such as Twinkies, candy bars, cupcakes, and Cokes, which caused a chemical imbalance in his brain. White said he therefore murdered because of his abnormally high blood **sugar**. Although this was a novel defense, White was still convicted. In 1981, Congress outlawed the Twinkie Defense. While many people are convinced that children's behavior is influenced by the large amounts of sweets they consume, little scholarly proof has been offered for this assertion.

Twinkies. © Kelly Fitzsimmons

Twinkies remain an American culinary icon. When health advocates have argued for a tax on the sale of junk and fast foods, they called it a fat tax or a Twinkie tax. Deep-Fried Twinkies became a cult favorite during the 1990s. In 1999, the White House Millennium Council selected Twinkies as one of the items to be preserved in the Nation's Millennium Time Capsule, representing "an object of enduring American symbolism." The manufacturer, **Hostess**, produces more than 500 million Twinkies a year.

SUGGESTED READING: The Twinkies Cookbook: an Inventive and Unexpected Recipe Collection (Berkeley: Ten Speed Press, 2006); Twinkies Web site: www.twinkies.com

U

Uniforms During the 1970s, Billy Ingram, owner of **White Castle**, the first nation's **fast food chain**, faced many problems, one of which was the reputation of **hamburger** stands as being greasy, unclean, and unhealthy. To overcome these widespread perceptions, he required all employees to maintain strict standards of cleanliness. At first he did not require employees to wear uniforms, but he did require them to wear white shirts. Eventually uniforms were required for all employees. The company supplied white wool caps, which changed size when they were washed. Then Ingram hit upon the idea of using white paper caps, which did not have to be washed and could be easily replaced. Over time, White Castle altered its uniforms to conform with changing fashions.

The pattern started by White Castle has been followed by other fast food chains. **McDonald's**, for instance, initially required all employees to be dressed in white. Its uniforms have remained standard but they have shifted to specific uniforms for each different outlet, thus reinforcing an image that the chain wished to convey. In addition to a clean appearance, uniforms give the outlet a semimilitary appearance reflecting good management and excellent organization, and create an egalitarian working atmosphere untroubled by the latest fashions.

Many **drive-ins** also required uniforms, but they were just the opposite of those developed by White Castle and other fast food chains. Rather than being plain and white, drive-in uniforms were often gaudy and flamboyant. **Carhops**, for instance, were often required to wear bright uniforms, military-style caps, and pants with stripes down the side. Others were required to wear costumes similar to those worn by movie ushers. Still others dressed women in sexually suggestive majorette costumes with white boots and abbreviated skirts.

SUGGESTED READING: John A. Jakle and Keith A. Sculle, Fast Food: *Roadside Restaurants in the Automobile Age* (Baltimore: Johns Hopkins University Press, 1999); Philip Langdon, *Orange Roofs, Golden Arches: The Architecture of American Chain Restaurants* (New York: Knopf, 1986).

Unilever Unilever was formed in 1930 when the Dutch margarine company Margarine Unie merged with British soap maker Lever Brothers. The resulting Anglo-Dutch multinational corporation has acquired many food companies. In the United States, these include **Ben & Jerry's**, Slim-Fast, Hellmann's, Birdseye, **Good Humor**, **Breyers**, and Gold Bond Ice Cream, makers of **Popsicle** and **Good Humor**, **Dove**, and **Klondike** bars.

SUGGESTED READING: Unilever Web site: www.unilever.com

Urban Blight **Fast food chains** are not the cause of urban blight, but they have contributed to it. During the 1920s, **drive-in** restaurants targeted customers driving **automobiles**. Drive-ins were usually constructed on the outskirts of cities where land prices were lower and automobile traffic was high, thus contributing to urban sprawl. Because automobiles sped along at a fast clip, drive-ins developed gaudy **architecture** and large signs to attract motorists. Citizens objected to these outlandish structures and promotions and considered them eyesores; these complaints have continued ever since.

After World War II, Americans began leaving inner cities and moving into suburbs. This movement created challenges and opportunities for fast food chains. Those fast food chains that had targeted inner cities, such as **White Castle** and **White Tower**, confronted a major loss of customers and a significant increase in **crime** and vagrancy. Without a large customer base, many fast food establishments in inner cities closed and their buildings deteriorated.

Other fast food chains, such as **McDonald's** and **Burger King**, initially targeted the suburbs. Some municipalities objected to them because of their architecture. McDonald's, for instance, was criticized because of the arches bursting through their roofs and others considered their slanted roofs an eyesore. Likewise, others objected to Burger King's handlebars on their roofs. Both McDonald's and Burger King redesigned their outlets to appear less gaudy in hopes of quashing criticism. However, the concerns do not just rest with the design of particular outlets; the massive collections of fast food outlets that have spread along highways passing through cities are considered objectionable, as well. These strips are visually unattractive.

In addition fast food chains have greatly contributed to the trash that is generated by their patrons. Of the garbage along city streets and along highways, it is estimated that 40 percent comes from fast food chains.

SUGGESTED READING: Philip Langdon, *Orange Roofs, Golden Arches: The Architecture of American Chain Restaurants* (New York: Knopf, 1986).

U.S. Department of Agriculture (USDA) The Bureau of Agriculture was established in 1862; in 1889, the Bureau became the U.S. Department of Agriculture with cabinet rank. The USDA administers thousands of programs related to food and agriculture and has sponsored extensive research to help farmers improve their crops. Critics have claimed that USDA programs have strongly supported **factory farms** and large commercial concerns at the expense of small, independent family farms.

The USDA also has responsibilities for food safety and **nutrition**. The USDA's Food Safety Inspection Service (FSIS) is charged with ensuring that all meat, poultry, and egg products in the United States are safe to consume and are accurately labeled. This includes all food products that contain more than 2 to 3 percent meat products. All other food products are regulated by the U.S. Food and Drug Administration (FDA). There are several ways by which unsafe or improperly labeled meat and poultry products are detected, including (a) those uncovered by the company that manufactured or distributed the food; (b) FSIS test results that indicate that the products are adulterated or misbranded; (c) when FSIS field inspectors discover unsafe or improperly labeled foods; or (d) when epidemiological data from local, state, or federal sources (such as the FDA or the Centers for Disease Control and Prevention) reveal unsafe, unwholesome, or inaccurately labeled food. When problems are discovered, manufacturers or distributors initiate a food recall to protect the public. If a company refuses to recall its products, then the FSIS has the legal authority to detain and seize those products. Once a recall has been issued, FSIS conducts effectiveness checks to verify that the product is removed from commerce. Critics believe that the FSIS does not have the funds necessary to properly inspect and test food, and therefore is not adequately meeting its responsibilities.

SUGGESTED READING: Food Safety and Inspection Service (FSIS) Web site: www.fsis.usda.gov; Marion Nestle, *Food Politics: How the Food Industry Influences Nutrition and Health* (Berkeley, CA: University of California Press, 2002); Marion Nestle, *Safe Food: Bacteria, Biotechnology, and Bioterrorism* (Berkeley, CA: University of California Press, 2003); Eric Schlosser, *Fast Food Nation: The Dark Side of the All-American Meal* (New York: Houghton Mifflin Company, 2001); U.S. Department of Agriculture (USDA) Web site: www.usda.gov

V

Valentine's Day Candies Valentine's Day is celebrated on February 14, traditionally in honor of a saint killed in Roman times. It was a popular holiday in medieval Europe. Precisely when candy became the traditional gift given on Valentine's Day is unclear. In the 1860s, Richard Cadbury introduced the first Valentine's Day box of **chocolates** in England. One of the earliest American Valentine's Day candies was invented by the one of the predecessors of the **New England Confectionery Company** (NECCO), which began manufacturing Conversation Hearts in the 1860s. These heart-shaped candies were renamed Sweethearts in 1902. By the twenty-first century, NECCO produces about 8 billion Sweethearts each year, virtually all within six weeks before Valentine's Day, and they are the best-selling Valentine's Day candy in the world.

By tradition, males give chocolates to their sweethearts, mothers, or wives on Valentine's Day. It is promoted as a day of Cupid and love, and candies have reflected this dimension. Chemicals found in small amounts in chocolate are anandamide, serotonin, endorphins, and phenylethylamine (PEA); in the human brain these chemicals create positive feelings. The aphrodisial effect of chocolate has been greatly exaggerated in advertisement imagery in order to increase sales.

According to the **National Confectioners Association** Americans annually spend just over $1 billion for Valentine's Day.

SUGGESTED READING: Jack Santino, *New Old-Fashioned Ways: Holidays and Popular Culture* (Knoxville, TN: The University of Tennessee Press, 1996).

Classic Valentine's Day candy. © Kelly Fitzsimmons

Vegetarianism/Veganism The term *vegetarian* was used in the United States by the 1830s, but it was popularized by Vegetarian Society of the United Kingdom at their first meeting in 1847 and by the American Vegetarian Society at its inaugural meeting in 1850. During the latter part of the nineteenth century, the Seventh-Day

Adventist Church strongly encouraged its members to become vegetarians for health reasons. John Harvey Kellogg, a Seventh-Day Adventist, became director of the Battle Creek sanitarium in Michigan, and he promoted vegetarianism throughout his entire life. He invented cold **cereal** such as Kellogg's Corn Flakes, as an alternative to the traditional **breakfast** of eggs and bacon. As part of his efforts to create an alternative to butter made from cow's milk, he invented peanut butter, which became popular during the early twentieth century. Peanut butter has been an important ingredient in many confections.

Vegetarianism has been variously defined, but it is generally considered the practice of not eating meat, poultry, or fish. Ovo vegetarians also do not eat eggs and lacto vegetarians do not eat dairy products. The word *vegan* was coined by Donald Watson, the founder of the Vegan Society, in 1944. A vegan eats neither meat nor meat byproducts, eggs or dairy products.

Vegetarianism became particularly popular in the late twentieth century. In 1960, there were an estimated 2 million vegetarians in the United States; by 1990, there were more than 6 million. Part of this growth can be attributed to the organizing efforts of the North American Vegetarian Society, which was founded in 1974, and the publication of several vegetarian magazines, such as *Vegetarian Times*.

Vegetarians have opposed **fast food** sales of meat, fish, or poultry and products that have been made with nonvegetarian byproducts. Vegetarians have challenged fast food operations, such as the way large-scale **suppliers** raise and slaughter animals. They have also opposed certain food preparation practices, such as using animal products in making **French fries**. Vegetarians have influenced fast food **chains**. **McDonald's** for instance, which once used animal byproducts in the oils used to cook French fries, has discontinued the practice. Some vegetarians have taken stronger action, as in 1999 when some vegetarians set fire to a McDonald's in Antwerp, Belgium, in protest.

Many fast food chains now offer vegetarian meals, such as veggie burgers and salads. In addition, many vegetarian products are now sold in stores. For instance, in 1993 Max Shondor, a Florida-based natural food restaurateur, introduced soy-based Boca Burgers; he subsequently expanded his line to include other flavors, meatless breakfast patties, and nuggets. Similar products are now sold in some fast food chains.

SUGGESTED READING: Myrna Chandler Goldstein and Mark A. Goldstein, *Controversies in Food and Nutrition* (Westport, CT: Greenwood Press, 2002); Eric Schlosser, *Fast Food Nation: The Dark Side of the All-American Meal* (New York: Houghton Mifflin Company, 2001).

Vending Machines Automatic vending machines were developed in the United Kingdom in the 1880s. The Thomas Adams Gum Company began selling **gum** in vending machines on New York's elevated train platforms. Previously, **penny candy**, gum and peanuts had been sold in glass jars by grocers. Coin-operated machines offered the means to sell **junk foods** in many other places without the need for a sales force. Vending machines took off nationally in 1901, when F. W. and H. S. Mills debuted penny-in-the-slot machines in Chicago. By the end of the decade, there were 30,000 machines selling penny candy, peanuts, and gum across America. During the early 1920s, vending machines dispensed soft drinks into cups.

By 1926, there was a vending machine for every 100 people in America. These machines generated a million dollars per day. At that time, the largest single operator was William Wrigley, who installed 10,000 slot machines in the New York City subway system.

Vending machines were also the core of **automats**, which dispensed more substantial food. These types of machines were also placed in offices and public areas. They sold **sandwiches**, pies, coffee, candy, **ice cream** and **soda**. Bottled **Coca-Cola** was sold in vending machines after World War II. In 1965, soft drinks in cans were dispensed from vending machines. In 1981, talking vending machines were introduced. Today, vending machines are a multibillion-dollar business, and many different products are sold in them. It is estimated that Coca-Cola products alone are sold in 1.4 million vending machines.

Vending machines became controversial when they were placed on public **school** campuses. In 2006, Faerie Films released a documentary film titled *Vending Machine*, which examined health issues as seen from the viewpoint of teenagers who have been targeted by fast food and junk food manufacturers. Efforts are underway to remove vending machines selling soda and junk foods from schools.

Vending machine. © Kelly Fitzsimmons

SUGGESTED READING: The Automatic Vending Machine Industry: Its Growth and Development (Washington, D.C.: U.S. Government Printing Office, 1962).

Vernor's Ginger Ale In 1866, James Vernor, a Detroit pharmacist, introduced Vernor's Ginger Ale, which is considered the first commercial carbonated soft drink. In 1896, Vernor established his own **soda fountain** to dispense it and he began selling the extract to drugstores in other cities, such as Buffalo, Toledo, and Cleveland. Today, Vernor's brand is owned by **Cadbury Schweppes** Americas Beverages.

SUGGESTED READING: Lawrence L. Rouch, *The Vernor's Story: From Gnomes to Now* (Ann Arbor, MI: University of Michigan Press, 2003).

Violence In addition to **crime**, **fast food chains** have been subjected to violence due to various political, economic, and social causes. An activist French farmer, José Bové, became upset in 1999 with tariffs placed on importation of Roquefort cheese into the United States, which he and fellow farmers made. As a result, also in 1999, he and his group, the radical Confédération Paysanne, decided to retaliate by bulldozing a local **McDonald's** restaurant under construction in Millau, France. He declared that his action was a challenge to globalism. When he went on trial, 30,000 people demonstrated on his behalf, carrying signs saying "Non à McMerde." Bové was convicted and served three months in a French prison. Subsequently, he and his supporters destroyed research plots with **genetically modified** crops in Brazil and have participated in demonstrations (some of which have turned violent) against **globalization**.

It addition to violent protests against globalism, fast food chains have been subjected to violence due to international events and causes. In 1979, Marxist guerrillas blew up a McDonald's outlet in San Salvador and announced that their act was intended as a blow against "imperialist America." When American aircraft accidentally bombed the Chinese embassy in Belgrade during the war in Yugoslavia in 1999, Chinese students ransacked the McDonald's in Beijing. During American bombing of Afghanistan in 2001, Pakistan's **Kentucky Fried Chicken** outlets were trashed. In 1996, a KFC in Bangalore, India, was looted by farmers who believed that the company threatened their agricultural practices. Anarchists destroyed a McDonald's in Copenhagen in 1995 and regularly protest at McDonald's locations in Paris and London. Bombs have destroyed McDonald's restaurants in St. Petersburg, Russia, Athens, Greece, and Rio de Janeiro, Brazil. Vegetarians set fire to McDonald's in Antwerp in 1999 and a McDonald's in London was trashed, also in 1999. In 2000, a bomb was set off in a McDonald's restaurant in Breton, France, killing a 27-year-old employee; five activists belonging to Emgann, a group considered a front for the Breton Revolutionary Army, were arrested in connection with that action. In 2001, 500 enraged Hindus ransacked a McDonald's in Bombay, India, and smeared cow dung all over a statue of **Ronald McDonald** because they wrongly thought that **French fries** served at Indian restaurants were being fried in beef tallow. In 2002, the McDonald's in Bali, Indonesia, was bombed by Indonesian terrorists. When American troops attacked Iraq in 2003, protests were held in many cities, and McDonald's was again the target of many demonstrators. In Moscow, a McDonald's restaurant was destroyed by a bomb in 2003. In 2005, a bomb destroyed a KFC restaurant in Karachi, Pakistan. Members of the Balochistan Liberation Army, an ethnic Baloch group in the Balochistan province, claimed responsibility and the suspects who were apprehended were members of that group.

Yet another cause of violence has been crime. In 2001, a bomb was set off in a Xian, China, McDonald's restaurant that killed two people. Two years later, a man was convicted of the bombing; prior to the bombing, he had sent threatening letters to the management, requesting money. The perpetrator was sent to prison.

SUGGESTED READING: José Bové, François Dufour, and Gilles Luneau, *The World Is Not for Sale: Farmers Against Junk Food* (New York: Verso, 2001); Eric Schlosser, *Fast Food Nation: The Dark Side of the All-American Meal* (New York: Houghton Mifflin Company, 2001).

Waste **Fast food chains package** their foods in disposable paper bags, wrappers, and cardboard and Styrofoam containers. Fast food outlets therefore do not have to clean utensils, ceramic cups, plates, or serving dishes. Although paper, plastic, and foam products cost money, they are not as expensive as the stolen and broken dishes that prevailed before the fast food industry shifted to disposable packaging. Many Americans believe that fast food generates vast amounts of trash. However studies have consistently shown that fast food establishments are responsible for less than 1 percent of landfill volumes. The problem with fast food trash has been the customers who toss their refuse onto highways and streets, making it highly visible. Fast food establishments have placed trash containers in convenient locations so they can be easily used. Chains have also encouraged customers to "put trash in its place." Also, most fast food chains have installed trash compactors in each outlet to limit the volume of trash generated at the outlet. To counteract the bad public relations due to its customers tossing trash onto streets, many fast food chains have contributed to local activities, such as sponsoring highway cleanups.

In addition to the waste generated at the fast food outlets, a great deal of secondary waste is generated by fast food **suppliers**, and this is a serious problem. Feedlots and slaughterhouses, for instance, produce vast amounts of waste, which greatly contribute to pollution.

A large volume of trash is generated by the **soda** industry. It is estimated that 44 billion soft drink cans and bottles are thrown into landfills annually. Many municipalities and states have required deposits on all bottles, and others have enacted laws requiring recycling. Soda manufacturing and bottling companies have opposed such laws, but because they found that they generate much more money from people who fail to redeem deposits than they lose on the recycling, they now strongly support such efforts.

SUGGESTED READING: Eric Schlosser, *Fast Food Nation: The Dark Side of the All-American Meal* (New York: Houghton Mifflin Company, 2001); Eric Schlosser and Charles Wilson, *Chew On This: Everything You Don't Want to Know about Fast Food* (Boston: Houghton Mifflin, 2006).

Wendy's International **Dave Thomas** worked for **Kentucky Fried Chicken** and **Arthur Treacher's** before he opened his first Wendy's restaurant in 1969 in Columbus, Ohio. Thomas believed that Americans wanted larger **hamburgers** than those offered by other

chains, so he created a square beef patty, which probably was influenced by **White Castle**'s square patty. He charged 55 cents for the large **sandwich**, which was a risk because at that time **McDonald's** charged 18 cents for its hamburgers. Wendy's claimed that Thomas's Old Fashioned Hamburger could be ordered in 256 different ways. Thomas concentrated on young adults for customers, as opposed to children whom other chains targeted. He correctly judged the willingness of young adults to purchase an expensive hamburger.

Beginning in 1970, Thomas expanded his operation in other cities in Ohio. In 1972, the first out-of-state Wendy's was opened in Indianapolis. Wendy's went from nine outlets in 1972 to 1,818 six years later. Wendy's went public in 1975. One reason for Wendy's early success was its **drive-thru** windows that were installed in 1971. Their advantage was that less space had to be used for parking lots or indoor eating space. McDonald's and **Burger King** followed Wendy's example.

In addition to hamburgers and **French fries**, Wendy's has diversified its **menu** to include **chicken sandwiches**, the Frosty (similar to a **milk shake**), baked potatoes, and chili. The salad bar was added in 1979. In September, 1986, Wendy's introduced the Big Classic, which was a quarter-pound hamburger on a Kaiser-style bun.

Wendy's, like other fast food chains, has **advertised** extensively on **television**. In 1984, the company launched its famous "Where's the Beef?" commercial. Later that year, the phrase ended up being used by Walter Mondale in his presidential campaign against Ronald Reagan. Dave Thomas appeared in Wendy's advertisements beginning in 1989.

Wendy's is the third-largest hamburger chain, with more than 6,600 outlets in the United States and 34 other countries. The company also owns the Tim Horton's and Baja Fresh Mexican Grill chains. The company also has extensive investments in Pasta Pomodoro and Café Express.

SUGGESTED READING: John A. Jakle and Keith A. Sculle, *Fast Food: Roadside Restaurants in the Automobile Age* (Baltimore: Johns Hopkins University Press, 1999); R. David Thomas, *Dave's Way: a New Approach to Old-fashioned Success* (New York: G. P. Putnam's Sons, 1991); R. David Thomas, *Dave Says—Well Done! The Common Guy's Guide to Everyday Success* (Grand Rapids, MI: Zondervan, 1994).

White Castle In 1916, J. Walter "Walt" Anderson, a short-order cook in a diner in Wichita, Kansas, purchased an old shoe repair building, which he converted into a **hamburger** stand. He sold his burgers for a nickel apiece, which his customers (mainly workers) could afford. At the time, hamburgers were commonly sold on the street but they did not have a particularly good reputation. The ground beef was frequently overcooked and tasteless, and everyone was worried about its composition. Anderson's burgers were different. His secret was to make thin, 1-inch square patties that permitted quick cooking. To ensure freshness, he arranged for beef and square buns to be delivered twice a day, and sometimes more often. To make sure that customers knew what was in his hamburgers, he ground his own beef so that customers could watch him do so through glass windows. It was so successful that he opened three additional stands, all with carry-out service. Additional stands were opened and in 1920 Anderson customers proclaimed him to be the "King of the Hamburger."

Anderson wanted to expand his operation even further, but he needed a partner with money. In 1921, he went into business with Edgar Waldo "Billy" Ingram, a real estate and insurance man who liked what Anderson had accomplished. Ingram also believed that

Anderson's operation could be greatly improved. The new joint venture was renamed White Castle. Ingram designed a new structure, complete with turrets, that imitated the Chicago Water Tower, which was one of the few structures to survive the Chicago fire of 1871. It was a symbol of permanence, which was quite different from the image of other low-cost hamburger stands that dotted the nation at the time. The dominant color of the new outlets was white, which was intended to represent purity and cleanliness. This new design was successful and White Castle expanded to Omaha, Kansas City, and St. Louis by 1924. In 1925, the company sold more than 84,000 hamburgers.

White Castle initially served only coffee, hamburgers, **Coca-Cola**, and pie, but this **menu** expanded over the years. Employees were required to observe high standards of cleanliness and had to wear **uniforms**. At first, Ingram made arrangements with local butchers to produce a particular meat product. As White Castle became larger, he established meat processing plants, paper suppliers, and bun baking operations to produce consistent products.

Anderson sold his portion of the operation to Ingram, who continued to expand it, particularly in urban areas near mass transit stops across the street from large factories. As White Castle expanded in various regions, it was possible for the company to advertise over a broad area, thus increasing the sales. White Castle advertised in newspapers and through **radio**. It offered a single **slogan** for all outlets: "Sell 'em by the sackful."

By 1931, the company owned 131 outlets. The Depression was not a major problem. The company restructured its operation by closing unprofitable outlets and opening new operations in more profitable areas. Because it sold its products at a low price, White Castle food was a luxury that Americans with jobs could afford. The company streamlined its operations further, and hamburgers were sold at an increasing rate. The company also advertised in newspapers and included coupons for reduced prices. The company also experimented with new products, such as **milk shakes**, which it decided not to continue because milk shakes took so long to make and the equipment frequently broke down and was difficult for operators to fix. White Castle management also believed that milk shakes ruined customer's appetites for hamburgers, the company's flagship product. In 1935, White Castle sold 40 million hamburgers.

During World War II, White Castle did face serious problems due to labor shortages and the lack of meat, which was rationed during the war. Likewise, **sugar** was also rationed and Coca-Cola was also in short supply. Ingram sought new potential products. One was the fried egg sandwich. Eggs were fried in a metal ring and were then served on a bun, much like **McDonald's** Egg McMuffin. Potatoes were another product that White Castle experimented with during the war. Potatoes were inexpensive, plentiful, and were not rationed. White Castle began serving **French fries**, which previously had not been served much at fast food operations.

White Castle continued to sell French fries after the war, but they were discontinued because many managers believed that deep-frying in hot grease was dangerous for operators and it was difficult for operators to know when the fries were properly cooked. In the 1950s, technological improvements made it possible for French fries to be easily and safely prepared, and so they were returned to the menu. Milk shake equipment also improved during the 1950s, so White Castle resumed selling them. In 1958, they test-marketed a King Size hamburger to compete with the increasing popularity of the Bob's **Big Boy**. It was not a success.

White Castle was confronted with a series of problems. Suburbs developed and highways permitted workers easy access to cities. As the number of **automobiles** sold skyrocketed during the 1940s and 1950s, car owners began frequenting **drive-ins.** Most White Castle outlets were located in urban areas and many outlets did not have parking lots. Another problem was the **crime** that affected inner cities; many White Castles were open 24 hours a day and were frequent targets of robbers late at night. In addition, many inner-city establishments became havens for the homeless. Many used White Castle's restrooms to bathe in and left messes, destroying White Castle's reputation for cleanliness. Finally, racial unrest hit the inner cities. Most Americans became weary of eating at White Castle. White Castle began to fade and by the 1960s there were only 90 White Castle outlets left.

In 1968, White Castle began a new construction program, locating many outlets in suburbs. While it could not compete with large chains such as McDonald's or **Burger King**, it could compete with smaller **chains**. Recently, White Castle has developed new partnerships with other chains, such as **Church's Chicken**, which has expanded White Castle's operations.

The White Castle system that Ingram developed had important differences from previous hamburger operations. Its formula had five components: efficiency and economy (nickel hamburgers), limited menu, mass volume, standardization, and simplification of processes of preparing the food; prominent locations (near mass transit stops); uniform and distinctive **architecture** (the white castle); aggressive expansion of outlets; and pleasant settings, which were especially good places for women and children. These characteristics, somewhat altered, became the basis for each subsequent fast food chain.

White Castle changed American culture dramatically. Hamburgers became one of America's most important foods during the 1920s, in part due to White Castle. Customer surveys indicated that they liked the taste of the hamburger, the low price, the quality of all the products served, the cleanliness of the outlets, and the convenience. That this system has survived for more than 80 years (even though throughout much of its history it was a small, family-owned business) is a credit to its model, which was duplicated by other fast food chains, such as McDonald's. Most fast food chains today are based on variations of the White Castle system. As a result of this system, millions of fast food hamburgers are sold, not just in the United States but throughout the world.

SUGGESTED READING: Paul Hirshorn and Steven Izenour, *White Towers* (Cambridge, MA: MIT Press, 1979); David Gerard Hogan, *Selling 'em by the Sack: White Castle and the Creation of American Food* (New York: New York University Press, 1997); Billy Ingram, *All this from a 5-cent Hamburger! The Story of the White Castle System* (New York: Newcomen Society in North America, 1964); John A. Jakle and Keith A. Sculle, *Fast Food: Roadside Restaurants in the Automobile Age* (Baltimore: Johns Hopkins University Press, 1999).

White Tower In the 1920s, John E. Saxe, his son, Thomas E. Saxe, and an associate, Daniel J. O'Connell, examined **White Castle** outlets in Minneapolis and concluded that **fast food** was an excellent idea and that White Castle had the right approach. In 1926, they opened their first White Tower restaurant near Marquette University in Milwaukee. It was a clone of White Castle. Like White Castle, White Tower located its outlets at subway, trolley, and bus stops frequented by workers going to or from large factories. It specialized in 5-cent **hamburgers**, which were almost the same as White Castle's, but it also sold ham **sandwiches**, **doughnuts**, pies, and **beverages**. The buildings were similar. White Tower's **slogan**, "Take Home a Bagful," was a take-off on White Castle's "Buy 'em by the Sack." Like

White Castle restaurants, White Tower outlets were white in color to assure customers of the purity and cleanliness of their restaurants. Unlike White Castle, White Tower **franchised** its operation and the **chain** expanded steadily throughout the Midwest. In the late 1920s, White Tower was one of the largest hamburger chains in America. In 1929, White Castle sued White Tower for trademark infringement and court ruled in favor of White Castle. White Tower was ordered to change its name and all resemblances to White Castle in its **architecture** and slogans. White Tower maintained its name by paying White Castle a large sum of money. After World War II, the chain began to falter as urban areas decayed and the suburbs began siphoning off the middle class. By 1979, White Tower had only 80 outlets, all of which were owned by Tombrock Corporation. White Tower slowly disappeared thereafter.

SUGGESTED READING: Anne Cooper Funderburg, *Sundae Best: A History of Soda Fountains* (Bowling Green, OH: Bowling Green State University Popular Press, 2002); Paul Hirshorn and Steven Izenour, *White Towers* (Cambridge, MA: MIT Press, 1979); David Gerard Hogan, *Selling 'em by the Sack: White Castle and the Creation of American Food* (New York: New York University Press, 1997); Harvey Levenstein, *Paradox of Plenty: A Social History of Eating in Modern America* (New York: Oxford University Press, 1993).

Wienerschnitzel Glen Bell, then an owner of a small chain of Mexican restaurants called El Taco, convinced John Galardi, a commissary manager for the company, to launch his own **fast food chain**. Bell invested in it and helped develop the idea. Martha Bell, Glen's wife, supplied the name for it, Der Wienerschnitzel. It derived from the traditional Austrian veal dish, *wiener schnitzel*, which has nothing to do with hot dogs. The "Der" was removed from the name in 1977. In 1961, the first outlet, featuring **hot dogs**, corn dogs, and chili dogs, opened in Newport Beach, California. Galardi's first stand was flat-roofed but he switched to an A-frame structure in which customers actually drove through the building. The chain's **mascot** is a hot dog that runs away from people who want to eat him. Wienerschnitzel remains privately owned; its parent company, the Galardi Group Franchise & Leasing, Inc., is headquartered in Newport Beach. Wienerschnitzel is the largest hot dog chain, with more than 360 outlets in 10 states and Guam. In 2005, the company co-branded with **Tastee-Freez** so that its menu now includes Taste-Freez items.

SUGGESTED READING: John A. Jakle and Keith A. Sculle, *Fast Food: Roadside Restaurants in the Automobile Age* (Baltimore: Johns Hopkins University Press, 1999); Philip Langdon, *Orange Roofs, Golden Arches: The Architecture of American Chain Restaurants* (New York: Knopf, 1986).

Wimpy Elzie Crisler Segar, a syndicated cartoonist for the King Features, created the Popeye the Sailor Man comics in 1929. In 1931, Segar introduced J. Wellington Wimpy, a fat cartoon character who loved to eat **hamburgers**. Wimpy was either too cheap or too poor to pay for them, and so he tried to con others into buying them for him. His immortal phrase was "I'd gladly pay you tomorrow for a hamburger today." The term *Wimpy* became synonymous with hamburger in the United States and later in the United Kingdom. This association was so close that it spawned Wimpy's Grills, a hamburger **chain** that was launched in 1934 by Edward Vale Gold of Chicago. The chain thrived in the United States for a decade and at its height had about 1,500 outlets. It featured a 10-cent hamburger, which was expensive for the time, as well as **sandwiches** made with roasted and toasted meats. The chain also **franchised** in the

United Kingdom, making it the first American **fast food** chain to operate outside the United States. The chain survived until 1978, when Gold died. In his will he stipulated that all Wimpy outlets be closed.

SUGGESTED READING: David Gerard Hogan, *Selling 'em by the Sack: White Castle and the Creation of American Food* (New York: New York University Press, 1997).

Winchell's Donut House In 1948, Verne H. Winchell founded Winchell's Donut House in Temple City, a suburb of Los Angeles. From Los Angeles, Winchell's spread northward to San Francisco, Portland, Seattle, and east to Phoenix and Denver. The company merged with the Denny's restaurant chain 20 years later. The trend toward healthier foods caused serious problems for **doughnut** sales beginning in the 1980s. Winchell's was sold to TW Services, which passed it along to a Canadian investment group. Many Winchell's **franchises** were sold to Cambodian immigrants, who established a special economic niche for themselves. By 1985, 80 percent of California's doughnut shops were Cambodian-owned. In celebration of its 50th anniversary in 1998, Winchell's in Pasadena, California, created the world's largest doughnut, weighing 5,000 pounds and measuring 95 feet in diameter.

The company has expanded its product line. It now includes 70 different varieties of doughnuts, croissants, cinnamon rolls, bagels, and muffins, as well as beverages including coffee, frozen cappuccinos, fruit juices, and **soda**. As of 2005, Winchell's Donut House had about 200 stores, mainly in western states, as well as in Guam, New Zealand, Saipan, and Saudi Arabia.

SUGGESTED READING: John A. Jakle and Keith A. Sculle, *Fast Food: Roadside Restaurants in the Automobile Age* (Baltimore: Johns Hopkins University Press, 1999).

Wrigley Co. In 1891, William Wrigley, Jr. moved to Chicago and began selling soap. To increase sales, he gave away **gum** to his customers. His gum was a hit and so he decided to make and sell gum. In 1893, he began manufacturing Juicy Fruit and Spearmint gums. Wrigley's gum was packaged in small containers with five sticks each and were distributed though confectioners and grocery stores. At the time, Wrigley was just one of hundreds of gum manufacturers in the United States.

Wrigley began promoting his gum through advertisements and he began to expand his operation. He was the first American gum manufacturer to begin selling his products abroad, first in Canada (1910), then in the United Kingdom (1911) and Australia (1915). In 1927, he opened up a factory in London. He also continued to create new products and innovate their distribution. For instance, the company released its Doublemint gum in 1914. Wrigley sold his gum through **vending machines** and in the 1920s he purchased the rights to 10,000 machines in the New York City subways.

During World War II, the Wrigley Company was contracted to pack K rations for soldiers. It inserted a sick of chewing gum in every ration. The company has continued to develop new gums; it introduced its Freedent Gum (designed to not stick to dentures) in 1977 and Extra Sugarfree Gum in 1984. Two years later it introduced Hubba Bubble bubble gum.

The Wrigley Company has engaged in extensive **advertising**. Its jingle "Double your pleasure, double your fun" for Doublemint Gum has been rated by *Advertising Age* in 2001 as one of the top ten advertising jingles of the twentieth century.

The Wrigley Company has factories in 10 other countries and its gum is distributed in 180 countries. It is the top-selling gum in China. The company is the world's largest maker of chewing and bubble gum; its headquarters are in Chicago. It has acquired other confections, such as **LifeSavers**. Today, Wrigley's gum is a $2 billion operation and remains family-owned.

SUGGESTED READING: Robert Hendrickson, *The Great American Chewing Gum Book* (Radnor, PA: Chilton Book Company, 1976); Michael R. Redclift, *Chewing Gum: The Fortunes of Taste* (New York: Routledge, 2004); Wrigley Web site: www.wrigley.com

Y

York Peppermint Patties. © Kelly Fitzsimmons

York Peppermint Patties The York Peppermint Pattie is a flat, round, dark **chocolate** with peppermint creme inside. It was formulated and launched in 1940 by the York Cone Company, which mainly manufactured **ice cream** cones. The company had been founded in 1920 in York, Pennsylvania; it mainly distributed its product in the Northeast, Ohio, Indiana, and Florida. In 1972, the company was acquired by **Peter Paul**, which expanded production and aggressively promoted it nationally beginning in 1975. Peter Paul was sold to **Cadbury** in 1978 and, 10 years later, the **Hershey Company** acquired York Peppermint Patties when it purchased the confectionery operations of **Cadbury Schweppes** in the United States. It is one of the best-selling **candies** in the United States.

SUGGESTED READING: York Peppermint Pattie Web site: www.hersheys.com/products/details/york.asp

Yum! Brands, Inc. Beginning in the 1970s, **PepsiCo** had acquired several **fast food** restaurant **chains**, including **Kentucky Fried Chicken**, **Pizza Hut**, and **Taco Bell**, as an adjunct to its **soda** business. It required that those chains serve only Pepsi-Cola. Other fast food chains, such as **McDonald's**, saw PepsiCo as a competitor and refused to sell PepsiCo products. PepsiCo finally concluded that it would be in the company's interest to spin off its restaurant businesses. Accordingly in 1997, Tricon Global Restaurants, Inc. was founded as an independent, publicly traded company. It was headquartered in Louisville, Kentucky. In 2002, Tricon announced the acquisition of Yorkshire Global

Restaurants with its two brands, **Long John Silver's** and **A&W** All-American Food. Tricon changed its name to Yum! Brands Inc. in 2003.As of 2005, Yum! Brands operated 33,000 restaurants in more than 100 countries. It is the world's largest fast food company.

SUGGESTED READING: Yum! Brands Web site: www.yum.com

Glossary

Aspartame: Marketed under the names NutraSweet and Equal, aspartame is an artificial sweetener that was discovered in 1965. It was first authorized to enter the U.S. market in 1974. Numerous allegations have been made against aspartame, none of which has been conclusively proven.

Bundling: The practice of joining related products together for the purpose of selling them as a single unit.

Calorie: In the 1890s, chemist Wilbur O. Atwater broke analyzed the nutritional components of food (proteins, fats, and carbohydrates) and measured the caloric value of each of the groups. In the early 1900s, Russell Chittenden, a chemist at Yale University, took Atwater's idea of assessing food in terms of calories—the amount of heat required to raise the temperature of 1 gram of water 1 degree Centigrade—and applied it not only to energy taken in but to energy burned in exercise. Calorie-counting was born. Lulu Hunt Peters's book, *Diet and Health, with Key to the Calories* (1917), advocated calorie-counting as a method of weight reduction. It introduced the so-called scientific principle that calorie control equated weight control. Those who were unable to control their weight were judged to have no self-discipline and obesity became a sign of moral weakness.

Carbohydrates: Carbohydrates are one of the major dietary components. Their primary function is to provide energy for the body. The most important carbohydrates include simple sugars, starches, glycogens, and fiber. Complex carbohydrates are ultimately broken down into simple sugars that the body can easily metabolize.

Chains: Multiple restaurants owned by the same company or franchisers.

Cholesterol (blood): The body manufactures cholesterol in the form of dietary cholesterol. High levels of blood cholesterol increase risk of heart disease; cholesterol travels in the blood in little packages of fat and protein called lipoproteins. Cholesterol in high-density lipoproteins (HDL), is the so-called good cholesterol; cholesterol in low-density lipoproteins (LDL) is bad because it is headed for your artery walls.

Cholesterol (dietary): A crystalline substance found in animal tissues. The body normally synthesized it in the liver. Its level in the bloodstream can be influenced by heredity and through the consumption of certain foods. Cholesterol can cause atherosclerotic plaque and heart disease.

Co-branding: The displaying of more than one brand name on a product; the marketing of co-branded products or services. A co-branding arrangement with potential benefits to be gained for both sides.

Electrolytes: Sodium and potassium salts that are lost due to exercise and other causes. Sports drinks with electrolytes are used to replenish the body's water and electrolyte levels after dehydration caused by exercise, diaphoresis, diarrhea, vomiting, or starvation. Giving pure water to such a person is not the best way to restore fluid levels because it dilutes the salts inside the body's cells and interferes with their chemical functions.

Encroachment: The awarding of a new franchise or the opening of a company store too close to an existing franchise.

Extruded: The process wherein hot foods are forced through an extruder and they puff up when they hit cool air.

Fat (Dietary): There are five major types of dietary fats: saturated, unsaturated, polyunsaturated, monounsaturated, and partially hydrogenated vegetable oil. Saturated fats are saturated with hydrogen atoms. In the United States, they are mainly found in dairy products, meat, poultry, and vegetable shortenings made with coconut oil, palm oil, and/or palm kernel oil. Saturated fats can raise blood cholesterol levels, whereas unsaturated fats do not. Polyunsaturated fat molecules are missing hydrogen atoms. Sources of polyunsaturated fats corn oil, cottonseed oil, safflower oil, soybean oil, and sunflower oil as well as some fish oils, margarines, mayonnaise, almonds, and pecans. Monounsaturated fats are dietary fats with one double-bonded carbon in the molecule; they are commonly found in poultry, shortening, meat, dairy products, and olive and canola oils. Partially hydrogenated vegetable oils are harder and more stable than other oils. Companies mix them with hydrogen, which increases the amount of saturated fat and creates trans fat, which raises blood cholesterol.

Fondant: A sweet, creamy sugar paste used in making candies and icings. It is composed of gelatin, confectioner's sugar, and water. It is a very smooth and malleable icing that dries hard. Bonbons are candies that frequently have fondant fillings.

Franchise: The authorization granted to an individual or group by a company to sell its products or services in a particular area.

Junk food: Foods high in calories, fat, caffeine, sugar, and/or salt, with little nutritional value.

Maltose: A disaccharide composed of two glucose residues. It is used as a nutrient and sweetener, particularly in China, where historically it has been extracted from sorghum grass.

Nougat: A chewy or hard confection made from sugar or honey, nuts such as almonds, walnuts, or pistachio, and occasionally fruit. Flavorings are added to produce nougats with different tastes. Nougats are used in the manufacture of many confections, including 3 Musketeers candy bars.

Obesity: A chronic condition characterized by excessive body fat. There are several different methods of determining obesity. A man is considered obese when his weight is 20 percent or more above the maximum recommended weight for his height (25 percent for women). Another method is the Body Mass Index (BMI) method. This calculation is weight (kg) / height (meters) × height (meters).

QSR: Quick Service Restaurant is the term used by many as an alternative to the term *fast food*, which now has pejorative connotations.

Saccharin: An artificial sweetener invented by a graduate student at Johns Hopkins University in 1879. This became the foundation for the megacorporation Monsanto. The long-term safety of saccharin was challenged in 1977, and the FDA placed a moratorium on its use until more studies were conducted. The ban was lifted in 1991, but by that time virtually all diet soda production had shifted to using aspartame.

Sugar: Common table sugar is sucrose, which is a disaccharide made up of one molecule each of two other common monosaccharides: fructose and glucose. All three are simple carbohydrates, easily absorbed and converted by the body into energy. Sucrose is the most adaptable for culinary purposes and it has been used for hundreds of years as a preservative and sweetener. It is also used as an aid to the fermentation of beer and wine, and because it encourages yeast growth it has been used in baking. It is present in all green plants but exists in sufficient quantities to be viable for commercial extraction only in sugarcane and sugar beets. Sugar has no nutritional value (no minerals, vitamins, protein, or fiber) other than providing calories.

Tie-in: An association between two publicity campaigns in the form of a theme common to both, or an advertisement that appears in two different media.

Selected Bibliography

Alfino, Mark, John S. Caputo, and Robin Wynyard, eds. *McDonaldization Revisited: Critical Essays on Consumer Culture.* Westport, CT: Greenwood Press, 1998.

Amos, Wally, with Leroy Robinson. *The Famous Amos Story: The Face That Launched a Thousand Chips.* Garden City, NY: Doubleday, 1983.

Bernstein, Charles, and Ron Paul. *Winning the Chain Restaurant Game: Eight Key Strategies.* New York: John Wiley & Sons, 1994.

Boas, Max, and Steve Chain. *Big Mac: The Unauthorized Story of McDonald's.* New York: Mentor Books, The New American Library, 1977.

Bové, José, François Dufour, and Gilles Luneau. *The World Is Not for Sale: Farmers Against Junk Food.* New York: Verso, 2001.

Bowers, Q. David. *The Moxie Encyclopedia.* Vestal, NY: Vestal Press, 1985.

Brenner, Joël Glenn. *The Emperors of Chocolate: Inside the Secret World of Hershey & Mars.* New York: Broadway Books, 2000.

Broekel, Ray. *The Chocolate Chronicles.* Lombard, IL: Wallace-Homestead Book Company, 1985.

Broekel, Ray. *The Great America Candy Bar Book.* Boston: Houghton Mifflin Company, 1982.

Butko, Brian. *Klondikes, Chipped Ham & Skyscraper Cones: The Story of Isaly's.* Mechanicsburg, PA: Stackpole Books, 2001.

Cahn, William. *Out of the Cracker Barrel: From Animal Crackers to ZuZu's.* New York: Simon and Schuster, 1969.

Campos, Paul. *The Obesity Myth: Why America's Obsession with Weight Is Hazardous to Your Health.* New York: Gotham Books, 2004.

Carlson, Laurie Winn. *Cattle: An informal Social History*. Chicago: Ivan R. Dee, 2001.

Cartensen, Laurence W. "The Burger Kingdom: Growth and Diffusion of McDonald's Restaurant's in the United States, 1955–1978," in George O. Carney, ed., *Fast Food, Stock Cars, and Rock 'N' Roll: Place and Space in American Pop Culture.* Lanham, MD: Rowman & Littlefield Publishers, 1995.

Coe, Sophie D., and Michael D. Coe. *The True History of Chocolate.* New York: Thames and Hudson, Inc., 1996.

Cohen, Gerald Leonard, Barry Popik, and David Shulman. *Origin of the Term "Hot Dog."* Rolla, MO: G. Cohen, 2004.

Cohon, George. *To Russia with Fries.* Toronto: McFarlane, 1997.

Consumers Union Education Services. *Captive Kids: A Report on Commercial Pressures on Kids at School.* Yonkers, NY: Consumers Union, 1998.

Consumers Union Education Services. *Selling America's Kids: Commercial Pressures on Kids of the 90's.* Mount Vernon, NY: Consumers Union, 1990. Consumers Union Web site: www.consumersunion.org/other/sellingkids/index.htm

Conza, Tony. *Success: It's a Beautiful Thing: Lessons on Life and Business from the Founder of Blimpie International.* New York: Wiley, 2000.

Décasy, Gyula. *Hamburger for America and the World: A Handbook of the Transworld Hamburger Culture.* Volume 3 of the Transworld Identity Series. Bloomington, IN: EUROPA, European Research Association, 1984.

Ellis, Harry E. *Dr Pepper: King of Beverages Centennial Edition* (Dallas: Dr Pepper Company, 1986.

Emerson, Robert L. *Fast Food: The Endless Shakeout.* New York: Lebhar-Friedman Books, 1979.

Emerson, Robert L. *The New Economics of Fast Food.* New York: Van Nostrand Reinhold, 1990.

Enrico, Roger, and Jesse Kornbluth. *The Other Guy Blinked: How Pepsi Won the Cola Wars.* New York: Bantam, 1986.

Feldman, Stanley A., and Vincent Marks, eds. *Panic Nation: Unpicking the Myths We're Told about Food and Health.* London: Blake, 2005.

Funderburg, Anne Cooper. *Chocolate, Strawberry, and Vanilla: A History of American Ice Cream.* Bowling Green, OH: Bowling Green State University Popular Press, 1995.

Funderburg, Anne Cooper. *Sundae Best: A History of Soda Fountains.* Bowling Green, OH: Bowling Green State University Popular Press, 2002.

Gould, William. *Business Portraits: McDonald's.* Lincolnwood, IL: VGM Career Horizons, 1996.

Gupta, B. S., and Uma Gupta, eds. *Caffeine and Behavior: Current Views and Research Trends.* Boca Raton, FL: CRC Press, 1999.

Heimann, Jim. *Car Hops and Curb Service: A History of American Drive-In Restaurants, 1920–1960.* San Francisco: Chronicle Books, 1996.

Heller, Richard F., and Rachael F. Heller. *Carbohydrate-addicted Kids: Help Your Child or Teen Break Free of Junk Food and Sugar Cravings—for Life!* New York: HarperCollins, 1997.

Hendrickson, Robert. *The Great American Chewing Gum Book.* Radnor, PA: Chilton Book Company, 1976.

Henriques, Gary, and Audre DuVall. *McDonald's Collectibles: Identification and Value Guide.* Paducah, KY: Collector Books, nd.

Hirshorn, Paul, and Steven Izenour. *White Towers.* Cambridge, MA: MIT Press, 1979.

Hogan, David Gerard. *Selling 'em by the Sack: White Castle and the Creation of American Food.* New York: New York University Press, 1997.

Ingram, Billy. *All This from a 5-cent Hamburger! The Story of the White Castle System.* New York: Newcomen Society in North America, 1964.

Jacobson, Michael F. *Liquid Candy: How Soft Drinks are Harming Americans' Health.* 2nd ed. Washington, D.C.: Center for Science in the Public Interest, 2005.

Jacobson, Michael F., and Sarah Fritschner. *Fast-Food Guide.* 2nd ed. New York: Workman Publishing, 1991.

Jacobson, Michael F., and Bruce Maxwell. *What Are We Feeding Our Kids?* New York: Workman Publishing, 1994.

Jakle, John A., and Keith A. Sculle. *Fast Food: Roadside Restaurants in the Automobile Age.* Baltimore: Johns Hopkins University Press, 1999.

Kahn, E. J., Jr. *The Big Drink: The Story of Coca-Cola.* New York: Random House, 1960.

Kant, Ashima K. "Consumption of Energy-dense, Nutrient-poor Foods by Adult Americans: Nutritional and Health Implications. The Third National Health and Nutrition Examination Survey, 1988–1994," *American Journal of Clinical Nutrition* 72 (October, 2000):929–936.

Kincheloe, Joe L. *The Sign of the Burger: McDonald's and the Culture of Power.* Philadelphia: Temple University Press, 2002.

Kiple, Kenneth F., and Kriemhid Conee Ornelas, eds. *The Cambridge World History of Food.* Two vols. New York: Cambridge University Press, 2000.

Kroc, Ray, with Robert Anderson. *Grinding It Out: The Making of McDonald's.* Chicago: Henry Regnery Company, 1977.

Langdon, Philip. *Orange Roofs, Golden Arches: The Architecture of American Chain Restaurants.* New York: Knopf, 1986.

Leidner, Robin. *Fast Food, Fast Talk: Service Work and the Routinization of Everyday Life.* Berkeley, CA: University of California Press, 1993.

Levine, Ed. *Pizza: A Slice of Heaven. The Ultimate Pizza Guide and Companion.* New York: Universe Publishing, 2005.

Libal, Autumn. *Fats, Sugars, and Empty Calories: The Fast Food Habit.* Philadelphia: Mason Crest Publishers, 2005.

Losonsky, Joyce, and Terry Losonsky. *McDonald's Pre-Happy Meal Toys from the Fifties, Sixties, and Seventies.* Atglen, PA: Schiffer Publishing, 1998.

Losonsky, Terry, and Joyce Losonsky. *McDonald's Happy Meal Toys around the World.* Atglen, PA: Schiffer Publishing, 1995.

Louis, J. C., and Harvey Yazijian. *The Cola Wars: The Story of the Global Corporate Battle between the Coca-Cola Company and PepsiCo.* New York: Everest House, 1980.

Love, John F. *McDonald's Behind the Arches.* Revised and updated. New York: Bantam Books, 1995.

Martin, Milward W. *Twelve Full Ounces.* 2nd ed. New York: Holt, Rinehart and Winston, 1969.

Matz, Samuel A. *Snack Food Technology.* 3rd ed. New York: AVI Van Nostrand Reinhold, 1993.

McDonald, Ronald L. *The Complete Hamburger: The History of America's Favorite Sandwich.* Secaucus, NJ: Carol Publishing Group, 1997.

McDonald, Ronald L. *Ronald McDonald's Franchise Buyers Guide: How to Buy a Fast Food Franchise.* Philadelphia, PA: Xlibris, 2003.

McDonald, Ronald L. *Ronald McDonald's International Burger Book.* Tucson, AZ: Hats Off Books, 2004.

McLamore, James W. *The Burger King: Jim McLamore and the Building of an Empire.* New York: McGraw-Hill, 1998.

Mecuri, Becky. *American Sandwich: Great East from All 50 States.* Layton, UT: Gibbs Smith, 2004.

Mintz, Sidney. "Fast Food Nation: What the All-American Meal Is Doing to the World," *Times Literary Supplement,* September 14, 2001: 7–9.

Monaghan, Tom, with Robert Anderson. *Pizza Tiger.* New York: Random House, 1986.

Morton, Marcia, and Frederic Morton. *Chocolate: An Illustrated History.* New York: Crown Publishers, 1986.

Oliver, J. Eric. *Fat Politics: The Real Story Behind America's Obesity Epidemic.* New York: Oxford University Press, 2005.

Otis, Caroline Hall. *The Cone with the Curl on Top: Celebrating Fifty Years 1940–1990* Minneapolis, MN: International Dairy Queen, 1990.

Pendergrast, Mark. *For God, Country and Coca-Cola.* New York: Scribner's, 1993.

Perl, Lila. *Junk Food, Fast Food, Health Food: What America Eats and Why.* New York: Houghton Mifflin/Clarion Books, 1980.

Potter, Frank N. *The Moxie Mystique.* Virginia Beach, VA: Donning Company, 1981.

Pottker, Janice. *Crisis in Candyland: Melting the Chocolate Shell of the Mars Family Empire.* Bethesda, MD: National Press Books, 1995.

Redclift, Michael R. *Chewing Gum: The Fortunes of Taste.* New York: Routledge, 2004.

Richardson, Tim. *Sweets: A History of Candy.* New York: Bloomsbury, 2002.

Ritzer, George, ed., *McDonaldization: the Reader.* 2nd ed. (Thousand Oaks, CA: Pine Forge Press, 2006)

Ritzer, George. *The McDonaldization of Society.* Revised ed. Thousand Oaks, CA: Pine Forge Press, 1996.

Ritzer, George. *The McDonaldization Thesis: Explorations and Extensions.* Thousand Oaks, CA: Sage Publications, 1998.

Ritzer, George, and Elizabeth Malone. "Globalization Theory: Lessons from the Exportation of McDonaldization and the New Means of Consumption," *American Studies* 41 (Summer-Fall, 2000): 97–99.

Roden, Steve, and Dan Goodsell. *Krazy Kid's Food! Vintage Food Graphics.* Köln, Germany: Taschen, 2002.

Rodengen, Jeffrey L. *The Legend of Dr. Pepper/Seven-up.* Ft. Lauderdale, FL: Write Stuff Syndicate, 1995.

Rouch, Lawrence L. *The Vernor's Story: From Gnomes to Now.* Ann Arbor, MI: University of Michigan Press, 2003.

Royle, Tony. *Working for McDonald's in Europe: The Unequal Struggle?* New York: Routledge, 2001.

Royle, Tony, and Brian Towers. *Labour Relations in the Global Fast Food Industry.* New York: Routledge, 2002.

Rubin, Charles J., David Rollert, John Farago, Rick Stark, and Jonathan Etra. *Junk Food.* New York: Dell Publishing Company, 1980.

Santino, Jack. *New Old-Fashioned Ways: Holidays and Popular Culture.* Knoxville, TN: The University of Tennessee Press, 1996.

Schlosser, Eric. *Fast Food Nation: The Dark Side of the All-American Meal.* New York: Houghton Mifflin Company, 2001.

Schlosser, Eric and Charles Wilson. *Chew On This: Everything You Don't Want to Know about Fast Food* (Boston: Houghton Mifflin, 2006)

Seago, Alex. "Where Hamburgers Sizzle on an Open Grill Night and Day": Global Pop Music and Americanization in the Year 2000," *American Studies* 41 (Summer-Fall, 2000).

Seixas, Judith S. *Junk Food–What It Is, What It Does.* New York: Greenwillow Books, 1984.

Smart, Barry, ed. *Resisting McDonaldization.* Thousand Oaks, CA: Sage Publications, 1999.

Smith, Andrew F., ed. *Oxford Encyclopedia of Food and Drink in America.* New York: Oxford University Press, 2004.

Smith, Andrew F. *Peanuts: The Illustrious History of the Goober Pea.* Urbana, IL: University of Illinois Press, 2002.

Smith, Andrew F. *Popped Culture: The Social History of Popcorn in America.* Columbia, SC: University of South Carolina Press, 1999.

Smith, Andrew F. "Tacos, Enchiladas and Refried Beans: The Invention of Mexican-American Cookery," in Mary Wallace Kelsey and ZoeAnn Holmes, eds., *Cultural and Historical Aspects of Foods.* Corvallis, OR: Oregon State University, 1999, 183–203.

Snack Food Association. *Fifty Years: A Foundation for the Future.* Alexandria, VA: Snack Food Association, 1987.

Snack Food Association. *Who's Who in the Snack Food Industry.* Alexandria, VA: Snack Food Association, 1996.

Spitznagel, Eric. *The Junk Food Companion: The Complete Guide to Eating Badly.* New York: Plume/Penguin Group, 1999.

Spurlock, Morgan. *Don't Eat this Book: Fast Food and the Supersizing of America.* New York: G. P. Putnam's Sons, 2005.

Striffler, Steve. *Chicken: The Dangerous Transformation of America's Favorite Food.* New Haven: Yale University Press, 2005.

Talwar, Jennifer Parker. *Fast Food, Fast Track: Immigrants, Big Business, and the American Dream.* Boulder, CO: Westview Press, 2002.

Tannock, Stuart. *Youth at Work: The Unionized Fast-food and Grocery Workplace.* Philadelphia: Temple University Press, 2001.

Tennyson, Jeffrey. *Hamburger Heaven: The Illustrated History of the Hamburger.* New York: Hyperion, 1993.

Thomas, R. David. *Dave Says—Well Done! The Common Guy's Guide to Everyday Success.* Grand Rapids, MI: Zondervan, 1994.

Thomas, R. David. *Dave's Way: A New Approach to Old-fashioned Success.* New York: G. P. Putnam's Sons, 1991.

Thomas, R. David, and Michael Seid. *Franchising for Dummies.* Foster City, CA: IDG Books Worldwide, 2000.

Thorner, Marvin Edward. *Convenience and Fast Food Handbook.* Westport, CT, AVI Publishing Company, 1973.

The Twinkies Cookbook: An Inventive and Unexpected Recipe Collection. Berkeley: Ten Speed Press, 2006.

Untermeyer, Louis. *A Century of Candymaking 1847–1947: The Story of the Origin and Growth of New England Confectionery Company.* Boston: The Barta Press, 1947.

Vaccaro, Pamela J. *Beyond the Ice Cream Cone: The Whole Scoop on Food at the 1904 World's Fair.* St Louis, MO: Enid Press, 2004.

Vidal, John. *McLibel: Burger Culture on Trial.* New York: The New Press, 1997.

Volpe, Tina. *The Fast Food Craze: Wreaking Havoc on Our Bodies and Our Animals.* Kagel Canyon, CA: Canyon Publishing, 2005.

Watson, James L., ed. *Golden Arches East: McDonald's in East Asia.* Stanford, CA: Stanford University Press, 1997.

Weinberg, Bennett Alan, and Bonnie K. Bealer. *The World of Caffeine: The Science and Culture of the World's Most Popular Drug.* New York: Routledge, 2001.

Williams, Meredith. *Tomart's Price Guide to McDonald's Happy Meal Collectibles.* Revised and updated. Dayton, OH: Tomart Publications, 1995.

Winchell, Lawrence, ed. *Drive-In Management Guidebook.* New York: Harcourt Brace, 1968.

Yates, Donald, and Elizabeth Yates, eds. *American Stone Ginger Beer & Root Beer Heritage, 1790 to 1920; Written by Numerous Authors and Historians.* Homerville, OH: Donald Yates Publishers, 2003.

Yu, Er. "Foreign Fast Foods Gobble Up Chinese-Style Fast Foods," *Chinese Sociology & Anthropology* 31 (Summer, 1999): 80–87.

Resource Guide

CDs, DVDs, Films, and Videos

The Adventures of Fat Albert and the Cosby Kids. With Bill Cosby. Videorecording: Animation: Juvenile audience: DVD (85 min.) Alexandria, VA: Time-Life Video, 2002.

American Eats: History on a Bun. Hosted by Peter Schillinger, Alan Goldberg, and Pamela Wolfe, producer/writers. Atlas Media Corporation for the History Channel, 1999.

Biography. Ray Kroc, Fast Food McMillionaire. Written and produced by Greg Weinstein, History Television Productions, A&E Television Network, 1996.

Crayhon, Robert. *Junk Food Nation.* CD. R. Crayhon; Pennsauken, NJ: Manufactured and printed by Disc Makers, 1998.

Fast Food Survival Guide. VHS tape (22 min.), with a teaching guide. Lake Zurich, IL: Learning Seed, 2005.

The Future of Food. Deborah Koons Garcia, director/writer/producer. Documentary film. Distributor: Cinema Libre Studio, 2005.

How to Create a Junk Food. With Julia Child. VHS, with a teaching guide. Boston: WGBH. Released by Coronet, 1988.

Junk Food: Nothing to Snickers About. Cambridge Career Products; Cambridge Educational; Motion Masters Film & Video Production; Charleston, WV: Cambridge Educational, 1991.

Junk Food & Nutrition. With Phil Donahue. VHS (28 min.). Produced by Multi-media Entertainment, Inc. Princeton, NJ: Films for the Humanities & Sciences, Inc., 1988.

Junk Food Junkie: The Effects of Diet on Health. VHS (68 min.) Mt. Kisco, NY: Guidance Associates; Indianapolis, IN: distributed by the Indiana Department of Education, 1990.

Nikkel, Evelyn. *Junk Food vs. the Right Stuff.* VHS (Tape 1, 100 min.) Des Moines, IA: Iowa Dept. of Management, 2001.

Super Size Me. Dir. Morgan Spurlock. Goldwyn Films, 2004.

Vending Machine. A documentary film released by Fairie Films, which is an independent film company located in Aliso Viejo, California. The film examines the lives of teenagers who have been targeted by junk food and fast food manufacturers. The film focuses on nutrition and health issues. Web site: www.vendingmachinemovie.com

Organizations

Center for Science in the Public Interest (CSPI)
1875 Connecticut Avenue N.W., Number 300
Washington, D.C. 20009
Phone: (202) 332-9110
Fax: (202) 265-4954
Web site: www.cspinet.org

Nutritional Resource Foundation
P.O. Box 730
Manitowoc, WI 54221-0730
Phone: (920) 758-2500
E-mail: nrf@naturalovens.com
Web site: www.naturalovens.com

People for the Ethical Treatment of Animals (PETA)
501 Front Street
Norfolk, VA 23510
Web site: www.peta.org

Physicians Committee for Responsible Medicine
5100 Wisconsin Ave., N.W., Ste. 400,
Washington, D.C. 20016
Phone: (202) 686-2210
Web site: www.pcrm.org

Slow Food U.S.A.
Phone: (718) 260-8000
Web site: www.slowfoodusa.org

Web Sites

California Healthy Kids Resource Center, a project funded in part by the state Department of Education, maintains an impressive collection of health education materials for preschool through 12th grade.
www.hkresources.org

California Project LEAN. Funded in part by the California Department of Health Services. Under Bright Ideas, it maintains an inspiring array of successful examples of healthy eating and physical activity strategies in schools. Case studies include how the San Francisco Unified School District developed policies to rid schools of soda and junk food in 2003.
www.californiaprojectlean.org

CSPI nutrition site for children.
www.smart-mouth.org

Farm to School. Programs in each state connect schools with local farms to serve healthy meals and provide health and nutrition education, all the while supporting small, local farmers.
www.farmtoschool.org

Feingold Association of the United States Web site dedicated to helping youth and adults apply dietary techniques for better.
health.www.feingold.org

Food Is Elementary. Authored by Cornell-trained food education expert Antonia Demas, who teaches about food and nutrition.
www.foodstudies.org

McSpotlight Web site focusing on the legal issues surrounding the McLibel court case in the United Kingdom from the defendants point of view.
www.mcspotlight.org

No Junk Food A resource for those interested in promoting a healthier environment for youth.
www.nojunkfood.org

Nutrition.gov U.S. Dept. of Agriculture Web site which covers nutritional information.
www.nutrition.gov

Super Size Me Web site for Morgan Spurlock's film about the effects of eating fast food.
www.supersizeme.com/

Index

Note: Pages in **boldface** refer to the main entry on the subject.

A&W Root Beer, **1–2**; first drive-in, 81; franchising by, 106, 109; globalization, 6; locations, 160, 232; secret formulas, 241
Adams, Thomas, 121
Adams Confectionery, 31
Advantica Restaurant Group, Inc., 216
Advertising, **2–6**; Battle of the Burgers, 20; to children, 65–67, 100; Christmas and, 50–51; for Coca-Cola, 53, 54, 56–57; conformity and, 59–60; consumerism and, 60; for Cracker Jack, 67; for Doublemint gum, 288; fast food and, 99; Hershey's Company and, 132; for Jell-O, 143; for junk food, 145; for Little Caesar's Pizza, 141; for M&M's, 163; newspapers and, 196–97; obesity and, 202; packaging and, 207; patriotism in, 210; for Planters Peanuts, 189–90; radio and, 225–26; for Reese's Peanut Butter Cups, 227; for snack foods, 246; sports sponsorships, 253–54; on television, 267; in theaters, 267–68; for 7-Up, 56
AFC Enterprises, **6,** 51
African-American populations, 77
Agatston, Arthur, 74
Alderton, Charles, 79
All-Bran, 148
Allen, Roy, 1, 82, 241
Allied Breweries, 20
Allied Lyon, 20, 84
AllSport athletic drinks, 253
Almond Joy, 188, 191, 213, 244
Alpha Beta Food Markets, 258
Altrie, 152
Aluminum cans, 208, 249
American Beverage Association, 100
American Biscuit Manufacturing Company, 193
American Bottlers of Carbonated Beverages, 249
American Caramel Company, 35, 130, 133
American Cereal Company, 2
American Cookery (Simmons), 63
American Council for Fitness and Nutrition (ACFN), 100, 195
American Federation of Labor, 131
American Graffiti, 36, 102
American Home Products, 261
American Junk Food and Fast Food in other Countries, **6–8**
American Licorice Company, 156
American School Food Association, 238
American Securities Capital Partners, 216
Amos, Wally, 97, 181
Amos Chocolate Cookie Company, 97
Amstar, 78
Anaya, Ignacio, 193
Anderson, J. Walter "Walt," 89, 125, 181, 240, 284–85
Anderson, Pamela, 26
Anderson, Robert, 78, 181
Animal Biscuits, 63
Animal Rights Movement, **8,** 214, 223–24
Anti-unionization, **9**
Arby's, 7, **9–10,** 11, 41, 65, 99
Arcapita Inc., 51
Archer, Frank M., 188–89
Architecture and Design, **10–12,** 70. *See also* Signage
Artesian Manufacturing & Bottling Company, 79
Arthur Treacher's, **12–13,** 103
Aspartame, 54, 72, 122, 251
Atkins, Robert C., 74
Atomic Fireballs, 120

Atwater, Wilbur O., 73
Automats, Cafeterias, Diners, and Lunchrooms, **13–15,** 281
Automobiles, 10, **15–16**
Avery, Tex, 112
Axene, Harry, 69, 265
Ayala, Anna, 156

Baby Ruth, 3, **17–18,** 34, 49
The Baby Ruth Hour, 18
Baci, 48
Baer Group, 97
Baker, I. L., 96
Baker, James, 33
Baker, Walter, 49, 129
Bakery and Confectionery Workers International Union, 131
Bakery Snacks, **18–19**
Baldassare, Angelo, 23, 255
Barber, Benjamin, 177
Bar codes, 209
Barnard, Neal D., 214
Barnum's Animals, 63
Barq, Edward Charles Edmond, 19
Barq's Root Beer, **19,** 232
Barrett Foods, 113
Baskin, Burt, 19
Baskin-Robbins, **19–20,** 98, 140
Bass Brothers Enterprises, 97
Battle, E. K., 265
Battle of the Burgers, **20**
Baumann, Emil, 270
Beatrice Foods Company, 52, 153, 185
Beef Jerky, **20**
Beeman, Edward, 121
Bell, Glen, 263, 287
Ben & Jerry's, **20–21,** 25, 140
Bent, Joshua, 62
Bent's water-crackers, 62
Berkshire Hathaway, Inc, 34, 70
Bertie Bott's Every Flavour Beans, 121, 144
Beverages, **21–22**
Bib-Label Lithiated Lemon-Lime Soda, 241
Big Boy, **22–23,** 125, 168
Big Drum, Inc., 83
Big Gulp, 241
Big M, 153
Big Mac, 174
Big Wheels, 18
Birdseye, Clarence, 61
Bit-O-Honey, **23**
Black Horse Pastry Company, 212
Blimpie International, Inc., **23–24,** 160, 255
Blue Bell Creameries, **24,** 92, 139, 140
Blumenthal Chocolate Company, 49
Bob's Big Boy, 23, 125, 222
Bob's Candies, Inc, 50
Boca Burgers, 280
Born, Samuel, 146, 160
Born Sucker Machine, 160
Boston Market, **24**
Bové, José, 117, 281
Bovine Growth Hormone (BGH), 21, **24–25**
Bovine spongiform encephalitis (BSE), 164
Bowman, Charles, 226
Boycotts, **25–26,** 223–24
Bozo's Circus, 4
Brach, Emil J., 33
Bradham, Caleb D., 53, 212
Bradley Smith Company, 160
Brad's Drink, 212
Breakfast Fast Foods, **26–27**
Breisch-Hine Company, 35, 130
Brenham Creamery Company, 24, 139
Breyer, William A., 27
Breyers, **27,** 140
Bridgforth, Bill, 188
Brock, Robert L., 51
Brock, William E., 33
Brock Candy Company, 33
Brown, John Y., 89, 149, 237
Brownell, Kelly, 265, 266
Bubbas Bubblegum, 31
Bubble gum, 122
Bubble Yum!, 34, 133
Buck, Peter, 256
Bugles, **27**
Burger Chef, 127, 182
Burger King, **27–28**; acquisitions, 99; architecture of, 12; Battle of the Burgers, 20; breakfast menus, 26; drive-thru operation, 82; egg fast food, 87; hamburgers, 126; King Size, 259; locations, 159; mascot, 168–69; menus, 182; movie tie-ins, 369; overseas boycott of, 25; pricing, 222; protests over, 223–24; slogans, 244; sports sponsorships, 254; training, 272
Burns, Matthew, 27
Burt, Harry, 119–20
Bushnell, Nolan, 51
Butterfinger, **28–29,** 34, 49

Cacao, 46–47
The Cactus and Randy Show, 4
Cadbury, **31**; acquisitions, 188, 213, 291; chocolate confections, 48; Schweppes and, 239; secret formulas, 240; Valentine's Day candy, 279
Cadbury, John, 31
Cadbury Beverages, Inc., 2
Cadbury Schweppes, **31**; A&W Beverages and, 2; acquisitions, 80, 134, 204, 223, 241, 242; lawsuit, 242; pricing, 223
Cade, Robert, 252

Cafeterias, 14
Caffeine, **31–32,** 46, 250
Cajun Kitchen, 220
Calcium, 197
California Pizza Kitchen, **32**
Callebaut, Barry, 34
Campbell Soup Company, 212
Canada Dry, 31, 32
Canada Dry Ginger Ale, **32–33**
Candy, **33–35**
Candy floss, 96
Candy Gulp, 43
Canning, Franklin V., 121
Caramels, **35,** 49
Carbohydrates, **35–36,** 197, 256–58
Carhops, 11, **36–37,** 81, 252, 275
Carl Karcher Enterprises, Inc., 37, 147
Carlow, Michael, 52
Carl's Jr., 26, **37,** 129
Carney, Dan, 214
Carney, Frank, 214
Carvel, Thomas, 140, 159, 272
Carvel College of Ice Cream Knowledge, 37, 272
Carvel Corporation, **37–38,** 108, 140, 272
Cellophane, 208
Center for Nutrition Policy and Promotion, 104
Center for Science in the Public Interest (CSPI), **38**; Ben & Jerry's and, 21; on fat consumption, 218; on food labeling, 235; lobbying by, 159; on nutrition in schools, 66; "Save Harry" campaign, 135; on soft drinks, 250; on sugar consumption, 258
Centers for Disease Control (CDC), 104, 201
Cereals (Breakfast), **38–40**
Chains, **40–41**
Chandler, Asa, 53
Channel One, 238
Chanukah Candy, **41**
Charities, **41–42,** 230–31
Charles E. Hires Co., 134, 204
Charles N. Miller Company, 168
Charms Company, 271
Chattanooga Bakery, 188
Cheese-based Snacks, **42,** 113
Cheetos, **42–43**
Cheez-It crackers, 42, 64, 148
Chef America, 196
Cheng, Andrew, 210
Chero-Cola, 53, 233
Chewy Candy, **43**
Chicken, **43–44,** 95
Chicken Delight, 6, **44–45,** 108, 244
Chicken McNuggets, **45–46,** 149, 174
Chicken on the Run, 219
Children: advertising to, 5–6, 100, 173–74, 250; obesity in, 202
Chipper, Bervie, 70
Chips Ahoy!, **46**
Chittenden, Russell, 73
Chocolate, 22, 33–34, 41, **46–47,** 85, 221
Chocolate Chip Cookies, **47–48**
Chocolate Confections, **48–49**
Chocolate Cup Cakes, 18
Chocolate Manufacturers Association, 194
Cholesterol, **50**
Christmas, **50–51**
Chuck E. Cheese Pizza, **51**
Church, George K., Sr., 51
Church's Chicken, 7, **51–52,** 98, 220
Cinnabon, **52**
Clabir Corporation, 150
Clark, David, 52
Clark Bar, 34, 47, **52**
Classic Caramel Company, 35
Clostridium perfringens, 104
Coca-Cola Company, **53–56**; acquisitions, 19, 134; advertising, 4, 250; boycott of, 25; charitable foundation, 42; Cola Wars, 56–57; collectibles, 57; diet sodas, 72; franchising by, 106; Gatorade, 253; globalization, 6, 117; holiday labels, 50–51; introduction of, 249; patriotism in, 210; pricing, 222–23; secret formulas, 240; slogans, 243; sponsorships, 253
Cod, 103
Cohen, Ben, 20
Cohon, George, 181
Cola, **56**
Cola Wars, **56–57**
Colgan, John, 121
Collectibles and Americana, **57–58**
Collins, James, 172
Colonel Sanders, 16, 89, 112, 148–49, 169, 180
Colorado Milling and Elevator Co., 242
Columbia Pictures, 134
Columbian Exposition, Chicago, 96
ConAgra Foods, 20, 219, 227, 261
Condiments, **59,** 126, 136, 235
Conformity, **59–60**
Consolidated Foods Corporation, 211, 220
Consumerism, **60**
Continental Baking Company, 18, 135, 273
Controversies, **60**
Convenience Foods/Drinks, **60–62**
Conza, Tony, 23, 181, 255
Cookies and Crackers, **62–64**
Cool Kids, 146
Copeland, Al, 149, 219
Cores, Arthur, 24
Corn Chips, **64**

Corn syrup, high-fructose, 251, 258
Corporate Concentration, **64–65**
Corporate Sponsorships and Programs in Schools, **65–67**
Cotton candy, 96
Country Time, 221
Coupons, 57
Cracker Jack, **67**; advertising, 3, 5; collectibles and Americana, 57–58; contents, 217, 271; coupons, 57; Frito-Lay and, 113; globalization, 6, 117; introduction, 96; packaging, 207; patriotism, 210; trademark for, 3
Cramer, Keith G., 27, 89, 172, 186
Crane, Clarence, 156
Crime, **67–68,** 142, 202, 281–82
Cronk, W. F., 80
Crosse & Blackwell, 196
Crum, George, 220
Crush International, 134
Crystal Light, 221
Curtiss Candy Company, 17, 28–29
Cyclamates, 72

Dad's Old-Fashioned Root Beer, 232
Dairy Queen, **69–70**; franchising by, 107; globalization, 6, 7; launch of, 98, 140; locations, 160; Slurpees and, 245
Davis, Fletcher, 124
DeCarlo, Peter, 23, 255
Deep-fried Mars Bars and Twinkies, **70–71,** 274
Del Monte Corporation, 150
Del Taco, **71,** 82
Delacre Company, 212
Delligati, Jim, 87
Delmonico brothers, 139
DeLuca, Frederick, 255, 256
DeNovo Corporation, 265
Denton, Camilla, 181
Dentyne, 31
Dewar, Jimmy, 273
Dexatrim, 75
Diabetes, 36, **71,** 201, 251
Diemer, Walter E., 122
Dietary Guidelines for Americans, 236
Diet Rite Cola, 72, 233, 250
Diet Soda, **71–73**
Dieting, **73–75,** 202
DiGiorno's pizza, 114, 152
Diners, 14
Ding Dongs, 18
Dips, **75–76**
Disclosure, **76–77,** 108
Discrimination, **77**
Dixie Wax Paper Company, 208
D. L. Clark Company, 52, 185
Doctor's Associates, Inc., 256
Doherty, James C., 92
Dolly Madison line, 18
Domino's Pizza, 41, 66, **77–78,** 99, 187
Don't Eat this Book (Spurlock), 260
Doolin, Elmer, 64, 113
Doritos, 64, **78,** 184
Doublemint Gum, 288
Doughnuts, **78–79**. *See specific doughnut brands*
Dove Bar, **79,** 140, 168
Dows, Gustavus D., 251
Dr Pepper, **79–80**; A&W Beverages and, 2; Cola Wars, 56–57; collectibles and Americana, 57; diet, 72; introduction of, 249; merger, 241; slogans, 243
Drake, Newman E., 18
Drake's Cakes, 18
Dreyer's/Edy's Ice Cream, **80**
Drive-ins, 10, 36, **80–82**
Drive-thrus, 16, **82–83**
Drumsticks, **83,** 140
Dryer's, 196
Dunkin' Donuts, 6–7, 26, 66, **83–84,** 98, 244

Eades, Michael R., 74
Easter Candy, **85–86**
Eat Your Heart Out (Hightower), 169
Edgerton, David R. Jr., 27–28, 89
Edy, Joseph, 80
Efficiency, **86**
Egg Fast Food, **86–87**
Egg McMuffin, 174
Elderly, **87**
Elias Brothers, 23
Employment, **87–89,** 92, 175–76, 187
Encroachment, 108–9
Entenmann, William, 19
Entrepreneurs, **89–90**
Environment, **90,** 176, 223–24, 260–61
Environmental Defense Fund, 260–61
Epperson, Frank, 220
Epsicles, 220
Escherichia coli, **90–91,** 104, 105, 180
Eskimo Pie, 24, 34, **91–92**
ET, The Extra-Terrestrial, 3–4, 102, 132, 134
Exploitation, **92**
Exposés, **92–93,** 101
Extra Sugarfree Gum, 288
Extruded Snacks, 42, **93**

Factory Farming, **95**
Fahnestock, Samuel, 248, 251
Fair Food, **95–96**
F. A. Martoccio Company, 211
Famous Amos, 63, **97**
Farley's & Sathers Candy Co., 43, 50
Farrell's Ice Cream Parlours, 165

Fast Food, **97–100**
Fast Food and Snack Food Associations, **100–101**
Fast Food Nation (Schlosser), **101**; on advertising to children, 250; film, 102; on foodborne illnesses, 104; on McDonald's fries, 111; publication, 93; on suppliers, 260; on unionization, 9
Fat Boy, 22–23
Fats, **101,** 197
Federal Trade Commission, 76–77, 108
Feltman, Charles, 136, 194, 254
Fernando's Foods Corporation, 20
Ferrara Pan Candy Company, 120, 128
Fiddle Faddle, 261
Fields, Debra "Debbi," 181, 190
Filler, Isadore J., 64
Film, **101–3**
Fish and Chips, **103**
Fish as Fast Food, **103**
Flagstar, 216
Flax, Larry, 32
Fobes, Daniel, 254
FOCUS Brands, 38
Fogle, Jared, 256
Food and Drug Administration, U. S., 179
Food Manufacturer's, Inc., 163, 165
Food Pyramid, **103–4,** 198, 216
Food Safety and Inspection System (FSIS), 105, 276
Foodborne Illnesses, 60, 87, **104–5,** 215, 235
Foodmaker, Inc., 143
Fortune Cookies, **105**
Foster, George, 105
Fosters Freeze, **105–6**
Franchising, 40–41, 98, **106–8,** 125, 172–73
Frankenfoods, 116
Franklin, Benjamin, 248
Franklin's Crunch 'n Munch, 261
Freedent Gum, 288
French Fries, **109–12,** 231
Fresca, 72
Fried Chicken, **112**
Frito Bandito, **112,** 114, 169
Frito-Lay, **112–13**; acquisition by PepsiCo, 212; advertising to children, 5; Big Grab size, 259; cheese-based snacks, 42–43, 78; corn chips, 64; lawsuit, 155; mascot, 169; Oh Boy! snacks, 20; patriotism, 210; Wow! line, 74
Frito-Lay Corn Chips, **113–14**
Fritos, 61, 64, 112, 113–14, 184, 210, 241
Frosted Flakes, 148
Frozen Drumstick Company, 83
Frozen Pizza, **114,** 214
Fruit Smack, 151
Frusen Glaje, 123
Fudge, 49
The Future of Food, 102
F. W. Rueckheim & Brother, 96, 254–55

Galardi, John, 82, 136, 287
Galardi Group Franchise & Leasing, 287
Galardi Group, Inc., 265
Garbage Pail Kids, 122
Gardner, James Carson, 128
Gatorade, 253
General Foods Corporation, **115**; acquisitions, 143, 264; Bugles, 27; convenience foods from, 61; origins of, 39
General Mills, 39, 40, **115,** 225
Genetically Modified Organisms (GMOs), **115–16,** 176–77, 281–82
Gentile, Anthony, 189
George F. Chester Seed Company, 226
George H. Ruth Candy Co., 17
George Weston Bakeries, 19
Ghirardelli, 34
Ghirardelli, Domingo, 49
Gibson, John, 4
Ginger Ale, **116,** 249
Gino's chain, 165
Girl Scout Cookies, 63, **116–17**
Globalization, **117–19**; of Coca-Cola, 55; of fast food establishments, 99; of Hershey's, 132; of Kentucky Fried Chicken, 149; of Mars, Inc., 168; of McDonald's, 174–75; menu changes and, 183; of popcorn, 219; of Popeyes, 220; protests and, 223–24, 281–82
Goelitz, Gustav, 144
Gold, Edward Vale, 125, 287
Gold Bond Ice Cream Company, 220
Gold Medal Flour, 115
Golden Arches East (Watson), 170, 175
Goldfish, 42, **119,** 155
Goldstein, Oscar, 4, 230
Goobers, 49
Good & Plenty, 34, **119,** 156
Good Humor, **119–20**
The Good Humor Man, 102, 120
Graham, Sylvester, 120
Graham Crackers, 62, 63, **120**
Grandma's brand cookies, 113
Granola, 39
Green, Adolphus, 193
Green, Robert, 185
Greenfield, Jerry, 20
Greenpeace, 178
Grigg, Charles Leiper, 241, 249
Grigg, F. Nephi, 265
Grigg, Golden, 265
Gross-out Candy, **120–21**
Guacamole, 75

100,000,000 Guinea Pigs (Kallet), 93, 124–25
Gum, **121–22,** 208
Gummi/Gummy Candy, 43
Guth, Charles, 212

Häagen-Dazs, 21, **123,** 140
Haas, Eduard, 213
Hackbarth, Ed, 71
Halajian, Peter Paul, 213
Hall, Jeanette, 36
Halloway Company, 185
Halloween, **123–24**
Halls, 31
Hamburger University, 173, 272
Hamburgers, 20, 117, **124–27**
Handwerker, Nathan, 136, 194
Happier Meals (Nierenberg), 93
Happy Meal, 5, **127–28,** 174, 209
Hard Candy, **128**
Hardart, Frank, 14
Hardee, Wilbur, 128
Hardee's, **128–29,** 147, 160
Hardtack, 62
Haribo, 43
Harkin, Tom, 239
Harmon, Pete, 148, 236
Harvey, Frederick Henry, 40
Hatcher, Claud A., 41–42, 53, 233
Hawaiian Punch, 31
Hay, William H., 73
H. B. Reese Candy Company, 34, 131, 227
Health Concerns, **129**
Heide, Henry, 43
Hemolytic uremic syndrome (HUS), 90
Henry Heide Candy Company, 43, 133
Herman Goelitz Candy Company, 144
Hershey, Milton S., 34, **129-30**; caramel manufacture, 35; charitable contributions, 41; entrepreneurship, 89; ideal community, 87–88; Mounds Bar and, 188; production of chocolates, 47
Hershey Chocolate Company, 49, 96
Hershey Company, **130–33**; acquisitions, 34, 43, 119, 291; advertising, 3; patriotism, 210; PayDay and, 211
Hershey's Chocolate Bar, **133,** 155
Heston, William, 38
Heublein Company, 149
Hightower, Jim, 59, 169
Highway Beautification Act of 1965, 243
Hines, Duncan, 236
Hires, Charles E., 133, 134, 204, 232, 249
Hires Root Beer, **133–34,** 204, 232, 249
Hirsch, Samuel, 155
Hirshfield, Leo, 271
H. J. Heinz Company, 24, 111, 150, 263, 265
Ho Jo, Jr., 107
Hokey-Pokies, 220
Holahan, John, 40
Hollywood Brands, Inc., 211
Hollywood, Movie Tie-ins, and Celebrity Endorsements, **134–35**
Homemade Ice Cream Company, 69
Honey Nut Cheerios, 40
Hong Kong Noodle Company, 105
Horlick, William, 185
Horn, Joseph, 14
Horton, J. M., 139
Horton, Tim, 79
Horton Ice Cream Company, 139
Host Marriott Corporation, 165
Hostess, 18, **135–36,** 274
Hot Dog, **136–37,** 254
Hot Tamales, 120
Howard Johnson chain, 165
Howdy Corporation, 241, 242
Howell, Clayton J., 204
Hubba Bubble bubble gum, 288
Hulman, Tony, 226
Hunt Brothers Packing Company, 150
Hunt-Wessen, 227
Hurtz, Gene, 1
Hydrox Cookies, 63, 147
Hyperactivity, **137**

Ice Cream, 139, **139–41,** 224
Ice Cream sodas. *See* Milk Shakes, Malts, and Ice Cream Sodas
Iconography. *See* Mascots, Logos, and Icons
Ilitch, Mike, **141,** 157
Imasco, 128, 233
Industrial Luncheon Services, 83
Ingram, Edgar Waldo "Billy," 89, 106, 125, 180, 275, 284–85
Ingram-White Castle Foundation, 41
Injury, **142**
In-N-Out Burger, 82, 88, 111–12, **141–42,** 183
Interstate Brands Corporation (IBC), 18, 135–36
I-Scream Bar, 91
Islay Dairy Company, 150
Italian Beef Sandwiches, 255

Jack in the Box, **143**; breakfast menus, 26; drive-thru operation, 82; *E. coli* outbreak, 91; egg fast food, 87; franchising agreements and, 108; hamburgers, 126; launch of, 98; pricing, 222
Jackson, James C., 39
Jacmar Companies, 242
Jacobs Suchard Company, 270
Jacobson, Michael F., 38, 235–36, 266

James O. Welch Company, 145, 160
Jell-O, **143–44**
Jelly Beans, **144**
Jelly Belly Candy Company, 144
Jelly Belly Company, 121
Jenny Craig, 74
Jerrico, Inc., 160
J. Hungerford Smith Company, 1
Jihad vs. McWorld (Barber), 177
J. L. Kraft & Brothers, 151
J. Lyons & Co., Ltd., 20
Joe Lowe Company, 220
John E. Marshall Company, 220, 245
Johnson, Howard, 106–7, 140
Johnson, Nancy, 139
Johnson, Sherwood, 242
Johnson Patent Ice-Cream Freezer, 139
Jones, Vess, 241
Joseph S. Fry & Sons, 31, 48
Judson, Stuart, 210
Juicy Fruit gum, 288
Jujubes, 43
Jung, Baker David, 105
The Jungle (Sinclair), 92, 124, 179
Junior Mints, **145**
Junk Foods, **145–46**
Just Born, 85, 144, **146,** 185

Kahala Group, 24
Kallet, Arthur, 93, 124–25
Kandy Kate, 17
Karcher, Carl N., 37, **147,** 172, 181
Keebler, **147–48,** 169
Keebler, Ernie, 147
Keebler, Godfrey, 147
Keebler Company, 97
Keebler Foods, 63
Kellogg, John Harvey, 39, 148
Kellogg, Will K., 39, 148
Kellogg Company, 27, 97, 147, **148,** 217
Kentucky Fried Chicken (KFC), **148–49**; acquisition by PepsiCo, 213; architecture of, 11–12; boycott of, 26; drive-thru operations, 83; fried chicken, 112; globalization, 6–7, 7; Harland Sanders and, 237; launch of, 98; mascot, 169; menus, 183; packaging, 209; PETA and, 261; pricing, 222; protests against, 282; slogans, 244; sports sponsorships, 254
Ketchup, **149–50**
Kirby, J. G., 80, 106
Kirsch, Hyman, 71–72
Kirsch Beverages, 72, 116, 250
Kit Kat bar, 131, 232
Klein, Steven, 41
Klondike Bar, 91, **150–51**
Knight, Carolyn B., 181
Knox, Charles B., 143
Koch, Otto, 45
Koerner, John, 10
Kolow, Steven, 24
Kool-Aid, 22, **151,** 221, 264
Korn Kurls, 42, 93
Krackel, 131
Kraft, James L., 151
Kraft Foods, **151–52**; acquisitions, 114, 157, 205, 264, 270–71; DiGiorno's pizza and, 114; Nabisco merger, 193; ownership of, 152
Kraft-Phenix Cheese Corporation, 152
Krispy Kreme, 19, **152**
Kroc, Ray, **152–53**; on advertising, 4; Dairy Queen and, 70; entrepreneurship, 89; McDonald's and, 107, 126, 172; memoirs, 180–81; Sonneborn and, 265
Kruppenbacher, William, 167

Labeling, 209, 235–36
Labor unions, 8
LaLanne, Jack, 73
Lancaster Caramel Company, 130, 133
LaPlante, Bruce, 86
Lawsuits, **155–56,** 180, 216
Lay, Herman W., 64, 112–13, 114
Lazenby, Robert S., 79–80
Leaf, Inc., 211
Leaf North America, 34, 133
Leahy, Patrick, 66
Lehmann, Johann Martin, 96, 129
Lemonheads, 120
Lewis, Tillie, 73
Libby's, 196
Licorice, **156**
Liebeck, Stella, 155
LifeSavers, **156–57,** 289
Liggett, Roberts, 23
Lincoln Snacks, 261
Lindt, Rodolphe, 48
Lippert, Albert, 74
Lippincott, Charles, 95
Liquid Candy (CSPI), 250, 258
Listeria monocytogenes, 104
Little Brownie Bakers, 63
Little Caesar's Pizza, 141, **157–58,** 169, 187
Little Debbie, 19, 158, 169
Lobbying, **158–59,** 195
Locations, **159–60**
Loft Candy Company, 41, 212
Lollipops and Suckers, 128, **160**
Long John Silver's, 2, **160–61**
Loose-Wiles Biscuit Company, 63
Lowney, Walter M., 49, 130
Lucky Charms, 40
Lunchrooms, 13

M&M's, 3, **163–64,** 244
Mad Cow Disease, **164,** 179
Maggi, 196
Make-A-Wish Foundation, 41
Malin, Joseph, 103
Malted milk, 185
Malts. *See* Milk Shakes, Malts, and Ice Cream Sodas
Mann, Pearl, 158
Mansfield Pure Milk Company, 150
Maranz, Leo, 265
Marathon Bars, 248
Marchiony, Italo, 139
Mariana, Vin, 53
Marriott, J. Willard, 106, 164–65
Marriott Corporation, 23, **164–65,** 233
Mars, Forrest, 6, 117, 163, **165–66**
Mars, Frank, 49, 89, **166,** 186, 247
Mars, Inc., **166–68**; advertising, 3; Food Manufacturer's, Inc. and, 165; globalization, 6, 117; ice cream bars, 140; M&M's and, 163; 3 Musketeers and, 269; patriotism, 210, 211; research facilities, 47; Rowntree and, 232; Universal Studios and, 134
Marshmallow Peeps, 146
Martin, Clovis, 255
Martin, John, 264
Martin Brothers Grocery, 255
Martinez, Mariano, 245
Martoccio, Frank, 211
Mary Jane Candies, 34, **168**
Mascots, Logos, and Icons, 100, **168–69**
Massy, Jack, 89, 149, 237
Mattus, Reuben, 123
Maxwell, Brian, 222
Maxwell, Jennifer, 222
Mayer, Oscar, 136
McCullough, H. A. "Alex," 69
McCullough, John F., 69
McDonald, Maurice, 81, 89, 125, 136, 170
McDonald, Richard, 81, 89, 125, 136, 170
McDonaldization, 59, 86, **169–70**
The McDonaldization of Society (Ritzer), 169, 177
McDonaldization Revisited (eds. Alfino, Caputo and Wynyard), 170
McDonald's, **170–78**; advertising, 4, 267; animal rights decisions, 8; Battle of the Burgers, 20; Boston Market and, 24; breakfast menus, 26; Chicken McNuggets, 45–46, 149; collectibles and Americana, 58; design of, 11, 12, 81, 83; egg fast food, 87; Fillet-O-Fish, 103; franchising by, 107; French fries profit, 110; globalization, 7, 117; Happy Meals, 271–72; labor unions and, 9; launch of, 98; lawsuit, 155; locations, 159, 239; mascot, 169; McLean, 74; menus, 182, 183; movie tie-ins, 369; pricing, 222; product placement, 134, 135; protests against, 223–24, 281–82; Ray Kroc and, 153–54; secret formulas, 240; self-service model, 36–37; slogans, 244; sponsorships, 253; supersizing and, 259; suppliers, 260–61; training, 272; uniforms, 275
McKee, O. D., 158
McKee Bakery Company, 19
McKee Foods, 158, 169
McKeesport Candy Company, 213
McLamore, James, 27–28, 89, 181
McLaughlin, John J., 32
McLibel, 156, **178–79**
Meatpacking Industry, 142, **179–80,** 203
Mecca Cola, 55
Meehan, Michael J., 120
Megarel, Roy C., 212
Memoirs, **180–82,** 237
Menus, **182–83**
Mexican Food, **184–85**
Microwave ovens, 61
Mike and Ike, 146, **185**
Milk, 22, 25
Milk Duds, **185**
Milk Shakes, Malts, and Ice Cream Sodas, 27, **185–86**
Milky Way, 165, 167, **186**
Millennium Time Capsule, 274
Miller, Charles N., 168
Mills, F. W., 280
Mills, H. S., 280
Milton Hershey Industrial School, 133
Milton Hershey School, 41
Minimum Wage, **187**
Minneapolis Mill Company, 115
Mint Products Company, 157
Minute Maid, 61
Miracle Insta Machines, 186
Mister Donut, 84
Mitchell, Earl, Sr., 188
Molasses, 257
Monaghan, James, 77
Monaghan, Thomas S., 77, **187,** 214
Monarch Company, 189
Monsanto Company, 116
Moon Pie, 18, **188**
Moore, William, 193
Morris, Dave, 156, 178–79
Morrison, Wade, 79
Mott, H. R., 233
Motts, 31
Mounds Bar, **188,** 213
Mountain Dew, 72, **188,** 212, 243
Moxie, **188–89,** 249

Mr. Goodbar, 131
Mr. Peanut, 169, **189–90**
Mrs. Fields Cookies, 63, **190**
Muckrakers, 92
Munchkin Bottling Company, 5
Murrie, Bruce, 165, 167
Murrie, William, 89, 131
Music, **190–91**
MyPyramid, 104

Nabisco, **193**; acquisitions, 18, 145, 203; Chips Ahoy!, 46; cookie output of, 63; formation of, 62; Graham Crackers, 120; lawsuit, 155; Oreos and, 205; Ritz Crackers, 62. *See also* National Biscuit Company
Nachos, 96, 184, **193–94**
Nadaff, George, 24
Nathan's Famous, 98, 136, **194**
National Biscuit Company, 3, 62, 120, 193, 229. *See also* Nabisco
National Confectioners Association, 100, 124, 158, **194–95,** 244
National Fast Food Corporation, 13
National Restaurant Association, 100
Naugules, 71
Nehi Corporation, 233
Neighborhoods, **195**
Neil, Florence E., 116
Nelson, Christian, 34, 91
Nelson-Mustard Cream Company, 91
Nestlé: acquisitions, 18, 23, 83, 203, 233; boycott of, 25; Butterfinger and, 28–29; chocolate, 48; secret formulas, 240
Nestlé, Henri, 48, 195
Nestlé SA, **195–96**
New England Confectionery Company (NECCO), 128, **196**; acquisitions, 34, 52, 168, 185; Fobes and, 254; Valentine's Day candies, 279
Newspapers, **196–97**
Nidetch, Jean, 74
Nierenberg, Danielle, 93
Nobel, Edward, 157
No-Cal, 72
North American Free Trade Agreement (NAFTA), 118, 132
NutriSystem Weight Loss, 74
Nutrition, **197,** 209, 215–16, 223–24, 256–58
Nutrition Labeling and Education Act (NLEA), 129
Nutritional Guidelines, **198**
Nuts, **198–99**

Oberto Sausage Company, 20
Obesity, **201–2**; Americanization and, 118; children and, 239; diets and, 74–75; junk food and, 145; politics of, 215; soft drinks and, 251; supersizing and, 260; taxing snack foods and, 265–66; trends, 129
Obici, Amedeo, 189
Occupational Safety and Health Administration (OSHA), 68, 180, **202–3**
O'Connell, Daniel J., 286
Oh Boy! snacks, 20
Oh Henry!, 49, **203–4**
Old El Paso, 75
Olestra (Olean), 75, 155, 223
Oltz, Harry M., 69
Onion Rings, **204**
Open Kettle, 83
OrangeCo, 13
Orange Crush, **204**
Orangina, 31
Ore-Ida, 111, 265
Oreos, 63, **205**
Ornish, Dean, 74
Ortega, 75
Oscar Mayer Wienermobile, 136
Oudt, John, 10
Ovaltine, 221, 225

Pace, Dave, 75
Pace Foods, 75
Packaging, 60–61, **207–9,** 221, 246–47, 283
Painter, William, 208, 249
Palmer Chocolates, 85
Panda Express, **210**
Pappe, Charlie, 252
Parker, J. T. "Stubby," 83, 140
Patriotism, **210–11**
Patton, Thomas, 96
PayDay, **211**
P. C. Wiest Company, 130
P. D. Saylor and Associates, 32
Pemberton, John Stith, 53, 56
Pemberton's French Wine Coca, 53
Pendergast Candy Company, 167
Penny Candy, **211**
People for the Ethical Treatment of Animals (PETA), 8, 261
Pepperidge Farm, 42, 119, 155, **211–12**
PepsiCo, 212–13; acquisitions, 41, 99, 113, 149, 188, 215, 263; advertising, 4–5; charitable foundation, 41; Cola Wars, 56–57; globalization, 6; pricing, 222–23; slogans, 243; sports sponsorships, 253
Pepsi-Cola, 53, 57
Pepsi-Cola Company, 212
Perkins, Edwin, 22, 151
Perkins Products Company, 22, 151
Pernod Ricard, 20, 84
Peruzzi, Mario, 189
Peter, Daniel, 48

Peter Paul Candy Company, 34, 132, 188, 191, **213,** 291
Peters, Lulu Hunt, 73
Peterson, Robert O., 143
PEZ, **213**
Pfefferminze, 213
Phenix Cheese Corporation, 152
Phenylpropanolamine (PPA), 74–75
Philadelphia Centennial Exposition, 1876, 95–96
Philip Morris, 115, 152, 193, 242
Physicians Committee for Responsible Medicine, **213–14**
Pichett-Hatcher Education Fund, 41–42
Pig Stand drive-in, 106
Pilgrim's Pride, 8, 26
Pillsbury Company: acquisitions, 28, 99; Ben & Jerry's lawsuit against, 21; convenience foods from, 61; Häagen-Dazs and, 123; purchase of, 115
Pittsburgh Food and Beverage Company, 52
Pizza, **214**. *See specific pizza brands*
Pizza Hut, **214–15**; architecture of, 12; Book It! program, 66; home delivery, 78; launch of, 98–99; mascot, 169; PepsiCo and, 213; pricing, 222; sports sponsorships, 254
Plamondon, Jim, Sr., 233
Planters Peanuts, 6, 58, 117, 189–90, 199, 207
Plummer, Ed, 242
Po'Boy, 255
Politics of Junk Food, **215–16**
El Pollo Loco, 105, **216**
Pollution, 90
Polyethylene terephthalate (PET), 208, 249
Pop Rocks, 120
Popcorn, **217–19,** 226–27, 254, 261, 267–68
Popeyes, 51, 109, **219**
Poppycock clusters, 261
Popsicle, **219–20**
Pop-Tarts, 27, **220**
Porter, William Sydney, 203
Post, Charles W., 39, 115
Post Cereals, 217
Postum Cereal Company, 39, 115, 143
Potato Chips, 113, **220–21,** 244
Potatoes, 109–12
Powdered Mixes, **221**
Power and Energy Bars, **222**
PowerBar, 222
President Baking Company, 97
Pretzels, **222**
Prevention of Childhood Obesity Act, 202
Pricing, **222–23**
Primedia, 238
Princeton Farms, 226
Pringles, 221, **223**
Pritikin, Nathan, 74
Proctor & Gamble, 204, 221, 223
Proteins, 197
Protests, **223–24,** 231, 281–82
Pure Food and Drug Act of 1906, 92, 179
Pure, White and Deadly: The Problem of Sugar (Yudkin), 258
Push-ups, **224**

Quaker City Confectionary Company, 119
Quaker Oats Company, 2–3, 38, 61
Quigley, Sam, 204
Quintillion (software), 159
Quiznos Sub, **225,** 255

Radio, 4, 39, **225–26**
Raffel, Forrest, 9–10
Raffel, Leroy, 9–10
Ralph's Grocery Company, 258
Ralston Purina, 108, 143, 196
Rapp, C. J., 250
Rawls, J. Leonard, 128
Read, George, 186
Reading Pretzel Machinery Company, 222
Red Baron Pizza, 114
Red-E-Foods Systems, Inc, 71
Redenbacher, Orville, 181, 218, **226–27**
Redhots, 120
Reese, Harry Burnett, 132, 227
Reese's Peanut Butter Cups, **227–28**
Reese's Pieces, 4, 102, 132, 134, 155, 164, 228, 241
Regional Fast Foods, **228–29**
Rice Krispies, 39–40, 148
Ridgway, Edmund, 241
Ring Dings, 18
Ritz, César, 229
Ritz Crackers, 62, **229–30**
Ritzer, George, 86, 169, 177
R. J. Reynolds, 149
Roark Capital Group, 38
Robbins, Irvine, 19
Rocket pops, 224
Rodda Candy Company, 85, 144, 146, 185
Rogers, T. Gary, 80
Ronald McDonald, 4, 41, 169, 174, 181, **230–31**
Root Beer, **231–32,** 249
Root-T-Toot, 146
Rosenfield, Rick, 32
Rosenfield, William, 83, 84
Rowntree, B. Seebohm, 232
Rowntree, Henry Isaac, 232
Rowntree, Joseph, 232
Rowntree & Co., 167
Rowntree's of York, 131–32, **232–33**
Roy Rogers, 106, 129, 165, **233**

Royal Crown Cola, 10, 41–42, 53, 72, 208, **233–34**
Rudkin, Margaret, 211–12
Rudolph, Vernon, 153
Rueckheim, Frederick, 67, 254–55
Rueckheim, Louis, 67
Ruffles, 221, 244
Rules, **234**
Russell Stover Candy Store, 91

Sagittarius Acquisitions, Inc, 2
Salisbury, James H., 124
Salisbury Steak, 124
Salmonella, 104, 105, 180, **235**
Salsa, 75
Salt, **235**
Sam's Onions, 204
Sanders, Harland, 89, 112, 148, 180, **236–37**
San Diego Commissary Company, 143
Sandoz-Wander, 261
Sandwiches, **237–38**
Sara Lee, 61
Saratoga Potatoes, 220
Saxe, John E., 286
Saxe, Thomas E., 286
Sbarro, **238**
Schlink, Frederick, 92–93
Schlosser, Eric: on advertising to children, 250; boycott of fast foods by, 26; on corporate sponsors in schools, 65–66; *Fast Food Nation,* 93, 101, 104, 111, 250; on McDonald's fries, 111; on suppliers, 260; on unionization, 9
Schnering, Otto Y., 3, 17–18, 28–29, 49
Schools, 65–67, 145, 202, **238–39,** 250. *See also* Advertising; Children; Sponsorships
Schutter-Johnson Company, 23
Schwan Food Company, 114
Schweppes, 31, **239**
Schweppes, Jean Jacob, 239, 248
Scott, Walter, 13
Scott, Willard, 230, 267
Screaming Yellow Zonkers, 261
Scudder, Laura, 208
Sears, Barry, 74
Seasonal Candy, **239–40**
Secret Formulas, **240–41**
See, Charles, 34
Segar, Elzie Crisler, 287
Sells, Christopher, 71
7-Eleven, 7, 43, 132, **241–42**
7-Up, 56, **241–42,** 250
Seymour, Henry D., 38
Shaden, Rick, 225
Shakey's Pizza, 6, 98, 214, **242–43**
Shansby Group, 97
Shattuck, Frank, 14
Shires, Dana, 252
Shondor, Max, 280
Signage, **243**
Simek Family, 270
Simmons, Amelia, 63
Simplot Potato Company, 110
Sinclair, Upton, 92, 124, 179
Sleeper, 102
Slogans and Jingles, 173, **243–44**
Slow Food, **244–45**
Slurpee, 241, **245**
Small Business Administration (SBA), 107
Smarties, 163, 232
Smith, George, 160
Smith, Richie, 123
Smith, Troy, 252
Snack Food Association, 100
Snack Foods, **245–47**
Snapple Beverage Group, 31
Snickerization, 170
Snickers, 18, 166, 167, **247–48**
Sno Balls, 18
Snyder, Esther, 141
Snyder, Harry, 141
Soda/Soft Drinks, 4–5, 32, 208–9, **248–51,** 250
Soda Fountains, 22, **251–52**
Sonic, 81, **252**
Sonneborn, Harry J., 107, 172, 265
Southland Ice Company, 241
Space Dust, 121
Spangler Candy Company, 160
Spearmint gum, 288
Sponsorships, 238, 253–54
Sports Beans, 144
Sports Drinks, **252–53**
Sports Sponsorships, **253–54**
Spurlock, Morgan, 102, 260
Standard Brands, 203
Staphylococcus aureus, 104
Stark Candy Company, 34, 168
Steel, Helen, 156, 178–79
Stefanos, Leo, 79
Stephen F. Whitman Company, 33–34
St. Louis Louisiana Purchase Exposition, 1904, 80, 96
Stokely-Van Camp, Inc, 253
Stouffer's, 196
Stover, Russell C., 34, 91
Street Vendors, **254–55**
Sturgis, Julius, 222
Subs/Grinders, **255**
Subway, 108, 255, **256**
Suckers. *See* Lollipops and Suckers
Sucralose, 72
Sugar Association, 100
Sugar Babies, 160
Sugar Daddies, 160

Sugar Pops, 40, 148
Sugars, 197, **256**
Sunshine Biscuit Company, 42, 63, 147
Super Size Me, 102
Supermarkets, **258–59**
Supersizing, 183, **259–60**
Suppliers, **260–61**
Swanson, 61
Sweet Popcorn, **261**
Sweethearts, 279
Sweets Company of America, 271

Tab, 72
El Taco, 263
Taco Bell, **263–64**; acquisition of, 213; boycott of, 25; drive-thru operations, 83; expansion, 184; launch of, 99; mascot, 169; slogans, 244; sports sponsorships, 254
Taco Tia, 263
Tacos, 184
Taggart Bakery, 18
Taggart Baking Company, 135
Tang, 26–27, 221, **264–65**
Tarnower, Herman, 74
Tastee-Freez, 140, **265,** 287
Tasti-Diet, 73
Tater Tots, **265**
Taubes, Gary, 74
Taubman, A. Alfred, 2
Taxing Snack Food, **265–66**
Tea, 22
Ted Bates & Co., 3
Teen Hangouts, **266–67**
Teenage Mutant Ninja Turtles, 102, 134–35
Teenee Beanee Jelly Beans, 144
Teenie Beanie Baby, 128, 272
Television, 4, 165, **267**
Theaters, 101, **267–68**
Thomas, Dave, 126, 149, 181, **269,** 283
Thomas Adams Gum Company, 280–81
Thomas J. Lipton Company, 75
Thompson, Augustin, 188
3 Musketeers, 166, 167, **269**
Tie-ins, 5, 101–3, **269–70,** 272, 273
Tierney, Patrick, 13
TJ Cinnamons Classic Bakery, 10
Toasted Corn Flakes Company, 39
Tobler, Jean, 48, 167
Tobler, Theodore, 270
Toblerone, 48, **270**
Toll House Cookies, 63
Toll House Inn, 47
Tombrock Corporation, 287
Tombstone Pizza, 114, 214, **270–71**
Tooth decay, 251
Tootsie Roll, 145, 160, 208, **271**
Tootsie Roll Company, 128
Top Hat Drive-In, 252
Tote'm stores, 241
Totino, Rose, 114
Tower-O-Matic restaurants, 14
Toys, **271–72**
Training, **272–73**
Trall, Russell Thacher, 62, 120
Tray-boys. *See* Carhops
Tray-girls. *See* Carhops
Tri-City Beverage, 188
Tricon Global Restaurants. *See* Yum! Brands, Inc.
Trident, 31
Trigg Candy Company, 33
Trimaran Capital Partners, 216
Triscuits, 62
Trix cereal, 40
Trolli, 43
Tufts, James W., 95, 251
Tunick, A. L. "Al," 44
Turner, Fred, 45
TV dinners, 61
Twinkies, 70–71, 135, **273–74**
Twitchell, George, 232
Tyson Foods, 45–46

Uncle Ben's Rice, 165, 167
Uncle Noname, 97
Uneeda Biscuits, 3, 62
Uniforms, **275**
Unilever, 21, 220, **275–76**
Union Bottling Works, 233
Unions, 131, 175–76, 223–24
United Brands Company, 1–2. *See also* United Fruit Company
United Cigar Store, 157
United Fruit Company, 1, 20. *See also* United Brands Company
United States Baking Company, 193
United States Caramel Company, 35
United States Foil Company, 91
Universal Studios, 3–4, 134
Urban Blight, **276**
U.S. Department of Agriculture (USDA), 66, 103–4, 198, 235, **276–77**

Vair, Howard, 261
Valentine's Day Candies, **279**
Van Houten, Coenraad, 48
Vegetarianism/Veganism, 111, **279–80**
Venable, Willis, 53
Vending Machines, **280–81,** 288
Vernor, James, 116, 249
Vernor's Ginger Ale, 116, **281**
Violence, **281–82**

Wakefield, Ruth, 47, 63

Wallach, Andrew, 189
Wal-Martization, 170
Walt Disney Company, 135
Wander, 261
Ward, Neil C., 204
Ward's Orange Crush, 204
Warner-Lambert Company, 145, 271
Washburn, Cadwallader C., 115
Washburn Crosby Company, 39
Washburn Mills Company, 115
Waste, **283**
Watson, James L., 170, 175
Waxed paper, 208
Weight Losers Institute, 74
Weight Watchers, 74
Welch's Grape Juice, 22
Wellington, J., 125
Wendy's International, **283–84**; Battle of the Burgers, 20; crime and, 68; Dave Thomas and, 269; drive-thru operation, 82; hamburgers, 126; lawsuit, 156; movie tie-ins, 369; slogans, 244
West, Arch, 78
W. F. Schrafft's, 14
Wheaties, 39, 115
White, Ellen, 39
White Castle, **284–86**; advertising, 4; architecture of, 11; breakfast menus, 26; charitable foundation, 41; crime problems, 67–68; design of, 81; efficiency studies, 86, 182; egg sandwiches, 182; employment benefits, 88; fast food and, 97–98; fish sandwich, 103; franchising and, 106; hamburgers, 125; locations, 159; opening of, 40; packaging, 209; pricing, 222; radio advertising, 225; secret formulas, 240; slogans, 244; uniforms, 275
White chocolate, 47
White Heat, 102
White Mountain Freezer Company, 139
White Tower, 40, 106, 159, 244, **286–87**
Whitman Sampler, 33–34
Whopper College, 272
Whopper hamburger, 27
Wian, Robert, 22, 125
Wienerschnitzel, 12, 136, 263, **287**
William Tuke and Sons, 232
Williamson, George H., 49, 203
Williamson Candy Company, 203
Wilson, Denny, 105
Wilson, Edward, 42, 93
Wilson, Ernest, 49
Wimpy, 125, **287–88**
Winchell, Verne H., 288
Winchell's Donut House, 26, 98, **288**
Winfrey, Oprah, 180
Woodward, Frank, 143
World Cocoa Foundation, 195
Wright, Frank, 1
Wrigley, Thomas, Jr., 121
Wrigley, William, 280, 288
Wrigley Co., 157, **288–89**
Wyandot Popcorn Company, 217–18
Wyeth, Nathan, 249

Yodels, 18
York Candy Kitchens, 35
York Cone Company, 213
York Peppermint Patties, 213, **291**
Yorkshire Global Restaurants, 161
Young, William, 139
Young and Smylie, 156
Young Women's Christian Association (YWCA), 14
Y & S Candies, 34, 132, 156
Yudkin, John, 197, 258
Yum! Brands, Inc., **291–92**; acquisitions, 2, 99, 161, 215, 264; creation of, 149, 213; locations, 160

Zein, Jim, 4
Zotz, 121
Zours, 146

About the Author

ANDREW F. SMITH is an independent scholar and speaker specializing in education, history, and culinary themes. He is the author of several books on popular foods, such as *Popped Culture: A Social History of Popcorn in America* (1999), *Souper Tomatoes: The Story of America's Favorite Food* (2000), and *Peanuts: The Illustrious History of the Goober Pea* (2002). He was also the editor in chief of *The Oxford Encyclopedia of Food and Drink in America* (2004).